JavaScript
The Definitive Guide

Other resources from O'Reilly

Related titles
Ajax Hacks™
Ajax Design Patterns
Dynamic HTML: The Definitive Guide
Head Rush Ajax

JavaScript and DHTML Cookbook™
JavaScript Application Cookbook™
JavaScript Pocket Reference
Learning JavaScript

oreilly.com
oreilly.com is more than a complete catalog of O'Reilly books. You'll also find links to news, events, articles, weblogs, sample chapters, and code examples.

oreillynet.com is the essential portal for developers interested in open and emerging technologies, including new platforms, programming languages, and operating systems.

Conferences
O'Reilly brings diverse innovators together to nurture the ideas that spark revolutionary industries. We specialize in documenting the latest tools and systems, translating the innovator's knowledge into useful skills for those in the trenches. Visit *conferences.oreilly.com* for our upcoming events.

Safari Bookshelf (*safari.oreilly.com*) is the premier online reference library for programmers and IT professionals. Conduct searches across more than 1,000 books. Subscribers can zero in on answers to time-critical questions in a matter of seconds. Read the books on your Bookshelf from cover to cover or simply flip to the page you need. Try it today with a free trial.

FIFTH EDITION

JavaScript
The Definitive Guide

David Flanagan

O'REILLY®

Beijing · Cambridge · Farnham · Köln · Paris · Sebastopol · Taipei · Tokyo

JavaScript: The Definitive Guide, Fifth Edition
by David Flanagan

Copyright © 2006, 2002, 1998, 1997, 1996 O'Reilly Media, Inc. All rights reserved.
Printed in the United States of America.

Published by O'Reilly Media, Inc., 1005 Gravenstein Highway North, Sebastopol, CA 95472.

O'Reilly books may be purchased for educational, business, or sales promotional use. Online editions are also available for most titles (*safari.oreilly.com*). For more information, contact our corporate/institutional sales department: (800) 998-9938 or *corporate@oreilly.com*.

Editor: Debra Cameron	**Indexer:** Ellen Troutman-Zaig
Production Editor: Sanders Kleinfeld	**Cover Designer:** Edie Freedman
Copyeditor: Mary Anne Weeks Mayo	**Interior Designer:** David Futato
Proofreader: Sanders Kleinfeld	**Illustrators:** Robert Romano and Jessamyn Read

Printing History:

August 1996:	Beta Edition.
January 1997:	Second Edition.
June 1998:	Third Edition.
January 2002:	Fourth Edition.
August 2006:	Fifth Edition.

Nutshell Handbook, the Nutshell Handbook logo, and the O'Reilly logo are registered trademarks of O'Reilly Media, Inc. *JavaScript: The Definitive Guide*, the image of a Javan rhinoceros, and related trade dress are trademarks of O'Reilly Media, Inc. Java™, all Java-based trademarks and logos, and JavaScript™ are trademarks or registered trademarks of Sun Microsystems, Inc., in the United States and other countries. O'Reilly Media, Inc. is independent of Sun Microsystems.

Mozilla and Firefox are registered trademarks of the Mozilla Foundation. Netscape and Netscape Navigator are registered trademarks of America Online, Inc. Internet Explorer and the Internet Explorer Logo are trademarks and tradenames of Microsoft Corporation. All other product names and logos are trademarks of their respective owners.

Many of the designations used by manufacturers and sellers to distinguish their products are claimed as trademarks. Where those designations appear in this book, and O'Reilly Media, Inc. was aware of a trademark claim, the designations have been printed in caps or initial caps.

While every precaution has been taken in the preparation of this book, the publisher and author assume no responsibility for errors or omissions, or for damages resulting from the use of the information contained herein.

ISBN-10: 0-596-10199-6
ISBN-13: 978-0-596-10199-2
[M]

This book is dedicated to all
who teach peace and resist violence.

Table of Contents

Part III. Core JavaScript Reference

Part IV. Client-Side JavaScript Reference

Preface

After the fourth edition of *JavaScript: The Definitive Guide* was published, the Document Object Model—the fundamental API for client-side JavaScript™ programming—became widely, if not completely, implemented in web browsers. This meant that web developers had a stable, mature language (JavaScript 1.5) and a common API for manipulating web pages on the client. Several years of stability followed.

But things have started to get interesting again. Developers are now using JavaScript to script HTTP, manipulate XML data, and even draw dynamic graphics in a web browser. Many JavaScript developers have also started to write longer programs and use more sophisticated programming techniques, such as closures and namespaces. This fifth edition has been fully revised for the new world of Ajax and Web 2.0 technologies.

What's New in the Fifth Edition

In Part I, *Core JavaScript*, the chapter on functions (Chapter 8) has been expanded, with particular emphasis on nested functions and closures. The material on defining your own classes has also been expanded and moved to a chapter of its own (Chapter 9). Chapter 10 is another new chapter that covers namespaces, which are essential for writing modular, reusable code. Finally, Chapter 12 demonstrates how to use JavaScript to actually script Java; it shows how to embed a JavaScript interpreter within a Java 6 application and how to use JavaScript to create Java objects and invoke methods on those objects.

In Part II, *Client-Side JavaScript*, the coverage of the legacy (Level 0) Document Object Model has been merged with the coverage of the W3C standard DOM. Because the DOM is now universally implemented, there is no need for two separate chapters on manipulating documents. The biggest change in Part II, however, is the amount of new material:

- Chapter 19, *Cookies and Client-Side Persistence*, has updated coverage of cookies and new coverage of other client-side persistence techniques.

- Chapter 20, *Scripting HTTP*, explains how to make scripted HTTP requests using the powerful XMLHttpRequest object, which is the enabling technology for Ajax-style web applications.

- Chapter 21, *JavaScript and XML*, demonstrates how to use JavaScript to create, load, parse, transform, query, serialize, and extract information from XML documents. It also introduces the E4X extension to the core JavaScript language.

- Chapter 22, *Scripted Client-Side Graphics*, explains JavaScript's graphics capabilities. It covers simple image rollovers and animations but also explains advanced scripted graphics using the cutting-edge <canvas> tag. It also demonstrates other ways to create dynamic, scripted client-side graphics using SVG, VML, the Flash plug-in, and the Java plug-in.

- Chapter 23, *Scripting Java Applets and Flash Movies*, has added coverage of the Flash plug-in to its coverage of the Java plug-in. It now explains how to script Flash movies as well as Java applets.

Part III, the reference section for the core JavaScript API, is little changed from the previous edition, because that API has remained stable. If you have used the fourth edition, you'll find this part of the book comfortably familiar.

The big change to the reference material is that the documentation of the DOM API, which was previously segregated into a section of its own, has been fully integrated into Part IV, the client-side JavaScript reference section. Now there is only one client-side reference section to consult. No more looking up the Document object in one reference section and then looking up the HTMLDocument object in the other. Reference material for DOM interfaces that were never (widely) implemented in web browsers has simply been cut. The NodeIterator interface, for example, is simply not available in web browsers, and it no longer clutters up this book. The focus has also been moved away from the awkwardly formal interfaces defined by the DOM specification and onto the JavaScript objects that actually implement those interfaces. So, for example, getComputedStyle( ) is now documented as a method of the Window object, where you'd expect it, rather than as a method of the AbstractView interface. There is no reason that client-side JavaScript programmers should care about AbstractView, and it has simply been removed from the reference. All these changes result in a simpler, easier-to-use client-side reference section.

Using This Book

Chapter 1 provides an introduction to JavaScript. The rest of the book is in four parts. Part I, which immediately follows this chapter, documents the core JavaScript language. Chapters 2 through 6 cover some bland but necessary reading; these chapters cover the basic information you need to understand when learning a new programming language:

- Chapter 2, *Lexical Structure*, explains the basic structure of the language.

- Chapter 3, *Datatypes and Values*, documents the datatypes supported by JavaScript.

- Chapter 4, *Variables*, covers variables, variable scope, and related topics.

- Chapter 5, *Expressions and Operators*, explains expressions in JavaScript and documents each operator supported by JavaScript. Because JavaScript syntax is modeled on Java, which is, in turn, modeled on C and C++, experienced C, C++, or Java programmers can skim much of this chapter.

- Chapter 6, *Statements*, describes the syntax and usage of each of the JavaScript statements. Again, experienced C, C++, and Java programmers can skim some, but not all, of this chapter.

The next six chapters of Part I become more interesting. They still cover the core of the JavaScript language, but they document parts of the language that will not be familiar to you even if you already know C or Java. These chapters must be studied carefully if you want to really understand JavaScript:

- Chapter 7, *Objects and Arrays*, explains objects and arrays in JavaScript.

- Chapter 8, *Functions*, documents how functions are defined, invoked, and manipulated in JavaScript. It also includes advanced material on closures.

- Chapter 9, *Classes, Constructors, and Prototypes*, covers OO programming in JavaScript, explaining how to define constructor functions for new classes of objects and how JavaScript's prototype-based inheritance works. This chapter also demonstrates how to simulate traditional class-based OO idioms in JavaScript.

- Chapter 10, *Modules and Namespaces*, shows how JavaScript objects define namespaces and explains programming practices that can protect your modules of JavaScript code from namespace collisions.

- Chapter 11, *Pattern Matching with Regular Expressions*, explains how to use regular expressions in JavaScript to perform pattern-matching and search-and-replace operations.

- Chapter 12, *Scripting Java*, demonstrates how to embed a JavaScript interpreter within a Java application and explains how JavaScript programs running within such an application can script Java objects. This chapter is of interest only to Java programmers.

Part II explains JavaScript in web browsers. The first six chapters cover the core features of client-side JavaScript:

- Chapter 13, *JavaScript in Web Browsers*, explains the integration of JavaScript with web browsers. It discusses the web browser as a programming environment and explains the various ways in which JavaScript is integrated into web pages for execution on the client side.

- Chapter 14, *Scripting Browser Windows*, documents the central object of client-side JavaScript—the Window object—and explains how you can use this object to control web browser windows.

- Chapter 15, *Scripting Documents*, covers the Document object and explains how JavaScript can script the content displayed within a web browser window. This is the most important chapter in Part II.

- Chapter 16, *Cascading Style Sheets and Dynamic HTML*, explains how JavaScript and CSS stylesheets interact. It demonstrates how JavaScript can manipulate the style, appearance, and position of elements within an HTML document to produce visual effects known as DHTML.

- Chapter 17, *Events and Event Handling*, covers JavaScript events and event handlers, which are central to all JavaScript programs that interact with the user.

- Chapter 18, *Forms and Form Elements*, explains how JavaScript can work with HTML forms and form elements. This is logically an extension of Chapter 15, but the topic is substantial enough that it deserves its own chapter.

These first six chapters of Part II are followed by five more that cover advanced topics in client-side JavaScript.

- Chapter 19, *Cookies and Client-Side Persistence*, covers client-side persistence: the ability of scripts to store data on the user's computer for later retrieval. This chapter explains how to script HTTP cookies for persistence and also how to achieve persistence using proprietary features of Internet Explorer and the Flash plug-in.

- Chapter 20, *Scripting HTTP*, shows how JavaScript can script the HTTP protocol, sending requests to and receiving responses from web servers using the XMLHttpRequest object. This capability is the cornerstone of a web application architecture known as Ajax.

- Chapter 21, *JavaScript and XML*, demonstrates how to use JavaScript to create, load, parse, transform, query, serialize, and extract information from XML documents.

- Chapter 22, *Scripted Client-Side Graphics*, explains JavaScript's graphics capabilities. It covers simple image rollovers and animations, as well as advanced graphics techniques using Scalable Vector Graphics (SVG), Vector Markup Language (VML), the <canvas> tag, the Flash plug-in, and the Java plug-in.

- Chapter 23, *Scripting Java Applets and Flash Movies*, explains how you can use JavaScript to communicate with and control Java applets and Flash movies. It also covers how you can do the reverse—invoke JavaScript code from Java applets and Flash movies.

Parts III and IV contain reference material covering core JavaScript and client-side JavaScript, respectively. These parts document relevant objects, methods, and properties alphabetically.

Conventions Used in This Book

The following formatting conventions are used in this book:

Bold

Is occasionally used to refer to particular keys on a computer keyboard or to portions of a user interface, such as the **Back** button or the **Options** menu.

Italic

Is used for emphasis and to indicate the first use of a term. *Italic* is also used for email addresses, web sites, FTP sites, file and directory names, and newsgroups. Finally, *italic* is used in this book for the names of Java classes, to help keep Java class names distinct from JavaScript names.

`Constant width`

Is used in all JavaScript code and HTML text listings, and generally for anything that you would type literally when programming.

`Constant width bold`

Is used to indicate command-line text that should be typed by the user.

`Constant width italic`

Is used for the names of function arguments, and generally as a placeholder to indicate an item that should be replaced with an actual value in your program.

Using Code Examples

This book is here to help you get your job done. In general, you may use the code in this book in your programs and documentation. You do not need to contact us for permission unless you're reproducing a significant portion of the code. For example, writing a program that uses several chunks of code from this book does not require permission. Selling or distributing a CD-ROM of examples from O'Reilly books *does* require permission. Answering a question by citing this book and quoting example code does not require permission. Incorporating a significant amount of example code from this book into your product's documentation *does* require permission.

We appreciate, but do not require, attribution. An attribution usually includes the title, author, publisher, and ISBN. For example: "*JavaScript: The Definitive Guide*, by David Flanagan. Copyright 2006 O'Reilly Media, Inc., 978-0-596-10199-2."

If you feel your use of code examples falls outside fair use of the permission given above, feel free to contact us at *permissions@oreilly.com*.

Safari® Enabled

 When you see a Safari® Enabled icon on the cover of your favorite technology book, that means the book is available online through the O'Reilly Network Safari Bookshelf.

Safari offers a solution that's better than e-books. It's a virtual library that lets you easily search thousands of top tech books, cut and paste code samples, download chapters, and find quick answers when you need the most accurate, current information. Try it for free at *http://safari.oreilly.com*.

How to Contact Us

Please address comments and questions concerning this book to the publisher:

> O'Reilly Media, Inc.
> 1005 Gravenstein Highway North
> Sebastopol, CA 95472
> 800-998-9938 (in the United States or Canada)
> 707-829-0515 (international or local)
> 707-829-0104 (fax)

We have a web page for this book that lists errata, examples, or any additional information. You can access this page at:

> *http://www.oreilly.com/catalog/jscript5*

You can also download the examples from the author's web site:

> *http://www.davidflanagan.com/javascript5*

To comment or ask technical questions about this book, send email to:

> *bookquestions@oreilly.com*

For more information about our books, conferences, Resource Centers, and the O'Reilly Network, see our web site at:

> *http://www.oreilly.com/*

Acknowledgments

Brendan Eich of the Mozilla organization is the originator and chief innovator of JavaScript. I, and many JavaScript developers, owe Brendan a tremendous debt of gratitude for developing JavaScript and for taking the time out of his crazy schedule to answer our questions and even solicit our input. Besides patiently answering my many questions, Brendan also read and provided very helpful comments on the first and third editions of this book.

This book has been blessed with top-notch technical reviewers whose comments have gone a long way toward making it a stronger and more accurate book. Aristotle Pagaltzis (*http://plasmasturm.org*) reviewed the new material on functions and the new chapters on classes and namespaces in this edition. He gave my code a particularly careful review and had many useful comments. Douglas Crockford (*http://www.crockford.com*) reviewed the new material on functions and classes. Norris Boyd, creator of the Rhino JavaScript interpreter, reviewed the chapter on embedding Java-Script in Java applications. Peter-Paul Koch (*http://www.quirksmode.org*), Christian Heilmann (*http://www.wait-till-i.com*), and Ken Cooper reviewed the Ajax-related chapters of the book. Ken was kind enough to pitch in at the end and help out with new client-side reference material. Todd Ditchendorf (*http://www.ditchnet.org*) and Geoff Stearns (*http://blog.deconcept.com*) reviewed the chapter on scripted client-side graphics. Todd was kind enough to find and isolate a bug for me, and Geoff helped me understand Flash and ActionScript. Finally, Sanders Kleinfeld reviewed the entire book with remarkable attention to detail. His suggestions and technical corrections have made the book clearer and more precise. My sincere thanks to each of them for their careful reviews. Any errors that remain are, of course, my own.

I am also grateful to the reviewers of the fourth edition. Waldemar Horwat at Netscape reviewed the new material on JavaScript 1.5. The new material on the W3C DOM was reviewed by Philippe Le Hegaret of the W3C and by Peter-Paul Koch, Dylan Schiemann, and Jeff Yates. Although he was not a reviewer, Joseph Kesselman of IBM Research was very helpful in answering my questions about the W3C DOM.

The third edition of the book was reviewed by Brendan Eich, Waldemar Horwat, and Vidur Apparao at Netscape; Herman Venter at Microsoft; and two independent JavaScript developers, Jay Hodges and Angelo Sirigos. Dan Shafer did some preliminary work on the third edition. Although his material was not used in this edition, his ideas and general outline were quite helpful. Norris Boyd and Scott Furman at Netscape also provided useful information for this edition, and Vidur Apparao of Netscape and Scott Issacs of Microsoft each took the time to talk to me about the forthcoming Document Object Model standard. Finally, Dr. Tankred Hirschmann provided challenging insights into the intricacies of JavaScript 1.2.

The second edition benefited greatly from the help and comments of Nick Thompson and Richard Yaker of Netscape; Dr. Shon Katzenberger, Larry Sullivan, and Dave C. Mitchell at Microsoft; and Lynn Rollins of R&B Communications. The first edition was reviewed by Neil Berkman of Bay Networks and by Andrew Schulman and Terry Allen of O'Reilly.

This book also gains strength from the diversity of editors it has had. Deb Cameron is the editor of this edition and has given the book a thorough edit and much-needed freshening, with special emphasis on removing outdated material. Paula Ferguson edited the third and fourth editions. Frank Willison edited the second edition, and Andrew Schulman edited the first.

Finally, my thanks, as always and for so many reasons, to Christie.

—David Flanagan
http://www.davidflanagan.com/
April 2006

CHAPTER 1

Introduction to JavaScript

JavaScript is an interpreted programming language with object-oriented (OO) capabilities. Syntactically, the core JavaScript language resembles C, C++, and Java, with programming constructs such as the if statement, the while loop, and the && operator. The similarity ends with this syntactic resemblance, however. JavaScript is a loosely typed language, which means that variables do not need to have a type specified. Objects in JavaScript map property names to arbitrary property values. In this way, they are more like hash tables or associative arrays (in Perl) than they are like structs (in C) or objects (in C++ or Java). The OO inheritance mechanism of JavaScript is prototype-based like that of the little-known language Self. This is quite different from inheritance in C++ and Java. Like Perl, JavaScript is an interpreted language, and it draws inspiration from Perl in a number of areas, such as its regular-expression and array-handling features.

The core JavaScript language supports numbers, strings, and Boolean values as primitive datatypes. It also includes built-in support for array, date, and regular-expression objects.

JavaScript is most commonly used in web browsers, and, in that context, the general-purpose core is extended with objects that allow scripts to interact with the user, control the web browser, and alter the document content that appears within the web browser window. This embedded version of JavaScript runs scripts embedded within HTML web pages. It is commonly called *client-side* JavaScript to emphasize that scripts are run by the client computer rather than the web server.

The core JavaScript language and its built-in datatypes are the subject of international standards, and compatibility across implementations is very good. Parts of client-side JavaScript are formally standardized, other parts are de facto standards, and other parts are browser-specific extensions. Cross-browser compatibility is often an important concern for client-side JavaScript programmers.

This chapter is a high-level overview of JavaScript; it provides the background information you need before embarking on a study of the language. As motivation and introduction, it includes some simple examples of client-side JavaScript code.

1.1 What Is JavaScript?

JavaScript is the subject of a fair bit of misinformation and confusion. Before proceeding any further, it is important to debunk two common and persistent myths about the language.

1.1.1 JavaScript Is Not Java

One of the most common misconceptions about JavaScript is that it is a simplified version of Java, the programming language from Sun Microsystems. Other than an incomplete syntactic resemblance and the fact that both Java and JavaScript can provide executable content in web browsers, the two languages are entirely unrelated. The similarity of names is purely a marketing ploy by Netscape and Sun (the language was originally called LiveScript; its name was changed to JavaScript at the last minute). However, JavaScript can, in fact, script Java (see Chapters 12 and 23).

1.1.2 JavaScript Is Not Simple

Because JavaScript is interpreted instead of compiled, it is often considered a scripting language instead of a true programming language. The implication is that scripting languages are simpler and that they are programming languages for nonprogrammers. The fact that JavaScript is loosely typed does make it somewhat more forgiving for unsophisticated programmers. And many web designers have been able to use JavaScript for limited, cookbook-style programming tasks.

Beneath its thin veneer of simplicity, however, JavaScript is a full-featured programming language, as complex as any and more complex than some. Programmers who attempt to use JavaScript for nontrivial tasks often find the process frustrating if they do not have a solid understanding of the language. This book documents JavaScript comprehensively so that you can develop a sophisticated understanding. If you are used to cookbook-style JavaScript tutorials, you may be surprised at the depth and detail of the chapters ahead.

1.2 Versions of JavaScript

Like any new technology, JavaScript evolved quickly when it was new. Previous editions of this book documented this evolution version by version, explaining exactly which language features were introduced in which version of the language. At the time of this writing, however, the language has stabilized and has been standardized by the European Computer Manufacturer's Association, or ECMA.* Implementations of this standard include the JavaScript 1.5 interpreter from Netscape and the Mozilla Foundation, and the JScript 5.5 interpreter from Microsoft. Any web browser newer than Netscape 4.5 or Internet Explorer 4 supports the latest version of the language. As a practical matter, you are unlikely to encounter a noncompliant interpreter.

Note that the official name of the language, according to the ECMA-262 standard, is ECMAScript. But this awkward name is normally used only when making explicit reference to the standard. Technically, the name "JavaScript" refers only to language implementations from Netscape and the Mozilla Foundation. In practice, however, everyone calls the language JavaScript.

After a long period of stability for JavaScript, there are now some signs of change. The Firefox 1.5 web browser from the Mozilla Foundation includes a new JavaScript interpreter with the version number 1.6. This version includes new (nonstandard) array manipulation methods described in Section 7.7.10, as well as support for E4X, which is described next.

In addition to the ECMA-262 specification that standardizes the core JavaScript language, ECMA has released another JavaScript-related standard. ECMA-357 standardizes an extension to JavaScript known as E4X, or ECMAScript for XML. This extension adds an XML datatype to the language along with operators and statements for manipulating XML values. At the time of this writing, E4X is implemented only by JavaScript 1.6 and Firefox 1.5. E4X is not documented formally in this book, but Chapter 21 includes an extended introduction in tutorial form.

Proposals for a fourth edition of the ECMA-262 specification, to standardize JavaScript 2.0, have been on the table for a number of years. These proposals describe a complete overhaul of the language, including strong typing and true class-based inheritance. To date, there has been little progress toward standardization of JavaScript 2.0. Nevertheless, implementations based on draft proposals include Microsoft's JScript.NET language and the ActionScript 2.0 and ActionScript 3.0 languages used in the Adobe (formerly Macromedia) Flash player. At the time of this writing, there are signs that work on JavaScript 2.0 is resuming, and the release of JavaScript 1.6 can be seen as a preliminary step in this direction. Any new version of the language is expected to be backward-compatible with the version documented here, of course. And even once JavaScript 2.0 is standardized, it will take a few years before it is universally deployed in web browsers.

---

* The standard is ECMA-262, version 3 (available at *http://www.ecma-international.org/publications/files/ecma-st/ECMA-262.pdf*).

1.3   Client-Side JavaScript

When a JavaScript interpreter is embedded in a web browser, the result is client-side JavaScript. This is by far the most common variant of JavaScript; when most people refer to JavaScript, they usually mean client-side JavaScript. This book documents client-side JavaScript, along with the core JavaScript language that client-side Java-Script incorporates.

Client-side JavaScript combines the scripting ability of a JavaScript interpreter with the Document Object Model (DOM) defined by a web browser. Documents may contain JavaScript scripts, and those scripts can use the DOM to modify the document or control the web browser that displays the document. Put another way, we can say that client-side JavaScript adds behavior to otherwise static web content. Client-side JavaScript is at the heart of web development techniques such as DHTML (see Chapter 16) and architectures such as Ajax (see Chapter 20). The introduction to Chapter 13 includes an overview of the many capabilities of client-side JavaScript.

Just as the ECMA-262 specification defines a standard version of the core JavaScript language, the World Wide Web Consortium (W3C) has published a DOM specification that standardizes the features a browser must support in its DOM. (You'll learn much more about this standard in Chapters 15, 16, and 17.) The core portions of the W3C DOM standard are well supported in all major web browsers. One notable exception is Microsoft Internet Explorer, which does not support the W3C standard for event handling.

1.3.1   Client-Side JavaScript Examples

When a web browser is augmented with a JavaScript interpreter, it allows executable content to be distributed over the Internet in the form of JavaScript scripts. Example 1-1 shows what this looks like: it is a simple JavaScript program, or script, embedded in an HTML file.

Example 1-1. A simple JavaScript program

```
<html>
<head><title>Factorials</title></head>
<body>
<h2>Table of Factorials</h2>
<script>
var fact = 1;
for(i = 1; i < 10; i++) {
    fact = fact*i;
    document.write(i + "! = " + fact + "<br>");
}
</script>
</body>
</html>
```

When loaded into a JavaScript-enabled browser, this script produces the output shown in Figure 1-1.

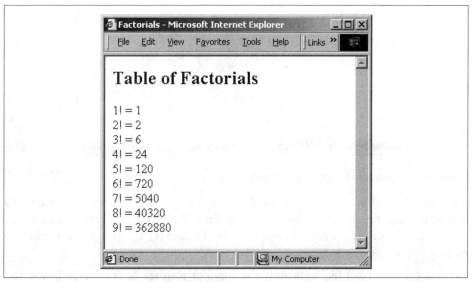

Figure 1-1. A web page generated with JavaScript

As you can see in this example, the <script> and </script> tags are used to embed JavaScript code in an HTML file. I'll describe the <script> tag further in Chapter 13. The main feature of JavaScript demonstrated by this example is the use of the document.write( ) method.* This method is used to dynamically output HTML text into an HTML document while it is being loaded into the browser.

JavaScript can control not only the content of HTML documents but also the behavior of those documents. That is, a JavaScript program might respond in some way when you enter a value in an input field or hover the mouse over an image in a document. JavaScript does this by defining *event handlers* for the document—pieces of JavaScript code that are executed when a particular event occurs, such as when the user clicks on a button. Example 1-2 shows a simple HTML fragment that includes an event handler executed in response to a button click.

Example 1-2. An HTML button with a JavaScript event handler defined

```
<button onclick="alert('You clicked the button');">
Click here
</button>
```

Figure 1-2 illustrates the result of clicking the button.

---

* "Method" is the OO term for function or procedure; you'll see it used throughout this book.

Figure 1-2. The JavaScript response to an event

The `onclick` attribute shown in Example 1-2 holds a string of JavaScript code that's executed when the user clicks the button. In this case, the `onclick` event handler calls the `alert()` function. As you can see in Figure 1-2, `alert()` pops up a dialog box to display the specified message.

Examples 1-1 and 1-2 highlight only the simplest features of client-side JavaScript. The real power of JavaScript on the client side is that scripts have access to the content of HTML documents. Example 1-3 contains a complete, nontrivial JavaScript program. The program computes the monthly payment on a home mortgage or other loan, given the amount of the loan, the interest rate, and the repayment period. It reads user input from HTML form fields, performs computations on that input, and then alters the document to display the results of the computation.

Figure 1-3 shows what the program looks like when displayed in a web browser. As you can see, it consists of an HTML form and some other text. But the figure captures only a static snapshot of the program. The addition of JavaScript code makes it dynamic: whenever the user changes the amount of the loan, the interest rate, or the number of payments, the JavaScript code recomputes the monthly payment, the total of all payments, and the total interest paid over the lifetime of the loan.

The first half of Example 1-3 is a simple CSS stylesheet and an HTML form, formatted within an HTML table. Note that the form elements define `onchange` or `onclick` event handlers. The web browser triggers these event handlers when the user changes the input or clicks on the **Compute** button displayed in the form, respectively. In each case, the value of the event handler attribute is a string of JavaScript code: `calculate()`. When the event handler is triggered, it executes this code, which calls the function `calculate()`.

The `calculate()` function is defined in the second half of the example, inside a `<script>` tag. The function reads the user's input from the form, does the math

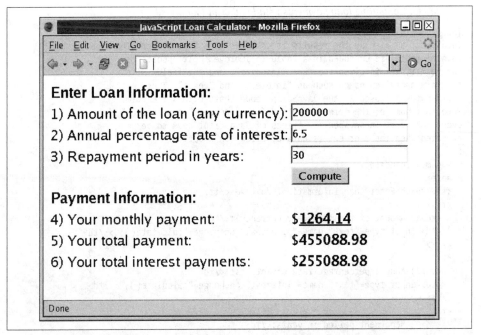

Figure 1-3. A JavaScript loan payment calculator

required to compute the loan payments, and inserts the results of these calculations into the document within <span> tags that are specially named with id attributes.

Example 1-3 is not a short example, but it is straightforward, and it is worth taking the time to look at it carefully. You shouldn't expect to understand all the code at this point, but the HTML, CSS, and JavaScript are all commented, and studying this example will give you the feel for client-side JavaScript.[*]

Example 1-3. Computing loan payments with JavaScript

```
<html>
<head>
<title>JavaScript Loan Calculator</title>
<style>
/* This is a CSS style sheet: it adds style to the program output */
.result { font-weight: bold; }  /* For elements with class="result" */
#payment { text-decoration: underline; } /* For element with id="payment" */
</style>
</head>
<body>
<!--
```

---

[*] If your intuition tells you that it is a bad idea to intermingle HTML markup, CSS styles, and JavaScript code like this, you are not alone. The trend in JavaScript programming and web design circles is to keep content, presentation, and behavior in separate files. Section 13.1.5 in Chapter 13 explains how to do this.

Example 1-3. Computing loan payments with JavaScript (continued)

```
This is an HTML form that allows the user to enter data and allows
JavaScript to display the results it computes back to the user. The
form elements are embedded in a table to improve their appearance.
The form itself is given the name "loandata", and the fields within
the form are given names such as "interest" and "years". These
field names are used in the JavaScript code that follows the form.
Note that some of the form elements define "onchange" or "onclick"
event handlers. These specify strings of JavaScript code to be
executed when the user enters data or clicks on a button.
-->
<form name="loandata">
  <table>
    <tr><td><b>Enter Loan Information:</b></td></tr>
    <tr>
      <td>1) Amount of the loan (any currency):</td>
      <td><input type="text" name="principal" onchange="calculate( );"></td>
    </tr>
    <tr>
      <td>2) Annual percentage rate of interest:</td>
      <td><input type="text" name="interest" onchange="calculate( );"></td>
    </tr>
    <tr>
      <td>3) Repayment period in years:</td>
      <td><input type="text" name="years" onchange="calculate( );"></td>
    </tr>
    <tr><td></td>
      <td><input type="button" value="Compute" onclick="calculate( );"></td>
    </tr>
    <tr><td><b>Payment Information:</b></td></tr>
    <tr>
      <td>4) Your monthly payment:</td>
      <td>$<span class="result" id="payment"></span></td>
    </tr>
    <tr>
      <td>5) Your total payment:</td>
      <td>$<span class="result" id="total"></span></td>
    </tr>
    <tr>
      <td>6) Your total interest payments:</td>
      <td>$<span class="result" id="totalinterest"></span></td>
    </tr>
  </table>
</form>

<script language="JavaScript">
/*
 * This is the JavaScript function that makes the example work. Note that
 * this script defines the calculate( ) function called by the event
 * handlers in the form. The function reads values from the form
 * <input> fields using the names defined in the previous HTML code.  It outputs
 * its results into the named <span> elements.
 */
```

Example 1-3. Computing loan payments with JavaScript (continued)

```javascript
function calculate( ) {
    // Get the user's input from the form. Assume it is all valid.
    // Convert interest from a percentage to a decimal, and convert from
    // an annual rate to a monthly rate. Convert payment period in years
    // to the number of monthly payments.
    var principal = document.loandata.principal.value;
    var interest = document.loandata.interest.value / 100 / 12;
    var payments = document.loandata.years.value * 12;

    // Now compute the monthly payment figure, using esoteric math.
    var x = Math.pow(1 + interest, payments);
    var monthly = (principal*x*interest)/(x-1);

    // Get named <span> elements from the form.
    var payment = document.getElementById("payment");
    var total = document.getElementById("total");
    var totalinterest = document.getElementById("totalinterest");

    // Check that the result is a finite number. If so, display the
    // results by setting the HTML content of each <span> element.
    if (isFinite(monthly)) {
        payment.innerHTML = monthly.toFixed(2);
        total.innerHTML = (monthly * payments).toFixed(2);
        totalinterest.innerHTML = ((monthly*payments)-principal).toFixed(2);
    }
    // Otherwise, the user's input was probably invalid, so display nothing.
    else {
        payment.innerHTML = "";
        total.innerHTML = ""
        totalinterest.innerHTML = "";
    }
}
</script>
</body>
</html>
```

1.4 JavaScript in Other Contexts

JavaScript is a general-purpose programming language, and its use is not restricted to web browsers. JavaScript was designed to be embedded within, and provide scripting capabilities for, any application. From the earliest days, in fact, Netscape's web servers included a JavaScript interpreter so that server-side scripts could be written in JavaScript. Similarly, Microsoft uses its JScript interpreter in its IIS web server and in its Windows Scripting Host product in addition to using it in Internet Explorer. Adobe uses a language derived from JavaScript for scripting its Flash player. And Sun bundles a JavaScript interpreter with its Java 6.0 distribution so that scripting capabilities can easily be added to any Java application (Chapter 12 shows how to do this).

Both Netscape and Microsoft have made their JavaScript interpreters available to companies and programmers who want to embed them in their applications. Netscape's interpreter was released as open source and is now available through the Mozilla organization (see *http://www.mozilla.org/js/*). Mozilla actually provides two different versions of the JavaScript 1.5 interpreter. One is written in C and is called SpiderMonkey. The other is written in Java and, in a flattering reference to this book, is called Rhino.

If you are writing scripts for an application that includes an embedded JavaScript interpreter, you'll find the first half of this book, documenting the core language, to be useful. The web-browser-specific chapters, however, will probably not be applicable to your scripts.

1.5   Exploring JavaScript

The way to really learn a new programming language is to write programs with it. As you read through this book, I encourage you to try out JavaScript features as you learn about them. A number of techniques make it easy to experiment with JavaScript.

The most obvious way to explore JavaScript is to write simple scripts. One of the nice things about client-side JavaScript is that anyone with a web browser and a simple text editor has a complete development environment; there is no need to buy or download special-purpose software in order to begin writing JavaScript scripts.

For example, you could modify Example 1-1 to display Fibonacci numbers instead of factorials:

```
<script>
document.write("<h2>Table of Fibonacci Numbers</h2>");
for (i=0, j=1, k=0, fib =0; i<50; i++, fib=j+k, j=k, k=fib){
    document.write("Fibonacci (" + i + ") = " + fib);
    document.write("<br>");
}
</script>
```

This code may be convoluted (and don't worry if you don't yet understand it), but the point is that when you want to experiment with short programs like this, you can simply type them up and try them out in your web browser using a local file: URL. Note that the code uses the document.write( ) method to display its HTML output so that you can see the results of its computations. This is an important technique for experimenting with JavaScript. As an alternative, you can also use the alert( ) method to display plain-text output in a dialog box:

```
 alert("Fibonacci (" + i + ") = " + fib);
```

Note also that for simple JavaScript experiments like this, you can omit the <html>, <head>, and <body> tags in your HTML file.

For even simpler experiments with JavaScript, you can sometimes use the javascript: URL pseudoprotocol to evaluate a JavaScript expression and return the result. A JavaScript URL consists of the javascript: protocol specifier followed by arbitrary JavaScript code (with statements separated from one another by semicolons). When the browser loads such a URL, it executes the JavaScript code. The value of the last expression in the URL is converted to a string, and this string is displayed by the web browser as its new document. For example, you might type the following JavaScript URLs into the **Location** field of your web browser to test your understanding of some of JavaScript's operators and statements:

```
javascript:5%2
javascript:x = 3; (x < 5)? "x is less": "x is greater"
javascript:d = new Date( ); typeof d;
javascript:for(i=0,j=1,k=0,fib=1; i<5; i++,fib=j+k,k=j,j=fib) alert(fib);
javascript:s=""; for(i in navigator) s+=i+":"+navigator[i]+"\n"; alert(s);
```

In the Firefox web browser, you can also type single-line experiments into the JavaScript console, which you access through the **Tools** menu. Simply type in an expression you want to evaluate or a statement you want to execute. When using the console instead of the location bar, you omit the javascript: prefix.

While exploring JavaScript, you'll probably write code that doesn't work as you expect it to, and you'll want to debug it. The basic debugging technique for JavaScript is like that in many other languages: insert statements into your code to print out the values of relevant variables so that you can try to figure out what is actually happening. As shown previously, you can use the document.write( ) or alert( ) methods to do this. (Example 15-9 provides a more sophisticated facility for logging debugging messages.)

The for/in loop (described in Chapter 6) is also useful for debugging. You can use it, along with the alert( ) method, to display a list of the names and values of all properties of an object, for example. This kind of function can be handy when exploring the language or trying to debug code.

If your JavaScript bugs are persistent and aggravating, you may be interested in an actual JavaScript debugger. In Internet Explorer, you can use Microsoft Script Debugger. In Firefox, you can use a debugger extension known as Venkman. Both tools are beyond the scope of this book, but you can find them easily with an Internet search. Another useful tool that is not strictly a debugger is *jslint*, which looks for common problems in JavaScript code (see *http://jslint.com*).

PART I

Core JavaScript

This part of the book, Chapters 2 though 12, documents the core JavaScript language and is meant to be a JavaScript language reference. After you read through it once to learn the language, you may find yourself referring back to it to refresh your memory about some of the trickier points of JavaScript:

Chapter 2, *Lexical Structure*

Chapter 3, *Datatypes and Values*

Chapter 4, *Variables*

Chapter 5, *Expressions and Operators*

Chapter 6, *Statements*

Chapter 7, *Objects and Arrays*

Chapter 8, *Functions*

Chapter 9, *Classes, Constructors, and Prototypes*

Chapter 10, *Modules and Namespaces*

Chapter 11, *Pattern Matching with Regular Expressions*

Chapter 12, *Scripting Java*

Lexical Structure

The lexical structure of a programming language is the set of elementary rules that specifies how you write programs in that language. It is the lowest-level syntax of a language; it specifies such things as what variable names look like, what characters are used for comments, and how one program statement is separated from the next. This short chapter documents the lexical structure of JavaScript.

2.1 Character Set

JavaScript programs are written using the Unicode character set. Unlike the 7-bit ASCII encoding, which is useful only for English, and the 8-bit ISO Latin-1 encoding, which is useful only for English and major Western European languages, the 16-bit Unicode encoding can represent virtually every written language in common use on the planet. This is an important feature for internationalization and is particularly important for programmers who do not speak English.

American and other English-speaking programmers typically write programs using a text editor that supports only the ASCII or Latin-1 character encodings, and thus they don't have easy access to the full Unicode character set. This is not a problem, however, because both the ASCII and Latin-1 encodings are subsets of Unicode, so any JavaScript program written using those character sets is perfectly valid. Programmers who are used to thinking of characters as 8-bit quantities may be disconcerted to know that JavaScript represents each character using 2 bytes, but this fact is actually transparent to the programmer and can simply be ignored.

Although the ECMAScript v3 standard allows Unicode characters anywhere in a JavaScript program, versions 1 and 2 of the standard allow Unicode characters only in comments and quoted string literals; all elements are restricted to the ASCII character set. Versions of JavaScript that predate ECMAScript standardization typically do not support Unicode at all.

2.2   Case Sensitivity

JavaScript is a case-sensitive language. This means that language keywords, variables, function names, and any other identifiers must always be typed with a consistent capitalization of letters. The `while` keyword, for example, must be typed "while," not "While" or "WHILE." Similarly, `online`, `Online`, `OnLine`, and `ONLINE` are four distinct variable names.

Note, however, that HTML is not case-sensitive (although XHTML is). Because of its close association with client-side JavaScript, this difference can be confusing. Many JavaScript objects and properties have the same names as the HTML tags and attributes they represent. While these tags and attribute names can be typed in any case in HTML, in JavaScript they typically must be all lowercase. For example, the HTML `onclick` event handler attribute is sometimes specified as `onClick` in HTML, but it must be specified as `onclick` in JavaScript code (or in XHTML documents).

2.3   Whitespace and Line Breaks

JavaScript ignores spaces, tabs, and newlines that appear between tokens in programs. Because you can use spaces, tabs, and newlines freely in your programs, you are free to format and indent your programs in a neat and consistent way that makes the code easy to read and understand. Note, however, that there is one minor restriction on the placement of line breaks; it is described in the following section.

2.4   Optional Semicolons

Simple statements in JavaScript are generally followed by semicolons (;), just as they are in C, C++, and Java. The semicolon serves to separate statements from each other. In JavaScript, however, you may omit the semicolon if each of your statements is placed on a separate line. For example, the following code could be written without semicolons:

```
a = 3;
b = 4;
```

But when formatted as follows, the first semicolon is required:

```
a = 3; b = 4;
```

Omitting semicolons is not a good programming practice; you should get in the habit of using them.

Although JavaScript theoretically allows line breaks between any two tokens, the fact that JavaScript automatically inserts semicolons for you causes some exceptions to this rule. Loosely, if you break a line of code in such a way that the line before the break appears to be a complete statement, JavaScript may think you omitted the semicolon and insert one for you, altering your meaning. Some places you should look out for this are with the return, break, and continue statements (which are described in Chapter 6). For example, consider the following:

```
return
true;
```

JavaScript assumes you meant:

```
return;
true;
```

However, you probably meant:

```
return true;
```

This is something to watch out for: this code does not cause a syntax error and will fail in a nonobvious way. A similar problem occurs if you write:

```
break
outerloop;
```

JavaScript inserts a semicolon after the break keyword, causing a syntax error when it tries to interpret the next line. For similar reasons, the ++ and -- postfix operators (see Chapter 5) must always appear on the same line as the expressions to which they are applied.

2.5 Comments

JavaScript, like Java, supports both C++ and C-style comments. Any text between a // and the end of a line is treated as a comment and is ignored by JavaScript. Any text between the characters /* and */ is also treated as a comment; these C-style comments may span multiple lines but may not be nested. The following lines of code are all legal JavaScript comments:

```
// This is a single-line comment.
/* This is also a comment */  // and here is another comment.
/*
 * This is yet another comment.
 * It has multiple lines.
 */
```

2.6 Literals

A *literal* is a data value that appears directly in a program. The following are all literals:

```
12               // The number twelve
1.2              // The number one point two
"hello world"    // A string of text
'Hi'             // Another string
true             // A Boolean value
false            // The other Boolean value
/javascript/gi   // A "regular expression" literal (for pattern matching)
null             // Absence of an object
```

In ECMAScript v3, expressions that serve as array and object literals are also supported. For example:

```
{ x:1, y:2 }    // An object initializer
[1,2,3,4,5]     // An array initializer
```

Literals are an important part of any programming language, because it is impossible to write a program without them. The various JavaScript literals are described in detail in Chapter 3.

2.7   Identifiers

An *identifier* is simply a name. In JavaScript, identifiers are used to name variables and functions, and to provide labels for certain loops in JavaScript code. The rules for legal identifier names are the same in JavaScript as they are in Java and many other languages. The first character must be a letter, an underscore (_), or a dollar sign ($).* Subsequent characters can be a letter, a digit, an underscore, or a dollar sign. (Digits are not allowed as the first character so that JavaScript can easily distinguish identifiers from numbers.) These are all legal identifiers:

```
i
my_variable_name
v13
_dummy
$str
```

In ECMAScript v3, identifiers can contain letters and digits from the complete Unicode character set. Prior to this version of the standard, JavaScript identifiers were restricted to the ASCII character set. ECMAScript v3 also allows Unicode escape sequences to appear in identifiers. A Unicode escape contains the characters \u followed by four hexadecimal digits that specify a 16-bit character encoding. For example, the identifier π can also be written as \u03c0. Although this is an awkward syntax, it makes it possible to translate JavaScript programs that contain Unicode characters into a form that allows them to be manipulated with text editors and other tools that do not support the full Unicode character set.

Finally, identifiers can't be the same as any of the keywords used for other purposes in JavaScript. The next section lists the special keywords that are reserved in JavaScript.

---

* Note that prior to JavaScript 1.1, dollar signs are not legal in identifiers. They are intended for use only by code-generation tools, so you should avoid using dollar signs in identifiers in the code you write yourself.

2.8 Reserved Words

JavaScript has a number of reserved keywords. These are words that you cannot use as identifiers (variable names, function names, and loop labels) in your JavaScript programs. Table 2-1 lists the keywords standardized by ECMAScript v3. These words have special meaning to JavaScript; they are part of the language syntax itself.

Table 2-1. Reserved JavaScript keywords

break	do	if	switch	typeof
case	else	in	this	var
catch	false	instanceof	throw	void
continue	finally	new	true	while
default	for	null	try	with
delete	function	return		

Table 2-2 lists other reserved keywords. These words are not currently used in Java-Script, but they are reserved by ECMAScript v3 as possible future extensions to the language.

Table 2-2. Words reserved for ECMA extensions

abstract	double	goto	native	static
boolean	enum	implements	package	super
byte	export	import	private	synchronized
char	extends	int	protected	throws
class	final	interface	public	transient
const	float	long	short	volatile
debugger				

In addition to some of the formally reserved words just listed, current drafts of the ECMAScript v4 standard are contemplating the use of the keywords as, is, namespace, and use. Current JavaScript interpreters will not prevent you from using these four words as identifiers, but you should avoid them anyway.

You should also avoid using as identifiers the names of global variables and functions that are predefined by JavaScript. If you create variables or functions with these names, either you will get an error (if the property is read-only) or you will redefine the existing variable or function—something you should not do unless you know exactly what you're doing. Table 2-3 lists global variables and functions defined by the ECMAScript v3 standard. Specific implementations may define other global properties, and each specific JavaScript embedding (client-side, server-side, etc.) will have its own extensive list of global properties.[*]

Table 2-3. Other identifiers to avoid

arguments	encodeURI	Infinity	Object	String
Array	Error	isFinite	parseFloat	SyntaxError
Boolean	escape	isNaN	parseInt	TypeError
Date	eval	Math	RangeError	undefined
decodeURI	EvalError	NaN	ReferenceError	unescape
decodeURIComponent	Function	Number	RegExp	URIError

[*] See the Window object in Part IV for a list of the additional global variables and functions defined by client-side JavaScript.

CHAPTER 3

Datatypes and Values

Computer programs work by manipulating *values*, such as the number 3.14 or the text "Hello World." The types of values that can be represented and manipulated in a programming language are known as *datatypes*, and one of the most fundamental characteristics of a programming language is the set of datatypes it supports. Java-Script allows you to work with three primitive datatypes: numbers, strings of text (known as *strings*), and Boolean truth values (known as *booleans*). JavaScript also defines two trivial datatypes, *null* and *undefined*, each of which defines only a single value.

In addition to these primitive datatypes, JavaScript supports a composite datatype known as an *object*. An object (that is, a member of the datatype *object*) represents a collection of values (either primitive values, such as numbers and strings, or composite values, such as other objects). Objects in JavaScript have a dual nature: an object can represent an unordered collection of named values or an ordered collection of numbered values. In the latter case, the object is called an *array*. Although objects and arrays are fundamentally the same datatype in JavaScript, they behave quite differently and will usually be considered distinct types throughout this book.

JavaScript defines another special kind of object, known as a *function*. A function is an object that has executable code associated with it. A function may be *invoked* to perform some kind of operation. Like arrays, functions behave differently from other kinds of objects, and JavaScript defines a special language syntax for working with them. Thus, we'll treat the function datatype independently of the object and array types.

In addition to functions and arrays, core JavaScript defines a few other specialized kinds of objects. These objects do not represent new datatypes, just new *classes* of objects. The Date class defines objects that represent dates, the RegExp class defines objects that represent regular expressions (a powerful pattern-matching tool described in Chapter 11), and the Error class defines objects that represent syntax and runtime errors that can occur in a JavaScript program.

The remainder of this chapter documents each of the primitive datatypes in detail. It also introduces the object, array, and function datatypes, which are fully documented in Chapters 7 and 8. Finally, it provides an overview of the Date, RegExp, and Error classes, which are documented in full detail in Part III of this book. The chapter concludes with some advanced details that you may want to skip on your first reading.

3.1 Numbers

Numbers are the most basic datatype; they require very little explanation. JavaScript differs from programming languages such as C and Java in that it does not make a distinction between integer values and floating-point values. All numbers in JavaScript are represented as floating-point values. JavaScript represents numbers using the 64-bit floating-point format defined by the IEEE 754 standard,* which means it can represent numbers as large as $\pm1.7976931348623157 \times 10^{308}$ and as small as $\pm5 \times 10^{-324}$.

When a number appears directly in a JavaScript program, it's called a *numeric literal*. JavaScript supports numeric literals in several formats, as described in the following sections. Note that any numeric literal can be preceded by a minus sign (–) to make the number negative. Technically, however, – is the unary negation operator (see Chapter 5) and is not part of the numeric literal syntax.

3.1.1 Integer Literals

In a JavaScript program, a base-10 integer is written as a sequence of digits. For example:

```
0
3
10000000
```

The JavaScript number format allows you to exactly represent all integers between –9007199254740992 (-2^{53}) and 9007199254740992 (2^{53}), inclusive. If you use integer values larger than this, you may lose precision in the trailing digits. Note, however, that certain integer operations in JavaScript (in particular the bitwise operators described in Chapter 5) are performed on 32-bit integers, which range from –2147483648 (-2^{31}) to 2147483647 ($2^{31}-1$).

---

* This format should be familiar to Java programmers as the format of the double type. It is also the double format used in almost all modern implementations of C and C++.

3.1.2 Hexadecimal and Octal Literals

In addition to base-10 integer literals, JavaScript recognizes hexadecimal (base-16) values. A hexadecimal literal begins with "0x" or "0X", followed by a string of hexadecimal digits. A hexadecimal digit is one of the digits 0 through 9 or the letters a (or A) through f (or F), which represent values 10 through 15. Here are examples of hexadecimal integer literals:

```
0xff  // 15*16 + 15 = 255 (base 10)
0xCAFE911
```

Although the ECMAScript standard does not support them, some implementations of JavaScript allow you to specify integer literals in octal (base-8) format. An octal literal begins with the digit 0 and is followed by a sequence of digits, each between 0 and 7. For example:

```
0377  // 3*64 + 7*8 + 7 = 255 (base 10)
```

Since some implementations support octal literals and some do not, you should never write an integer literal with a leading zero; you cannot know in this case whether an implementation will interpret it as an octal or decimal value.

3.1.3 Floating-Point Literals

Floating-point literals can have a decimal point; they use the traditional syntax for real numbers. A real value is represented as the integral part of the number, followed by a decimal point and the fractional part of the number.

Floating-point literals may also be represented using exponential notation: a real number followed by the letter e (or E), followed by an optional plus or minus sign, followed by an integer exponent. This notation represents the real number multiplied by 10 to the power of the exponent.

More succinctly, the syntax is:

```
[digits][.digits][(E|e)[(+|-)]digits]
```

For example:

```
3.14
2345.789
.333333333333333333
6.02e23        // 6.02 × 10²³
1.4738223E-32  // 1.4738223 × 10⁻³²
```

Note that there are infinitely many real numbers, but only a finite number of them (18437736874454810627, to be exact) can be represented exactly by the JavaScript floating-point format. This means that when you're working with real numbers in JavaScript, the representation of the number will often be an approximation of the actual number. The approximation is usually good enough, however, and this is rarely a practical problem.

3.1.4 Working with Numbers

JavaScript programs work with numbers using the arithmetic operators that the language provides. These include + for addition, - for subtraction, * for multiplication, and / for division. Full details on these and other arithmetic operators can be found in Chapter 5.

In addition to these basic arithmetic operations, JavaScript supports more complex mathematical operations through a large number of mathematical functions that are a core part of the language. For convenience, these functions are all stored as properties of a single Math object, so you always use the literal name Math to access them. For example, here's how to compute the sine of the numeric value x:

```
sine_of_x = Math.sin(x);
```

And to compute the square root of a numeric expression:

```
hypot = Math.sqrt(x*x + y*y);
```

See the Math object and subsequent listings in Part III for full details on all the mathematical functions supported by JavaScript.

3.1.5 Numeric Conversions

JavaScript can format numbers as strings and parse strings into numbers. The conversion of numbers to and from strings is described in Section 3.2.

3.1.6 Special Numeric Values

JavaScript uses several special numeric values. When a floating-point value becomes larger than the largest representable finite number, the result is a special infinity value, which JavaScript prints as Infinity. Similarly, when a negative value becomes lower than the last representable negative number, the result is negative infinity, printed as -Infinity.

Another special JavaScript numeric value is returned when a mathematical operation (such as division of zero by zero) yields an undefined result or an error. In this case, the result is the special not-a-number value, printed as NaN. The not-a-number value behaves unusually: it does not compare equal to any number, including itself! For this reason, a special function, isNaN( ), is required to test for this value. A related function, isFinite( ), tests whether a number is not NaN and is not positive or negative infinity.

Table 3-1 lists several constants that JavaScript defines to represent these special numeric values.

Table 3-1. Special numeric constants

Constant	Meaning
Infinity	Special value to represent infinity
NaN	Special not-a-number value
Number.MAX_VALUE	Largest representable number
Number.MIN_VALUE	Smallest (closest to zero) representable number
Number.NaN	Special not-a-number value
Number.POSITIVE_INFINITY	Special value to represent infinity
Number.NEGATIVE_INFINITY	Special value to represent negative infinity

The Infinity and NaN constants are defined by the ECMAScript v1 standard and are not implemented prior to JavaScript 1.3. The various Number constants, however, have been implemented since JavaScript 1.1.

3.2 Strings

A *string* is a sequence of Unicode letters, digits, punctuation characters, and so on; it is the JavaScript datatype for representing text. As you'll see shortly, you can include string literals in your programs by enclosing them in matching pairs of single or double quotation marks. Note that JavaScript does not have a character datatype such as char, as C, C++, and Java do. To represent a single character, you simply use a string that has a length of 1.

3.2.1 String Literals

A string comprises a sequence of zero or more Unicode characters enclosed within single or double quotes (' or "). Double-quote characters may be contained within strings delimited by single-quote characters, and single-quote characters may be contained within strings delimited by double quotes. String literals must be written on a single line; they may not be broken across two lines. If you need to include a newline character in a string literal, use the character sequence \n, which is documented in the next section. Here are examples of string literals:

```
""   // The empty string: it has zero characters
'testing'
"3.14"
'name="myform"'
"Wouldn't you prefer O'Reilly's book?"
"This string\nhas two lines"
"π is the ratio of a circle's circumference to its diameter"
```

As illustrated in the last example string shown, the ECMAScript v1 standard allows Unicode characters within string literals. Implementations prior to JavaScript 1.3, however, typically support only ASCII or Latin-1 characters in strings. As explained in the next section, you can also include Unicode characters in your string literals using special *escape sequences*. This is useful if your text editor does not provide complete Unicode support.

Note that when you use single quotes to delimit your strings, you must be careful with English contractions and possessives, such as *can't* and *O'Reilly's*. Since the apostrophe is the same as the single-quote character, you must use the backslash character (\) to escape any apostrophes that appear in single-quoted strings (this is explained in the next section).

In client-side JavaScript programming, JavaScript code often contains strings of HTML code, and HTML code often contains strings of JavaScript code. Like JavaScript, HTML uses either single or double quotes to delimit its strings. Thus, when combining JavaScript and HTML, it is a good idea to use one style of quotes for JavaScript and the other style for HTML. In the following example, the string "Thank you" is single-quoted within a JavaScript expression, which is double-quoted within an HTML event-handler attribute:

```
<a href="" onclick="alert('Thank you')">Click Me</a>
```

3.2.2   Escape Sequences in String Literals

The backslash character (\) has a special purpose in JavaScript strings. Combined with the character that follows it, it represents a character that is not otherwise representable within the string. For example, \n is an *escape sequence* that represents a newline character.[*]

Another example, mentioned in the previous section, is the \' escape, which represents the single quote (or apostrophe) character. This escape sequence is useful when you need to include an apostrophe in a string literal that is contained within single quotes. You can see why these are called escape sequences: the backslash allows you to escape from the usual interpretation of the single-quote character. Instead of using it to mark the end of the string, you use it as an apostrophe:

```
'You\'re right, it can\'t be a quote'
```

Table 3-2 lists the JavaScript escape sequences and the characters they represent. Two escape sequences are generic and can be used to represent any character by specifying its Latin-1 or Unicode character code as a hexadecimal number. For example, the sequence \xA9 represents the copyright symbol, which has the Latin-1 encoding given by the hexadecimal number A9. Similarly, the \u escape represents an arbitrary Unicode character specified by four hexadecimal digits; \u03c0 represents the character π, for example. Note that Unicode escapes are required by the

---

[*] C, C++, and Java programmers will already be familiar with this and other JavaScript escape sequences.

ECMAScript v1 standard but are not typically supported in implementations prior to JavaScript 1.3. Some implementations of JavaScript also allow a Latin-1 character to be specified by three octal digits following a backslash, but this escape sequence is not supported in the ECMAScript v3 standard and should no longer be used.

Table 3-2. JavaScript escape sequences

Sequence	Character represented
\0	The NUL character (\u0000).
\b	Backspace (\u0008).
\t	Horizontal tab (\u0009).
\n	Newline (\u000A).
\v	Vertical tab (\u000B).
\f	Form feed (\u000C).
\r	Carriage return (\u000D).
\"	Double quote (\u0022).
\'	Apostrophe or single quote (\u0027).
\\	Backslash (\u005C).
\x*XX*	The Latin-1 character specified by the two hexadecimal digits *XX*.
\u*XXXX*	The Unicode character specified by the four hexadecimal digits *XXXX*.
XXX	The Latin-1 character specified by the octal digits *XXX*, between 1 and 377. Not supported by ECMA-Script v3; do not use this escape sequence.

Finally, note that the backslash escape cannot be used before a line break to continue a string (or other JavaScript) token across two lines or to include a literal line break in a string. If the \ character precedes any character other than those shown in Table 3-2, the backslash is simply ignored (although future versions of the language may, of course, define new escape sequences). For example, \# is the same as #.

3.2.3 Working with Strings

One of the built-in features of JavaScript is the ability to *concatenate* strings. If you use the + operator with numbers, it adds them. But if you use this operator on strings, it joins them by appending the second to the first. For example:

```
msg = "Hello, " + "world";   // Produces the string "Hello, world"
greeting = "Welcome to my blog," + " " + name;
```

To determine the length of a string—the number of characters it contains—use the length property of the string. If the variable s contains a string, you access its length like this:

```
s.length
```

You can use a number of methods to operate on strings. For example, to get the last character of a string s:

```
last_char = s.charAt(s.length - 1)
```

To extract the second, third, and fourth characters from a string s:

```
sub = s.substring(1,4);
```

To find the position of the first letter "a" in a string s:

```
i = s.indexOf('a');
```

You can use quite a few other methods to manipulate strings. You'll find full documentation of these methods in Part III, under the String object and subsequent listings.

As you can tell from the previous examples, JavaScript strings (and JavaScript arrays, as we'll see later) are indexed starting with zero. That is, the first character in a string is character 0. C, C++, and Java programmers should be perfectly comfortable with this convention, but programmers familiar with languages that have 1-based strings and arrays may find that it takes some getting used to.

In some implementations of JavaScript, individual characters can be read from strings (but not written into strings) using array notation, so the earlier call to charAt( ) can also be written like this:

```
last_char = s[s.length - 1];
```

Note, however, that this syntax is not part of the ECMAScript v3 standard, is not portable, and should be avoided.

When we discuss the object datatype, you'll see that object properties and methods are used in the same way that string properties and methods are used in the previous examples. This does not mean that strings are a type of object. In fact, strings are a distinct JavaScript datatype: they use object syntax for accessing properties and methods, but they are not themselves objects. You'll see just why this is so at the end of this chapter.

3.2.4 Converting Numbers to Strings

Numbers are automatically converted to strings when needed. If a number is used in a string concatenation expression, for example, the number is converted to a string first:

```
var n = 100;
var s = n + " bottles of beer on the wall.";
```

This conversion-through-concatenation feature of JavaScript results in an idiom that you may occasionally see: to convert a number to a string, simply add the empty string to it:

```
var n_as_string = n + "";
```

To make number-to-string conversions more explicit, use the String( ) function:

```
var string_value = String(number);
```

Another technique for converting numbers to strings uses the toString( ) method:

```
string_value = number.toString( );
```

The toString( ) method of the Number object (primitive numbers are converted to Number objects so that this method can be called) takes an optional argument that specifies a radix, or base, for the conversion. If you do not specify the argument, the conversion is done in base 10. However, you can also convert numbers in other bases (between 2 and 36).[*] For example:

```
var n = 17;
binary_string = n.toString(2);       // Evaluates to "10001"
octal_string = "0" + n.toString(8);  // Evaluates to "021"
hex_string = "0x" + n.toString(16);  // Evaluates to "0x11"
```

A shortcoming of JavaScript prior to JavaScript 1.5 is that there is no built-in way to convert a number to a string and specify the number of decimal places to be included, or to specify whether exponential notation should be used. This can make it difficult to display numbers that have traditional formats, such as numbers that represent monetary values.

ECMAScript v3 and JavaScript 1.5 solve this problem by adding three new number-to-string methods to the Number class. toFixed( ) converts a number to a string and displays a specified number of digits after the decimal point. It does not use exponential notation. toExponential( ) converts a number to a string using exponential notation, with one digit before the decimal point and a specified number of digits after the decimal point. toPrecision( ) displays a number using the specified number of significant digits. It uses exponential notation if the number of significant digits is not large enough to display the entire integer portion of the number. Note that all three methods round the trailing digits of the resulting string as appropriate. Consider the following examples:

```
var n = 123456.789;
n.toFixed(0);          // "123457"
n.toFixed(2);          // "123456.79"
n.toExponential(1);    // "1.2e+5"
n.toExponential(3);    // "1.235e+5"
n.toPrecision(4);      // "1.235e+5"
n.toPrecision(7);      // "123456.8"
```

[*] The ECMAScript specification supports the radix argument to the toString( ) method, but it allows the method to return an implementation-defined string for any radix other than 10. Thus, conforming implementations may simply ignore the argument and always return a base-10 result. In practice, however, implementations do honor the requested radix.

3.2.5 Converting Strings to Numbers

When a string is used in a numeric context, it is automatically converted to a number. This means, for example, that the following code actually works:

```
var product = "21" * "2"; // product is the number 42.
```

You can take advantage of this fact to convert a string to a number by simply subtracting zero from it:

```
var number = string_value - 0;
```

(Note, however that adding zero to a string value results in string concatenation rather than type conversion.)

A less tricky and more explicit way to convert a string to a number is to call the Number( ) constructor as a function:

```
var number = Number(string_value);
```

The trouble with this sort of string-to-number conversion is that it is overly strict. It works only with base-10 numbers, and although it allows leading and trailing spaces, it does not allow any nonspace characters to appear in the string following the number.

To allow more flexible conversions, you can use parseInt( ) and parseFloat( ). These functions convert and return any number at the beginning of a string, ignoring any trailing nonnumbers. parseInt( ) parses only integers, while parseFloat( ) parses both integers and floating-point numbers. If a string begins with "0x" or "0X", parseInt( ) interprets it as a hexadecimal number.[*] For example:

```
parseInt("3 blind mice");       // Returns 3
parseFloat("3.14 meters");      // Returns 3.14
parseInt("12.34");              // Returns 12
parseInt("0xFF");               // Returns 255
```

parseInt( ) can even take a second argument specifying the radix (base) of the number to be parsed. Legal values are between 2 and 36. For example:

```
parseInt("11", 2);      // Returns 3 (1*2 + 1)
parseInt("ff", 16);     // Returns 255 (15*16 + 15)
parseInt("zz", 36);     // Returns 1295 (35*36 + 35)
parseInt("077", 8);     // Returns 63 (7*8 + 7)
parseInt("077", 10);    // Returns 77 (7*10 + 7)
```

If parseInt( ) or parseFloat( ) cannot convert the specified string to a number, it returns NaN:

```
parseInt("eleven");     // Returns NaN
parseFloat("$72.47");   // Returns NaN
```

---

[*] The ECMAScript specification says that if a string begins with "0" (but not "0x" or "0X"), parseInt( ) may parse it as an octal number or as a decimal number. Because the behavior is unspecified, you should never use parseInt( ) to parse numbers with leading zeros, unless you explicitly specify the radix to be used!

3.3   Boolean Values

The number and string datatypes have a large or infinite number of possible values. The boolean datatype, on the other hand, has only two. These two values are represented by the literals true and false. A value of type boolean represents a truth value; it says whether something is true or not.

Boolean values are generally the result of comparisons you make in your JavaScript programs. For example:

```
a == 4
```

This code tests to see whether the value of the variable a is equal to the number 4. If it is, the result of this comparison is the boolean value true. If a is not equal to 4, the result of the comparison is false.

Boolean values are typically used in JavaScript control structures. For example, the if/else statement in JavaScript performs one action if a boolean value is true and another action if the value is false. You usually combine a comparison that creates a boolean value directly with a statement that uses it. The result looks like this:

```
if (a == 4)
    b = b + 1;
else
    a = a + 1;
```

This code checks whether a equals 4. If so, it adds 1 to b; otherwise, it adds 1 to a.

Instead of thinking of the two possible boolean values as true and false, it is sometimes convenient to think of them as on (true) and off (false), or yes (true) and no (false).

3.3.1   Boolean Type Conversions

Boolean values are easily convertible to and from other types and are often automatically converted.* If a boolean value is used in a numeric context, true converts to the number 1 and false converts to the number 0. If a boolean value is used in a string context, true converts to the string "true" and false converts to the string "false".

If a number is used where a boolean value is expected, the number is converted to true unless the number is 0 or NaN, which are converted to false. If a string is used where a boolean value is expected, it is converted to true except for the empty string,

---

* C programmers should note that JavaScript has a distinct boolean datatype, unlike C, which simply uses integer values to simulate Boolean values. Java programmers should note that although JavaScript has a boolean type, it is not nearly as pure as the Java boolean datatype; JavaScript boolean values are easily converted to and from other datatypes, and so in practice, the use of boolean values in JavaScript is much more like their use in C than in Java.

which is converted to false. null and the undefined value convert to false, and any non-null object, array, or function converts to true.

If you prefer to make your type conversions explicit, you can use the Boolean( ) function:

```
var x_as_boolean = Boolean(x);
```

Another technique is to use the Boolean NOT operator twice:

```
var x_as_boolean = !!x;
```

3.4   Functions

A *function* is a piece of executable code that is defined by a JavaScript program or predefined by the JavaScript implementation. Although a function is defined only once, a JavaScript program can execute or invoke it any number of times. A function may be passed *arguments*, or *parameters*, specifying the value or values upon which it is to perform its computation, and it may also return a value that represents the results of that computation. JavaScript implementations provide many predefined functions, such as the Math.sin( ) function that computes the sine of an angle.

JavaScript programs may also define their own functions with code that looks like this:

```
function square(x) // The function is named square. It expects one argument, x.
{                  // The body of the function begins here.
  return x*x;      // The function squares its argument and returns that value.
}                  // The function ends here.
```

Once a function is defined, you can invoke it by following the function's name with an optional comma-separated list of arguments within parentheses. The following lines are function invocations:

```
y = Math.sin(x);
y = square(x);
d = compute_distance(x1, y1, z1, x2, y2, z2);
move( );
```

An important feature of JavaScript is that functions are values that can be manipulated by JavaScript code. In many languages, including Java, functions are only a syntactic feature of the language: they can be defined and invoked, but they are not datatypes. The fact that functions are true values in JavaScript gives a lot of flexibility to the language. It means that functions can be stored in variables, arrays, and objects, and it means that functions can be passed as arguments to other functions. This can quite often be useful. Defining and invoking functions, as well as how to use them as data values, are discussed in Chapter 8.

Since functions are values just like numbers and strings, they can be assigned to object properties just as other values can. When a function is assigned to a property of an object (the object datatype and object properties are described in Section 3.5), it is often referred to as a *method* of that object. Methods are an important part of object-oriented programming. You'll see more about them in Chapter 7.

3.4.1 Function Literals

The preceding section defined a function called square( ). The syntax shown there is used to define most functions in most JavaScript programs. However, JavaScript also provides a syntax for defining function literals. A function literal is defined with the function keyword, followed by an optional function name, followed by a parenthesized list of function arguments, and then the body of the function within curly braces. In other words, a function literal looks just like a function definition, except that it does not have to have a name. The big difference is that function literals can appear within other JavaScript expressions. Thus, instead of defining the function square( ) with a function definition:

```
function square(x) { return x*x; }
```

it can be defined with a function literal:

```
var square = function(x) { return x*x; }
```

Functions defined in this way are sometimes called *lambda functions* in homage to the Lisp programming language, which was one of the first to allow unnamed functions to be embedded as literal data values within a program. Although it is not immediately obvious why you might choose to use function literals in a program, I'll show you later how in advanced scripts, they can be quite convenient and useful.

There is one other way to define a function: you can pass the argument list and the body of the function as strings to the Function( ) constructor. For example:

```
var square = new Function("x", "return x*x;");
```

Defining a function in this way is not often useful. It is usually awkward to express the function body as a string, and in many JavaScript implementations, functions defined in this way are less efficient than functions defined in either of the other two ways.

3.5 Objects

An *object* is a collection of named values. These named values are usually referred to as *properties* of the object. (Sometimes they are called *fields* of the object, but this usage can be confusing.) To refer to a property of an object, you refer to the object, followed by a period and the name of the property. For example, if an object named image has properties named width and height, you can refer to those properties like this:

```
image.width
image.height
```

Properties of objects are, in many ways, just like JavaScript variables; they can contain any type of data, including arrays, functions, and other objects. Thus, you might see JavaScript code like this:

```
document.myform.button
```

This code refers to the button property of an object that is itself stored in the myform property of an object named document.

As mentioned earlier, when a function value is stored in a property of an object, that function is often called a method, and the property name becomes the method name. To invoke a method of an object, use the . syntax to extract the function value from the object and then use the ( ) syntax to invoke that function. For example, to invoke the write( ) method of an object named document, you can use code like this:

```
document.write("this is a test");
```

Objects in JavaScript can serve as associative arrays; that is, they can associate arbitrary data values with arbitrary strings. When an object is used in this way, a different syntax is generally required to access the object's properties: a string containing the name of the desired property is enclosed within square brackets. Using this syntax, you can access the properties of the image object mentioned previously with code like this:

```
image["width"]
image["height"]
```

Associative arrays are a powerful datatype; they are useful for a number of programming techniques. I describe objects in their traditional and associative array usages in Chapter 7.

3.5.1 Creating Objects

As you'll see in Chapter 7, objects are created by invoking special *constructor* functions. For example, the following lines all create new objects:

```
var o = new Object();
var now = new Date();
var pattern = new RegExp("\\sjava\\s", "i");
```

Once you have created an object of your own, you can use and set its properties however you desire:

```
var point = new Object();
point.x = 2.3;
point.y = -1.2;
```

3.5.2 Object Literals

JavaScript defines an object literal syntax that allows you to create an object and specify its properties. An object literal (also called an object initializer) consists of a comma-separated list of colon-separated property/value pairs, all enclosed within curly braces. Thus, the object point in the previous code can also be created and initialized with this line:

```
var point = { x:2.3, y:-1.2 };
```

Object literals can also be nested. For example:

```
var rectangle = { upperLeft: { x: 2, y: 2 },
                  lowerRight: { x: 4, y: 4}
                };
```

Finally, the property values used in object literals need not be constants; they can be arbitrary JavaScript expressions. Also, the property names in object literals may be strings rather than identifiers:

```
var square = { "upperLeft": { x:point.x, y:point.y },
               'lowerRight': { x:(point.x + side), y:(point.y+side) }};
```

3.5.3 Object Conversions

When a non-null object is used in a Boolean context, it converts to true. When an object is used in a string context, JavaScript calls the toString( ) method of the object and uses the string value returned by that method. When an object is used in a numeric context, JavaScript first calls the valueOf( ) method of the object. If this method returns a primitive value, that value is used. In most cases, however, the valueOf( ) method returns the object itself. In this case, JavaScript first converts the object to a string with the toString( ) method and then attempts to convert the string to a number.

Object-to-primitive type conversion has some quirks, and we'll return to this topic at the end of this chapter.

3.6   Arrays

An *array* is a collection of data values, just as an object is. While each data value contained in an object has a name, each data value in an array has a number, or *index*. In JavaScript, you retrieve a value from an array by enclosing an index in square brackets after the array name. For example, if an array is named a and i is a nonnegative integer, a[i] is an element of the array. Array indexes begin with zero; thus, a[2] refers to the *third* element of the array a.

Arrays may contain any type of JavaScript data, including references to other arrays or to objects or functions. For example:

```
document.images[1].width
```

This code refers to the width property of an object stored in the second element of an array stored in the images property of the document object.

Note that the arrays described here differ from the associative arrays described in Section 3.5. The regular arrays we are discussing here are indexed by nonnegative integers. Associative arrays are indexed by strings. Also note that JavaScript does not support multidimensional arrays, except as arrays of arrays. Finally, because Java-Script is an untyped language, the elements of an array do not all need to be of the same type, as they do in typed languages like Java. Arrays are discussed further in Chapter 7.

3.6.1   Creating Arrays

Arrays can be created with the Array( ) constructor function. Once created, any number of indexed elements can easily be assigned to the array:

```
var a = new Array( );
a[0] = 1.2;
a[1] = "JavaScript";
a[2] = true;
a[3] = { x:1, y:3 };
```

Arrays can also be initialized by passing array elements to the Array( ) constructor. Thus, the previous array creation and initialization code can also be written:

```
var a = new Array(1.2, "JavaScript", true, { x:1, y:3 });
```

If you pass only a single number to the Array( ) constructor, it specifies the length of the array. Thus:

```
var a = new Array(10);
```

creates a new array with 10 undefined elements.

3.6.2   Array Literals

JavaScript defines a literal syntax for creating and initializing arrays. An array literal (or array initializer) is a comma-separated list of values contained within square brackets. The values within the brackets are assigned sequentially to array indexes starting with zero. For example, the array creation and initialization code in the previous section can also be written as:

```
var a = [1.2, "JavaScript", true, { x:1, y:3 }];
```

Like object literals, array literals can be nested:

```
var matrix = [[1,2,3], [4,5,6], [7,8,9]];
```

Also, as with object literals, the elements in array literals can be arbitrary expressions and need not be restricted to constants:

```
var base = 1024;
var table = [base, base+1, base+2, base+3];
```

Undefined elements can be included in an array literal by simply omitting a value between commas. For example, the following array contains five elements, including three undefined elements:

```
var sparseArray = [1,,,,5];
```

3.7   null

The JavaScript keyword null is a special value that indicates no value. null is usually considered a special value of object type—a value that represents no object. null is a unique value, distinct from all other values. When a variable holds the value null, you know that it does not contain a valid object, array, number, string, or boolean value.[*]

When null is used in a Boolean context, it converts to false. When used in a numeric context, it converts to 0. And when used in a string context, it converts to "null".

3.8   undefined

Another special value used occasionally by JavaScript is the undefined value. undefined is returned when you use either a variable that has been declared but never had a value assigned to it or an object property that does not exist. Note that this special undefined value is not the same as null.

Although null and the undefined value are distinct, the == equality operator considers them equal to one another. Consider the following:

```
my.prop == null
```

This comparison is true if either the my.prop property does not exist or it does exist but contains the value null. Since both null and the undefined value indicate an absence of value, this equality is often what we want. However, if you truly must distinguish between a null value and an undefined value, use the === identity operator or the typeof operator (see Chapter 5 for details).

Unlike null, undefined is not a reserved word in JavaScript. The ECMAScript v3 standard specifies that there is always a global variable named undefined whose initial value is the undefined value. Thus, in a conforming implementation, you can treat undefined as a keyword, as long as you don't assign a value to the variable.

If you are not sure that your implementation has the undefined variable, you can simply declare your own:

```
var undefined;
```

---

[*] C and C++ programmers should note that null in JavaScript is not the same as 0, as it is in those languages. null is automatically converted to 0, but the two are not equivalent.

By declaring but not initializing the variable, you assure your implementation has the undefined value. The void operator (see Chapter 5) provides another way to obtain the undefined value.

When the undefined value is used in a Boolean context, it converts to false. When used in a numeric context, it converts to NaN. And when used in a string context, it converts to "undefined".

3.9   The Date Object

The previous sections have described all the fundamental datatypes supported by JavaScript. Date and time values are not one of these fundamental types, but JavaScript does provide a class of object that represents dates and times and can be used to manipulate this type of data. A Date object in JavaScript is created with the new operator and the Date() constructor (the new operator is introduced in Chapter 5, and you'll learn more about object creation in Chapter 7):

```
var now = new Date();  // Create an object holding the current date and time.
// Create a Date object representing Christmas.
// Note that months are zero-based, so December is month 11!
var xmas = new Date(2006, 11, 25);
```

Methods of the Date object allow you to get and set the various date and time values and to convert the Date to a string, using either local time or GMT time. For example:

```
xmas.setFullYear(xmas.getFullYear() + 1); // Change the date to next Christmas.
var weekday = xmas.getDay();              // It falls on a Tuesday in 2007.
document.write("Today is: " + now.toLocaleString());  // Current date/time.
```

The Date object also defines functions (not methods; they are not invoked through a Date object) to convert a date specified in string or numeric form to an internal millisecond representation that is useful for some kinds of date arithmetic.

You can find full documentation on the Date object and its methods in Part III.

3.10   Regular Expressions

Regular expressions provide a rich and powerful syntax for describing textual patterns; they are used for pattern matching and for implementing search and replace operations. JavaScript has adopted the Perl programming language syntax for expressing regular expressions.

Regular expressions are represented in JavaScript by the RegExp object and may be created using the RegExp() constructor. Like the Date object, the RegExp object is not one of the fundamental datatypes of JavaScript; it is simply a specialized kind of object provided by all conforming JavaScript implementations.

Unlike the Date object, however, RegExp objects have a literal syntax and can be encoded directly into JavaScript programs. Text between a pair of slashes constitutes a regular expression literal. The second slash in the pair can also be followed by one or more letters, which modify the meaning of the pattern. For example:

```
/^HTML/
/[1-9][0-9]*/
/\bjavascript\b/i
```

The regular-expression grammar is complex and is documented in detail in Chapter 11. At this point, you need only know what a regular expression literal looks like in JavaScript code.

3.11 Error Objects

ECMAScript v3 defines a number of classes that represent errors. The JavaScript interpreter "throws" an object of one of these types when a runtime error occurs. (See the throw and try statements in Chapter 6 for a discussion of throwing and catching errors.) Each error object has a message property that contains an implementation-specific error message. The types of predefined error objects are Error, EvalError, RangeError, ReferenceError, SyntaxError, TypeError, and URIError. You can find out more about these classes in Part III.

3.12 Type Conversion Summary

As each datatype has been described in the previous sections, I've discussed how values of each type convert into values of other types. The basic rule is that when a value of one type is used in a context that requires a value of some other type, Java-Script automatically attempts to convert the value as needed. So, for example, if a number is used in a Boolean context, it is converted to a boolean. If an object is used in a string context, it is converted to a string. If a string is used in a numeric context, JavaScript attempts to convert it to a number. Table 3-3 summarizes each of these conversions and shows the conversion that is performed when a particular type of value is used in a particular context.

Table 3-3. Automatic datatype conversions

Value	Context in which value is used			
	String	**Number**	**Boolean**	**Object**
Undefined value	`"undefined"`	NaN	`false`	Error
null	`"null"`	0	`false`	Error
Nonempty string	As is	Numeric value of string or NaN	`true`	String object
Empty string	As is	0	`false`	String object
0	`"0"`	As is	`false`	Number object
NaN	`"NaN"`	As is	`false`	Number object

Table 3-3. Automatic datatype conversions (continued)

Value	Context in which value is used			
	String	Number	Boolean	Object
Infinity	`"Infinity"`	As is	true	Number object
Negative infinity	`"-Infinity"`	As is	true	Number object
Any other number	String value of number	As is	true	Number object
true	`"true"`	1	As is	Boolean object
false	`"false"`	0	As is	Boolean object
Object	`toString()`	`valueOf()`, `toString()`, or NaN	true	As is

3.13 Primitive Datatype Wrapper Objects

When we discussed strings earlier in this chapter, I pointed out a strange feature of that datatype: to operate on strings, you use object notation.[*] For example, a typical operation involving strings might look like the following:

```
var s = "These are the times that try people's souls.";
var last_word = s.substring(s.lastIndexOf(" ")+1, s.length);
```

If you didn't know better, it would appear that s was an object and that you were invoking methods and reading property values of that object.

What's going on? Are strings objects, or are they primitive datatypes? The typeof operator (see Chapter 5) assures us that strings have the datatype "string", which is distinct from the datatype "object". Why, then, are strings manipulated using object notation?

The truth is that a corresponding object class is defined for each of the three key primitive datatypes. That is, besides supporting the number, string, and boolean datatypes, JavaScript also supports Number, String, and Boolean classes. These classes are wrappers around the primitive datatypes. A *wrapper* contains the same primitive data value, but it also defines properties and methods that can be used to manipulate that data.

JavaScript can flexibly convert values from one type to another. When you use a string in an object context—i.e., when you try to access a property or method of the string—JavaScript internally creates a String wrapper object for the string value. This String object is used in place of the primitive string value. The object has properties and methods defined, so the use of the primitive value in an object context succeeds. The same is true, of course, for the other primitive types and their corresponding

[*] This section covers advanced material, which you may want to skip on your first reading.

wrapper objects; you just don't use the other types in an object context nearly as often as you use strings in that context.

Note that the String object created when you use a string in an object context is a transient one; it allows you to access a property or method, and then it is no longer needed, so it is reclaimed by the system. Suppose s is a string and the length of the string is determined with a line like this:

```
var len = s.length;
```

In this case, s remains a string; the original string value itself is not changed. A new transient String object is created, which allows you to access the length property, and then the transient object is discarded, with no change to the original value s. If you think this scheme sounds elegant and bizarrely complex at the same time, you are right. Typically, however, JavaScript implementations perform this internal conversion very efficiently, and it is not something you should worry about.

If you want to use a String object explicitly in your program, you have to create a nontransient one that is not automatically discarded by the system. String objects are created just like other objects, with the new operator. For example:

```
var s = "hello world";          // A primitive string value
var S = new String("Hello World");  // A String object
```

Once you've created a String object S, what can you do with it? Nothing that can't be done with the corresponding primitive string value. If you use the typeof operator, it says that S is indeed an object and not a string value, but except for that case, you'll find that you can't normally distinguish between a primitive string and the String object.* As I've already shown, strings are automatically converted to String objects whenever necessary. It turns out that the reverse is also true. Whenever you use a String object where a primitive string value is expected, JavaScript automatically converts the String to a string. So if you use a String object with the + operator, a transient primitive string value is created so that the string concatenation operation can be performed:

```
msg = S + '!';
```

Bear in mind that everything discussed in this section about string values and String objects applies also to number and boolean values, and their corresponding Number and Boolean objects. You can learn more about the Number and Boolean classes from their respective entries in Part III.

Finally, note that any number, string, or boolean value can be converted to its corresponding wrapper object with the Object( ) function:

```
var number_wrapper = Object(3);
```

---

* Note, however, that the eval( ) method treats string values and String objects differently, and it will not behave as you expect it to if you inadvertently pass it a String object instead of a primitive string value.

3.14 Object-to-Primitive Conversion

Objects can usually be converted to primitive values in the straightforward way described in Section 3.5.3. Several details of this conversion require additional discussion, however.[*]

First, note that whenever a non-null object is used in a Boolean context, it converts to true. This is true for all objects (including arrays and functions), even for all wrapper objects that represent primitive values that convert to false. For example, all the following objects convert to true when used in a Boolean context:

```
new Boolean(false)  // Internal value is false, but object converts to true
new Number(0)
new String("")
new Array()
```

Table 3-3 showed that objects are converted to numbers by first calling the valueOf( ) method of the object. Most objects inherit the default valueOf( ) method of Object, which simply returns the object itself. Since the default valueOf( ) method does not return a primitive value, JavaScript next tries to convert the object to a number by calling its toString( ) method and converting the resulting string to a number.

This leads to interesting results for arrays. The toString( ) method of arrays converts the array elements to strings, then returns the result of concatenating these strings, with commas in between. Therefore, an array with no elements converts to the empty string, which converts to the number zero! Also, if an array has a single element that is a number n, the array converts to a string representation of n, which is then converted back to n itself. If an array contains more than one element, or if its one element is not a number, the array converts to NaN.

The conversion of a value depends on the context in which it is used. There are a couple of circumstances in JavaScript in which the context is ambiguous. The + operator and the comparison operators (<, <=, >, and >=) operate on both numbers and strings, so when an object is used with one of these operators, it is not clear whether it should be converted to a number or a string. In most cases, JavaScript first attempts to convert the object by calling its valueOf( ) method. If this method returns a primitive value (usually a number), that value is used. Often, however, valueOf( ) simply returns the unconverted object; in this case, JavaScript then tries to convert the object to a string by calling its toString( ) method.

But there is one exception to this conversion rule: when a Date object is used with the + operator, the conversion is performed with the toString( ) method. This exception exists because Date has both toString( ) and valueOf( ) methods. When a Date is used with +, you almost always want to perform a string concatenation. But when

---

[*] This section covers advanced material, which you may want to skip on your first reading.

using a Date with the comparison operators, you almost always want to perform a numeric comparison to determine which of two times is earlier than the other.

Most objects either don't have valueOf( ) methods or don't have valueOf( ) methods that return useful results. When you use an object with the + operator, you usually get string concatenation rather than addition. When you use an object with a comparison operator, you usually get string comparison rather than numeric comparison.

An object that defines a custom valueOf( ) method may behave differently. If you define a valueOf( ) method that returns a number, you can use arithmetic and other operators with your object, but adding your object to a string may not achieve the desired result: the toString( ) method is no longer called, and a string representation of the number returned by valueOf( ) is concatenated to the string.

Finally, remember that valueOf( ) is not called toNumber( ); strictly speaking, its job is to convert an object to a reasonable primitive value, so some objects may have valueOf( ) methods that return strings.

3.15 By Value Versus by Reference

In JavaScript, as in all programming languages, you can manipulate a data value in three important ways.[*] First, you can copy it. For example, you might assign it to a new variable. Second, you can pass it as an argument to a function or method. Third, you can compare it with another value to see whether the two values are equal. To understand any programming language, you must understand how these three operations are performed in that language.

There are two fundamentally distinct ways to manipulate data values. These techniques are called *by value* and *by reference*. When a datum is manipulated by value, it is the *value* of the datum that matters. In an assignment, a copy of the actual value is made, and that copy is stored in a variable, object property, or array element; the copy and the original are two totally independent values that are stored separately. When a datum is passed by value to a function, a copy of the datum is passed to the function; if the function modifies the value, the change affects only the function's copy of the datum—it does not affect the original datum. Finally, when a datum is compared by value to another datum, the two distinct pieces of data must represent exactly the same value (which usually means that a byte-by-byte comparison finds them to be equal).

The other way to manipulate a value is by reference. With this technique, there is only one actual copy of the value; references to that value are manipulated.[†] If a

---

[*] This section covers advanced material, which you may want to skip on your first reading.

[†] C programmers and anyone else familiar with the concept of pointers should understand the idea of a reference in this context. Note, however, that JavaScript does not support pointers.

value is manipulated by reference, variables do not hold that value directly; they hold only references to it. It is these references that are copied, passed, and compared. So, in an assignment made by reference, it is the reference to the value that is assigned, not a copy of the value and not the value itself. After the assignment, the new variable refers to the same value that the original variable refers to. Both references are equally valid, and both can be used to manipulate the value; if the value is changed through one reference, that change also appears through the original reference. The situation is similar when a value is passed to a function by reference. A reference to the value is passed to the function, and the function can use that reference to modify the value itself; any such modifications are visible outside the function. Finally, when a value is compared to another by reference, the two references are compared to see if they refer to the same unique copy of a value; references to two distinct values that happen to be equivalent (i.e., consist of the same bytes) are not treated as equal.

These are two very different ways of manipulating values, and they have important implications that you should understand. Table 3-4 summarizes these implications. This discussion of manipulating data by value and by reference has been a general one, but the distinctions apply to all programming languages. The sections that follow explain how these distinctions apply specifically to JavaScript; they discuss which datatypes are manipulated by value and which are manipulated by reference.

Table 3-4. By value versus by reference

	By value	By reference
Copy	The value is actually copied; there are two distinct, independent copies.	Only a reference to the value is copied. If the value is modified through the new reference, that change is also visible through the original reference.
Pass	A distinct copy of the value is passed to the function; changes to it have no effect outside the function.	A reference to the value is passed to the function. If the function modifies the value through the passed reference, the modification is visible outside the function.
Compare	Two distinct values are compared (often byte by byte) to see if they are the same value.	Two references are compared to see if they refer to the same value. Two references to distinct values are not equal, even if the two values consist of the same bytes.

3.15.1 Primitive Types and Reference Types

The basic rule in JavaScript is this: *primitive types* are manipulated by value, and *reference types*, as the name suggests, are manipulated by reference. Numbers and booleans are primitive types in JavaScript—primitive because they consist of nothing more than a small, fixed number of bytes that are easily manipulated at the low levels of the JavaScript interpreter. Objects, on the other hand, are reference types. Arrays and functions, which are specialized types of objects, are therefore also reference types. These datatypes can contain arbitrary numbers of properties or elements, so they cannot be manipulated as easily as fixed-size primitive values can.

Since object and array values can become quite large, it doesn't make sense to manipulate these types by value, because this could involve the inefficient copying and comparing of large amounts of memory.

What about strings? A string can have an arbitrary length, so it would seem that strings should be reference types. In fact, though, they are usually considered primitive types in JavaScript simply because they are not objects. Strings don't actually fit into the primitive-versus-reference type dichotomy. I'll explain more about strings and their behavior a little later.

The best way to explore the differences between data manipulation by value and by reference is through example. Study the following examples carefully, paying attention to the comments. Example 3-1 copies, passes, and compares numbers. Since numbers are primitive types, this example illustrates data manipulation by value.

Example 3-1. Copying, passing, and comparing by value

```
// First we illustrate copying by value
var n = 1;  // Variable n holds the value 1
var m = n;  // Copy by value: variable m holds a distinct value 1

// Here's a function we'll use to illustrate passing by value
// As we'll see, the function doesn't work the way we'd like it to
function add_to_total(total, x)
{
    total = total + x;  // This line changes only the internal copy of total
}

// Now call the function, passing the numbers contained in n and m by value.
// The value of n is copied, and that copied value is named total within the
// function. The function adds a copy of m to that copy of n. But adding
// something to a copy of n doesn't affect the original value of n outside
// of the function. So calling this function doesn't accomplish anything.
add_to_total(n, m);

// Now, we'll look at comparison by value.
// In the following line of code, the literal 1 is clearly a distinct numeric
// value encoded in the program. We compare it to the value held in variable
// n. In comparison by value, the bytes of the two numbers are checked to
// see if they are the same.
if (n == 1) m = 2;  // n contains the same value as the literal 1; m is now 2
```

Now, consider Example 3-2. This example copies, passes, and compares an object. Since objects are reference types, these manipulations are performed by reference. This example uses Date objects, which you can read more about in Part III.

Example 3-2. Copying, passing, and comparing by reference

```
// Here we create an object representing the date of Christmas, 2007
// The variable xmas contains a reference to the object, not the object itself
var xmas = new Date(2007, 11, 25);
```

Example 3-2. Copying, passing, and comparing by reference (continued)

```
// When we copy by reference, we get a new reference to the original object
var solstice = xmas;  // Both variables now refer to the same object value

// Here we change the object through our new reference to it
solstice.setDate(21);

// The change is visible through the original reference, as well
xmas.getDate();  // Returns 21, not the original value of 25

// The same is true when objects and arrays are passed to functions.
// The following function adds a value to each element of an array.
// A reference to the array is passed to the function, not a copy of the array.
// Therefore, the function can change the contents of the array through
// the reference, and those changes will be visible when the function returns.
function add_to_totals(totals, x)
{
    totals[0] = totals[0] + x;
    totals[1] = totals[1] + x;
    totals[2] = totals[2] + x;
}

// Finally, we'll examine comparison by reference.
// When we compare the two variables defined above, we find they are
// equal, because they refer to the same object, even though we were trying
// to make them refer to different dates:
(xmas == solstice)  // Evaluates to true

// The two variables defined next refer to two distinct objects, both
// of which represent exactly the same date.
var xmas = new Date(2007, 11, 25);
var solstice_plus_4 = new Date(2007, 11, 25);

// But, by the rules of "compare by reference," distinct objects are not equal!
(xmas != solstice_plus_4)  // Evaluates to true
```

Before we leave the topic of manipulating objects and arrays by reference, let's clear up a point of nomenclature. The phrase "pass by reference" can have several meanings. To some readers, the phrase refers to a function-invocation technique that allows a function to assign new values to its arguments and to have those modified values visible outside the function. This is not the way the term is used in this book. Here, I mean simply that a reference to an object or array—not the object itself—is passed to a function. A function can use the reference to modify properties of the object or elements of the array. But if the function overwrites the reference with a reference to a new object or array, that modification is not visible outside the function. Readers familiar with the other meaning of this term may prefer to say that objects and arrays are passed by value, but the value that is passed is actually a reference rather than the object itself. Example 3-3 illustrates this issue.

..

Example 3-3. References themselves are passed by value

```
// This is another version of the add_to_totals() function. It doesn't
// work, though, because instead of changing the array itself, it tries to
// change the reference to the array.
function add_to_totals2(totals, x)
{
    newtotals = new Array(3);
    newtotals[0] = totals[0] + x;
    newtotals[1] = totals[1] + x;
    newtotals[2] = totals[2] + x;
    totals = newtotals;  // This line has no effect outside of the function
}
```

3.15.2 Copying and Passing Strings

As mentioned earlier, JavaScript strings don't fit neatly into the primitive-versus-reference type dichotomy. Since strings are not objects, it is natural to assume that they are primitive. If they are primitive types, then by the rules given above, they should be manipulated by value. But since strings can be arbitrarily long, it would seem inefficient to copy, pass, and compare them byte by byte. Therefore, it would also be natural to assume that strings are implemented as reference types.

Instead of making assumptions about strings, let's write some JavaScript code to experiment with string manipulation. If strings are copied and passed by reference, you should be able to modify the contents of a string through the reference stored in another variable or passed to a function.

When setting out to write the code to perform this experiment, however, you'll run into a major stumbling block: there is no way to modify the contents of a string. The charAt( ) method returns the character at a given position in a string, but there is no corresponding setCharAt( ) method. This is not an oversight. JavaScript strings are intentionally *immutable*—that is, there is no JavaScript syntax, method, or property that allows you to change the characters in a string.

Since strings are immutable, the original question is moot: there is no way to tell whether strings are passed by value or by reference. You can assume that, for efficiency, JavaScript is implemented so that strings are passed by reference, but in actuality it doesn't matter, because it has no practical bearing on the code you write.

3.15.3 Comparing Strings

Despite the fact that you cannot determine whether strings are copied and passed by value or by reference, you can write JavaScript code to determine whether they are compared by value or by reference. Example 3-4 shows the code that can make this determination.

Example 3-4. Are strings compared by value or by reference?

```
// Determining whether strings are compared by value or reference is easy.
// We compare two clearly distinct strings that happen to contain the same
// characters. If they are compared by value they will be equal, but if they
// are compared by reference, they will not be equal:
var s1 = "hello";
var s2 = "hell" + "o";
if (s1 == s2) document.write("Strings compared by value");
```

This experiment demonstrates that strings are compared by value. This may be surprising to some programmers. In C, C++, and Java, strings are reference types and are compared by reference. If you want to compare the actual contents of two strings, you must use a special method or function. JavaScript, however, is a higher-level language and recognizes that when you compare strings, you most often want to compare them by value. Thus, despite the fact that, for efficiency, JavaScript strings are (presumably) copied and passed by reference, they are compared by value.

3.15.4 By Value Versus by Reference: Summary

Table 3-5 summarizes the way that the various JavaScript types are manipulated.

Table 3-5. Datatype manipulation in JavaScript

Type	Copied by	Passed by	Compared by
number	Value	Value	Value
boolean	Value	Value	Value
string	Immutable	Immutable	Value
object	Reference	Reference	Reference

CHAPTER 4

Variables

A *variable* is a name associated with a value; we say that the variable stores or contains the value. Variables allow you to store and manipulate data in your programs. For example, the following line of JavaScript assigns the value 2 to a variable named i:

```
i = 2;
```

And the following line adds 3 to i and assigns the result to a new variable, sum:

```
var sum = i + 3;
```

These two lines of code demonstrate just about everything you need to know about variables. However, to fully understand how variables work in JavaScript, you need to master a few more concepts. Unfortunately, these concepts require more than a couple of lines of code to explain! The rest of this chapter explains the typing, declaration, scope, contents, and resolution of variables. It also explores garbage collection and the variable/property duality.*

4.1 Variable Typing

An important difference between JavaScript and languages such as Java and C is that JavaScript is *untyped*. This means, in part, that a JavaScript variable can hold a value of any datatype, unlike a Java or C variable, which can hold only the one particular type of data for which it is declared. For example, it is perfectly legal in JavaScript to assign a number to a variable and then later assign a string to that variable:

```
i = 10;
i = "ten";
```

In C, C++, Java, or any other strongly typed language, code like this is illegal.

---

* These are tricky concepts, and a complete understanding of this chapter requires an understanding of concepts introduced in later chapters of the book. If you are relatively new to programming, you may want to read only the first two sections of this chapter and then move on to Chapters 5, 6, and 7 before returning to finish up the remainder of this chapter.

A feature related to JavaScript's lack of typing is that the language conveniently and automatically converts values from one type to another, as necessary. If you attempt to append a number to a string, for example, JavaScript automatically converts the number to the corresponding string so that it can be appended. Datatype conversion is covered in detail in Chapter 3.

JavaScript is obviously a simpler language for being untyped. The advantage of strongly typed languages such as C++ and Java is that they enforce rigorous programming practices, which makes it easier to write, maintain, and reuse long, complex programs. Since many JavaScript programs are shorter scripts, this rigor is not necessary, and we benefit from the simpler syntax.

4.2   Variable Declaration

Before you use a variable in a JavaScript program, you must *declare* it.* Variables are declared with the var keyword, like this:

```
var i;
var sum;
```

You can also declare multiple variables with the same var keyword:

```
var i, sum;
```

And you can combine variable declaration with variable initialization:

```
var message = "hello";
var i = 0, j = 0, k = 0;
```

If you don't specify an initial value for a variable with the var statement, the variable is declared, but its initial value is undefined until your code stores a value into it.

Note that the var statement can also appear as part of the for and for/in loops (introduced in Chapter 6), allowing you to succinctly declare the loop variable as part of the loop syntax itself. For example:

```
for(var i = 0; i < 10; i++) document.write(i, "<br>");
for(var i = 0, j=10; i < 10; i++,j--) document.write(i*j, "<br>");
for(var i in o) document.write(i, "<br>");
```

Variables declared with var are *permanent*: attempting to delete them with the delete operator causes an error. (The delete operator is introduced in Chapter 5.)

---

* If you don't declare a variable explicitly, JavaScript will declare it implicitly for you.

4.2.1 Repeated and Omitted Declarations

It is legal and harmless to declare a variable more than once with the var statement. If the repeated declaration has an initializer, it acts as if it were simply an assignment statement.

If you attempt to read the value of an undeclared variable, JavaScript generates an error. If you assign a value to a variable that you have not declared with var, Java-Script implicitly declares that variable for you. Note, however, that implicitly declared variables are always created as global variables, even if they are used within the body of a function. To prevent the creation of a global variable (or the use of an existing global variable) when you meant to create a local variable to use within a single function, you must always use the var statement within function bodies. It's best to use var for all variables, whether global or local. (The distinction between local and global variables is explored in more detail in the next section.)

4.3 Variable Scope

The *scope* of a variable is the region of your program in which it is defined. A *global* variable has global scope; it is defined everywhere in your JavaScript code. On the other hand, variables declared within a function are defined only within the body of the function. They are *local* variables and have local scope. Function parameters also count as local variables and are defined only within the body of the function.

Within the body of a function, a local variable takes precedence over a global variable with the same name. If you declare a local variable or function parameter with the same name as a global variable, you effectively hide the global variable. For example, the following code prints the word "local":

```
var scope = "global";        // Declare a global variable
function checkscope() {
    var scope = "local";     // Declare a local variable with the same name
    document.write(scope);   // Use the local variable, not the global one
}
checkscope();                // Prints "local"
```

Although you can get away with not using the var statement when you write code in the global scope, you must always use var to declare local variables. Consider what happens if you don't:

```
scope = "global";            // Declare a global variable, even without var
function checkscope() {
    scope = "local";         // Oops! We just changed the global variable
    document.write(scope);   // Uses the global variable
    myscope = "local";       // This implicitly declares a new global variable
    document.write(myscope); // Uses the new global variable
}
checkscope();                // Prints "locallocal"
document.write(scope);       // This prints "local"
document.write(myscope);     // This prints "local"
```

In general, functions do not know what variables are defined in the global scope or what they are being used for. Thus, if a function uses a global variable instead of a local one, it runs the risk of changing a value on which some other part of the program relies. Fortunately, avoiding this problem is simple: declare all variables with var.

Function definitions can be nested. Each function has its own local scope, so it is possible to have several nested layers of local scope. For example:

```
var scope = "global scope";      // A global variable
function checkscope() {
    var scope = "local scope";   // A local variable
    function nested() {
        var scope = "nested scope";  // A nested scope of local variables
        document.write(scope);       // Prints "nested scope"
    }
    nested();
}
checkscope();
```

4.3.1 No Block Scope

Note that unlike C, C++, and Java, JavaScript does not have block-level scope. All variables declared in a function, no matter where they are declared, are defined *throughout* the function. In the following code, the variables i, j, and k all have the same scope: all three are defined throughout the body of the function. This would not be the case if the code were written in C, C++, or Java:

```
function test(o) {
    var i = 0;                  // i is defined throughout function
    if (typeof o == "object") {
        var j = 0;              // j is defined everywhere, not just block
        for(var k=0; k < 10; k++) { // k is defined everywhere, not just loop
            document.write(k);
        }
        document.write(k);      // k is still defined: prints 10
    }
    document.write(j);          // j is defined, but may not be initialized
}
```

The rule that all variables declared in a function are defined throughout the function can cause surprising results. The following code illustrates this:

```
var scope = "global";
function f() {
    alert(scope);              // Displays "undefined", not "global"
    var scope = "local";       // Variable initialized here, but defined everywhere
    alert(scope);              // Displays "local"
}
f();
```

You might think that the first call to alert( ) would display "global", because the var statement declaring the local variable has not yet been executed. Because of the scope rules, however, this is not what happens. The local variable is defined throughout the body of the function, which means the global variable by the same name is hidden throughout the function. Although the local variable is defined throughout, it is not actually initialized until the var statement is executed. Thus, the function f in the previous example is equivalent to the following:

```
function f() {
    var scope;       // Local variable is declared at the start of the function
    alert(scope);    // It exists here, but still has "undefined" value
    scope = "local"; // Now we initialize it and give it a value
    alert(scope);    // And here it has a value
}
```

This example illustrates why it is good programming practice to place all your variable declarations together at the start of any function.

4.3.2   Undefined Versus Unassigned

The examples in the previous section demonstrate a subtle point in JavaScript programming: there are two different kinds of undefined variables. The first kind of undefined variable is one that has never been declared. An attempt to read the value of such an *undeclared variable* causes a runtime error. Undeclared variables are undefined because they simply do not exist. As described earlier, assigning a value to an undeclared variable does not cause an error; instead, it implicitly declares the variable in the global scope.

The second kind of undefined variable is one that has been declared but has never had a value assigned to it. If you read the value of one of these variables, you obtain its default value, undefined. This type of undefined variable might more usefully be called *unassigned*, to distinguish it from the more serious kind of undefined variable that has not even been declared and does not exist.

The following code fragment illustrates some of the differences between truly undefined and merely unassigned variables:

```
var x;      // Declare an unassigned variable. Its value is undefined.
alert(u);   // Using an undeclared variable causes an error.
u = 3;      // Assigning a value to an undeclared variable creates the variable.
```

4.4   Primitive Types and Reference Types

The next topic we need to consider is the content of variables. We often say that variables have or contain values. But just what is it that they contain? To answer this seemingly simple question, we must look again at the datatypes supported by JavaScript. The types can be divided into two groups: primitive types and reference types.

Numbers, boolean values, and the null and undefined types are primitive. Objects, arrays, and functions are reference types.

A primitive type has a fixed size in memory. For example, a number occupies eight bytes of memory, and a boolean value can be represented with only one bit. The number type is the largest of the primitive types. If each JavaScript variable reserves eight bytes of memory, the variable can directly hold any primitive value.*

Reference types are another matter, however. Objects, for example, can be of any length: they do not have a fixed size. The same is true of arrays: an array can have any number of elements. Similarly, a function can contain any amount of JavaScript code. Since these types do not have a fixed size, their values cannot be stored directly in the eight bytes of memory associated with each variable. Instead, the variable stores a *reference* to the value. Typically, this reference is some form of pointer or memory address. It is not the data value itself, but it tells the variable where to look to find the value.

The distinction between primitive and reference types is an important one because they behave differently. Consider the following code that uses numbers (a primitive type):

```
var a = 3.14;   // Declare and initialize a variable
var b = a;      // Copy the variable's value to a new variable
a = 4;          // Modify the value of the original variable
alert(b)        // Displays 3.14; the copy has not changed
```

There is nothing surprising about this code. Now consider what happens if we change the code slightly so that it uses arrays (a reference type) instead of numbers:

```
var a = [1,2,3];  // Initialize a variable to refer to an array
var b = a;        // Copy that reference into a new variable
a[0] = 99;        // Modify the array using the original reference
alert(b);         // Display the changed array [99,2,3] using the new reference
```

If this result does not seem surprising to you, you're already well familiar with the distinction between primitive and reference types. If it does seem surprising, take a closer look at the second line. Note that it is the reference to the array value, not the array itself, that is being assigned in this statement. After that second line of code, we still have only one array object; there just happens to be two references to it.

If the primitive-versus-reference type distinction is new to you, just try to keep the variable contents in mind. Variables hold the actual values of primitive types, but they hold only references to the values of reference types. The differing behavior of primitive and reference types is explored in more detail in Section 3.15.

You may have noticed that I did not specify whether strings are primitive or reference types in JavaScript. Strings are an unusual case. They have variable sizes, so obviously they cannot be stored directly in fixed-size variables. For efficiency, you

---

* This is an oversimplification and is not intended as a description of an actual JavaScript implementation.

would expect JavaScript to copy references to strings, not the actual contents of strings. On the other hand, strings behave like a primitive type in many ways. The question of whether strings are a primitive or reference type is actually moot because strings are *immutable*: there is no way to change the contents of a string value. This means that you cannot construct an example like the previous one that demonstrates that arrays are copied by reference. In the end, it doesn't matter much whether you think of strings as an immutable reference type that behaves like a primitive type or as a primitive type implemented with the internal efficiency of a reference type.

4.5 Garbage Collection

Reference types do not have a fixed size; indeed, some of them can become quite large. As we've already discussed, variables do not directly hold reference values. The value is stored at some other location, and the variables merely hold a reference to that location. Now let's focus briefly on the actual storage of the value.

Since strings, objects, and arrays do not have a fixed size, storage for them must be allocated dynamically, when the size is known. Every time a JavaScript program creates a string, array, or object, the interpreter must allocate memory to store that entity. Whenever memory is dynamically allocated like this, it must eventually be freed up for reuse, or the JavaScript interpreter will use up all the available memory on the system and crash.

In languages such as C and C++, memory must be freed manually. It is the programmer's responsibility to keep track of all objects that are created and to destroy them (freeing their memory) when they are no longer needed. This can be an onerous task and is often the source of bugs.

Instead of requiring manual deallocation, JavaScript relies on a technique called *garbage collection*. The JavaScript interpreter can detect when an object will never again be used by the program. When it determines that an object is unreachable (i.e., there is no longer any way to refer to it using the variables in the program), it knows that the object is no longer needed and its memory can be reclaimed. Consider the following lines of code, for example:

```
var s = "hello";            // Allocate memory for a string
var u = s.toUpperCase();    // Create a new string
s = u;                      // Overwrite reference to original string
```

After this code runs, the original string "hello" is no longer reachable; there are no references to it in any variables in the program. The system detects this fact and frees up its storage space for reuse.

Garbage collection is automatic and is invisible to the programmer. You need to know only enough about garbage collection to trust that it works: to know you can create all the garbage objects you want, and the system will clean up after you!

4.6   Variables as Properties

You may have noticed by now that there are a lot of similarities in JavaScript between variables and the properties of objects. They are both assigned the same way, they are used the same way in JavaScript expressions, and so on. Is there really any fundamental difference between the variable i and the property i of an object o? The answer is no. Variables in JavaScript are fundamentally the same as object properties.

4.6.1   The Global Object

When the JavaScript interpreter starts up, one of the first things it does, before executing any JavaScript code, is create a *global object*. The properties of this object are the global variables of JavaScript programs. When you declare a global JavaScript variable, what you are actually doing is defining a property of the global object.

The JavaScript interpreter initializes the global object with a number of properties that refer to predefined values and functions. For example, the Infinity, parseInt, and Math properties refer to the number infinity, the predefined parseInt( ) function, and the predefined Math object, respectively. You can read about these global values in Part III.

In top-level code (i.e., JavaScript code that is not part of a function), you can use the JavaScript keyword this to refer to the global object. Within functions, this has a different use, which is described in Chapter 8.

In client-side JavaScript, the Window object serves as the global object for all JavaScript code contained in the browser window it represents. This global Window object has a self-referential window property that can be used instead of this to refer to the global object. The Window object defines the core global properties, such as parseInt and Math, and also global client-side properties, such as navigator and screen.

4.6.2   Local Variables: The Call Object

If global variables are properties of the special global object, then what are local variables? They too are properties of an object. This object is known as the *call object*. The call object has a shorter lifespan than the global object, but it serves the same purpose. While the body of a function is executing, the function arguments and local variables are stored as properties of this call object. The use of an entirely separate object for local variables is what allows JavaScript to keep local variables from overwriting the value of global variables with the same name.

4.6.3   JavaScript Execution Contexts

Each time the JavaScript interpreter begins to execute a function, it creates a new *execution context* for that function. An execution context is, obviously, the context in which any piece of JavaScript code executes. An important part of the context is the object in which variables are defined. Thus, JavaScript code that is not part of any function runs in an execution context that uses the global object for variable definitions. And every JavaScript function runs in its own unique execution context with its own call object in which local variables are defined.

An interesting point to note is that JavaScript implementations may allow multiple global execution contexts, each with a *different* global object.[*] (Although, in this case, each global object is not entirely global.) The obvious example is client-side JavaScript, in which each separate browser window, or each frame within a window, defines a separate global execution context. Client-side JavaScript code in each frame or window runs in its own execution context and has its own global object. However, these separate client-side global objects have properties that link them. Thus, JavaScript code in one frame might refer to another frame with the expression `parent.frames[1]`, and the global variable x in the first frame might be referenced by the expression `parent.frames[0].x` in the second frame.

You don't need to fully understand just yet how separate window and frame execution contexts are linked together in client-side JavaScript. That topic is covered in detail in the discussion on the integration of JavaScript with web browsers in Chapter 13. What you should understand now is that JavaScript is flexible enough that a single JavaScript interpreter can run scripts in different global execution contexts and that those contexts need not be entirely separate; they can refer back and forth to each other.

This last point requires additional consideration. When JavaScript code in one execution context can read and write property values and execute functions that are defined in another execution context, you've reached a level of complexity that requires consideration of security issues. Take client-side JavaScript as an example. Suppose browser window A is running a script or contains information from your local intranet, and window B is running a script from some random site out on the Internet. In general, you do not want to allow the code in window B to be able to access the properties of window A. If you do allow it to do so, window B might be able to read sensitive company information and steal it, for example. Thus, in order to safely run JavaScript code, there must be a security mechanism that prevents access from one execution context to another when such access should not be permitted. We'll return to this topic in Section 13.8.

4.7 Variable Scope Revisited

When we first discussed the notion of variable scope, I based the definition solely on the lexical structure of JavaScript code: global variables have global scope, and

---

[*] This is merely an aside; if it does not interest you, feel free to move on to the next section.

variables declared in functions have local scope. If one function definition is nested within another, variables declared within that nested function have a nested local scope. Now that you know that global variables are properties of a global object and that local variables are properties of a special call object, we can return to the notion of variable scope and reconceptualize it. This new description of scope offers a useful way to think about variables in many contexts; it provides a powerful new understanding of how JavaScript works.

Every JavaScript execution context has a *scope chain* associated with it. This scope chain is a list or chain of objects. When JavaScript code needs to look up the value of a variable *x* (a process called *variable name resolution*), it starts by looking at the first object in the chain. If that object has a property named *x*, the value of that property is used. If the first object does not have a property named *x*, JavaScript continues the search with the next object in the chain. If the second object does not have a property named *x*, the search moves on to the next object, and so on.

In top-level JavaScript code (i.e., code not contained within any function definitions), the scope chain consists of a single object, the global object. All variables are looked up in this object. If a variable does not exist, the variable value is undefined. In a (nonnested) function, however, the scope chain consists of two objects. The first is the function's call object, and the second is the global object. When the function refers to a variable, the call object (the local scope) is checked first, and the global object (the global scope) is checked second. A nested function would have three or more objects in its scope chain. Figure 4-1 illustrates the process of looking up a variable name in the scope chain of a function.

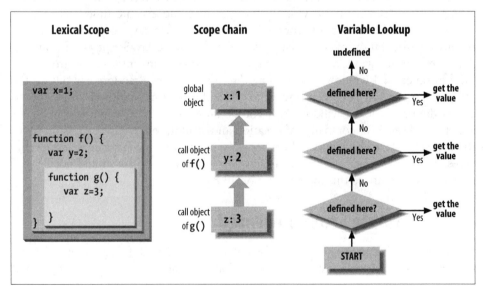

Figure 4-1. The scope chain and variable resolution

CHAPTER 5

Expressions and Operators

This chapter explains how expressions and operators work in JavaScript. If you are familiar with C, C++, or Java, you'll notice that the expressions and operators in JavaScript are very similar, and you'll be able to skim this chapter quickly. If you are not a C, C++, or Java programmer, this chapter tells you everything you need to know about expressions and operators in JavaScript.

5.1 Expressions

An *expression* is a phrase of JavaScript that a JavaScript interpreter can *evaluate* to produce a value. The simplest expressions are literals or variable names, like these:

```
1.7                     // A numeric literal
"JavaScript is fun!"    // A string literal
true                    // A boolean literal
null                    // The literal null value
/java/                  // A regular-expression literal
{ x:2, y:2 }            // An object literal
[2,3,5,7,11,13,17,19]   // An array literal
function(x) {return x*x;} // A function literal
i                       // The variable i
sum                     // The variable sum
```

The value of a literal expression is simply the literal value itself. The value of a variable expression is the value that the variable contains or refers to.

These expressions are not particularly interesting. More complex (and interesting) expressions can be created by combining simple expressions. For example, the previous examples show that 1.7 is an expression and i is an expression. The following is also an expression:

```
i + 1.7
```

The value of this expression is determined by adding the values of the two simpler expressions. The + in this example is an *operator* that combines two expressions into a more complex expression. Another operator is -, which combines expressions by subtraction. For example:

```
(i + 1.7) - sum
```

This expression uses the - operator to subtract the value of the sum variable from the value of the previous expression, i + 1.7. JavaScript supports a number of other operators besides + and -, as you'll see in the next section.

5.2   Operator Overview

If you are a C, C++, or Java programmer, most of the JavaScript operators should already be familiar to you. Table 5-1 summarizes the operators; you can use this table as a reference. Note that most operators are represented by punctuation characters such as + and =. Some, however, are represented by keywords such as delete and instanceof. Keyword operators are regular operators, just like those expressed with punctuation; they are simply expressed using a more readable and less succinct syntax.

In this table, the column labeled "P" gives the operator precedence, and the column labeled "A" gives the operator associativity, which can be L (left-to-right) or R (right-to-left). If you do not already understand precedence and associativity, the subsections that follow the table explain these concepts. The operators themselves are documented following that discussion.

Table 5-1. JavaScript operators

P	A	Operator	Operand type(s)	Operation performed
15	L	.	object, identifier	Property access
	L	[]	array, integer	Array index
	L	( )	function, arguments	Function call
	R	new	constructor call	Create new object
14	R	++	lvalue	Pre- or post-increment (unary)
	R	--	lvalue	Pre- or post-decrement (unary)
	R	-	number	Unary minus (negation)
	R	+	number	Unary plus (no-op)
	R	~	integer	Bitwise complement (unary)
	R	!	boolean	Logical complement (unary)
	R	delete	lvalue	Undefine a property (unary)
	R	typeof	any	Return datatype (unary)
	R	void	any	Return undefined value (unary)
13	L	*, /, %	numbers	Multiplication, division, remainder
12	L	+, -	numbers	Addition, subtraction

Table 5-1. JavaScript operators (continued)

P	A	Operator	Operand type(s)	Operation performed
	L	+	strings	String concatenation
11	L	<<	integers	Left shift
	L	>>	integers	Right shift with sign extension
	L	>>>	integers	Right shift with zero extension
10	L	<, <=	numbers or strings	Less than, less than or equal
	L	>, >=	numbers or strings	Greater than, greater than or equal
	L	instanceof	object, constructor	Check object type
	L	in	string, object	Check whether property exists
9	L	==	any	Test for equality
	L	!=	any	Test for inequality
	L	===	any	Test for identity
	L	!==	any	Test for nonidentity
8	L	&	integers	Bitwise AND
7	L	^	integers	Bitwise XOR
6	L	|	integers	Bitwise OR
5	L	&&	booleans	Logical AND
4	L	||	booleans	Logical OR
3	R	?:	boolean, any, any	Conditional operator (three operands)
2	R	=	lvalue, any	Assignment
	R	*=, /=, %=, +=, -=, <<=, >>=, >>>=, &=, ^=, |=	lvalue, any	Assignment with operation
1	L	,	any	Multiple evaluation

5.2.1 Number of Operands

Operators can be categorized based on the number of operands they expect. Most JavaScript operators, like the + operator shown earlier, are *binary operators* that combine two expressions into a single, more complex expression. That is, they operate on two operands. JavaScript also supports a number of *unary operators*, which convert a single expression into a single, more complex expression. The - operator in the expression -3 is a unary operator that performs the operation of negation on the operand 3. Finally, JavaScript supports one *ternary operator*, the conditional operator ?:, which combines the value of three expressions into a single expression.

5.2.2 Type of Operands

When constructing JavaScript expressions, you must pay attention to the datatypes that are being passed to operators and to the datatypes that are returned. Different operators expect their operands' expressions to evaluate to values of a certain datatype. For example, it is not possible to multiply strings, so the expression "a" * "b" is not legal in JavaScript. Note, however, that JavaScript tries to convert expressions to the appropriate type whenever possible, so the expression "3" * "5" is legal. Its value is the number 15, not the string "15". JavaScript type conversions are covered in more detail in Section 3.12.

Furthermore, some operators behave differently depending on the type of the operands used with them. Most notably, the + operator adds numeric operands but concatenates string operands. Also, if passed one string and one number, it converts the number to a string and concatenates the two resulting strings. For example, "1" + 0 yields the string "10".

Notice that the assignment operators, as well as a few other operators, expect their left-side expressions to be lvalues. *lvalue* is a historical term that means "an expression that can legally appear on the left side of an assignment expression." In JavaScript, variables, properties of objects, and elements of arrays are lvalues. The ECMAScript specification allows built-in functions to return lvalues but does not define any built-in functions that behave that way.

Finally, note that operators do not always return the same type as their operands. The comparison operators (less than, equal to, greater than, etc.) take operands of various types, but when comparison expressions are evaluated, they always yield a primitive boolean value that indicates whether the comparison is true or not. For example, the expression a < 3 returns true if the value of variable a is in fact less than 3. As you'll see, the boolean values returned by comparison operators are used in if statements, while loops, and for loops: JavaScript statements that control the execution of a program based on the results of evaluating expressions that contain comparison operators.

5.2.3 Operator Precedence

In Table 5-1, the column labeled "P" specifies the *precedence* of each operator. Operator precedence controls the order in which operations are performed. Operators with higher numbers in the "P" column are performed before those with lower numbers.

Consider the following expression:

```
w = x + y*z;
```

The multiplication operator * has a higher precedence than the addition operator +, so the multiplication is performed before the addition. Furthermore, the assignment operator = has the lowest precedence, so the assignment is performed after all the operations on the right side are completed.

Operator precedence can be overridden with the explicit use of parentheses. To force the addition in the previous example to be performed first, write:

```
w = (x + y)*z;
```

In practice, if you are at all unsure about the precedence of your operators, the simplest thing to do is to use parentheses to make the evaluation order explicit. The only rules that are important to know are these: multiplication and division are performed before addition and subtraction, and assignment has very low precedence and is almost always performed last.

5.2.4 Operator Associativity

In Table 5-1, the column labeled "A" specifies the *associativity* of the operator. A value of L specifies left-to-right associativity, and a value of R specifies right-to-left associativity. The associativity of an operator specifies the order in which operations of the same precedence are performed. Left-to-right associativity means that operations are performed from left to right. For example, the addition operator has left-to-right associativity, so:

```
w = x + y + z;
```

is the same as:

```
w = ((x + y) + z);
```

On the other hand, the following (almost nonsensical) expressions:

```
x = ~-~y;
w = x = y = z;
q = a?b:c?d:e?f:g;
```

are equivalent to:

```
x = ~(-(~y));
w = (x = (y = z));
q = a?b:(c?d:(e?f:g));
```

because the unary, assignment, and ternary conditional operators have right-to-left associativity.

5.3 Arithmetic Operators

Having explained operator precedence, associativity, and other background material, it's time to discuss the operators themselves. This section details the arithmetic operators:

Addition (+)

The + operator adds numeric operands or concatenates string operands. If one operand is a string, the other is converted to a string, and the two strings are then concatenated. Object operands are converted to numbers or strings that can be added or concatenated. The conversion is performed by the valueOf( ) method and/or the toString( ) method of the object.

Subtraction (-)

When - is used as a binary operator, it subtracts its second operand from its first operand. If used with nonnumeric operands, it attempts to convert them to numbers.

Multiplication (*)

The * operator multiplies its two operands. If used with nonnumeric operands, it attempts to convert them to numbers.

Division (/)

The / operator divides its first operand by its second. If used with nonnumeric operands, it attempts to convert them to numbers. If you are used to programming languages that distinguish between integer and floating-point numbers, you might expect to get an integer result when you divide one integer by another. In JavaScript, however, all numbers are floating-point, so all division operations have floating-point results: 5/2 evaluates to 2.5, not 2. Division by zero yields positive or negative infinity, while 0/0 evaluates to NaN.

Modulo (%)

The % operator computes the first operand modulo the second operand. In other words, it returns the remainder when the first operand is divided by the second operand a certain number of times. If used with nonnumeric operands, the modulo operator attempts to convert them to numbers. The sign of the result is the same as the sign of the first operand. For example, 5 % 2 evaluates to 1.

While the modulo operator is typically used with integer operands, it also works for floating-point values. For example, -4.3 % 2.1 evaluates to -0.1.

Unary minus (-)

When - is used as a unary operator, before a single operand, it performs unary negation. In other words, it converts a positive value to an equivalently negative value, and vice versa. If the operand is not a number, this operator attempts to convert it to one.

Unary plus (+)

For symmetry with the unary minus operator, JavaScript also has a unary plus operator. This operator allows you to explicitly specify the sign of numeric literals, if you feel that this will make your code clearer:

```
var profit = +1000000;
```

In code like this, the + operator does nothing; it simply evaluates to the value of its argument. Note, however, that for nonnumeric arguments, the + operator has the effect of converting the argument to a number. It returns NaN if the argument cannot be converted.

Increment (++)

The ++ operator increments (i.e., adds 1 to) its single operand, which must be a variable, an element of an array, or a property of an object. If the value of this variable, element, or property is not a number, the operator first attempts to convert it to one. The precise behavior of this operator depends on its position relative to the operand. When used before the operand, where it is known as the pre-increment operator, it increments the operand and evaluates to the incremented value of that operand. When used after the operand, where it is known as the post-increment operator, it increments its operand but evaluates to the *unincremented* value of that operand. If the value to be incremented is not a number, it is converted to one by this process.

For example, the following code sets both i and j to 2:

```
i = 1;
j = ++i;
```

But these lines set i to 2 and j to 1:

```
i = 1;
j = i++;
```

This operator, in both of its forms, is most commonly used to increment a counter that controls a loop. Note that, because of JavaScript's automatic semicolon insertion, you may not insert a line break between the post-increment or post-decrement operator and the operand that precedes it. If you do so, JavaScript will treat the operand as a complete statement by itself and insert a semicolon before it.

Decrement (--)

The -- operator decrements (i.e., subtracts 1 from) its single numeric operand, which must be a variable, an element of an array, or a property of an object. If the value of this variable, element, or property is not a number, the operator first attempts to convert it to one. Like the ++ operator, the precise behavior of -- depends on its position relative to the operand. When used before the operand, it decrements and returns the decremented value. When used after the operand, it decrements the operand but returns the *undecremented* value.

5.4   Equality Operators

This section describes the JavaScript equality and inequality operators. These operators compare two values to determine whether they are the same or different and return a boolean value (true or false) depending on the result of the comparison. As shown in Chapter 6, they are most commonly used in such structures as if statements and for loops to control the flow of program execution.

5.4.1   Equality (==) and Identity (===)

The == and === operators check whether two values are the same, using two different definitions of sameness. Both operators accept operands of any type, and both return true if their operands are the same and false if they are different. The === operator is known as the identity operator, and it checks whether its two operands are "identical" using a strict definition of sameness. The == operator is known as the equality operator; it checks whether its two operands are "equal" using a more relaxed definition of sameness that allows type conversions.

The identity operator is standardized by ECMAScript v3 and implemented in JavaScript 1.3 and later. With the introduction of the identity operator, JavaScript supports =, ==, and === operators. Be sure you understand the differences between the assignment, equality, and identity operators, and be careful to use the correct one when coding! Although it is tempting to call all three operators "equals," it may help to reduce confusion if you read "gets or is assigned" for =, "is equal to" for ==, and "is identical to" for ===.

In JavaScript, numbers, strings, and boolean values are compared *by value*. In this case, two separate values are involved, and the == and === operators check that these two values are identical. This means that two variables are equal or identical only if they contain the same value. For example, two strings are equal only if they each contain exactly the same characters.

On the other hand, objects, arrays, and functions are compared *by reference*. This means that two variables are equal only if they *refer to* the same object. Two separate arrays are never equal or identical, even if they contain equal or identical elements. Two variables that contain references to objects, arrays, or functions are equal only if they refer to the same object, array, or function. If you want to test that two distinct objects contain the same properties or that two distinct arrays contain the same elements, you'll have to check the properties or elements individually for equality or identity. (And, if any of the properties or elements are themselves objects or arrays, you'll have to decide how deep you want the comparison to go.)

The following rules determine whether two values are identical according to the === operator:

- If the two values have different types, they are not identical.
- If both values are numbers and have the same value, they are identical, unless either or both values are NaN, in which case they are not identical. The NaN value is never identical to any other value, including itself! To check whether a value is NaN, use the global isNaN( ) function.
- If both values are strings and contain exactly the same characters in the same positions, they are identical. If the strings differ in length or content, they are not identical. Note that in some cases, the Unicode standard allows more than one way to encode the same string. For efficiency, however, JavaScript's string comparison compares strictly on a character-by-character basis, and it assumes that all strings have been converted to a "normalized form" before they are compared. See the String.localeCompare( ) reference page in Part III for another way to compare strings.

- If both values are the boolean value `true` or both are the boolean value `false`, they are identical.
- If both values refer to the same object, array, or function, they are identical. If they refer to different objects (or arrays or functions) they are not identical, even if both objects have identical properties or both arrays have identical elements.
- If both values are `null` or both values are `undefined`, they are identical.

The following rules determine whether two values are equal according to the `==` operator:

- If the two values have the same type, test them for identity. If the values are identical, they are equal; if they are not identical, they are not equal.
- If the two values do not have the same type, they may still be equal. Use the following rules and type conversions to check for equality:
  — If one value is `null` and the other is `undefined`, they are equal.
  — If one value is a number and the other is a string, convert the string to a number and try the comparison again, using the converted value.
  — If either value is `true`, convert it to 1 and try the comparison again. If either value is `false`, convert it to 0 and try the comparison again.
  — If one value is an object and the other is a number or string, convert the object to a primitive and try the comparison again. An object is converted to a primitive value by either its `toString( )` method or its `valueOf( )` method. The built-in classes of core JavaScript attempt `valueOf( )` conversion before `toString( )` conversion, except for the Date class, which performs `toString( )` conversion. Objects that are not part of core JavaScript may convert themselves to primitive values in an implementation-defined way.
  — Any other combinations of values are not equal.

As an example of testing for equality, consider the comparison:

```
"1" == true
```

This expression evaluates to `true`, indicating that these very different-looking values are in fact equal. The boolean value `true` is first converted to the number 1, and the comparison is done again. Next, the string `"1"` is converted to the number 1. Since both numbers are now the same, the comparison returns true.

5.4.2 Inequality (!=) and Nonidentity (!==)

The `!=` and `!==` operators test for the exact opposite of the `==` and `===` operators. The `!=` inequality operator returns `false` if two values are equal to each other and returns true otherwise. The `!==` nonidentity operator returns `false` if two values are identical to each other and returns true otherwise. Note that this operator is standardized by ECMAScript v3 and implemented in JavaScript 1.3 and later.

As you'll see, the ! operator computes the Boolean NOT operation. This makes it easy to remember that != stands for "not equal to" and !== stands for "not identical to." See the previous section for details on how equality and identity are defined for different datatypes.

5.5   Relational Operators

This section describes the JavaScript relational operators. These operators test for a relationship (such as "less than" or "property of") between two values and return true or false depending on whether that relationship exists. As shown in Chapter 6, they are most commonly used to control the flow of program execution in structures, such as if statements and while loops.

5.5.1   Comparison Operators

The most commonly used types of relational operators are the comparison operators, which determine the relative order of two values. Here are the comparison operators:

Less than (<)
> The < operator evaluates to true if its first operand is less than its second operand; otherwise it evaluates to false.

Greater than (>)
> The > operator evaluates to true if its first operand is greater than its second operand; otherwise it evaluates to false.

Less than or equal (<=)
> The <= operator evaluates to true if its first operand is less than or equal to its second operand; otherwise it evaluates to false.

Greater than or equal (>=)
> The >= operator evaluates to true if its first operand is greater than or equal to its second operand; otherwise it evaluates to false.

The operands of these comparison operators may be of any type. Comparison can be performed only on numbers and strings, however, so operands that are not numbers or strings are converted. Comparison and conversion occur as follows:

- If both operands are numbers, or if both convert to numbers, they are compared numerically.
- If both operands are strings or convert to strings, they are compared as strings.
- If one operand is or converts to a string, and one is or converts to a number, the operator attempts to convert the string to a number and performs a numerical comparison. If the string does not represent a number, it converts to NaN, and the comparison is false. (In JavaScript 1.1, the string-to-number conversion causes an error instead of yielding NaN.)

- If an object can be converted to either a number or a string, JavaScript performs the numerical conversion. This means, for example, that Date objects are compared numerically, and it is meaningful to compare two dates to see whether one is earlier than the other.
- If the operands of the comparison operators cannot both be successfully converted to numbers or to strings, these operators always return false.
- If either operand is or converts to NaN, the comparison operator always yields false.

Keep in mind that string comparison is done on a strict character-by-character basis using the numerical value of each character from the Unicode encoding. Although in some cases the Unicode standard allows equivalent strings to be encoded using different sequences of characters, the JavaScript comparison operators do not detect these encoding differences; they assume that all strings are expressed in normalized form. Note in particular that string comparison is case-sensitive, and in the Unicode encoding (at least for the ASCII subset), all capital letters are "less than" all lowercase letters. This rule can cause confusing results if you do not expect it. For example, according to the < operator, the string "Zoo" is less than the string "aardvark".

For a more robust string-comparison algorithm, see the String.localeCompare() method, which also takes locale-specific definitions of alphabetical order into account. For case-insensitive comparisons, you must first convert the strings to all lowercase or all uppercase using String.toLowerCase() or String.toUpperCase().

The <= (less-than-or-equal) and >= (greater-than-or-equal) operators do not rely on the equality or identity operators for determining whether two values are "equal." Instead, the less-than-or-equal operator is simply defined as "not greater than," and the greater-than-or-equal operator is defined as "not less than." The one exception occurs when either operand is (or converts to) NaN, in which case all four comparison operators return false.

5.5.2   The in Operator

The in operator expects a left-side operand that is or can be converted to a string. It expects a right-side operand that is an object (or array). It evaluates to true if the left-side value is the name of a property of the right-side object. For example:

```
var point = { x:1, y:1 };       // Define an object
var has_x_coord = "x" in point; // Evaluates to true
var has_y_coord = "y" in point; // Evaluates to true
var has_z_coord = "z" in point; // Evaluates to false; not a 3-D point
var ts = "toString" in point;   // Inherited property; evaluates to true
```

5.5.3 The instanceof Operator

The `instanceof` operator expects a left-side operand that is an object and a right-side operand that is the name of a class of objects. The operator evaluates to `true` if the left-side object is an instance of the right-side class and evaluates to `false` otherwise. Chapter 9 shows that, in JavaScript, classes of objects are defined by the constructor function that initializes them. Thus, the right-side operand of `instanceof` should be the name of a constructor function. Note that all objects are instances of `Object`. For example:

```
var d = new Date();  // Create a new object with the Date() constructor
d instanceof Date;   // Evaluates to true; d was created with Date()
d instanceof Object; // Evaluates to true; all objects are instances of Object
d instanceof Number; // Evaluates to false; d is not a Number object
var a = [1, 2, 3];   // Create an array with array literal syntax
a instanceof Array;  // Evaluates to true; a is an array
a instanceof Object; // Evaluates to true; all arrays are objects
a instanceof RegExp; // Evaluates to false; arrays are not regular expressions
```

If the left-side operand of `instanceof` is not an object, or if the right-side operand is an object that is not a constructor function, `instanceof` returns `false`. However, it returns a runtime error if the right-side operand is not an object at all.

5.6 String Operators

As discussed in the previous sections, several operators have special effects when their operands are strings.

The + operator concatenates two string operands—that is, it creates a new string that consists of the first string followed by the second. For example, the following expression evaluates to the string "hello there":

```
"hello" + " " + "there"
```

And the following lines produce the string "22":

```
a = "2"; b = "2";
c = a + b;
```

The <, <=, >, and >= operators compare two strings to determine their order. The comparison uses alphabetical order. As noted in Section 5.5.1, however, this alphabetical order is based on the Unicode character encoding used by JavaScript. In this encoding, all capital letters in the Latin alphabet come before (are less than) all lowercase letters, which can cause unexpected results.

The == and != operators work on strings, but, as you've seen, these operators work for all datatypes, and they do not have any special behavior when used with strings.

The + operator is a special one: it gives priority to string operands over numeric operands. As noted earlier, if either operand to + is a string (or an object), the other operand is converted to a string (or both operands are converted to strings) and concatenated, rather than added. On the other hand, the comparison operators perform string comparison only if *both* operands are strings. If only one operand is a string, JavaScript attempts to convert it to a number. The following lines illustrate:

```
1 + 2          // Addition. Result is 3.
"1" + "2"      // Concatenation. Result is "12".
"1" + 2        // Concatenation; 2 is converted to "2". Result is "12".
11 < 3         // Numeric comparison. Result is false.
"11" < "3"     // String comparison. Result is true.
"11" < 3       // Numeric comparison; "11" converted to 11. Result is false.
"one" < 3      // Numeric comparison; "one" converted to NaN. Result is false.
```

Finally, it is important to note that when the + operator is used with strings and numbers, it may not be associative. That is, the result may depend on the order in which operations are performed. This can be seen with examples like these:

```
s = 1 + 2 + " blind mice";   // Yields "3 blind mice"
t = "blind mice: " + 1 + 2;  // Yields "blind mice: 12"
```

The reason for this surprising difference in behavior is that the + operator works from left to right, unless parentheses change this order. Thus, the last two examples are equivalent to these:

```
s = (1 + 2) + "blind mice";   // 1st + yields number; 2nd yields string
t = ("blind mice: " + 1) + 2; // Both operations yield strings
```

5.7 Logical Operators

The logical operators typically perform Boolean algebra. They are often used in conjunction with comparison operators to express complex comparisons that involve more than one variable, and are also frequently used with the if, while, and for statements.

5.7.1 Logical AND (&&)

When used with Boolean operands, the && operator performs the Boolean AND operation on the two values: it returns true if and only if both its first operand *and* its second operand are true. If one or both of these operands is false, it returns false.

The actual behavior of this operator is somewhat more complicated. It starts by evaluating its first operand, the expression on its left. If the value of this expression can be converted to false (for example, if the left operand evaluates to null, 0, "", or undefined), the operator returns the value of the left-side expression. Otherwise, it evaluates its second operand, the expression on its right, and returns the value of that expression.[*]

Note that, depending on the value of the left-side expression, this operator may or may not evaluate the right-side expression. You may occasionally see code that purposely exploits this feature of the && operator. For example, the following two lines of JavaScript code have equivalent effects:

```
if (a == b) stop( );
(a == b) && stop( );
```

While some programmers (particularly Perl programmers) find this a natural and useful programming idiom, I recommend against using it. The fact that the right side is not guaranteed to be evaluated is a frequent source of bugs. Consider the following code, for example:

```
if ((a == null) && (b++ > 10)) stop( );
```

This statement probably does not do what the programmer intended because the increment operator on the right side is not evaluated whenever the comparison on the left side is false. To avoid this problem, do not use expressions with side effects (assignments, increments, decrements, and function calls) on the right side of && unless you are quite sure you know exactly what you are doing.

Despite the fairly confusing way that this operator actually works, it is easiest, and perfectly safe, to think of it as merely a Boolean algebra operator. Although it does not actually return a boolean value, the value it returns can always be converted to a boolean value.

5.7.2 Logical OR (||)

When used with Boolean operands, the || operator performs the Boolean OR operation on the two values: it returns true if either the first operand *or* the second operand is true, or if both are true. If both operands are false, it returns false.

Although the || operator is most often used simply as a Boolean OR operator, it, like the && operator, has more complex behavior. It starts by evaluating its first operand, the expression on its left. If the value of this expression can be converted to true, it returns the unconverted value of the left-side expression. Otherwise, it evaluates its second operand, the expression on its right, and returns the value of that expression.[†]

---

[*] In JavaScript 1.0 and JavaScript 1.1, if the left-side expression evaluates to false, the && operator returns false rather than returning the unconverted value of the left-side expression.

[†] In JavaScript 1.0 and JavaScript 1.1, if the left-side expression can be converted to true, the operator returns true and doesn't return the unconverted value of the left-side expression.

Core JavaScript

As with the && operator, you should avoid right-side operands that include side effects, unless you purposely want to use the fact that the right-side expression may not be evaluated.

Even when the || operator is used with operands that are not boolean values, it can still be considered a Boolean OR operator because its return value, whatever the type, can be converted to a boolean value.

On the other hand, you may sometimes see code that uses || with nonboolean operands and takes advantage of the fact that its return value is not a boolean. An idiomatic usage of this operator is to select the first value in a set of alternatives that is defined and non-null (that is, the first value that does not convert to false). Here is an example:

```
// If max_width is defined, use that.  Otherwise look for a value in
// the preferences object.  If that is not defined use a hard-coded constant.
var max = max_width || preferences.max_width || 500;
```

5.7.3   Logical NOT (!)

The ! operator is a unary operator; it is placed before a single operand. Its purpose is to invert the boolean value of its operand. For example, if the variable a has the value true (or is a value that converts to true), !a has the value false. And if the expression p && q evaluates to false (or to a value that converts to false), !(p && q) evaluates to true.

The ! operator converts its operand to a boolean value (using the rules described in Chapter 3) if necessary before inverting the converted value. This means that you can convert any value x to its equivalent boolean value by applying this operator twice: !!x.

5.8   Bitwise Operators

Despite the fact that all numbers in JavaScript are floating-point numbers, the bitwise operators require numeric operands that have integer values. They operate on these integer operands using a 32-bit integer representation instead of the equivalent floating-point representation. Four of these operators perform Boolean algebra on the individual bits of the operands, behaving as if each bit in each operand were a boolean value and performing similar operations to those performed by the logical operators shown earlier. The other three bitwise operators are used to shift bits left and right.

If the bitwise operators are used with operands that are not integers or are too large to fit in a 32-bit integer representation, they simply coerce the operands to 32-bit integers by dropping any fractional part of the operand or any bits beyond the 32nd. The shift operators require a right-side operand between 0 and 31. After converting this operand to a 32-bit integer, they drop any bits beyond the 5th, which yields a number in the appropriate range.

If you are not familiar with binary numbers and the binary representation of decimal integers, you can skip the operators described in this section. The purpose of these operators is not described here; they are needed for low-level manipulation of binary numbers and are not commonly used in JavaScript programming. Here are the bitwise operators:

Bitwise AND (&)
> The & operator performs a Boolean AND operation on each bit of its integer arguments. A bit is set in the result only if the corresponding bit is set in both operands. For example, 0x1234 & 0x00FF evaluates to 0x0034.

Bitwise OR (|)
> The | operator performs a Boolean OR operation on each bit of its integer arguments. A bit is set in the result if the corresponding bit is set in one or both of the operands. For example, 9 | 10 evaluates to 11.

Bitwise XOR (^)
> The ^ operator performs a Boolean exclusive OR operation on each bit of its integer arguments. Exclusive OR means that either operand one is true or operand two is true, but not both. A bit is set in this operation's result if a corresponding bit is set in one (but not both) of the two operands. For example, 9 ^ 10 evaluates to 3.

Bitwise NOT (~)
> The ~ operator is a unary operator that appears before its single integer argument. It operates by reversing all bits in the operand. Because of the way signed integers are represented in JavaScript, applying the ~ operator to a value is equivalent to changing its sign and subtracting 1. For example ~0x0f evaluates to 0xfffffff0, or −16.

Shift left (<<)
> The << operator moves all bits in its first operand to the left by the number of places specified in the second operand, which should be an integer between 0 and 31. For example, in the operation a << 1, the first bit (the ones bit) of a becomes the second bit (the twos bit), the second bit of a becomes the third, etc. A zero is used for the new first bit, and the value of the 32nd bit is lost. Shifting a value left by one position is equivalent to multiplying by 2, shifting two positions is equivalent to multiplying by 4, etc. For example, 7 << 1 evaluates to 14.

Shift right with sign (>>)
> The >> operator moves all bits in its first operand to the right by the number of places specified in the second operand (an integer between 0 and 31). Bits that are shifted off the right are lost. The bits filled in on the left depend on the sign

bit of the original operand, in order to preserve the sign of the result. If the first operand is positive, the result has zeros placed in the high bits; if the first operand is negative, the result has ones placed in the high bits. Shifting a value right one place is equivalent to dividing by 2 (discarding the remainder), shifting right two places is equivalent to integer division by 4, and so on. For example, 7 >> 1 evaluates to 3, and -7 >> 1 evaluates to -4.

Shift right with zero fill (>>>)

The >>> operator is just like the >> operator, except that the bits shifted in on the left are always zero, regardless of the sign of the first operand. For example, -1 >> 4 evaluates to -1, but -1 >>> 4 evaluates to 268435455 (0x0fffffff).

5.9   Assignment Operators

As shown in the discussion of variables in Chapter 4, = is used in JavaScript to assign a value to a variable. For example:

```
i = 0
```

While you might not normally think of such a line of JavaScript as an expression that can be evaluated, it is in fact an expression, and technically speaking, = is an operator.

The = operator expects its left-side operand to be either a variable, the element of an array, or a property of an object. It expects its right-side operand to be an arbitrary value of any type. The value of an assignment expression is the value of the right-side operand. As a side effect, the = operator assigns the value on the right to the variable, element, or property on the left so that future uses of the variable, element, or property refer to the value.

Because = is defined as an operator, you can include it in more complex expressions. For example, you can assign and test a value in the same expression with code like this:

```
(a = b) == 0
```

If you do this, be sure you are clear on the difference between the = and == operators!

The assignment operator has right-to-left associativity, which means that when multiple assignment operators appear in an expression, they are evaluated from right to left. Thus, you can write code like this to assign a single value to multiple variables:

```
i = j = k = 0;
```

Remember that each assignment expression has a value that is the value of the right side. So in the above code, the value of the first assignment (the rightmost one) becomes the right side for the second assignment (the middle one), and this value becomes the right side for the last (leftmost) assignment.

5.9.1 Assignment with Operation

Besides the normal = assignment operator, JavaScript supports a number of other assignment operators that provide shortcuts by combining assignment with some other operation. For example, the += operator performs addition and assignment. The following expression:

```
total += sales_tax
```

is equivalent to this one:

```
total = total + sales_tax
```

As you might expect, the += operator works for numbers or strings. For numeric operands, it performs addition and assignment; for string operands, it performs concatenation and assignment.

Similar operators include -=, *=, &=, and so on. Table 5-2 lists them all.

Table 5-2. Assignment operators

Operator	Example	Equivalent
+=	a += b	a = a + b
-=	a -= b	a = a - b
*=	a *= b	a = a * b
/=	a /= b	a = a / b
%=	a %= b	a = a % b
<<=	a <<= b	a = a << b
>>=	a >>= b	a = a >> b
>>>=	a >>>= b	a = a >>> b
&=	a &= b	a = a & b
|=	a |= b	a = a | b
^=	a ^= b	a = a ^ b

In most cases, the expression:

```
a op= b
```

where *op* is an operator, is equivalent to the expression:

```
a = a op b
```

These expressions differ only if a contains side effects such as a function call or an increment operator.

5.10   Miscellaneous Operators

JavaScript supports a number of other miscellaneous operators, described in the following sections.

5.10.1 The Conditional Operator (?:)

The conditional operator is the only ternary operator (three operands) in JavaScript and is sometimes actually called the ternary operator. This operator is sometimes written ?:, although it does not appear quite that way in code. Because this operator has three operands, the first goes before the ?, the second goes between the ? and the :, and the third goes after the :. It is used like this:

```
x > 0 ? x*y : -x*y
```

The first operand of the conditional operator must be (or be convertible to) a boolean value—usually this is the result of a comparison expression. The second and third operands may have any value. The value returned by the conditional operator depends on the boolean value of the first operand. If that operand is true, the value of the conditional expression is the value of the second operand. If the first operand is false, the value of the conditional expression is the value of the third operand.

While you can achieve similar results using the if statement, the ?: operator often provides a handy shortcut. Here is a typical usage, which checks to be sure that a variable is defined, uses it if so, and provides a default value if not:

```
greeting = "hello " + (username != null ? username : "there");
```

This is equivalent to, but more compact than, the following if statement:

```
greeting = "hello ";
if (username != null)
    greeting += username;
else
    greeting += "there";
```

5.10.2 The typeof Operator

typeof is a unary operator that is placed before its single operand, which can be of any type. Its value is a string indicating the datatype of the operand.

The typeof operator evaluates to "number", "string", or "boolean" if its operand is a number, string, or boolean value. It evaluates to "object" for objects, arrays, and (surprisingly) null. It evaluates to "function" for function operands and to "undefined" if the operand is undefined.

typeof evaluates to "object" when its operand is a Number, String, or Boolean wrapper object. It also evaluates to "object" for Date and RegExp objects. typeof evaluates to an implementation-dependent value for objects that are not part of core JavaScript but are provided by the context in which JavaScript is embedded. In client-side JavaScript, however, typeof typically evaluates to "object" for all client-side objects, just as it does for all core objects.

You might use the typeof operator in expressions like these:

```
typeof i
(typeof value == "string") ? "'" + value + "'" : value
```

Note that you can place parentheses around the operand to typeof, which makes typeof look like the name of a function rather than an operator keyword:

```
typeof(i)
```

Because typeof evaluates to "object" for all object and array types, it is useful only to distinguish objects from other, primitive types. In order to distinguish one object type from another, you must use other techniques, such as the instanceof operator (see Section 5.5.3) or the constructor property (see the Object.constructor entry in the core reference section).

The typeof operator is defined by the ECMAScript v1 specification and is implemented in JavaScript 1.1 and later.

5.10.3 The Object-Creation Operator (new)

The new operator creates a new object and invokes a constructor function to initialize it. new is a unary operator that appears before a constructor invocation. It has the following syntax:

```
new constructor(arguments)
```

constructor must be an expression that evaluates to a constructor function, and it should be followed by zero or more comma-separated arguments enclosed in parentheses. As a special case, for the new operator only, JavaScript simplifies the grammar by allowing the parentheses to be omitted if the function call has no arguments. Here are some examples using the new operator:

```
o = new Object;      // Optional parentheses omitted here
d = new Date();      // Returns a Date object representing the current time
c = new Rectangle(3.0, 4.0, 1.5, 2.75);  // Create an object of class Rectangle
obj[i] = new constructors[i]();
```

The new operator first creates a new object with no properties defined. Next, it invokes the specified constructor function, passing the specified arguments and also passing the newly created object as the value of the this keyword. The constructor function can then use the this keyword to initialize the new object in any way desired. You'll learn more about the new operator, the this keyword, and constructor functions in Chapter 7.

The new operator can also create arrays using the new Array( ) syntax. You'll see more about creating and working with objects and arrays in Chapter 7.

5.10.4 The delete Operator

delete is a unary operator that attempts to delete the object property, array element, or variable specified as its operand.* It returns true if the deletion was successful and false if the operand could not be deleted. Not all variables and properties can be deleted: some built-in core and client-side properties are immune from deletion, and user-defined variables declared with the var statement cannot be deleted. If delete is invoked on a nonexistent property, it returns true. (Surprisingly, the ECMAScript standard specifies that delete also evaluates to true if the operand is not a property, array element, or variable.) Here are some examples that use this operator:

```
var o = {x:1, y:2};  // Define a variable; initialize it to an object
delete o.x;          // Delete one of the object properties; returns true
typeof o.x;          // Property does not exist; returns "undefined"
delete o.x;          // Delete a nonexistent property; returns true
delete o;            // Can't delete a declared variable; returns false
delete 1;            // Can't delete an integer; returns true
x = 1;               // Implicitly declare a variable without var keyword
delete x;            // Can delete this kind of variable; returns true
x;                   // Runtime error: x is not defined
```

Note that a deleted property, variable, or array element is not merely set to the undefined value. When a property is deleted, the property ceases to exist. See the related discussion in Section 4.3.2.

It is important to understand that delete affects only properties, not objects referred to by those properties. Consider the following code:

```
var my = new Object( );    // Create an object named "my"
my.hire = new Date( );     // my.hire refers to a Date object
my.fire = my.hire;         // my.fire refers to the same object
delete my.hire;            // hire property is deleted; returns true
document.write(my.fire);   // But my.fire still refers to the Date object
```

5.10.5 The void Operator

void is a unary operator that appears before its single operand, which may be of any type. The purpose of this operator is an unusual one: it discards its operand value and returns undefined. The most common use for this operator is in a client-side

---

* If you are a C++ programmer, note that the delete operator in JavaScript is nothing like the delete operator in C++. In JavaScript, memory deallocation is handled automatically by garbage collection, and you never have to worry about explicitly freeing up memory. Thus, there is no need for a C++-style delete to delete entire objects.

javascript: URL, where it allows you to evaluate an expression for its side effects without the browser displaying the value of the evaluated expression.

For example, you might use the void operator in an HTML tag as follows:

```
<a href="javascript:void window.open( );">Open New Window</a>
```

Another use for void is to purposely generate the undefined value. void is specified by ECMAScript v1 and implemented in JavaScript 1.1. The global undefined property, however, is specified by ECMAScript v3 and implemented in JavaScript 1.5. Thus, for backward compatibility, you may find it useful to use an expression such as void 0 instead of relying on the undefined property.

5.10.6 The Comma Operator (,)

The comma operator is a simple one. It evaluates its left argument, evaluates its right argument, and then returns the value of its right argument. Thus, the following line:

```
i=0, j=1, k=2;
```

evaluates to 2 and is basically equivalent to:

```
i = 0;
j = 1;
k = 2;
```

This strange operator is useful only in a few limited circumstances, primarily when you need to evaluate several independent expressions with side effects in a situation where only a single expression is allowed. In practice, the comma operator is really used only in conjunction with the for loop statement, which is discussed in Chapter 6.

5.10.7 Array and Object Access Operators

As noted briefly in Chapter 3, you can access elements of an array using square brackets ([ ]), and you can access elements of an object using a dot (.). Both [ ] and . are treated as operators in JavaScript.

The . operator expects an object as its left-side operand and an identifier (a property name) as its right-side operand. The right-side operand should not be a string or a variable that contains a string; it should be the literal name of the property or method, without quotes of any kind. Here are some examples:

```
document.lastModified
navigator.appName
frames[0].length
document.write("hello world")
```

If the specified property does not exist in the object, JavaScript does not issue an error but instead simply returns undefined as the value of the expression.

Most operators allow arbitrary expressions for either operand, as long as the type of the operand is suitable. The . operator is an exception: the right-side operand must be an identifier. Nothing else is allowed.

The [] operator allows access to array elements. It also allows access to object properties without the restrictions that the . operator places on the right-side operand. If the first operand (which goes before the left bracket) refers to an array, the second operand (which goes between the brackets) should be an expression that evaluates to an integer. For example:

```
frames[1]
document.forms[i + j]
document.forms[i].elements[j++]
```

If the first operand to the [] operator is a reference to an object, the second operand should be an expression that evaluates to a string that names a property of the object. Note that in this case, the second operand is a string, not an identifier. It should be a constant in quotes or a variable or expression that refers to a string. For example:

```
document["lastModified"]
frames[0]['length']
data["val" + i]
```

The [] operator is typically used to access the elements of an array. It is less convenient than the . operator for accessing properties of an object because of the need to quote the name of the property. When an object is used as an associative array, however, and the property names are dynamically generated, the . operator cannot be used; only the [] operator will do. This is commonly the case when you use the for/in loop, which is introduced in Chapter 6. For example, the following JavaScript code uses a for/in loop and the [] operator to print out the names and values of all of the properties in an object o:

```
for (f in o) {
    document.write('o.' + f + ' = ' + o[f]);
    document.write('<br>');
}
```

5.10.8 The Function Call Operator

The ( ) operator is used to invoke functions in JavaScript. This is an unusual operator because it does not have a fixed number of operands. The first operand is always the name of a function or an expression that refers to a function. It is followed by the left parenthesis and any number of additional operands, which may be arbitrary expressions, each separated from the next with a comma. The right parenthesis follows the final operand. The ( ) operator evaluates each of its operands and then invokes the function specified by the first operand, with the values of the remaining operands passed as arguments. For example:

```
document.close()
Math.sin(x)
alert("Welcome " + name)
Date.UTC(2000, 11, 31, 23, 59, 59)
funcs[i].f(funcs[i].args[0], funcs[i].args[1])
```

CHAPTER 6

Statements

As shown in the last chapter, expressions are JavaScript phrases that can be evaluated to yield a value. Operators within an expression may have side effects, but in general, expressions don't do anything. To make something happen, you use a JavaScript *statement*, which is akin to a complete sentence or command. This chapter describes the various statements in JavaScript and explains their syntax. A JavaScript program is simply a collection of statements, so once you are familiar with the statements of JavaScript, you can begin writing JavaScript programs.

Before getting into JavaScript statements, recall from Section 2.4 that statements in JavaScript are separated from each other with semicolons. If you place each statement on a separate line, however, JavaScript allows you to leave out the semicolons. Nevertheless, it is a good idea to get in the habit of using semicolons everywhere.

6.1   Expression Statements

The simplest kinds of statements in JavaScript are expressions that have side effects. This sort of statement was shown in Chapter 5. Assignment statements are one major category of expression statements. For example:

```
s = "Hello " + name;
i *= 3;
```

The increment and decrement operators, ++ and --, are related to assignment statements. These have the side effect of changing a variable value, just as if an assignment had been performed:

```
counter++;
```

The delete operator has the important side effect of deleting an object property. Thus, it is almost always used as a statement, rather than as part of a larger expression:

```
delete o.x;
```

Function calls are another major category of expression statements. For example:

```
alert("Welcome, " + name);
window.close();
```

These client-side function calls are expressions, but they also affect the web browser, so they are statements, too.

If a function does not have any side effects, there is no sense in calling it, unless it is part of an assignment statement. For example, you wouldn't just compute a cosine and discard the result:

```
Math.cos(x);
```

Instead, you'd compute the value and assign it to a variable for future use:

```
cx = Math.cos(x);
```

Again, please note that each line of code in each of these examples is terminated with a semicolon.

6.2   Compound Statements

Chapter 5 described how the comma operator can combine a number of expressions into a single expression. JavaScript also has a way to combine a number of statements into a single statement, or *statement block*. This is done simply by enclosing any number of statements within curly braces. Thus, the following lines act as a single statement and can be used anywhere that JavaScript expects a single statement:

```
{
    x = Math.PI;
    cx = Math.cos(x);
    alert("cos(" + x + ") = " + cx);
}
```

Note that although this statement block acts as a single statement, it does *not* end with a semicolon. The primitive statements within the block end in semicolons, but the block itself does not.

Although combining expressions with the comma operator is an infrequently used technique, combining statements into larger statement blocks is extremely common. As you'll see in the following sections, a number of JavaScript statements themselves contain statements (just as expressions can contain other expressions); these statements are *compound statements*. Formal JavaScript syntax specifies that each of these compound statements contains a single substatement. Using statement blocks, you can place any number of statements within this single allowed substatement.

To execute a compound statement, the JavaScript interpreter simply executes the statements that comprise it one after another, in the order in which they are written. Normally, the JavaScript interpreter executes all of the statements. In some circumstances, however, a compound statement may terminate abruptly. This termination occurs if the compound statement contains a break, continue, return, or throw statement; if it causes an error; or if it calls a function that causes an uncaught error or throws an uncaught exception. You'll learn more about these abrupt terminations in later sections.

6.3   if

The if statement is the fundamental control statement that allows JavaScript to make decisions, or, more precisely, to execute statements conditionally. This statement has two forms. The first is:

```
if (expression)
    statement
```

In this form, *expression* is evaluated. If the resulting value is true or can be converted to true, *statement* is executed. If *expression* is false or converts to false, *statement* is not executed. For example:

```
if (username == null)        // If username is null or undefined,
    username = "John Doe";   // define it
```

Or similarly:

```
// If username is null, undefined, 0, "", or NaN, it converts to false,
// and this statement will assign a new value to it.
if (!username) username = "John Doe";
```

Although they look extraneous, the parentheses around the expression are a required part of the syntax for the if statement.

As mentioned in the previous section, you can always replace a single statement with a statement block. So the if statement might also look like this:

```
if ((address == null) || (address == "")) {
    address = "undefined";
    alert("Please specify a mailing address.");
}
```

The indentation used in these examples is not mandatory. Extra spaces and tabs are ignored in JavaScript, and since semicolons are used after all the primitive statements, these examples could have been written all on one line. Using line breaks and indentation as shown here, however, makes the code easier to read and understand.

The second form of the if statement introduces an else clause that is executed when *expression* is false. Its syntax is:

```
if (expression)
    statement1
else
    statement2
```

In this form of the statement, *expression* is evaluated, and if it is true, `statement1` is executed; otherwise, `statement2` is executed. For example:

```
if (username != null)
    alert("Hello " + username + "\nWelcome to my blog.");
else {
    username = prompt("Welcome!\n What is your name?");
    alert("Hello " + username);
}
```

When you have nested `if` statements with `else` clauses, some caution is required to ensure that the `else` clause goes with the appropriate `if` statement. Consider the following lines:

```
i = j = 1;
k = 2;
if (i == j)
    if (j == k)
        document.write("i equals k");
else
    document.write("i doesn't equal j");    // WRONG!!
```

In this example, the inner `if` statement forms the single statement allowed by the syntax of the outer `if` statement. Unfortunately, it is not clear (except from the hint given by the indentation) which `if` the `else` goes with. And in this example, the indenting hint is wrong, because a JavaScript interpreter actually interprets the previous example as:

```
if (i == j) {
    if (j == k)
        document.write("i equals k");
    else
    document.write("i doesn't equal j");    // OOPS!
}
```

The rule in JavaScript (as in most programming languages) is that by default an `else` clause is part of the nearest `if` statement. To make this example less ambiguous and easier to read, understand, maintain, and debug, you should use curly braces:

```
if (i == j) {
    if (j == k) {
        document.write("i equals k");
    }
}
else {  // What a difference the location of a curly brace makes!
    document.write("i doesn't equal j");
}
```

Although it is not the style used in this book, many programmers make a habit of enclosing the bodies of `if` and `else` statements (as well as other compound statements, such as `while` loops) within curly braces, even when the body consists of only a single statement. Doing so consistently can prevent the sort of problem just shown.

6.4   else if

I've shown that the if/else statement can test a condition and execute one of two
pieces of code, depending on the outcome. But what about when you need to execute one of many pieces of code? One way to do this is with an else if statement.
else if is not really a JavaScript statement, but simply a frequently used programming idiom that results when repeated if/else statements are used:

```
if (n == 1) {
    // Execute code block #1
}
else if (n == 2) {
    // Execute code block #2
}
else if (n == 3) {
    // Execute code block #3
}
else {
    // If all else fails, execute block #4
}
```

There is nothing special about this code. It is just a series of if statements, where
each following if is part of the else clause of the previous statement. Using the else
if idiom is preferable to, and more legible than, writing these statements out in their
syntactically equivalent, fully nested form:

```
if (n == 1) {
    // Execute code block #1
}
else {
    if (n == 2) {
        // Execute code block #2
    }
    else {
        if (n == 3) {
            // Execute code block #3
        }
        else {
            // If all else fails, execute block #4
        }
    }
}
```

6.5   switch

An if statement causes a branch in the flow of a program's execution. You can use
multiple if statements, as in the previous section, to perform a multiway branch.
However, this is not always the best solution, especially when all of the branches
depend on the value of a single variable. In this case, it is wasteful to repeatedly
check the value of the same variable in multiple if statements.

The switch statement handles exactly this situation, and it does so more efficiently than repeated if statements. The JavaScript switch statement is quite similar to the switch statement in Java or C. The switch keyword is followed by an expression and a block of code, much like the if statement:

```
switch(expression) {
    statements
}
```

However, the full syntax of a switch statement is more complex than this. Various locations in the block of code are labeled with the case keyword followed by a value and a colon. When a switch executes, it computes the value of *expression* and then looks for a case label that matches that value. If it finds one, it starts executing the block of code at the first statement following the case label. If it does not find a case label with a matching value, it starts execution at the first statement following a special default: label. Or, if there is no default: label, it skips the block of code altogether.

switch is a confusing statement to explain; its operation becomes much clearer with an example. The following switch statement is equivalent to the repeated if/else statements shown in the previous section:

```
switch(n) {
    case 1:                            // Start here if n == 1
        // Execute code block #1.
        break;                         // Stop here
    case 2:                            // Start here if n == 2
        // Execute code block #2.
        break;                         // Stop here
    case 3:                            // Start here if n == 3
        // Execute code block #3.
        break;                         // Stop here
    default:                           // If all else fails...
        // Execute code block #4.
        break;                         // stop here
}
```

Note the break keyword used at the end of each case in the code above. The break statement, described later in this chapter, causes execution to jump to the end of a switch statement or loop. The case clauses in a switch statement specify only the *starting point* of the desired code; they do not specify any ending point. In the absence of break statements, a switch statement begins executing its block of code at the case label that matches the value of its *expression* and continues executing statements until it reaches the end of the block. On rare occasions, it is useful to write code like this that falls through from one case label to the next, but 99 percent of the time you should be careful to end every case within a switch with a break statement. (When using switch inside a function, however, you may use a return statement instead of a break statement. Both serve to terminate the switch statement and prevent execution from falling through to the next case.)

Here is a more realistic example of the switch statement; it converts a value to a string in a way that depends on the type of the value:

```
function convert(x) {
    switch(typeof x) {
        case 'number':          // Convert the number to a hexadecimal integer
            return x.toString(16);
        case 'string':          // Return the string enclosed in quotes
            return '"' + x + '"';
        case 'boolean':         // Convert to TRUE or FALSE, in uppercase
            return x.toString().toUpperCase();
        default:                // Convert any other type in the usual way
            return x.toString()
    }
}
```

Note that in the two previous examples, the case keywords are followed by number and string literals, respectively. This is how the switch statement is most often used in practice, but note that the ECMAScript standard allows each case to be followed by an arbitrary expression.* For example:

```
case 60*60*24:
case Math.PI:
case n+1:
case a[0]:
```

The switch statement first evaluates the expression that follows the switch keyword and then evaluates the case expressions, in the order in which they appear, until it finds a value that matches.† The matching case is determined using the === identity operator, not the == equality operator, so the expressions must match without any type conversion.

Note that it is not good programming practice to use case expressions that contain side effects such as function calls or assignments, because not all of the case expressions are evaluated each time the switch statement is executed. When side effects occur only sometimes, it can be difficult to understand and predict the correct behavior of your program. The safest course is simply to limit your case expressions to constant expressions.

As explained earlier, if none of the case expressions match the switch expression, the switch statement begins executing its body at the statement labeled default:. If there is no default: label, the switch statement skips its body altogether. Note that in the

---

* This makes the JavaScript switch statement much different from the switch statement of C, C++, and Java. In those languages, the case expressions must be compile-time constants, must evaluate to integers or other integral types, and must all evaluate to the same type.

† This means that the JavaScript switch statement is not nearly as efficient as the switch statement in C, C++, and Java. Since the case expressions in those languages are compile-time constants, they never need to be evaluated at runtime as they are in JavaScript. Furthermore, since the case expressions are integral values in C, C++, and Java, the switch statement can often be implemented using a highly efficient *jump table*.

earlier examples, the `default:` label appears at the end of the `switch` body, following all the case labels. This is a logical and common place for it, but it can actually appear anywhere within the body of the statement.

6.6   while

Just as the `if` statement is the basic control statement that allows JavaScript to make decisions, the `while` statement is the basic statement that allows JavaScript to perform repetitive actions. It has the following syntax:

```
while (expression)
    statement
```

The `while` statement works by first evaluating *expression*. If it is `false`, JavaScript moves on to the next statement in the program. If it is `true`, the *statement* that forms the body of the loop is executed, and *expression* is evaluated again. Again, if the value of *expression* is `false`, JavaScript moves on to the next statement in the program; otherwise, it executes *statement* again. This cycle continues until *expression* evaluates to `false`, at which point the `while` statement ends and JavaScript moves on. Note that you can create an infinite loop with the syntax `while(true)`.

Usually, you do not want JavaScript to perform exactly the same operation over and over again. In almost every loop, one or more variables change with each *iteration* of the loop. Since the variables change, the actions performed by executing *statement* may differ each time through the loop. Furthermore, if the changing variable or variables are involved in *expression*, the value of the expression may be different each time through the loop. This is important; otherwise, an expression that starts off `true` would never change, and the loop would never end! Here is an example of a `while` loop:

```
var count = 0;
while (count < 10) {
    document.write(count + "<br>");
    count++;
}
```

As you can see, the variable `count` starts off at 0 in this example and is incremented each time the body of the loop runs. Once the loop has executed 10 times, the expression becomes `false` (i.e., the variable `count` is no longer less than 10), the `while` statement finishes, and JavaScript can move on to the next statement in the program. Most loops have a counter variable like `count`. The variable names `i`, `j`, and `k` are commonly used as loop counters, though you should use more descriptive names if it makes your code easier to understand.

6.7   do/while

The do/while loop is much like a while loop, except that the loop expression is tested at the bottom of the loop rather than at the top. This means that the body of the loop is always executed at least once. The syntax is:

```
do
    statement
while (expression);
```

The do/while loop is less commonly used than its while cousin. This is because, in practice, it is somewhat uncommon to encounter a situation in which you are always sure that you want a loop to execute at least once. Here's an example of a do/while loop:

```
function printArray(a) {
    if (a.length == 0)
        document.write("Empty Array");
    else {
        var i = 0;
        do {
            document.write(a[i] + "<br>");
        } while (++i < a.length);
    }
}
```

There are a couple of syntactic differences between the do/while loop and the ordinary while loop. First, the do loop requires both the do keyword (to mark the beginning of the loop) and the while keyword (to mark the end and introduce the loop condition). Also, unlike the while loop, the do loop is terminated with a semicolon. This is because the do loop ends with the loop condition, rather than simply with a curly brace that marks the end of the loop body.

6.8   for

The for statement provides a looping construct that is often more convenient than the while statement. The for statement takes advantage of a pattern common to most loops (including the earlier while loop example). Most loops have a counter variable of some kind. This variable is initialized before the loop starts and is tested as part of the *expression* evaluated before each iteration of the loop. Finally, the counter variable is incremented or otherwise updated at the end of the loop body, just before *expression* is evaluated again.

The initialization, the test, and the update are the three crucial manipulations of a loop variable; the for statement makes these three steps an explicit part of the loop syntax. This makes it especially easy to understand what a for loop is doing and prevents mistakes such as forgetting to initialize or increment the loop variable. Here's the syntax of the for statement:

```
for(initialize ; test ; increment)
    statement
```

The simplest way to explain what this for loop does is to show the equivalent while loop:[*]

```
initialize;
while(test) {
    statement
    increment;
}
```

In other words, the *initialize* expression is evaluated once, before the loop begins. To be useful, this expression must have side effects (usually an assignment). JavaScript also allows *initialize* to be a var variable declaration statement so that you can declare and initialize a loop counter at the same time. The *test* expression is evaluated before each iteration and controls whether the body of the loop is executed. If the *test* expression is true, the *statement* that is the body of the loop is executed. Finally, the *increment* expression is evaluated. Again, this must be an expression with side effects in order to be useful. Generally, either it is an assignment expression, or it uses the ++ or -- operators.

The while loop example in the previous section can be rewritten as the following for loop, which counts from 0 to 9:

```
for(var count = 0 ; count < 10 ; count++)
    document.write(count + "<br>");
```

Notice that this syntax places all the important information about the loop variable on a single line, which makes it clear how the loop executes. Also note that placing the *increment* expression in the for statement itself simplifies the body of the loop to a single statement; you don't even need to use curly braces to produce a statement block.

Loops can become a lot more complex than these simple examples, of course, and sometimes multiple variables change with each iteration of the loop. This situation is the only place that the comma operator is commonly used in JavaScript; it provides a way to combine multiple initialization and increment expressions into a single expression suitable for use in a for loop. For example:

```
for(i = 0, j = 10 ; i < 10 ; i++, j--)
    sum += i * j;
```

[*] As you will see when you consider the continue statement in Section 6.12, this while loop is not an exact equivalent of the for loop.

6.9 for/in

The for keyword is used in two ways in JavaScript. You've just seen how it is used in the for loop. It is also used in the for/in statement. This statement is a somewhat different kind of loop with the following syntax:

```
for (variable in object)
    statement
```

variable should be either the name of a variable, a var statement declaring a variable, an element of an array, or a property of an object (i.e., it should be something suitable as the left side of an assignment expression). *object* is the name of an object or an expression that evaluates to an object. As usual, *statement* is the statement or statement block that forms the body of the loop.

You can loop through the elements of an array by simply incrementing an index variable each time through a while or for loop. The for/in statement provides a way to loop through the properties of an object. The body of the for/in loop is executed once for each property of *object*. Before the body of the loop is executed, the name of one of the object's properties is assigned to *variable*, as a string. Within the body of the loop, you can use this variable to look up the value of the object's property with the [] operator. For example, the following for/in loop prints the name and value of each property of an object:

```
for (var prop in my_object) {
    document.write("name: " + prop + "; value: " + my_object[prop], "<br>");
}
```

Note that the *variable* in the for/in loop may be an arbitrary expression, as long as it evaluates to something suitable for the left side of an assignment. This expression is evaluated each time through the loop, which means that it may evaluate differently each time. For example, you can use code like the following to copy the names of all object properties into an array:

```
var o = {x:1, y:2, z:3};
var a = new Array();
var i = 0;
for(a[i++] in o) /* empty loop body */;
```

JavaScript arrays are simply a specialized kind of object. Therefore, the for/in loop enumerates array indexes as well as object properties. For example, following the previous code block with this line enumerates the array "properties" 0, 1, and 2:

```
for(i in a) alert(i);
```

The for/in loop does not specify the order in which the properties of an object are assigned to the variable. There is no way to tell what the order will be in advance, and the behavior may differ among implementations or versions of JavaScript. If the body of a for/in loop deletes a property that has not yet been enumerated, that property will not be enumerated. If the body of the loop defines new properties, whether or not those properties will be enumerated by the loop is implementation-dependent.

The for/in loop does not actually loop through all possible properties of all objects. In the same way that some object properties are flagged to be read-only or permanent (nondeletable), certain properties are flagged to be nonenumerable. These properties are not enumerated by the for/in loop. While all user-defined properties are enumerated, many built-in properties, including all built-in methods, are not enumerated. As you'll see in Chapter 7, objects can inherit properties from other objects. Inherited properties that are user-defined are also enumerated by the for/in loop.

6.10 Labels

The case and default: labels used with the switch statement are a special case of a more general label statement. Any statement may be labeled by preceding it with an identifier name and a colon:

```
identifier: statement
```

The identifier can be any legal JavaScript identifier that is not a reserved word. Label names are distinct from variable and function names, so you do not need to worry about name collisions if you give a label the same name as a variable or function. Here is an example of a labeled while statement:

```
parser:
  while(token != null) {
      // Code omitted here
  }
```

By labeling a statement, you give it a name that you can use to refer to it elsewhere in your program. You can label any statement, although the only statements that are commonly labeled are loops: while, do/while, for, and for/in. By giving a loop a name, you can use break and continue to exit the loop or to exit a single iteration of the loop (see the following two sections).

6.11 break

The break statement causes the innermost enclosing loop or a switch statement to exit immediately. Its syntax is simple:

```
break;
```

Because it causes a loop or switch to exit, this form of the break statement is legal only if it appears within one of these statements.

JavaScript allows the break keyword to be followed by the name of a label:

```
break labelname;
```

Note that *labelname* is simply an identifier; it is not followed by a colon, as it would be when defining a labeled statement.

When break is used with a label, it jumps to the end of, or terminates, the named statement, which may be any enclosing statement. The named statement need not be a loop or switch; a break statement used with a label need not even be contained within a loop or switch. The only restriction on the label of the break statement is that it name an *enclosing* statement. The label can name an if statement, for example, or even a block of statements grouped within curly braces, for the sole purpose of naming the block with a label.

As discussed in Chapter 2, a newline is not allowed between the break keyword and the *labelname*. This is an oddity of JavaScript syntax caused by its automatic insertion of omitted semicolons. If you break a line of code between the break keyword and the following label, JavaScript assumes you meant to use the simple, unlabeled form of the statement and adds a semicolon for you.

I've already shown examples of the break statement within a switch statement. In loops, it is typically used to exit prematurely when, for whatever reason, there is no longer any need to complete the loop. When a loop has complex termination conditions, it is often easier to implement some of these conditions with break statements rather than trying to express them all in a single loop expression.

The following code searches the elements of an array for a particular value. The loop terminates naturally when it reaches the end of the array; it terminates with a break statement if it finds what it is looking for in the array:

```
for(i = 0; i < a.length; i++) {
    if (a[i] == target)
        break;
}
```

You need the labeled form of the break statement only when you are using nested loops or switch statements and need to break out of a statement that is not the innermost one.

The following example shows labeled for loops and labeled break statements. See if you can figure out what its output will be:

```
outerloop:
  for(var i = 0; i < 10; i++) {
    innerloop:
      for(var j = 0; j < 10; j++) {
          if (j > 3) break;               // Quit the innermost loop
          if (i == 2) break innerloop;    // Do the same thing
          if (i == 4) break outerloop;    // Quit the outer loop
          document.write("i = " + i + " j = " + j + "<br>");
      }
  }
  document.write("FINAL i = " + i + " j = " + j + "<br>");
```

6.12 continue

The continue statement is similar to the break statement. Instead of exiting a loop, however, continue restarts a loop in a new iteration. The continue statement's syntax is just as simple as the break statement's:

```
continue;
```

The continue statement can also be used with a label:

```
continue labelname;
```

The continue statement, in both its labeled and unlabeled forms, can be used only within the body of a while, do/while, for, or for/in loop. Using it anywhere else causes a syntax error.

When the continue statement is executed, the current iteration of the enclosing loop is terminated, and the next iteration begins. This means different things for different types of loops:

- In a while loop, the specified *expression* at the beginning of the loop is tested again, and if it's true, the loop body is executed starting from the top.

- In a do/while loop, execution skips to the bottom of the loop, where the loop condition is tested again before restarting the loop at the top.

- In a for loop, the *increment* expression is evaluated, and the *test* expression is tested again to determine if another iteration should be done.

- In a for/in loop, the loop starts over with the next property name being assigned to the specified variable.

Note the difference in behavior of the continue statement in the while and for loops: a while loop returns directly to its condition, but a for loop first evaluates its *increment* expression and then returns to its condition. Previously, in the discussion of the for loop, I explained the behavior of the for loop in terms of an equivalent while loop. Because the continue statement behaves differently for these two loops, it is not possible to perfectly simulate a for loop with a while loop.

The following example shows an unlabeled continue statement being used to exit the current iteration of a loop when an error occurs:

```
for(i = 0; i < data.length; i++) {
    if (data[i] == null)
        continue;  // Can't proceed with undefined data
    total += data[i];
}
```

Like the break statement, the continue statement can be used in its labeled form within nested loops, when the loop to be restarted is not the immediately enclosing loop. Also, like the break statement, line breaks are not allowed between the continue statement and its *labelname*.

6.13 var

The var statement allows you to explicitly declare a variable or variables. Here's the syntax of this statement:

```
var name_1 [ = value_1] [ ,..., name_n [= value_n]]
```

The var keyword is followed by a comma-separated list of variables to declare; each variable in the list may optionally have an initializer expression that specifies its initial value. For example:

```
var i;
var j = 0;
var p, q;
var greeting = "hello" + name;
var x = 2.34, y = Math.cos(0.75), r, theta;
```

The var statement defines each named variable by creating a property with that name either in the call object of the enclosing function or, if the declaration does not appear within a function body, in the global object. The property or properties created by a var statement cannot be deleted with the delete operator. Note that enclosing a var statement in a with statement (see Section 6.18) does not change its behavior.

If no initial value is specified for a variable with the var statement, the variable is defined, but its initial value is undefined.

Note that the var statement can also appear as part of the for and for/in loops. For example:

```
for(var i = 0; i < 10; i++) document.write(i, "<br>");
for(var i = 0, j=10; i < 10; i++,j--) document.write(i*j, "<br>");
for(var i in o) document.write(i, "<br>");
```

Chapter 4 contains much more information on JavaScript variables and variable declarations.

6.14 function

The function statement defines a JavaScript function. It has the following syntax:

```
function funcname([arg1 [,arg2 [..., argn]]]) {
    statements
}
```

funcname is the name of the function being defined. This must be an identifier, not a string or an expression. The function name is followed by a comma-separated list of argument names in parentheses. These identifiers can be used within the body of the function to refer to the argument values passed when the function is invoked.

The body of the function is composed of any number of JavaScript statements, contained within curly braces. These statements are not executed when the function is defined. Instead, they are compiled and associated with the new function object for execution when the function is invoked with the ( ) function call operator. Note that the curly braces are a required part of the function statement. Unlike statement blocks used with while loops and other statements, a function body requires curly braces, even if the body consists of only a single statement.

A function definition creates a new function object and stores that object in a newly created property named *funcname*. Here are some examples of function definitions:

```
function welcome() { alert("Welcome to my blog!"); }

function print(msg) {
    document.write(msg, "<br>");
}

function hypotenuse(x, y) {
    return Math.sqrt(x*x + y*y);   // return is documented in the next section
}

function factorial(n) {          // A recursive function
    if (n <= 1) return 1;
    return n * factorial(n - 1);
}
```

Function definitions usually appear in top-level JavaScript code. They may also be nested within other function definitions, but only at the "top level" of those functions—that is, function definitions may not appear within if statements, while loops, or any other statements.

Technically speaking, the function statement is not a statement. Statements cause dynamic behavior in a JavaScript program, while function definitions describe the static structure of a program. Statements are executed at runtime, but functions are defined when JavaScript code is parsed, or compiled, before it is actually run. When the JavaScript parser encounters a function definition, it parses and stores (without executing) the statements that comprise the body of the function. Then it defines a property (in the call object if the function definition is nested in another function; otherwise, in the global object) with the same name as the function to hold the function.

The fact that function definitions occur at parse time rather than at runtime causes some surprising effects. Consider the following code:

```
alert(f(4));      // Displays 16. f() can be called before it is defined.
var f = 0;        // This statement overwrites the property f.
function f(x) {   // This "statement" defines the function f before either
    return x*x;   // of the lines above are executed.
}
alert(f);         // Displays 0. f() has been overwritten by the variable f.
```

These unusual results occur because function definition occurs at a different time than variable definition. Fortunately, these situations do not arise very often.

You'll learn more about functions in Chapter 8.

6.15 return

As you'll recall, a function invocation using the ( ) operator is an expression. All expressions have values; the return statement specifies the value returned by a function, which is thus the value of the function-invocation expression. Here's the syntax of the return statement:

```
return expression;
```

A return statement may appear only within the body of a function. It is a syntax error for it to appear anywhere else. When the return statement is executed, *expression* is evaluated and returned as the value of the function. Execution of the function stops when the return statement is executed, even if there are other statements remaining in the function body. The return statement can be used to return a value like this:

```
function square(x) { return x*x; }
```

The return statement may also be used without an *expression* to simply terminate execution of the function without returning a value. For example:

```
function display_object(obj) {
    // First make sure our argument is valid
    // Skip the rest of the function if it is not
    if (obj == null) return;
    // Rest of function goes here...
}
```

If a function executes a return statement with no *expression*, or if it returns because it reaches the end of the function body, the value of the function-call expression is undefined.

Because of JavaScript's automatic semicolon insertion, you may not include a line break between the return keyword and the expression that follows it.

6.16 throw

An *exception* is a signal that indicates that some sort of exceptional condition or error has occurred. To *throw* an exception is to signal such an error or exceptional condition. To *catch* an exception is to handle it—to take whatever actions are necessary or appropriate to recover from the exception. In JavaScript, exceptions are thrown whenever a runtime error occurs and whenever the program explicitly throws one using the throw statement. Exceptions are caught with the try/catch/finally statement, which is described in the next section.[*]

---

[*] The JavaScript throw and try/catch/finally statements are similar to, but not exactly the same as, the corresponding statements in C++ and Java.

The throw statement has the following syntax:

```
throw expression;
```

expression may evaluate to a value of any type. Commonly, however, it is an Error object or an instance of one of the subclasses of Error. It can also be useful to throw a string that contains an error message, or a numeric value that represents some sort of error code. Here is some sample code that uses the throw statement to throw an exception:

```
function factorial(x) {
    // If the input argument is invalid, throw an exception!
    if (x < 0) throw new Error("x must not be negative");
    // Otherwise, compute a value and return normally
    for(var f = 1; x > 1; f *= x, x--) /* empty */ ;
    return f;
}
```

When an exception is thrown, the JavaScript interpreter immediately stops normal program execution and jumps to the nearest exception handler. Exception handlers are written using the catch clause of the try/catch/finally statement, which is described in the next section. If the block of code in which the exception was thrown does not have an associated catch clause, the interpreter checks the next highest enclosing block of code to see if it has an exception handler associated with it. This continues until a handler is found. If an exception is thrown in a function that does not contain a try/catch/finally statement to handle it, the exception propagates up to the code that invoked the function. In this way, exceptions propagate up through the lexical structure of JavaScript methods and up the call stack. If no exception handler is ever found, the exception is treated as an error and is reported to the user.

The throw statement is standardized by ECMAScript v3 and implemented in JavaScript 1.4. The Error class and its subclasses are also part of ECMAScript v3, but they were not implemented until JavaScript 1.5.

6.17   try/catch/finally

The try/catch/finally statement is JavaScript's exception-handling mechanism. The try clause of this statement simply defines the block of code whose exceptions are to be handled. The try block is followed by a catch clause, which is a block of statements that are invoked when an exception occurs anywhere within the try block. The catch clause is followed by a finally block containing cleanup code that is guaranteed to be executed, regardless of what happens in the try block. Both the catch and finally blocks are optional, but a try block must be accompanied by at least one of these blocks. The try, catch, and finally blocks all begin and end with curly braces. These braces are a required part of the syntax and cannot be omitted, even if a clause contains only a single statement. Like the throw statement, the try/catch/finally statement is standardized by ECMAScript v3 and implemented in JavaScript 1.4.

The following code illustrates the syntax and purpose of the try/catch/finally statement. In particular, note that the catch keyword is followed by an identifier in parentheses. This identifier is like a function argument. It names a local variable that exists only within the body of the catch block. JavaScript assigns whatever exception object or value was thrown to this variable:

```
try {
    // Normally, this code runs from the top of the block to the bottom
    // without problems. But it can sometimes throw an exception,
    // either directly, with a throw statement, or indirectly, by calling
    // a method that throws an exception.
}
catch (e) {
    // The statements in this block are executed if, and only if, the try
    // block throws an exception. These statements can use the local variable
    // e to refer to the Error object or other value that was thrown.
    // This block may handle the exception somehow, may ignore the
    // exception by doing nothing, or may rethrow the exception with throw.
}
finally {
    // This block contains statements that are always executed, regardless of
    // what happens in the try block. They are executed whether the try
    // block terminates:
    //    1) normally, after reaching the bottom of the block
    //    2) because of a break, continue, or return statement
    //    3) with an exception that is handled by a catch clause above
    //    4) with an uncaught exception that is still propagating
}
```

Here is a realistic example of the try/catch statement. It uses the factorial( ) method defined in the previous section and the client-side JavaScript methods prompt( ) and alert( ) for input and output:

```
try {
    // Ask the user to enter a number
    var n = prompt("Please enter a positive integer", "");
    // Compute the factorial of the number, assuming that the user's
    // input is valid
    var f = factorial(n);
    // Display the result
    alert(n + "! = " + f);
}
catch (ex) {  // If the user's input was not valid, we end up here
    // Tell the user what the error is
    alert(ex);
}
```

This example is a try/catch statement with no finally clause. Although finally is not used as often as catch, it can often be useful. However, its behavior requires additional explanation. The finally clause is guaranteed to be executed if any portion of the try block is executed, regardless of how the code in the try block completes. It is generally used to clean up after the code in the try clause.

In the normal case, control reaches the end of the try block and then proceeds to the finally block, which performs any necessary cleanup. If control leaves the try block because of a return, continue, or break statement, the finally block is executed before control transfers to its new destination.

If an exception occurs in the try block and there is an associated catch block to handle the exception, control transfers first to the catch block and then to the finally block. If there is no local catch block to handle the exception, control transfers first to the finally block and then propagates up to the nearest containing catch clause that can handle the exception.

If a finally block itself transfers control with a return, continue, break, or throw statement, or by calling a method that throws an exception, the pending control transfer is abandoned, and this new transfer is processed. For example, if a finally clause throws an exception, that exception replaces any exception that was in the process of being thrown. If a finally clause issues a return statement, the method returns normally, even if an exception has been thrown and has not yet been handled.

try and finally can be used together without a catch clause. In this case, the finally block is simply cleanup code that is guaranteed to be executed, regardless of any break, continue, or return statements within the try clause. For example, the following code uses a try/finally statement to ensure that a loop counter variable is incremented at the end of each iteration, even when an iteration terminates abruptly because of a continue statement:

```
var i = 0, total = 0;
while(i < a.length) {
    try {
        if ((typeof a[i] != "number") || isNaN(a[i])) // If it is not a number,
            continue;   // go on to the next iteration of the loop.
        total += a[i];  // Otherwise, add the number to the total.
    }
    finally {
        i++;  // Always increment i, even if we used continue above.
    }
}
```

6.18 with

In Chapter 4, we discussed variable scope and the scope chain—a list of objects that are searched, in order, to perform variable name resolution. The with statement is used to temporarily modify the scope chain. It has the following syntax:

```
with (object)
    statement
```

This statement effectively adds object to the front of the scope chain, executes statement, and then restores the scope chain to its original state.

In practice, you can use the with statement to save yourself a lot of typing. In client-side JavaScript, for example, it is common to work with deeply nested object hierarchies. For instance, you may have to type expressions like this one to access elements of an HTML form:

```
frames[1].document.forms[0].address.value
```

If you need to access this form a number of times, you can use the with statement to add the form to the scope chain:

```
with(frames[1].document.forms[0]) {
    // Access form elements directly here. For example:
    name.value = "";
    address.value = "";
    email.value = "";
}
```

This reduces the amount of typing you have to do; you no longer need to prefix each form property name with frames[1].document.forms[0]. That object is temporarily part of the scope chain and is automatically searched when JavaScript needs to resolve an identifier such as address.

Despite its occasional convenience, use of the with statement is frowned upon. JavaScript code that uses with is difficult to optimize and may therefore run more slowly than the equivalent code written without the with statement. Furthermore, function definitions and variable initializations within the body of a with statement can have surprising and counterintuitive behavior.[*] For these reasons, it is recommended that you avoid the with statement.

Note that there are other perfectly legitimate ways to save yourself some typing. For instance, you can rewrite the previous example as follows:

```
var form = frames[1].document.forms[0];
form.name.value = "";
form.address.value = "";
form.email.value = "";
```

6.19 The Empty Statement

One final legal statement in JavaScript is the empty statement. It looks like this:

```
;
```

Executing the empty statement obviously has no effect and performs no action. You might think there would be little reason to ever use such a statement, but the empty statement is occasionally useful when you want to create a loop that has an empty body. For example:

```
// Initialize an array a
for(i=0; i < a.length; a[i++] = 0) ;
```

[*] This behavior, and the reasons behind it, are too complicated to explain here.

Note that the accidental inclusion of a semicolon after the right parenthesis of a for loop, while loop, or if statement can cause frustrating bugs that are difficult to detect. For example, the following code probably does not do what the author intended:

```
if ((a == 0) || (b == 0));    // Oops! This line does nothing...
    o = null;                 // and this line is always executed.
```

When you intentionally use the empty statement, it is a good idea to comment your code in a way that makes it clear that you are doing it on purpose. For example:

```
for(i=0; i < a.length; a[i++] = 0) /* Empty */ ;
```

6.20   Summary of JavaScript Statements

This chapter introduced each of the JavaScript language's statements. Table 6-1 summarizes them, listing the syntax and purpose of each.

Table 6-1. JavaScript statement syntax

Statement	Syntax	Purpose
break	break; break *label*;	Exit from the innermost loop or switch statement or from the statement named by *label*
case	case *expression*:	Label a statement within a switch statement
continue	continue; continue *label*;	Restart the innermost loop or the loop named by *label*
default	default:	Label the default statement within a switch statement
do/while	do *statement* while (*expression*);	An alternative to the while loop
empty	;	Do nothing
for	for (*initialize* ; *test* ; *increment*) *statement*	An easy-to-use loop
for/in	for (*variable* in *object*) *statement*	Loop through the properties of an object

function	function *funcname*([*arg1*[..., *argn*]])
	{
	    statements
	}
		Declare a function

if/else	if (*expression*) *statement1* [else *statement2*]	Conditionally execute code
label	*identifier*: *statement*	Give *statement* the name *identifier*
return	return [*expression*];	Return from a function or return the value of *expression* from a function

Table 6-1. JavaScript statement syntax (continued)

Statement	Syntax	Purpose

switch	switch (*expression*) {
	    statements
	}
		Multiway branch to statements labeled with case or default:

throw	throw *expression*;	Throw an exception

try	try {
	    statements
	}
	catch (*identifier*) {
	    statements
	}
	finally {
	    statements
	}
		Catch an exception

var	var *name_1* [= *value_1*] [,..., *name_n* [= *value_n*]];	Declare and initialize variables
while	while (*expression*) *statement*	A basic loop construct
with	with (*object*) *statement*	Extend the scope chain (deprecated)

CHAPTER 7

Objects and Arrays

Chapter 3, explained that objects and arrays are two fundamental datatypes in Java-Script. They are also two of the most important. Objects and arrays differ from primitive datatypes such as strings and numbers: instead of representing a single value, they are instead collections of values. An object is a collection of named values, and an array is a specialized kind of object that behaves as an ordered collection of numbered values. This chapter describes JavaScript objects and arrays in detail.

7.1 Creating Objects

Objects are composite datatypes: they aggregate multiple values into a single unit and allow you to store and retrieve those values by name. Another way to explain this is to say that an object is an unordered collection of *properties*, each of which has a name and a value. The named values held by an object may be primitive values, such as numbers and strings, or they may themselves be objects.

The easiest way to create an object is to include an object literal in your JavaScript code. An *object literal* is a comma-separated list of property name/value pairs, enclosed within curly braces. Each property name can be a JavaScript identifier or a string, and each property value can be a constant or any JavaScript expression. Here are some examples:

```
var empty = {};  // An object with no properties
var point = { x:0, y:0 };
var circle = { x:point.x, y:point.y+1, radius:2 };
var homer = {
    "name": "Homer Simpson",
    "age": 34,
    "married": true,
    "occupation": "plant operator",
    'email': "homer@example.com"
};
```

An object literal is an expression that creates and initializes a new and distinct object each time it is evaluated. That is, a single object literal can create many new objects if it appears within the body of a loop in a function that is called repeatedly.

The new operator can create specialized kinds of objects. You follow it with an invocation of a constructor function that initializes the properties of the object. For example:

```
var a = new Array( ); // Create an empty array
var d = new Date( );  // Create an object representing the current date and time
var r = new RegExp("javascript", "i");  // Create a pattern-matching object
```

The Array( ), Date( ), and RegExp( ) constructors shown above are a built-in part of core JavaScript. (The Array( ) constructor is described later in this chapter, and you can look up the others in Part III.) The Object( ) constructor creates an empty object, just as the literal {} does.

It is also possible to define your own constructor functions in order to initialize newly created objects in whatever way you'd like. You'll learn how to do this in Chapter 9.

7.2 Object Properties

You normally use the . operator to access the value of an object's properties. The value on the left of the . should be the object whose property you want to access. Usually, this is just the name of the variable that contains the object reference, but it can be any JavaScript expression that evaluates to an object. The value on the right of the . should be the name of the property. This must be an identifier, not a string or an expression. For example, you would refer to the property p in object o with o.p or to the property radius in the object circle with circle.radius. Object properties work like variables: you can store values in them and read values from them. For example:

```
// Create an object. Store a reference to it in a variable.
var book = {};

// Set a property in the object.
book.title = "JavaScript: The Definitive Guide"

// Set some more properties. Note the nested objects.
book.chapter1 = new Object( );
book.chapter1.title = "Introduction to JavaScript";
book.chapter1.pages = 11;
book.chapter2 = { title: "Lexical Structure", pages: 6 };

// Read some property values from the object.
alert("Outline: " + book.title + "\n\t" +
    "Chapter 1 " + book.chapter1.title + "\n\t" +
    "Chapter 2 " + book.chapter2.title);
```

An important point to notice about this example is that you can create a new property of an object simply by assigning a value to it. Although you declare variables with the var keyword, there is no need (and no way) to do so with object properties. Furthermore, once you have created an object property by assigning a value to it, you can change the value of the property at any time simply by assigning a new value:

```
book.title = "JavaScript: The Rhino Book"
```

7.2.1   Enumerating Properties

The for/in loop discussed in Chapter 6 provides a way to loop through, or enumerate, the properties of an object. This can be useful when debugging scripts or when working with objects that may have arbitrary properties whose names you do not know in advance. The following code shows a function you can use to list the property names of an object:

```
function DisplayPropertyNames(obj) {
    var names = "";
    for(var name in obj) names += name + "\n";
    alert(names);
}
```

Note that the for/in loop does not enumerate properties in any specific order, and although it enumerates all user-defined properties, it does not enumerate certain predefined properties or methods.

7.2.2   Checking Property Existence

The in operator (see Chapter 5) can be used to test for the existence of a property. The left side of this operator should be the name of the property as a string. The right side should be the object to be tested. For example:

```
// If o has a property named "x", then set it
if ("x" in o) o.x = 1;
```

The in operator is not often needed, however, because if you query a property that does not exist, the undefined value is returned. Thus, the above code can usually be written like this:

```
// If the property x exists and is not undefined, set it.
if (o.x !== undefined) o.x = 1;
```

Note that it is possible for a property to exist but still be undefined. For example, if you write:

```
o.x = undefined
```

the property x exists but has no value. In this situation, the first line of code in the previous paragraph sets x to 1, but the second line of code does nothing.

Note also that the !== operator was used earlier instead of the more common != operator. !== and === distinguish between undefined and null. Sometimes, however, you don't want to make this distinction:

```
// If the doSomething property exists and is not null or undefined,
// then assume it is a function and invoke it!
if (o.doSomething) o.doSomething();
```

7.2.3 Deleting Properties

You can use the delete operator to delete a property of an object:

```
delete book.chapter2;
```

Note that deleting a property does not merely set the property to undefined; it actually removes the property from the object. After deletion, for/in will not enumerate the property and the in operator will not detect it.

7.3   Objects as Associative Arrays

You've seen the . operator used to access the properties of an object. It is also possible to use the [] operator, which is more commonly used with arrays, to access these properties. Thus, the following two JavaScript expressions have the same value:

```
object.property
object["property"]
```

The important difference to note between these two syntaxes is that in the first, the property name is an identifier, and in the second, the property name is a string. You'll see why this is so important shortly.

In C, C++, Java, and similar strongly typed languages, an object can have only a fixed number of properties, and the names of these properties must be defined in advance. Since JavaScript is a loosely typed language, this rule does not apply: a program can create any number of properties in any object. When you use the . operator to access a property of an object, however, the name of the property is expressed as an identifier. Identifiers must be typed literally into your JavaScript program; they are not a datatype, so they cannot be manipulated by the program.

On the other hand, when you access a property of an object with the [] array notation, the name of the property is expressed as a string. Strings are JavaScript datatypes, so they can be manipulated and created while a program is running. So, for example, you can write the following code in JavaScript:

```
var addr = "";
for(i = 0; i < 4; i++) {
    addr += customer["address" + i] + '\n';
}
```

This code reads and concatenates the address0, address1, address2, and address3 properties of the customer object.

This brief example demonstrates the flexibility of using array notation to access properties of an object with string expressions. This example can be written using the . notation, but there are cases in which only the array notation will do. Suppose, for example, that you are writing a program that uses network resources to compute the current value of the user's stock market investments. The program allows the user to type in the name of each stock she owns as well as the number of shares of each stock. You might use an object named portfolio to hold this information. The object has one property for each stock. The name of the property is the name of the stock, and the property value is the number of shares of that stock. So, for example, if a user holds 50 shares of stock in IBM, the portfolio.ibm property has the value 50.

Part of this program needs to have a loop that prompts the user to enter the name of a stock she owns and then asks her to enter the number of shares she owns of that stock. Inside the loop, you'd have code something like this:

```
var stock_name = get_stock_name_from_user();
var shares = get_number_of_shares();
portfolio[stock_name] = shares;
```

Since the user enters stock names at runtime, there is no way that you can know the property names ahead of time. Since you can't know the property names when you write the program, there is no way you can use the . operator to access the properties of the portfolio object. You can use the [] operator, however, because it uses a string value (which is dynamic and can change at runtime) rather than an identifier (which is static and must be hardcoded in the program) to name the property.

When an object is used in this fashion, it is often called an *associative array*—a data structure that allows you to dynamically associate arbitrary values with arbitrary strings. The term *map* is often used to describe this situation as well: JavaScript objects map strings (property names) to values.

The . notation for accessing properties makes JavaScript objects seem like the static objects of C++ and Java, and they work perfectly well in that capacity. But they also have the powerful ability to associate values with arbitrary strings. In this respect, JavaScript objects are much more like Perl hashes than C++ or Java objects.

Chapter 6 introduced the for/in loop. The real power of this JavaScript statement becomes clear when you consider its use with associative arrays. To return to the stock portfolio example, you can use the following code after the user has entered her portfolio to compute its current total value:

```
var value = 0;
for (stock in portfolio) {
    // For each stock in the portfolio, get the per share value
    // and multiply it by the number of shares.
    value += get_share_value(stock) * portfolio[stock];
}
```

This code cannot be written without the for/in loop because the names of the stocks aren't known in advance. This is the only way to extract those property names from the associative array (or JavaScript object) named portfolio.

7.4   Universal Object Properties and Methods

As discussed earlier, all objects in JavaScript inherit from the Object class. While more specialized categories of objects, such as those created with the Date( ) and RegExp( ) constructors define properties and methods of their own, all objects, however created, also support the properties and methods defined by Object. Because of their universality, these properties and methods are of particular interest.

7.4.1   The constructor Property

In JavaScript, every object has a constructor property that refers to the constructor function that initializes the object. For example, if I create an object d with the Date( ) constructor, the property d.constructor refers to Date:

```
var d = new Date( );
d.constructor == Date;   // Evaluates to true
```

Since constructor functions define new categories or classes of objects, the constructor property can help determine the type of an object. For example, you might use code like the following to determine the type of an unknown value:

```
if ((typeof o == "object") && (o.constructor == Date))
    // Then do something with the Date object...
```

The instanceof operator checks the value of the constructor property, so the code above could also be written:

```
if ((typeof o == "object") && (o instanceof Date))
    // Then do something with the Date object...
```

7.4.2   The toString( ) Method

The toString( ) method takes no arguments; it returns a string that somehow represents the value of the object on which it is invoked. JavaScript invokes this method of an object whenever it needs to convert the object to a string. This occurs, for example, when you use the + operator to concatenate a string with an object or when you pass an object to a method such as alert( ) that expects a string.

The default toString( ) method is not very informative. For example, the following lines of code simply evaluate to the string "[object Object]":

```
var s = { x:1, y:1 }.toString( );
```

Because this default method does not display much useful information, many classes define their own versions of toString( ). For example, when an array is converted to a string, you obtain a list of the array elements, themselves each converted to a string, and when a function is converted to a string, you obtain the source code for the function.

Chapter 9 describes how to define a custom toString( ) method for your own object types.

7.4.3   The toLocaleString( ) Method

In ECMAScript v3 and JavaScript 1.5, the Object class defines a toLocaleString( ) method in addition to its toString( ) method. The purpose of this method is to return a localized string representation of the object. The default toLocaleString( ) method defined by Object doesn't do any localization itself; it always returns exactly the same thing as toString( ). Subclasses, however, may define their own versions of toLocaleString( ). In ECMAScript v3, the Array, Date, and Number classes do define toLocaleString( ) methods that return localized values.

7.4.4   The valueOf( ) Method

The valueOf( ) method is much like the toString( ) method, but it is called when JavaScript needs to convert an object to some primitive type other than a string— typically, a number. JavaScript calls this method automatically if an object is used in a context where a primitive value is required. The default valueOf( ) method does nothing interesting, but some of the built-in categories of objects define their own valueOf( ) method (see Date.valueOf( ), for example). Chapter 9 explains how to define a valueOf( ) method for custom object types you define.

7.4.5   The hasOwnProperty( ) Method

The hasOwnProperty( ) method returns true if the object locally defines a noninherited property with the name specified by the single string argument. Otherwise, it returns false. For example:

```
var o = {};
o.hasOwnProperty("undef");      // false: the property is not defined
o.hasOwnProperty("toString");   // false: toString is an inherited property
Math.hasOwnProperty("cos");     // true: the Math object has a cos property
```

Property inheritance is explained in Chapter 9.

This method is defined in ECMAScript v3 and implemented in JavaScript 1.5 and later.

7.4.6   The propertyIsEnumerable( ) Method

The propertyIsEnumerable( ) method returns true if the object defines a noninherited property with the name specified by the single string argument to the method and if that property would be enumerated by a for/in loop. Otherwise, it returns false. For example:

```
var o = { x:1 };
o.propertyIsEnumerable("x");       // true: property exists and is enumerable
o.propertyIsEnumerable("y");       // false: property doesn't exist
o.propertyIsEnumerable("valueOf"); // false: property is inherited
```

This method is defined in ECMAScript v3 and implemented in JavaScript 1.5 and later.

Note that all user-defined properties of an object are enumerable. Nonenumerable properties are typically inherited properties (see Chapter 9 for a discussion of property inheritance), so this method almost always returns the same result as hasOwnProperty( ).

7.4.7 The isPrototypeOf( ) Method

The isPrototypeOf( ) method returns true if the object to which the method is attached is the prototype object of the argument. Otherwise, it returns false. For example:

```
var o = {}
Object.prototype.isPrototypeOf(o);       // true: o.constructor == Object
Object.isPrototypeOf(o);                 // false
o.isPrototypeOf(Object.prototype);       // false
Function.prototype.isPrototypeOf(Object); // true: Object.constructor==Function
```

Prototype methods are documented in Chapter 9.

7.5 Arrays

An *array* is an ordered collection of values. Each value is called an *element*, and each element has a numeric position in the array, known as its *index*. Because JavaScript is an untyped language, an element of an array may be of any type, and different elements of the same array may be of different types. Array elements may even contain other arrays, which allows you to create data structures that are arrays of arrays.

Throughout this book, objects and arrays are often treated as distinct datatypes. This is a useful and reasonable simplification; you can treat objects and arrays as separate types for most of your JavaScript programming. To fully understand the behavior of objects and arrays, however, you have to know the truth: an array is nothing more than an object with a thin layer of extra functionality. You can see this with the typeof operator: applied to an array value, it returns the string "object".

The easiest way to create an array is with an array literal, which is simply a comma-separated list of array elements within square brackets. For example:

```
var empty = [];              // An array with no elements
var primes = [2, 3, 5, 7, 11]; // An array with 5 numeric elements
var misc = [ 1.1, true, "a", ]; // 3 elements of various types
```

The values in an array literal need not be constants; they may be arbitrary expressions:

```
var base = 1024;
var table = [base, base+1, base+2, base+3];
```

Array literals can contain object literals or other array literals:

```
var b = [[1,{x:1, y:2}], [2, {x:3, y:4}]];
```

The first value in an array literal is stored at index 0 of the newly created array. The second value is stored at index 1, and so on. Undefined elements are created by simply omitting the element value between commas:

```
var count = [1,,3]; // An array with 3 elements, the middle one undefined.
var undefs = [,,];  // An array with 2 elements, both undefined.
```

Another way to create an array is with the Array( ) constructor. You can invoke this constructor in three distinct ways:

- Call it with no arguments:

    ```
    var a = new Array( );
    ```

    This method creates an empty array with no elements and is equivalent to the array literal [ ].

- Explicitly specify values for the first *n* elements of an array:

    ```
    var a = new Array(5, 4, 3, 2, 1, "testing, testing");
    ```

    In this form, the constructor takes a list of arguments. Each argument specifies an element value and may be of any type. Elements are assigned to the array starting with element 0. The length property of the array is set to the number of arguments passed to the constructor. Using an array literal is almost always simpler than this usage of the Array( ) constructor.

- Call it with a single numeric argument, which specifies a length:

    ```
    var a = new Array(10);
    ```

    This technique creates an array with the specified number of elements (each of which has the undefined value) and sets the array's length property to the value specified. This form of the Array( ) constructor can be used to preallocate an array when you know in advance how many elements will be required. Array literals are not typically useful in this case.

7.6   Reading and Writing Array Elements

You access an element of an array using the [] operator. A reference to the array should appear to the left of the brackets. An arbitrary expression that has a nonnegative integer value should be inside the brackets. You can use this syntax to both read and write the value of an element of an array. Thus, the following are all legal JavaScript statements:

```
value = a[0];
a[1] = 3.14;
i = 2;
a[i] = 3;
a[i + 1] = "hello";
a[a[i]] = a[0];
```

In some languages, the first element of an array is at index 1. In JavaScript (as in C, C++, and Java), however, the first element of an array is at index 0.

As noted earlier, the [] operator can also be used to access named properties of objects.

```
my['salary'] *= 2;
```

Because arrays are a specialized kind of object, you can define nonnumeric object properties on an array and access those properties using the . or [] syntax.

Note that array indexes must be integers greater than or equal to 0 and less than $2^{32}-1$. If you use a number that is too large, a negative number, or a floating-point number (or a boolean, an object, or other value), JavaScript converts it to a string and uses the resulting string as the name of an object property, not as an array index. Thus, the following line creates a new property named "-1.23"; it does not define a new array element:

```
a[-1.23] = true;
```

7.6.1 Adding New Elements to an Array

In languages such as C and Java, an array has a fixed number of elements that must be specified when you create the array. This is not the case in JavaScript; an array can have any number of elements, and you can change the number of elements at any time.

To add a new element to an array, simply assign a value to it:

```
a[10] = 10;
```

Arrays in JavaScript may be *sparse*. This means that array indexes need not fall into a contiguous range of numbers; a JavaScript implementation may allocate memory only for those array elements that are actually stored in the array. Thus, when you execute the following lines of code, the JavaScript interpreter will typically allocate memory only for array indexes 0 and 10,000, not for the 9,999 indexes between:

```
a[0] = 1;
a[10000] = "this is element 10,000";
```

Note that array elements can also be added to objects:

```
var c = new Circle(1,2,3);
c[0] = "this is an array element of an object!"
```

This example merely defines a new object property named "0", however. Adding array elements to an object does not make it an array.

7.6.2 Deleting Array Elements

The delete operator sets an array element to the undefined value, but the element itself continues to exist. To actually delete an element, so that all elements above it are shifted down to lower indexes, you must use an array method. Array.shift() deletes the first element of an array, Array.pop() deletes the last element, and Array.splice() deletes a contiguous range of elements from an array. These functions are described later in this chapter and also in Part III.

7.6.3 Array Length

All arrays, whether created with the Array() constructor or defined with an array literal, have a special length property that specifies how many elements the array contains. More precisely, since arrays can have undefined elements, the length property is *always* one larger than the largest element number in the array. Unlike regular object properties, the length property of an array is automatically updated to maintain this invariant when new elements are added to the array. The following code illustrates:

```
var a = new Array();    // a.length == 0  (no elements defined)
a = new Array(10);      // a.length == 10 (empty elements 0-9 defined)
a = new Array(1,2,3);   // a.length == 3  (elements 0-2 defined)
a = [4, 5];             // a.length == 2  (elements 0 and 1 defined)
a[5] = -1;              // a.length == 6  (elements 0, 1, and 5 defined)
a[49] = 0;              // a.length == 50 (elements 0, 1, 5, and 49 defined)
```

Remember that array indexes must be less than $2^{32}-1$, which means that the largest possible value for the length property is $2^{32}-1$.

7.6.4 Iterating Through Arrays

Probably the most common use of the length property of an array is to allow you to loop through the elements of an array:

```
var fruits = ["mango", "banana", "cherry", "pear"];
for(var i = 0; i < fruits.length; i++)
    alert(fruits[i]);
```

This example assumes, of course, that elements of the array are contiguous and begin at element 0. If this is not the case, you should test that each array element is defined before using it:

```
for(var i = 0; i < fruits.length; i++)
    if (fruits[i]) alert(fruits[i]);
```

You can use this same looping syntax to initialize the elements of an array created with the Array( ) constructor:

```
var lookup_table = new Array(1024);
for(var i = 0; i < lookup_table.length; i++)
    lookup_table[i] = i * 512;
```

7.6.5   Truncating and Enlarging Arrays

The length property of an array is a read/write value. If you set length to a value smaller than its current value, the array is truncated to the new length; any elements that no longer fit are discarded, and their values are lost.

If you make length larger than its current value, new, undefined elements are added at the end of the array to increase it to the newly specified size.

Note that although objects can be assigned array elements, they do not have a length property. The length property, with its special behavior, is the most important feature of arrays. The other features that make arrays different from objects are the various methods defined by the Array class, which are described in Section 7.7.

7.6.6   Multidimensional Arrays

JavaScript does not support true multidimensional arrays, but it does allow you to approximate them quite nicely with arrays of arrays. To access a data element in an array of arrays, simply use the [] operator twice. For example, suppose the variable matrix is an array of arrays of numbers. Every element in matrix[x] is an array of numbers. To access a particular number within this array, you would write matrix[x][y]. Here is a concrete example that uses a two-dimensional array as a multiplication table:

```
// Create a multidimensional array
var table = new Array(10);          // 10 rows of the table
for(var i = 0; i < table.length; i++)
    table[i] = new Array(10);       // Each row has 10 columns

// Initialize the array
for(var row = 0; row < table.length; row++) {
    for(col = 0; col < table[row].length; col++) {
        table[row][col] = row*col;
    }
}

// Use the multidimensional array to compute 5*7
var product = table[5][7];  // 35
```

7.7   Array Methods

In addition to the [] operator, arrays can be manipulated through various methods provided by the Array class. The following sections introduce these methods. Many of the methods were inspired in part by the Perl programming language; Perl programmers may find them comfortingly familiar. As usual, this is only an overview; complete details can be found in Part III.

7.7.1   join( )

The Array.join( ) method converts all the elements of an array to strings and concatenates them. You can specify an optional string that separates the elements in the resulting string. If no separator string is specified, a comma is used. For example, the following lines of code produce the string "1,2,3":

```
var a = [1, 2, 3];    // Create a new array with these three elements
var s = a.join();     // s == "1,2,3"
```

The following invocation specifies the optional separator to produce a slightly different result:

```
s = a.join(", ");    // s == "1, 2, 3"
```

Notice the space after the comma.

The Array.join( ) method is the inverse of the String.split( ) method, which creates an array by breaking a string into pieces.

7.7.2   reverse( )

The Array.reverse( ) method reverses the order of the elements of an array and returns the reversed array. It does this in place; in other words, it doesn't create a new array with the elements rearranged but instead rearranges them in the already existing array. For example, the following code, which uses the reverse( ) and join( ) methods, produces the string "3,2,1":

```
var a = new Array(1,2,3); // a[0] = 1, a[1] = 2, a[2] = 3
a.reverse();              // now a[0] = 3, a[1] = 2, a[2] = 1
var s = a.join();         // s == "3,2,1"
```

7.7.3   sort( )

Array.sort( ) sorts the elements of an array in place and returns the sorted array. When sort( ) is called with no arguments, it sorts the array elements in alphabetical order (temporarily converting them to strings to perform the comparison, if necessary):

```
var a = new Array("banana", "cherry", "apple");
a.sort();
var s = a.join(", "); // s == "apple, banana, cherry"
```

If an array contains undefined elements, they are sorted to the end of the array.

To sort an array into some order other than alphabetical, you must pass a comparison function as an argument to sort( ). This function decides which of its two arguments should appear first in the sorted array. If the first argument should appear before the second, the comparison function should return a number less than zero. If the first argument should appear after the second in the sorted array, the function should return a number greater than zero. And if the two values are equivalent (i.e., if their order is irrelevant), the comparison function should return 0. So, for example, to sort array elements into numerical rather than alphabetical order, you might do this:

```
var a = [33, 4, 1111, 222];
a.sort();              // Alphabetical order: 1111, 222, 33, 4
a.sort(function(a,b) { // Numerical order: 4, 33, 222, 1111
           return a-b; // Returns < 0, 0, or > 0, depending on order
       });
```

Note the convenient use of a function literal in this code. Since the comparison function is used only once, there is no need to give it a name.

As another example of sorting array items, you might perform a case-insensitive alphabetical sort on an array of strings by passing a comparison function that converts both of its arguments to lowercase (with the toLowerCase( ) method) before comparing them. You can probably think of other comparison functions that sort numbers into various esoteric orders: reverse numerical order, odd numbers before even numbers, etc. The possibilities become more interesting, of course, when the array elements you are comparing are objects rather than simple types such as numbers or strings.

7.7.4 concat( )

The Array.concat( ) method creates and returns a new array that contains the elements of the original array on which concat( ) was invoked, followed by each of the arguments to concat( ). If any of these arguments is itself an array, it is flattened, and its elements are added to the returned array. Note, however, that concat( ) does not recursively flatten arrays of arrays. Here are some examples:

```
var a = [1,2,3];
a.concat(4, 5)         // Returns [1,2,3,4,5]
a.concat([4,5]);       // Returns [1,2,3,4,5]
a.concat([4,5],[6,7])  // Returns [1,2,3,4,5,6,7]
a.concat(4, [5,[6,7]]) // Returns [1,2,3,4,5,[6,7]]
```

7.7.5 slice( )

The Array.slice( ) method returns a *slice*, or subarray, of the specified array. Its two arguments specify the start and end of the slice to be returned. The returned array contains the element specified by the first argument and all subsequent elements up to, but not including, the element specified by the second argument. If only one argument is specified, the returned array contains all elements from the start position to the end of the array. If either argument is negative, it specifies an array element relative to the last element in the array. An argument of –1, for example, specifies the last element in the array, and an argument of –3 specifies the third from last element of the array. Here are some examples:

```
var a = [1,2,3,4,5];
a.slice(0,3);    // Returns [1,2,3]
a.slice(3);      // Returns [4,5]
a.slice(1,-1);   // Returns [2,3,4]
a.slice(-3,-2);  // Returns [3]
```

7.7.6 splice( )

The Array.splice( ) method is a general-purpose method for inserting or removing elements from an array. splice( ) modifies the array in place; it does not return a new array, as slice( ) and concat( ) do. Note that splice( ) and slice( ) have very similar names but perform substantially different operations.

splice( ) can delete elements from an array, insert new elements into an array, or perform both operations at the same time. Array elements that appear after the insertion or deletion are moved as necessary so that they remain contiguous with the rest of the array. The first argument to splice( ) specifies the array position at which the insertion and/or deletion is to begin. The second argument specifies the number of elements that should be deleted from (spliced out of) the array. If this second argument is omitted, all array elements from the start element to the end of the array are removed. splice( ) returns an array of the deleted elements, or an empty array if no elements were deleted. For example:

```
var a = [1,2,3,4,5,6,7,8];
a.splice(4);     // Returns [5,6,7,8]; a is [1,2,3,4]
a.splice(1,2);   // Returns [2,3]; a is [1,4]
a.splice(1,1);   // Returns [4]; a is [1]
```

The first two arguments to splice( ) specify which array elements are to be deleted. These arguments may be followed by any number of additional arguments that specify elements to be inserted into the array, starting at the position specified by the first argument. For example:

```
var a = [1,2,3,4,5];
a.splice(2,0,'a','b');   // Returns []; a is [1,2,'a','b',3,4,5]
a.splice(2,2,[1,2],3);   // Returns ['a','b']; a is [1,2,[1,2],3,3,4,5]
```

Note that, unlike concat( ), splice( ) does not flatten array arguments that it inserts. That is, if it is passed an array to insert, it inserts the array itself, not the elements of that array.

7.7.7 push( ) and pop( )

The push( ) and pop( ) methods allow you to work with arrays as if they were stacks. The push( ) method appends one or more new elements to the end of an array and returns the new length of the array. The pop( ) method does the reverse: it deletes the last element of an array, decrements the array length, and returns the value that it removed. Note that both methods modify the array in place rather than produce a modified copy of the array. The combination of push( ) and pop( ) allows you to use a JavaScript array to implement a first-in, last-out stack. For example:

```
var stack = [];          // stack: []
stack.push(1,2);         // stack: [1,2]      Returns 2
stack.pop();             // stack: [1]        Returns 2
stack.push(3);           // stack: [1,3]      Returns 2
stack.pop();             // stack: [1]        Returns 3
stack.push([4,5]);       // stack: [1,[4,5]]  Returns 2
stack.pop()              // stack: [1]        Returns [4,5]
stack.pop();             // stack: []         Returns 1
```

7.7.8 unshift( ) and shift( )

The unshift( ) and shift( ) methods behave much like push( ) and pop( ), except that they insert and remove elements from the beginning of an array rather than from the end. unshift( ) adds an element or elements to the beginning of the array, shifts the existing array elements up to higher indexes to make room, and returns the new length of the array. shift( ) removes and returns the first element of the array, shifting all subsequent elements down one place to occupy the newly vacant space at the start of the array. For example:

```
var a = [];              // a:[]
a.unshift(1);            // a:[1]            Returns: 1
a.unshift(22);           // a:[22,1]         Returns: 2
a.shift();               // a:[1]            Returns: 22
a.unshift(3,[4,5]);      // a:[3,[4,5],1]    Returns: 3
a.shift();               // a:[[4,5],1]      Returns: 3
a.shift();               // a:[1]            Returns: [4,5]
a.shift();               // a:[]             Returns: 1
```

Note the possibly surprising behavior of unshift( ) when it's invoked with multiple arguments. Instead of being inserted into the array one at a time, arguments are inserted all at once (as with the splice( ) method). This means that they appear in the resulting array in the same order in which they appeared in the argument list. Had the elements been inserted one at a time, their order would have been reversed.

7.7.9 toString( ) and toLocaleString( )

An array, like any JavaScript object, has a toString( ) method. For an array, this method converts each of its elements to a string (calling the toString( ) methods of its elements, if necessary) and outputs a comma-separated list of those strings. Note that the output does not include square brackets or any other sort of delimiter around the array value. For example:

```
[1,2,3].toString()          // Yields '1,2,3'
["a", "b", "c"].toString()  // Yields 'a,b,c'
[1, [2,'c']].toString()     // Yields '1,2,c'
```

Note that the join() method returns the same string when it is invoked with no arguments.

toLocaleString() is the localized version of toString(). It converts each array element to a string by calling the toLocaleString() method of the element, and then it concatenates the resulting strings using a locale-specific (and implementation-defined) separator string.

7.7.10 Array Extras

The Firefox 1.5 browser bumps its JavaScript version number to 1.6 and adds a bundle of additional native array methods known as *array extras*. Notably, they include indexOf() and lastIndexOf() methods for quickly searching an array for a given value (see String.indexOf() in Part III for a similar method). Other methods include forEach(), which invokes a specified function for each element in the array; map(), which returns an array of the results obtained by passing each element in the array to a specified function; and filter(), which returns an array of elements for which a supplied predicate function returned true.

At the time of this writing, these extra array functions are available only in Firefox and are not yet official or de facto standards. They are not documented here. If, however, you are explicitly targeting the Firefox browser, or if you are using a compatibility layer that provides these easily emulated array methods, you can find their documentation online at *http://developer.mozilla.org*.

See Chapter 8 for some sample implementations of array utility methods.

7.8 Array-Like Objects

A JavaScript array is special because its length property behaves specially:

- Its value is automatically updated as new elements are added to the list.
- Setting this property expands or truncates the array.

JavaScript arrays are also instanceof Array, and the various Array methods can be invoked through them.

These are the unique features of JavaScript arrays. But they are not the essential features that define an array. It is often perfectly reasonable to treat any object with a length property and corresponding nonnegative integer properties as a kind of array.

These "array-like" objects actually do occasionally appear in practice, and although you cannot invoke array methods on them or expect special behavior from the length property, you can still iterate through them with the same code you'd use for a true array. It turns out that many array algorithms work just as well with array-like objects as they do with real arrays. As long as you don't try to add elements to the array or change the length property, you can treat array-like objects as real arrays.

The following code takes a regular object, adds properties to make it an array-like object, and then iterates through the "elements" of the resulting pseudo-array:

```
var a = {};  // Start with a regular empty object

// Add properties to make it "array-like"
var i = 0;
while(i < 10) {
    a[i] = i * i;
    i++;
}
a.length = i;

// Now iterate through it as if it were a real array
var total = 0;
for(var j = 0; j < a.length; j++)
    total += a[j];
```

The Arguments object that's described in Section 8.2.2 is an array-like object. In client-side JavaScript, a number of DOM methods, such as document.getElementsByTagName( ), return array-like objects.

CHAPTER 8

Functions

A *function* is a block of JavaScript code that is defined once but may be *invoked*, or executed, any number of times. Functions may have *parameters*, or *arguments*—local variables whose value is specified when the function is invoked. Functions often use these arguments to compute a *return value* that becomes the value of the function-invocation expression. When a function is invoked *on* an object, the function is called a *method*, and the object on which it is invoked is passed as an implicit argument of the function. You may already be familiar with the concept of a function under a name such as *subroutine* or *procedure*.

This chapter focuses on defining and invoking your own JavaScript functions. It is important to remember that JavaScript supports quite a few built-in functions, such as eval( ), parseInt( ), and the sort( ) method of the Array class. Client-side JavaScript defines others, such as document.write( ) and alert( ). Built-in functions in JavaScript can be used in exactly the same ways as user-defined functions. You can find more information about the built-in functions mentioned here in Parts III and IV of this book.

Functions and objects are intertwined in JavaScript. For this reason, I'll defer discussion of some features of functions until Chapter 9.

8.1 Defining and Invoking Functions

As shown in Chapter 6, the most common way to define a function is with the function statement. This statement consists of the function keyword followed by:

- The name of the function
- Zero or more parameter names contained within parenthesis, each separated by commas
- The JavaScript statements that comprise the body of the function, contained within curly braces

Example 8-1 shows the definitions of several functions. Although these functions are short and simple, they all contain each of the elements just listed. Note that functions may be defined to expect varying numbers of arguments and that they may or may not contain a return statement. The return statement was introduced in Chapter 6; it causes the function to stop executing and to return the value of its expression (if any) to the caller. If the return statement does not have an associated expression, it returns the undefined value. If a function does not contain a return statement, it simply executes each statement in the function body and returns the undefined value to the caller.

Example 8-1. Defining JavaScript functions

```
// A shortcut function, sometimes useful instead of document.write()
// This function has no return statement, so it returns undefined.
function print(msg) {
    document.write(msg, "<br>");
}

// A function that computes and returns the distance between two points
function distance(x1, y1, x2, y2) {
    var dx = x2 - x1;
    var dy = y2 - y1;
    return Math.sqrt(dx*dx + dy*dy);
}

// A recursive function (one that calls itself) that computes factorials
// Recall that x! is the product of x and all positive integers less than it
function factorial(x) {
    if (x <= 1)
        return 1;
    return x * factorial(x-1);
}
```

Once a function has been defined, it may be invoked with the ( ) operator, introduced in Chapter 5. Recall that the parentheses appear after the name of the function (actually, any JavaScript expression that evaluates to a function value may be followed by parentheses) and that an optional comma-separated list of argument values (or expressions) appears within the parentheses. The functions defined in Example 8-1 can be invoked with code like the following:

```
print("Hello, " + name);
print("Welcome to my blog!");
total_dist = distance(0,0,2,1) + distance(2,1,3,5);
print("The probability of that is: " + factorial(5)/factorial(13));
```

When you invoke a function, each expression you specify between the parentheses is evaluated, and the resulting value is used as an argument of the function. These values are assigned to the parameters named when the function was defined, and the function operates on its parameters by referring to them by name. Note that these parameter variables are normally available only within the body of the executing function: they cannot normally be accessed outside the body of the function or after the function has returned. (But see Section 8.8 for an important exception.)

Since JavaScript is a loosely typed language, you are not expected to specify a datatype for function parameters, and JavaScript does not check whether you have passed the type of data that the function expects. If the datatype of an argument is important, you can test it yourself with the typeof operator. JavaScript does not check whether you have passed the correct number of arguments either. If you pass more arguments than the function expects, the function ignores the extra arguments. If you pass fewer than expected, the parameters you omit are given the undefined value. Some functions are written to tolerate omitted arguments, and others behave incorrectly if you don't pass all the arguments they expect. Later in this chapter, you'll learn how a function can determine exactly how many arguments it was passed and can access those arguments by their position in the argument list rather than by name.

Note that the print( ) function defined in Example 8-1 does not contain a return statement, so it always returns the undefined value and cannot meaningfully be used as part of a larger expression. The distance( ) and factorial( ) functions, on the other hand, can be invoked as parts of larger expressions, as shown in the previous examples.

8.1.1   Nested Functions

In JavaScript, functions may be nested within other functions. For example:

```
function hypotenuse(a, b) {
    function square(x) { return x*x; }
    return Math.sqrt(square(a) + square(b));
}
```

Nested functions may be defined only at the top level of the function within which they are nested. That is, they may not be defined within statement blocks, such as the body of an if statement or while loop.* Note that this restriction applies only to functions defined with the function *statement*. Function literal expressions, which are described in the next section, may appear anywhere.

Some interesting programming techniques involve nested functions, and I'll have more to say about them later in the chapter.

---

* Different implementations of JavaScript may be more relaxed about function definitions than the standard requires. For example, Netscape's implementation of JavaScript 1.5 allows "conditional function definitions" that appear within if statements.

8.1.2 Function Literals

JavaScript allows functions to be defined with *function literals*. As discussed in Chapter 3, a function literal is an expression that defines an unnamed function. The syntax for a function literal is much like that of the function statement, except that it is used as an expression rather than as a statement and no function name is required. The following two lines of code define two more or less identical functions using a function statement and a function literal, respectively:

```
function f(x) { return x*x; }          // function statement
var f = function(x) { return x*x; };   // function literal
```

Although function literals create unnamed functions, the syntax allows a function name to be optionally specified, which is useful when writing recursive functions that call themselves. For example:

```
var f = function fact(x) { if (x <= 1) return 1; else return x*fact(x-1); };
```

This line of code defines an unnamed function and stores a reference to it in the variable f. It does *not* store a reference to the function into a variable named *fact*, but it does allow the body of the function to refer to itself using that name. Note, however, that this type of named function literal was not properly implemented before JavaScript 1.5.

Because function literals are created by JavaScript expressions rather than statements, they are quite flexible and are particularly well suited for functions that are used only once and need not be named. For example, the function specified by a function literal expression can be stored into a variable, passed to another function, or even invoked directly:

```
f[0] = function(x) { return x*x; };  // Define a function and store it
a.sort(function(a,b){return a-b;});  // Define a function; pass it to another
var tensquared = (function(x) {return x*x;})(10);  // Define and invoke
```

8.1.3 Naming Functions

Any legal JavaScript identifier can be a function name. Try to choose function names that are descriptive but concise. Striking the right balance is an art that comes with experience. Well-chosen function names can make a big difference in the readability (and thus maintainability) of your code.

Function names are often verbs or phrases that begin with verbs. It is a common convention to begin function names with a lowercase letter. When a name includes multiple words, one convention is to separate words with underscores like_this(); another convention is to begin all words after the first with an uppercase letter likeThis(). Functions that are supposed to be internal or hidden are sometimes given names that begin with an underscore.

In some styles of programming, or within well-defined programming frameworks, it can be useful to give frequently used functions very short names. The client-side JavaScript framework Prototype (*http://prototype.conio.net*), for example, elegantly uses a function named $( ) (yes, just the dollar sign) as an intelligent replacement for the very common but hard-to-type document.getElementById( ). (Recall from Chapter 2 that dollar signs and underscores are the two characters besides letters and numbers that are legal in JavaScript identifiers.)

8.2 Function Arguments

JavaScript functions can be invoked with any number of arguments, regardless of the number of arguments named in the function definition. Because a function is loosely typed, there is no way for it to declare the type of arguments it expects, and it is legal to pass values of any type to any function. The following subsections discuss these issues.

8.2.1 Optional Arguments

When a function is invoked with fewer arguments than are declared, the additional arguments have the undefined value. It is often useful to write functions so that some arguments are optional and may be omitted when the function is invoked. To do this, you must be able to assign a reasonable default value to arguments that are omitted (or specified as null). Here is an example:

```
// Append the names of the enumerable properties of object o to the
// array a, and return a.  If a is omitted or null, create and return
// a new array
function copyPropertyNamesToArray(o, /* optional */ a) {
    if (!a) a = [];  // If undefined or null, use a blank array
    for(var property in o) a.push(property);
    return a;
}
```

With the function defined this way, you have flexibility in how it is invoked:

```
// Get property names of objects o and p
var a = copyPropertyNamesToArray(o); // Get o's properties into a new array
copyPropertyNamesToArray(p,a);       // append p's properties to that array
```

Instead of using an if statement in the first line of this function, you can use the || operator in this idiomatic way:

```
a = a || [];
```

Recall from Chapter 5 that the || operator returns its first argument if that argument is true or a value that converts to true. Otherwise it returns its second argument. In this case, it returns a if a is defined and non-null, even if a is empty. Otherwise, it returns a new, empty array.

Note that when designing functions with optional arguments, you should be sure to put the optional ones at the end of the argument list so that they can be omitted. The programmer who calls your function cannot omit the first argument and pass the second, for example. In this case, he would have to explicitly pass undefined or null as the first argument.

8.2.2   Variable-Length Argument Lists: The Arguments Object

Within the body of a function, the identifier arguments has special meaning. arguments is a special property that refers to an object known as the Arguments object. The Arguments object is an array-like object (see Section 7.8) that allows the argument values passed to the function to be retrieved by number, rather than by name. The Arguments object also defines an additional callee property, described in the next section.

Although a JavaScript function is defined with a fixed number of named arguments, it can be passed any number of arguments when it is invoked. The Arguments object allows full access to these argument values, even when some or all are unnamed. Suppose you define a function f that expects to be passed one argument, x. If you invoke this function with two arguments, the first argument is accessible within the function by the parameter name x or as arguments[0]. The second argument is accessible only as arguments[1]. Furthermore, like true arrays, arguments has a length property that specifies the number of elements it contains. Thus, within the body of the function f, invoked with two arguments, arguments.length has the value 2.

The arguments object is useful in a number of ways. The following example shows how you can use it to verify that a function is invoked with the correct number of arguments, since JavaScript doesn't do this for you:

```
function f(x, y, z)
{
    // First, verify that the right number of arguments was passed
    if (arguments.length != 3) {
        throw new Error("function f called with " + arguments.length +
                        "arguments, but it expects 3 arguments.");
    }
    // Now do the actual function...
}
```

The arguments object also opens up an important possibility for JavaScript functions: they can be written so that they work with any number of arguments. Here's an example that shows how you can write a simple max( ) function that accepts any number of arguments and returns the value of the largest argument it is passed (see also the built-in function Math.max( ), which behaves the same way):

```
function max(/* ... */)
{
    var m = Number.NEGATIVE_INFINITY;
```

```
    // Loop through all the arguments, looking for, and
    // remembering, the biggest
    for(var i = 0; i < arguments.length; i++)
        if (arguments[i] > m) m = arguments[i];
    // Return the biggest
    return m;
}

var largest = max(1, 10, 100, 2, 3, 1000, 4, 5, 10000, 6);
```

Functions like this one that can accept any number of arguments are called *variadic functions*, *variable arity functions*, or *varargs functions*. This book uses the most colloquial term, *varargs*, which dates to the early days of the C programming language.

Note that varargs functions need not allow invocations with zero arguments. It is perfectly reasonable to use the arguments[] object to write functions that expect some fixed number of named and required arguments followed by an arbitrary number of unnamed optional arguments.

Remember that arguments is not really an array; it is an Arguments object. Each Arguments object defines numbered array elements and a length property, but it is not technically an array; it is better to think of it as an object that happens to have some numbered properties. The ECMAScript specification does not require the Arguments object to implement any of the special behavior that arrays do. Although you can assign a value to the arguments.length property, for example, ECMAScript does not actually alter the number of array elements defined in the object. (See Section 7.6.3 for an explanation of the special behavior of the length property of true Array objects.)

The Arguments object has one *very* unusual feature. When a function has named arguments, the array elements of the Arguments object are synonyms for the local variables that hold the function arguments. The arguments[] array and the named arguments are two different ways of referring to the same variable. Changing the value of an argument with an argument name changes the value that is retrieved through the arguments[] array. Conversely, changing the value of an argument through the arguments[] array changes the value that is retrieved by the argument name. For example:

```
function f(x) {
    print(x);             // Displays the initial value of the argument
    arguments[0] = null;  // Changing the array element also changes x!
    print(x);             // Now displays "null"
}
```

This is emphatically not the behavior you would see if the Arguments object were an ordinary array. In that case, arguments[0] and x could refer initially to the same value, but a change to one reference would have no effect on the other reference.

Finally, bear in mind that arguments is just an ordinary JavaScript identifier, not a reserved word. If a function has an argument or local variable with that name, it hides the reference to the Arguments object. For this reason, it is a good idea to treat arguments as a reserved word and avoid using it as a variable name.

8.2.2.1 The callee Property

In addition to its array elements, the Arguments object defines a callee property that refers to the function that is currently being executed. This property is rarely useful, but it can be used to allow unnamed functions to invoke themselves recursively. For instance, here is an unnamed function literal that computes factorials:

```
function(x) {
    if (x <= 1) return 1;
    return x * arguments.callee(x-1);
}
```

8.2.3   Using Object Properties as Arguments

When a function requires more than about three arguments, it becomes difficult for the programmer who invokes the function to remember the correct order in which to pass arguments. In order to save the programmer the trouble of consulting the documentation each time she uses the function, it would be nice to allow arguments to be passed as name/value pairs in any order. To implement this style of method invocation, define your function to expect a single object as its argument and then have users of the function pass an object literal that defines the required name/value pairs. The following code gives an example and also demonstrates that this style of function invocation allows the function to specify defaults for any arguments that are omitted:

```
// Copy length elements of the array from to the array to.
// Begin copying with element from_start in the from array
// and copy that element to to_start in the to array.
// It is hard to remember the order of the arguments.
function arraycopy(/* array */ from, /* index */ from_start,
                   /* array */ to,   /* index */ to_start,
                   /* integer */ length)
{
    // code goes here
}

// This version is a little less efficient, but you don't have to
// remember the order of the arguments, and from_start and to_start
// default to 0.
function easycopy(args) {
    arraycopy(args.from,
              args.from_start || 0,  // Note default value provided
              args.to,
              args.to_start || 0,
              args.length);
}
```

```
// Here is how you might invoke easycopy():
var a = [1,2,3,4];
var b = new Array(4);
easycopy({from: a, to: b, length: 4});
```

8.2.4 Argument Types

Since JavaScript is loosely typed, method arguments have no declared types, and no
type checking is performed on the values you pass to a function. You can help to
make your code self-documenting by choosing descriptive names for function arguments and also by including argument types in comments, as in the arraycopy()
method just shown. For arguments that are optional, you can include the word
"optional" in the comment. And when a method can accept any number of arguments, you can use an ellipsis:

```
function max(/* number... */) { /* code here */ }
```

As described in Chapter 3, JavaScript performs liberal type conversion as needed. So
if you write a function that expects a string argument and then call that function with
a value of some other type, the value you passed will simply be converted to a string
when the function tries to use it as a string. All primitive types can be converted to
strings, and all objects have toString() methods (if not necessarily useful ones), so
an error never occurs in this case.

This is not always the case, however. Consider again the arraycopy() method shown
earlier. It expects an array as its first argument. Any plausible implementation will
fail if that first argument is anything but an array (or possibly an array-like object).
Unless you are writing a "throwaway" function that will be called only once or twice,
it is worth adding code to check the types of arguments like this. If arguments of the
wrong type are passed, throw an exception that reports the fact. It is better for a
function to fail immediately and predictably when passed bad data than to begin executing and fail later when you try to access an array element of a number, for example, as in this code snippet:

```
// Return the sum of the elements of array (or array-like object) a.
// The elements of a must all be numbers, but null and undefined
// elements are ignored.
function sum(a) {
    if ((a instanceof Array) ||                       // if array
        (a && typeof a == "object" && "length" in a)) { // or array like
        var total = 0;
        for(var i = 0; i < a.length; i++) {
            var element = a[i];
            if (!element) continue;  // ignore null and undefined elements
            if (typeof element == "number") total += element;
            else throw new Error("sum(): all array elements must be numbers");
        }
        return total;
    }
    else throw new Error("sum(): argument must be an array");
}
```

This sum( ) method is fairly strict about the argument it accepts and throws suitably informative errors if it is passed bad values. It does offer a bit of flexibility, however, by working with array-like objects as well as true arrays and by ignoring null and undefined array elements.

JavaScript is a very flexible and loosely typed language, and sometimes it is appropriate to write functions that are flexible about the number and type of arguments they are passed. The following flexisum( ) method takes this approach (and arguably takes it to an extreme). For example, it accepts any number of arguments but recursively processes any arguments that are arrays. In this way, it can be used as a varargs method or with an array argument. Furthermore, it tries its best to convert nonnumeric values to numbers before throwing an error:

```javascript
function flexisum(a) {
    var total = 0;
    for(var i = 0; i < arguments.length; i++) {
        var element = arguments[i];
        if (!element) continue;  // Ignore null and undefined arguments

        // Try to convert the argument to a number n,
        // based on its type
        var n;
        switch(typeof element) {
        case "number":
            n = element;                  // No conversion needed here
            break;
        case "object":
            if (element instanceof Array) // Recurse for arrays
                n = flexisum.apply(this, element);
            else n = element.valueOf();   // valueOf method for other objects
            break;
        case "function":
            n = element( );               // Try to invoke functions
            break;
        case "string":
            n = parseFloat(element);      // Try to parse strings
            break;
        case "boolean":
            n = NaN;                      // Can't convert boolean values
            break;
        }

        // If we got a valid number, add it to the total.
        if (typeof n == "number" && !isNaN(n)) total += n;
        // Otherwise report an error
        else throw new Error("sum( ): can't convert " + element + " to number");
    }
    return total;
}
```

8.3   Functions as Data

The most important features of functions are that they can be defined and invoked, as shown in the previous section. Function definition and invocation are syntactic features of JavaScript and of most other programming languages. In JavaScript, however, functions are not only syntax but also data, which means that they can be assigned to variables, stored in the properties of objects or the elements of arrays, passed as arguments to functions, and so on.[*]

To understand how functions can be JavaScript data as well as JavaScript syntax, consider this function definition:

```
function square(x) { return x*x; }
```

This definition creates a new function object and assigns it to the variable square. The name of a function is really immaterial; it is simply the name of a variable that refers to the function. The function can be assigned to another variable and still work the same way:

```
var a = square(4);  // a contains the number 16
var b = square;     // Now b refers to the same function that square does
var c = b(5);       // c contains the number 25
```

Functions can also be assigned to object properties rather than global variables. When you do this, they're called methods:

```
var o = new Object;
o.square = function(x) { return x*x; }      // function literal
y = o.square(16);                           // y equals 256
```

Functions don't even require names at all, as when they're assigned to array elements:

```
var a = new Array(3);
a[0] = function(x) { return x*x; }
a[1] = 20;
a[2] = a[0](a[1]);                // a[2] contains 400
```

The function-invocation syntax in this last example looks strange, but it is still a legal use of the JavaScript ( ) operator!

Example 8-2 is a detailed example of the things that can be done when functions are used as data. It demonstrates how functions can be passed as arguments to other functions. This example may be a little tricky, but the comments explain what is going on; it is worth studying carefully.

---

[*] This may not seem like a particularly interesting point unless you are familiar with languages such as Java, in which functions are part of a program but cannot be manipulated by the program.

Example 8-2. Using functions as data

```
// We define some simple functions here
function add(x,y) { return x + y; }
function subtract(x,y) { return x - y; }
function multiply(x,y) { return x * y; }
function divide(x,y) { return x / y; }

// Here's a function that takes one of the above functions
// as an argument and invokes it on two operands
function operate(operator, operand1, operand2)
{
    return operator(operand1, operand2);
}

// We could invoke this function like this to compute the value (2+3) + (4*5):
var i = operate(add, operate(add, 2, 3), operate(multiply, 4, 5));

// For the sake of the example, we implement the simple functions again, this time
// using function literals within an object literal;
var operators = {
    add:      function(x,y) { return x+y; },
    subtract: function(x,y) { return x-y; },
    multiply: function(x,y) { return x*y; },
    divide:   function(x,y) { return x/y; },
    pow:      Math.pow  // Works for predefined functions too
};

// This function takes the name of an operator, looks up that operator
// in the object, and then invokes it on the supplied operands. Note
// the syntax used to invoke the operator function.
function operate2(op_name, operand1, operand2)
{
    if (typeof operators[op_name] == "function")
        return operators[op_name](operand1, operand2);
    else throw "unknown operator";
}

// We could invoke this function as follows to compute
// the value ("hello" + " " + "world"):
var j = operate2("add", "hello", operate2("add", " ", "world"))
// Using the predefined Math.pow() function:
var k = operate2("pow", 10, 2)
```

If the preceding example does not convince you of the utility of being able to pass functions as arguments to other functions and otherwise treat functions as data values, consider the `Array.sort()` function. This function sorts the elements of an array. Because there are many possible orders to sort by (numerical order, alphabetical order, date order, ascending, descending, and so on), the `sort()` function optionally takes another function as an argument to tell it how to perform the sort. This function has a simple job: it takes two elements of the array, compares them, and then returns a value that specifies which element comes first. This function argument makes the `Array.sort( )` method perfectly general and infinitely flexible; it can sort any type of data into any conceivable order! (An example using `Array.sort( )` is in Section 7.7.3.)

8.4   Functions as Methods

A *method* is nothing more than a JavaScript function that is stored in a property of an object and invoked through that object. Recall that functions are data values and that there is nothing special about the names with which they are defined; a function can be assigned to any variable, or even to any property of an object. If you have a function f and an object o, you can define a method named m with the following line:

```
o.m = f;
```

Having defined the method m( ) of the object o, invoke it like this:

```
o.m( );
```

Or, if m( ) expects two arguments, you can invoke it like this:

```
o.m(x, x+2);
```

Methods have one very important property: the object through which a method is invoked becomes the value of the this keyword within the body of the method. Thus, when you invoke o.m( ), the body of the method can refer to the object o with the this keyword. Here is a concrete example:

```
var calculator = {  // An object literal
    operand1: 1,
    operand2: 1,
    compute: function( ) {
        this.result = this.operand1 + this.operand2;
    }
};
calculator.compute( );        // What is 1+1?
print(calculator.result);     // Display the result
```

The this keyword is important. Any function that is used as a method is effectively passed an implicit argument—the object through which it is invoked. Typically, a method performs some sort of operation on that object, so the method-invocation syntax is a particularly elegant way to express the fact that a function is operating on an object. Compare the following two lines of code:

```
rect.setSize(width, height);
setRectSize(rect, width, height);
```

The hypothetical functions invoked in these two lines of code may perform exactly the same operation on the (hypothetical) object rect, but the method-invocation syntax in the first line more clearly indicates the idea that it is the object rect that is the primary focus of the operation. (If the first line does not seem a more natural syntax to you, you are probably new to object-oriented programming.)

When a function is invoked as a function rather that as a method, the this keyword refers to the global object. Confusingly, this is true even when a nested function is invoked (as a function) within a containing method that was invoked as a method: the this keyword has one value in the containing function but (counterintuitively) refers to the global object within the body of the nested function.

Note that this is a keyword, not a variable or property name. JavaScript syntax does not allow you to assign a value to this.

8.5 Constructor Functions

A *constructor* function is a function that initializes the properties of an object and is intended for use with the new operator. Constructors are covered in detail in Chapter 9. Briefly, however: the new operator creates a new object and then invokes the constructor function, passing the newly created object as the value of the this keyword.

8.6 Function Properties and Methods

We've seen that functions can be used as data values in JavaScript programs. The typeof operator returns the string "function" when applied to a function, but functions are really a specialized kind of JavaScript object. Since functions are objects, they have properties and methods, just like the Date and RegExp objects, for example.

8.6.1 The length Property

As shown previously, within the body of a function, the length property of the arguments array specifies the number of arguments that were passed to the function. The length property of a function itself, however, has a different meaning. This read-only property returns the number of arguments that the function *expects* to be passed—that is, the number of parameters it declares in its parameter list. Recall that a function can be invoked with any number of arguments, which it can retrieve through the arguments array, regardless of the number of parameters it declares. The length property of the Function object specifies exactly how many declared parameters a function has. Note that unlike arguments.length, this length property is available both inside and outside of the function body.

The following code defines a function named check( ) that is passed the arguments array from another function. It compares the arguments.length property to the Function.length property (which it accesses as arguments.callee.length) to see if the function was passed the number of arguments it expected. If not, it throws an exception. The check( ) function is followed by a test function f( ) that demonstrates how check( ) can be used:

```
function check(args) {
    var actual = args.length;           // The actual number of arguments
    var expected = args.callee.length;  // The expected number of arguments
    if (actual != expected) {  // Throw an exception if they don't match
        throw new Error("Wrong number of arguments: expected: " +
                        expected + "; actually passed " + actual);
    }
}

function f(x, y, z) {
    // Check that the actual # of args matches the expected # of args
    // Throw an exception if they don't match
    check(arguments);
    // Now do the rest of the function normally
    return x + y + z;
}
```

8.6.2   The prototype Property

Every function has a prototype property that refers to a predefined *prototype object*. This prototype object comes into play when the function is used as a constructor with the new operator; it plays an important role in the process of defining new object types. This property is explored in detail in Chapter 9.

8.6.3   Defining Your Own Function Properties

When a function needs to use a variable whose value persists across invocations, it is often convenient to use a property of the Function object, instead of cluttering up the namespace by defining a global variable. For example, suppose you want to write a function that returns a unique integer whenever it is invoked. The function must never return the same value twice. In order to manage this, the function needs to keep track of the values it has already returned, and this information must persist across function invocations. You could store this information in a global variable, but that is unnecessary because the information is used only by the function itself. It is better to store the information in a property of the Function object. Here is an example that returns a unique integer whenever it is called:

```
// Create and initialize the "static" variable.
// Function declarations are processed before code is executed, so
// we really can do this assignment before the function declaration.
uniqueInteger.counter = 0;

// Here's the function. It returns a different value each time
// it is called and uses a "static" property of itself to keep track
// of the last value it returned.
function uniqueInteger( ) {
```

```
    // Increment and return our "static" variable
    return uniqueInteger.counter++;
}
```

8.6.4 The apply( ) and call( ) Methods

ECMAScript specifies two methods that are defined for all functions, call( ) and apply( ). These methods allow you to invoke a function as if it were a method of some other object. The first argument to both call( ) and apply( ) is the object on which the function is to be invoked; this argument becomes the value of the this keyword within the body of the function. Any remaining arguments to call( ) are the values that are passed to the function that is invoked. For example, to pass two numbers to the function f( ) and invoke it as if it were a method of the object o, you could use code like this:

```
f.call(o, 1, 2);
```

This is similar to the following lines of code:

```
o.m = f;
o.m(1,2);
delete o.m;
```

The apply( ) method is like the call( ) method, except that the arguments to be passed to the function are specified as an array:

```
f.apply(o, [1,2]);
```

For example, to find the largest number in an array of numbers, you could use the apply( ) method to pass the elements of the array to the Math.max( ) function:

```
var biggest = Math.max.apply(null, array_of_numbers);
```

8.7 Utility Function Examples

This section includes a few useful example functions for manipulating objects, arrays, and functions. Let's begin with some object utilities in Example 8-3.

Example 8-3. Object utility functions

```
// Return an array that holds the names of the enumerable properties of o
function getPropertyNames(/* object */o) {
    var r = [];
    for(name in o) r.push(name);
    return r;
}

// Copy the enumerable properties of the object from to the object to.
// If to is null, a new object is created.  The function returns to or the
// newly created object.
function copyProperties(/* object */ from, /* optional object */ to) {
    if (!to) to = {};
```

Example 8-3. Object utility functions (continued)

```
    for(p in from) to[p] = from[p];
    return to;
}


// Copy the enumerable properties of the object from to the object to,
// but only the ones that are not already defined by to.
// This is useful, for example, when from contains default values that
// we want to use if they are not already defined in to.
function copyUndefinedProperties(/* object */ from, /* object */ to) {
    for(p in from) {
        if (!p in to) to[p] = from[p];
    }
}
```

Next, here are some array utilities in Example 8-4.

Example 8-4. Array utility functions

```
// Pass each element of the array a to the specified predicate function.
// Return an array that holds the elements for which the predicate
// returned true
function filterArray(/* array */ a, /* boolean function */ predicate) {
    var results = [];
    var length = a.length;   // In case predicate changes the length!
    for(var i = 0; i < length; i++) {
        var element = a[i];
        if (predicate(element)) results.push(element);
    }
    return results;
}


// Return the array of values that result when each of the elements
// of the array a are passed to the function f
function mapArray(/* array */a, /* function */ f) {
    var r = [];              // to hold the results
    var length = a.length;   // In case f changes the length!
    for(var i = 0; i < length; i++) r[i] = f(a[i]);
    return r;
}
```

Finally, the functions in Example 8-5 are utilities for working with functions. They actually use and return nested functions. Nested functions returned in this way are sometimes called closures, and they can be confusing. Closures are discussed in the next section.

Example 8-5. Utility functions for functions

```
// Return a standalone function that invokes the function f as a method of
// the object o.  This is useful when you need to pass a method to a function.
// If you don't bind it to its object, the association will be lost and
// the method you passed will be invoked as a regular function.
function bindMethod(/* object */ o, /* function */ f) {
```

Example 8-5. Utility functions for functions (continued)

```
    return function( ) { return f.apply(o, arguments) }
}

// Return a function that invokes the function f with the
// specified arguments and also any additional arguments that are
// passed to the returned function. (This is sometimes called "currying".)
function bindArguments(/* function */ f /*, initial arguments... */) {
    var boundArgs = arguments;
    return function( ) {
        // Build up an array of arguments.  It starts with the previously
        // bound arguments and is extended with the arguments passed now
        var args = [];
        for(var i = 1; i < boundArgs.length; i++) args.push(boundArgs[i]);
        for(var i = 0; i < arguments.length; i++) args.push(arguments[i]);

        // Now invoke the function with these arguments
        return f.apply(this, args);
    }
}
```

8.8   Function Scope and Closures

As described in Chapter 4, the body of a JavaScript function executes in a local scope that differs from the global scope. This section explains these and related scoping issues, including closures.*

8.8.1   Lexical Scoping

Functions in JavaScript are lexically rather than dynamically scoped. This means that they run in the scope in which they are defined, not the scope from which they are executed. When a function is defined, the current scope chain is saved and becomes part of the internal state of the function. At the top level, the scope chain simply consists of the global object, and lexical scoping is not particularly relevant. When you define a nested function, however, the scope chain includes the containing function. This means that nested functions can access all of the arguments and local variables of the containing function.

Note that although the scope chain is fixed when a function is defined, the properties defined in that scope chain are not fixed. The scope chain is "live," and a function has access to whatever bindings are current when it is invoked.

---

* This section covers advanced material that you may want to skip on your first reading.

8.8.2　The Call Object

When the JavaScript interpreter invokes a function, it first sets the scope to the scope chain that was in effect when the function was defined. Next, it adds a new object, known as the *call object* (the ECMAScript specification uses the term *activation object*) to the front of the scope chain. The call object is initialized with a property named arguments that refers to the Arguments object for the function. Named parameters of the function are added to the call object next. Any local variables declared with the var statement are also defined within this object. Since this call object is at the head of the scope chain, local variables, function parameters, and the Arguments object are all in scope within the function. This also means that they hide any properties with the same name that are further up the scope chain, of course.

Note that unlike arguments, this is a keyword, not a property in the call object.

8.8.3　The Call Object as a Namespace

It is sometimes useful to define a function simply to create a call object that acts as a temporary namespace in which you can define variables and create properties without corrupting the global namespace. Suppose, for example, you have a file of JavaScript code that you want to use in a number of different JavaScript programs (or, for client-side JavaScript, on a number of different web pages). Assume that this code, like most code, defines variables to store the intermediate results of its computation. The problem is that since this code will be used in many different programs, you don't know whether the variables it creates will conflict with variables used by the programs that import it.

The solution, of course, is to put the code into a function and then invoke the function. This way, variables are defined in the call object of the function:

```
function init() {
    // Code goes here.
    // Any variables declared become properties of the call
    // object instead of cluttering up the global namespace.
}
init();  // But don't forget to invoke the function!
```

The code adds only a single property to the global namespace: the property "init", which refers to the function. If defining even a single property is too much, you can define and invoke an anonymous function in a single expression. The code for this JavaScript idiom looks like this:

```
(function() {  // This function has no name.
    // Code goes here.
    // Any variables declared become properties of the call
    // object instead of cluttering up the global namespace.
})();          // end the function literal and invoke it now.
```

Note that the parentheses around the function literal are required by JavaScript syntax.

8.8.4 Nested Functions as Closures

The facts that JavaScript allows nested functions, allows functions to be used as data, and uses lexical scoping interact to create surprising and powerful effects. To begin exploring this, consider a function g defined within a function f. When f is invoked, the scope chain consists of the call object for that invocation of f followed by the global object. g is defined within f, so this scope chain is saved as part of the definition of g. When g is invoked, the scope chain includes three objects: its own call object, the call object of f, and the global object.

Nested functions are perfectly understandable when they are invoked in the same lexical scope in which they are defined. For example, the following code does not do anything particularly surprising:

```
var x = "global";
function f() {
    var x = "local";
    function g() { alert(x); }
    g();
}
f();  // Calling this function displays "local"
```

In JavaScript, however, functions are data just like any other value, so they can be returned from functions, assigned to object properties, stored in arrays, and so on. This does not cause anything particularly surprising either, except when nested functions are involved. Consider the following code, which includes a function that returns a nested function. Each time it is called, it returns a function. The JavaScript code of the returned function is always the same, but the scope in which it is created differs slightly on each invocation because the values of the arguments to the outer function differ on each invocation. (That is, there is a different call object on the scope chain for each invocation of the outer function.) If you save the returned functions in an array and then invoke each one, you'll see that each returns a different value. Since each function consists of identical JavaScript code, and each is invoked from exactly the same scope, the only factor that could be causing the differing return values is the scope in which the functions were defined:

```
// This function returns a function each time it is called
// The scope in which the function is defined differs for each call
function makefunc(x) {
    return function() { return x; }
}

// Call makefunc() several times, and save the results in an array:
var a = [makefunc(0), makefunc(1), makefunc(2)];

// Now call these functions and display their values.
// Although the body of each function is the same, the scope is
// different, and each call returns a different value:
alert(a[0]());  // Displays 0
alert(a[1]());  // Displays 1
alert(a[2]());  // Displays 2
```

The results of this code are exactly what you would expect from a strict application of the lexical scoping rule: a function is executed in the scope in which it was defined. The reason that these results are surprising, however, is that you expect local scopes to cease to exist when the function that defines them exits. This is, in fact, what normally happens. When a function is invoked, a call object is created for it and placed on the scope chain. When the function exits, the call object is removed from the scope chain. When no nested functions are involved, the scope chain is the only reference to the call object. When the object is removed from the chain, there are no more references to it, and it ends up being garbage collected.

But nested functions change the picture. If a nested function is created, the definition of that function refers to the call objects because that call object is the top of the scope chain in which the function was defined. If the nested function is used only within the outer function, however, the only reference to the nested function is in the call object. When the outer function returns, the nested function refers to the call object, and the call object refers to nested function, but there are no other references to either one, and so both objects become available for garbage collection.

Things are different if you save a reference to the nested function in the global scope. You do so by using the nested function as the return value of the outer function or by storing the nested function as the property of some other object. In this case, there is an external reference to the nested function, and the nested function retains its reference to the call object of the outer function. The upshot is that the call object for that one particular invocation of the outer function continues to live, and the names and values of the function arguments and local variables persist in this object. JavaScript code cannot directly access the call object in any way, but the properties it defines are part of the scope chain for any invocation of the nested function. (Note that if an outer function stores global references to two nested functions, these two nested functions share the same call object, and changes made by an invocation of one function are visible to invocations of the other function.)

JavaScript functions are a combination of code to be executed and the scope in which to execute them. This combination of code and scope is known as a *closure* in the computer science literature. All JavaScript functions are closures. These closures are only interesting, however, in the case discussed above: when a nested function is exported outside the scope in which it is defined. When a nested function is used in this way, it is often explicitly called a closure.

Closures are an interesting and powerful technique. Although they are not commonly used in day-to-day JavaScript programming, it is still worth working to understand them. If you understand closures, you understand the scope chain and function call objects, and can truly call yourself an advanced JavaScript programmer.

8.8.4.1 Closure examples

Occasionally you'll want to write a function that can remember a value across invocations. The value cannot be stored in a local variable because the call object does not persist across invocations. A global variable would work, but that pollutes the global namespace. In Section 8.6.3, I presented a function named uniqueInteger( ) that used a property of itself to store the persistent value. You can use a closure to take this a step further and create a persistent and *private* variable. Here's how to write a function without a closure:

```
// Return a different integer each time we're called
uniqueID = function( ) {
    if (!arguments.callee.id) arguments.callee.id = 0;
    return arguments.callee.id++;
};
```

The problem with this approach is that anyone can set uniqueID.id back to 0 and break the contract of the function that says that it never returns the same value twice. You can prevent that by storing the persistent value in a closure that only your function has access to:

```
uniqueID = (function( ) {  // The call object of this function holds our value
    var id = 0;          // This is the private persistent value
    // The outer function returns a nested function that has access
    // to the persistent value.  It is this nested function we're storing
    // in the variable uniqueID above.
    return function( ) { return id++; };  // Return and increment
})( ); // Invoke the outer function after defining it.
```

Example 8-6 is a second closure example. It demonstrates that private persistent variables like the one used above can be shared by more than one function.

Example 8-6. Private properties with closures

```
// This function adds property accessor methods for a property with
// the specified name to the object o.  The methods are named get<name>
// and set<name>.  If a predicate function is supplied, the setter
// method uses it to test its argument for validity before storing it.
// If the predicate returns false, the setter method throws an exception.
//
// The unusual thing about this function is that the property value
// that is manipulated by the getter and setter methods is not stored in
// the object o.  Instead, the value is stored only in a local variable
// in this function.  The getter and setter methods are also defined
// locally to this function and therefore have access to this local variable.
// Note that the value is private to the two accessor methods, and it cannot
// be set or modified except through the setter.
function makeProperty(o, name, predicate) {
    var value;  // This is the property value

    // The setter method simply returns the value.
    o["get" + name] = function( ) { return value; };

    // The getter method stores the value or throws an exception if
    // the predicate rejects the value.
    o["set" + name] = function(v) {
        if (predicate && !predicate(v))
```

Example 8-6. Private properties with closures (continued)

```
            throw "set" + name + ": invalid value " + v;
        else
            value = v;
    };
}

// The following code demonstrates the makeProperty() method.
var o = {};  // Here is an empty object

// Add property accessor methods getName and setName()
// Ensure that only string values are allowed
makeProperty(o, "Name", function(x) { return typeof x == "string"; });

o.setName("Frank");  // Set the property value
print(o.getName());  // Get the property value
o.setName(0);        // Try to set a value of the wrong type
```

The most useful and least contrived example using closures that I am aware of is the breakpoint facility created by Steve Yen and published on *http://trimpath.com* as part of the TrimPath client-side framework. A *breakpoint* is a point in a function at which code execution stops and the programmer is given the opportunity to inspect the value of variables, evaluate expressions, call functions, and so on. Steve's breakpoint technique uses a closure to capture the current scope within a function (including local variables and function arguments) and combines this with the global eval() function to allow that scope to be inspected. eval() evaluates a string of JavaScript code and returns its result (you can read more about it in Part III). Here is a nested function that works as a self-inspecting closure:

```
// Capture current scope and allow it to be inspected with eval()
var inspector = function($) { return eval($); }
```

This function uses the uncommon identifier $ as its argument name to reduce the possibility of naming conflicts with the scope it is intended to inspect.

You can create a breakpoint within a function by passing this closure to a function like the one in Example 8-7.

Example 8-7. Breakpoints using closures

```
// This function implements a breakpoint. It repeatedly prompts the user
// for an expression, evaluates it with the supplied self-inspecting closure,
// and displays the result. It is the closure that provides access to the
// scope to be inspected, so each function must supply its own closure.
//
// Inspired by Steve Yen's breakpoint() function at
// http://trimpath.com/project/wiki/TrimBreakpoint
function inspect(inspector, title) {
    var expression, result;

    // You can use a breakpoint to turn off subsequent breakpoints by
    // creating a property named "ignore" on this function.
```

Example 8-7. Breakpoints using closures (continued)

```
    if ("ignore" in arguments.callee) return;

    while(true) {
        // Figure out how to prompt the user
        var message = "";
        // If we were given a title, display that first
        if (title) message = title + "\n";
        // If we've already evaluated an expression, display it and its value
        if (expression) message += "\n" + expression + " ==> " + result + "\n";
        else expression = "";
        // We always display at least a basic prompt:
        message += "Enter an expression to evaluate:";

        // Get the user's input, displaying our prompt and using the
        // last expression as the default value this time.
        expression = prompt(message, expression);

        // If the user didn't enter anything (or clicked Cancel),
        // they're done, and so we return, ending the breakpoint.
        if (!expression) return;

        // Otherwise, use the supplied closure to evaluate the expression
        // in the scope that is being inspected.
        // The result will be displayed on the next iteration.
        result = inspector(expression);
    }
}
```

Note that the inspect( ) function of Example 8-7 uses the Window.prompt( ) method to display text to the user and allow him to enter a string (see Window.prompt( ) in Part IV for further details).

Here is a function for computing factorials that uses this breakpointing technique:

```
function factorial(n) {
    // Create a closure for this function
    var inspector = function($) { return eval($); }
    inspect(inspector, "Entering factorial()");

    var result = 1;
    while(n > 1) {
        result = result * n;
        n--;
        inspect(inspector, "factorial() loop");
    }

    inspect(inspector, "Exiting factorial()");
    return result;
}
```

8.8.4.2 Closures and memory leaks in Internet Explorer

Microsoft's Internet Explorer web browser uses a weak form of garbage collection for ActiveX objects and client-side DOM elements. These client-side objects are reference-counted and freed when their reference count reaches zero. This scheme fails when there are circular references, such as when a core JavaScript object refers to a document element and that document element has a property (such as an event handler) that refers back to the core JavaScript object.

This kind of circular reference frequently occurs when closures are used with client-side programming in IE. When you use a closure, remember that the call object of the enclosing function, including all function arguments and local variables, will last as long as the closure does. If any of those function arguments or local variables refer to a client-side object, you may be creating a memory leak.

A full discussion of this problem is beyond the scope of this book. See *http://msdn. microsoft.com/library/en-us/IETechCol/dnwebgen/ie_leak_patterns.asp* for details.

8.9 The Function( ) Constructor

As explained earlier, functions are usually defined using the function keyword, either in the form of a function definition statement or a function literal expression. Functions can also be defined with the Function( ) constructor. Using the Function( ) constructor is typically harder than using a function literal, and so this technique is not commonly used. Here is an example that creates a function with the Function( ) constructor:

```
var f = new Function("x", "y", "return x*y;");
```

This line of code creates a new function that is more or less equivalent to a function defined with the familiar syntax:

```
function f(x, y) { return x*y; }
```

The Function( ) constructor expects any number of string arguments. The last argument is the body of the function; it can contain arbitrary JavaScript statements, separated from each other by semicolons. All other arguments to the constructor are strings that specify the names of the parameters to the function being defined. If you are defining a function that takes no arguments, you simply pass a single string—the function body—to the constructor.

Notice that the Function( ) constructor is not passed any argument that specifies a name for the function it creates. Like function literals, the Function( ) constructor creates anonymous functions.

There are a few points that are important to understand about the Function( ) constructor:

- The Function( ) constructor allows JavaScript code to be dynamically created and compiled at runtime. It is like the global eval( ) function (see Part III) in this way.

- The Function( ) constructor parses the function body and creates a new function object each time it is called. If the call to the constructor appears within a loop or within a frequently called function, this process can be inefficient. By contrast, a function literal or nested function that appears within a loop or function is not recompiled each time it is encountered. Nor is a different function object created each time a function literal is encountered. (Although, as noted earlier, a new closure may be required to capture differences in the lexical scope in which the function is defined.)

- A last, very important point about the Function( ) constructor is that the functions it creates do not use lexical scoping; instead, they are always compiled as if they were top-level functions, as the following code demonstrates:

```
var y = "global";
function constructFunction( ) {
    var y = "local";
    return new Function("return y");  // Does not capture the local scope!
}
// This line displays "global" because the function returned by the
// Function( ) constructor does not use the local scope. Had a function
// literal been used instead, this line would have displayed "local".
alert(constructFunction( )( ));  // Displays "global"
```

CHAPTER 9
Classes, Constructors, and Prototypes

JavaScript objects were introduced in Chapter 7. That chapter treated each object as a unique set of properties, different from every other object. In many object-oriented programming languages, it is possible to define a *class* of objects and then create individual objects that are *instances* of that class. You might define a class named Complex to represent and perform arithmetic on complex numbers, for example. A Complex object would represent a single complex number and would be an instance of that class.

JavaScript does not support true classes the way that languages like Java, C++, and C# do.[*] Still, however, it is possible to define pseudoclasses in JavaScript. The tools for doing this are constructor functions and prototype objects. This chapter explains constructors and prototypes and includes examples of several JavaScript pseudoclasses and even pseudosubclasses.

For lack of a better term, I use the word "class" informally in this chapter. Be careful, however, that you don't confuse these informal classes with the true classes of JavaScript 2 and other languages.

9.1 Constructors

Chapter 7 showed you how to create a new, empty object either with the object literal {} or with the following expression:

```
new Object()
```

You have also seen other kinds of JavaScript objects created with a similar syntax:

```
var array = new Array(10);
var today = new Date();
```

---

[*] True classes are planned for JavaScript 2.0, however.

The new operator must be followed by a function invocation. It creates a new object, with no properties and then invokes the function, passing the new object as the value of the this keyword. A function designed to be used with the new operator is called a *constructor* function or simply a constructor. A constructor's job is to initialize a newly created object, setting any properties that need to be set before the object is used. You can define your own constructor function, simply by writing a function that adds properties to this. The following code defines a constructor and then invokes it twice with the new operator to create two new objects:

```
// Define the constructor.
// Note how it initializes the object referred to by "this".
function Rectangle(w, h) {
    this.width = w;
    this.height = h;
    // Note: no return statement here
}

// Invoke the constructor to create two Rectangle objects.
// We pass the width and height to the constructor
// so that it can initialize each new object appropriately.
var rect1 = new Rectangle(2, 4);    // rect1 = { width:2, height:4 };
var rect2 = new Rectangle(8.5, 11); // rect2 = { width:8.5, height:11 };
```

Notice how the constructor uses its arguments to initialize properties of the object referred to by the this keyword. You have defined a class of objects simply by defining an appropriate constructor function; all objects created with the Rectangle() constructor are now guaranteed to have initialized width and height properties. This means that you can write programs that rely on this fact and treat all Rectangle objects uniformly. Because every constructor defines a class of objects, it is stylistically important to give a constructor function a name that indicates the class of objects it creates. Creating a rectangle with new Rectangle(1,2) is a lot more intuitive than with new init_rect(1,2), for example.

Constructor functions typically do not have return values. They initialize the object passed as the value of this and return nothing. However, a constructor is allowed to return an object value, and, if it does so, that returned object becomes the value of the new expression. In this case, the object that was the value of this is simply discarded.

9.2   Prototypes and Inheritance

Recall from Chapter 8 that a *method* is a function that is invoked as a property of an object. When a function is invoked in this way, the object through which it is accessed becomes the value of the this keyword. Suppose you'd like to compute the area of the rectangle represented by a Rectangle object. Here is one way to do it:

```
function computeAreaOfRectangle(r) { return r.width * r.height; }
```

This works, but it is not object-oriented. When using objects, it is better to invoke a method on the object rather than passing the object to a function. Here's how to do that:

```
// Create a Rectangle object
var r = new Rectangle(8.5, 11);
// Add a method to it
r.area = function() { return this.width * this.height; }
// Now invoke the method to compute the area
var a = r.area();
```

Having to add a method to an object before you can invoke it is silly, of course. You can improve the situation by initializing the area property to refer to the area computing function in the constructor. Here is an improved Rectangle() constructor:

```
function Rectangle(w, h) {
    this.width = w;
    this.height = h;
    this.area = function() { return this.width * this.height; }
}
```

With this new version of the constructor, you can write code like this:

```
// How big is a sheet of U.S. Letter paper in square inches?
var r = new Rectangle(8.5, 11);
var a = r.area();
```

This solution works better but is still not optimal. Every rectangle created will have three properties. The width and height properties may be different for each rectangle, but the area of every single Rectangle object always refers to the same function (someone might change it, of course, but you usually intend the methods of an object to be constant). It is inefficient to use regular properties for methods that are intended to be shared by all objects of the same class (that is, all objects created with the same constructor).

There is a solution, however. It turns out that every JavaScript object includes an internal reference to another object, known as its prototype object. Any properties of the prototype appear to be properties of an object for which it is the prototype. Another way of saying this is that a JavaScript object *inherits* properties from its prototype.

In the previous section, I showed that the new operator creates a new, empty object and then invokes a constructor function as a method of that object. This is not the complete story, however. After creating the empty object, new sets the prototype of that object. The prototype of an object is the value of the prototype property of its constructor function. All functions have a prototype property that is automatically created and initialized when the function is defined. The initial value of the prototype property is an object with a single property. This property is named constructor and refers back to the constructor function with which the prototype is associated. (You may recall the constructor property from Chapter 7; this is why every object has a constructor property.) Any properties you add to this prototype object will appear to be properties of objects initialized by the constructor.

This is clearer with an example. Here again is the `Rectangle( )` constructor:

```
// The constructor function initializes those properties that
// will be different for each instance.
function Rectangle(w, h) {
    this.width = w;
    this.height = h;
}

// The prototype object holds methods and other properties that
// should be shared by each instance.
Rectangle.prototype.area = function() { return this.width * this.height; }
```

A constructor provides a name for a "class" of objects and initializes properties, such as width and height, that may be different for each instance of the class. The prototype object is associated with the constructor, and each object initialized by the constructor inherits exactly the same set of properties from the prototype. This means that the prototype object is an ideal place for methods and other constant properties.

Note that inheritance occurs automatically as part of the process of looking up a property value. Properties are *not* copied from the prototype object into new objects; they merely appear as if they were properties of those objects. This has two important implications. First, the use of prototype objects can dramatically decrease the amount of memory required by each object because the object can inherit many of its properties. The second implication is that an object inherits properties even if they are added to its prototype *after* the object is created. This means that it is possible (though not necessarily a good idea) to add new methods to existing classes.

Inherited properties behave just like regular properties of an object. They are enumerated by the `for/in` loop and can be tested with the `in` operator. You can distinguish them only with the `Object.hasOwnProperty( )` method:

```
var r = new Rectangle(2, 3);
r.hasOwnProperty("width");    // true: width is a direct property of r
r.hasOwnProperty("area");     // false: area is an inherited property of r
"area" in r;                  // true: "area" is a property of r
```

9.2.1   Reading and Writing Inherited Properties

Each class has one prototype object, with one set of properties. But there are potentially many instances of a class, each of which inherits those prototype properties. Because one prototype property can be inherited by many objects, JavaScript must enforce a fundamental asymmetry between reading and writing property values. When you read property p of an object o, JavaScript first checks to see if o has a property named p. If it does not, it next checks to see if the prototype object of o has a property named p. This is what makes prototype-based inheritance work.

When you write the value of a property, on the other hand, JavaScript does not use the prototype object. To see why, consider what would happen if it did: suppose you try to set the value of the property o.p when the object o does not have a property named p. Further suppose that JavaScript goes ahead and looks up the property p in the prototype object of o and allows you to set the property of the prototype. Now you have changed the value of p for a whole class of objects—not at all what you intended.

Therefore, property inheritance occurs only when you read property values, not when you write them. If you set the property p in an object o that inherits that property from its prototype, what happens is that you create a new property p directly in o. Now that o has its own property named p, it no longer inherits the value of p from its prototype. When you read the value of p, JavaScript first looks at the properties of o. Since it finds p defined in o, it doesn't need to search the prototype object and never finds the value of p defined there. We sometimes say that the property p in o "shadows" or "hides" the property p in the prototype object. Prototype inheritance can be a confusing topic. Figure 9-1 illustrates the concepts discussed here.

Because prototype properties are shared by all objects of a class, it generally makes sense to use them to define only properties that are the same for all objects within the class. This makes prototypes ideal for defining methods. Other properties with constant values (such as mathematical constants) are also suitable for definition with prototype properties. If your class defines a property with a very commonly used default value, you might define this property and its default value in a prototype object. Then, the few objects that want to deviate from the default value can create their own private, unshared copies of the property and define their own nondefault values.

9.2.2 Extending Built-in Types

It is not only user-defined classes that have prototype objects. Built-in classes, such as String and Date, have prototype objects too, and you can assign values to them. For example, the following code defines a new method that is available for all String objects:

```
// Returns true if the last character is c
String.prototype.endsWith = function(c) {
    return (c == this.charAt(this.length-1))
}
```

Having defined the new endsWith( ) method in the String prototype object, you can use it like this:

```
var message = "hello world";
message.endsWith('h')  // Returns false
message.endsWith('d')  // Returns true
```

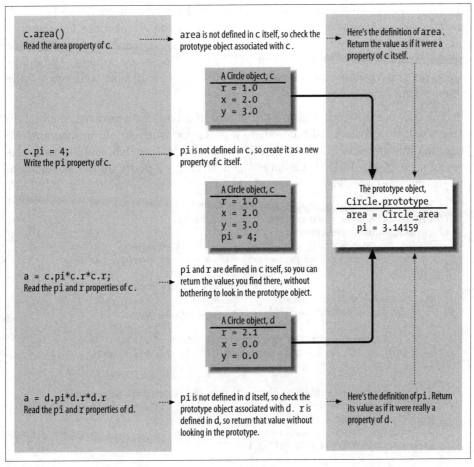

Figure 9-1. Objects and prototypes

There is a strong argument against extending built-in types with your own methods; if you do so, you are essentially creating your own custom version of the core Java-Script API. Any other programmers who have to read or maintain your code will likely find it confusing if your code includes methods they have never heard of. Unless you are creating a low-level JavaScript framework that you expect to be adopted by many other programmers, it is probably best to stay away from the prototype objects of the built-in types.

Note that you must *never* add properties to Object.prototype. Any properties or methods you add are enumerable with a for/in loop, and adding them to Object.prototype makes them visible in every single JavaScript object. An empty object, {}, is expected to have no enumerable properties. Anything added to Object.prototype becomes an enumerable property of the empty object and will likely break code that uses objects as associative arrays.

The technique shown here for extending built-in object types is guaranteed to work only for core JavaScript "native objects." When JavaScript is embedded in some context, such as a web browser or a Java application, it has access to additional "host objects" such as objects that represent web browser document content. These host objects do not typically have constructors and prototype objects, and you usually cannot extend them.

There is one case in which it is safe and useful to extend the prototype of a built-in native class: to add standard methods to a prototype when an old or incompatible JavaScript implementation lacks them. For example, the Function.apply() method is missing in Microsoft Internet Explorer 4 and 5. This is a pretty important function, and you may see code like this to replace it:

```
// IE 4 & 5 don't implement Function.apply().
// This workaround is based on code by Aaron Boodman.
if (!Function.prototype.apply) {
    // Invoke this function as a method of the specified object,
    // passing the specified parameters.  We have to use eval() to do this
    Function.prototype.apply = function(object, parameters) {
        var f = this;                   // The function to invoke
        var o = object || window;       // The object to invoke it on
        var args = parameters || [];    // The arguments to pass

        // Temporarily make the function into a method of o
        // To do this we use a property name that is unlikely to exist
        o._$_apply_$_ = f;

        // We will use eval() to invoke the method. To do this we've got
        // to write the invocation as a string. First build the argument list.
        var stringArgs = [];
        for(var i = 0; i < args.length; i++)
            stringArgs[i] = "args[" + i + "]";

        // Concatenate the argument strings into a comma-separated list.
        var arglist = stringArgs.join(",");

        // Now build the entire method call string
        var methodcall = "o._$_apply_$_(" + arglist + ");";

        // Use the eval() function to make the methodcall
        var result = eval(methodcall);

        // Unbind the function from the object
        delete o._$_apply_$_;

        // And return the result
        return result;
    };
}
```

As another example, consider the new array methods implemented in Firefox 1.5 (see Section 7.7.10). If you want to use the new Array.map() method but also want your code to work on platforms that do not support this method natively, you can use this code for compatibility:

```
// Array.map() invokes a function f on each element of the array,
// returning a new array of the values that result from each function
// call. If map() is called with two arguments, the function f
// is invoked as a method of the second argument. When invoked, f()
// is passed 3 arguments. The first is the value of the array
// element. The second is the index of the array element, and the
// third is the array itself. In most cases it needs to use only the
// first argument.
if (!Array.prototype.map) {
    Array.prototype.map = function(f, thisObject) {
        var results = [];
        for(var len = this.length, i = 0; i < len; i++) {
            results.push(f.call(thisObject, this[i], i, this));
        }
        return results;
    }
}
```

9.3   Simulating Classes in JavaScript

Although JavaScript supports a datatype called an object, it does not have a formal notion of a class. This makes it quite different from classic object-oriented languages such as C++ and Java. The common conception about object-oriented programming languages is that they are strongly typed and support class-based inheritance. By these criteria, it is easy to dismiss JavaScript as not being a true object-oriented language. On the other hand, you've seen that JavaScript makes heavy use of objects, and it has its own type of prototype-based inheritance. JavaScript is a true object-oriented language. It draws inspiration from a number of other (relatively obscure) object-oriented languages that use prototype-based inheritance instead of class-based inheritance.

Although JavaScript is not a class-based object-oriented language, it does a good job of simulating the features of class-based languages such as Java and C++. I've been using the term *class* informally throughout this chapter. This section more formally explores the parallels between JavaScript and true class-based inheritance languages such as Java and C++.[*]

Let's start by defining some basic terminology. An *object*, as you've already seen, is a data structure that contains various pieces of named data and may also contain various methods to operate on those pieces of data. An object groups related values and methods into a single convenient package, which generally makes programming

---

[*] You should read this section even if you are not familiar with those languages and that style of object-oriented programming.

easier by increasing the modularity and reusability of code. Objects in JavaScript may have any number of properties, and properties may be dynamically added to an object. This is not the case in strictly typed languages such as Java and C++. In those languages, each object has a predefined set of properties,[*] where each property is of a predefined type. When you use JavaScript objects to simulate object-oriented programming techniques, you generally define in advance the set of properties for each object and the type of data that each property holds.

In Java and C++, a *class* defines the structure of an object. The class specifies exactly what fields an object contains and what types of data each holds. It also defines the methods that operate on an object. JavaScript does not have a formal notion of a class, but, as shown earlier, it approximates classes with its constructors and their prototype objects.

In both JavaScript and class-based object-oriented languages, there may be multiple objects of the same class. We often say that an object is an *instance* of its class. Thus, there may be many instances of any class. Sometimes the term *instantiate* is used to describe the process of creating an object (i.e., an instance of a class).

In Java, it is a common programming convention to name classes with an initial capital letter and to name objects with lowercase letters. This convention helps keep classes and objects distinct from each other in code, and it is useful to follow in JavaScript programming as well. Previous sections of this chapter, for example, have defined a Rectangle class and created instances of that class with names such as rect.

The members of a Java class may be of four basic types: instance properties, instance methods, class properties, and class methods. In the following sections, we'll explore the differences between these types and show how they are simulated in JavaScript.

9.3.1   Instance Properties

Every object has its own separate copies of its *instance properties*. In other words, if there are 10 objects of a given class, there are 10 copies of each instance property. In our Rectangle class, for example, every Rectangle object has a property width that specifies the width of the rectangle. In this case, width is an instance property. Since each object has its own copy of the instance properties, these properties are accessed through individual objects. If r is an object that is an instance of the Rectangle class, for example, its width is referred to as:

```
r.width
```

By default, any object property in JavaScript is an instance property. To truly simulate traditional class-based object-oriented programming, however, we will say that

---

[*] They are usually called "fields" in Java and C++, but I'll refer to them as properties here since that is the JavaScript terminology.

instance properties in JavaScript are those properties that are created and initialized by the constructor function.

9.3.2 Instance Methods

An *instance method* is much like an instance property, except that it is a method rather than a data value. (In Java, functions and methods are not data, as they are in JavaScript, so this distinction is more clear.) Instance methods are invoked on a particular object, or instance. The area( ) method of our Rectangle class is an instance method. It is invoked on a Rectangle object r like this:

```
a = r.area( );
```

The implementation of an instance method uses the this keyword to refer to the object or instance on which it is invoked. An instance method can be invoked for any instance of a class, but this does not mean that each object contains its own private copy of the method, as it does with instance properties. Instead, each instance method is shared by all instances of a class. In JavaScript, an instance method for a class is defined by setting a property in the constructor's prototype object to a function value. This way, all objects created by that constructor share an inherited reference to the function and can invoke it using the method-invocation syntax shown earlier.

9.3.2.1 Instance methods and this

If you are a Java or C++ programmer, you may have noticed an important difference between instance methods in those languages and instance methods in JavaScript. In Java and C++, the scope of instance methods includes the this object. The body of an area method in Java, for example might simply be:

```
return width * height;
```

In JavaScript, however, you've seen that you must explicitly specify the this keyword for these properties:

```
return this.width * this.height;
```

If you find it awkward to have to prefix each instance field with this, you can use the with statement (covered in Section 6.18) in each of your methods. For example:

```
Rectangle.prototype.area = function( ) {
    with(this) {
        return width*height;
    }
}
```

9.3.3 Class Properties

A *class property* in Java is a property that is associated with a class itself, rather than with each instance of a class. No matter how many instances of the class are created, there is only one copy of each class property. Just as instance properties are accessed through an instance of a class, class properties are accessed through the class itself. `Number.MAX_VALUE` is an example of a class property in JavaScript: the `MAX_VALUE` property is accessed through the Number class. Because there is only one copy of each class property, class properties are essentially global. What is nice about them, however, is that they are associated with a class, and they have a logical niche—a position in the JavaScript namespace where they are not likely to be overwritten by other properties with the same name. As is probably clear, you simulate a class property in JavaScript simply by defining a property of the constructor function itself. For example, to create a class property `Rectangle.UNIT` to store a special 1x1 rectangle, you can do the following:

```
Rectangle.UNIT = new Rectangle(1,1);
```

Rectangle is a constructor function, but because JavaScript functions are objects, you can create properties of a function just as you can create properties of any other object.

9.3.4 Class Methods

A *class method* is associated with a class rather than with an instance of a class. Class methods are invoked through the class itself, not through a particular instance of the class. The `Date.parse( )` method (which you can look up in Part III) is a class method. You always invoke it through the Date constructor object rather than through a particular instance of the Date class.

Because class methods are invoked through a constructor function, the this keyword does not refer to any particular instance of the class. Instead, it refers to the constructor function itself. (Typically, a class method does not use this at all.)

Like class properties, class methods are global. Because they do not operate on a particular object, class methods are generally more easily thought of as functions that happen to be invoked through a class. Again, associating these functions with a class gives them a convenient niche in the JavaScript namespace and prevents namespace collisions. To define a class method in JavaScript, simply make the appropriate function a property of the constructor.

9.3.5 Example: A Circle Class

The code in Example 9-1 is a constructor function and prototype object for creating objects that represent circles. It contains examples of instance properties, instance methods, class properties, and class methods.

Example 9-1. A circle class

```
// We begin with the constructor
function Circle(radius) {
```

Example 9-1. A circle class (continued)

```
    // r is an instance property, defined and initialized in the constructor.
    this.r = radius;
}

// Circle.PI is a class property--it is a property of the constructor function.
Circle.PI = 3.14159;

// Here is an instance method that computes a circle's area.
Circle.prototype.area = function() { return Circle.PI * this.r * this.r; }

// This class method takes two Circle objects and returns the
// one that has the larger radius.
Circle.max = function(a,b) {
    if (a.r > b.r) return a;
    else return b;
}

// Here is some code that uses each of these fields:
var c = new Circle(1.0);        // Create an instance of the Circle class
c.r = 2.2;                      // Set the r instance property
var a = c.area();               // Invoke the area() instance method
var x = Math.exp(Circle.PI);    // Use the PI class property in our own computation
var d = new Circle(1.2);        // Create another Circle instance
var bigger = Circle.max(c,d);   // Use the max() class method
```

9.3.6   Example: Complex Numbers

Example 9-2 is another example, somewhat more formal than the last, that defines a
class of objects in JavaScript. The code and the comments are worth careful study.

Example 9-2. A complex number class

```
/*
 * Complex.js:
 * This file defines a Complex class to represent complex numbers.
 * Recall that a complex number is the sum of a real number and an
 * imaginary number and that the imaginary number i is the
 * square root of -1.
 */

/*
 * The first step in defining a class is defining the constructor
 * function of the class. This constructor should initialize any
 * instance properties of the object. These are the essential
 * "state variables" that make each instance of the class different.
 */
function Complex(real, imaginary) {
    this.x = real;        // The real part of the number
    this.y = imaginary;   // The imaginary part of the number
}

/*
```

Example 9-2. A complex number class (continued)

```
 * The second step in defining a class is defining its instance
 * methods (and possibly other properties) in the prototype object
 * of the constructor. Any properties defined in this object will
 * be inherited by all instances of the class. Note that instance
 * methods operate on the this keyword. For many methods,
 * no other arguments are needed.
 */

// Return the magnitude of a complex number. This is defined
// as its distance from the origin (0,0) of the complex plane.
Complex.prototype.magnitude = function() {
    return Math.sqrt(this.x*this.x + this.y*this.y);
};

// Return a complex number that is the negative of this one.
Complex.prototype.negative = function() {
    return new Complex(-this.x, -this.y);
};

// Add a complex number to this one and return the sum in a new object.
Complex.prototype.add = function(that) {
    return new Complex(this.x + that.x, this.y + that.y);
}

// Multiply this complex number by another and return the product as a
// new Complex object.
Complex.prototype.multiply = function(that) {
    return new Complex(this.x * that.x - this.y * that.y,
                       this.x * that.y + this.y * that.x);
}

// Convert a Complex object to a string in a useful way.
// This is invoked when a Complex object is used as a string.
Complex.prototype.toString = function() {
    return "{" + this.x + "," + this.y + "}";
};

// Test whether this Complex object has the same value as another.
Complex.prototype.equals = function(that) {
    return this.x == that.x && this.y == that.y;
}

// Return the real portion of a complex number. This function
// is invoked when a Complex object is treated as a primitive value.
Complex.prototype.valueOf = function() { return this.x; }

/*
 * The third step in defining a class is to define class methods,
 * constants, and any needed class properties as properties of the
 * constructor function itself (instead of as properties of the
 * prototype object of the constructor). Note that class methods
 * do not use the this keyword: they operate only on their arguments.
```

Example 9-2. A complex number class (continued)

```
 */
// Add two complex numbers and return the result.
// Contrast this with the instance method add( )
Complex.sum = function (a, b) {
    return new Complex(a.x + b.x, a.y + b.y);
};

// Multiply two complex numbers and return the product.
// Contrast with the instance method multiply( )
Complex.product = function(a, b) {
    return new Complex(a.x * b.x - a.y * b.y,
                       a.x * b.y + a.y * b.x);
};

// Here are some useful predefined complex numbers.
// They are defined as class properties, and their names are in uppercase
// to indicate that they are intended to be constants (although it is not
// possible to make JavaScript properties read-only).
Complex.ZERO = new Complex(0,0);
Complex.ONE = new Complex(1,0);
Complex.I = new Complex(0,1);
```

9.3.7 Private Members

A common feature of traditional object-oriented languages such as Java and C++ is that the properties of a class can be declared private so that they are available only to the methods of the class and cannot be manipulated by code outside of the class. A common programming technique called *data encapsulation* makes properties private and allows read and write access to them only through special accessor methods. JavaScript can simulate this using closures (an advanced topic, covered in Section 8.8), but to do so, the accessor methods must be stored on each object instance; they cannot be inherited from the prototype object.

The following code illustrates how this is done. It implements an immutable Rectangle object whose width and height can never be changed and are available only through accessor methods:

```
function ImmutableRectangle(w, h) {
    // This constructor does not store the width and height properties
    // in the object it initializes. Instead, it simply defines
    // accessor methods in the object. These methods are closures and
    // the width and height values are captured in their scope chains.
    this.getWidth = function() { return w; }
    this.getHeight = function() { return h; }
}

// Note that the class can have regular methods in the prototype object.
ImmutableRectangle.prototype.area = function() {
    return this.getWidth() * this.getHeight();
};
```

Douglas Crockford is generally credited as the first person to discover (or at least to publish) this technique for defining private properties. His original discussion is at *http://www.crockford.com/javascript/private.html*.

9.4 Common Object Methods

When defining a new JavaScript class, there are several methods that you should always consider defining. These methods are detailed in the subsections that follow.

9.4.1 The toString( ) Method

The idea behind toString( ) is that each class of objects has its own particular string representation, so it should define an appropriate toString( ) method to convert objects to that string form. When you define a class, you should define a toString( ) method for it so that instances of the class can be converted to meaningful strings. The string should contain information about the object being converted because this is useful for debugging purposes. If the string representation is chosen carefully, it can also be useful in programs themselves. Additionally, you might consider adding a static parse( ) method to your class to parse a string output by toString( ) back into object form.

The Complex class of Example 9-2 includes a toString( ) method, and the following code shows a toString( ) method you can define for a Circle class:

```
Circle.prototype.toString = function () {
    return "[Circle of radius " + this.r + ", centered at ("
        + this.x + ", " + this.y + ").]";
}
```

With this toString( ) method defined, a typical Circle object might be converted to the string "[Circle of radius 1, centered at (0, 0).]".

9.4.2 The valueOf( ) Method

The valueOf( ) method is much like the toString( ) method, but it is called when JavaScript needs to convert an object to some primitive type other than a string—typically, a number. Where possible, the function should return a primitive value that somehow represents the value of the object referred to by the this keyword.

By definition, objects are not primitive values, so most objects do not have a primitive equivalent. Thus, the default valueOf( ) method defined by the Object class performs no conversion and simply returns the object on which it is invoked. Classes such as Number and Boolean have obvious primitive equivalents, so they override the valueOf( ) method to return appropriate primitive values. This is why Number and Boolean objects can behave so much like their equivalent primitive values.

Occasionally, you may define a class that has some reasonable primitive equivalent. In this case, you may want to define a custom valueOf( ) method for the class. In the Complex class of Example 9-2, you'll see that a valueOf( ) method was defined that returned the real part of the complex number. Thus, when a Complex object is used in a numeric context, it behaves as if it were a real number without its imaginary component. For example, consider the following code:

```
var a = new Complex(5,4);
var b = new Complex(2,1);
var c = Complex.sum(a,b);   // c is the complex number {7,5}
var d = a + b;              // d is the number 7
```

One note of caution about defining a valueOf( ) method: the valueOf( ) method can, in some circumstances, take priority over the toString( ) method when converting an object to a string. Thus, when you define a valueOf( ) method for a class, you may need to be more explicit about calling the toString( ) method when you want to force an object of that class to be converted to a string. To continue with the Complex example:

```
alert("c = " + c);              // Uses valueOf(); displays "c = 7"
alert("c = " + c.toString());   // Displays "c = {7,5}"
```

9.4.3 Comparison Methods

JavaScript equality operators compare objects by reference, not by value. That is, given two object references, they look to see if both references are to the same object. They do not check to see if two different objects have the same property names and values. It is often useful to be able to compare two objects for equality or even for relative order (as the < and > operators do). If you define a class and want to be able to compare instances of that class, you should define appropriate methods to perform those comparisons.

The Java programming language uses methods for object comparison, and adopting the Java conventions is a common and useful thing to do in JavaScript. To enable instances of your class to be tested for equality, define an instance method named equals( ). It should take a single argument and return true if that argument is equal to the object it is invoked on. Of course it is up to you to decide what "equal" means in the context of your own class. Typically, you simply compare the instance properties of the two objects to ensure that they have the same values. The Complex class in Example 9-2 has an equals( ) method of this sort.

It is sometimes useful to compare objects according to some ordering. That is, for some classes, it is possible to say that one instance is "less than" or "greater than" another instance. You might order Complex numbers based on their magnitude( ), for example. On the other hand, it is not clear that there is a meaningful ordering of Circle objects: do you compare them based on radius, X coordinate and Y coordinate, or some combination of these?

If you try to use objects with JavaScript's relation operators such as < and <=, JavaScript first calls the valueOf( ) method of the objects and, if this method returns a primitive value, compares those values. Since our Complex class has a valueOf( ) method that returns the real part of a complex number, instances of the Complex class can be compared as if they were real numbers with no imaginary part. This may or may not be what you actually want. To compare objects according to an explicitly defined ordering of your own choosing, you can (again, following Java convention) define a method named compareTo( ).

The compareTo( ) method should accept a single argument and compare it to the object on which the method is invoked. If the this object is less than the argument object, compareTo( ) should return a value less that zero. If the this object is greater than the argument object, the method should return a value greater than zero. And if the two objects are equal, the method should return zero. These conventions about the return value are important, and they allow you to substitute the following expressions for relational and equality operators:

Replace this	With this
a < b	a.compareTo(b) < 0
a <= b	a.compareTo(b) <= 0
a > b	a.compareTo(b) > 0
a >= b	a.compareTo(b) >= 0
a == b	a.compareTo(b) == 0
a != b	a.compareTo(b) != 0

Here is a compareTo( ) method for the Complex class in Example 9-2 that compares complex numbers by magnitude:

```
Complex.prototype.compareTo = function(that) {
    // If we aren't given an argument, or are passed a value that
    // does not have a magnitude() method, throw an exception
    // An alternative would be to return -1 or 1 in this case to say
    // that all Complex objects are always less than or greater than
    // any other values.
    if (!that || !that.magnitude || typeof that.magnitude != "function")
        throw new Error("bad argument to Complex.compareTo()");

    // This subtraction trick returns a value less than, equal to, or
    // greater than zero.  It is useful in many compareTo() methods.
    return this.magnitude() - that.magnitude();
}
```

One reason to compare instances of a class is so that arrays of those instances can be sorted into some order. The Array.sort( ) method accepts as an optional argument a comparison function that uses the same return-value conventions as the compareTo( ) method. Given the compareTo( ) method shown, it is easy to sort an array of Complex objects with code like this:

```
complexNumbers.sort(new function(a,b) { return a.compareTo(b); });
```

Sorting is important enough that you should consider adding a static `compare()` method to any class for which you define a `compareTo()` instance method. One can easily be defined in terms of the other. For example:

```
Complex.compare = function(a,b) { return a.compareTo(b); };
```

With a method like this defined, sorting becomes simpler:

```
complexNumbers.sort(Complex.compare);
```

Notice that the `compareTo()` and `compare()` methods shown here were not included in the original Complex class of Example 9-2. That is because they are not *consistent with* the `equals()` method that was defined in that example. The `equals()` method says that two Complex objects are equal only if both their real and imaginary parts are the same. But the `compareTo()` method returns zero for any two complex numbers that have the same magnitude. Both the numbers $1+0i$ and $0+1i$ have the same magnitude, and these two values are equal according to `compareTo()` but not according to `equals()`. If you write `equals()` and `compareTo()` methods for the same Class, it is a good idea to make them consistent. Inconsistent notions of equality can be a pernicious source of bugs. Here is a `compareTo()` method that defines an ordering consistent with the existing `equals()` method:

```
// Compare complex numbers first by their real part.  If their real
// parts are equal, compare them by complex part
Complex.prototype.compareTo = function(that) {
    var result = this.x - that.x;   // compare real using subtraction
    if (result == 0)                // if they are equal...
        result = this.y - that.y;   //   then compare imaginary parts
    // Now our result is 0 if and only if this.equals(that)
    return result;
};
```

9.5 Superclasses and Subclasses

Java, C++, and other class-based object-oriented languages have an explicit concept of the *class hierarchy*. Every class can have a *superclass* from which it inherits properties and methods. Any class can be extended, or subclassed, so that the resulting *subclass* inherits its behavior. As shown previously, JavaScript supports prototype inheritance instead of class-based inheritance. Still, JavaScript analogies to the class hierarchy can be drawn. In JavaScript, the Object class is the most generic, and all other classes are specialized versions, or subclasses, of it. Another way to say this is that Object is the superclass of all the built-in classes, and all classes inherit a few basic methods from Object.

Recall that objects inherit properties from the prototype object of their constructor. How do they also inherit properties from the Object class? Remember that the prototype object is itself an object; it is created with the `Object()` constructor. This means the prototype object itself inherits properties from `Object.prototype`! Prototype-based inheritance is not limited to a single prototype object; instead, a chain of prototype objects is involved. Thus, a Complex object inherits properties from Complex.prototype and from Object.prototype. When you look up a property in a Complex object, the object itself is searched first. If the property is not found, the Complex.prototype object is searched next. Finally, if the property is not found in that object, the Object. prototype object is searched.

Note that because the Complex prototype object is searched before the Object prototype object, properties of Complex.prototype hide any properties with the same name in Object.prototype. For example, in the Complex class of Example 9-2, a toString( ) method was defined in the Complex.prototype object. Object.prototype also defines a method with this name, but Complex objects never see it because the definition of toString( ) in Complex.prototype is found first.

The classes shown so far in this chapter are all direct subclasses of Object. When necessary, however, it is possible to subclass any other class. Recall the Rectangle class shown earlier in the chapter, for example. It had properties that represent the width and height of the rectangle but no properties describing its position. Suppose you want to create a subclass of Rectangle in order to add fields and methods related to the position of the rectangle. To do this, simply make sure that the prototype object of the new class is itself an instance of Rectangle so that it inherits all the properties of Rectangle.prototype. Example 9-3 repeats the definition of a simple Rectangle class and then extends it to define a PositionedRectangle class.

Example 9-3. Subclassing a JavaScript class

```
// Here is a simple Rectangle class.
// It has a width and height and can compute its own area
function Rectangle(w, h) {
    this.width = w;
    this.height = h;
}
Rectangle.prototype.area = function( ) { return this.width * this.height; }

// Here is how we might subclass it
function PositionedRectangle(x, y, w, h) {
    // First, invoke the superclass constructor on the new object
    // so that it can initialize the width and height.
    // We use the call method so that we invoke the constructor as a
    // method of the object to be initialized.
    // This is called constructor chaining.
    Rectangle.call(this, w, h);

    // Now store the position of the upper-left corner of the rectangle
    this.x = x;
    this.y = y;
}

// If we use the default prototype object that is created when we
// define the PositionedRectangle( ) constructor, we get a subclass of Object.
```

Example 9-3. Subclassing a JavaScript class (continued)

```
// To subclass Rectangle, we must explicitly create our prototype object.
PositionedRectangle.prototype = new Rectangle();

// We create this prototype object for inheritance purposes, but we
// don't actually want to inherit the width and height properties that
// each Rectangle object has, so delete them from the prototype.
delete PositionedRectangle.prototype.width;
delete PositionedRectangle.prototype.height;

// Since the prototype object was created with the Rectangle() constructor,
// it has a constructor property that refers to that constructor.  But
// we want PositionedRectangle objects to have a different constructor
// property, so we've got to reassign this default constructor property.
PositionedRectangle.prototype.constructor = PositionedRectangle;

// Now that we've configured the prototype object for our subclass,
// we can add instance methods to it.
PositionedRectangle.prototype.contains = function(x,y) {
    return (x > this.x && x < this.x + this.width &&
            y > this.y && y < this.y + this.height);
}
```

As you can see from Example 9-3, creating a subclass in JavaScript is not as simple as creating a class that inherits directly from Object. First, there is the issue of invoking the superclass constructor from the subclass constructor. Take care when you do this that the superclass constructor is invoked as a method of the newly created object. Next, there are the tricks required to set the prototype object of the subclass constructor. You must explicitly create this prototype object as an instance of the superclass, then explicitly set the constructor property of the prototype object.* Optionally, you may also want to delete any properties that the superclass constructor created in the prototype object because what's important are the properties that the prototype object inherits from *its* prototype.

Having defined this PositionedRectangle class, you can use it with code like this:

```
var r = new PositionedRectangle(2,2,2,2);
print(r.contains(3,3));   // invoke an instance method
print(r.area());          // invoke an inherited instance method

// Use the instance fields of the class:
print(r.x + ", " + r.y + ", " + r.width + ", " + r.height);

// Our object is an instance of all 3 of these classes
```

---

* There is a bug in Rhino (the Java-based JavaScript interpreter) in version 1.6r1 and earlier that makes the constructor property read-only and nondeletable. In these versions of Rhino, the code to set the constructor property of the prototype object fails silently, and instances of the PositionedRectangle class inherit a constructor property that refers to the Rectangle() constructor. In practice, this bug is not severe because property inheritance works correctly, and the instanceof operator also works correctly for Rectangle and PositionedRectangle objects.

```
    print(r instanceof PositionedRectangle &&
          r instanceof Rectangle &&
          r instanceof Object);
```

9.5.1   Constructor Chaining

In the example just shown, the `PositionedRectangle()` constructor function needed to explicitly invoke the superclass constructor function. This is called *constructor chaining* and is quite common when creating subclasses. You can simplify the syntax for constructor chaining by adding a property named `superclass` to the prototype object of the subclass:

```
// Store a reference to our superclass constructor.
PositionedRectangle.prototype.superclass = Rectangle;
```

With this property defined, the syntax for constructor chaining is simpler:

```
function PositionedRectangle(x, y, w, h) {
    this.superclass(w,h);
    this.x = x;
    this.y = y;
}
```

Note that the superclass constructor function is explicitly invoked through the `this` object. This means that you no longer need to use `call()` or `apply()` to invoke the superclass constructor as a method of that object.

9.5.2   Invoking Overridden Methods

When a subclass defines a method that has the same name as a method in the super-class, the subclass *overrides* that method. This is a relatively common thing to do when creating subclasses of existing classes. Anytime you define a `toString()` method for a class, you override the `toString()` method of Object, for example.

A method that overrides another often wants to augment the functionality of the overridden method instead of replacing it altogether. To do that, a method must be able to invoke the method that it overrides. In a sense, this is a kind of method chaining, as described for constructors earlier in this chapter. Invoking an overridden method is more awkward than invoking a superclass constructor, however.

Let's consider an example. Suppose the Rectangle class had defined a `toString()` method (as it should have in the first place):

```
Rectangle.prototype.toString = function() {
    return "[" + this.width + "," + this.height + "]";
}
```

If you give Rectangle a `toString()` method, you really must override that method in PositionedRectangle so that instances of the subclass have a string representation that reflects all their properties, not just their width and height properties. PositionedRectangle is a simple enough class that its `toString()` method can just return the values of all properties. But for the sake of example, let's handle the position properties and delegate to its superclass for the `width` and `height` properties. Here is what the code might look like:

```
PositionedRectangle.prototype.toString = function() {
    return "(" + this.x + "," + this.y + ") " +      // our fields
        Rectangle.prototype.toString.apply(this);    // chain to superclass
}
```

The superclass's implementation of `toString()` is a property of the superclass's prototype object. Note that you can't invoke it directly. Invoke it with `apply()` so that you can specify the object on which it should be called.

If you add a `superclass` property to `PositionedRectangle.prototype`, this code can be rewritten in a superclass-independent way:

```
PositionedRectangle.prototype.toString = function() {
    return "(" + this.x + "," + this.y + ") " +      // our fields
        this.superclass.prototype.toString.apply(this);
}
```

9.6   Extending Without Inheriting

The discussion of creating subclasses earlier in this chapter explains how to create a new class that inherits the methods of another. JavaScript is such a flexible language that subclassing and inheritance is not the only way to extend a class. Since JavaScript functions are data values, you can simply copy (or "borrow") the functions from one class for use in another. Example 9-4 shows a function that borrows all the methods in one class and makes copies in the prototype object of another class.

Example 9-4. Borrowing methods from one class for use by another

```
// Borrow methods from one class for use by another.
// The arguments should be the constructor functions for the classes.
// Methods of built-in types such as Object, Array, Date, and RegExp are
// not enumerable and cannot be borrowed with this method.
function borrowMethods(borrowFrom, addTo) {
    var from = borrowFrom.prototype;  // prototype object to borrow from
    var to = addTo.prototype;         // prototype object to extend

    for(m in from) {  // Loop through all properties of the prototye
        if (typeof from[m] != "function") continue; // ignore nonfunctions
        to[m] = from[m];  // borrow the method
    }
}
```

Many methods are tied strongly to the class that defines them, and it makes no sense to try to use them in other classes. But it is possible to write some methods generically so that they are suitable for use by any class, or by any class that defines certain properties. Example 9-5 includes two classes that do nothing but define useful methods that other classes can borrow. Classes like these that are designed for borrowing are called *mixin classes* or *mixins*.

Example 9-5. Mixin classes with generic methods for borrowing

```
// This class isn't good for much on its own. But it does define a
// generic toString() method that may be of interest to other classes.
function GenericToString() {}
GenericToString.prototype.toString = function() {
    var props = [];
    for(var name in this) {
        if (!this.hasOwnProperty(name)) continue;
        var value = this[name];
        var s = name + ":"
        switch(typeof value) {
        case 'function':
            s += "function";
            break;
        case 'object':
            if (value instanceof Array) s += "array"
            else s += value.toString();
            break;
        default:
            s += String(value);
            break;
        }
        props.push(s);
    }
    return "{" + props.join(", ") + "}";
}

// This mixin class defines an equals() method that can compare
// simple objects for equality.
function GenericEquals() {}
GenericEquals.prototype.equals = function(that) {
    if (this == that) return true;

    // this and that are equal only if this has all the properties of
    // that and doesn't have any additional properties
    // Note that we don't do deep comparison.  Property values
    // must be === to each other.  So properties that refer to objects
    // must refer to the same object, not objects that are equals()
    var propsInThat = 0;
    for(var name in that) {
        propsInThat++;
        if (this[name] !== that[name]) return false;
    }

    // Now make sure that this object doesn't have additional props
    var propsInThis = 0;
    for(name in this) propsInThis++;

    // If this has additional properties, then they are not equal
    if (propsInThis != propsInThat) return false;
```

Example 9-5. Mixin classes with generic methods for borrowing (continued)

```
    // The two objects appear to be equal.
    return true;
}
```

Here is a simple Rectangle class that borrows the toString( ) and equals( ) methods defined by the mixin classes:

```
    // Here is a simple Rectangle class.
    function Rectangle(x, y, w, h) {
        this.x = x;
        this.y = y;
        this.width = w;
        this.height = h;
    }
    Rectangle.prototype.area = function() { return this.width * this.height; }

    // Borrow some more methods for it
    borrowMethods(GenericEquals, Rectangle);
    borrowMethods(GenericToString, Rectangle);
```

Neither of the mixins shown have a constructor function, but it is possible to borrow constructors as well. In the following code, a new class is created named ColoredRectangle. It inherits rectangle functionality from Rectangle and borrows a constructor and a method from a mixin named Colored:

```
    // This mixin has a method that depends on its constructor.  Both the
    // constructor and the method must be borrowed.
    function Colored(c) { this.color = c; }
    Colored.prototype.getColor = function() { return this.color; }

    // Define the constructor for a new class.
    function ColoredRectangle(x, y, w, h, c) {
        this.superclass(x, y, w, h);  // Invoke superclass constructor
        Colored.call(this, c);        // and borrow the Colored constructor
    }

    // Set up the prototype object to inherit methods from Rectangle
    ColoredRectangle.prototype = new Rectangle();
    ColoredRectangle.prototype.constructor = ColoredRectangle;
    ColoredRectangle.prototype.superclass = Rectangle;

    // And borrow the methods of Colored for our new class
    borrowMethods(Colored, ColoredRectangle);
```

The ColoredRectangle class extends (and inherits methods from) Rectangle and borrows methods from Colored. Rectangle itself inherits from Object and borrows from GenericEquals and GenericToString. Although any kind of strict analogy is impossible, you can think of this as a kind of multiple inheritance. Since the ColoredRectangle class borrows the methods of Colored, instances of ColoredRectangle can be considered instances of Colored as well. The instanceof operator will not report this, but in Section 9.7.3, we'll develop a more general method for determining whether an object inherits from *or* borrows from a specified class.

9.7 Determining Object Type

JavaScript is loosely typed, and JavaScript objects are even more loosely typed. There are a number of techniques you can use to determine the type of an arbitrary value in JavaScript.

The most obvious technique is the typeof operator, of course (see Section 5.10.2 for details). typeof is useful primarily for distinguishing primitive types from objects. There are a few quirks to typeof. First, remember that typeof null is "object", while typeof undefined is "undefined". Also, the type of any array is "object" because all arrays are objects. However, the type of any function is "function", even though functions are objects, too.

9.7.1 instanceof and constructor

Once you have determined that a value is an object rather than a primitive value or a function, you can use the instanceof operator to learn more about it. For example, if x is an array, the following evaluates to true:

```
x instanceof Array
```

The left side of instanceof is the value to be tested, and the right side should be a constructor function that defines a class. Note that an object is an instance of its own class and of any superclasses. So, for any object o, o instanceof Object is always true. Interestingly, instanceof works for functions, so for any function f, all these expressions are true:

```
typeof f == "function"
f instanceof Function
f instanceof Object
```

If you want to test whether an object is an instance of one specific class and not an instance of some subclass, you can check its constructor property. Consider the following code:

```
var d = new Date();                        // A Date object; Date extends Object
var isobject = d instanceof Object;        // evaluates to true
var realobject = d.constructor==Object;    // evaluates to false
```

9.7.2 Object.toString() for Object Typing

One shortcoming of the instanceof operator and the constructor property is that they allow you to test an object only against classes you already know about. They aren't useful to inspect unknown objects, as you might do when debugging, for example. A useful trick that uses the default implementation of the Object.toString() method can help in this case.

As shown in Chapter 7, Object defines a default toString() method. Any class that does not define its own method inherits this default implementation. An interesting feature of the default toString( ) method is that it reveals some internal type information about built-in objects. The ECMAScript specification requires that this default toString( ) method always returns a string of the form:

```
[object class]
```

class is the internal type of the object and usually corresponds to the name of the constructor function for the object. For example, arrays have a *class* of "Array", functions have a *class* of "Function", and Date objects have a *class* of "Date". The built-in Math object has a *class* of "Math", and all Error objects (including instances of the various Error subclasses) have a *class* of "Error". Client-side JavaScript objects and any other objects defined by the JavaScript implementation have an implementation-defined *class* (such as "Window", "Document", or "Form"). Objects of user-defined types, such as the Circle and Complex classes defined earlier in this chapter, always have a *class* of "Object", however, so this toString( ) technique is useful only for built-in object types.

Since most classes override the default toString( ) method, you can't invoke it directly on an object and expect to find its class name. Instead, you refer to the default function explicitly in Object.prototype and use apply( ) to invoke it on the object whose type you're interested in:

```
Object.prototype.toString.apply(o); // Always invokes the default toString( )
```

This technique is used in Example 9-6 to define a function that provides enhanced "type of" functionality. As noted earlier, the toString( ) method does not work for user-defined classes, so in this case, the function checks for a string-value property named classname and returns its value if it exists.

Example 9-6. Enhanced typeof testing

```
function getType(x) {
    // If x is null, return "null"
    if (x == null) return "null";

    // Next try the typeof operator
    var t = typeof x;
    // If the result is not vague, return it
    if (t != "object")  return t;

    // Otherwise, x is an object. Use the default toString( ) method to
    // get the class value of the object.
    var c = Object.prototype.toString.apply(x);  // Returns "[object class]"
    c = c.substring(8, c.length-1);               // Strip off "[object" and "]"

    // If the class is not a vague one, return it.
    if (c != "Object") return c;

    // If we get here, c is "Object".  Check to see if
    // the value x is really just a generic object.
    if (x.constructor == Object) return c;  // Okay the type really is "Object"
```

Example 9-6. Enhanced typeof testing (continued)

```
    // For user-defined classes, look for a string-valued property named
    // classname, that is inherited from the object's prototype
    if ("classname" in x.constructor.prototype &&  // inherits classname
        typeof x.constructor.prototype.classname == "string") // its a string
        return x.constructor.prototype.classname;

    // If we really can't figure it out, say so.
    return "<unknown type>";
}
```

9.7.3   Duck Typing

There is an old saying: "If it walks like a duck and quacks like a duck, it's a duck!" Translated into JavaScript, this aphorism is not nearly so evocative. Try it this way: "If it implements all the methods defined by a class, it is an instance of that class." In flexible, loosely typed languages like JavaScript, this is called *duck typing*: if an object has the properties defined by class X, you can treat it as an instance of class X, even if it was not actually created with the X( ) constructor function.[*]

Duck typing is particularly useful in conjunction with classes that "borrow" methods from other classes. Earlier in the chapter, a Rectangle class borrowed the implementation of an equals( ) method from another class named GenericEquals. Thus, you can consider any Rectangle instance to also be an instance of GenericEquals. The instanceof operator will not report this, but you can define a method that will. Example 9-7 shows how.

Example 9-7. Testing whether an object borrows the methods of a class

```
// Return true if each of the method properties in c.prototype have been
// borrowed by o. If o is a function rather than an object, we
// test the prototype of o rather than o itself.
// Note that this function requires methods to be copied, not
// reimplemented.  If a class borrows a method and then overrides it,
// this method will return false.
function borrows(o, c) {
    // If we are an instance of something, then of course we have its methods
    if (o instanceof c) return true;

    // It is impossible to test whether the methods of a built-in type have
    // been borrowed, since the methods of built-in types are not enumerable.
    // We return undefined in this case as a kind of "I don't know" answer
    // instead of throwing an exception. Undefined behaves much like false,
    // but can be distinguished from false if the caller needs to.
    if (c == Array || c == Boolean || c == Date || c == Error ||
```

---

[*] The term "duck typing" has been popularlized by the Ruby programming language. A more formal name is *allomorphism*.

Example 9-7. Testing whether an object borrows the methods of a class (continued)

```
            c == Function || c == Number || c == RegExp || c == String)
            return undefined;

    if (typeof o == "function") o = o.prototype;
    var proto = c.prototype;
    for(var p in proto) {
        // Ignore properties that are not functions
        if (typeof proto[p] != "function") continue;
        if (o[p] != proto[p]) return false;
    }
    return true;
}
```

The borrows( ) method of Example 9-7 is relatively strict: it requires the object o to have exact copies of the methods defined by the class c. True duck typing is more flexible: o should be considered an instance of c as long as it provides methods that look like methods of c. In JavaScript, "look like" means "have the same name as" and (perhaps) "are declared with the same number of arguments as." Example 9-8 shows a method that tests for this.

Example 9-8. Testing whether an object provides methods

```
// Return true if o has methods with the same name and arity as all
// methods in c.prototype. Otherwise, return false.  Throws an exception
// if c is a built-in type with nonenumerable methods.
function provides(o, c) {
    // If o actually is an instance of c, it obviously looks like c
    if (o instanceof c) return true;

    // If a constructor was passed instead of an object, use its prototype
    if (typeof o == "function") o = o.prototype;

    // The methods of built-in types are not enumerable, and we return
    // undefined.  Otherwise, any object would appear to provide any of
    // the built-in types.
    if (c == Array || c == Boolean || c == Date || c == Error ||
        c == Function || c == Number || c == RegExp || c == String)
        return undefined;

    var proto = c.prototype;
    for(var p in proto) {  // Loop through all properties in c.prototype
        // Ignore properties that are not functions
        if (typeof proto[p] != "function") continue;
        // If o does not have a property by the same name, return false
        if (!(p in o)) return false;
        // If that property is not a function, return false
        if (typeof o[p] != "function") return false;
        // If the two functions are not declared with the same number
        // of arguments, return false.
        if (o[p].length != proto[p].length) return false;
    }
```

Example 9-8. Testing whether an object provides methods (continued)

```
    // If all the methods check out, we can finally return true.
    return true;
}
```

As an example of when duck typing and the provides( ) method are useful, consider the compareTo( ) method described in Section 9.4.3. compareTo( ) is not a method that lends itself to borrowing, but it would still be nice if we could easily test for objects that are comparable with the compareTo( ) method. To do this, define a Comparable class:

```
function Comparable() {}
Comparable.prototype.compareTo = function(that) {
    throw "Comparable.compareTo() is abstract.  Don't invoke it!";
}
```

This Comparable class is *abstract*: its method isn't designed to actually be invoked but simply to define an API. With this class defined, however, you can check if two objects can be compared like this:

```
// Check whether objects o and p can be compared
// They must be of the same type, and that type must be comparable
if (o.constructor == p.constructor && provides(o, Comparable)) {
    var order = o.compareTo(p);
}
```

Note that both the borrows( ) and provides( ) functions presented in this section return undefined if passed any core JavaScript built-in type, such as Array. This is because the properties of the prototype objects of the built-in types are not enumerable with a for/in loop. If those functions did not explicitly check for built-in types and return undefined, they would think that these built-in types have no methods and would always return true for built-in types.

The Array type is one that is worth considering specially, however. Recall from Section 7.8 that many array algorithms (such as iterating over the elements) can work fine on objects that are not true arrays but are array-like. Another application of duck typing is to determine which objects look like arrays. Example 9-9 shows one way to do it.

Example 9-9. Testing for array-like objects

```
function isArrayLike(x) {
    if (x instanceof Array) return true;    // Real arrays are array-like
    if (!("length" in x)) return false;     // Arrays must have a length property
    if (typeof x.length != "number") return false;  // Length must be a number
    if (x.length < 0) return false;                  // and nonnegative
    if (x.length > 0) {
        // If the array is nonempty, it must at a minimum
        // have a property defined whose name is the number length-1
        if (!((x.length-1) in x)) return false;
    }
    return true;
}
```

9.8   Example: A defineClass( ) Utility Method

This chapter ends with a defineClass( ) utility method that ties together the previous discussions of constructors, prototypes, subclassing, and borrowing and providing methods. Example 9-10 shows the code.

Example 9-10. A utility function for defining classes

```
/**
 * defineClass() -- a utility function for defining JavaScript classes.
 *
 * This function expects a single object as its only argument.  It defines
 * a new JavaScript class based on the data in that object and returns the
 * constructor function of the new class.  This function handles the repetitive
 * tasks of defining classes: setting up the prototype object for correct
 * inheritance, copying methods from other types, and so on.
 *
 * The object passed as an argument should have some or all of the
 * following properties:
 *
 *      name: The name of the class being defined.
 *            If specified, this value will be stored in the classname
 *            property of the prototype object.
 *
 *    extend: The constructor of the class to be extended. If omitted,
 *            the Object() constructor will be used. This value will
 *            be stored in the superclass property of the prototype object.
 *
 * construct: The constructor function for the class. If omitted, a new
 *            empty function will be used. This value becomes the return
 *            value of the function, and is also stored in the constructor
 *            property of the prototype object.
 *
 *   methods: An object that specifies the instance methods (and other shared
 *            properties) for the class. The properties of this object are
 *            copied into the prototype object of the class. If omitted,
 *            an empty object is used instead. Properties named
 *            "classname", "superclass", and "constructor" are reserved
 *            and should not be used in this object.
 *
 *   statics: An object that specifies the static methods (and other static
 *            properties) for the class. The properties of this object become
 *            properties of the constructor function. If omitted, an empty
 *            object is used instead.
 *
 *   borrows: A constructor function or array of constructor functions.
 *            The instance methods of each of the specified classes are copied
 *            into the prototype object of this new class so that the
 *            new class borrows the methods of each specified class.
 *            Constructors are processed in the order they are specified,
 *            so the methods of a class listed at the end of the array may
 *            overwrite the methods of those specified earlier. Note that
 *            borrowed methods are stored in the prototype object before
 *            the properties of the methods object above. Therefore,
```

Example 9-10. A utility function for defining classes (continued)

```
 *              methods specified in the methods object can overwrite borrowed
 *              methods. If this property is not specified, no methods are
 *              borrowed.
 *
 * provides: A constructor function or array of constructor functions.
 *              After the prototype object is fully initialized, this function
 *              verifies that the prototype includes methods whose names and
 *              number of arguments match the instance methods defined by each
 *              of these classes. No methods are copied; this is simply an
 *              assertion that this class "provides" the functionality of the
 *              specified classes. If the assertion fails, this method will
 *              throw an exception. If no exception is thrown, any
 *              instance of the new class can also be considered (using "duck
 *              typing") to be an instance of these other types.  If this
 *              property is not specified, no such verification is performed.
 **/
function defineClass(data) {
    // Extract the fields we'll use from the argument object.
    // Set up default values.
    var classname = data.name;
    var superclass = data.extend || Object;
    var constructor = data.construct || function() {};
    var methods = data.methods || {};
    var statics = data.statics || {};
    var borrows;
    var provides;

    // Borrows may be a single constructor or an array of them.
    if (!data.borrows) borrows = [];
    else if (data.borrows instanceof Array) borrows = data.borrows;
    else borrows = [ data.borrows ];

    // Ditto for the provides property.
    if (!data.provides) provides = [];
    else if (data.provides instanceof Array) provides = data.provides;
    else provides = [ data.provides ];

    // Create the object that will become the prototype for our class.
    var proto = new superclass();

    // Delete any noninherited properties of this new prototype object.
    for(var p in proto)
        if (proto.hasOwnProperty(p)) delete proto[p];

    // Borrow methods from "mixin" classes by copying to our prototype.
    for(var i = 0; i < borrows.length; i++) {
        var c = data.borrows[i];
        borrows[i] = c;
        // Copy method properties from prototype of c to our prototype
        for(var p in c.prototype) {
            if (typeof c.prototype[p] != "function") continue;
            proto[p] = c.prototype[p];
        }
    }
}
```

Example 9-10. A utility function for defining classes (continued)

```
    // Copy instance methods to the prototype object
    // This may overwrite methods of the mixin classes
    for(var p in methods) proto[p] = methods[p];

    // Set up the reserved "constructor", "superclass", and "classname"
    // properties of the prototype.
    proto.constructor = constructor;
    proto.superclass = superclass;
    // classname is set only if a name was actually specified.
    if (classname) proto.classname = classname;

    // Verify that our prototype provides all of the methods it is supposed to.
    for(var i = 0; i < provides.length; i++) {  // for each class
        var c = provides[i];
        for(var p in c.prototype) {    // for each property
            if (typeof c.prototype[p] != "function") continue;  // methods only
            if (p == "constructor" || p == "superclass") continue;
            // Check that we have a method with the same name and that
            // it has the same number of declared arguments.  If so, move on
            if (p in proto &&
                typeof proto[p] == "function" &&
                proto[p].length == c.prototype[p].length) continue;
            // Otherwise, throw an exception
            throw new Error("Class " + classname + " does not provide method "+
                            c.classname + "." + p);
        }
    }

    // Associate the prototype object with the constructor function
    constructor.prototype = proto;

    // Copy static properties to the constructor
    for(var p in statics) constructor[p] = data.statics[p];

    // Finally, return the constructor function
    return constructor;
}
```

Example 9-11 shows sample code that uses the defineClass( ) method.

Example 9-11. Using the defineClass() method

```
// A Comparable class with an abstract method
// so that we can define classes that "provide" Comparable.
var Comparable = defineClass({
    name: "Comparable",
    methods: { compareTo: function(that) { throw "abstract"; } }
});

// A mixin class with a usefully generic equals() method for borrowing
var GenericEquals = defineClass({
    name: "GenericEquals",
    methods: {
```

Example 9-11. Using the defineClass( ) method (continued)

```
        equals: function(that) {
            if (this == that) return true;
            var propsInThat = 0;
            for(var name in that) {
                propsInThat++;
                if (this[name] !== that[name]) return false;
            }

            // Now make sure that this object doesn't have additional props
            var propsInThis = 0;
            for(name in this) propsInThis++;

            // If this has additional properties, then they are not equal
            if (propsInThis != propsInThat) return false;

            // The two objects appear to be equal.
            return true;
        }
    }
});
// A very simple Rectangle class that provides Comparable
var Rectangle = defineClass({
    name: "Rectangle",
    construct: function(w,h) { this.width = w; this.height = h; },
    methods: {
        area: function() { return this.width * this.height; },
        compareTo: function(that) { return this.area() - that.area(); }
    },
    provides: Comparable
});
// A subclass of Rectangle that chains to its superclass constructor,
// inherits methods from its superclass, defines an instance method and
// a static method of its own, and borrows an equals() method.
var PositionedRectangle = defineClass({
    name: "PositionedRectangle",
    extend: Rectangle,
    construct: function(x,y,w,h) {
        this.superclass(w,h);  // chain to superclass
        this.x = x;
        this.y = y;
    },
    methods: {
        isInside: function(x,y) {
            return x > this.x && x < this.x+this.width &&
                y > this.y && y < this.y+this.height;
        }
    },
    statics: {
        comparator: function(a,b) { return a.compareTo(b); }
    },
    borrows: [GenericEquals]
});
```

CHAPTER 10

Modules and Namespaces

In JavaScript's early years, it was often used in small, simple scripts embedded directly in web pages. As web browsers and web standards have matured, JavaScript programs have become longer and more complex. Today, many JavaScript scripts depend on external *modules* or libraries of JavaScript code.[*]

At the time of this writing, there is an effort underway to create a collection of reusable, open source JavaScript modules. The JavaScript Archive Network (JSAN) is fashioned after the Comprehensive Perl Archive Network (CPAN) and hopes to do for JavaScript what CPAN did for the Perl language and community. See *http://www.openjsan.org* to learn more and find code.

JavaScript does not provide any language features for creating or managing modules, so writing portable, reusable modules of JavaScript code is largely a matter of following some basic conventions, which are described in this chapter.

The most important convention involves the use of *namespaces* to prevent namespace collisions—which is what happens when two modules define global properties with the same name: one module overwrites the properties of another, and one or both modules operate incorrectly.

Another convention involves module initialization code. This is particularly important in client-side JavaScript because modules that manipulate a document in a web browser often need to have code triggered when the document finishes loading.

The following sections discuss namespaces and initialization, and the chapter concludes with an extended example of a module of utility functions for working with modules.

---

[*] Core JavaScript does not have any mechanism for loading or including an external module of code. This is the responsibility of whatever environment the JavaScript interpreter is embedded within. In client-side JavaScript, it is done with the `<script src=>` tag (see Chapter 13). Other embeddings may provide a simple `load( )` function for loading modules.

10.1 Creating Modules and Namespaces

If you want to write a module of JavaScript code that can be used by any script and can be used with any other module, the most important rule you must follow is to avoid defining global variables. Anytime you define a global variable, you run the risk of having that variable overwritten by another module or by the programmer who is using your module. The solution instead is to define all the methods and properties for your module inside a namespace that you create specifically for the module.

JavaScript does not have any specific language support for namespaces, but Java-Script objects work quite well for this purpose. Consider the provides() and defineClass() utility methods developed in Examples 9-8 and 9-10, respectively. Both method names are global symbols. If you want to create a module of functions for working with JavaScript classes, you don't define these methods in the global namespace. Instead, write code like this:

```
// Create an empty object as our namespace
// This single global symbol will hold all of our other symbols
var Class = {};
// Define functions within the namespace
Class.define = function(data) { /* code goes here */ }
Class.provides = function(o, c) { /* code goes here */ }
```

Note that you're not defining instance methods (or even static methods) of a Java-Script class here. You are defining ordinary functions and storing references to them within a specially created object instead of in the global object.

This code demonstrates the first rule of JavaScript modules: *a module should never add more than a single symbol to the global namespace*. Here are two suggestions that are good common-sense adjuncts to this rule:

- If a module adds a symbol to the global namespace, its documentation should clearly state what that symbol is.

- If a module adds a symbol to the global namespace, there should be a clear relationship between the name of that symbol and the name of the file from which the module is loaded.

In the case of the class module, you can put the code in a file named *Class.js* and begin that file with a comment that looks like this:

```
/**
 * Class.js: A module of utility functions for working with classes.
 *
 *   This module defines a single global symbol named "Class".
 *   Class refers to a namespace object, and all utility functions
 *   are stored as properties of this namespace.
 **/
```

Classes are pretty important in JavaScript, and there is certain to be more than one useful module for working with them. What happens if two modules both use the global symbol Class to refer to their namespace? If this happens, you're back where you started, with a namespace collision. By using a namespace you've reduced the likelihood of a collision but have not eliminated it entirely. Following a filenaming convention helps a lot. If two conflicting modules are both named *Class.js*, they cannot be stored in the same directory. The only way that a script could include two different *Class.js* files is if they were stored in different directories, such as *utilities/Class.js* and *flanagan/Class.js*.

And if scripts are stored in subdirectories, the subdirectory names should probably be part of the module name. That is, the "Class" module defined here should really be called flanagan.Class. Here's what the code might look like:

```
/**
 * flanagan/Class.js: A module of utility functions for working with classes.
 *
 *   This module creates a single global symbol named "flanagan" if it
 *   does not already exist. It then creates a namespace object and stores
 *   it in the Class property of the flanagan object.  All utility functions
 *   are placed in the flanagan.Class namespace.
 **/
var flanagan;                   // Declare a single global symbol "flanagan"
if (!flanagan) flanagan = {};   // If undefined, make it an object
flanagan.Class = {}             // Now create the flanagan.Class namespace
// Now populate the namespace with our utility methods
flanagan.Class.define = function(data) { /* code here */ };
flanagan.Class.provides = function(o, c) { /* code here */ };
```

In this code, the global flanagan object is a namespace for namespaces. If I wrote another module to hold utility functions for working with dates, I could store those utilities in the flanagan.Date namespace. Notice that this code declares the global symbol flanagan with a var statement before testing for the presence of that symbol. This is because attempting to read an undeclared global symbol throws an exception, whereas attempting to read a declared but undefined symbol simply returns the undefined value. This is a special behavior of the global object only. If you attempt to read a nonexistent property of a namespace object, you simply get the undefined value with no exception.

With a two-level namespace like flanagan.Class, we now seem pretty safe from name collisions. If some other JavaScript developer whose last name is Flanagan decides to write a module of class-related utilities, a programmer who wanted to use both modules would find herself in trouble. But this seems pretty unlikely. For complete certainty, however, you can adopt a convention from the Java programming language for globally unique package name prefixes: start with the name of an Internet domain that you own. Reverse it so that the top-level domain (*.com*, or whatever) comes first, and use this as the prefix for all your JavaScript modules. Since my web site is at *davidflanagan.com*, I would store my modules in the file *com/davidflanagan/Class.js* and use the namespace com.davidflanagan.Class. If all JavaScript developers follow this convention, no one else will define anything in the com.davidflanagan namespace because no one else owns the *davidflanagan.com* domain.

This convention may be overkill for most JavaScript modules, and you don't need to follow it yourself. But you should be aware of it. Don't accidentally create namespaces that might be someone else's domain name: *never define a namespace using a reversed domain name unless you own the domain yourself.*

Example 10-1 demonstrates the creation of a com.davidflanagan.Class namespace. It adds error checking that was missing from the previous examples and throws an exception if com.davidflanagan.Class already exists, or if com or com.davidflanagan already exists but does not refer to an object. It also demonstrates that you can create and populate a namespace with a single object literal rather than doing so in separate steps.

Example 10-1. Creating a namespace based on a domain name

```
// Create the global symbol "com" if it doesn't exist
// Throw an error if it does exist but is not an object
var com;
if (!com) com = {};
else if (typeof com != "object")
    throw new Error("com already exists and is not an object");

// Repeat the creation and type-checking code for the next level
if (!com.davidflanagan) com.davidflanagan = {}
else if (typeof com.davidflanagan != "object")
    throw new Error("com.davidflanagan already exists and is not an object");

// Throw an error if com.davidflanagan.Class already exists
if (com.davidflanagan.Class)
    throw new Error("com.davidflanagan.Class already exists");

// Otherwise, create and populate the namespace with one big object literal
com.davidflanagan.Class = {
    define: function(data) { /* code here */ },
    provides: function(o, c) { /* code here */ }
};
```

10.1.1 Testing the Availability of a Module

If you are writing code that depends on an external module, you can test for the presence of that module simply by checking for its namespace. The code for doing this is a little tricky because it requires you to test for each component of the namespace. Notice that this code declares the global symbol com before testing for its presence. You have to do this just as you do when defining the namespace:

```
    var com;  // Declare global symbol before testing for its presence
    if (!com || !com.davidflanagan || !com.davidflanagan.Class)
        throw new Error("com/davidflanagan/Class.js has not been loaded");
```

If module authors follow a consistent versioning convention, such as making the version number of a module available through the VERSION property of the module's namespace, it is possible to test for the presence not just of the module, but of a specific version of the module. At the end of this chapter, I'll provide an example that does just this.

10.1.2 Classes as Modules

The "Class" module used in Example 10-1 is simply a cooperating set of utility functions. There is no restriction on what a module may be, however. It might be a single function, a JavaScript class, or even a set of cooperating classes and functions.

Example 10-2 shows code that creates a module consisting of a single class. The module relies on our hypothetical Class module and its define( ) function. (See Example 9-10 if you've forgotten how this utility function works.)

Example 10-2. A complex-number class as a module

```
/**
 * com/davidflanagan/Complex.js: a class representing complex numbers
 *
 * This module defines the constructor function com.davidflanagan.Complex( )
 * This module requires the com/davidflanagan/Class.js module
 **/
// First, check for the Class module
var com;  // Declare global symbol before testing for its presence
if (!com || !com.davidflanagan || !com.davidflanagan.Class)
    throw new Error("com/davidflanagan/Class.js has not been loaded");

// We know from this test that the com.davidflanagan namespace
// exists, so we don't have to create it here.  We'll just define
// our Complex class within it
com.davidflanagan.Complex = com.davidflanagan.Class.define({
    name: "Complex",
    construct: function(x,y) { this.x = x; this.y = y; },
    methods: {
        add: function(c) {
            return new com.davidflanagan.Complex(this.x + c.x,
                                                 this.y + c.y);
        }
    },
});
```

You can also define a module that consists of more than one class. Example 10-3 is a sketch of a module that defines various classes representing geometric shapes.

Example 10-3. A module of shapes classes

```
/**
 * com/davidflanagan/Shapes.js: a module of classes representing shapes
 *
 * This module defines classes within the com.davidflanagan.shapes namespace
 * This module requires the com/davidflanagan/Class.js module
 **/
// First, check for the Class module
var com;  // Declare global symbol before testing for its presence
if (!com || !com.davidflanagan || !com.davidflanagan.Class)
    throw new Error("com/davidflanagan/Class.js has not been loaded");

// Import a symbol from that module
var define = com.davidflanagan.Class.define;

// We know from the test for the Class module that the com.davidflanagan
// namespace exists, so we don't have to create it here.
// We just create our shapes namespace within it.
if (com.davidflanagan.shapes)
    throw new Error("com.davidflanagan.shapes namespace already exists");

// Create the namespace
com.davidflanagan.shapes = {};

// Now define classes, storing their constructor functions in our namespace
com.davidflanagan.shapes.Circle = define({ /* class data here */ });
com.davidflanagan.shapes.Rectangle = define({ /* class data here */ });
com.davidflanagan.shapes.Triangle = define({ /* class data here */});
```

10.1.3 Module Initialization Code

We tend to think of JavaScript modules as collections of functions (or classes). But, as is clear from the previous examples, modules do more than just define functions to be invoked later. They also run code when first loaded to set up and populate their namespace. A module can run any amount of this kind of one-shot code, and it is perfectly acceptable to write modules that define no functions or classes and simply run some code. The only rule is that they must not clutter the global namespace. The best way to structure a module of this sort is to put the code inside an anonymous function that is invoked immediately after being defined:

```
(function() {  // Define an anonymous function.  No name means no global symbol
    // Code goes here
    // Any variables are safely nested within the function,
    // so no global symbols are created.
})();          // End the function definition and invoke it.
```

Some modules can run their own initialization code when they are loaded. Others need to have an initialization function invoked at a later time. This is common in client-side JavaScript: modules designed to operate on HTML documents usually need initialization code triggered when the HTML document has finished loading into the web browser.

A module can take a passive approach to the initialization problem by simply defining and documenting an initialization function and having the user of the module invoke the function at an appropriate time. This is a safe and conservative approach, but it requires an HTML document to have enough JavaScript code within it to at least initialize the modules that will be acting on it.

There is a school of thought (called *unobtrusive JavaScript* and described in Section 13.1.5) that says that modules should be completely self-contained and that HTML documents should not contain any JavaScript code. To write modules that are unobtrusive to this degree, modules must be able to actively register their initialization functions so they are invoked at the appropriate time.

Example 10-5 at the end of this chapter includes an initialization solution that allows modules to actively register initialization functions. When run in a web browser, all registered functions are automatically invoked in response to the "onload" event sent by the web browser. (You'll learn about client-side events and event handlers in Chapter 17.)

10.2 Importing Symbols from Namespaces

The problem with unique namespace names such as com.davidflanagan.Class is that they lead to even longer function names—e.g., com.davidflanagan.Class.define(). This is the fully qualified named of the function, but you don't have to type it this way all the time. Since JavaScript functions are data, you can put them where you want. After loading the com.davidflanagan.Class module, for example, a user of that module might write the following:

```
// This is an easier name, to save typing.
var define = com.davidflanagan.Class.define;
```

It is the module developer's responsibility to use namespaces to prevent collisions. But it is the module user's prerogative to import symbols from the module's namespace into the global namespace. The programmer using the module will know what other modules are in use and what all the potential name collisions are. She can determine what symbols to import and how to import them to prevent collisions.

Note that the previous code snippet uses the global symbol define for a class-definition utility function. This is not a good choice for a global function because it doesn't say what is being defined. An alternative is to change the name:

```
var defineClass = com.davidflanagan.Class.define;
```

But changing method names is not fully satisfactory, either. Another programmer who has used the module before might find the name defineClass() confusing because he is familiar with the function under the name define(). Also, module developers often put quite a bit of thought into their function names, and changing these names may not do justice to the module. Another alternative is not to use the global namespace but to import symbols into an easier-to-type namespace:

```
// Create a simple namespace. No error checking required.  The
// module user knows that this symbol does not exist yet.
var Class = {};
// Now import a symbol into this new namespace.
Class.define = com.davidflanagan.Class.define;
```

There are some important things to understand about importing symbols like this. First: *you can import only symbols that refer to a function, object, or array.* If you import a symbol whose value is a primitive type such as a number or a string, you simply get a static copy of the value. Any changes to the value occur in the namespace and are not reflected in an imported copy of the value. Suppose that the Class.define( ) method keeps track of the number of classes it has defined and increments the value com.davidflanagan.Class.counter each time it is called. If you attempt to import this value, you merely get a static copy of its current value:

```
// Make a static copy only. Changes in the namespace are not
// reflected in the imported property since this is a primitive value.
Class.counter = com.davidflanagan.Class.counter;
```

The lesson for module developers is if your module defines properties that refer to primitive values, you should provide accessor methods that can be imported:

```
// A property of primitive type; cannot be imported
com.davidflanagan.Class.counter = 0;

// Here is an accessor method that can be imported
com.davidflanagan.Class.getCounter = function( ) {
    return com.davidflanagan.Class.counter;
}
```

The second important point to understand about imports is that they are for the users of a module. *Module developers must always use the fully qualified name of their symbols.* You can see this in the getCounter( ) method just shown. Since JavaScript has no built-in support for modules and namespaces, there are no shortcuts here, and you must type the fully qualified name of the counter property even though that property and the getCounter( ) accessor method are both part of the same namespace. Module writers must not assume that their functions will be imported into the global namespace. Functions that call other functions in the module must use their fully qualified name so that they work correctly even when invoked without having been imported. (An exception to this rule, involving closures, is discussed in Section 10.2.2.)

10.2.1 Public and Private Symbols

Not all the symbols defined in a module's namespace are intended for external use. A module may have its own internal functions and variables that are not intended to be used directly by the scripts that use the module. JavaScript does not have any way to specify that some properties in a namespace are public and that some are not, and so, again, we rely on convention to prevent inappropriate use of a module's private properties from outside the module.

The most straightforward approach is simple documentation. The module developer should clearly document which functions and other properties make up the public API of the module. Conversely, the module user should restrict his use of the module to this public API, resisting the temptation to call any other function or access any other property.

A convention that can help to make the public/private distinction clear, even without reference to the documentation is to prefix private symbols with an underscore. In the discussion of the getCounter( ) accessor function, you can make it clear that the counter property is private by changing its name to _counter. This does not prevent external code from using the property, but it makes it difficult for a programmer to inadvertently use a private property.

Modules distributed through JSAN go a step further. The module definition includes arrays that list the public symbols. The JSAN module named *JSAN* includes utility functions for importing symbols from a module, and these functions refuse to import symbols that are not explicitly listed as public.

10.2.2 Closures as Private Namespace and Scope

Recall from Section 8.8 that a closure is a function plus the scope that was in effect when the function was defined.[*] By defining a function, therefore, you can use its local scope as a private namespace. Nested functions defined within the outer function have access to this private namespace. The advantages of this are twofold. First, since the private namespace is also the first object on the scope chain, functions in the namespace can refer to other functions and properties in the namespace without requiring a fully qualified name.

The second advantage to using a function to define a private namespace has to do with the fact that it is truly private. There is no way to access the symbols defined within the function from outside the function. Those symbols become available only if the function that contains them exports them to an external, public namespace. What this means is that a module can choose to export only its public functions, leaving implementation details such as helper methods and variables locked up in the privacy of the closure.

---

[*] Closures are an advanced feature, and if you skipped over their discussion in Chapter 8, you should return to this section after you read about closures.

Example 10-4 helps to illustrate this point. It uses a closure to create a private namespace, and then exports its public methods to a public namespace.

Example 10-4. Defining a private namespace with a closure

```
// Create the namespace object.  Error checking omitted here for brevity.
var com;
if (!com) com = {};
if (!com.davidflanagan) com.davidflanagan = {};
com.davidflanagan.Class = {};

// Don't stick anything into the namespace directly.
// Instead we define and invoke an anonymous function to create a closure
// that serves as our private namespace. This function will export its
// public symbols from the closure into the com.davidflanagan.Class object
// Note that we use an unnamed function so we don't create any other
// global symbols.
(function() {  // Begin anonymous function definition
    // Nested functions create symbols within the closure
    function define(data) { counter++; /* more code here */ }
    function provides(o, c) { /* code here */ }

    // Local variable are symbols within the closure.
    // This one will remain private within the closure
    var counter = 0;

    // This function can refer to the variable with a simple name
    // instead of having to qualify it with a namespace
    function getCounter() { return counter; }

    // Now that we've defined the properties we want in our private
    // closure, we can export the public ones to the public namespace
    // and leave the private ones hidden here.
    var ns = com.davidflanagan.Class;
    ns.define = define;
    ns.provides = provides;
    ns.getCounter = getCounter;
})();          // End anonymous function definition and invoke it
```

10.3   Module Utilities

This section presents an extended example (Example 10-5) of a module of module-related utilities. The Module.createNamespace() utility handles namespace creation and error checking. A module author might use it like this:

```
// Create a namespace for our module
Module.createNamespace("com.davidflanagan.Class");

// Now start populating the namespace
com.davidflanagan.Class.define = function(data) { /* code here */ };
com.davidflanagan.Class.provides = function(o, c) { /* code here */ };
```

The `Module.require()` function checks for the presence of the specified version (or later) of a named module and throws an error if it does not exist. Use it like this:

```
// This Complex module requires the Class module to be loaded first
Module.require("com.davidflanagan.Class", 1.0);
```

The `Module.importSymbols()` function simplifies the task of importing symbols into the global namespace or another specified namespace. Here are examples of its use:

```
// Import the default set of Module symbols to the global namespace
// One of these defualt symbols is importSymbols itself
Module.importSymbols(Module); // Note we pass the namespace, not module name

// Import the Complex class into the global namespace
importSymbols(com.davidflanagan.Complex);

// Import the com.davidflanagan.Class.define() method to a Class object
var Class = {};
importSymbols(com.davidflanagan.Class, Class, "define");
```

Finally, the `Module.registerInitializationFunction()` allows a module to register a function of initialization code to be run at some later time.[*] When this function is used in client-side JavaScript, an event handler is automatically registered to invoke all initialization functions for all loaded modules when the document finishes loading. When used in other, nonclient-side contexts, the initialization functions are not automatically invoked, but can be explicitly invoked with `Module.runInitializationFunctions()`.

The Module module is shown in Example 10-5. This example is a long one, but the code repays careful study. Documentation and full details of each utility function are found in the code.

Example 10-5. A module of module-related utilities

```
/**
 * Module.js: module and namspace utilities
 *
 * This is a module of module-related utility functions that are
 * compatible with JSAN-type modules.
 * This module defines the namespace Module.
 */

// Make sure we haven't already been loaded
var Module;
if (Module && (typeof Module != "object" || Module.NAME))
    throw new Error("Namespace 'Module' already exists");

// Create our namespace
Module = {};

// This is some metainformation about this namespace
```

---

[*] See also Example 17-6 for a similar initialization function registration utility.

Example 10-5. A module of module-related utilities (continued)

```
Module.NAME = "Module";      // The name of this namespace
Module.VERSION = 0.1;        // The version of this namespace

// This is the list of public symbols that we export from this namespace.
// These are of interest to programers who use modules.
Module.EXPORT = ["require", "importSymbols"];

// These are other symbols we are willing to export. They are ones normally
// used only by module authors and are not typically imported.
Module.EXPORT_OK = ["createNamespace", "isDefined",
                    "registerInitializationFunction",
                    "runInitializationFunctions",
                    "modules", "globalNamespace"];


// Now start adding symbols to the namespace
Module.globalNamespace = this;  // So we can always refer to the global scope
Module.modules = { "Module": Module };  // Module name->namespace map.

/**
 * This function creates and returns a namespace object for the
 * specified name and does useful error checking to ensure that the
 * name does not conflict with any previously loaded module. It
 * throws an error if the namespace already exists or if any of the
 * property components of the namespace exist and are not objects.
 *
 * Sets a NAME property of the new namespace to its name.
 * If the version argument is specified, set the VERSION property
 * of the namespace.
 *
 * A mapping for the new namespace is added to the Module.modules object
 */
Module.createNamespace = function(name, version) {
    // Check name for validity.  It must exist, and must not begin or
    // end with a period or contain two periods in a row.
    if (!name) throw new Error("Module.createNamespace(): name required");
    if (name.charAt(0) == '.' ||
        name.charAt(name.length-1) == '.' ||
        name.indexOf("..") != -1)
        throw new Error("Module.createNamespace(): illegal name: " + name);

    // Break the name at periods and create the object hierarchy we need
    var parts = name.split('.');

    // For each namespace component, either create an object or ensure that
    // an object by that name already exists.
    var container = Module.globalNamespace;
    for(var i = 0; i < parts.length; i++) {
        var part = parts[i];
        // If there is no property of container with this name, create
        // an empty object.
        if (!container[part]) container[part] = {};
```

Example 10-5. A module of module-related utilities (continued)

```
        else if (typeof container[part] != "object") {
            // If there is already a property, make sure it is an object
            var n = parts.slice(0,i).join('.');
            throw new Error(n + " already exists and is not an object");
        }
        container = container[part];
    }

    // The last container traversed above is the namespace we need.
    var namespace = container;

    // It is an error to define a namespace twice. It is okay if our
    // namespace object already exists, but it must not already have a
    // NAME property defined.
    if (namespace.NAME) throw new Error("Module "+name+" is already defined");

    // Initialize name and version fields of the namespace
    namespace.NAME = name;
    if (version) namespace.VERSION = version;

    // Register this namespace in the map of all modules
    Module.modules[name] = namespace;

    // Return the namespace object to the caller
    return namespace;
}
/**
 * Test whether the module with the specified name has been defined.
 * Returns true if it is defined and false otherwise.
 */
Module.isDefined = function(name) {
    return name in Module.modules;
};

/**
 * This function throws an error if the named module is not defined
 * or if it is defined but its version is less than the specified version.
 * If the namespace exists and has a suitable version, this function simply
 * returns without doing anything. Use this function to cause a fatal
 * error if the modules that your code requires are not present.
 */
Module.require = function(name, version) {
    if (!(name in Module.modules)) {
        throw new Error("Module " + name + " is not defined");
    }

    // If no version was specified, there is nothing to check
    if (!version) return;

    var n = Module.modules[name];

    // If the defined version is less than the required version or if
```

Example 10-5. A module of module-related utilities (continued)

```
            // the namespace does not declare any version, throw an error.
            if (!n.VERSION || n.VERSION < version)
            throw new Error("Module " + name + " has version " +
                            n.VERSION + " but version " + version +
                            " or greater is required.");
};


/**
 * This function imports symbols from a specified module.  By default, it
 * imports them into the global namespace, but you may specify a different
 * destination as the second argument.
 *
 * If no symbols are explicitly specified, the symbols in the EXPORT
 * array of the module will be imported. If no such array is defined,
 * and no EXPORT_OK is defined, all symbols from the module will be imported.
 *
 * To import an explicitly specified set of symbols, pass their names as
 * arguments after the module and the optional destination namespace. If the
 * modules defines an EXPORT or EXPORT_OK array, symbols will be imported
 * only if they are listed in one of those arrays.
 */
Module.importSymbols = function(from) {
    // Make sure that the module is correctly specified. We expect the
    // module's namespace object but will try with a string, too
    if (typeof from == "string") from = Module.modules[from];
    if (!from || typeof from != "object")
        throw new Error("Module.importSymbols( ): " +
                        "namespace object required");

    // The source namespace may be followed by an optional destination
    // namespace and the names of one or more symbols to import;
    var to = Module.globalNamespace; // Default destination
    var symbols = [];                // No symbols by default
    var firstsymbol = 1;             // Index in arguments of first symbol name

    // See if a destination namespace is specified
    if (arguments.length > 1 && typeof arguments[1] == "object") {
        if (arguments[1] != null) to = arguments[1];
        firstsymbol = 2;
    }

    // Now get the list of specified symbols
    for(var a = firstsymbol; a < arguments.length; a++)
        symbols.push(arguments[a]);

    // If we were not passed any symbols to import, import a set defined
    // by the module, or just import all of them.
    if (symbols.length == 0) {
        // If the module defines an EXPORT array, import
        // the symbols in that array.
        if (from.EXPORT) {
            for(var i = 0; i < from.EXPORT.length; i++) {
```

Example 10-5. A module of module-related utilities (continued)

```
                var s = from.EXPORT[i];
                to[s] = from[s];
            }
            return;
        }
        // Otherwise if the modules does not define an EXPORT_OK array,
        // just import everything in the module's namespace
        else if (!from.EXPORT_OK) {
            for(s in from) to[s] = from[s];
            return;
        }
    }

    // If we get here, we have an explicitly specified array of symbols
    // to import. If the namespace defines EXPORT and/or EXPORT_OK arrays,
    // ensure that each symbol is listed before importing it.
    // Throw an error if a requested symbol does not exist or if
    // it is not allowed to be exported.
    var allowed;
    if (from.EXPORT || from.EXPORT_OK) {
        allowed = {};
        // Copy allowed symbols from arrays to properties of an object.
        // This allows us to test for an allowed symbol more efficiently.
        if (from.EXPORT)
            for(var i = 0; i < from.EXPORT.length; i++)
                allowed[from.EXPORT[i]] = true;
        if (from.EXPORT_OK)
            for(var i = 0; i < from.EXPORT_OK.length; i++)
                allowed[from.EXPORT_OK[i]] = true;
    }

    // Import the symbols
    for(var i = 0; i < symbols.length; i++) {
        var s = symbols[i];              // The name of the symbol to import
        if (!(s in from))                // Make sure it exists
            throw new Error("Module.importSymbols(): symbol " + s +
                            " is not defined");
        if (allowed && !(s in allowed))  // Make sure it is a public symbol
            throw new Error("Module.importSymbols(): symbol " + s +
                            " is not public and cannot be imported.");
        to[s] = from[s];                 // Import it
    }
};


// Modules use this function to register one or more initialization functions
Module.registerInitializationFunction = function(f) {
    // Store the function in the array of initialization functions
    Module._initfuncs.push(f);
    // If we have not yet registered an onload event handler, do so now.
    Module._registerEventHandler();
}
```

Example 10-5. A module of module-related utilities (continued)

```
// A function to invoke all registered initialization functions.
// In client-side JavaScript, this will automatically be called in
// when the document finished loading. In other contexts, you must
// call it explicitly.
Module.runInitializationFunctions = function() {
    // Run each initialization function, catching and ignoring exceptions
    // so that a failure by one module does not prevent other modules
    // from being initialized.
    for(var i = 0; i < Module._initfuncs.length; i++) {
        try { Module._initfuncs[i](); }
        catch(e) { /* ignore exceptions */}
    }
    // Erase the array so the functions are never called more than once.
    Module._initfuncs.length = 0;
}

// A private array holding initialization functions to invoke later
Module._initfuncs = [];

// If we are loaded into a web browser, this private function registers an
// onload event handler to run the initialization functions for all loaded
// modules. It does not allow itself to be called more than once.
Module._registerEventHandler = function() {
    var clientside =     // Check for well-known client-side properties
        "window" in Module.globalNamespace &&
        "navigator" in window;

    if (clientside) {
        if (window.addEventListener) {  // W3C DOM standard event registration
            window.addEventListener("load", Module.runInitializationFunctions,
                                    false);
        }
        else if (window.attachEvent) {  // IE5+ event registration
            window.attachEvent("onload", Module.runInitializationFunctions);
        }
        else {
            // IE4 and old browsers
            // If the <body> defines an onload tag, this event listener
            // will be overwritten and never get called.
            window.onload = Module.runInitializationFunctions;
        }
    }

    // The function overwrites itself with an empty function so it never
    // gets called more than once.
    Module._registerEventHandler = function() {};
}
```

CHAPTER 11

Pattern Matching with Regular Expressions

A *regular expression* is an object that describes a pattern of characters. The Java-Script RegExp class represents regular expressions, and both String and RegExp define methods that use regular expressions to perform powerful pattern-matching and search-and-replace functions on text.*

JavaScript regular expressions were standardized in ECMAScript v3. JavaScript 1.2 implements a subset of the regular-expression features required by ECMAScript v3, and JavaScript 1.5 implements the full standard. JavaScript regular expressions are strongly based on the regular-expression facilities of the Perl programming language. Roughly speaking, you can say that JavaScript 1.2 implements Perl 4 regular expressions and JavaScript 1.5 implements a large subset of Perl 5 regular expressions.

This chapter begins by defining the syntax that regular expressions use to describe textual patterns. It then moves on to describe the String and RegExp methods that use regular expressions.

11.1 Defining Regular Expressions

In JavaScript, regular expressions are represented by RegExp objects. RegExp objects may be created with the RegExp( ) constructor, of course, but they are more often created using a special literal syntax. Just as string literals are specified as characters within quotation marks, regular expression literals are specified as characters within a pair of slash (/) characters. Thus, your JavaScript code may contain lines like this:

```
var pattern = /s$/;
```

This line creates a new RegExp object and assigns it to the variable pattern. This particular RegExp object matches any string that ends with the letter "s." (I'll get into

---

* The term "regular expression" is an obscure one that dates back many years. The syntax used to describe a textual pattern is indeed a type of expression. However, as you'll see, that syntax is far from regular! A regular expression is sometimes called a "regexp" or even an "RE."

the grammar for defining patterns shortly.) This regular expression could have equivalently been defined with the RegExp( ) constructor like this:

```
var pattern = new RegExp("s$");
```

Creating a RegExp object, either literally or with the RegExp( ) constructor, is the easy part. The more difficult task is describing the desired pattern of characters using regular expression syntax. JavaScript adopts a fairly complete subset of the regular-expression syntax used by Perl, so if you are an experienced Perl programmer, you already know how to describe patterns in JavaScript.

Regular-expression pattern specifications consist of a series of characters. Most characters, including all alphanumeric characters, simply describe characters to be matched literally. Thus, the regular expression /java/ matches any string that contains the substring "java". Other characters in regular expressions are not matched literally but have special significance. For example, the regular expression /s$/ contains two characters. The first, "s", matches itself literally. The second, "$", is a special metacharacter that matches the end of a string. Thus, this regular expression matches any string that contains the letter "s" as its last character.

The following sections describe the various characters and metacharacters used in JavaScript regular expressions. Note, however, that a complete tutorial on regular-expression grammar is beyond the scope of this book. For complete details of the syntax, consult a book on Perl, such as *Programming Perl* by Larry Wall et al. (O'Reilly). *Mastering Regular Expressions* by Jeffrey E.F. Friedl (O'Reilly) is another excellent source of information on regular expressions.

11.1.1 Literal Characters

As noted earlier, all alphabetic characters and digits match themselves literally in regular expressions. JavaScript regular-expression syntax also supports certain non-alphabetic characters through escape sequences that begin with a backslash (\). For example, the sequence \n matches a literal newline character in a string. Table 11-1 lists these characters.

Table 11-1. Regular-expression literal characters

Character	Matches
Alphanumeric character	Itself
\0	The NUL character (\u0000)
\t	Tab (\u0009)
\n	Newline (\u000A)
\v	Vertical tab (\u000B)
\f	Form feed (\u000C)
\r	Carriage return (\u000D)

Table 11-1. Regular-expression literal characters (continued)

Character	Matches
\x*nn*	The Latin character specified by the hexadecimal number *nn*; for example, \x0A is the same as \n
\u*xxxx*	The Unicode character specified by the hexadecimal number *xxxx*; for example, \u0009 is the same as \t
\c*X*	The control character ^*X*; for example, \cJ is equivalent to the newline character \n

A number of punctuation characters have special meanings in regular expressions. They are:

```
^ $ . * + ? = ! : | \ / ( ) [ ] { }
```

The meanings of these characters are discussed in the sections that follow. Some of these characters have special meaning only within certain contexts of a regular expression and are treated literally in other contexts. As a general rule, however, if you want to include any of these punctuation characters literally in a regular expression, you must precede them with a \. Other punctuation characters, such as quotation marks and @, do not have special meaning and simply match themselves literally in a regular expression.

If you can't remember exactly which punctuation characters need to be escaped with a backslash, you may safely place a backslash before any punctuation character. On the other hand, note that many letters and numbers have special meaning when preceded by a backslash, so any letters or numbers that you want to match literally should not be escaped with a backslash. To include a backslash character literally in a regular expression, you must escape it with a backslash, of course. For example, the following regular expression matches any string that includes a backslash: /\\/.

11.1.2 Character Classes

Individual literal characters can be combined into *character classes* by placing them within square brackets. A character class matches any one character that is contained within it. Thus, the regular expression /[abc]/ matches any one of the letters a, b, or c. Negated character classes can also be defined; these match any character except those contained within the brackets. A negated character class is specified by placing a caret (^) as the first character inside the left bracket. The regexp /[^abc]/ matches any one character other than a, b, or c. Character classes can use a hyphen to indicate a range of characters. To match any one lowercase character from the Latin alphabet, use /[a-z]/ and to match any letter or digit from the Latin alphabet, use /[a-zA-Z0-9]/.

Because certain character classes are commonly used, the JavaScript regular-expression syntax includes special characters and escape sequences to represent these common classes. For example, \s matches the space character, the tab character, and any other Unicode whitespace character; \S matches any character that is *not* Unicode whitespace. Table 11-2 lists these characters and summarizes character-class syntax. (Note that several of these character-class escape sequences match only ASCII characters and have not been extended to work with Unicode characters. You can, however, explicitly define your own Unicode character classes; for example, /[\u0400-\u04FF]/ matches any one Cyrillic character.)

Table 11-2. Regular expression character classes

Character	Matches
[...]	Any one character between the brackets.
[^...]	Any one character not between the brackets.
.	Any character except newline or another Unicode line terminator.
\w	Any ASCII word character. Equivalent to [a-zA-Z0-9_].
\W	Any character that is not an ASCII word character. Equivalent to [^a-zA-Z0-9_].
\s	Any Unicode whitespace character.
\S	Any character that is not Unicode whitespace. Note that \w and \S are not the same thing.
\d	Any ASCII digit. Equivalent to [0-9].
\D	Any character other than an ASCII digit. Equivalent to [^0-9].
[\b]	A literal backspace (special case).

Note that the special character-class escapes can be used within square brackets. \s matches any whitespace character, and \d matches any digit, so /[\s\d]/ matches any one whitespace character or digit. Note that there is one special case. As you'll see later, the \b escape has a special meaning. When used within a character class, however, it represents the backspace character. Thus, to represent a backspace character literally in a regular expression, use the character class with one element: /[\b]/.

11.1.3 Repetition

With the regular expression syntax you've learned so far, you can describe a two-digit number as /\d\d/ and a four-digit number as /\d\d\d\d/. But you don't have any way to describe, for example, a number that can have any number of digits or a string of three letters followed by an optional digit. These more complex patterns use regular-expression syntax that specifies how many times an element of a regular expression may be repeated.

The characters that specify repetition always follow the pattern to which they are being applied. Because certain types of repetition are quite commonly used, there are special characters to represent these cases. For example, + matches one or more occurrences of the previous pattern. Table 11-3 summarizes the repetition syntax.

Table 11-3. Regular expression repetition characters

Character	Meaning
{n,m}	Match the previous item at least *n* times but no more than *m* times.
{n,}	Match the previous item *n* or more times.
{n}	Match exactly *n* occurrences of the previous item.
?	Match zero or one occurrences of the previous item. That is, the previous item is optional. Equivalent to {0,1}.
+	Match one or more occurrences of the previous item. Equivalent to {1,}.
*	Match zero or more occurrences of the previous item. Equivalent to {0,}.

The following lines show some examples:

```
/\d{2,4}/       // Match between two and four digits
/\w{3}\d?/      // Match exactly three word characters and an optional digit
/\s+java\s+/    // Match "java" with one or more spaces before and after
/[^"]*/         // Match zero or more non-quote characters
```

Be careful when using the * and ? repetition characters. Since these characters may match zero instances of whatever precedes them, they are allowed to match nothing. For example, the regular expression /a*/ actually matches the string "bbbb" because the string contains zero occurrences of the letter a!

11.1.3.1 Nongreedy repetition

The repetition characters listed in Table 11-3 match as many times as possible while still allowing any following parts of the regular expression to match. We say that this repetition is "greedy." It is also possible (in JavaScript 1.5 and later; this is one of the Perl 5 features not implemented in JavaScript 1.2) to specify that repetition should be done in a nongreedy way. Simply follow the repetition character or characters with a question mark: ??, +?, *?, or even {1,5}?. For example, the regular expression /a+/ matches one or more occurrences of the letter a. When applied to the string "aaa", it matches all three letters. But /a+?/ matches one or more occurrences of the letter a, matching as few characters as necessary. When applied to the same string, this pattern matches only the first letter a.

Using nongreedy repetition may not always produce the results you expect. Consider the pattern /a*b/, which matches zero or more letter a's, followed by the letter b. When applied to the string "aaab", it matches the entire string. Now let's use the nongreedy version: /a*?b/. This should match the letter b preceded by the fewest number of a's possible. When applied to the same string "aaab", you might expect it to match only the last letter b. In fact, however, this pattern matches the entire string as well, just like the greedy version of the pattern. This is because regular-expression pattern matching is done by finding the first position in the string at which a match is possible. The nongreedy version of our pattern does match at the first character of the string, so this match is returned; matches at subsequent characters are never even considered.

11.1.4 Alternation, Grouping, and References

The regular-expression grammar includes special characters for specifying alternatives, grouping subexpressions, and referring to previous subexpressions. The | character separates alternatives. For example, /ab|cd|ef/ matches the string "ab" or the string "cd" or the string "ef". And /\d{3}|[a-z]{4}/ matches either three digits or four lowercase letters.

Note that alternatives are considered left to right until a match is found. If the left alternative matches, the right alternative is ignored, even if it would have produced a "better" match. Thus, when the pattern /a|ab/ is applied to the string "ab", it matches only the first letter.

Parentheses have several purposes in regular expressions. One purpose is to group separate items into a single subexpression so that the items can be treated as a single unit by |, *, +, ?, and so on. For example, /java(script)?/ matches "java" followed by the optional "script". And /(ab|cd)+|ef)/ matches either the string "ef" or one or more repetitions of either of the strings "ab" or "cd".

Another purpose of parentheses in regular expressions is to define subpatterns within the complete pattern. When a regular expression is successfully matched against a target string, it is possible to extract the portions of the target string that matched any particular parenthesized subpattern. (You'll see how these matching substrings are obtained later in the chapter.) For example, suppose you are looking for one or more lowercase letters followed by one or more digits. You might use the pattern /[a-z]+\d+/. But suppose you only really care about the digits at the end of each match. If you put that part of the pattern in parentheses (/[a-z]+(\d+)/), you can extract the digits from any matches you find, as explained later.

A related use of parenthesized subexpressions is to allow you to refer back to a subexpression later in the same regular expression. This is done by following a \ character by a digit or digits. The digits refer to the position of the parenthesized subexpression within the regular expression. For example, \1 refers back to the first subexpression, and \3 refers to the third. Note that, because subexpressions can be nested within others, it is the position of the left parenthesis that is counted. In the following regular expression, for example, the nested subexpression ([Ss]cript) is referred to as \2:

```
/([Jj]ava([Ss]cript)?)\sis\s(fun\w*)/
```

A reference to a previous subexpression of a regular expression does *not* refer to the pattern for that subexpression but rather to the text that matched the pattern. Thus, references can be used to enforce a constraint that separate portions of a string contain exactly the same characters. For example, the following regular expression matches zero or more characters within single or double quotes. However, it does not require the opening and closing quotes to match (i.e., both single quotes or both double quotes):

```
/['"][^'"]*['"]/
```

To require the quotes to match, use a reference:

```
/(['"])[^'"]*\1/
```

The \1 matches whatever the first parenthesized subexpression matched. In this example, it enforces the constraint that the closing quote match the opening quote. This regular expression does not allow single quotes within double-quoted strings or vice versa. It is not legal to use a reference within a character class, so you cannot write:

```
/(['"])[^\1]*\1/
```

Later in this chapter, you'll see that this kind of reference to a parenthesized subexpression is a powerful feature of regular-expression search-and-replace operations.

In JavaScript 1.5 (but not JavaScript 1.2), it is possible to group items in a regular expression without creating a numbered reference to those items. Instead of simply grouping the items within (and), begin the group with (?: and end it with). Consider the following pattern, for example:

```
/([Jj]ava(?:[Ss]cript)?)\sis\s(fun\w*)/
```

Here, the subexpression (?:[Ss]cript) is used simply for grouping, so the ? repetition character can be applied to the group. These modified parentheses do not produce a reference, so in this regular expression, \2 refers to the text matched by (fun\w*).

Table 11-4 summarizes the regular-expression alternation, grouping, and referencing operators.

Table 11-4. Regular expression alternation, grouping, and reference characters

Character	Meaning
|	Alternation. Match either the subexpression to the left or the subexpression to the right.
(...)	Grouping. Group items into a single unit that can be used with *, +, ?, |, and so on. Also remember the characters that match this group for use with later references.
(?:...)	Grouping only. Group items into a single unit, but do not remember the characters that match this group.
\n	Match the same characters that were matched when group number *n* was first matched. Groups are subexpressions within (possibly nested) parentheses. Group numbers are assigned by counting left parentheses from left to right. Groups formed with (?: are not numbered.

11.1.5 Specifying Match Position

As described earlier, many elements of a regular expression match a single character in a string. For example, \s matches a single character of whitespace. Other regular expression elements match the positions between characters, instead of actual characters. \b, for example, matches a word boundary—the boundary between a \w (ASCII word character) and a \W (nonword character), or the boundary between an

ASCII word character and the beginning or end of a string.[*] Elements such as \b do not specify any characters to be used in a matched string; what they do specify, however, is legal positions at which a match can occur. Sometimes these elements are called *regular-expression anchors* because they anchor the pattern to a specific position in the search string. The most commonly used anchor elements are ^, which ties the pattern to the beginning of the string, and $, which anchors the pattern to the end of the string.

For example, to match the word "JavaScript" on a line by itself, you can use the regular expression /^JavaScript$/. If you want to search for "Java" used as a word by itself (not as a prefix, as it is in "JavaScript"), you can try the pattern /\sJava\s/, which requires a space before and after the word. But there are two problems with this solution. First, it does not match "Java" if that word appears at the beginning or the end of a string, but only if it appears with space on either side. Second, when this pattern does find a match, the matched string it returns has leading and trailing spaces, which is not quite what's needed. So instead of matching actual space characters with \s, match (or anchor to) word boundaries with \b. The resulting expression is /\bJava\b/. The element \B anchors the match to a location that is not a word boundary. Thus, the pattern /\B[Ss]cript/ matches "JavaScript" and "postscript", but not "script" or "Scripting".

In JavaScript 1.5 (but not JavaScript 1.2), you can also use arbitrary regular expressions as anchor conditions. If you include an expression within (?= and) characters, it is a lookahead assertion, and it specifies that the enclosed characters must match, without actually matching them. For example, to match the name of a common programming language, but only if it is followed by a colon, you could use /[Jj]ava([Ss]cript)?(?=\:)/. This pattern matches the word "JavaScript" in "JavaScript: The Definitive Guide", but it does not match "Java" in "Java in a Nutshell" because it is not followed by a colon.

If you instead introduce an assertion with (?!, it is a negative lookahead assertion, which specifies that the following characters must not match. For example, /Java(?!Script)([A-Z]\w*)/ matches "Java" followed by a capital letter and any number of additional ASCII word characters, as long as "Java" is not followed by "Script". It matches "JavaBeans" but not "Javanese", and it matches "JavaScrip" but not "JavaScript" or "JavaScripter".

Table 11-5 summarizes regular-expression anchors.

Table 11-5. Regular-expression anchor characters

Character	Meaning
^	Match the beginning of the string and, in multiline searches, the beginning of a line.
$	Match the end of the string and, in multiline searches, the end of a line.

---

[*] Except within a character class (square brackets), where \b matches the backspace character.

Table 11-5. Regular-expression anchor characters (continued)

Character	Meaning
\b	Match a word boundary. That is, match the position between a \w character and a \W character or between a \w character and the beginning or end of a string. (Note, however, that [\b] matches backspace.)
\B	Match a position that is not a word boundary.
(?=p)	A positive lookahead assertion. Require that the following characters match the pattern p , but do not include those characters in the match.
(?!p)	A negative lookahead assertion. Require that the following characters do not match the pattern p .

11.1.6 Flags

There is one final element of regular-expression grammar. Regular-expression flags specify high-level pattern-matching rules. Unlike the rest of regular-expression syntax, flags are specified outside the / characters; instead of appearing within the slashes, they appear following the second slash. JavaScript 1.2 supports two flags. The i flag specifies that pattern matching should be case-insensitive. The g flag specifies that pattern matching should be global—that is, all matches within the searched string should be found. Both flags may be combined to perform a global case-insensitive match.

For example, to do a case-insensitive search for the first occurrence of the word "java" (or "Java", "JAVA", etc.), you can use the case-insensitive regular expression /\bjava\b/i. And to find all occurrences of the word in a string, you can add the g flag: /\bjava\b/gi.

JavaScript 1.5 supports an additional flag: m. The m flag performs pattern matching in multiline mode. In this mode, if the string to be searched contains newlines, the ^ and $ anchors match the beginning and end of a line in addition to matching the beginning and end of a string. For example, the pattern /Java$/im matches "java" as well as "Java\nis fun".

Table 11-6 summarizes these regular-expression flags. Note that you'll see more about the g flag later in this chapter, when the String and RegExp methods are used to actually perform matches.

Table 11-6. Regular-expression flags

Character	Meaning
i	Perform case-insensitive matching.
g	Perform a global match—that is, find all matches rather than stopping after the first match.
m	Multiline mode. ^ matches beginning of line or beginning of string, and $ matches end of line or end of string.

11.1.7 Perl RegExp Features Not Supported in JavaScript

ECMAScript v3 specifies a relatively complete subset of the regular-expression facilities from Perl 5. Advanced Perl features that are not supported by ECMAScript include the following:

- The s (single-line mode) and x (extended syntax) flags
- The \a, \e, \l, \u, \L, \U, \E, \Q, \A, \Z, \z, and \G escape sequences
- The (?<= positive look-behind anchor and the (?<! negative look-behind anchor
- The (?# comment and the other extended (? syntaxes

11.2 String Methods for Pattern Matching

Until now, this chapter has discussed the grammar used to create regular expressions, but it hasn't examined how those regular expressions can actually be used in JavaScript code. This section discusses methods of the String object that use regular expressions to perform pattern matching and search-and-replace operations. The sections that follow this one continue the discussion of pattern matching with JavaScript regular expressions by discussing the RegExp object and its methods and properties. Note that the discussion that follows is merely an overview of the various methods and properties related to regular expressions. As usual, complete details can be found in Part III.

Strings support four methods that use regular expressions. The simplest is search(). This method takes a regular-expression argument and returns either the character position of the start of the first matching substring or −1 if there is no match. For example, the following call returns 4:

```
"JavaScript".search(/script/i);
```

If the argument to search() is not a regular expression, it is first converted to one by passing it to the RegExp constructor. search() does not support global searches; it ignores the g flag of its regular expression argument.

The replace() method performs a search-and-replace operation. It takes a regular expression as its first argument and a replacement string as its second argument. It searches the string on which it is called for matches with the specified pattern. If the regular expression has the g flag set, the replace() method replaces all matches in the string with the replacement string; otherwise, it replaces only the first match it finds. If the first argument to replace() is a string rather than a regular expression, the method searches for that string literally rather than converting it to a regular expression with the RegExp() constructor, as search() does. As an example, you can use replace() as follows to provide uniform capitalization of the word "JavaScript" throughout a string of text:

```
// No matter how it is capitalized, replace it with the correct capitalization
text.replace(/javascript/gi, "JavaScript");
```

replace( ) is more powerful than this, however. Recall that parenthesized subexpressions of a regular expression are numbered from left to right and that the regular expression remembers the text that each subexpression matches. If a $ followed by a digit appears in the replacement string, replace( ) replaces those two characters with the text that matches the specified subexpression. This is a very useful feature. You can use it, for example, to replace straight quotes in a string with curly quotes, simulated with ASCII characters:

```
// A quote is a quotation mark, followed by any number of
// nonquotation-mark characters (which we remember), followed
// by another quotation mark.
var quote = /"([^"]*)"/g;
// Replace the straight quotation marks with "curly quotes,"
// and leave the contents of the quote (stored in $1) unchanged.
text.replace(quote, "``$1''");
```

The replace( ) method has other important features as well, which are described in the String.replace( ) reference page in Part III. Most notably, the second argument to replace( ) can be a function that dynamically computes the replacement string.

The match( ) method is the most general of the String regular-expression methods. It takes a regular expression as its only argument (or converts its argument to a regular expression by passing it to the RegExp( ) constructor) and returns an array that contains the results of the match. If the regular expression has the g flag set, the method returns an array of all matches that appear in the string. For example:

```
"1 plus 2 equals 3".match(/\d+/g)   // returns ["1", "2", "3"]
```

If the regular expression does not have the g flag set, match( ) does not do a global search; it simply searches for the first match. However, match( ) returns an array even when it does not perform a global search. In this case, the first element of the array is the matching string, and any remaining elements are the parenthesized subexpressions of the regular expression. Thus, if match( ) returns an array a, a[0] contains the complete match, a[1] contains the substring that matched the first parenthesized expression, and so on. To draw a parallel with the replace( ) method, a[n] holds the contents of $n.

For example, consider parsing a URL with the following code:

```
var url = /(\w+):\/\/([\w.]+)\/(\S*)/;
var text = "Visit my blog at http://www.example.com/~david";
var result = text.match(url);
if (result != null) {
    var fullurl = result[0];   // Contains "http://www.example.com/~david"
    var protocol = result[1];  // Contains "http"
    var host = result[2];      // Contains "www.example.com"
    var path = result[3];      // Contains "~david"
}
```

Finally, you should know about one more feature of the match( ) method. The array it returns has a length property, as all arrays do. When match( ) is invoked on a nonglobal regular expression, however, the returned array also has two other properties: the index property, which contains the character position within the string at which the match begins, and the input property, which is a copy of the target string. So in the previous code, the value of the result.index property would be 17 because the matched URL begins at character position 17 in the text. The result.input property holds the same string as the text variable. For a regular expression r and string s that does not have the g flag set, calling s.match(r) returns the same value as r.exec(s). The RegExp.exec( ) method is discussed a little later in this chapter.

The last of the regular-expression methods of the String object is split( ). This method breaks the string on which it is called into an array of substrings, using the argument as a separator. For example:

```
"123,456,789".split(",");  // Returns ["123","456","789"]
```

The split( ) method can also take a regular expression as its argument. This ability makes the method more powerful. For example, you can now specify a separator character that allows an arbitrary amount of whitespace on either side:

```
"1,2, 3 , 4 ,5".split(/\s*,\s*/); // Returns ["1","2","3","4","5"]
```

The split( ) method has other features as well. See the String.split( ) entry in Part III for complete details.

11.3 The RegExp Object

As mentioned at the beginning of this chapter, regular expressions are represented as RegExp objects. In addition to the RegExp( ) constructor, RegExp objects support three methods and a number of properties. An unusual feature of the RegExp class is that it defines both class (or static) properties and instance properties. That is, it defines global properties that belong to the RegExp( ) constructor as well as other properties that belong to individual RegExp objects. RegExp pattern-matching methods and properties are described in the next two sections.

The RegExp( ) constructor takes one or two string arguments and creates a new RegExp object. The first argument to this constructor is a string that contains the body of the regular expression—the text that would appear within slashes in a regular-expression literal. Note that both string literals and regular expressions use the \ character for escape sequences, so when you pass a regular expression to RegExp( ) as a string literal, you must replace each \ character with \\. The second argument to RegExp( ) is optional. If supplied, it indicates the regular-expression flags. It should be g, i, m, or a combination of those letters. For example:

```
// Find all five-digit numbers in a string. Note the double \\ in this case.
var zipcode = new RegExp("\\d{5}", "g");
```

The RegExp( ) constructor is useful when a regular expression is being dynamically created and thus cannot be represented with the regular-expression literal syntax.

For example, to search for a string entered by the user, a regular expression must be created at runtime with RegExp( ).

11.3.1 RegExp Methods for Pattern Matching

RegExp objects define two methods that perform pattern-matching operations; they behave similarly to the String methods described earlier. The main RegExp pattern-matching method is exec( ). It is similar to the String match( ) method described in Section 11.2, except that it is a RegExp method that takes a string, rather than a String method that takes a RegExp. The exec( ) method executes a regular expression on the specified string. That is, it searches the string for a match. If it finds none, it returns null. If it does find one, however, it returns an array just like the array returned by the match( ) method for nonglobal searches. Element 0 of the array contains the string that matched the regular expression, and any subsequent array elements contain the substrings that matched any parenthesized subexpressions. Furthermore, the index property contains the character position at which the match occurred, and the input property refers to the string that was searched.

Unlike the match( ) method, exec( ) returns the same kind of array whether or not the regular expression has the global g flag. Recall that match( ) returns an array of matches when passed a global regular expression. exec( ), by contrast, always returns a single match and provides complete information about that match. When exec( ) is called on a regular expression that has the g flag, it sets the lastIndex property of the regular-expression object to the character position immediately following the matched substring. When exec( ) is invoked a second time for the same regular expression, it begins its search at the character position indicated by the lastIndex property. If exec( ) does not find a match, it resets lastIndex to 0. (You can also set lastIndex to 0 at any time, which you should do whenever you quit a search before you find the last match in one string and begin searching another string with the same RegExp object.) This special behavior allows you to call exec( ) repeatedly in order to loop through all the regular expression matches in a string. For example:

```
var pattern = /Java/g;
var text = "JavaScript is more fun than Java!";
var result;
while((result = pattern.exec(text)) != null) {
    alert("Matched `" + result[0] + "'" +
        " at position " + result.index +
        "; next search begins at " + pattern.lastIndex);
}
```

The other RegExp method is test( ). test( ) is a much simpler method than exec( ). It takes a string and returns true if the string contains a match for the regular expression:

```
var pattern = /java/i;
pattern.test("JavaScript");  // Returns true
```

Calling test( ) is equivalent to calling exec( ) and returning true if the return value of exec( ) is not null. Because of this equivalence, the test( ) method behaves the same way as the exec( ) method when invoked for a global regular expression: it begins searching the specified string at the position specified by lastIndex, and if it finds a match, it sets lastIndex to the position of the character immediately following the match. Thus, you can loop through a string using the test( ) method just as you can with the exec( ) method.

The String methods search( ), replace( ), and match( ) do not use the lastIndex property as exec( ) and test( ) do. In fact, the String methods simply reset lastIndex( ) to 0. If you use exec( ) or test( ) on a pattern that has the g flag set, and you are searching multiple strings, you must either find all the matches in each string so that lastIndex is automatically reset to zero (this happens when the last search fails), or you must explicitly set the lastIndex property to 0 yourself. If you forget to do this, you may start searching a new string at some arbitrary position within the string rather than from the beginning. Finally, remember that this special lastIndex behavior occurs only for regular expressions with the g flag. exec( ) and test( ) ignore the lastIndex property of RegExp objects that do not have the g flag.

11.3.2 RegExp Instance Properties

Each RegExp object has five properties. The source property is a read-only string that contains the text of the regular expression. The global property is a read-only boolean value that specifies whether the regular expression has the g flag. The ignoreCase property is a read-only boolean value that specifies whether the regular expression has the i flag. The multiline property is a read-only boolean value that specifies whether the regular expression has the m flag. The final property is lastIndex, a read/write integer. For patterns with the g flag, this property stores the position in the string at which the next search is to begin. It is used by the exec( ) and test( ) methods, as described in the previous section.

CHAPTER 12

Scripting Java

Despite its name, the JavaScript programming language is unrelated to the Java programming language. There is a superficial syntactical resemblance because they both use syntax of the C programming language, but beneath that they are very different. Nevertheless, JavaScript has evolved and can now actually be used to script Java.[*] Java 6 recognizes this fact and ships with a bundled JavaScript interpreter so that scripting capability can easily be embedded into any Java application. Furthermore, some JavaScript interpreters (such as the one bundled with Java 6) support a feature set that allows JavaScript to interact with Java objects, setting and querying fields and invoking methods.

This chapter first explains how to embed a JavaScript interpreter into a Java 6 application and how to run JavaScript scripts from that application. It then turns things around and demonstrates how those scripts can script Java objects directly.

I'll return to the topic of Java scripting again in Chapter 23, which covers Java applets and the Java plug-in in the context of a web browser.

12.1 Embedding JavaScript

We are nearing the end of the Core JavaScript section of this book. Part II of this book is entirely devoted to JavaScript as it is used in web browsers. Before beginning that discussion, however, let's briefly look at how JavaScript can be embedded into other applications. The motivation for embedding JavaScript within applications is typically to allow users to customize the application with scripts. The Firefox web browser, for example, uses JavaScript scripts to control the behavior of its user interface. Many other highly configurable applications use scripting languages of some sort or another.

---

[*] This chapter is written for Java programmers, and many of the examples in this chapter are written partially or entirely in Java. Unless you already know how to program in Java, you should skip this chapter.

Two open source JavaScript interpreters are available from the Mozilla project. SpiderMonkey is the original JavaScript interpreter and is written in C. Rhino is an implementation in Java. Both have embedding APIs. If you want to add scripting to a C application, you can use Spidermonkey; if you want to add scripting to a Java application, you can use Rhino. You can learn more about using these interpreters in your own applications at *http://www.mozilla.org/js/spidermonkey* and *http://www. mozilla.org/rhino*.

With the advent of Java 6.0, it becomes particularly easy to add JavaScript scripting functionality to your Java applications, and this is what is discussed here. Java 6 introduces a new javax.script package that provides a generic interface to scripting languages and is bundled with a version of Rhino that uses the new package.[*]

Example 12-1 demonstrates the basic use of the javax.script package: it obtains a ScriptEngine object that represents an instance of a JavaScript interpreter and a Bindings object that holds JavaScript variables. It then runs a script stored in an external file by passing a java.io.Reader stream and the bindings to the eval() method of the ScriptEngine. The eval() method returns the result of the script or throws a ScriptException if something goes wrong.

Example 12-1. A Java program for running JavaScript scripts

```
import javax.script.*;
import java.io.*;

// Evaluate a file of JavaScript and print its result
public class RunScript {
    public static void main(String[] args) throws IOException {
        // Obtain an interpreter or "ScriptEngine" to run the script.
        ScriptEngineManager scriptManager = new ScriptEngineManager();
        ScriptEngine js = scriptManager.getEngineByExtension("js");

        // The script file we are going to run
        String filename = null;

        // A Bindings object is a symbol table for or namespace for the
        // script engine. It associates names and values and makes
        // them available to the script.
        Bindings bindings = js.createBindings();

        // Process the arguments. They may include any number of
        // -Dname=value arguments, which define variables for the script.
        // Any argument that does not begin with -D is taken as a filename
        for(int i = 0; i < args.length; i++) {
            String arg = args[i];
```

---

[*] At the time of this writing, Java 6 is still under development. The javax.script package appears to be stable enough to document, but there is a chance that the APIs documented here may change before the final release.

Example 12-1. A Java program for running JavaScript scripts (continued)

```
                if (arg.startsWith("-D")) {
                    int pos = arg.indexOf('=');
                    if (pos == -1) usage();
                    String name = arg.substring(2, pos);
                    String value = arg.substring(pos+1);
                    // Note that all the variables we define are strings.
                    // Scripts can convert them to other types if necessary.
                    // We could also pass a java.lang.Number, a java.lang.Boolean
                    // or any Java object or null.
                    bindings.put(name, value);
                }
                else {
                    if (filename != null) usage(); // only one file please
                    filename = arg;
                }
            }
            // Make sure we got a file out of the arguments.
            if (filename == null) usage();

            // Add one more binding using a special reserved variable name
            // to tell the script engine the name of the file it will be executing.
            // This allows it to provide better error messages.
            bindings.put(ScriptEngine.FILENAME, filename);

            // Get a stream to read the script.
            Reader in = new FileReader(filename);

            try {
                // Evaluate the script using the bindings and get its result.
                Object result = js.eval(in, bindings);
                // Display the result.
                System.out.println(result);
            }
            catch(ScriptException ex) {
                // Or display an error message.
                System.out.println(ex);
            }
        }

    static void usage() {
        System.err.println(
                "Usage: java RunScript [-Dname=value...] script.js");
        System.exit(1);
    }
}
```

The Bindings object created in this code snippet is not static: any variables created by the JavaScript script are stored there as well. Example 12-2 is a more realistic example of scripting Java. It stores its Bindings object in a ScriptContext object in a higher scope so that the variables can be read, but new variables are not stored into the Bindings object. The example implements a simple configuration file utility: a text file is used to define name/value pairs, which can be queried through the Configuration class defined here. Values may be strings, numbers, or booleans, and if a value is enclosed in curly braces, it is passed to a JavaScript interpreter for evaluation. Interestingly, the java.util.Map object that holds these name/value pairs is wrapped in a SimpleBindings object so that the JavaScript interpreter can also access the value of other variables defined in the same file.[*]

Example 12-2. A Java configuration file utility that interprets JavaScript expressions

```java
import javax.script.*;
import java.util.*;
import java.io.*;

/**
 * This class is like java.util.Properties but allows property values to
 * be determined by evaluating JavaScript expressions.
 */
public class Configuration {
    // Here is where we store name/value pairs of defaults.
    Map<String,Object> defaults = new HashMap<String,Object>();

    // Accessors for getting and setting values in the map
    public Object get(String key) { return defaults.get(key); }
    public void put(String key, Object value) { defaults.put(key, value); }

    // Initialize the contents of the Map from a file of name/value pairs.
    // If a value is enclosed in curly braces, evaluate it as JavaScript.
    public void load(String filename) throws IOException, ScriptException {
        // Get a JavaScript interpreter.
        ScriptEngineManager manager = new ScriptEngineManager();
        ScriptEngine engine = manager.getEngineByExtension("js");

        // Use our own name/value pairs as JavaScript variables.
        Bindings bindings = new SimpleBindings(defaults);

        // Create a context for evaluating scripts.
        ScriptContext context = new SimpleScriptContext();

        // Set those Bindings in the Context so that they are readable
        // by the scripts but so that variables defined by the scripts do
        // not get placed into our Map object.
        context.setBindings(bindings, ScriptContext.GLOBAL_SCOPE);

        BufferedReader in = new BufferedReader(new FileReader(filename));
        String line;
        while((line = in.readLine()) != null) {
            line = line.trim();  // strip leading and trailing space
```

---

[*] As shown later in this chapter, JavaScript code can use any public members of any public class. For this reason, you will typically run any Java code that executes a user-defined script with a restricted set of security permissions. A discussion of the Java security framework is beyond the scope of this chapter, however.

```java
            if (line.length( ) == 0) continue;      // skip blank lines
            if (line.charAt(0) == '#') continue; // skip comments

            int pos = line.indexOf(":");
            if (pos == -1)
                throw new IllegalArgumentException("syntax: " + line);

            String name = line.substring(0, pos).trim( );
            String value = line.substring(pos+1).trim( );
            char firstchar = value.charAt(0);
            int len = value.length( );
            char lastchar = value.charAt(len-1);

            if (firstchar == '"' && lastchar == '"') {
                // Double-quoted quoted values are strings
                defaults.put(name, value.substring(1, len-1));
            }
            else if (Character.isDigit(firstchar)) {
                // If it begins with a number, try to parse a number
                try {
                    double d = Double.parseDouble(value);
                    defaults.put(name, d);
                }
                catch(NumberFormatException e) {
                    // Oops.  Not a number.  Store as a string
                    defaults.put(name, value);
                }
            }
            else if (value.equals("true"))          // handle boolean values
                defaults.put(name, Boolean.TRUE);
            else if (value.equals("false"))
                defaults.put(name, Boolean.FALSE);
            else if (value.equals("null"))
                defaults.put(name, null);
            else if (firstchar == '{' && lastchar == '}') {
                // If the value is in curly braces, evaluate as JavaScript code
                String script = value.substring(1, len-1);
                Object result = engine.eval(script, context);
                defaults.put(name, result);
            }
            else {
                // In the default case, just store the value as a string.
                defaults.put(name, value);
            }
        }
    }

    // A simple test program for the class
    public static void main(String[] args) throws IOException, ScriptException
    {
        Configuration defaults = new Configuration( );
        defaults.load(args[0]);
```

Example 12-2. A Java configuration file utility that interprets JavaScript expressions (continued)

```
        Set<Map.Entry<String,Object>> entryset = defaults.defaults.entrySet();
        for(Map.Entry<String,Object> entry : entryset) {
            System.out.printf("%s: %s%n", entry.getKey(), entry.getValue());
        }
    }
}
```

12.1.1 Type Conversion with javax.script

Whenever one language is invoked from another, you must consider the question of how the types of one language are mapped to the types of the other language. Suppose you bind a java.lang.String and a java.lang.Integer to variables in a Bindings object. When a JavaScript script uses those variables, what are the types of the values it sees? And if the result of evaluating the script is a JavaScript boolean value, what is the type of object returned by the eval( ) method?

In the case of Java and JavaScript, the answer is fairly straightforward. When you store a Java object (there is no way to store primitive values) in a Bindings object, it converts to JavaScript as follows:

- Boolean objects convert to JavaScript booleans.
- All java.lang.Number objects convert to Java numbers.
- Java Character and String objects convert to JavaScript strings.
- The Java null value converts to the JavaScript null value.
- Any other Java object is simply wrapped in a JavaScript JavaObject object. You'll learn more about the JavaObject type when I discuss how JavaScript can script Java later in the chapter.

There are a few additional details to understand about number conversion. All Java numbers convert to JavaScript numbers. This includes Byte, Short, Integer, Long, Float, Double, and also java.math.BigInteger and java.math.BigDouble. Special floating-point values such as Infinity and NaN are supported in both languages and convert from one to the other. Note that the JavaScript number type is based on a 64-bit floating-point value akin to Java's double type. Not all long values can be precisely represented within a double, so if you pass a Java long to JavaScript, you may lose data. The same caution applies when using BigInteger and BigDecimal: trailing digits may be lost if the Java value has more precision than JavaScript can represent. Or if the Java value is larger than Double.MAX_VALUE, it will be converted to a JavaScript Infinity value.

Conversions in the other direction are similarly straightforward. When a JavaScript script stores a value in a variable (and therefore in a Bindings object) or when a JavaScript expression is evaluated, JavaScript values are converted to Java values as follows:

- JavaScript boolean values are converted to Java Boolean objects.

- JavaScript string values are converted to Java String objects.

- JavaScript numbers are converted to Java Double objects. Infinity and NaN values are properly converted.

- The JavaScript null and undefined values convert to the Java null value.

- JavaScript objects and arrays convert to Java objects of opaque type. These values can be passed back to JavaScript but have an unpublished API that is not intended for use by Java programs. Note that JavaScript wrapper objects of type String, Boolean, and Number are converted to opaque Java objects rather than to their corresponding Java types.

12.1.2 Compiling Scripts

If you want to execute the same script repeatedly (presumably using different bindings each time), it is more efficient to compile the script first and then invoke the compiled version. You can do this with code like this:

```
// This is the text of the script we want to compile.
String scripttext = "x * x";

// Get the script engine.
ScriptEngineManager scriptManager = new ScriptEngineManager();
ScriptEngine js = scriptManager.getEngineByExtension("js");

// Cast it to the Compilable interface to get compilation functionality.
Compilable compiler = (Compilable)js;

// Compile the script to a form that we can execute repeatedly.
CompiledScript script = compiler.compile(scripttext);

// Now execute the script five times, using a different value for the
// variable x each time.
Bindings bindings = js.createBindings();
for(int i = 0; i < 5; i++) {
    bindings.put("x", i);
    Object result = script.eval(bindings);
    System.out.printf("f(%d) = %s%n", i, result);
}
```

12.1.3 Invoking JavaScript Functions

The javax.script package also allows you to evaluate a script once, and then repeatedly invoke the functions defined by that script. You can do so like this:

```
// Obtain an interpreter or "ScriptEngine" to run the script
ScriptEngineManager scriptManager = new ScriptEngineManager();
ScriptEngine js = scriptManager.getEngineByExtension("js");

// Evaluate the script. We discard the result since we only
```

```
    // care about the function definition.
    js.eval("function f(x) { return x*x; }");

    // Now, invoke a function defined by the script.
    try {
        // Cast the ScriptEngine to the Invokable interface to
        // access its invocation functionality.
        Invocable invocable = (Invocable) js;
        for(int i = 0; i < 5; i++) {
            Object result = invocable.invoke("f", i);      // Compute f(i)
            System.out.printf("f(%d) = %s%n", i, result); // Print result
        }
    }
    catch(NoSuchMethodException e) {
        // This happens if the script did not define a function named "f".
        System.out.println(e);
    }
```

12.1.4 Implementing Interfaces in JavaScript

The Invocable interface demonstrated in the previous section also provides the ability to implement interfaces in JavaScript. Example 12-3 uses the JavaScript code in the file *listener.js* to implement the java.awt.event.KeyListener interface:

Example 12-3. Implementing a Java interface with JavaScript code

```
import javax.script.*;
import java.io.*;
import java.awt.event.*;
import javax.swing.*;

public class Keys {
    public static void main(String[] args) throws ScriptException, IOException
    {
        // Obtain an interpreter or "ScriptEngine" to run the script.
        ScriptEngineManager scriptManager = new ScriptEngineManager();
        ScriptEngine js = scriptManager.getEngineByExtension("js");

        // Evaluate the script. We discard the result since we only
        // care about the function definitions in it.
        js.eval(new FileReader("listener.js"));

        // Cast to Invocable and get an object that implements KeyListener.
        Invocable invocable = (Invocable) js;
        KeyListener listener = invocable.getInterface(KeyListener.class);

        // Now use that KeyListener in a very simple GUI.
        JFrame frame = new JFrame("Keys Demo");
        frame.addKeyListener(listener);
        frame.setSize(200, 200);
        frame.setVisible(true);
    }
}
```

Implementing an interface in JavaScript simply means defining a function with the same name as each method defined by the interface. Here, for example, is a simple script that implements KeyListener:

```
function keyPressed(e) {
    print("key pressed: " + String.fromCharCode(e.getKeyChar()));
}
function keyReleased(e) { /* do nothing */ }
function keyTyped(e) { /* do nothing */ }
```

Note that the JavaScript keyPressed() method defined here accepts a java.awt. event.KeyEvent object as its argument and actually invokes a method on that Java object. The next section explains how this is done.

12.2 Scripting Java

JavaScript interpreters often include a feature that allows JavaScript code to query and set the fields and invoke the methods of Java objects. If a script has access to an object through a method argument or a Bindings object, it can operate on that Java object almost as if it were a JavaScript object. And even if a script is not passed any references to Java objects, it can create its own. Netscape was the first to implement Java scripting with JavaScript when they enabled their Spidermonkey interpreter to script applets in a web browser. Netscape called their technology LiveConnect. The Rhino interpreter and Microsoft's JScript interpreter have adopted LiveConnect syntax, and the name LiveConnect is used throughout this chapter to refer to any implementation of JavaScript-to-Java scripting.

Let's begin this section with an overview of LiveConnect features. This overview is followed by subsections that explain LiveConnect in detail.

Note that Rhino and Spidermonkey implement somewhat different versions of LiveConnect. The features described here are Rhino features that can be used in scripts embedded in Java 6. Spidermonkey implements a subset of these features, and this is discussed in Chapter 23.

When a Java object is passed to a JavaScript script through a Bindings object or passed to a JavaScript function, JavaScript can manipulate that object almost as if it were a native JavaScript object. All the public fields and methods of the Java object are exposed as properties of the JavaScript wrapper object. For example, suppose a script is passed a reference to a Java object that draws charts. Now, suppose this object defines a field named lineColor whose type is String and that the JavaScript script stores its reference to the charting object in a variable named chart. JavaScript code can then query and set this field with code like this:

```
var chartcolor = chart.lineColor;  // Read a Java field.
chart.lineColor = "#ff00ff";        // Set a Java field.
```

JavaScript can even query and set the values of fields that are arrays. Suppose that the chart object defines two fields declared as follows (Java code):

```
public int numPoints;
public double[] points;
```

A JavaScript program might use these fields with code like this:

```
for(var i = 0; i < chart.numPoints; i++)
    chart.points[i] = i*i;
```

In addition to querying and setting the fields of a Java object, JavaScript can also invoke the methods of an object. Suppose, for example, that the chart object defines a method named redraw( ). This method takes no arguments and simply serves to tell the object that its points[] array has been modified and it should redraw itself. Java-Script can invoke this method just as if it were a JavaScript method:

```
chart.redraw( );
```

JavaScript can also call methods that take arguments and return values. Type conversions are performed as necessary on the method arguments and return values. Suppose the chart object defines Java methods like these:

```
public void setDomain(double xmin, double xmax);
public void setChartTitle(String title);
public String getXAxisLabel( );
```

JavaScript can call these methods with code like this:

```
chart.setDomain(0, 20);
chart.setChartTitle("y = x*x");
var label = chart.getXAxisLabel( );
```

Finally, note that Java methods can return Java objects as their return values, and JavaScript can read and write the public fields and invoke the public methods of these objects as well. JavaScript can also use Java objects as arguments to Java methods. Suppose the chart object defines a method named getXAxis( ) that returns another Java object that is an instance of a class named Axis. Suppose that the chart object also defines a method named setYAxis( ) that takes an Axis argument. Now, suppose further that Axis has a method named setTitle( ). You might use these methods with JavaScript code like this:

```
var xaxis = chart.getXAxis( );   // Get an Axis object.
var newyaxis = xaxis.clone( );    // Make a copy of it.
newyaxis.setTitle("Y");           // Call a method of it...
chart.setYAxis(newyaxis);         // ...and pass it to another method
```

LiveConnect allows JavaScript code to create its own Java objects so that JavaScript can script Java even if no Java objects are passed to it.

The global symbol Packages provides access to all the Java packages that the JavaScript interpreter knows about. The expression Packages.java.lang refers to the *java.lang* package, and the expression Packages.java.lang.System refers to the *java.lang.System* class. For convenience, the global symbol java is a shortcut for Packages.java. Java-Script code might invoke a static method of this *java.lang.System* class as follows:

```
// Invoke the static Java method System.getProperty()
var javaVersion = java.lang.System.getProperty("java.version");
```

This use of LiveConnect is not limited to system classes because LiveConnect allows you to use the JavaScript new operator to create new instances of Java classes. As an example, consider the following JavaScript code that creates and displays Java Swing GUI components:

```
// Define a shortcut to the javax.* package hierarchy.
var javax = Packages.javax;

// Create some Java objects.
var frame = new javax.swing.JFrame("Hello World");
var button = new javax.swing.JButton("Hello World");
var font = new java.awt.Font("SansSerif", java.awt.Font.BOLD, 24);

// Invoke methods on the new objects.
frame.add(button);
button.setFont(font);
frame.setSize(200, 200);
frame.setVisible(true);
```

To understand how LiveConnect does its job of connecting JavaScript to Java, you have to understand the JavaScript datatypes that LiveConnect uses. The following sections explain these JavaScript datatypes.

12.2.1 The JavaPackage Class

A *package* in Java is a collection of related Java classes. The JavaPackage class is a JavaScript datatype that represents a Java package. The properties of a JavaPackage are the classes that the package contains (classes are represented by the JavaClass class, which you'll see shortly), as well as any other packages that the package contains. The classes in a JavaPackage are not enumerable, so you cannot use a for/in loop to inspect package contents.

All JavaPackage objects are contained within a parent JavaPackage; the global property named Packages is a top-level JavaPackage that serves as the root of this package hierarchy. It has properties such as java and javax, which are JavaPackage objects that represent the various hierarchies of Java classes that are available to the interpreter. For example, the JavaPackage Packages.java contains the JavaPackage Packages.java.awt. For convenience, the global object also has a java property that is a shortcut to Packages.java. Thus, instead of typing Packages.java.awt, you can simply type java.awt.

To continue with the example, java.awt is a JavaPackage object that contains Java-Class objects such as java.awt.Button, which represents the *java.awt.Button* class.

But it also contains yet another JavaPackage object, java.awt.image, which represents the *java.awt.image* package in Java.

The JavaPackage class has a few shortcomings. There is no way for LiveConnect to tell in advance whether a property of a JavaPackage refers to a Java class or to another Java package, so JavaScript assumes that it is a class and tries to load a class. Thus, when you use an expression such as java.awt, LiveConnect first looks for a class by that name. If LiveConnect does not find a class, it assumes that the property refers to a package, but it has no way to ascertain that the package actually exists and has real classes in it. This causes the second shortcoming: if you misspell a class name, LiveConnect happily treats it as a package name, rather than telling you that the class you are trying to use does not exist.

12.2.2 The JavaClass Class

The JavaClass class is a JavaScript datatype that represents a Java class. A JavaClass object does not have any properties of its own: all of its properties represent (and have the same name as) the public static fields and methods of the represented Java class. These public static fields and methods are sometimes called *class fields* and *class methods* to indicate they are associated with a class rather than an object instance. Unlike the JavaPackage class, JavaClass does allow the use of the for/in loop to enumerate its properties. Note that JavaClass objects do not have properties representing the instance fields and methods of a Java class; individual instances of a Java class are represented by the JavaObject class, which is documented in the next section.

As shown earlier, JavaClass objects are contained in JavaPackage objects. For example, java.lang is a JavaPackage that contains a System property. Thus, java.lang.System is a JavaClass object, representing the Java class *java.lang.System*. This Java-Class object, in turn, has properties such as out and in that represent static fields of the *java.lang.System* class. You can use JavaScript to refer to any of the standard Java system classes in this same way. The *java.lang.Double* class is named java.lang.Double (or Packages.java.lang.Double), for example, and *javax.swing.JButton* class is Packages.javax.swing.JButton.

Another way to obtain a JavaClass object in JavaScript is to use the getClass( ) function. Given any JavaObject object, you can obtain a JavaClass object that represents the class of that Java object by passing the JavaObject to getClass( ).[*]

Once you have a JavaClass object, you can do several things with it. The JavaClass class implements the LiveConnect functionality that allows JavaScript programs to read and write the public static fields of Java classes and invoke the public static

---

[*] Don't confuse the JavaScript getClass( ) function, which returns a JavaClass object, with the Java getClass( ) method, which returns a java.lang.Class object.

methods of Java classes. For example, java.lang.System is a JavaClass. You can read the value of a static field of java.lang.System like this:

```
var java_console = java.lang.System.out;
```

Similarly, you can invoke a static method of java.lang.System with a line like this:

```
var java_version = java.lang.System.getProperty("java.version");
```

Recall that Java is a typed language: all fields and method arguments have types. If you attempt to set a field or pass an argument of the wrong type, an exception is thrown.

The JavaClass class has one more important feature. You can use JavaClass objects with the JavaScript new operator to create new instances of Java classes—i.e., to create JavaObject objects. The syntax for doing so is just as it is in JavaScript (and just as it is in Java):

```
var d = new java.lang.Double(1.23);
```

Finally, having created a JavaObject in this way, we can return to the getClass() function and show an example of its use:

```
var d = new java.lang.Double(1.23);   // Create a JavaObject.
var d_class = getClass(d);            // Obtain the JavaClass of the JavaObject.
if (d_class == java.lang.Double) ...; // This comparison will be true.
```

Instead of referring to a JavaClass with a cumbersome expression such as java.lang.Double, you can define a variable that serves as a shortcut:

```
var Double = java.lang.Double;
```

This mimics the Java import statement and can improve the efficiency of your program because LiveConnect does not have to look up the lang property of java and the Double property of java.lang.

12.2.3 Importing Packages and Classes

The Rhino version of LiveConnect defines global functions for importing Java packages and classes. To import a package, pass a JavaPackage object to importPackage(). To import a class, pass a JavaClass object to importClass():

```
importPackage(java.util);
importClass(java.awt.List);
```

importClass() copies a single JavaClass object from its JavaPackage object into the global object. The importClass() call above is equivalent to this code:

```
var List = java.awt.List;
```

importPackage() does not actually copy all JavaClass objects out of a JavaPackage and into the global object. Instead (and with much the same effect), it adds the package to an internal list of packages to search when unresolved identifiers are encountered and copies only the JavaClass objects that are actually used. Thus, after making the importPackage( ) call shown above, you might use the JavaScript identifier Map. If this is not the name of a declared variable or function, it is resolved as the JavaClass java.util.Map and then stored in a newly defined Map property of the global object.

Note that it is a bad idea to call importPackage( ) on the java.lang package because java.lang defines a number of classes with the same name as built-in JavaScript constructors and conversion functions. As an alternative to importing packages, you simply copy the JavaPackage object to a more convenient place:

```
var swing = Packages.javax.swing;
```

The importPackage( ) and importClass( ) functions are not available in Spidermonkey, but single-class importing is easy to simulate and is safer than cluttering up the global namespace with imported packages.

12.2.4 The JavaObject Class

The JavaObject class is a JavaScript datatype that represents a Java object. The JavaObject class is, in many ways, analogous to the JavaClass class. As with JavaClass, a JavaObject has no properties of its own; all of its properties represent (and have the same names as) the public instance fields and public instance methods of the Java object it represents. As with JavaClass, you can use a JavaScript for/in loop to enumerate all the properties of a JavaObject object. The JavaObject class implements the LiveConnect functionality that allows you to read and write the public instance fields and invoke the public methods of a Java object.

For example, if d is a JavaObject that represents an instance of the *java.lang.Double* class, you can invoke a method of that Java object with JavaScript code like this:

```
n = d.doubleValue( );
```

As shown earlier, the *java.lang.System* class also has a static field out. This field refers to a Java object of class *java.io.PrintStream*. In JavaScript, the corresponding JavaObject is referred to as:

```
java.lang.System.out
```

and a method of this object can be invoked like this:

```
java.lang.System.out.println("Hello world!");
```

A JavaObject object also allows you to read and write the public instance fields of the Java object it represents. Neither the *java.lang.Double* class nor the *java.io.PrintStream* class used in the preceding examples has any public instance fields, however. But suppose you use JavaScript to create an instance of the *java.awt.Rectangle* class:

```
r = new java.awt.Rectangle( );
```

You can then read and write its public instance fields with JavaScript code like the following:

```
r.x = r.y = 0;
r.width = 4;
```

```
r.height = 5;
var perimeter = 2*r.width + 2*r.height;
```

The beauty of LiveConnect is that it allows a Java object, r, to be used just as if it were a JavaScript object. Some caution is required, however: r is a JavaObject and does not behave identically to regular JavaScript objects. The differences will be detailed later. Also, remember that unlike JavaScript, the fields of Java objects and the arguments of their methods are typed. If you do not specify JavaScript values of the correct types, you cause JavaScript exceptions.

12.2.5 Java Methods

Because LiveConnect makes Java methods accessible through JavaScript properties, you can treat those methods as data values, just as you can with JavaScript functions. Note, however, that Java instance methods are in fact methods and not functions, and they must be invoked through a Java object. Static Java methods can be treated like JavaScript functions, however, and may be imported into the global namespace for convenience:

```
var isDigit = java.lang.Character.isDigit;
```

12.2.5.1 Property accessor methods

In the Rhino version of LiveConnect, if a Java object has instance methods that look like property accessor (getter/setter) methods according to the JavaBeans naming conventions, LiveConnect makes the property exposed by those methods available directly as a JavaScript property. For example, consider the javax.swing.JFrame and javax.swing.JButton objects shown earlier. JButton has setFont( ) and getFont( ) methods, and JFrame has setVisible( ) and isVisible( ) methods. LiveConnect makes these methods available, but it also defines a font property for JButton objects and a visible property for JFrame objects. As a result, you can replace lines of code like these:

```
button.setFont(font);
frame.setVisible(true);
```

with lines like these:

```
button.font = font;
frame.visible = true;
```

12.2.5.2 Overloaded methods

Java classes can define more than one method by the same name. If you enumerate the properties of a JavaObject that has an overloaded instance method, you will see only a single property with the overloaded name. Usually, LiveConnect will invoke the correct method for you, based on the types of arguments you are supplying.

Occasionally, however, you may need to explicitly refer to a single overloading of a method. JavaObject and JavaClass make overloaded methods available through special properties that include the method name and the method argument types. Suppose you have a JavaObject o that has two methods named f, one that accepts an int argument and another that accepts a boolean argument. o.f is a function that invokes whichever Java method better matches its own argument. However, you can explicitly distinguish between the two Java methods with code like this:

```
var f = o['f'];                 // either method
var boolfunc = o['f(boolean)'];  // boolean method
var intfunc = o['f(int)'];       // int method
```

When you specify parentheses as part of a property name, you cannot use the regular "." notation to access it and must express it as a string within square brackets.

Note that the JavaClass type can also distinguish overridden static methods.

12.2.6 The JavaArray Class

The final LiveConnect datatype for JavaScript is the JavaArray class. As you might expect by now, instances of this class represent Java arrays and provide the Live-Connect functionality that allows JavaScript to read the elements of Java arrays. Like JavaScript arrays (and like Java arrays), a JavaArray object has a length property that specifies the number of elements it contains. The elements of a JavaArray object are read with the standard JavaScript [ ] array index operator. They can also be enumerated with a for/in loop. You can use JavaArray objects to access multidimensional arrays (actually arrays of arrays), just as in JavaScript or Java.

For example, let's create an instance of the *java.awt.Polygon* class:

```
p = new java.awt.Polygon();
```

The JavaObject p has properties xpoints and ypoints that are JavaArray objects representing Java arrays of integers. (To learn the names and types of these properties, look up the documentation for *java.awt.Polygon* in a Java reference manual.) You can use these JavaArray objects to randomly initialize the Java polygon with code like this:

```
for(var i = 0; i < p.xpoints.length; i++)
    p.xpoints[i] = Math.round(Math.random()*100);
for(var i = 0; i < p.ypoints.length; i++)
    p.ypoints[i] = Math.round(Math.random()*100);
```

12.2.6.1 Creating Java arrays

LiveConnect has no built-in syntax for creating Java arrays or for converting Java-Script arrays to Java arrays. If you need to create a Java array, you must do so explicitly with the java.lang.reflect package:

```
var p = new java.awt.Polygon();
p.xpoints = java.lang.reflect.Array.newInstance(java.lang.Integer.TYPE,5);
p.ypoints = java.lang.reflect.Array.newInstance(java.lang.Integer.TYPE,5);
for(var i = 0; i < p.xpoints.length; i++) {
    p.xpoints[i] = i;
    p.ypoints[i] = i * i;
}
```

12.2.7 Implementing Interfaces with LiveConnect

Rhino LiveConnect allows JavaScript scripts to implement Java interfaces using a simple syntax: simply treat the interface's JavaClass object as a constructor and pass a JavaScript object that has properties for each of the interface's methods. You can use this feature, for example, to add an event handler to the GUI creation code shown earlier:

```
// Import the stuff we'll need.
importClass(Packages.javax.swing.JFrame);
importClass(Packages.javax.swing.JButton);
importClass(java.awt.event.ActionListener);

// Create some Java objects.
var frame = new JFrame("Hello World");
var button = new JButton("Hello World");

// Implement the ActionListener interface.
var listener = new ActionListener({
        actionPerformed: function(e) { print("Hello!"); }
    });

// Tell the button what to do when clicked.
button.addActionListener(listener);

// Put the button in its frame and display.
frame.add(button);
frame.setSize(200, 200);
frame.setVisible(true);
```

12.2.8 LiveConnect Data Conversion

Java is a strongly typed language with a relatively large number of datatypes, while JavaScript is an untyped language with a relatively small number of types. Because of this major structural difference between the two languages, one of the central responsibilities of LiveConnect is data conversion. When JavaScript sets a Java field or passes an argument to a Java method, a JavaScript value must be converted to an equivalent Java value, and when JavaScript reads a Java field or obtains the return value of a Java method, that Java value must be converted to a compatible JavaScript value. Unfortunately, LiveConnect data conversion is done somewhat differently than the data conversion that is performed by the javax.script package.

Figures 12-1 and 12-2 illustrate how data conversion is performed when JavaScript writes Java values and when it reads them, respectively.

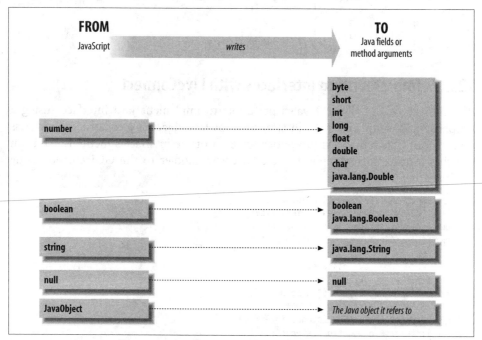

Figure 12-1. Data conversions performed when JavaScript writes Java values

Note the following points about the data conversions illustrated in Figure 12-1:

- Figure 12-1 does not show all possible conversions from JavaScript types to Java types. This is because JavaScript-to-JavaScript type conversions can occur before the JavaScript-to-Java conversion takes place. For example, if you pass a Java-Script number to a Java method that expects a *java.lang.String* argument, Java-Script first converts that number to a JavaScript string, which can then be converted to a Java string.

- A JavaScript number can be converted to any of the primitive Java numeric types. The actual conversion performed depends, of course, on the type of the Java field being set or the method argument being passed. Note that you can lose precision doing this, for example, when you pass a large number to a Java field of type short or when you pass a floating-point value to a Java integral type.

- A JavaScript number can also be converted to an instance of the Java class *java.lang.Double* but not to an instance of a related class, such as *java.lang.Integer* or *java.lang.Float*.

- JavaScript does not have any representation for character data, so a JavaScript number may also be converted to the Java primitive char type.

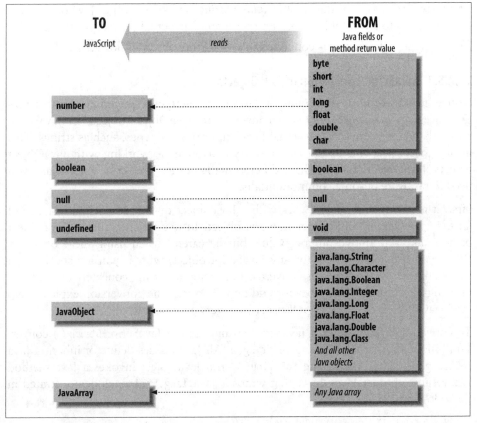

Figure 12-2. Data conversions performed when JavaScript reads Java values

- A JavaObject in JavaScript is "unwrapped" when passed to Java—that is, it is converted to the Java object it represents. Note, however, that JavaClass objects in JavaScript are not converted to instances of *java.lang.Class*, as might be expected.

- JavaScript arrays are not converted to Java arrays. JavaScript objects, arrays, and functions are converted to Java objects that do not have a standardized API and are usually considered opaque.

Also note these points about the conversions illustrated in Figure 12-2:

- Since JavaScript does not have a type for character data, the Java primitive char type is converted to a JavaScript number, not a string, as might be expected.

- A Java instance of *java.lang.Double*, *java.lang.Integer*, or a similar class is not converted to a JavaScript number. Like any Java object, it is converted to a Java-Object object in JavaScript.

- A Java string is an instance of *java.lang.String*, so like any other Java object, it is converted to a JavaObject object rather than to an actual JavaScript string.
- Any type of Java array is converted to a JavaArray object in JavaScript.

12.2.8.1 JavaScript conversion of JavaObjects

Notice in Figure 12-2 that quite a few Java datatypes, including Java strings (instances of *java.lang.String*), are converted to JavaObject objects in JavaScript rather than being converted to actual JavaScript primitive types, such as strings. This means that when you use LiveConnect, you'll often be working with JavaObject objects. JavaObject objects behave differently than other JavaScript objects, and you need to be aware of some common pitfalls.

First, it is not uncommon to work with a JavaObject that represents an instance of *java.lang.Double* or some other numeric object. In many ways, such a JavaObject behaves like a primitive number value, but be careful when using the + operator. When you use a JavaObject (or any JavaScript object) with +, you are specifying a string context, so the object is converted to a string for string concatenation instead of being converted to a number for addition. To make the conversion explicit, pass the JavaObject to the JavaScript Number( ) conversion function.

To convert a JavaObject to a JavaScript string, use the JavaScript String( ) conversion function rather than calling toString( ). All Java classes define or inherit a Java toString( ) method, so calling toString( ) on a JavaObject invokes a Java method and returns another JavaObject that wraps a java.lang.String, as demonstrated in the following code:

```
var d = new java.lang.Double(1.234);
var s = d.toString();   // Converts to a java.lang.String, not a JavaScript string
print(typeof s);        // Prints "object" since s is a JavaObject
s = String(d);          // Now convert to a JavaScript string
print(typeof s);        // Displays "string".
```

Note also that JavaScript strings have a length property that is a number. A JavaObject that wraps a java.lang.String, on the other hand, has a length property that is a function representing the length( ) method of the Java string.

Another strange case is the JavaObject java.lang.Boolean.FALSE. Used in a string context, this value converts to false. Used in a Boolean context, however, it converts to true! This is because the JavaObject is non-null. The value held by the object simply does not matter for this conversion.

PART II

Client-Side JavaScript

This part of the book, Chapters 13 through 23, documents JavaScript as it is implemented in web browsers. These chapters introduce a variety of scriptable objects that represent the web browser and the contents of HTML and XML documents:

Part (IV)

Client-Side JavaScript

CHAPTER 13

JavaScript in Web Browsers

The first part of this book described the core JavaScript language. Part II moves on to JavaScript as used within web browsers, commonly called client-side JavaScript.[*] Most of the examples you've seen so far, while legal JavaScript code, have no particular context; they are JavaScript fragments that run in no specified environment. This chapter provides that context. It starts with an overview of the web browser programming environment. Next, it discusses how to actually embed JavaScript code within HTML documents, using `<script>` tags, HTML event handler attributes, and JavaScript URLs. These sections on embedding JavaScript are followed by a section that explains the client-side JavaScript execution model: how and when web browsers run JavaScript code. Next are sections that cover three important topics in JavaScript programming: compatibility, accessibility, and security. The chapter concludes with an short description of web-related embeddings of the JavaScript language other than client-side JavaScript.

When JavaScript is embedded in a web browser, the browser exposes a powerful and diverse set of capabilities and allows them to be scripted. The chapters that follow Chapter 13 each focus on one major area of client-side JavaScript functionality:

- Chapter 14, *Scripting Browser Windows*, explains how JavaScript can script web browser windows by, for example, opening and closing windows, displaying dialog boxes, causing windows to load specified URLs, or causing windows to go back or forward in their browsing history. This chapter also covers other, miscellaneous features of client-side JavaScript that happen to be associated with the Window object in client-side JavaScript.

- Chapter 15, *Scripting Documents*, explains how JavaScript can interact with the document content displayed within a web browser window and how it can find, insert, delete, or alter content within a document.

---

[*] The term *client-side JavaScript* is left over from the days when JavaScript was used in only two places: web browsers (clients) and web servers. As JavaScript is adopted as a scripting language in more and more environments, the term *client-side* makes less and less sense because it doesn't specify the client side of *what*. Nevertheless, I'll continue to use the term in this book.

- Chapter 16, *Cascading Style Sheets and Dynamic HTML*, covers the interaction of JavaScript and CSS and shows how JavaScript code can alter the presentation of a document by scripting CSS styles, classes, and stylesheets. One particularly potent result of combining scripting with CSS is Dynamic HTML (or DHTML) in which HTML content can be hidden and shown, moved, and even animated.

- Chapter 17, *Events and Event Handling*, explains events and event handling and shows how JavaScript adds interactivity to a web page by allowing it to respond to a user's input.

- Chapter 18, *Forms and Form Elements*, covers forms within HTML documents and shows how JavaScript can gather, validate, process, and submit user input with forms.

- Chapter 19, *Cookies and Client-Side Persistence*, shows how JavaScript scripts can persistently store data using HTTP cookies.

- Chapter 20, *Scripting HTTP*, introduces HTTP scripting (commonly known as Ajax) and demonstrates how JavaScript can communicate with web servers.

- Chapter 21, *JavaScript and XML*, shows how JavaScript can create, load, parse, transform, query, serialize, and extract information from XML documents.

- Chapter 22, *Scripted Client-Side Graphics*, demonstrates common JavaScript image-manipulation techniques that can create image rollovers and animations in web pages. It also demonstrates several techniques for dynamically drawing vector graphics under JavaScript control.

- Chapter 23, *Scripting Java Applets and Flash Movies*, explains how JavaScript can interact with Java applets and Flash movies embedded in a web page.

13.1 The Web Browser Environment

To understand client-side JavaScript, you must understand the programming environment provided by a web browser. The following sections introduce three important features of that programming environment:

- The Window object that serves as the global object and global execution context for client-side JavaScript code

- The client-side object hierarchy and the Document Object Model that forms a part of it

- The event-driven programming model

These sections are followed by a discussion of the proper role of JavaScript in web application development.

13.1.1 The Window as Global Execution Context

The primary task of a web browser is to display HTML documents in a window. In client-side JavaScript, the Document object represents an HTML document, and the Window object represents the browser window (or frame) that displays the document. While the Document and Window objects are both important to client-side JavaScript, the Window object is more important for one substantial reason: the Window object is the global object in client-side programming.

Recall from Chapter 4 that in every implementation of JavaScript there is always a global object at the head of the scope chain; the properties of this global object are global variables. In client-side JavaScript, the Window object is the global object. The Window object defines a number of properties and methods that allow you to manipulate the web browser window. It also defines properties that refer to other important objects, such as the document property for the Document object. Finally, the Window object has two self-referential properties, window and self. You can use either global variable to refer directly to the Window object.

Since the Window object is the global object in client-side JavaScript, all global variables are defined as properties of the window. For example, the following two lines of code perform essentially the same function:

```
var answer = 42;      // Declare and initialize a global variable
window.answer = 42;   // Create a new property of the Window object
```

The Window object represents a web browser window (or a frame within a window; in client-side JavaScript, top-level windows and frames are essentially equivalent). It is possible to write applications that use multiple windows (or frames). Each window involved in an application has a unique Window object and defines a unique execution context for client-side JavaScript code. In other words, a global variable declared by JavaScript code in one window is not a global variable within a second window. However, JavaScript code in the second window *can* access a global variable of the first window, subject to certain security restrictions. These issues are considered in detail in Chapter 14.

13.1.2 The Client-Side Object Hierarchy and the DOM

The Window object is the key object in client-side JavaScript. All other client-side objects are accessed via this object. For example, every Window object defines a document property that refers to the Document object associated with the window and a location property that refers to the Location object associated with the window. When a web browser displays a framed document, the frames[] array of the top-level Window object contains references to the Window objects that represent the frames. Thus, in client-side JavaScript, the expression document refers to the Document object of the current window; the expression frames[1].document refers to the Document object of the second frame of the current window.

The Document object (and other client-side JavaScript objects) also have properties that refer to other objects. For example, every Document object has a forms[] array containing Form objects that represent any HTML forms appearing in the document. To refer to one of these forms, you might write:

```
window.document.forms[0]
```

To continue with the same example, each Form object has an elements[] array containing objects that represent the various HTML form elements (input fields, buttons, etc.) that appear within the form. In extreme cases, you can write code that refers to an object at the end of a whole chain of objects, ending up with expressions as complex as this one:

```
parent.frames[0].document.forms[0].elements[3].options[2].text
```

As shown earlier, the Window object is the global object at the head of the scope chain, and all client-side objects in JavaScript are accessible as properties of other objects. This means that there is a hierarchy of JavaScript objects, with the Window object at its root. Figure 13-1 shows this hierarchy.

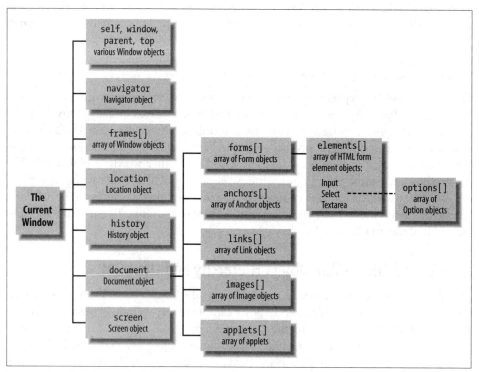

Figure 13-1. The client-side object hierarchy and Level 0 DOM

Note that Figure 13-1 shows just the object properties that refer to other objects. Most of the objects shown in the diagram have methods and properties other than those shown.

Many of the objects pictured in Figure 13-1 descend from the Document object. This subtree of the larger client-side object hierarchy is known as the document object model (DOM), which is interesting because it has been the focus of a standardization effort. Figure 13-1 illustrates the Document objects that have become de facto standards because they are consistently implemented by all major browsers. Collectively, they are known as the Level 0 DOM because they form a base level of document functionality that JavaScript programmers can rely on in all browsers. These basic Document objects are covered in Chapter 15, which also explains a more advanced document object model that has been standardized by the W3C. HTML forms are part of the DOM but are specialized enough that they are covered in their own chapter, Chapter 18.

13.1.3 The Event-Driven Programming Model

In the early days of computing, computer programs often ran in batch mode; they read in a batch of data, did some computation on that data, and then wrote out the results. Later, with time-sharing and text-based terminals, limited kinds of interactivity became possible; the program could ask the user for input, and the user could type in data. The computer then processed the data and displayed the results onscreen.

Nowadays, with graphical displays and pointing devices such as mice, the situation is different. Programs are generally event-driven; they respond to asynchronous user input in the form of mouse clicks and keystrokes in a way that depends on the position of the mouse pointer. A web browser is just such a graphical environment. An HTML document contains an embedded graphical user interface (GUI), so client-side JavaScript uses the event-driven programming model.

It is perfectly possible to write a static JavaScript program that does not accept user input and does exactly the same thing every time it is run. Sometimes this sort of program is useful. More often, however, you'll want to write dynamic programs that interact with the user. To do this, you must be able to respond to user input.

In client-side JavaScript, the web browser notifies programs of user input by generating *events*. There are various types of events, such as keystroke events, mouse motion events, and so on. When an event occurs, the web browser attempts to invoke an appropriate *event handler* function to respond to the event. Thus, to write dynamic, interactive client-side JavaScript programs, you must define appropriate event handlers and register them with the system, so that the browser can invoke them at appropriate times.

If you are not already accustomed to the event-driven programming model, it can take a little getting used to. In the old model, you wrote a single, monolithic block of code that followed some well-defined flow of control and ran to completion from beginning to end. Event-driven programming stands this model on its head. In event-driven programming, you write a number of independent (but mutually interacting) event handlers. You do not invoke these handlers directly but allow the system to invoke them at the appropriate times. Since they are triggered by the user's input, the handlers are invoked at unpredictable, asynchronous times. Much of the time, your program is not running at all but merely sitting, waiting for the system to invoke one of its event handlers.

The sections that follow explain how JavaScript code is embedded within HTML files. It shows how to define both static blocks of code that run synchronously from start to finish and event handlers that are invoked asynchronously by the system. Events and event handling are discussed again in Chapter 15, and then events are covered in detail in Chapter 17.

13.1.4 The Role of JavaScript on the Web

The introduction to this chapter included a list of the web browser capabilities that can be scripted with client-side JavaScript. Note, however, that listing what JavaScript *can* be used for is not the same as explaining what JavaScript *ought* to be used for. This section attempts to explain the proper role of JavaScript in web application development.

Web browsers display HTML-structured text styled with CSS stylesheets. HTML defines the content, and CSS supplies the presentation. Properly used, JavaScript adds *behavior* to the content and its presentation. The role of JavaScript is to enhance a user's browsing experience, making it easier to obtain or transmit information. The user's experience should not be dependent on JavaScript, but JavaScript can serve to facilitate that experience. JavaScript can do this in any number of ways. Here are some examples:

- Creating visual effects such as image rollovers that subtly guide a user and help with page navigation
- Sorting the columns of a table to make it easier for a user to find what he needs
- Hiding certain content and revealing details selectively as the user "drills down" into that content
- Streamlining the browsing experience by communicating directly with a web server so that new information can be displayed without requiring a complete page reload

13.1.5 Unobtrusive JavaScript

A new client-side programming paradigm known as *unobtrusive JavaScript* has been gaining currency within the web development community. As its name implies, this paradigm holds that JavaScript should not draw attention to itself; it should not obtrude.[*] It should not obtrude on users viewing a web page, on content authors creating HTML markup, or on web designers creating HTML templates or CSS stylesheets.

There is no specific formula for writing unobtrusive JavaScript code. However, a number of helpful practices, discussed elsewhere in this book, will put you on the right track.

The first goal of unobtrusive JavaScript is to keep JavaScript code separate from HTML markup. This keeps content separate from behavior in the same way that putting CSS in external stylesheets keeps content separate from presentation. To achieve this goal, you put all your JavaScript code in external files and include those files into your HTML pages with `<script src=>` tags (see Section 13.2.2 for details). If you are strict about the separation of content and behavior, you won't even include JavaScript code in the event-handler attributes of your HTML files. Instead, you will write JavaScript code (in an external file) that registers event handlers on the HTML elements that need them (Chapter 17 describes how to do this).

As a corollary to this goal, you should strive to make your external files of JavaScript code as modular as possible using techniques described in Chapter 10. This allows you to include multiple independent modules of code into the same web page without worrying about the variables and functions of one module overwriting the variables and functions of another.

The second goal of unobtrusive JavaScript is that it must degrade gracefully. Your scripts should be conceived and designed as enhancements to HTML content, but that content should still be available without your JavaScript code (as will happen, for example, when a user disables JavaScript in her browser). An important technique for graceful degradation is called *feature testing*: before taking any actions, your JavaScript modules should first ensure that the client-side features they require are available in the browser in which the code is running. Feature testing is a compatibility technique described in more detail in Section 13.6.3.

A third goal of unobtrusive JavaScript is that it must not degrade the accessibility of an HTML page (and ideally it should enhance accessibility). If the inclusion of JavaScript code reduces the accessibility of web pages, that JavaScript code has obtruded on the disabled users who rely on accessible web pages. JavaScript accessibility is described in more detail in Section 13.7.

---

[*] "Obtrude" is an obscure synonym for "intrude." The American Heritage dictionary cites: "To impose…on others with undue insistence or without invitation."

Other formulations of unobtrusive JavaScript may include other goals in addition to the three described here. One primary source from which to learn more about unobtrusive scripting is "The JavaScript Manifesto," published by the DOM Scripting Task Force at *http://domscripting.webstandards.org/?page_id=2*.

13.2 Embedding Scripts in HTML

Client-side JavaScript code is embedded within HTML documents in a number of ways:

- Between a pair of <script> and </script> tags
- From an external file specified by the src attribute of a <script> tag
- In an event handler, specified as the value of an HTML attribute such as onclick or onmouseover
- In a URL that uses the special javascript: protocol

This section covers <script> tags. Event handlers and JavaScript URLs are covered later in the chapter.

13.2.1 The <script> Tag

Client-side JavaScript scripts are part of an HTML file and are coded within <script> and </script> tags:

```
<script>
// Your JavaScript code goes here
</script>
```

In XHTML, the content of a <script> tag is treated like any other content. If your JavaScript code contains the < or & characters, these characters are interpreted as XML markup. For this reason, it is best to put all JavaScript code within a CDATA section if you are using XHTML:

```
<script><![CDATA[// Your JavaScript code goes here
]]></script>
```

A single HTML document may contain any number of <script> elements. Multiple, separate scripts are executed in the order in which they appear within the document (see the defer attribute in Section 13.2.4 for an exception, however). While separate scripts within a single file are executed at different times during the loading and parsing of the HTML file, they constitute part of the same JavaScript program: functions and variables defined in one script are available to all scripts that follow in the same file. For example, you can have the following script in the <head> of an HTML page:

```
<script>function square(x) { return x*x; }</script>
```

Later in the same HTML page, you can refer to the `square()` function, even though it's in a different script block. The context that matters is the HTML page, not the script block:[*]

```
<script>alert(square(2));</script>
```

Example 13-1 shows a sample HTML file that includes a simple JavaScript program. Note the difference between this example and many of the code fragments shown earlier in this book: this one is integrated with an HTML file and has a clear context in which it runs. Note also the use of a `language` attribute in the `<script>` tag; this is explained in Section 13.2.3.

Example 13-1. A simple JavaScript program in an HTML file

```
<html>
<head>
<title>Today's Date</title>
<script language="JavaScript">
// Define a function for later use
function print_todays_date() {
    var d = new Date();                       // Get today's date and time
    document.write(d.toLocaleString());       // Insert it into the document
}
</script>
</head>
<body>
The date and time are:<br>
<script language="JavaScript">
  // Now call the function we defined above
  print_todays_date();
</script>
</body>
</html>
```

Example 13-1 also demonstrates the `document.write()` function. Client-side Java-Script code can use this function to output HTML text into the document at the location of the script (see Chapter 15 for further details on this method). Note that the possibility that scripts can generate output for insertion into the HTML document means that the HTML parser must interpret JavaScript scripts as part of the parsing process. It is not possible to simply concatenate all script text in a document and run it as one large script after the document has been parsed because any script within a document may alter the document (see the discussion of the `defer` attribute in Section 13.2.4).

---

[*] The `alert()` function used here is a simple way to display output in client-side JavaScript: it converts its argument to a string and displays that string in a pop-up dialog box. See Section 14.5 for details on the `alert()` method, and see Example 15-9 for an alternative to `alert()` that does not pop up a dialog box that must be clicked away.

13.2.2 Scripts in External Files

The `<script>` tag supports a `src` attribute that specifies the URL of a file containing JavaScript code. It is used like this:

```
<script src="../../scripts/util.js"></script>
```

A JavaScript file typically has a *.js* extension and contains pure JavaScript, without `<script>` tags or any other HTML.

A `<script>` tag with the `src` attribute specified behaves exactly as if the contents of the specified JavaScript file appeared directly between the `<script>` and `</script>` tags. Any code or markup that appears between these tags is ignored. Note that the closing `</script>` tag is required even when the `src` attribute is specified, and there is no JavaScript between the `<script>` and `</script>` tags.

There are a number of advantages to using the `src` attribute:

- It simplifies your HTML files by allowing you to remove large blocks of Java-Script code from them—that is, it helps keep content and behavior separate. Using the `src` attribute is the cornerstone of unobtrusive JavaScript programming. (See Section 13.1.5 for more on this programming philosophy.)

- When you have a function or other JavaScript code used by several different HTML files, you can keep it in a single file and read it into each HTML file that needs it. This makes code maintenance much easier.

- When JavaScript functions are used by more than one page, placing them in a separate JavaScript file allows them to be cached by the browser, making them load more quickly. When JavaScript code is shared by multiple pages, the time savings of caching more than outweigh the small delay required for the browser to open a separate network connection to download the JavaScript file the first time it is requested.

- Because the `src` attribute takes an arbitrary URL as its value, a JavaScript program or web page from one web server can employ code exported by other web servers. Much Internet advertising relies on this fact.

This last point has important security implications. The same-origin security policy described in Section 13.8.2 prevents JavaScript in a document from one domain from interacting with content from another domain. However, notice that the origin of the script itself does not matter: only the origin of the document in which the script is embedded. Therefore, the same-origin policy does not apply in this case: JavaScript code can interact with the document in which it is embedded, even when the code has a different origin than the document. When you use the `src` attribute to include a script in your page, you are giving the author of that script (and the webmaster of the domain from which the script is loaded) complete control over your web page.

13.2.3 Specifying the Scripting Language

Although JavaScript was the original scripting language for the Web and remains the most common by far, it is not the only one. The HTML specification is language-agnostic, and browser vendors can support whatever scripting languages they choose. In practice, the only alternative to JavaScript is Microsoft's Visual Basic Scripting Edition,* which is supported by Internet Explorer.

Since there is more than one possible scripting language, you must tell the web browser what language your scripts are written in. This enables it to interpret the scripts correctly and to skip scripts written in languages that it does not know how to interpret. You can specify the default scripting language for a file with the HTTP Content-Script-Type header, and you can simulate this header with the HTML <meta> tag. To specify that all your scripts are in JavaScript (unless specified otherwise), just put the following tag in the <head> of all your HTML documents:

```
<meta http-equiv="Content-Script-Type" content="text/javascript">
```

In practice, browsers assume that JavaScript is the default scripting language even if your server omits the Content-Script-Type header and your pages omit the <meta> tag. If you do not specify a default scripting language, however, or wish to override your default, you should use the type attribute of the <script> tag:

```
<script type="text/javascript"></script>
```

The traditional MIME type for JavaScript programs is "text/javascript". Another type that has been used is "application/x-javascript" (the "x-" prefix indicates that it is an experimental, nonstandard type). RFC 4329 standardizes the "text/javascript" type because it is in common use. However, because JavaScript programs are not really text documents, it marks this type as obsolete and recommends "application/javascript" (without the "x-") instead. At the time of this writing, "application/javascript" is not well supported, however. Once it has become well supported, the most appropriate <script> and <meta> tags will be:

```
<script type="application/javascript"></script>
<meta http-equiv="Content-Script-Type" content="application/javascript">
```

When the <script> tag was first introduced, it was a nonstandard extension to HTML and did not support the type attribute. Instead, the scripting language was defined with the language attribute. This attribute simply specifies the common name of the scripting language. If you are writing JavaScript code, use the language attribute as follows:

```
<script language="JavaScript">
    // JavaScript code goes here
</script>
```

---

* Also known as VBScript. The only browser that supports VBScript is Internet Explorer, so scripts written in this language are not portable. VBScript interfaces with HTML objects the same way JavaScript does, but the core language itself has a different syntax than JavaScript. VBScript is not documented in this book.

And if you are writing a script in VBScript, use the attribute like this:

```
<script language="VBScript">
    ' VBScript code goes here (' is a comment character like // in JavaScript)
</script>
```

The HTML 4 specification standardized the `<script>` tag, but it deprecated the language attribute because there is no standard set of names for scripting languages. Sometimes you'll see `<script>` tags that use the type attribute for standards compliance and the language attribute for backward compatibility with older browsers:

```
<script type="text/javascript" language="JavaScript"></script>
```

The language attribute is sometimes used to specify the version of JavaScript in which a script is written, with tags like these:

```
<script language="JavaScript1.2"></script>
<script language="JavaScript1.5"></script>
```

In theory, web browsers ignore scripts written in versions of JavaScript that they do not support. That is, an old browser that does not support JavaScript 1.5 will not attempt to run a script that has a language attribute of "JavaScript1.5". Older web browsers respect this version number, but because the core JavaScript language has remained stable for a number of years, many newer browsers ignore any version number specified with the language attribute.

13.2.4 The defer Attribute

As mentioned earlier, a script may call the `document.write()` method to dynamically add content to a document. Because of this, when the HTML parser encounters a script, it must normally stop parsing the document and wait for the script to execute. The HTML 4 standard defines a defer attribute of the `<script>` tag to address this problem.

If you write a script that does not produce any document output—for example, a script that defines a function but never calls `document.write()`—you may use the defer attribute in the `<script>` tag as a hint to the browser that it is safe to continue parsing the HTML document and defer execution of the script until it encounters a script that cannot be deferred. Deferring a script is particularly useful when it is loaded from an external file; if it is not deferred, the browser must wait until the script has loaded before it can resume parsing the containing document. Deferring may result in improved performance in browsers that take advantage of the defer attribute. In HTML the defer attribute does not have a value; it simply must be present in the tag:

```
<script defer>
    // Any JavaScript code that does not call document.write()
</script>
```

In XHTML, however, a value is required:

```
<script defer="defer"></script>
```

At the time of this writing, Internet Explorer is the only browser that uses the defer attribute. It does this when it is combined with the src attribute. It does not implement it quite correctly, however, because deferred scripts are always deferred until the end of the document, instead of simply being deferred until the next nondeferred script is encountered. This means that deferred scripts in IE are executed out of order and must not define any functions or set any variables that are required by the non-deferred scripts that follow.

13.2.5 The <noscript> Tag

HTML defines the <noscript> element to hold content that should be rendered only if JavaScript has been disabled in the browser. Ideally, you should to craft your web pages so that JavaScript serves as an enhancement only, and the pages "degrade gracefully" and still function without JavaScript. When this is not possible, however, you can use <noscript> to notify the users that JavaScript is required and possibly to provide a link to alternative content.

13.2.6 The </script> Tag

You may at some point find yourself writing a script that uses the document.write( ) method or innerHTML property to output some other script (typically into another window or frame). If you do this, you'll need to output a </script> tag to terminate the script you are creating. You must be careful, though: the HTML parser makes no attempt to understand your JavaScript code, and if it sees the string "</script>" in your code, even if it appears within quotes, it assumes that it has found the closing tag of the currently running script. To avoid this problem, simply break up the tag into pieces and write it out using an expression such as "</" + "script>":

```
<script>
f1.document.write("<script>");
f1.document.write("document.write('<h2>This is the quoted script</h2>')");
f1.document.write("</" + "script>");
</script>
```

Alternatively, you can escape the / in </script> with a backslash:

```
f1.document.write("<\/script>");
```

In XHTML, scripts are enclosed in CDATA sections, and this problem with closing </script> tags does not occur.

13.2.7 Hiding Scripts from Old Browsers

When JavaScript was new, some browsers did not recognize the <script> tag and would therefore (correctly) render the content of this tag as text. The user visiting the web page would see JavaScript code formatted into big meaningless paragraphs and presented as web page content! The workaround to this problem was a simple hack that used HTML comments inside the script tag. JavaScript programmers habitually wrote their scripts like this:

```
<script language="JavaScript">
<!-- Begin HTML comment that hides the script
    // JavaScript statements go here
    //           .
    //           .
// End HTML comment that hides the script -->
</script>
```

Or, more compactly, like this:

```
<script><!--
// script body goes here
//--></script>
```

In order to make this work, client-side JavaScript tweaks the core JavaScript language slightly so that the character sequence <!-- at the beginning of a script behaves just like //: it introduces a single-line comment.

The browsers that required this commenting hack are long gone, but you will probably still encounter the hack in existing web pages.

13.2.8 Nonstandard Script Attributes

Microsoft has defined two completely nonstandard attributes for the <script> tag that work only in Internet Explorer. The event and for attributes allow you to define event handlers using the <script> tag. The event attribute specifies the name of the event to be handled, and the for attribute specifies the name or ID of the element for which the event is to be handled. The content of the script is executed when the specified event occurs on the specified element.

These attributes work only in IE, and their functionality can easily be achieved in other ways. You should never use them; they are mentioned here only so that you will know what they are if you encounter them in existing web pages.

13.3 Event Handlers in HTML

JavaScript code in a script is executed once: when the HTML file that contains it is read into the web browser. A program that uses only this sort of static script cannot dynamically respond to the user. More dynamic programs define event handlers that are automatically invoked by the web browser when certain events occur—for example, when the user clicks on a button within a form. Because events in client-side JavaScript originate from HTML objects (such as buttons), event handlers can be defined as attributes of those objects. For example, to define an event handler that is invoked when the user clicks on a checkbox in a form, you specify the handler code as an attribute of the HTML tag that defines the checkbox:

```
<input type="checkbox" name="options" value="giftwrap"
    onclick="giftwrap = this.checked;"
>
```

What's of interest here is the onclick attribute. The string value of the onclick attribute may contain one or more JavaScript statements. If there is more than one statement, the statements must be separated from each other with semicolons. When the specified event—in this case, a click—occurs on the checkbox, the JavaScript code within the string is executed.

While you can include any number of JavaScript statements within an event-handler definition, a common technique is to simply use event-handler attributes to invoke functions that are defined elsewhere within <script> tags. This keeps most of your actual JavaScript code within scripts and reduces the need to mingle JavaScript and HTML.

Note that HTML event-handler attributes are not the only way to define JavaScript event handlers. Chapter 17 shows that it is possible to specify JavaScript event handlers for HTML elements using JavaScript code in a <script> tag. Some JavaScript developers argue that HTML event-handler attributes should never be used—that truly unobtrusive JavaScript requires a complete separation of content from behavior. According to this style of JavaScript coding, all JavaScript code should be placed in external files, referenced from HTML with the src attribute of <script> tags. This external JavaScript code can define whatever event handlers it needs when it runs.

Events and event handlers are covered in much more detail in Chapter 17, but you'll see them used in a variety of examples before then. Chapter 17 includes a comprehensive list of event handlers, but these are the most common:

onclick

> This handler is supported by all button-like form elements, as well as <a> and <area> tags. It is triggered when the user clicks on the element. If an onclick handler returns false, the browser does not perform any default action associated with the button or link; for example, it doesn't follow a hyperlink (for an <a> tag) or submit a form (for a **Submit** button).

onmousedown, onmouseup

> These two event handlers are a lot like onclick, but they are triggered separately when the user presses and releases a mouse button, respectively. Most document elements support these handlers.

onmouseover, onmouseout

> These two event handlers are triggered when the mouse pointer moves over or out of a document element, respectively.

onchange

> This event handler is supported by the <input>, <select>, and <textarea> elements. It is triggered when the user changes the value displayed by the element and then tabs or otherwise moves focus out of the element.

onload

> This event handler may appear on the <body> tag and is triggered when the document and its external content (such as images) are fully loaded. The onload handler is often used to trigger code that manipulates the document content because it indicates that the document has reached a stable state and is safe to modify.

For a realistic example of the use of event handlers, take another look at the interactive loan-payment script in Example 1-3. The HTML form in this example contains a number of event-handler attributes. The body of these handlers is simple: they simply call the calculate( ) function defined elsewhere within a <script>.

13.4   JavaScript in URLs

Another way that JavaScript code can be included on the client side is in a URL following the javascript: pseudoprotocol specifier. This special protocol type specifies that the body of the URL is an arbitrary string of JavaScript code to be run by the JavaScript interpreter. It is treated as a single line of code, which means that statements must be separated by semicolons and that /* */ comments must be used in place of // comments. A JavaScript URL might look like this:

```
javascript:var now = new Date( ); "<h1>The time is:</h1>" + now;
```

When the browser loads one of these JavaScript URLs, it executes the JavaScript code contained in the URL and uses the value of the last JavaScript statement or expression, converted to a string, as the contents of the new document to display. This string value may contain HTML tags and is formatted and displayed just like any other document loaded into the browser.

JavaScript URLs may also contain JavaScript statements that perform actions but return no value. For example:

```
javascript:alert("Hello World!")
```

When this sort of URL is loaded, the browser executes the JavaScript code, but because there is no value to display as the new document, it does not modify the currently displayed document.

Often, you'll want to use a JavaScript URL to execute some JavaScript code without altering the currently displayed document. To do this, be sure that the last statement in the URL has no return value. One way to ensure this is to use the void operator to explicitly specify an undefined return value. Simply use the statement void 0; at the end of your JavaScript URL. For example, here is a URL that opens a new, blank browser window without altering the contents of the current window:

```
javascript:window.open("about:blank"); void 0;
```

Without the void operator in this URL, the return value of the Window.open() method call would be converted to a string and displayed, and the current document would be overwritten by a document that appears something like this:

```
[object Window]
```

You can use a JavaScript URL anywhere you'd use a regular URL. One handy way to use this syntax is to type it directly into the **Location** field of your browser, where you can test arbitrary JavaScript code without having to open your editor and create an HTML file containing the code.

The javascript: pseudoprotocol can be used with HTML attributes whose value should be a URL. The href attribute of a hyperlink is one such case. When the user clicks on such a link, the specified JavaScript code is executed. In this context, the JavaScript URL is essentially a substitute for an onclick event handler. (Note that using either an onclick handler or a JavaScript URL with an HTML link is normally a bad design choice; use a button instead, and reserve links for loading new documents.) Similarly, a JavaScript URL can be used as the value of the action attribute of a <form> tag so that the JavaScript code in the URL is executed when the user submits the form.

JavaScript URLs can also be passed to methods, such as Window.open() (see Chapter 14), that expect URL arguments.

13.4.1 Bookmarklets

One particularly important use of javascript: URLs is in bookmarks, where they form useful mini-JavaScript programs, or *bookmarklets*, that can be easily launched from a menu or toolbar of bookmarks. The following HTML snippet includes an <a> tag with a javascript: URL as the value of its href attribute. Clicking the link opens a simple JavaScript expression evaluator that allows you to evaluate expressions and execute statements in the context of the page:

```
<a href='javascript:
var e = "", r = ""; /* Expression to evaluate and the result */
do {
    /* Display expression and result and ask for a new expression */
    e = prompt("Expression: " + e + "\n" + r + "\n", e);
    try { r = "Result: " + eval(e); } /* Try to evaluate the expression */
    catch(ex) { r = ex; }            /* Or remember the error instead  */
} while(e); /* Continue until no expression entered or Cancel clicked */
void 0;     /* This prevents the current document from being overwritten */
'>
JavaScript Evaluator
</a>
```

Note that even though this JavaScript URL is written across multiple lines, the HTML parser treats it as a single line, and single-line // comments will not work in it. Here's what the link looks like with comments and whitespace stripped out:

```
<a href='javascript:var e="",r="";do{e=prompt("Expression: "+e+"\n"+r+"\n",e);
try{r="Result: "+eval(e);}catch(ex){r=ex;}}while(e);void 0;'>JS Evaluator</a>
```

A link like this is useful when hardcoded into a page that you are developing but becomes much more useful when stored as a bookmark that you can run on any page. Typically you can store a bookmark by right-clicking on the link and selecting **Bookmark This Link** or some similar option. In Firefox, you can simply drag the link to your bookmarks toolbar.

The client-side JavaScript techniques covered in this book are all applicable to the creation of bookmarklets, but bookmarklets themselves are not covered in any detail. If you are intrigued by the possibilities of these little programs, try an Internet search for "bookmarklets". You will find a number of sites that host many interesting and useful bookmarklets.

13.5 Execution of JavaScript Programs

The previous sections discussed the mechanics of integrating JavaScript code into an HTML file. Now the following sections discuss exactly how and when that integrated JavaScript code is executed by the JavaScript interpreter.

13.5.1 Executing Scripts

JavaScript statements that appear between <script> and </script> tags are executed in the order that they appear in the script. When a file has more than one script, the scripts are executed in the order in which they appear (with the exception of scripts with the defer attribute, which IE executes out of order). The JavaScript code in <script> tags is executed as part of the document loading and parsing process.

Any <script> element that does not have a defer attribute may call the document.write() method (described in detail in Chapter 15). The text passed to this method is inserted into the document at the location of the scripts. When the script is finished executing, the HTML parser resumes parsing the document, starting with any text output by the script.

Scripts can appear in the <head> or the <body> of an HTML document. Scripts in the <head> typically define functions to be called by other code. They may also declare and initialize variables that other code will use. It is common for scripts in the <head> of a document to define a single function and then register that function as an onload event handler for later execution. It is legal, but uncommon, to call document.write() in the <head> of a document.

Scripts in the <body> of a document can do everything that scripts in the <head> can do. It is more common to see calls to document.write( ) in these scripts, however. Scripts in the <body> of a document may also (using techniques described in Chapter 15) access and manipulate document elements and document content that appear before the script. As described later in this chapter, however, document elements are not guaranteed to be available and stable when the scripts in the <body> are executed. If a script simply defines functions and variables to be used later and does not call document.write( ) or otherwise attempt to modify document content, convention dictates that it should appear in the <head> of the document instead of the <body>.

As previously mentioned, IE executes scripts with the defer attribute out of order. These scripts are run after all nondeferred scripts and after the document is fully parsed, but before the onload event handler is triggered.

13.5.2 The onload Event Handler

After the document is parsed, all scripts have run, and all auxiliary content (such as images) has loaded, the browser fires the onload event and runs any JavaScript code that has been registered with the Window object as an onload event handler. An onload handler can be registered by setting the onload attribute of the <body> tag. It is also possible (using techniques shown in Chapter 17) for separate modules of JavaScript code to register their own onload event handlers. When more than one onload handler is registered, the browser invokes all handlers, but there is no guarantee about the order in which they are invoked.

When the onload handler is triggered, the document is fully loaded and parsed, and any document element can be manipulated by JavaScript code. For this reason, JavaScript modules that modify document content typically contain a function to perform the modification and event-registration code that arranges for the function to be invoked when the document is fully loaded.

Because onload event handlers are invoked after document parsing is complete, they must not call document.write( ). Instead of appending to the current document, any such call would instead begin a new document and overwrite the current document before the user even had a chance to view it.

13.5.3 Event Handlers and JavaScript URLs

When document loading and parsing ends, the onload handler is triggered, and JavaScript execution enters its event-driven phase. During this phase, event handlers are executed asynchronously in response to user input such as mouse motion, mouse clicks, and key presses. JavaScript URLs may be invoked asynchronously during this phase as well, if, for example, the user clicks on a link whose href attribute uses the javascript: pseudoprotocol.

`<script>` elements are typically used to define functions, and event handlers are typically used to invoke those functions in response to user input. Event handlers can define functions, of course, but this is an uncommon (and not very useful) thing to do.

If an event handler calls `document.write()` on the document of which it is a part, it will overwrite that document and begin a new one. This is almost never what is intended, and, as a rule of thumb, event handlers should never call this method. Nor should they call functions that call this method. The exception, however, is in multi-window applications in which an event handler in one window invokes the `write()` method of the document of a different window. (See Section 14.8 for more on multi-window JavaScript applications.)

13.5.4 The onunload Event Handler

When the user navigates away from a web page, the browser triggers the `onunload` event handler, giving the JavaScript code on that page one final chance to run. You can define an `onunload` handler by setting the `onunload` attribute of the `<body>` tag or with other event-handler registration techniques described in Chapter 17.

The `onunload` event enables you to undo the effects of your `onload` handler or other scripts in your web page. For example, if your application opens up a secondary browser window, the `onunload` handler provides an opportunity to close that window when the user leaves your main page. The `onunload` handler should not run any time-consuming operation, nor should it pop up a dialog box. It exists simply to perform a quick cleanup operation; running it should not slow down or impede the user's transition to a new page.

13.5.5 The Window Object as Execution Context

All scripts, event handlers, and JavaScript URLs in a document share the same Window object as their global object. JavaScript variables and functions are nothing more than properties of the global object. This means that a function declared in one `<script>` can be invoked by the code in any subsequent `<script>`.

Since the onload event is not triggered until after all scripts have executed, every onload event handler has access to all functions defined and variables declared by all scripts in the document.

Whenever a new document is loaded into a window, the Window object for that window is restored to its default state: any properties and functions defined by a script in the previous document are deleted, and any of the standard system properties that may have been altered or overwritten are restored. Every document begins with a clean slate. Your scripts can rely on this; they will not inherit a corrupted environment from the previous document. This also means that any variables and functions your scripts define persist only until the document is replaced with a new one.

The properties of a Window object have the same lifetime as the document that contains the JavaScript code that defined those properties. A Window object itself has a longer lifetime; it exists as long as the window it represents exists. A reference to a Window object remains valid regardless of how many web pages the window loads and unloads. This is relevant only for web applications that use multiple windows or frames. In this case, JavaScript code in one window or frame may maintain a reference to another window or frame. That reference remains valid even if the other window or frame loads a new document.

13.5.6 Client-Side JavaScript Threading Model

The core JavaScript language does not contain any threading mechanism, and client-side JavaScript does not add any. Client-side JavaScript is (or behaves as if it is) single-threaded. Document parsing stops while scripts are loaded and executed, and web browsers stop responding to user input while event handlers are being executed.

Single-threaded execution makes for much simpler scripting: you can write code with the assurance that two event handlers will never run at the same time. You can manipulate document content knowing that no other thread is attempting to modify it at the same time.

Single-threaded execution also places a burden on JavaScript programmers: it means that JavaScript scripts and event handlers must not run for too long. If a script performs a computationally intensive task, it will introduce a delay into document loading, and the user will not see the document content until the script completes. If an event handler performs a computationally intensive task, the browser may become nonresponsive, possibly causing the user to think that it has crashed.*

If your application must perform enough computation to cause a noticeable delay, you should allow the document to load fully before performing that computation, and you should be sure to notify the user that computation is underway and that the browser is not hung. If it is possible to break your computation down into discrete subtasks, you can use methods such as setTimeout() and setInterval() (see Chapter 14) to run the subtasks in the background while updating a progress indicator that displays feedback to the user.

13.5.7 Manipulating the Document During Loading

While a document is being loaded and parsed, JavaScript code in a <script> element can insert content into the document with document.write(). Other kinds of document manipulation, using DOM scripting techniques shown in Chapter 15, may or may not be allowed in <script> tags.

---

* Some browsers, such as Firefox, guard against denial-of-service attacks and accidental infinite loops, and prompt the user if a script or event handler takes too long to run. This gives the user the chance to abort a runaway script.

Most browsers seem to allow scripts to manipulate any document elements that appear before the <script> tag. Some JavaScript coders do this routinely. However, no standard requires it to work, and there is a persistent, if vague, belief among some experienced JavaScript coders that placing document manipulation code within <script> tags can cause problems (perhaps only occasionally, only with some browsers, or only when a document is reloaded or revisited with the browser's **Back** button).

The only consensus that exists in this gray area is that it is safe to manipulate the document once the onload event has been triggered, and this is what most JavaScript applications do: they use the onload handler to trigger all document modifications. I present a utility routine for registering onload event handlers in Example 17-7.

In documents that contain large images or many images, the main document may be parsed well before the images are loaded and the onload event is triggered. In this case, you might want to begin manipulating the document before the onload event. One technique (whose safety is debated) is to place the manipulation code at the end of the document. An IE-specific technique is to put the document manipulation code in a <script> that has both defer and src attributes. A Firefox-specific technique is to make the document-manipulation code an event handler for the undocumented DOMContentLoaded event, which is fired when the document is parsed but before external objects, such as images, are fully loaded.

Another gray area in the JavaScript execution model is the question of whether event handlers can be invoked before the document is fully loaded. Our discussion of the JavaScript execution model has so far concluded that all event handlers are always triggered after all scripts have been executed. While this typically happens, it is not required by any standard. If a document is very long or is being loaded over a slow network connection, the browser might partially render the document and allow the user to begin interacting with it (and triggering event handlers) before all scripts and onload handlers have run. If such an event handler invokes a function that is not yet defined, it will fail. (This is one reason to define all functions in scripts in the <head> of a document.) And if such an event handler attempts to manipulate a part of the document that has not yet been parsed, it will fail. This scenario is uncommon in practice, and it is not usually worth the extra coding effort required to aggressively protect against it.

13.6 Client-Side Compatibility

The web browser is a universal platform for hosting applications, and JavaScript is the language in which those applications are developed. Fortunately, the JavaScript language is standardized and well-supported: all modern web browsers support ECMAScript v3. The same can not be said for the platform itself. All web browsers display HTML, of course, but they differ in their support for other standards such as

CSS (Cascading Style Sheets) and the DOM. And although all modern browsers include a compliant JavaScript interpreter, they differ in the APIs they make available to client-side JavaScript code.

Compatibility issues are simply an unpleasant fact of life for client-side JavaScript programmers. The JavaScript code you write and deploy may be run in various versions of various browsers running on various operating systems. Consider the permutations of popular operating systems and browsers: Internet Explorer on Windows and Mac OS;* Firefox on Windows, Mac OS, and Linux; Safari on Mac OS; and Opera on Windows, Mac OS, and Linux. If you want to support the current version of each browser plus the previous two versions, multiply these nine browser/OS pairs by three, for a total of 27 browser/version/OS combinations. The only way to be absolutely sure that your web application runs on all 27 combinations is to test it in each. This is a daunting task, and in practice, the testing is often done by the users after the application is deployed!

Before you reach the testing phase of application development, you must write the code. When programming in JavaScript, knowledge of the incompatibilities among browsers is crucial for creating compatible code. Unfortunately, producing a definitive listing of all known vendor, version, and platform incompatibilities would be an enormous task. It is beyond the scope and mission of this book, and to my knowledge, no comprehensive client-side JavaScript test suite has ever been developed. You can find browser compatibility information online, and here are two sites that I have found useful:

http://www.quirksmode.org/dom/
  This is freelance web developer Peter-Paul Koch's web site. His DOM compatibility tables show the compatibility of various browsers with the W3C DOM.

http://webdevout.net/browser_support.php
  This site by David Hammond is similar to *quirksmode.org*, but its compatibility tables are more comprehensive and (at the time of this writing) somewhat more up-to-date. In addition to DOM compatibility, it also rates browser compliance with the HTML, CSS, and ECMAScript standards.

Awareness of incompatibilities is only the first step, of course. The subsections that follow demonstrate techniques you can use to work around the incompatibilities you encounter.

13.6.1 The History of Incompatibility

Client-side JavaScript programming has always been about coping with incompatibility. Knowing the history provides some useful context. The early days of web programming were marked by the "browser wars" between Netscape and Microsoft.

---

* IE for Mac is being phased out, which is a blessing because it is substantially different from IE for Windows.

This was an intense burst of development, in often incompatible directions, of the browser environment and client-side JavaScript APIs. Incompatibility problems were at their worst at this point, and some web sites simply gave up and told their visitors which browser they needed to use to access the site.

The browser wars ended, with Microsoft holding a dominant market share, and web standards, such as the DOM and CSS, started to take hold. A period of stability (or stagnation) followed while the Netscape browser slowly morphed into the Firefox browser and Microsoft made a few incremental improvements to its browser. Standards support in both browsers was good, or at least good enough for compatible web applications to be written.

At the time of this writing, we seem to be at the start of another burst of browser innovation. For example, all major browsers now support scripted HTTP requests, which form the cornerstone of the new Ajax web application architecture (see Chapter 20). Microsoft is working on Internet Explorer 7, which will address a number of long-standing security and CSS compatibility issues. IE 7 will have many user-visible changes but will not, apparently, break new ground for web developers. Other browsers are breaking new ground, however. For example, Safari and Firefox support a <canvas> tag for scripted client-side graphics (see Chapter 22). A consortium of browser vendors (with the notable absence of Microsoft) known as WHATWG (*whatwg.org*) is working to standardize the <canvas> tag and many other extensions to HTML and the DOM.

13.6.2 A Word about "Modern Browsers"

Client-side JavaScript is a moving target, especially if we're indeed entering a period of rapid evolution. For this reason, I shy away in this book from making narrow statements about particular versions of particular browsers. Any such claims are likely to be outdated before I can write a new edition of the book. A printed book like this simply cannot be updated as often as necessary to provide a useful guide to the compatibility issues that affect the current crop of browsers.

You'll find, therefore, that I often hedge my statements with purposely vague language like "all modern browsers" (or sometimes "all modern browsers except IE"). At the time of this writing, the loose set of "modern browsers" includes: Firefox 1.0, Firefox 1.5, IE 5.5, IE 6.0, Safari 2.0, Opera 8, and Opera 8.5. This is not a guarantee that every statement in this book about "modern browsers" is true for each of these specific browsers. However, it allows you to know what browsers were current technology when this book was written.

13.6.3 Feature Testing

Feature testing (sometimes called *capability testing*) is a powerful technique for coping with incompatibilities. If you want to use a feature or capability that may not be supported by all browsers, include code in your script that tests to see whether that feature is supported. If the desired feature is not supported on the current platform, either do not use it on that platform or provide alternative code that works on all platforms.

You'll see feature testing again and again in the chapters that follow. In Chapter 17, for example, there is code that looks like this:

```
if (element.addEventListener) { // Test for this W3C method before using it
    element.addEventListener("keydown", handler, false);
    element.addEventListener("keypress", handler, false);
}
else if (element.attachEvent) { // Test for this IE method before using it
    element.attachEvent("onkeydown", handler);
    element.attachEvent("onkeypress", handler);
}
else {  // Otherwise, fall back on a universally supported technique
    element.onkeydown = element.onkeypress = handler;
}
```

Chapter 20 describes yet another approach to feature testing: keep trying alternatives until you find one that does not throw an exception! And, when you find an alternative that works, remember it for future use. Here is a preview of code from Example 20-1:

```
// This is a list of XMLHttpRequest creation functions to try
HTTP._factories = [
    function() { return new XMLHttpRequest(); },
    function() { return new ActiveXObject("Msxml2.XMLHTTP"); },
    function() { return new ActiveXObject("Microsoft.XMLHTTP"); }
];

// When we find a factory that works, store it here
HTTP._factory = null;

// Create and return a new XMLHttpRequest object.
//
// The first time we're called, try the list of factory functions until
// we find one that returns a nonnull value and does not throw an
// exception. Once we find a working factory, remember it for later use.
HTTP.newRequest = function() { /* fuction body omitted */ }
```

A common, but outdated, example of feature testing that you may still encounter in existing code is used to determine which DOM a browser supports. It often occurs in DHTML code and usually looks something like this:

```
if (document.getElementById) {  // If the W3C DOM API is supported,
    // do our DHTML using the W3C DOM API
}
else if (document.all) {        // If the IE 4 API is supported,
    // do our DHTML using the IE 4 API
}
else if (document.layers) {     // If the Netscape 4 API is supported,
```

```
        // do the DHTML effect (as best we can) using the Netscape 4 API
    }
    else {                         // Otherwise, DHTML is not supported,
        // so provide a static alternative to DHTML
    }
```

Code like this is outdated because almost all browsers deployed today support the W3C DOM and its document.getElementById( ) function.

The important thing about the feature-testing technique is that it results in code that is not tied to a specific list of browser vendors or browser version numbers. It works with the set of browsers that exist today and should continue to work with future browsers, whatever feature sets they implement. Note, however, that it requires browser vendors not to define a property or method unless that property or method is fully functional. If Microsoft were to define an addEventHandler( ) method that only partially implemented the W3C specification, it would break a lot of code that uses feature testing before calling addEventHandler( ).

The document.all property shown in this example deserves a special mention here. The document.all[] array was introduced by Microsoft in IE 4. It allowed JavaScript code to refer to all elements of a document and ushered in a new era of client-side programming. It was never standardized and was superseded by document.getElementById( ). It is still used in existing code and has often been used (incorrectly) to determine whether a script is running in IE with code like this:

```
if (document.all) {
    // We're running in IE
}
else {
    // We're in some other browser
}
```

Because there is still a lot of extant code that uses document.all, the Firefox browser has added support for it so that Firefox can work with sites that were previously IE-dependent. Because the presence of the all property is often used for browser detection, Firefox pretends that it does not support the property. So even though Firefox does support document.all, the if statement in the following script behaves as if the all property does not exist, and the script displays a dialog box containing the text "Firefox":

```
if (document.all) alert("IE"); else alert("Firefox");
```

This example illustrates that the feature-testing approach does not work if the browser actively lies to you! It also shows that web developers are not the only ones plagued by compatibility issues. Browser vendors must also go through contortions for compatibility.

13.6.4 Browser Testing

Feature testing is well suited to checking for support of large functional areas. You can use it to determine whether a browser supports the W3C event-handling model or the IE event-handling model, for example. On the other hand, sometimes you may need to work around individual bugs or quirks in a particular browser, and there may be no easy way to test for the existence of the bug. In this case, you need to create a platform-specific workaround that is tied to a particular browser vendor, version, or operating system (or some combination of the three).

The way to do this in client-side JavaScript is with the Navigator object, which you'll learn about in Chapter 14. Code that determines the vendor and version of the current browser is often called a *browser sniffer* or a *client sniffer*. A simple example is shown in Example 14-3. Client sniffing was a common client-side programming technique in the early days of the Web when the Netscape and IE platforms were incompatible and diverging. Now that the compatibility situation has stabilized, client sniffing has fallen out of favor and should be used only when absolutely necessary.

Note that client sniffing can be done on the server side as well, with the web server choosing what JavaScript code to send based on how the browser identifies itself in its User-Agent header.

13.6.5 Conditional Comments in Internet Explorer

In practice, you'll find that many of the incompatibilities in client-side JavaScript programming turn out to be IE-specific. That is, you must write code in one way for IE and in another way for all other browsers. Although you should normally avoid browser-specific extensions that are not likely to be standardized, IE supports conditional comments in both HTML and JavaScript code that can be useful.

Here is what conditional comments in HTML look like. Notice the tricks played with the closing delimiter of HTML comments:

```
<!--[if IE]>
This content is actually inside an HTML comment.
It will only be displayed in IE.
<![endif]-->

<!--[if gte IE 6]>
This content will only be displayed by IE 6 and later.
<![endif]-->

<!--[if !IE]> <-->
This is normal HTML content, but IE will not display it
because of the comment above and the comment below.
<!--> <![endif]-->

This is normal content, displayed by all browsers.
```

Conditional comments are also supported by IE's JavaScript interpreter, and C and C++ programmers may find them similar to the #ifdef/#endif functionality of the C preprocessor. A JavaScript conditional comment in IE begins with the text /*@cc_on and ends with the text @*/. (The cc in cc_on stands for conditional compilation.) The following conditional comment includes code that is executed only in IE:

```
/*@cc_on
  @if (@_jscript)

      // This code is inside a JS comment but is executed in IE.
      alert("In IE");

  @end
  @*/
```

Inside a conditional comment, the keywords @if, @else, and @end delimit the code that is to be conditionally executed by IE's JavaScript interpreter. Most of the time, you need only the simple conditional shown above: @if (@_jscript). JScript is Microsoft's name for its JavaScript interpreter, and the @_jscript variable is always true in IE.

With clever interleaving of conditional comments and regular JavaScript comments, you can set up one block of code to run in IE and a different block to run in all other browsers:

```
/*@cc_on
  @if (@_jscript)
      // This code is inside a conditional comment, which is also a
      // regular JavaScript comment. IE runs it but other browsers ignore it.
      alert('You are using Internet Explorer);
  @else*/
      // This code is no longer inside a JavaScript comment, but is still
      // inside the IE conditional comment.  This means that all browsers
      // except IE will run this code.
      alert('You are not using Internet Explorer');
  /*@end
  @*/
```

Conditional comments, in both their HTML and JavaScript forms, are completely nonstandard. They are sometimes a useful way to achieve compatibility with IE, however.

13.7 Accessibility

The Web is a wonderful tool for disseminating information, and JavaScript programs can enhance access to that information. JavaScript programmers must be careful, however: it is easy to write JavaScript code that inadvertently denies information to visitors with visual or physical handicaps.

Blind users may use a form of "assistive technology" known as a screen reader to convert written words to spoken words. Some screen readers are JavaScript-aware, and others work best when JavaScript is turned off. If you design a web site that requires JavaScript to display its information, you exclude the users of these screen readers. (And you have also excluded anyone who browses with a mobile device, such as a cell phone, that does not have JavaScript support, as well as anyone else who intentionally disables JavaScript in his browser.) The proper role of JavaScript is to enhance the presentation of information, not to take over the presentation of that information. A cardinal rule of JavaScript accessibility is to design your code so that the web page on which it is used will still function (at least in some form) with the JavaScript interpreter turned off.

Another important accessibility concern is for users who can use the keyboard but cannot use (or choose not to use) a pointing device such as a mouse. If you write JavaScript code that relies on mouse-specific events, you exclude users who do not use the mouse. Web browsers allow keyboard traversal and activation of a web page, and your JavaScript code should as well. And at the same time, you should not write code that requires keyboard input either, or you will exclude users who cannot use a keyboard as well as many users of tablet PCs and cell phone browsers. As shown in Chapter 17, JavaScript supports device-independent events, such as onfocus and onchange, as well as device-dependent events, such as onmouseover and onmousedown. For accessibility, you should favor the device-independent events whenever possible.

Creating accessible web pages is a nontrivial problem without clear-cut solutions. At the time of this writing, debate continues on how to best use JavaScript to foster, rather than degrade, accessibility. A full discussion of JavaScript and accessibility is beyond the scope of this book. An Internet search will yield a lot of information on this topic, much of it couched in the form of recommendations from authoritative sources. Keep in mind that both client-side JavaScript programming practices and assistive technologies are evolving, and accessibility guidelines do not always keep up.

13.8   JavaScript Security

Internet security is a broad and complex field. This section focuses on client-side JavaScript security issues.

13.8.1 What JavaScript Can't Do

The introduction of JavaScript interpreters into web browsers means that loading a web page can cause arbitrary JavaScript code to be executed on your computer. Secure web browsers—and commonly used modern browsers appear to be relatively secure—restrict scripts in various ways to prevent malicious code from reading confidential data, altering your data, or compromising your privacy.

JavaScript's first line of defense against malicious code is that the language simply does not support certain capabilities. For example, client-side JavaScript does not provide any way to read, write, or delete files or directories on the client computer. With no File object and no file-access functions, a JavaScript program cannot delete a user's data or plant viruses on a user's system.

The second line of defense is that JavaScript imposes restrictions on certain features that it does support. For example, client-side JavaScript can script the HTTP protocol to exchange data with web servers, and it can even download data from FTP and other servers. But JavaScript does not provide general networking primitives and cannot open a socket to, or accept a connection from, another host.

The following list includes other features that may be restricted. Note that this is not a definitive list. Different browsers have different restrictions, and many of these restrictions may be user-configurable:

- A JavaScript program can open new browser windows, but, to prevent pop-up abuse by advertisers, many browsers restrict this feature so that it can happen only in response to a user-initiated event such as a mouse click.

- A JavaScript program can close browser windows that it opened itself, but it is not allowed to close other windows without user confirmation. This prevents malicious scripts from calling self.close() to close the user's browsing window, thereby causing the program to exit.

- A JavaScript program cannot obscure the destination of a link by setting the status line text when the mouse moves over the link. (It was common in the past to provide additional information about a link in the status line. Abuse by phishing scams has caused many browser vendors to disable this capability.)

- A script cannot open a window that is too small (typically smaller than 100 pixels on a side) or shrink a window too small. Similarly, a script cannot move a window off the screen or create a window that is larger than the screen. This prevents scripts from opening windows that the user cannot see or could easily overlook; such windows could contain scripts that keep running after the user thinks they have stopped. Also, a script may not create a browser window without a titlebar or status line because such a window could spoof an operating dialog box and trick the user into entering a sensitive password, for example.

- The value property of HTML FileUpload elements cannot be set. If this property could be set, a script could set it to any desired filename and cause the form to upload the contents of any specified file (such as a password file) to the server.

- A script cannot read the content of documents loaded from different servers than the document that contains the script. Similarly, a script cannot register event listeners on documents from different servers. This prevents scripts from snooping on the user's input (such as the keystrokes that constitute a password entry) to other pages. This restriction is known as the *same-origin policy* and is described in more detail in the next section.

13.8.2 The Same-Origin Policy

The *same-origin policy* is a sweeping security restriction on what web content Java-Script code can interact with. It typically comes into play when a web page uses multiple frames, includes <iframe> tags, or opens other browser windows. In this case, the same-origin policy governs the interactions of JavaScript code in one window or frame with other windows and frames. Specifically, a script can read only the properties of windows and documents that have the same origin as the document that contains the script (see Section 14.8 to learn how to use JavaScript with multiple windows and frames).

The same-origin policy also comes up when scripting HTTP with the XMLHttpRequest object. This object allows client-side JavaScript code to make arbitrary HTTP requests but only to the web server from which the containing document was loaded (see Chapter 20 for more on the XMLHttpRequest object).

The *origin* of a document is defined as the protocol, host, and port of the URL from which the document was loaded. Documents loaded from different web servers have different origins. Documents loaded through different ports of the same host have different origins. And a document loaded with the http: protocol has a different origin than one loaded with the https: protocol, even if they come from the same web server.

It is important to understand that the origin of the script itself is not relevant to the same-origin policy: what matters is the origin of the document in which the script is embedded. Suppose, for example, that a script from domain A is included (using the src property of the <script> tag) in a web page in domain B. That script has full access to the content of the document that contains it. If the script opens a new window and loads a second document from domain B, the script also has full access to the content of that second document. But if the script opens a third window and loads a document from domain C (or even from domain A) into it, the same-origin policy comes into effect and prevents the script from accessing this document.

The same-origin policy does not actually apply to all properties of all objects in a window from a different origin. But it does apply to many of them, and, in particular, it applies to practically all the properties of the Document object (see Chapter 15). Furthermore, different browser vendors implement this security policy somewhat differently. (For example, Firefox 1.0 allows a script to call history.back( ) on different-origin windows, but IE 6 does not.) For all intents and purposes, therefore, you should consider any window that contains a document from another server to be off-limits to your scripts. If your script opened the window, your script can close it, but it cannot "look inside" the window in any way.

The same-origin policy is necessary to prevent scripts from stealing proprietary information. Without this restriction, a malicious script (loaded through a firewall into a browser on a secure corporate intranet) might open an empty window, hoping to trick the user into using that window to browse files on the intranet. The malicious script would then read the content of that window and send it back to its own server. The same-origin policy prevents this kind of behavior.

In some circumstances, the same-origin policy is too restrictive. It poses particular problems for large web sites that use more than one server. For example, a script from *home.example.com* might legitimately want to read properties of a document loaded from *developer.example.com*, or scripts from *orders.example.com* might need to read properties from documents on *catalog.example.com*. To support large web sites of this sort, you can use the domain property of the Document object. By default, the domain property contains the hostname of the server from which the document was loaded. You can set this property, but only to a string that is a valid domain suffix of itself. Thus, if domain is originally the string "home.example.com", you can set it to the string "example.com", but not to "home.example" or "ample.com". Furthermore, the domain value must have at least one dot in it; you cannot set it to "com" or any other top-level domain.

If two windows (or frames) contain scripts that set domain to the same value, the same-origin policy is relaxed for these two windows, and each window can interact with the other. For example, cooperating scripts in documents loaded from *orders.example.com* and *catalog.example.com* might set their document.domain properties to "example.com", thereby making the documents appear to have the same origin and enabling each document to read properties of the other.

13.8.3 Scripting Plug-ins and ActiveX Controls

Although the core JavaScript language and the basic client-side object model lack the filesystem and networking features that most malicious code requires, the situation is not quite as simple as it appears. In many web browsers, JavaScript is used as a "script engine" for other software components, such as ActiveX controls in Internet Explorer and plug-ins in other browsers. This exposes important and powerful features to client-side scripts. You'll see examples in Chapter 20, where an ActiveX control is used for scripting HTTP, and in Chapters 19 and 22, where the Java and Flash plug-ins are used for persistence and advanced client-side graphics.

There are security implications to being able to script ActiveX controls and plug-ins. Java applets, for example, have access to low-level networking capabilities. The Java security "sandbox" prevents applets from communicating with any server other than the one from which they were loaded, so this does not open a security hole. But it exposes the basic problem: if plug-ins are scriptable, you must trust not just the web browser's security architecture, but also the plug-in's security architecture. In practice, the Java and Flash plug-ins seem to have robust security and do not appear to introduce security issues into client-side JavaScript. ActiveX scripting has had a more checkered past, however. The IE browser has access to a variety of scriptable ActiveX controls that are part of the Windows operating system, and in the past some of these scriptable controls have included exploitable security holes. At the time of this writing, however, these problems appear to have been resolved.

13.8.4 Cross-Site Scripting

Cross-site scripting, or XSS, is a term for a category of security issues in which an attacker injects HTML tags or scripts into a target web site. Defending against XSS attacks is typically the job of server-side web developers. However, client-side Java-Script programmers must also be aware of, and defend against, cross-site scripting.

A web page is vulnerable to cross-site scripting if it dynamically generates document content and bases that content on user-submitted data without first "sanitizing" that data by removing any embedded HTML tags from it. As a trivial example, consider the following web page that uses JavaScript to greet the user by name:

```
<script>
var name = decodeURIComponent(window.location.search.substring(6)) || "";
document.write("Hello " + name);
</script>
```

This two-line script uses `window.location.search` to obtain the portion of its own URL that begins with ?. It uses `document.write( )` to add dynamically generated content to the document. This page is intended to be invoked with a URL like this:

```
http://www.example.com/greet.html?name=David
```

When used like this, it displays the text "Hello David". But consider what happens when it is invoked with this URL:

```
http://www.example.com/greet.html?name=%3Cscript%3Ealert('David')%3C/script%3E
```

With this URL, the script dynamically generates another script (%3C and %3E are codes for angle brackets)! In this case, the injected script simply displays a dialog box, which is relatively benign. But consider this case:

```
http://siteA/greet.html?name=%3Cscript src=siteB/evil.js%3E%3C/script%3E
```

Cross-site scripting attacks are so called because more than one site is involved. Site B (or even site C) includes a specially crafted link (like the one above) to site A that injects a script from site B. The script *evil.js* is hosted by the evil site B, but it is now embedded in site A, and can do absolutely anything it wants with site A's content. It might deface the page or cause it to malfunction (such as by initiating one of the denial-of-service attacks described in the next section). This would be bad for site A's customer relations. More dangerously, the malicious script can read cookies stored by site A (perhaps account numbers or other personally identifying information) and send that data back to site B. The injected script can even track the user's keystrokes and send that data back to site B.

In general, the way to prevent XSS attacks is to remove HTML tags from any untrusted data before using it to create dynamic document content. You can fix the *greet.html* file shown earlier by adding this line of code to remove the angle brackets around <script> tags.

```
name = name.replace(/</g, "&lt;").replace(/>/g, "&gt;");
```

Cross-site scripting enables a pernicious vulnerability whose roots go deep into the architecture of the Web. It is worth understanding this vulnerability in depth, but further discussion is beyond the scope of this book. There are many online resources to help you defend against cross-site scripting. One important primary source is the original CERT Advisory about this problem: *http://www.cert.org/advisories/CA-2000-02.html*.

13.8.5 Denial-of-Service Attacks

The same-origin policy and other security restrictions described here do a good job of preventing malicious code from damaging your data or compromising your privacy. They do not protect against brute-force denial-of-service attacks, however. If you visit a malicious web site with JavaScript enabled, that site can tie up your browser with an infinite loop of alert( ) dialog boxes, forcing you to use, for example, the Unix kill command or the Windows Task Manager to shut your browser down.

A malicious site can also attempt to tie up your CPU with an infinite loop or meaningless computation. Some browsers (such as Firefox) detect long-running scripts and give the user the option to stop them. This defends against accidental infinite loops, but malicious code can use techniques such as the window.setInterval( ) command to avoid being shut down. A similar attack ties up your system by allocating lots of memory.

There is no general way that web browsers can prevent this kind of ham-handed attack. In practice, this is not a common problem on the Web since no one returns to a site that engages in this kind of scripting abuse!

13.9   Other Web-Related JavaScript Embeddings

In addition to client-side JavaScript, the JavaScript language has other web-related embeddings. This book does not cover these other embeddings, but you should know enough about them so that you don't confuse them with client-side JavaScript:

User scripting

User scripting is an innovation in which user-defined scripts are applied to HTML documents before they are rendered by the browser. Rather than being solely under the control of the page author, web pages can now be controlled by the page visitor as well. The best-known example of user scripting is enabled by the Greasemonkey extension to the Firefox web browser (*http://greasemonkey.mozdev.org*). The programming environment exposed to user scripts is similar to, but not the same as, the client-side programming environment. This book will not teach you how to write Greasemonkey user scripts, but learning client-side JavaScript programming can be considered a prerequisite to learning user scripting.

SVG

SVG (Scalable Vector Graphics) is an XML-based graphics format that permits embedded JavaScript scripts. Client-side JavaScript can script the HTML document within which it is embedded, and JavaScript code embedded in an SVG file can script the XML elements of that document. The material in Chapters 15 and 17 is relevant to SVG scripting but is not sufficient: the DOM for SVG differs substantially from the HTML DOM.

The SVG specification is at *http://www.w3.org/TR/SVG*. Appendix B of this specification defines the SVG DOM. Chapter 22 uses client-side JavaScript embedded in an HTML document to create an SVG document that is embedded in an HTML document. Since the JavaScript code is outside the SVG document, this is an example of regular client-side JavaScript rather than SVG embedding of JavaScript.

XUL

XUL is an XML-based grammar for describing user interfaces. The GUI of the Firefox web browser is defined with XUL documents. Like SVG, the XUL grammar allows JavaScript scripts. As with SVG, the material in Chapters 15 and 17 is relevant to XUL programming. However, JavaScript code in a XUL document has access to different objects and APIs, and is subject to a different security model than client-side JavaScript code. Learn more about XUL at *http://www.mozilla.org/projects/xul* and *http://www.xulplanet.com*.

ActionScript

ActionScript is a JavaScript-like language (descended from the same ECMA-Script specification but evolved in an object-oriented direction) used in Flash movies. Most of the core JavaScript material in Part I of this book is relevant to ActionScript programming. Flash is not XML- or HTML-based, and the APIs exposed by Flash are unrelated to those discussed in this book. This book includes examples of how client-side JavaScript can script Flash movies in Chapters 19, 22, and 23. These examples necessarily include small snippets of Action-Script code, but the focus is on the use of regular client-side JavaScript to interact with that code.

CHAPTER 14

Scripting Browser Windows

Chapter 13 described the Window object and the central role it plays in client-side JavaScript: it is the global object for client-side JavaScript programs. This chapter explores the properties and methods of the Window object that allow you to control the browser and its windows and frames.

Here, you'll find out how to:

- Register JavaScript code to be executed in the future, either once or repeatedly
- Get the URL of the document displayed in a window and parse query arguments out of that URL
- Make the browser load and display a new document
- Tell the browser to go back or forward in its history and learn to control other browser functions such as printing
- Open new browser windows, manipulate them, and close them
- Display simple dialog boxes
- Determine what browser your JavaScript code is running in and obtain other information about the client-side environment
- Display arbitrary text in the status line of a browser window
- Handle uncaught JavaScript errors that occur in a window
- Write JavaScript code that interacts with multiple windows or frames

You'll notice that this chapter is all about manipulating browser windows but does not have anything to say about the *content* displayed within those windows. When JavaScript was young, document content was scriptable only in very limited ways, and the window scripting techniques described in this chapter were exciting and fresh. Today, with fully scriptable documents (see Chapter 15), scripting the browser is no longer cutting-edge. Furthermore, some of the techniques shown in this chapter are hampered with security restrictions and do not function as well as they once did. Other techniques still function, but have fallen out of favor with web designers and are no longer commonly used.

Although this chapter is less relevant today, it is not altogether irrelevant, and I do not recommend that you skip it. The chapter is organized so that (most of) the most important material comes first. This is followed by less important or less commonly used techniques. One important, but more complicated, section on the use of Java-Script to interact with multiple windows and frames is deferred until the end of the chapter, and the chapter concludes with a useful example.

14.1 Timers

An important feature of any programming environment is the ability to schedule code to be executed at some point in the future. The core JavaScript language does not provide any such feature, but client-side JavaScript does provide it in the form of the global functions setTimeout( ), clearTimeout( ), setInterval( ), and clearInterval( ). These functions don't really have anything to do with the Window object, but they are documented in this chapter because the Window object is the global object in client-side JavaScript and these global functions are therefore methods of that object.

The setTimeout( ) method of the Window object schedules a function to run after a specified number of milliseconds elapses. setTimeout( ) returns an opaque value that can be passed to clearTimeout( ) to cancel the execution of the scheduled function.

setInterval( ) is like setTimeout( ) except that the specified function is invoked repeatedly at intervals of the specified number of milliseconds. Like setTimeout( ), setInterval( ) returns an opaque value that can be passed to clearInterval( ) to cancel any future invocations of the scheduled function.

Although the preferred way to invoke setTimeout( ) and setInterval( ) is to pass a function as the first argument, it is also legal to pass a string of JavaScript code instead. If you do this, the string is evaluated (once or repeatedly) after the specified amount of time. In old browsers, such as IE 4, functions are not supported, and you must invoke these methods with a string as the first argument.

setTimeout( ) and setInterval( ) are useful in a variety of situations. If you want to display a tool tip when a user hovers her mouse over some document element for more than half a second, you can use setTimeout( ) to schedule the tool tip display code. If the mouse moves away before the code is triggered, you can use clearTimeout( ) to cancel the scheduled code. setTimeout( ) is demonstrated later in Example 14-7. Whenever you perform any kind of animation, you typically use setInterval( ) to schedule the code that performs the animation. You'll see demonstrations of this in Examples 14-4 and 14-6.

One useful trick with setTimeout( ) is to register a function to be invoked after a delay of 0 milliseconds. The code isn't invoked right away but is run "as soon as possible." In practice, setTimeout( ) tells the browser to invoke the function when it has finished running the event handlers for any currently pending events and has finished updating the current state of the document. Event handlers (see Chapter 17) that query or modify document content (see Chapter 15) must sometimes use this trick to defer execution of their code until the document is in a stable state.

You can find reference information on these timer functions in the Window object section of Part IV.

14.2   Browser Location and History

This section discusses a window's Location and History objects. These objects provide access to the URL of the currently displayed document and enable you to load new documents or make the browser go back (or forward) to a previously viewed document.

14.2.1   Parsing URLs

The location property of a window (or frame) is a reference to a Location object; it represents the URL of the document currently being displayed in that window. The href property of the Location object is a string that contains the complete text of the URL. The toString( ) method of the Location object returns the value of the href property, so you can use location in place of location.href.

Other properties of this object—such as protocol, host, pathname, and search—specify the various individual parts of the URL (see the Location object in Part IV for full details).

The search property of the Location object is an interesting one. It contains the portion, if any, of a URL following (and including) a question mark, which is often some sort of query string. In general, the question-mark syntax in a URL is a technique for embedding arguments in the URL. While these arguments are usually intended for scripts run on a server, there is no reason why they cannot also be used in JavaScript-enabled pages. Example 14-1 shows the definition of a general-purpose getArgs( ) function you can use to extract arguments from the search property of a URL.

Example 14-1. Extracting arguments from a URL

```
/*
 * This function parses ampersand-separated name=value argument pairs from
 * the query string of the URL. It stores the name=value pairs in
 * properties of an object and returns that object. Use it like this:
 *
 * var args = getArgs( );  // Parse args from URL
 * var q = args.q || "";   // Use argument, if defined, or a default value
 * var n = args.n ? parseInt(args.n) : 10;
 */
function getArgs( ) {
    var args = new Object( );
    var query = location.search.substring(1);    // Get query string
    var pairs = query.split("&");                // Break at ampersand
```

Example 14-1. Extracting arguments from a URL (continued)

```
for(var i = 0; i < pairs.length; i++) {
    var pos = pairs[i].indexOf('=');        // Look for "name=value"
    if (pos == -1) continue;                // If not found, skip
    var argname = pairs[i].substring(0,pos); // Extract the name
    var value = pairs[i].substring(pos+1);  // Extract the value
    value = decodeURIComponent(value);      // Decode it, if needed
    args[argname] = value;                  // Store as a property
}
return args;                                // Return the object
}
```

14.2.2 Loading New Documents

Although the location property of a window refers to a Location object, you can assign a string value to the property. When you do this, the browser interprets the string as a URL and attempts to load and display the document at that URL. For example, you might assign a URL to the location property like this:

```
// If the browser does not support the Document.getElementById function,
// redirect to a static page that does not require that function.
if (!document.getElementById) location = "staticpage.html";
```

Notice that the URL assigned to the location property in this example is a relative one. Relative URLs are interpreted relative to the page in which they appear, just as they would be if they were used in a hyperlink.

Example 14-7, at the end of this chapter, also uses the location property to load a new document.

It is surprising that there is not a method of the Window object that makes the browser load and display a new page. Historically, assigning a URL to the location property of a window has been the supported technique for loading new pages. The Location object does have two methods with related purposes, however. The reload( ) method reloads the currently displayed page from the web server; the replace( ) method loads and displays a URL that you specify. However, invoking the latter method for a given URL is different from assigning that URL to the location property of a window. When you call replace( ), the specified URL replaces the current one in the browser's history list rather than creating a new entry in that history list. Therefore, if you use replace( ) to overwrite one document with a new one, the **Back** button does not take the user back to the original document, as it does if you load the new document by assigning a URL to the location property. For web sites that use frames and display a lot of temporary pages (perhaps generated by a server-side script), replace( ) is often useful. Since temporary pages are not stored in the history list, the **Back** button is more useful to the user.

Finally, don't confuse the location property of the Window object, which refers to a Location object, with the location property of the Document object, which is simply a read-only string with none of the special features of the Location object. `document.location` is a synonym for `document.URL`, which is the preferred name for this property (because it avoids potential confusion). In most cases, `document.location` is the same as `location.href`. When there is a server redirect, however, `document.location` contains the URL as loaded, and `location.href` contains the URL as originally requested.

14.2.3 The History Object

The `history` property of the Window object refers to the History object for the window. The History object was originally designed to model the browsing history of a window as an array of recently visited URLs. This turned out to be a poor design choice, however. For important security and privacy reasons, it is almost never appropriate to give a script access to the list of web sites that the user has previously visited. Thus, the array elements of the History object are never actually accessible to scripts.

Although its array elements are inaccessible, the History object supports three methods. The `back()` and `forward()` methods move backward or forward in a window's (or frame's) browsing history, replacing the currently displayed document with a previously viewed one. This is similar to what happens when the user clicks on the **Back** and **Forward** browser buttons. The third method, `go()`, takes an integer argument and can skip any number of pages forward (for positive arguments) or backward (for negative arguments) in the history list. Example 14-7, at the end of this chapter, demonstrates the `back()` and `forward()` methods of the History object.

Netscape and Mozilla-based browsers also support `back()` and `forward()` methods on the Window object itself. These nonportable methods perform the same action as the browser's **Back** and **Forward** buttons. When frames are used, `window.back()` may perform a different action than `history.back()`.

14.3 Obtaining Window, Screen, and Browser Information

Scripts sometimes need to obtain information about the window, desktop, or browser in which they are running. This section describes properties of the Window, Screen, and Navigator objects that allow you to determine things such as the size of the browser window, the size of the desktop, and the version number of the web browser. This information allows a script to customize its behavior based on its environment.

14.3.1 Window Geometry

Most browsers (the only notable exception is Internet Explorer) support a simple set of properties on the Window object that obtain information about the window's size and position:

```
// The overall size of the browser window on the desktop
var windowWidth = window.outerWidth;
var windowHeight = window.outerHeight;

// This is the position of the browser window on the desktop
var windowX = window.screenX
var windowY = window.screenY

// The size of the viewport in which the HTML document is displayed
// This is the window size minus the menu bars, toolbars, scrollbars, etc.
var viewportWidth = window.innerWidth;
var viewportHeight = window.innerWidth;

// These values specify the horizontal and vertical scrollbar positions.
// They are used to convert between document coordinates and window coordinates.
// These values specify what part of the document appears in the
// upper-left corner of the screen.
var horizontalScroll = window.pageXOffset;
var verticalScroll = window.pageYOffset;
```

Note that these properties are read-only. Window-manipulation methods that allow you to move, resize, and scroll the window are described later in this chapter. Also note that there are several different coordinate systems you must be aware of. *Screen coordinates* describe the position of a browser window on the desktop; they are measured relative to the upper-left corner of the desktop. *Window coordinates* describe a position within the web browser's viewport; they are measured relative to the upper-left corner of the viewport. *Document coordinates* describe a position within an HTML document; they are measured relative to the upper-left corner of the document. When the document is longer or wider than the viewport (as web pages often are), document coordinates and window coordinates are not the same, and you'll need to take the position of the scrollbars into account when converting between these two coordinate systems. There's more about document coordinates in Chapters 15 and 16.

As mentioned earlier, the properties of the Window object listed here are not defined in Internet Explorer. For some reason, IE places these window geometry properties on the <body> of the HTML document. And, further confusing matters, IE 6, when displaying a document with a <!DOCTYPE> declaration, places the properties on the document.documentElement element instead of document.body.

Example 14-2 provides the details. It defines a Geometry object with methods for portably querying the viewport size, scrollbar position, and screen position.

Example 14-2. Portably querying window geometry

```
/**
 * Geometry.js: portable functions for querying window and document geometry
 *
 * This module defines functions for querying window and document geometry.
 *
 * getWindowX/Y( ): return the position of the window on the screen
 * getViewportWidth/Height( ): return the size of the browser viewport area
 * getDocumentWidth/Height( ): return the size of the document
 * getHorizontalScroll( ): return the position of the horizontal scrollbar
 * getVerticalScroll( ): return the position of the vertical scrollbar
 *
 * Note that there is no portable way to query the overall size of the
 * browser window, so there are no getWindowWidth/Height( ) functions.
 *
 * IMPORTANT: This module must be included in the <body> of a document
 *            instead of the <head> of the document.
 */
var Geometry = {};

if (window.screenLeft) { // IE and others
    Geometry.getWindowX = function() { return window.screenLeft; };
    Geometry.getWindowY = function() { return window.screenTop; };
}
else if (window.screenX) { // Firefox and others
    Geometry.getWindowX = function() { return window.screenX; };
    Geometry.getWindowY = function() { return window.screenY; };
}

if (window.innerWidth) { // All browsers but IE
    Geometry.getViewportWidth = function() { return window.innerWidth; };
    Geometry.getViewportHeight = function() { return window.innerHeight; };
    Geometry.getHorizontalScroll = function() { return window.pageXOffset; };
    Geometry.getVerticalScroll = function() { return window.pageYOffset; };
}
else if (document.documentElement && document.documentElement.clientWidth) {
    // These functions are for IE 6 when there is a DOCTYPE
    Geometry.getViewportWidth =
        function() { return document.documentElement.clientWidth; };
    Geometry.getViewportHeight =
        function() { return document.documentElement.clientHeight; };
    Geometry.getHorizontalScroll =
        function() { return document.documentElement.scrollLeft; };
    Geometry.getVerticalScroll =
        function() { return document.documentElement.scrollTop; };
}
else if (document.body.clientWidth) {
    // These are for IE4, IE5, and IE6 without a DOCTYPE
    Geometry.getViewportWidth =
        function() { return document.body.clientWidth; };
    Geometry.getViewportHeight =
        function() { return document.body.clientHeight; };
    Geometry.getHorizontalScroll =
```

Example 14-2. Portably querying window geometry (continued)

```
        function( ) { return document.body.scrollLeft; };
    Geometry.getVerticalScroll =
        function( ) { return document.body.scrollTop; };
}

// These functions return the size of the document. They are not window
// related, but they are useful to have here anyway.
if (document.documentElement && document.documentElemnet.scrollWidth) {
    Geometry.getDocumentWidth =
        function( ) { return document.documentElement.scrollWidth; };
    Geometry.getDocumentHeight =
        function( ) { return document.documentElement.scrollHeight; };
}
else if (document.body.scrollWidth) {
    Geometry.getDocumentWidth =
        function( ) { return document.body.scrollWidth; };
    Geometry.getDocumentHeight =
        function( ) { return document.body.scrollHeight; };
}
```

14.3.2 The Screen Object

The screen property of a Window object refers to a Screen object that provides information about the size of the user's display and the number of colors available on it. The width and height properties specify the size of the display in pixels. You might use these properties to help decide what size images to include in a document, for example.

The availWidth and availHeight properties specify the display size that is actually available; they exclude the space required by features such as a desktop taskbar. Firefox and related browsers (but not IE) also define availLeft and availTop properties of the screen object. These properties specify the coordinates of the first available position on the screen. If you are writing a script that opens a new browser window (you'll learn how to do this later in the chapter), you might use properties like these to help you center it on the screen.

Example 14-4, later in this chapter, illustrates the use of the Screen object.

14.3.3 The Navigator Object

The navigator property of a Window object refers to a Navigator object that contains information about the web browser as a whole, such as the version and a list of the data formats it can display. The Navigator object is named after Netscape Navigator, but it is also supported by all other browsers. (IE also supports clientInformation as a vendor-neutral synonym for navigator. Unfortunately, other browsers have not adopted this more sensibly named property.)

In the past, the Navigator object was commonly used by scripts to determine if they were running in Internet Explorer or Netscape. This browser-sniffing approach is problematic because it requires constant tweaking as new browsers and new versions of existing browsers are introduced. Today, a *capability-testing* approach is preferred. Rather than making assumptions about particular browsers and their capabilities, you simply test for the capability (i.e., the method) you need. For example, here is how you use the capability-testing approach with event-handler registration methods (which are discussed in Chapter 17):

```
if (window.addEventListener) {
    // If the addEventListener( ) method is supported, use that.
    // This covers the case of standards-compliant browsers like
    // Netscape/Mozilla/Firefox.
}
else if (window.attachEvent) {
    // Otherwise, if the attachEvent( ) method exists, use it.
    // This covers IE and any nonstandard browser that decides to emulate it.
}
else {
    // Otherwise, neither method is available.
    // This happens in old browsers that don't support DHTML.
}
```

Browser sniffing is sometimes still valuable, however. One such case is when you need to work around a specific bug that exists in a specific version of a specific browser. The Navigator object lets you do this.

The Navigator object has five properties that provide version information about the browser that is running:

appName

The simple name of the web browser. In IE, this is "Microsoft Internet Explorer". In Firefox and other browsers derived from the Netscape codebase (such as Mozilla and Netscape itself), this property is "Netscape".

appVersion

The version number and/or other version information for the browser. Note that this should be considered an internal version number since it does not always correspond to the version number displayed to the user. For example, Netscape 6 and subsequent releases of Mozilla and Firefox report a version number of 5.0. Also, IE versions 4 through 6 all report a version number of 4.0 to indicate compatibility with the baseline functionality of fourth-generation browsers.

userAgent

The string that the browser sends in its USER-AGENT HTTP header. This property typically contains all the information in both appName and appVersion and may often contain additional details as well. There is no standard formatting for this information, however, so parsing it in a browser-independent way isn't possible.

appCodeName

The code name of the browser. Netscape uses the code name "Mozilla" as the value of this property. For compatibility, IE does the same thing.

platform

The hardware platform on which the browser is running. This property was added in JavaScript 1.2.

The following lines of JavaScript code display each Navigator object property in a dialog box:

```
var browser = "BROWSER INFORMATION:\n";
for(var propname in navigator) {
    browser += propname + ": " + navigator[propname] + "\n"
}
alert(browser);
```

Figure 14-1 shows the dialog box displayed when the code is run on IE 6.

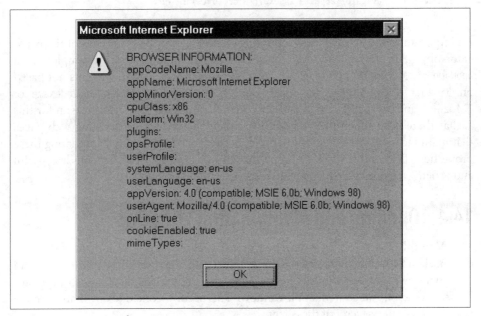

Figure 14-1. Navigator object properties

As you can see from Figure 14-1, the properties of the Navigator object have values that are sometimes more complex than what you need. You may be interested in only the first digit of the appVersion property, for example. When using the Navigator object to test browser information, you can use methods such as parseInt( ) and String.indexOf( ) to extract only the information you want. Example 14-3 shows some code that does this: it processes the properties of the Navigator object and stores them in an object named browser. These properties, in their processed form, are easier to use than the raw navigator properties. The general term for code like this is a *client sniffer*, and you can find more complex and general-purpose sniffer code on the Internet. (See, for example, *http://www.mozilla.org/docs/web-developer/ sniffer/browser_type.html*.) For many purposes, however, code as simple as that shown in Example 14-3 works just fine.

Example 14-3. Determining browser vendor and version

```
/**
 * browser.js: a simple client sniffer
 *
 * This module defines an object named "browser" that is easier to use than
 * the "navigator" object.
 */
var browser = {
    version: parseInt(navigator.appVersion),
    isNetscape: navigator.appName.indexOf("Netscape") != -1,
    isMicrosoft: navigator.appName.indexOf("Microsoft") != -1
};
```

An important point to take away from this section is that the properties of the Navigator object do not reliably describe the browser. Firefox 1.0, for example, has a appName of "Netscape" and a appVersion that begins "5.0". Safari, which is not based on Mozilla code, returns the same values! And IE 6.0 has an appCodeName of "Mozilla" and an appVersion that begins with the number "4.0". The reason for this is that there is so much browser-sniffing code deployed in old, existing web pages that manufacturers cannot afford to break backward compatibility by updating these properties. This is one of the reasons that browser sniffing has become less useful and is being superseded by capability testing.

14.4   Opening and Manipulating Windows

The Window object defines several methods that allow high-level control of the window itself. The following sections explore how these methods allow you to open and close windows, control window position and size, request and relinquish keyboard focus, and scroll the contents of a window. This section concludes with an example that demonstrates several of these features.

14.4.1 Opening Windows

You can open a new web browser window with the open( ) method of the Window object.

Window.open( ) is the method by which advertisements are made to "pop up" or "pop under" while you browse the Web. Because of this flood of annoying pop ups, most web browsers have now instituted some kind of pop-up-blocking system. Typically, calls to the open( ) method are successful only if they occur in response to a user action such as clicking on a button or a link. JavaScript code that tries to open a pop-up window when the browser first loads (or unloads) a page will fail.

`Window.open()` takes four optional arguments and returns a Window object that represents the newly opened window. The first argument to `open()` is the URL of the document to display in the new window. If this argument is omitted (or is `null` or the empty string), the window will be empty.

The second argument to `open()` is the name of the window. As discussed later in the chapter, this name can be useful as the value of the `target` attribute of a `<form>` or `<a>` tag. If you specify the name of a window that already exists, `open()` simply returns a reference to that existing window, rather than opening a new one.

The third optional argument to `open()` is a list of features that specify the window size and GUI decorations. If you omit this argument, the new window is given a default size and has a full set of standard features: a menu bar, status line, toolbar, and so on. On the other hand, if you specify this argument, you can explicitly specify the size of the window and the set of features it includes. For example, to open a small, resizeable browser window with a status bar but no menu bar, toolbar, or location bar, you can use the following line of JavaScript:

```
var w = window.open("smallwin.html", "smallwin",
                    "width=400,height=350,status=yes,resizable=yes");
```

Note that when you specify this third argument, any features you do not explicitly specify are omitted. See `Window.open()` in Part IV for the full set of available features and their names. For various security reasons, browsers include restrictions on the features you may specify. You are typically not allowed to specify a window that is too small or is positioned offscreen, for example, and some browsers will not allow you to create a window without a status line. As spammers, phishers, and other denizens of the dark side of the Web find new ways to spoof users, browser manufactures will place more and more restrictions on the use of the `open()` method.

The fourth argument to `open()` is useful only when the second argument names an existing window. This fourth argument is a boolean value that specifies whether the URL specified as the first argument should replace the current entry in the window's browsing history (`true`) or create a new entry in the window's browsing history (`false`), which is the default behavior.

The return value of the `open()` method is the Window object that represents the newly created window. You can use this Window object in your JavaScript code to refer to the new window, just as you use the implicit Window object `window` to refer to the window within which your code is running. But what about the reverse situation? What if JavaScript code in the new window wants to refer back to the window that opened it? The opener property of a window refers to the window from which it was opened. If the window was created by the user instead of by JavaScript code, the opener property is `null`.

14.4.2 Closing Windows

Just as the open( ) method opens a new window, the close( ) method closes one. If you create a Window object w, you can close it with:

```
w.close();
```

JavaScript code running within that window itself can close it with:

```
window.close();
```

Note the explicit use of the window identifier to distinguish the close( ) method of the Window object from the close( ) method of the Document object.

Most browsers allow you to automatically close only those windows that your own JavaScript code has created. If you attempt to close any other window, the request either fails or the user is presented with a dialog box that asks him to confirm (or cancel) that request to close the window. This precaution prevents inconsiderate scripters from writing code to close a user's main browsing window.

A Window object continues to exist after the window it represents has been closed. You should not attempt to use any of its properties or methods, however, except to test the closed property; this property is true if the window has been closed. Remember that the user can close any window at any time, so to avoid errors, it is a good idea to check periodically that the window you are trying to use is still open.

14.4.3 Window Geometry

The Window object defines methods that move and resize a window. Using these methods is typically considered very poor form: the user should have exclusive control of the size and position of all windows on her desktop. Modern browsers typically have an option to prevent JavaScript from moving and resizing windows, and you should expect this option to be on in a sizable percentage of browsers. Furthermore, in order to thwart malicious scripts that rely on code running in small or off-screen windows that the user does not notice, browsers usually restrict your ability to move windows offscreen or to make them too small. If, after all these caveats, you still want to move or resize a window, read on.

moveTo( ) moves the upper-left corner of the window to the specified coordinates. Similarly, moveBy( ) moves the window a specified number of pixels left or right and up or down. resizeTo( ) and resizeBy( ) resize the window by an absolute or relative amount. Details are in Part IV.

14.4.4 Keyboard Focus and Visibility

The focus( ) and blur( ) methods also provide high-level control over a window. Calling focus( ) requests that the system give keyboard focus to the window, and calling blur( ) relinquishes keyboard focus. In addition, the focus( ) method ensures that the window is visible by moving it to the top of the stacking order. When you use the `Window.open( )` method to open a new window, the browser automatically creates that window on top. But if the second argument specifies the name of a window that already exists, the `open( )` method does not automatically make that window visible. Thus, it is common practice to follow calls to `open( )` with a call to `focus( )`.

14.4.5 Scrolling

The Window object also contains methods that scroll the document within the window or frame. `scrollBy( )` scrolls the document displayed in the window by a specified number of pixels left or right and up or down. `scrollTo( )` scrolls the document to an absolute position. It moves the document so that the specified document coordinates are displayed in the upper-left corner of the document area within the window.

In modern browsers the HTML elements of a document (see Chapter 15) have `offsetLeft` and `offsetTop` properties that specify the X and Y coordinates of the element (see Section 16.2.3 for methods you can use to determine the position of any element). Once you have determined element position, you can use the `scrollTo( )` method to scroll a window so that any specified element is at the upper-left corner of the window.

Another approach to scrolling is to call the `focus( )` method of document elements (such as form fields and buttons) that can accept keyboard focus. As part of transferring focus to the element, the document is scrolled to make the element visible. Note that this does not necessarily put the specified element at the top left of the window but does ensure that it is visible somewhere in the window.

Most modern browsers support another useful scrolling method: calling `scrollIntoView( )` on any HTML element to make that element visible. This method attempts to position the element at the top of the window, but it can't do that if the element is near the end of the document, of course. `scrollIntoView( )` is less widely implemented then the `focus( )` method but works on any HTML element, not just those that can accept keyboard focus. Read more about this method in the HTMLElement section in Part IV.

One final way you can scroll a window under script control is to define anchors with `<a name=>` tags at all locations to which you may want to scroll the document. Then, use these anchor names with the `hash` property of the Location object. For example, if you define an anchor named "top" at the start of your document, you can jump back to the top like this:

```
window.location.hash = "#top";
```

This technique leverages HTML's ability to navigate within a document using named anchors. It makes the current document position visible in the browser's location bar, makes that location bookmarkable, and allows the user to go back to his previous position with the **Back** button, which can be an attractive feature.

On the other hand, cluttering up the user's browsing history with script-generated named anchors could be considered a nuisance in some situations. To scroll to a named anchor without (in most browsers) generating a new history entry, use the Location.replace( ) method instead:

```
window.location.replace("#top");
```

14.4.6 Window Methods Example

Example 14-4 demonstrates the Window open( ), close( ), and moveTo( ) methods and several other window-programming techniques discussed in this chapter. It creates a new window and then uses setInterval( ) to repeatedly call a function that moves it around the screen. It determines the size of the screen with the Screen object and then uses this information to make the window bounce when it reaches any edge of the screen.

Example 14-4. Creating and manipulating windows

```
<script>
var bounce = {
    x:0, y:0, w:200, h:200,   // Window position and size
    dx:5, dy:5,                // Window velocity
    interval: 100,             // Milliseconds between updates
    win: null,                 // The window we will create
    timer: null,               // Return value of setInterval( )

    // Start the animation
    start: function( ) {
        // Start with the window in the center of the screen
        bounce.x = (screen.width - bounce.w)/2;
        bounce.y = (screen.height - bounce.h)/2;

        // Create the window that we're going to move around
        // The javascript: URL is simply a way to display a short document
        // The final argument specifies the window size
        bounce.win = window.open('javascript:"<h1>BOUNCE!</h1>"', "",
                        "left=" + bounce.x + ",top=" + bounce.y +
                        ",width=" + bounce.w + ",height=" +bounce.h+
                        ",status=yes");

        // Use setInterval( ) to call the nextFrame( ) method every interval
        // milliseconds. Store the return value so that we can stop the
        // animation by passing it to clearInterval( ).
        bounce.timer  = setInterval(bounce.nextFrame, bounce.interval);
    },

    // Stop the animation
    stop: function( ) {
```

Example 14-4. Creating and manipulating windows (continued)

```
            clearInterval(bounce.timer);              // Cancel timer
            if (!bounce.win.closed) bounce.win.close(); // Close window
    },

    // Display the next frame of the animation.  Invoked by setInterval()
    nextFrame: function() {
        // If the user closed the window, stop the animation
        if (bounce.win.closed) {
            clearInterval(bounce.timer);
            return;
        }

        // Bounce if we have reached the right or left edge
        if ((bounce.x+bounce.dx > (screen.availWidth - bounce.w)) ||
            (bounce.x+bounce.dx < 0)) bounce.dx = -bounce.dx;

        // Bounce if we have reached the bottom or top edge
        if ((bounce.y+bounce.dy > (screen.availHeight - bounce.h)) ||
            (bounce.y+bounce.dy < 0)) bounce.dy = -bounce.dy;

        // Update the current position of the window
        bounce.x += bounce.dx;
        bounce.y += bounce.dy;

        // Finally, move the window to the new position
        bounce.win.moveTo(bounce.x,bounce.y);

        // Display current position in window status line
        bounce.win.defaultStatus = "(" + bounce.x + "," + bounce.y + ")";
    }
}
</script>
<button onclick="bounce.start()">Start</button>
<button onclick="bounce.stop()">Stop</button>
```

14.5 Simple Dialog Boxes

The Window object provides three methods for displaying simple dialog boxes to the user. alert( ) displays a message to the user and waits for the user to dismiss the dialog. confirm( ) asks the user to click an **OK** or **Cancel** button to confirm or cancel an operation. And prompt( ) asks the user to enter a string.

Although these dialog methods are extremely simple and easy to use, good design dictates that you use them sparingly, if at all. Dialog boxes like these are not a common feature of the web paradigm, and they have become much less common now that more capable web browsers support scripting of the document content itself. Most users will find the dialog boxes produced by the alert( ), confirm( ), and prompt( ) methods disruptive to their browsing experience. The only common use for these methods today is for debugging: JavaScript programmers often insert alert( )

methods in code that is not working in an attempt to diagnose the problem. (See Example 15-9 for a debugging alternative.)

Note that the text displayed by these dialog boxes is plain text, not HTML-formatted text. You can format these dialog boxes only with spaces, newlines, and various punctuation characters.

Some browsers display the word "JavaScript" in the titlebar or upper-left corner of all dialog boxes produced by alert( ), confirm( ), and prompt( ). Although designers find this annoying, it should be considered a feature instead of a bug: it is there to make the origin of the dialog box clear to users and to prevent crackers from writing Trojan-horse code that spoofs system dialog boxes and tricks users into entering their passwords or doing other things they shouldn't do.

The confirm( ) and prompt( ) methods *block*—that is, these methods do not return until the user dismisses the dialog boxes they display. This means that when you pop up one of these boxes, your code stops running, and the currently loading document, if any, stops loading until the user responds with the requested input. There is no alternative to blocking for these methods; their return value is the user's input, so the methods must wait for the user before they can return. In most browsers, the alert( ) method also blocks and waits for the user to dismiss the dialog box.

Example 14-5 shows one possible use of the confirm( ) method, which produces the dialog box shown in Figure 14-2.

Example 14-5. Using the confirm() method

```
function submitQuery( ) {
    // This is what we want to ask the user.
    // Limited formatting is possible with underscores and newlines.
    var message = "\n\n\n\n" +
         "_____\n\n" +
         "Please be aware that complex queries such as yours\n"      +
         "may require a minute or more of search time.\n"     +
         "_____\n\n\n"     +
         "Click Ok to proceed or Cancel to abort";

    // Ask for confirmation, and abort if we don't get it.
    if (!confirm(message)) return;

    /* The code to perform the query would go here */
}
```

14.6   Scripting the Status Line

Web browsers typically display a *status line* at the bottom of every window in which the browser can display messages to the user. When the user moves the mouse over a hypertext link, for example, a browser typically displays the URL to which the link points.

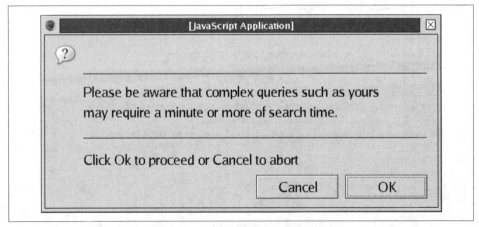

Figure 14-2. A confirm() dialog box

In old browsers, you can set the status property to specify text that the browser should temporarily display in the status line. This property was typically used when the user hovered the mouse over a hyperlink to display a human-readable description of the linked document instead of the machine-readable URL of the document. Code that did this typically looked like this:

```
Confused? Try the
<a href="help.html" onmouseover="status='Click here for help!'; return true;">
Online Help</a>.
```

When the mouse moves over this hyperlink, the JavaScript code in the onmouseover attribute is evaluated. It sets the status property of the window and then returns true to tell the browser not to take its own action (displaying the URL of the hyperlink).

This code snippet no longer works. Code like this was too often used to intentionally deceive users about the destination of a link (in phishing scams, for example), and modern browsers have disabled the ability to set the status property.

The Window object also defines a defaultStatus property that specifies text to be displayed in the status line when the browser doesn't have anything else (such as hyperlink URLs) to display there. defaultStatus still works in some browsers (but not all: Firefox 1.0, for example, disables the defaultStatus property along with the status property).

Historically, one use of the defaultStatus property was to produce status line animations. In the old days, when document content was not yet scriptable, but the defaultStatus property and the setInterval() method were available, web developers proved unable to resist the temptation to create a variety of distracting and gaudy marquee-style animations that scrolled a message across the status line. Fortunately, those days are gone. There are still occasional reasons to use the status line, however, and even to use it with setInterval(), as Example 14-6 demonstrates.

Example 14-6. A tasteful status-line animation

```
<script>
var WastedTime = {
    start: new Date(),    // Remember the time we started
    displayElapsedTime: function() {
        var now = new Date();  // What time is it now
        // compute elapsed minutes
        var elapsed = Math.round((now - WastedTime.start)/60000);
        // And try to display this in the status bar
        window.defaultStatus = "You have wasted " + elapsed + " minutes.";
    }
}
// Update the status line every minute
setInterval(WastedTime.displayElapsedTime, 60000);
</script>
```

14.7 Error Handling

The onerror property of a Window object is special. If you assign a function to this property, the function is invoked whenever a JavaScript error occurs in that window: the function you assign becomes an error handler for the window. (Note that you ought to be able to simply define a global function named onerror( ), as this should be equivalent to assigning a function to the onerror property of a Window object. Defining a global onerror( ) function does not work in IE, however.)

Three arguments are passed to an error handler when a JavaScript error occurs. The first is a message describing the error. This may be something like "missing operator in expression", "self is read-only", or "myname is not defined". The second argument is a string that contains the URL of the document containing the JavaScript code that caused the error. The third argument is the line number within the document where the error occurred. An error handler can use these arguments for any purpose; a typical error handler might display the error message to the user, log it somewhere, or force the error to be ignored. Prior to JavaScript 1.5, the onerror handler can also be used as a poor substitute for try/catch (see Chapter 6) exception handling.

In addition to those three arguments, the return value of the onerror handler is significant. If the onerror handler returns true, it tells the browser that the handler has handled the error and that no further action is necessary—in other words, the browser should not display its own error message.

Browsers have changed the way they handle JavaScript errors over the years. When JavaScript was new, and web browsers were young, it was typical for the browser to pop up a dialog box every time a JavaScript error occurred. These dialogs are useful to developers but disruptive to end users. To prevent an end user from ever seeing an error dialog on a production web site (many web sites cause JavaScript errors, at least in some browsers), you can simply define an error handler that handles all errors silently:

```
// Don't bother the user with error reports
window.onerror = function( ) { return true; }
```

As poorly written and incompatible JavaScript code proliferated on the Web, and JavaScript errors became commonplace, web browsers began to log errors unobtrusively. This is better for end users but more difficult for JavaScript developers, who (in Firefox, for example) have to open up a JavaScript Console window to see whether errors have occurred. To simplify matters during code development, you might define an error handler like this:

```
// Display error messages in a dialog box, but never more than 3
window.onerror = function(msg, url, line) {
    if (onerror.num++ < onerror.max) {
        alert("ERROR: " + msg + "\n" + url + ":" + line);
        return true;
    }
}
onerror.max = 3;
onerror.num = 0;
```

14.8 Multiple Windows and Frames

Most web applications run in a single window, or perhaps open up small auxiliary windows for displaying help. But it is also possible to create applications that use two or more frames or windows and use JavaScript code to make those windows or frames interact with one another. This section explains how it is done.[*]

Before starting the discussion of multiple windows or frames, it is worth reviewing the implications of the same-origin security policy described in Section 13.8.2. Under this policy, JavaScript code can interact only with content from the same web server as the document in which the JavaScript code is embedded. Any attempt to read content or properties of a document from a different web server will fail. This means, for example, that you can write a JavaScript program that indexes its own web site to make a list of all links that appear on the site. However, you cannot extend the program to follow those links and index other sites: your attempt to obtain the list of links in an off-site document will fail. You'll see code that does not work because of the same-origin policy later in Example 14-7.

---

[*] In the early days of JavaScript, multiframe and multiwindow web applications were fairly common. Now, web design consensus has turned strongly against the use of frames (but not inline frames, called *iframes*), and it is less common to see web sites that use interacting windows.

14.8.1 Relationships Between Frames

Recall that the open( ) method of the Window object returns a new Window object representing the newly created window and that this new window has an opener property that refers back to the original window. In this way, the two windows can refer to each other, and each can read properties and invoke methods of the other. The same thing is possible with frames. Any frame in a window can refer to any other frame through the use of the frames, parent, and top properties of the Window object.

The JavaScript code in any window or frame can refer to its own window or frame as window or self. Since every window and frame is a global object for its own code, it is necessary to use window or self only when you need to refer to this global object itself. If you want to refer to a method or property of the window or frame, it is not necessary (although it is sometimes stylistically useful) to prefix the property or method name with window or self.

Every window has a frames property. This property refers to an array of Window objects, each of which represents a frame contained within the window. (If a window does not have any frames, the frames[] array is empty and frames.length is zero.) Thus, a window (or frame) can refer to its first frame as frames[0], its second frame as frames[1], and so on. Similarly, JavaScript code running in a window can refer to the third subframe of its second frame like this:

```
frames[1].frames[2]
```

Every window also has a parent property, which refers to the Window object in which it is contained. Thus, the first frame within a window might refer to its sibling frame (the second frame within the window) like this:

```
parent.frames[1]
```

If a window is a top-level window and not a frame, parent simply refers to the window itself:

```
parent == self;  // For any top-level window
```

If a frame is contained within another frame that is contained within a top-level window, that frame can refer to the top-level window as parent.parent. The top property is a general-case shortcut, however: no matter how deeply a frame is nested, its top property refers to the top-level containing window. If a Window object represents a top-level window, top simply refers to that window itself. For frames that are direct children of a top-level window, the top property is the same as the parent property.

Frames are typically created with <frameset> and <frame> tags. In HTML 4, however, the <iframe> tag can also be used to create an *inline frame* within a document. As far as JavaScript is concerned, frames created with <iframe> are the same as frames created with <frameset> and <frame>. Everything discussed here applies to both kinds of frames.

Figure 14-3 illustrates these relationships between frames and shows how code running in any one frame can refer to any other frame through the use of the frames, parent, and top properties. The figure shows a browser window that contains two frames, one on top of the other. The second frame (the larger one on the bottom) itself contains three subframes, side by side.

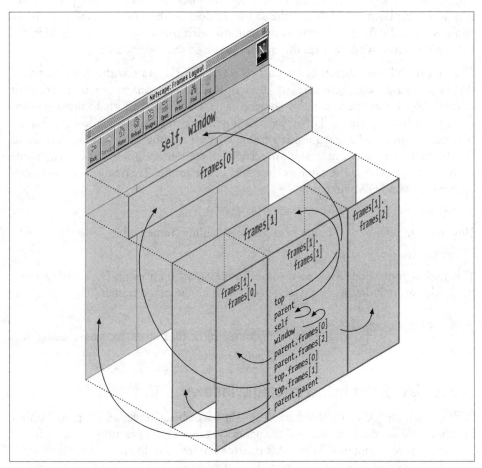

Figure 14-3. Relationships between frames

14.8.2 Window and Frame Names

The second, optional argument to the Window.open( ) method discussed earlier is a name for the newly created window. When you create a frame with the HTML <frame> tag, you can specify a name with the name attribute. An important reason to specify names for windows and frames is that those names can be used as the value of the target attribute of the `<a>` and `<form>` tags, telling the browser where you want to display the results of activating a link or submitting a form.

For example, if you have two windows, one named `table_of_contents` and the other `mainwin`, you might have HTML like the following in the `table_of_contents` window:

```
<a href="chapter01.html" target="mainwin">Chapter 1, Introduction</a>
```

The browser loads the specified URL when the user clicks on this hyperlink, but instead of displaying the URL in the same window as the link, it displays it in the window named `mainwin`. If there is no window with the name `mainwin`, clicking the link creates a new window with that name and loads the specified URL into it.

The target and name attributes are part of HTML and operate without the intervention of JavaScript, but there are also JavaScript-related reasons to give names to your frames. Recall that every Window object has a `frames[]` array that contains references to each of its frames. This array contains all the frames in a window (or frame), whether or not they have names. If a frame is given a name, however, a reference to that frame is also stored in a new property of the parent Window object. The name of that new property is the same as the name of the frame. Therefore, you might create a frame with HTML like this:

```
<frame name="table_of_contents" src="toc.html">
```

Now you can refer to that frame from another, sibling frame with:

```
parent.table_of_contents
```

This makes your code easier to read and understand than using (and relying on) a hardcoded array index, as you'd have to do with an unnamed frame:

```
parent.frames[1]
```

Example 14-7, at the end of this chapter, refers to frames by name using this technique.

14.8.3 JavaScript in Interacting Windows

Back in Chapter 13, you learned that the Window object serves as the global object for client-side JavaScript code, and the window serves as the execution context for all JavaScript code it contains. This holds true for frames as well: every frame is an independent JavaScript execution context. Because every Window object is its own global object, each window defines its own namespace and its own set of global variables. When viewed from the perspective of multiple frames or windows, global variables do not seem all that global, after all!

Although each window and frame defines an independent JavaScript execution context, this does not mean that JavaScript code running in one window is isolated from code running in other windows. Code running in one frame has a different Window object at the top of its scope chain than code running in another frame. However, the code from both frames is executed by the same JavaScript interpreter, in the same JavaScript environment. As you've seen, one frame can refer to any other frame using the frames, parent, and top properties. So, although JavaScript code in different frames is executed with different scope chains, the code in one frame can still refer to and use the variables and functions defined by code in another frame.

For example, suppose code in frame A defines a variable i:

```
var i = 3;
```

That variable is nothing more than a property of the global object—a property of the Window object. Code in frame A can refer to the variable explicitly as such a property with either of these two expressions:

```
window.i
self.i
```

Now suppose that frame A has a sibling frame B that wants to set the value of the variable i defined by the code in frame A. If frame B just sets a variable i, it merely succeeds in creating a new property of its own Window object. So instead, it must explicitly refer to the property i in its sibling frame with code like this:

```
parent.frames[0].i = 4;
```

Recall that the function keyword that defines functions declares a variable just like the var keyword does. If JavaScript code in frame A declares a function f, that function is defined only within frame A. Code in frame A can invoke f like this:

```
f();
```

Code in frame B, however, must refer to f as a property of the Window object of frame A:

```
parent.frames[0].f();
```

If the code in frame B needs to use this function frequently, it might assign the function to a variable of frame B so that it can more conveniently refer to the function:

```
var f = parent.frames[0].f;
```

Now code in frame B can invoke the function as f( ), just as code in frame A does.

When you share functions between frames or windows like this, it is very important to keep the rules of lexical scoping in mind. A function is executed in the scope in which it was defined, not in the scope from which it is invoked. Thus, to continue with the previous example, if the function f refers to global variables, these variables are looked up as properties of frame A, even when the function is invoked from frame B.

If you don't pay careful attention to this, you can end up with programs that behave in unexpected and confusing ways. For example, suppose you define the following function in the <head> section of a multiframe document, with the idea that it will help with debugging:

```
function debug(msg) {
    alert("Debugging message from frame: " + name + "\n" + msg);
}
```

The JavaScript code in each of your frames can refer to this function as `top.debug( )`. Whenever this function is invoked, however, it looks up the variable `name` in the context of the top-level window in which the function is defined, rather than the context of the frame from which it is invoked. Thus, the debugging messages always carry the name of the top-level window rather than the name of the frame that sent the message, as was intended.

Remember that constructors are also functions, so when you define a class of objects with a constructor function and an associated prototype object, that class is defined only for a single window. Recall the Complex class defined in Chapter 9, and consider the following multiframe HTML document:

```
<head>
<script src="Complex.js"></script>
</head>
<frameset rows="50%,50%">
  <frame name="frame1" src="frame1.html">
  <frame name="frame2" src="frame2.html">
</frameset>
```

JavaScript code in the files *frame1.html* and *frame2.html* cannot create a Complex object with an expression like this:

```
var c = new Complex(1,2);  // Won't work from either frame
```

Instead, code in these files must explicitly refer to the constructor function:

```
var c = new top.Complex(3,4);
```

Alternatively, code in either frame can define its own variable to refer more conveniently to the constructor function:

```
var Complex = top.Complex;
var c = new Complex(1,2);
```

Unlike user-defined constructors, predefined constructors are automatically predefined in all windows. Note, however, that each window has an independent copy of the constructor and an independent copy of the constructor's prototype object. For example, each window has its own copy of the `String( )` constructor and the `String.prototype` object. So, if you write a new method for manipulating JavaScript strings and then make it a method of the String class by assigning it to the `String.prototype` object in the current window, all strings in that window can use the new method. However, the new method is not accessible to strings defined in other windows. Note that it does not matter which window holds a reference to the string; only the window in which the string was actually created matters.

14.9   Example: A Navigation Bar in a Frame

This chapter ends with an example that demonstrates many of the more important window scripting techniques described here:

- Querying the current URL with `location.href` and loading new documents by setting the `location` property
- Using the `back( )` and `forward( )` methods of the History object
- Using `setTimeout( )` to defer the invocation of a function
- Opening a new browser window with `window.open( )`
- Using JavaScript in one frame to interact with another frame
- Coping with the restrictions imposed by the same-origin policy

Example 14-7 is a script and simple HTML form designed to be used in a framed document. It creates a simple navigation bar in one frame and uses that bar to control the content of another frame. The navigation bar includes a **Back** button, a **Forward** button, and a text field in which the user can type a URL. You can see the navigation bar near the bottom of Figure 14-4.

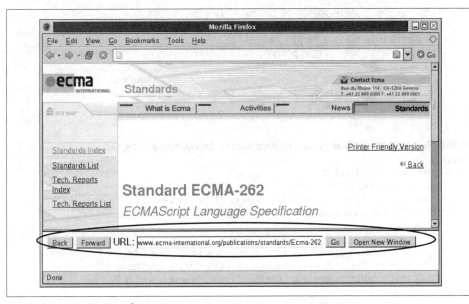

Figure 14-4. A navigation bar

Example 14-7 defines JavaScript functions in a `<script>` and buttons and a URL-entry text field in a `<form>` tag. It uses HTML event handlers to invoke functions when the buttons are clicked. I haven't yet discussed event handlers or HTML forms in detail, but these aspects of the code are not important here. In this example, you'll find uses of the Location and History objects, the `setTimeout( )` function, and the

Window.open( ) function. You'll see how the JavaScript code in the navigation bar frame refers to the other frame by name and also see the use of try/catch blocks in places where the same-origin policy may cause the code to fail.

Example 14-7. A navigation bar

```
<!--
    This file implements a navigation bar, designed to go in a frame.
    Include it in a frameset like the following:

        <frameset rows="*,75">
          <frame src="about:blank" name="main">
          <frame src="navigation.html">
        </frameset>

    The code in this file will control the contents of the frame named "main"
-->
<script>
// The function is invoked by the Back button in our navigation bar
function back() {
    // First, clear the URL entry field in our form
    document.navbar.url.value = "";

    // Then use the History object of the main frame to go back
    // Unless the same-origin policy thwarts us
    try { parent.main.history.back(); }
    catch(e) { alert("Same-origin policy blocks History.back(): " + e.message); }

    // Display the URL of the document we just went back to, if we can.
    // We have to defer this call to updateURL() to allow it to work.
    setTimeout(updateURL, 1000);
}

// This function is invoked by the Forward button in the navigation bar.
function forward() {
    document.navbar.url.value = "";
    try { parent.main.history.forward(); }
    catch(e) { alert("Same-origin policy blocks History.forward(): "+e.message);}
    setTimeout(updateURL, 1000);
}

// This private function is used by back() and forward() to update the URL
// text field in the form. Usually the same-origin policy prevents us from
// querying the location property of the main frame, however.
function updateURL() {
    try { document.navbar.url.value = parent.main.location.href; }
    catch(e) {
        document.navbar.url.value = "<Same-origin policy prevents URL access>";
    }
}

// Utility function: if the url does not begin with "http://", add it.
function fixup(url) {
```

Example 14-7. A navigation bar (continued)

```
    if (url.substring(0,7) != "http://") url = "http://" + url;
    return url;
}

// This function is invoked by the Go button in the navigation bar and also
// when the user submits the form
function go() {
    // And load the specified URL into the main frame.
    parent.main.location = fixup(document.navbar.url.value);
}

// Open a new window and display the URL specified by the user in it
function displayInNewWindow() {
    // We're opening a regular, unnamed, full-featured window, so we just
    // need to specify the URL argument. Once this window is opened, our
    // navigation bar will not have any control over it.
    window.open(fixup(document.navbar.url.value));
}
</script>

<!-- Here's the form, with event handlers that invoke the functions above -->
<form name="navbar" onsubmit="go(); return false;">
  <input type="button" value="Back" onclick="back();">
  <input type="button" value="Forward" onclick="forward();">
  URL: <input type="text" name="url" size="50">
  <input type="button" value="Go" onclick="go();">
  <input type="button" value="Open New Window" onclick="displayInNewWindow();">
</form>
```

CHAPTER 15

Scripting Documents

Client-side JavaScript exists to turn static HTML documents into interactive web applications. Scripting the content of web pages is the raison d'être of JavaScript. This chapter—the most important in Part II—explains how to do this.

Every web browser window (or frame) displays an HTML document. The Window object that represents that window has a document property that refers to a Document object. This Document object is the subject of this chapter, which begins by studying properties and methods of the Document object itself. These are interesting, but they are only the beginning.

More interesting than the Document object itself are the objects that represent the *content* of the document. HTML documents can contain text, images, hyperlinks, form elements, and so on. JavaScript code can access and manipulate the objects that represent each document element. Being able to directly access the objects that represent the content of a document is very powerful, but this is also where things start to get complicated.

A Document Object Model, or DOM, is an API that defines how to access the objects that compose a document. The W3C defines a standard DOM that is reasonably well supported in all modern web browsers. Unfortunately, this has not always been the case. The history of client-side JavaScript programming is really the history of the evolution (sometimes in incompatible ways) of the DOM. In the early days of the Web, Netscape was the leading browser vendor, and it defined the APIs for client-side scripting. Netscape 2 and 3 supported a simple DOM that provided access only to special document elements such as links, images, and form elements. This legacy DOM was adopted by all browser vendors and has been formally incorporated into the W3C standard as the "Level 0" DOM. This legacy DOM still works in all browsers, and I'll cover it first.

With Internet Explorer 4, Microsoft took control of the Web. IE 4 had a revolutionary new DOM: it allowed access to all elements in a document and allowed you to script many of them in interesting ways. It even allowed you to alter the text of a document, reflowing paragraphs of the document as needed. Microsoft's API is known as the IE 4 DOM. It was never standardized, and IE 5 and later adopted the W3C DOM while retaining support for the IE 4 DOM. Portions of the IE 4 DOM were adopted by other browsers, and it is still in use on the Web. I'll discuss it at the end of this chapter, after covering the standard alternative to it.

Netscape 4 took a very different approach to the DOM, based on dynamically positioned scriptable elements known as *layers*. This Netscape 4 DOM was an evolutionary dead end, supported only in Netscape 4 and dropped from the Mozilla and Firefox browsers that sprang from the Netscape codebase. Coverage of the Netscape 4 DOM has been removed from this edition of the book.

The bulk of this chapter covers the W3C DOM standard. Note, however, that I present only the core parts of the standard here. Scripting document content is the reason for client-side JavaScript, and most of the remaining chapters of this book are really continuations of this chapter. Chapter 16 covers the W3C DOM standard for working with CSS styles and stylesheets. Chapter 17 covers the the W3C DOM standard for handling events (as well as legacy and IE-specific techniques for doing those things). Chapter 18 explains the DOM for interacting with HTML form elements, and Chapter 22 explains how to script the <img> tags of an HTML document and how to add scripted drawings to client-side web pages.

The Level 0 DOM defines only a single Document class, and this chapter often refers informally to the Document object. The W3C DOM, however, defines a Document API that provides general document functionality applicable to HTML and XML documents, and a specialized HTMLDocument API that adds HTML-specific properties and methods. The reference material in Part IV of this book follows the W3C convention: if you are looking up HTML-specific document features, look under HTMLDocument. Most of the features of the Level 0 DOM are HTML-specific, and you must look them up under HTMLDocument, even though this chapter refers to them as properties and methods of Document.

15.1 Dynamic Document Content

Let's begin exploring the Document object with its write( ) method, which allows you to write content into the document. This method is part of the legacy DOM and has been around since the very earliest releases of JavaScript. document.write( ) can be used in two ways. The first and simplest way to use it is within a script, to output HTML into the document that is currently being parsed. Consider the following code, which uses write( ) to add the current date to an otherwise static HTML document:

```
<script>
  var today = new Date( );
  document.write("<p>Document accessed on: " + today.toString( ));
</script>
```

Be aware, however, that you can use the write( ) method to output HTML to the current document only while that document is being parsed. That is, you can call document.write( ) from within top-level code in <script> tags only because these scripts are executed as part of the document parsing process. If you place a document.write( ) call within a function definition and then call that function from an event handler, it will not work as you expect—in fact, it will erase the current document and the scripts it contains! (You'll see why shortly.)

document.write( ) inserts text into an HTML document at the location of the <script> tag that contains the invocation of the method. If a <script> tag has a defer attribute, it may not contain any calls to document.write( ). The defer attribute tells the web browser that it is safe to defer execution of the script until the document is fully loaded. And once that has happened, it is too late for document.write( ) to insert content into the document while it is being parsed.

Using the write( ) method to generate document content while the document is being parsed used to be an extremely common JavaScript programming technique. The W3C DOM now allows you to insert content (using techniques you'll learn about later) into any part of a document after the document has been parsed. Nevertheless, this use of document.write( ) is still fairly common.

You can also use the write( ) method (in conjunction with the open( ) and close( ) methods of the Document object) to create entirely new documents in other windows or frames. Although you cannot usefully write to the current document from an event handler, there is no reason why you can't write to a document in another window or frame; doing so can be a useful technique with multiwindow or multi-frame web sites. For example, you might create a pop-up window and write some HTML to it with code like this:

```
// This function opens a pop-up window. Invoke it from an event handler
// or the pop up will probably be blocked.
function hello( ) {
    var w = window.open( );            // Create a new window with no content
    var d = w.document;                // Get its Document object
    d.open( );                         // Start a new document (optional)
    d.write("<h1>Hello world!</h1>");  // Output document content
    d.close( );                        // End the document
}
```

To create a new document, you first call the open( ) method of the Document object, then call write( ) any number of times to output the contents of the document, and finally call the close( ) method of the Document object to indicate that you're finished. This last step is important; if you forget to close the document, the browser does not stop the document-loading animation it displays. Also, the browser may buffer the HTML you have written; it is not required to display the buffered output until you explicitly end the document by calling close( ).

In contrast to the close( ) call, which is required, the open( ) call is optional. If you call the write( ) method on a document that has already been closed, JavaScript implicitly opens a new HTML document, as if you had called the open( ) method. This explains what happens when you call document.write( ) from an event handler within the same document: JavaScript opens a new document. In the process, however, the current document (and its contents, including scripts and event handlers) is discarded. As a general rule of thumb, a document should never call write( ) on itself from within an event handler.

A couple of final notes about the write( ) method. First, many people do not realize that the write( ) method can take more than one argument. When you pass multiple arguments, they are output one after another, just as if they had been concatenated. So instead of writing:

```
document.write("Hello, "  + username + " Welcome to my blog!");
```

you might equivalently write:

```
var greeting = "Hello, ";
var welcome = " Welcome to my blog!";
document.write(greeting, username, welcome);
```

The second point to note about the write( ) method is that the Document object also supports a writeln( ) method, which is identical to the write( ) method in every way except that it appends a newline after outputting its arguments. This can be useful if you are outputting preformatted text within a <pre> tag, for example.

See HTMLDocument in Part IV for complete details on the write( ), writeln( ), open( ), and close( ) methods.

15.2 Document Properties

Having considered the legacy methods of the Document object, let's now turn to its legacy properties:

bgColor
> The background color of the document. This property corresponds to the (deprecated) bgcolor attribute of the <body> tag.

cookie
> A special property that allows JavaScript programs to read and write HTTP cookies. This property is the topic of its very own chapter, Chapter 19.

domain
> A property that allows mutually trusted web servers within the same Internet domain to collaboratively relax same-origin policy security restrictions on interactions between their web pages (see Section 13.8.2).

lastModified
> A string that contains the modification date of the document.

location
> A deprecated synonym for the URL property.

referrer
> The URL of the document containing the link, if any, that brought the browser to the current document.

title
> The text between the `<title>` and `</title>` tags for this document.

URL
> A string specifying the URL from which the document was loaded. The value of this property is the same as the `location.href` property of the Window object, except when a server redirect has occurred.

Several of these properties provide information about the document as a whole. You can place code like the following at the bottom of each of your web documents to provide a useful automated footer that allows users to judge how up-to-date (or out-of-date) a document is when it is printed:

```
<hr><font size="1">
  Document: <i><script>document.write(document.title);</script></i><br>
  URL: <i><script>document.write(document.URL);</script></i><br>
  Last Update: <i><script>document.write(document.lastModified);</script></i>
</font>
```

referrer is another interesting property: it contains the URL of the document from which the user linked to the current document. You can use this property to prevent deep-linking to your site. If you want all visitors to arrive via your own home page, you can redirect them by placing this code at the top of all pages except the home page:

```
<script>
// If linked from somewhere offsite, go to home page first
if (document.referrer == "" || document.referrer.indexOf("mysite.com") == -1)
    window.location = "http://home.mysite.com";
</script>
```

Don't consider this trick to be any kind of serious security measure, of course. It obviously doesn't work for users who have disabled JavaScript in their web browsers.

One final Document property of interest is bgColor. This property corresponds to an HTML attribute whose use is deprecated, but it is listed here because of its history: changing the background color of a document was one of the first applications of client-side JavaScript. Even very, very old web browsers will change the background color of the document if you set document.bgColor to an HTML color string, such as "pink" or "#FFAAAA".

See HTMLDocument in Part IV for complete details on these legacy properties of the Document object.

The Document object has other important properties whose values are arrays of document objects. These document collections are the subject of the next section.

15.3 Legacy DOM: Document Object Collections

The list of Document object properties in the previous section omitted an important category of properties: document object collections. These array-valued properties are the heart of the legacy DOM. They are the properties that give you access to certain special elements of the document:

anchors[]

An array of Anchor objects that represent the anchors in the document. (An *anchor* is a named position in the document; it is created with an <a> tag that has a name attribute instead of an href attribute.) The name property of an Anchor object holds the value of the name attribute. See Part IV for complete details on the Anchor object.

applets[]

An array of Applet objects that represent the Java applets in the document. Applets are discussed in Chapter 23.

forms[]

An array of Form objects that represent the <form> elements in the document. Each Form object has its own collection property named elements[] that contains objects representing the form elements contained in the form. Form objects trigger an onsubmit event handler before the form is submitted. This handler can perform client-side form validation: if it returns false, the browser will not submit the form. The form[] collection is easily the most important one of the legacy DOM, and forms and form elements are the subject of Chapter 18.

images[]

An array of Image objects that represent the <img> elements in the document. The src property of an Image object is read/write, and assigning a URL to this property causes the browser to read and display a new image (in older browsers it must be the same size as the original). Scripting the src property of an Image object allows image-rollover effects and simple animations. These are covered in Chapter 22.

links[]

An array of Link objects that represent the hypertext links in the document. Hypertext links are created in HTML with <a> tags and occasionally with <area> tags in client-side image maps. The href property of a Link object corresponds to the href attribute of the <a> tag: it holds the URL of the link. Link objects also make the various components of a URL available through properties such as protocol, hostname, and pathname. In this way, the Link object is similar to the Location object discussed in Chapter 14. A Link object triggers an onmouseover event handler when the mouse pointer moves over it and an onmouseout handler when the pointer moves off. It triggers an onclick handler when the mouse is clicked over a link. If the event handler returns false, the browser will not follow the link. See Part IV for complete details on Link objects.

As their names imply, these properties are collections of all the links, images, forms, etc., that appear in a document. Their elements are in the same order as in the document source code. `document.forms[0]` refers to the first `<form>` tag in the document, and `document.images[4]` refers to the fifth `<img>` tag, for example.

The objects contained by these legacy DOM collections are scriptable, but it is important to understand that none of them allows you to alter the *structure* of the document. You can inspect and alter link destinations, read and write values from form elements, and even swap one image for another image, but you can't change the text of the document. Old browsers, such as Netscape 2, 3, and 4 and IE 3, were not able to reflow (or relayout) a document once it had been parsed and displayed. For this reason, the legacy DOM did not (and does not) allow document changes that require a reflow. For example, the legacy DOM includes an API for adding new `<option>` elements within a `<select>` element. It can do this because HTML forms display `<select>` elements as pull-down menus, and adding new items to such a menu does not alter the layout of rest of the form. There is no API in the legacy DOM for adding a new radio button to a form or adding a new row to a table, however, because changes like these would require a reflow.

15.3.1 Naming Document Objects

The problem with numerically indexed document object collections is that position-based indexes are brittle: small document changes that reorder document elements can break code that relies on their order. A more robust solution is to assign names to important document elements and to refer to those elements by name. In the legacy DOM, you do this with the name attribute of forms, form elements, images, applets, and links.

When the name attribute is present, its value is used to expose the corresponding object by name. So, for example, suppose an HTML document contains the following form:

```
<form name="f1"><input type="button" value="Push Me"></form>
```

Assuming that the `<form>` is the first one in the document, your JavaScript code can refer to the resulting Form object with any of the following three expressions:

```
document.forms[0]      // Refer to the form by position within the document
document.forms.f1      // Refer to the form by name as a property
document.forms["f1"]   // Refer to the form by name as an array index
```

In fact, setting the name attribute of a `<form>`, `<img>`, or `<applet>` (but not of an `<a>` tag) also makes the corresponding Form, Image, or Applet object (but not Link or Anchor object) accessible as a named property of the document object itself. Thus, you can also refer to the form as:

```
document.f1
```

The elements within a form may also be given names. If you set the name attribute of a form element, the object that represents that form element becomes accessible through a property of the Form object itself. So suppose you have a form that looks like this:

```
<form name="shipping">
  ...
  <input type="text" name="zipcode">
  ...
</form>
```

You can refer to the text input field element of this form with an intuitive syntax:

```
document.shipping.zipcode
```

One final note is necessary about the naming of document elements in the legacy DOM. What happens if two document elements have name attributes with the same value? If a <form> and <img> tag both have the name "n", for example, the document.n property becomes an array that holds references to both elements.

Typically, you should strive to ensure that your name attributes are unique so that this situation does not arise. It is common in one case, however. In HTML forms, convention dictates that groups of related radio buttons and checkboxes are given the same name. When you do this, that name becomes a property of the containing Form object, and the property value is an array that holds references to the various radio button or checkbox objects. You'll learn more about this in Chapter 18.

15.3.2 Event Handlers on Document Objects

To be interactive, an HTML document and the elements within it must respond to user events. You learned a bit about events and event handlers in Chapter 13, and you've seen several examples that use simple event handlers. There are many more examples of event handlers in this chapter because they are the link between document objects and JavaScript code.

I'll defer a complete discussion of events and event handlers until Chapter 17. For now, remember that event handlers are defined by attributes of HTML elements, such as onclick and onmouseover. The values of these attributes should be strings of JavaScript code. This code is executed whenever the specified event occurs on the HTML element.

Document objects accessed through collections such as document.links have properties that correspond to the attributes of the HTML tag. A Link object, for example, has an href tag that mirrors the href attribute of the <a> tag. This holds for event handlers as well. You can define an onclick event handler for a hyperlink either by setting the onclick attribute on the <a> tag or by setting the onclick property of the

Link object. As another example, consider the onsubmit attribute of the <form> element. In JavaScript, the Form object has a corresponding onsubmit property. (Remember that HTML is not case-sensitive, and attributes can be written in uppercase, lowercase, or mixed case. In JavaScript, all event handler properties must be written in lowercase.)

In HTML, event handlers are defined by assigning a string of JavaScript code to an event-handler attribute. In JavaScript, however, they are defined by assigning a function to an event-handler property. Consider the following <form> and its onsubmit event handler:

```
<form name="myform" onsubmit="return validateform( );">...</form>
```

In JavaScript, instead of using a string of JavaScript code that invokes a function and returns its result, simply assign the function directly to the event-handler property like this:

```
document.myform.onsubmit = validateform;
```

Note that there are no parentheses after the function name. This is because you don't want to invoke the function here; you just want to assign a reference to it.

See Chapter 17 for a complete discussion of event handlers.

15.3.3 Legacy DOM Example

Example 15-1 shows a listanchors( ) function that opens a new window and uses document.write( ) to output a list of all the anchors in the original document. Each entry in this list is a link with an event handler that causes the original window to scroll to the location of the specified anchor. The code in this example is particularly useful if you write your HTML documents so that all section headings are enclosed in anchors like this:

```
<a name="sect14.6"><h2>The Anchor Object</h2></a>
```

Note that the listanchors( ) function uses the Window.open( ) method. As shown in Chapter 14, browsers typically block pop-up windows unless they are created in response to a user action. Call listanchors( ) when the user clicks on a link or button; don't do it automatically when your web page loads.

Example 15-1. Listing all anchors

```
/*
 * listanchors.js: Create a simple table of contents with document.anchors[].
 *
 * The function listanchors( ) is passed a document as its argument and opens
 * a new window to serve as a "navigation window" for that document. The new
 * window displays a list of all anchors in the document. Clicking on any
 * anchor in the list causes the document to scroll to that anchor.
 */
```

Example 15-1. Listing all anchors (continued)

```
function listanchors(d) {
    // Open a new window
    var newwin = window.open("", "navwin",
                            "menubar=yes,scrollbars=yes,resizable=yes," +
                            "width=500,height=300");

    // Give it a title
    newwin.document.write("<h1>Navigation Window: " + d.title + "</h1>");

    // List all anchors
    for(var i = 0; i < d.anchors.length; i++) {
        // For each anchor object, determine the text to display.
        // First, try to get the text between <a> and </a> using a
        // browser-dependent property. If none, use the name instead.
        var a = d.anchors[i];
        var text = null;
        if (a.text) text = a.text;                     // Netscape 4
        else if (a.innerText) text = a.innerText;      // IE 4+
        if ((text == null) || (text == '')) text = a.name;  // Default

        // Now output that text as a link. The href property of this link
        // is never used: the onclick handler does the work, setting the
        // location.hash property of the original window to make that
        // window jump to display the named anchor. See Window.opener,
        // Window.location and Location.hash, and Link.onclick.
        newwin.document.write('<a href="#' + a.name + '"' +
                              ' onclick="opener.location.hash=\'' + a.name +
                              '\'; return false;">');
        newwin.document.write(text);
        newwin.document.write('</a><br>');
    }
    newwin.document.close();  // Never forget to close the document!
}
```

15.4   Overview of the W3C DOM

Having examined the simple legacy DOM, let's now move on to the powerful and standardized W3C DOM that extends and replaces it. The API of the W3C DOM is not particularly complicated, but before beginning the discussion of programming with the DOM, there are a number of things you should understand about the DOM architecture.

15.4.1 Representing Documents as Trees

HTML documents have a hierarchical structure of nested tags that is represented in the DOM as a tree of objects. The tree representation of an HTML document contains nodes representing HTML tags or elements, such as <body> and <p>, and nodes representing strings of text. An HTML document may also contain nodes representing HTML comments.[*] Consider the following simple HTML document:

```
<html>
  <head>
    <title>Sample Document</title>
  </head>
  <body>
    <h1>An HTML Document</h1>
    <p>This is a <i>simple</i> document.
  </body>
</html>
```

The DOM representation of this document is the tree pictured in Figure 15-1.

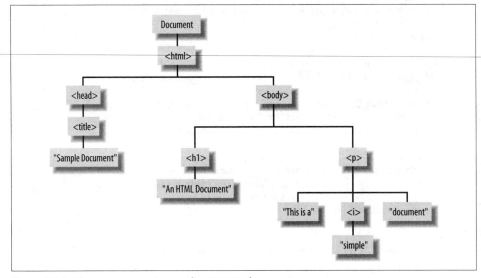

Figure 15-1. The tree representation of an HTML document

If you are not already familiar with tree structures in computer programming, it is helpful to know that they borrow terminology from family trees. The node directly above a node is the *parent* of that node. The nodes one level directly below another node are the *children* of that node. Nodes at the same level, and with the same parent, are *siblings*. The set of nodes any number of levels below another node are the *descendants* of that node. And the parent, grandparent, and all other nodes above a node are the *ancestors* of that node.

---

[*] The DOM can also be used to represent XML documents, which have a more complex syntax than HTML documents, and the tree representation of such a document may contain nodes that represent XML entity references, processing instructions, CDATA sections, and so on. For more about using the DOM with XML, see Chapter 21.

15.4.2 Nodes

The DOM tree structure illustrated in Figure 15-1 is represented as a tree of various types of Node objects. The Node interface[*] defines properties and methods for traversing and manipulating the tree. The childNodes property of a Node object returns a list of children of the node, and the firstChild, lastChild, nextSibling, previousSibling, and parentNode properties provide a way to traverse the tree of nodes. Methods such as appendChild( ), removeChild( ), replaceChild( ), and insertBefore( ) enable you to add and remove nodes from the document tree. You'll see examples of the use of these properties and methods later in this chapter.

15.4.2.1 Types of nodes

Different types of nodes in the document tree are represented by specific subinterfaces of Node. Every Node object has a nodeType property that specifies what kind of node it is. If the nodeType property of a node equals the constant Node.ELEMENT_NODE, for example, you know the Node object is also an Element object, and you can use all the methods and properties defined by the Element interface with it. Table 15-1 lists the node types commonly encountered in HTML documents and the nodeType value for each one.

Table 15-1. Common node types

Interface	nodeType constant	nodeType value
Element	Node.ELEMENT_NODE	1
Text	Node.TEXT_NODE	3
Document	Node.DOCUMENT_NODE	9
Comment	Node.COMMENT_NODE	8
DocumentFragment	Node.DOCUMENT_FRAGMENT_NODE	11
Attr	Node.ATTRIBUTE_NODE	2

The Node at the root of the DOM tree is a Document object. The documentElement property of this object refers to an Element object that represents the root element of the document. For HTML documents, this is the <html> tag that is either explicit or implicit in the document. (The Document node may have other children, such as Comment nodes, in addition to the root element.) In HTML documents, you'll typically be more interested in the <body> element than in the <html> element, and as a convenience, you can use document.body to refer to this element.

---

[*] The DOM standard defines interfaces, not classes. If you are not familiar with the term *interface* in object-oriented programming, think of it as an abstract kind of class. I'll describe the difference in more detail later in this DOM overview.

There is only one Document object in a DOM tree. Most nodes in the tree are Element objects, which represent tags such as <html> and <i>, and Text objects, which represent strings of text. If the document parser preserves comments, those comments are represented in the DOM tree by Comment objects. Figure 15-2 shows a partial class hierarchy for these and other core DOM interfaces.

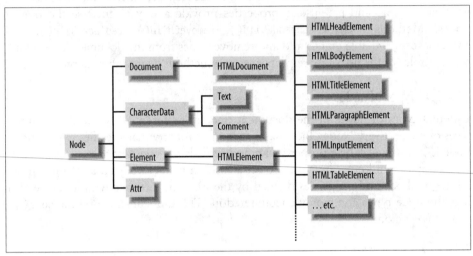

Figure 15-2. A partial class hierarchy of the core DOM API

15.4.2.2 Attributes

The attributes of an element (such as the src and width attributes of an <img> tag) may be queried, set, and deleted using the getAttribute( ), setAttribute( ), and removeAttribute( ) methods of the Element interface. As shown later, standard attributes of HTML tags are available as properties of the Element nodes that represent those tags.

Another, more awkward way to work with attributes is with the getAttributeNode( ) method, which returns an Attr object representing an attribute and its value. (One reason to use this more awkward technique is that the Attr interface defines a specified property that allows you to determine whether the attribute is literally specified in the document or whether its value is a default value.) The Attr interface appears in Figure 15-2 and is a type of node. Note, however, that Attr objects do not appear in the childNodes[ ] array of an element and are not directly part of the document tree in the way that Element and Text nodes are. The DOM specification allows Attr nodes to be accessed through the attributes[ ] array of the Node interface, but Internet Explorer defines a different and incompatible attributes[ ] array that makes it impossible to use this feature portably.

15.4.3 The DOM HTML API

The DOM standard was designed for use with both XML and HTML documents. The core DOM API—the Node, Element, Document, and other interfaces—is relatively generic and applies to both types of documents. The DOM standard also includes interfaces that are specific to HTML documents. As you can see from Figure 15-2, HTMLDocument is an HTML-specific subinterface of Document and HTMLElement is an HTML-specific subinterface of Element. Furthermore, the DOM defines tag-specific interfaces for many HTML elements. These tag-specific interfaces, such as HTMLBodyElement and HTMLTitleElement, typically define a set of properties that mirror the HTML tag's attributes.

The HTMLDocument interface defines various document properties and methods that were supported by browsers prior to W3C standardization. These include the location property, forms[] array, and write() method, which were described earlier in this chapter.

The HTMLElement interface defines id, style, title, lang, dir, and className properties. These properties allow convenient access to the values of the id, style, title, lang, dir, and class attributes, which are allowed on all HTML tags. ("class" is a reserved word in JavaScript, so the class attribute in HTML becomes the className property in JavaScript.) Some HTML tags, listed in Table 15-2, accept no attributes other than these six and so are fully represented by the HTMLElement interface.

Table 15-2. Simple HTML tags

<abbr>	<acronym>	<address>	<b>	<bdo>
<big>	<center>	<cite>	<code>	<dd>
<dfn>	<dt>	<em>	<i>	<kbd>
<noframes>	<noscript>	<s>	<samp>	<small>
<span>	<strike>	<strong>	<sub>	<sup>
<tt>	<u>	<var>		

All other HTML tags have corresponding interfaces defined by the HTML portion of the DOM specification. For many HTML tags, these interfaces do nothing more than provide a set of properties that mirror their HTML attributes. For example, the <ul> tag has a corresponding HTMLULListElement interface, and the <body> tag has a corresponding HTMLBodyElement interface. Because these interfaces simply define properties that are part of the HTML standard, they are not documented in detail in this book. You can safely assume that the HTMLElement object that represents a particular HTML tag has properties for each standard attribute of that tag (but see the naming conventions described in the next section). See the HTMLElement entry in Part IV for a table of HTML tags and their corresponding JavaScript properties.

Note that the DOM standard defines properties for HTML attributes as a convenience for script writers. The general way to query and set attribute values is with the getAttribute( ) and setAttribute( ) methods of the Element object, and you need to use these methods when working with attributes that are not part of the HTML standard.

Some of the interfaces specified by the HTML DOM define properties or methods other than those that simply mirror HTML attribute values. For example, the HTMLInputElement interface defines focus( ) and blur( ) methods and a form property, and the HTMLFormElement interface defines submit( ) and reset( ) methods and a length property. When the JavaScript representation of an HTML element includes properties or methods that do more than simply mirror an HTML attribute, those elements are documented in Part IV. Note, however, that the reference section does not use the verbose interface names defined by the DOM. Instead, for simplicity (and backward compatibility with historical usage); they are documented under simpler names. See, for example, the reference entries for Anchor, Image, Input, Form, Link, Option, Select, Table, and Textarea.

15.4.3.1 HTML naming conventions

When working with the HTML-specific portions of the DOM standard, you should be aware of some simple naming conventions. First, remember that although HTML is not case-sensitive, JavaScript is. Properties of the HTML-specific interfaces begin with lowercase letters. If the property name consists of multiple words, the first letters of the second and subsequent words are capitalized. Thus, the maxlength attribute of the <input> tag translates into the maxLength property of HTMLInputElement.

When an HTML attribute name conflicts with a JavaScript keyword, it is prefixed with the string "html" to avoid the conflict. Thus, the for attribute of the <label> tag translates to the htmlFor property of the HTMLLabelElement. An exception to this rule is the class attribute (which can be specified for any HTML element); it translates to the className property of HTMLElement.*

15.4.4 DOM Levels and Features

There are two versions, or "levels," of the DOM standard. DOM Level 1 was standardized in October 1998. It defines the core DOM interfaces, such as Node, Element, Attr, and Document, and also defines various HTML-specific interfaces. DOM Level 2 was standardized in November 2000. In addition to some updates to the core interfaces, this new version of the DOM is greatly expanded to define standard APIs

---

* The term className is misleading because in addition to specifying a single class name, this property (and the HTML attribute it represents) can also specify a space-separated list of class names.

for working with document events and CSS stylesheets and to provide additional tools for working with ranges of documents.

As of Level 2, the DOM standard has been "modularized." The Core module, which defines the basic tree structure of a document with the Document, Node, Element, and Text interfaces (among others), is the only required module. All other modules are optional and may or may not be supported, depending on the needs of the implementation. The DOM implementation of a web browser would obviously support the HTML module because web documents are written in HTML. Browsers that support CSS stylesheets typically support the StyleSheets and CSS modules because (as shown in Chapter 16) CSS styles play a crucial role in Dynamic HTML programming. Similarly, since almost all interesting client-side JavaScript programming requires event-handling capabilities, you would expect web browsers to support the Events module of the DOM specification. Unfortunately, Microsoft has never implemented the DOM Events module for Internet Explorer, and, as described in Chapter 17, events are handled differently in the legacy DOM, the W3C DOM, and the IE DOM.

This book documents DOM levels 1 and 2; you can find the corresponding reference material in Part IV.

The W3C has continued to refine and expand the DOM standard and has released specifications for several Level 3 modules, including the Level 3 version of the Core module. Level 3 features are not yet widely supported by web browsers (although Firefox has partial support) and are not documented in this edition of this book.

In addition to DOM Levels 1, 2, and 3, you may also sometimes see a reference to DOM Level 0. This term does not refer to any formal standard but does refer informally to the common features of the HTML document object models implemented by Netscape and Internet Explorer prior to W3C standardization. That is, "DOM Level 0" is a synonym for the "legacy DOM."

15.4.5 DOM Conformance

At the time of this writing, recent releases of modern browsers such as Firefox, Safari, and Opera have good or excellent support of the DOM Level 2 standard. Internet Explorer 6 is compliant with the Level 1 DOM but does not support the Level 2 DOM nearly as well. In addition to incomplete support of the Level 2 Core, it has no support at all for the Level 2 Events module, which is the topic of Chapter 17. Internet Explorer 5 and 5.5 have substantial gaps in their Level 1 conformance but support key DOM Level 1 methods well enough to run most of the examples in this chapter.

The number of available browsers has become too large and the rate of change in the area of standards support has grown too fast for this book to even attempt to provide definitive statements about which browsers support which particular DOM features. Therefore, you'll have to rely on other information sources to determine exactly how conformant the DOM implementation is in any particular web browser.

One source for conformance information is the implementation itself. In a conformant implementation, the implementation property of the Document object refers to a DOMImplementation object that defines a method named hasFeature( ). You can use this method (if it exists) to ask an implementation whether it supports a specific feature (or module) of the DOM standard. For example, to determine whether the DOM implementation in a web browser supports the basic DOM Level 1 interfaces for working with HTML documents, you can use the following code:

```
if (document.implementation &&
    document.implementation.hasFeature &&
    document.implementation.hasFeature("html", "1.0")) {
        // The browser claims to support Level 1 Core and HTML interfaces
}
```

The hasFeature( ) method takes two arguments: the name of the feature to check and a version number, both expressed as a string. It returns true if the specified version of the specified feature is supported. Table 15-3 lists the feature name/version number pairs that are defined by the DOM Level 1 and Level 2 standards. Note that the feature names are case-insensitive: you can capitalize them any way you choose. The fourth column of the table specifies what other features are required for support of a feature and are therefore implied by a return value of true. For example, if hasFeature( ) indicates that the MouseEvents module is supported, this implies that UIEvents is also supported, which in turn implies that the Events, Views, and Core modules are supported.

Table 15-3. Features that can be tested with hasFeature()

Feature name	Version	Description	Implies
HTML	1.0	Level 1 Core and HTML interfaces	
XML	1.0	Level 1 Core and XML interfaces	
Core	2.0	Level 2 Core interfaces	
HTML	2.0	Level 2 HTML interfaces	Core
XML	2.0	Level 2 XML-specific interfaces	Core
Views	2.0	AbstractView interface	Core
StyleSheets	2.0	Generic stylesheet traversal	Core
CSS	2.0	CSS styles	Core, Views
CSS2	2.0	CSS2Properties interface	CSS
Events	2.0	Event-handling infrastructure	Core
UIEvents	2.0	User-interface events (plus Events and Views)	Events, Views
MouseEvents	2.0	Mouse events	UIEvents
HTMLEvents	2.0	HTML events	Events

In Internet Explorer 6, hasFeature( ) returns true only for the feature HTML and version 1.0. It does not report compliance to any of the other features listed in Table 15-3 (although, as shown in Chapter 16, it supports the most common uses of the CSS2 module).

This book documents the interfaces that make up all the DOM modules listed in Table 15-3. The Core and HTML modules are covered in this chapter. The StyleSheets, CSS, and CSS2 modules are covered in Chapter 16, and the various Event modules are covered in Chapter 17. Part IV includes complete coverage of all modules.

The hasFeature( ) method is not always perfectly reliable. As previously noted, IE 6 reports Level 1 compliance to HTML features even though there are some problems with its compliance. On the other hand, Netscape 6.1 reported noncompliance to the Level 2 Core feature even though it was mostly compliant. In both cases, you need fine-grained information about exactly what is and is not compliant. This is exactly the type of information that is too voluminous and volatile to include in a printed book.

If you are an active web developer, you undoubtedly already know or will discover many browser-specific support details on your own. There are also resources on the Web that can help you. The W3C has published a partial test suite for certain DOM modules at *http://www.w3c.org/DOM/Test/*. Unfortunately, it has not published its results from applying this suite to common browsers.

Perhaps the best place to find compatibility and compliance information is at independent sites on the Web. One notable site is *http://www.quirksmode.org* by Peter-Paul Koch; it includes the results of the author's extensive research into browser compatibility with the DOM and CSS standards. Another is *http://webdevout.net/browser_support.php* by David Hammond.

15.4.5.1 DOM conformance in Internet Explorer

Because IE is the most widely used web browser, a few special notes about its compliance to the DOM specifications are appropriate here. IE 5 and later support the Level 1 Core and HTML features well enough to run the examples in this chapter, and they support the key Level 2 CSS features well enough to run most of the examples in Chapter 16. Unfortunately, IE 5, 5.5, and 6 do not support the DOM Level 2 Events module, even though Microsoft participated in the definition of this module and had ample time to implement it for IE 6. IE's lack of support for the standard event model impedes the development of advanced client-side web applications.

Although IE 6 claims (through its hasFeature( ) method) to support the Core and HTML interfaces of the DOM Level 1 standard, this support is actually incomplete. The most egregious problem, and the one you are most likely to encounter, is a minor but annoying one: IE does not support the node-type constants defined by the

Node interface. Recall that each node in a document has a nodeType property that specifies what type of node it is. The DOM specification also says that the Node interface defines constants that represent each defined node type. For example, the constant Node.ELEMENT_NODE represents an Element node. In IE (at least as high as version 6), these constants simply do not exist.

The examples in this chapter have been modified to work around this problem by using integer literals instead of the corresponding symbolic constants. For example, you'll see code like this:

```
if (n.nodeType == 1 /*Node.ELEMENT_NODE*/)  // Check if n is an Element
```

It is good programming style to use constants instead of hardcoded integer literals in your code, and if you'd like to do this portably, you can include the following code in your programs to define these constants if they are missing:

```
if (!window.Node) {
    var Node = {                     // If there is no Node object, define one
        ELEMENT_NODE: 1,             // with the following properties and values.
        ATTRIBUTE_NODE: 2,           // Note that these are HTML node types only.
        TEXT_NODE: 3,                // For XML-specific nodes, you need to add
        COMMENT_NODE: 8,             // other constants here.
        DOCUMENT_NODE: 9,
        DOCUMENT_FRAGMENT_NODE: 11
    };
}
```

15.4.6 Language-Independent DOM Interfaces

Although the DOM standard grew out of a desire to have a common API for dynamic HTML programming, the DOM is not of interest only to web scripters. In fact, the standard is currently most heavily used by server-side Java and C++ programs that parse and manipulate XML documents. Because of its many uses, the DOM standard is defined as language-independent. This book describes only the JavaScript binding of the DOM API, but you should be aware of a few other points. First, note that object properties in the JavaScript binding are typically mapped to pairs of get/set methods in other language bindings. Thus, when a Java programmer asks you about the getFirstChild( ) method of the Node interface, you need to understand that the JavaScript binding of the Node API doesn't define a getFirstChild( ) method. Instead, it simply defines a firstChild property, and reading the value of this property in JavaScript is equivalent to calling getFirstChild( ) in Java.

Another important feature of the JavaScript binding of the DOM API is that certain DOM objects behave like JavaScript arrays. If an interface defines a method named item( ), objects that implement that interface behave like read-only numerical arrays. For example, suppose you've obtained a NodeList object by reading the childNodes property of a node. You can obtain the individual Node objects in the list by passing the desired node number to the item( ) method, or, more simply, you can simply treat the NodeList object as an array and index it directly. The following code illustrates these two options:

```
var n = document.documentElement;   // This is a Node object.
var children = n.childNodes;        // This is a NodeList object.
var head = children.item(0);        // Here is one way to use a NodeList.
var body = children[1];             // But this way is easier!
```

Similarly, if a DOM object has a namedItem( ) method, passing a string to this method is the same as using the string as an array index for the object. For example, the following lines of code are all equivalent ways to access a form element:

```
var f = document.forms.namedItem("myform");
var g = document.forms["myform"];
var h = document.forms.myform;
```

Although you can use array notation to access the elements of a NodeList, it is important to remember that a NodeList is simply an array-like object (see Section 7.8), not a true Array. A NodeList does not have a sort( ) method, for example.

Because the DOM standard may be used in a variety of ways, the architects of the standard were careful to define the DOM API in a way that would not restrict the ability of others to implement the API as they saw fit. Specifically, the DOM standard defines interfaces instead of classes. In object-oriented programming, a class is a fixed data type that must be implemented exactly as specified. An interface, on the other hand, is a collection of methods and properties that must be implemented together. Thus, an implementation of the DOM is free to define whatever classes it sees fit, but those classes must define the methods and properties of the various DOM interfaces.

This architecture has a couple of important implications. First, the class names used in an implementation might not correspond directly to the interface names used in the DOM standard. Second, a single class may implement more than one interface. For example, consider the Document object. This object is an instance of some class defined by the web browser implementation. We don't know what the specific class is, but we do know that it implements the DOM Document interface—that is, all methods and properties defined by Document are available to us through the Document object. Since web browsers work with HTML documents, we also know that the Document object implements the HTMLDocument interface and that all methods and properties defined by that interface are available to us as well. Furthermore, since web browsers support CSS, the Document object also implements the DocumentStyle and DocumentCSS DOM interfaces. And if the web browser supports the DOM Events and Views modules, Document implements the DocumentEvent and DocumentView interfaces as well.

In general, Part IV focuses on the objects that client-side JavaScript programmers actually interact with, rather than the more abstract interfaces that specify the API of those objects. Therefore, you'll find that the reference section contains entries for Document and HTMLDocument, but not for the minor add-on interfaces like DocumentCSS and DocumentView. The methods defined by those interfaces are simply integrated into the entry for the Document object.

Another important fact you need to understand is that because the DOM standard defines interfaces instead of classes, it does not define any constructor methods. If you want to create a new Text object to insert into a document, for example, you cannot write:

```
var t = new Text("this is a new text node");  // No such constructor!
```

Since it cannot define constructors, the DOM standard instead defines a number of useful *factory methods* in the Document interface. So, to create a new Text node for a document, you would write the following:

```
var t = document.createTextNode("this is a new text node");
```

Factory methods defined by the DOM have names that begin with the word "create". In addition to the factory methods defined by Document, a few others are defined by DOMImplementation and available through `document.implementation`.

15.5 Traversing a Document

With the preceding overview of the W3C DOM under your belt, you are now ready to start using the DOM API. This section and the sections that follow it demonstrate how to traverse DOM trees, find specific elements within a document, modify document content, and add new content to a document.

As already discussed, the DOM represents an HTML document as a tree of Node objects. With any tree structure, one of the most common things to do is traverse the tree, examining each node of the tree in turn. Example 15-2 shows one way to do this. It is a JavaScript function that recursively examines a node and all its children, adding up the number of HTML tags (i.e., Element nodes) it encounters in the course of the traversal. Note the use of the `childNodes` property of a node. The value of this property is a NodeList object, which behaves (in JavaScript) like an array of Node objects. Thus, the function can enumerate all the children of a given node by looping through the elements of the `childNodes[]` array. By recursing, the function enumerates not just all children of a given node, but all nodes in the tree of nodes. Note that this function also demonstrates the use of the `nodeType` property to determine the type of each node.

Example 15-2. Traversing the nodes of a document

```
<head>
<script>
// This function is passed a DOM Node object and checks to see if that node
// represents an HTML tag—i.e., if the node is an Element object. It
```

Example 15-2. Traversing the nodes of a document (continued)

```
// recursively calls itself on each of the children of the node, testing
// them in the same way. It returns the total number of Element objects
// it encounters. If you invoke this function by passing it the
// Document object, it traverses the entire DOM tree.
function countTags(n) {                        // n is a Node
    var numtags = 0;                           // Initialize the tag counter
    if (n.nodeType == 1 /*Node.ELEMENT_NODE*/) // Check if n is an Element
        numtags++;                             // Increment the counter if so
    var children = n.childNodes;               // Now get all children of n
    for(var i=0; i < children.length; i++) {   // Loop through the children
        numtags += countTags(children[i]);     // Recurse on each one
    }
    return numtags;                            // Return the total
}
</script>
</head>
<!-- Here's an example of how the countTags() function might be used -->
<body onload="alert('This document has ' + countTags(document) + ' tags')">
This is a <i>sample</i> document.
</body>
```

Another point to notice about Example 15-2 is that the countTags( ) function it defines is invoked from the onload event handler so that it is not called until the document is completely loaded. This is a general requirement when working with the DOM: you cannot traverse or manipulate the document tree until the document has been fully loaded. (See Section 13.5.7 for further details on this requirement. Also see Example 17-7 for a utility function that allows multiple modules to register onload event handlers.)

In addition to the childNodes property, the Node interface defines a few other useful properties. firstChild and lastChild refer to the first and last children of a node, and nextSibling and previousSibling refer to adjacent siblings of a node. (Two nodes are siblings if they have the same parent node.) These properties provide another way to loop through the children of a node, demonstrated in Example 15-3. This example defines a function named getText( ) that finds all Text nodes at or beneath a specified node. It extracts and concatenates the textual content of the nodes and returns it as a single JavaScript string. The need for a utility function like this arises surprisingly frequently in DOM programming.

Example 15-3. Obtaining all text beneath a DOM node

```
/**
 * getText(n): Find all Text nodes at or beneath the node n.
 * Concatenate their content and return it as a string.
 */
function getText(n) {
    // Repeated string concatenation can be inefficient, so we collect
    // the value of all text nodes into an array, and then concatenate
    // the elements of that array all at once.
```

Example 15-3. Obtaining all text beneath a DOM node (continued)

```
var strings = [];
getStrings(n, strings);
return strings.join("");

// This recursive function finds all text nodes and appends
// their text to an array.
function getStrings(n, strings) {
    if (n.nodeType == 3 /* Node.TEXT_NODE */)
        strings.push(n.data);
    else if (n.nodeType == 1 /* Node.ELEMENT_NODE */) {
        // Note iteration with firstChild/nextSibling
        for(var m = n.firstChild; m != null; m = m.nextSibling) {
            getStrings(m, strings);
        }
    }
}
}
```

15.6 Finding Elements in a Document

The ability to traverse all nodes in a document tree gives you the power to find specific nodes. When programming with the DOM API, it is quite common to need a particular node within the document or a list of nodes of a specific type within the document. Fortunately, the DOM API provides functions that make this easy.

The Document object is the root of every DOM tree, but it does not represent an HTML element in that tree. The document.documentElement property refers to the <html> tag that serves as the root element of the document. And the document.body property refers to the <body> tag which is more commonly useful than its <html> parent.

The body property of the HTMLDocument object is a convenient special-case property. If it did not exist, however, you could also refer to the <body> tag like this:

```
document.getElementsByTagName("body")[0]
```

This expression calls the Document object's getElementsByTagName( ) method and selects the first element of the returned array. The call to getElementsByTagName( ) returns an array of all <body> elements within the document. Since HTML documents can have only one <body>, you're interested in the first element of the returned array.[*]

You can use getElementsByTagName( ) to obtain a list of any type of HTML element. For example, to find all the tables within a document, you'd do this:

```
var tables = document.getElementsByTagName("table");
alert("This document contains " + tables.length + " tables");
```

---

[*] Technically, getElementsByTagName( ) returns a NodeList, which is an array-like object. In this book, I use array notation for indexing them and informally refer to them as "arrays."

Note that since HTML tags are not case-sensitive, the strings passed to getElementsByTagName( ) are also not case-sensitive. That is, the previous code finds `<table>` tags even if they are coded as `<TABLE>`. getElementsByTagName( ) returns elements in the order in which they appear in the document. Finally, if you pass the special string "*" to getElementsByTagName( ), it returns a list of all elements in the document, in the order in which they appear. (This special usage is not supported in IE 5 and IE 5.5. See instead the IE-specific HTMLDocument.all[ ] in Part IV.)

Sometimes you don't want a list of elements but instead want to operate on a single specific element of a document. If you know a lot about the structure of the document, you may still be able to use getElementsByTagName( ). For example, if you want to do something to the fourth paragraph in a document, you might use this code:

```
var myParagraph = document.getElementsByTagName("p")[3];
```

This typically is not the best (nor the most efficient) technique, however, because it depends so heavily on the structure of the document; a new paragraph inserted at the beginning of the document would break the code. Instead, when you need to manipulate specific elements of a document, it is best to give those elements an id attribute that specifies a unique (within the document) name for the element. You can then look up your desired element by its ID. For example, you might code the special fourth paragraph of your document with a tag like this:

```
<p id="specialParagraph">
```

You can then look up the node for that paragraph with JavaScript code like this:

```
var myParagraph = document.getElementById("specialParagraph");
```

Note that the getElementById( ) method does not return an array of elements as getElementsByTagName( ) does. Because the value of every id attribute is (or is supposed to be) unique, getElementById( ) returns only the single element with the matching id attribute.

getElementById( ) is an important method, and its use is extremely common in DOM programming. It is so commonly used that you may want to define a utility function with a shorter name. For example:

```
// If x is a string, assume it is an element id and look up the named element.
// Otherwise, assume x is already an element and just return it.
function id(x) {
    if (typeof x == "string") return document.getElementById(x);
    return x;
}
```

With a function like this defined, your DOM manipulation methods can be written to accept elements or element IDs as their arguments. For each such argument x, simply write x = id(x) before use. One well-known client-side JavaScript toolkit[*] defines a utility method like this but gives it an even shorter name: $( ).

---

[*] The Prototype library by Sam Stephenson, available from *http://prototype.conio.net*.

getElementById( ) and getElementsByTagName( ) are both methods of the Document object. Element objects also define a getElementsByTagName( ) method, however. This method of the Element object behaves just like the method of the Document object, except that it returns only elements that are descendants of the element on which it is invoked. Instead of searching the entire document for elements of a specific type, it searches only within the given element. This makes it possible, for example, to use getElementById( ) to find a specific element and then to use getElementsByTagName( ) to find all descendants of a given type within that specific tag. For example:

```
// Find a specific Table element within a document and count its rows
var tableOfContents = document.getElementById("TOC");
var rows = tableOfContents.getElementsByTagName("tr");
var numrows = rows.length;
```

Finally, note that for HTML documents, the HTMLDocument object also defines a getElementsByName( ) method. This method is like getElementById( ), but it looks at the name attribute of elements rather than the id attribute. Also, because the name attribute is not expected to be unique within a document (for example, radio buttons within HTML forms usually have the same name), getElementsByName( ) returns an array of elements rather than a single element. For example:

```
// Find <a name="top">
var link = document.getElementsByName("top")[0];
// Find all <input type="radio" name="shippingMethod"> elements
var choices = document.getElementsByName("shippingMethod");
```

In addition to selecting document elements by tag name or ID, it is also often useful to select elements that are members of a class. The HTML class attribute and the corresponding JavaScript className property assign an element to one or more named (and whitespace delimited) classes. These classes are intended for use with CSS stylesheets (see Chapter 16) but that need not be their only purpose. Suppose you code important warnings in an HTML document like this:

```
<div class="warning">
This is a warning
</div>
```

You can then use a CSS stylesheet to specify the colors, margins, borders, and other presentational attributes of those warnings. But what if you also wanted to write JavaScript code that could find and operate on <div> tags that are members of the "warning" class? Example 15-4 has a solution. This example defines a getElements( ) method that allows you to select elements by class and/or tag name. Note that the className property is a tricky one because an HTML element can be a member of more than one class. getElements( ) includes a nested isMember( ) method that tests whether a specified HTML element is a member of a specified class.

Example 15-4. Selecting HTML elements by class or tag name

```
/**
 * getElements(classname, tagname, root):
 * Return an array of DOM elements that are members of the specified class,
```

Example 15-4. Selecting HTML elements by class or tag name (continued)

```
 * have the specified tagname, and are descendants of the specified root.
 *
 * If no classname is specified, elements are returned regardless of class.
 * If no tagname is specified, elements are returned regardless of tagname.
 * If no root is specified, the document object is used. If the specified
 * root is a string, it is an element id, and the root
 * element is looked up using getElementsById( )
 */
function getElements(classname, tagname, root) {
    // If no root was specified, use the entire document
    // If a string was specified, look it up
    if (!root) root = document;
    else if (typeof root == "string") root = document.getElementById(root);

    // if no tagname was specified, use all tags
    if (!tagname) tagname = "*";

    // Find all descendants of the specified root with the specified tagname
    var all = root.getElementsByTagName(tagname);

    // If no classname was specified, we return all tags
    if (!classname) return all;

    // Otherwise, we filter the element by classname
    var elements = [];  // Start with an empty array
    for(var i = 0; i < all.length; i++) {
        var element = all[i];
        if (isMember(element, classname)) // isMember( ) is defined below
            elements.push(element);         // Add class members to our array
    }

    // Note that we always return an array, even if it is empty
    return elements;

    // Determine whether the specified element is a member of the specified
    // class. This function is optimized for the common case in which the
    // className property contains only a single classname. But it also
    // handles the case in which it is a list of whitespace-separated classes.
    function isMember(element, classname) {
        var classes = element.className;  // Get the list of classes
        if (!classes) return false;              // No classes defined
        if (classes == classname) return true;  // Exact match

        // We didn't match exactly, so if there is no whitespace, then
        // this element is not a member of the class
        var whitespace = /\s+/;
        if (!whitespace.test(classes)) return false;

        // If we get here, the element is a member of more than one class and
        // we've got to check them individually.
        var c = classes.split(whitespace);  // Split with whitespace delimiter
        for(var i = 0; i < c.length; i++) { // Loop through classes
```

Example 15-4. Selecting HTML elements by class or tag name (continued)

```
        if (c[i] == classname) return true;  // and check for matches
    }

    return false;  // None of the classes matched
  }
}
```

15.7 Modifying a Document

Traversing the nodes of a document can be useful, but the real power of the Core DOM API lies in the features that allow you to use JavaScript to dynamically modify documents. The following examples demonstrate the basic techniques of modifying documents and illustrate some of the possibilities.

Example 15-5 includes a JavaScript function named sortkids( ), a sample document, and an HTML button that, when pressed, calls the sortkids( ) function, passing it the ID of a <ul> tag. The sortkids( ) function finds the element children of the specified node, sorts them based on the text they contain, and rearranges them in the document (using appendChild( )) so that they appear in alphabetical order.

Example 15-5. Alphabetizing the elements of a list

```
<script>
function sortkids(e) {
    // This is the element whose children we are going to sort
    if (typeof e == "string") e = document.getElementById(e);

    // Transfer the element (but not text node) children of e to a real array
    var kids = [];
    for(var x = e.firstChild; x != null; x = x.nextSibling)
        if (x.nodeType == 1 /* Node.ELEMENT_NODE */) kids.push(x);

    // Now sort the array based on the text content of each kid.
    // Assume that each kid has only a single child and it is a Text node
    kids.sort(function(n, m) { // This is the comparator function for sorting
                var s = n.firstChild.data; // text of node n
                var t = m.firstChild.data; // text of node m
                if (s < t) return -1;      // n comes before m
                else if (s > t) return 1;  // n comes after m
                else return 0;             // n and m are equal
            });

    // Now append the kids back into the parent in their sorted order.
    // When we insert a node that is already part of the document, it is
    // automatically removed from its current position, so reinserting
    // these nodes automatically moves them from their old position
    // Note that any text nodes we skipped get left behind, however.
    for(var i = 0; i < kids.length; i++) e.appendChild(kids[i]);
}
</script>
```

Example 15-5. Alphabetizing the elements of a list (continued)

```
<ul id="list"> <!-- This is the list we'll sort -->
<li>one<li>two<li>three<li>four <!-- items are not in alphabetical order -->
</ul>
<!-- this is the button that sorts the list -->
<button onclick="sortkids('list')">Sort list</button>
```

The result of Example 15-5, illustrated in Figure 15-3, is that when the user clicks the button, the list items are alphabetized.

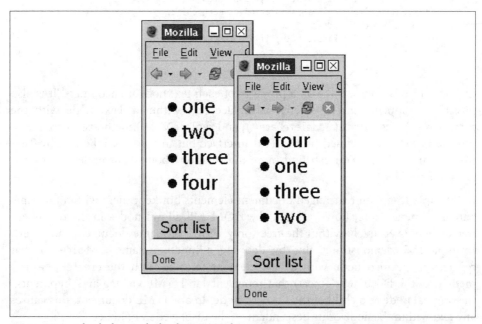

Figure 15-3. A list before and after being sorted

Note that Example 15-5 copied the nodes it was going to sort to a separate array. This enables you to easily sort the array but has another benefit as well. The NodeList objects that are the value of the childNodes property and that are returned by getElementsByTagName( ) are "live": any changes to the document are immediately reflected in the NodeList. This can be a source of difficulty if you insert or delete nodes from a list while iterating through that list. Thus it is often safest to take a "snapshot" of the nodes, by transferring them to a true array before looping through them.

Example 15-5 altered the structure of a document by rearranging elements. Example 15-6 alters the content of a document by changing its text. This example defines a function upcase( ) that recursively descends from a specified Node and converts the content of any Text nodes it finds to uppercase.

Example 15-6. Converting document content to uppercase

```
// This function recursively looks at Node n and its descendants,
// converting all Text node data to uppercase
function upcase(n) {
    if (n.nodeType == 3 /*Node.TEXT_NODE*/) {
        // If the node is a Text node, change its text to uppercase.
        n.data = n.data.toUpperCase();
    }
    else {
        // If the node is not a Text node, loop through its children
        // and recursively call this function on each child.
        var kids = n.childNodes;
        for(var i = 0; i < kids.length; i++) upcase(kids[i]);
    }
}
```

Example 15-6 simply sets the data property of each text node it encounters. It is also possible to append, insert, delete, or replace text within a Text node with the appendData( ), insertData( ), deleteData( ), and replaceData( ) methods. These methods are not directly defined by the Text interface but instead are inherited by Text from CharacterData. You can find more information about them under Character-Data in Part IV.

In Example 15-5, you rearranged document elements but kept them within the same parent element. Note, however, that the DOM API allows nodes in the document tree to be moved freely within the tree (only within the same document, however). Example 15-7 demonstrates this by defining a function named embolden( ) that replaces a specified node with a new element (created with the createElement( ) method of the Document object) that represents an HTML <b> tag and "reparents" the original node as a child of the new <b> node. In an HTML document, this causes any text within the node or its descendants to be displayed in boldface.

Example 15-7. Reparenting a node to a <b> element

```
<script>
// This function takes a Node n, replaces it in the tree with an Element node
// that represents an HTML <b> tag, and then makes the original node the
// child of the new <b> element.
function embolden(n) {
    if (typeof n == "string") n = document.getElementById(n); // Lookup node
    var b = document.createElement("b"); // Create a new <b> element
    var parent = n.parentNode;            // Get the parent of the node
    parent.replaceChild(b, n);            // Replace the node with the <b> tag
    b.appendChild(n);                     // Make the node a child of the <b> element
}
</script>

<!-- A couple of sample paragraphs -->
<p id="p1">This <i>is</i> paragraph #1.</p>
<p id="p2">This <i>is</i> paragraph #2.</p>
```

Example 15-7. Reparenting a node to a <b> element (continued)

```
<!-- A button that invokes the embolden( ) function on the element named p1 -->
<button onclick="embolden('p1');">Embolden</button>
```

15.7.1 Modifying Attributes

In addition to modifying documents by altering text and reparenting or otherwise rearranging nodes, it is also possible to make substantial changes to a document simply by setting attribute values on document elements. One way to do this is with the element.setAttribute( ) method. For example:

```
var headline = document.getElementById("headline");  // Find named element
headline.setAttribute("align", "center");              // Set align='center'
```

The DOM elements that represent HTML attributes define JavaScript properties that correspond to each of their standard attributes (even deprecated attributes such as align), so you can also achieve the same effect with this code:

```
var headline = document.getElementById("headline");
headline.align = "center";  // Set alignment attribute.
```

As shown in Chapter 16, you can achieve a whole world of useful effects by altering the CSS style properties of HTML elements in this way. Doing so does not alter the document structure or content, but instead alters its *presentation*.

15.7.2 Working with Document Fragments

A DocumentFragment is a special type of node that does not appear in a document itself but serves as a temporary container for a sequential collection of nodes and allows those nodes to be manipulated as a single object. When a DocumentFragment is inserted into a document (using any of the appendChild( ), insertBefore( ), or replaceChild( ) methods of the Node object), it is not the DocumentFragment itself that is inserted, but each of its children.

You can create a DocumentFragment with document.createDocumentFragment( ). You can add nodes to a DocumentFragment with appendChild( ) or any of the related Node methods. Then, when you are ready to add those nodes to the document, add the DocumentFragment itself. After you do this, the fragment is empty and cannot be reused unless you first add new children to it. Example 15-8 demonstrates this process. It defines a reverse( ) function that uses a DocumentFragment as a temporary container while reversing the order of the children of a Node.

Example 15-8. Using a DocumentFragment

```
// Reverse the order of the children of Node n
function reverse(n) {
    // Create an empty DocumentFragment as a temporary container
    var f = document.createDocumentFragment( );
```

Example 15-8. Using a DocumentFragment (continued)

```
    // Now loop backward through the children, moving each one to the fragment.
    // The last child of n becomes the first child of f, and vice-versa.
    // Note that appending a child to f automatically removes it from n.
    while(n.lastChild) f.appendChild(n.lastChild);

    // Finally, move the children of f all at once back to n, all at once.
    n.appendChild(f);
}
```

15.8 Adding Content to a Document

The methods Document.createElement( ) and Document.createTextNode( ) create new
Element and Text nodes, and the methods Node.appendChild( ), Node.insertBefore( ),
and Node.replaceChild( ) can be used to add them to a document. With these methods, you can build up a DOM tree of arbitrary document content.

Example 15-9 is an extended example that defines a log( ) function for message and
object logging. The example also includes a log.debug( ) utility function that can be
a helpful alternative to inserting alert( ) calls when debugging JavaScript code. The
"message" passed to the log( ) function can be either a string of plain text or a Java-
Script object. When a string is logged, it is simply displayed as it is. When an object
is logged, it is displayed as a table of property names and property values. In either
case, the createElement( ) and createTextNode( ) functions create the new content.

With an appropriate CSS stylesheet (which is shown in the example), the log( ) function of Example 15-9 generates output like that shown in Figure 15-4.

Example 15-9 is a long one, but it is well commented and worth studying carefully.
Pay attention, in particular, to the calls to createElement( ), createTextNode( ), and
appendChild( ). The private function log.makeTable( ) shows how these functions are
used to create the relatively complex structure of an HTML table.

Example 15-9. A logging facility for client-side JavaScript

```
/*
 * Log.js: Unobtrusive logging facility
 *
 * This module defines a single global symbol: a function named log( ).
 * Log a message by calling this function with 2 or 3 arguments:
 *
 *   category: the type of the message. This is required so that messages
 *     of different types can be selectively enabled or disabled and so
 *     that they can be styled independently. See below.
 *
 *   message: the text to be logged. May be empty if an object is supplied
 *
 *   object: an object to be logged. This argument is optional.  If passed,
 *     the properties of the object will be logged in the form of a table.
 *     Any property whose value is itself an object may be logged recursively.
```

Example 15-9. A logging facility for client-side JavaScript (continued)

```
 *
 * Utility Functions:
 *
 *   The log.debug( ) and log.warn( ) functions are utilities that simply
 *   call the log( ) function with hardcoded categories of "debug" and
 *   "warning".  It is trivial to define a utility that replaces the built-in
 *   alert( ) method with one that calls log( ).
 *
 * Enabling Logging
 *
 *   Log messages are *not* displayed by default.  You can enable the
 *   display of messages in a given category in one of two ways. The
 *   first is to create a <div> or other container element with an id
 *   of "<category>_log". For messages whose category is "debug", you might
 *   place the following in the containing document:
 *
 *       <div id="debug_log"></div>
 *
 *   In this case, all messages of the specified category are appended
 *   to this container, which can be styled however you like.
 *
 *   The second way to enable messages for a given category is to
 *   set an appropriate logging option. To enable the category
 *   "debug", you'd set log.options.debugEnabled = true. When you
 *   do this, a <div class="log"> is created for the logging messages.
 *   If you want to disable the display of log messages, even if a container
 *   with a suitable id exists, set another option:
 *   log.options.debugDisabled=true. Set this option back to false to
 *   re-enable log messages of that category.
 *
 * Styling Log Messages
 *
 *   In addition to styling the log container, you can use CSS to
 *   style the display of individual log messages. Each log message
 *   is placed in a <div> tag, and given a CSS class of
 *   <category>_message. Debugging messages would have a class "debug_message"
 *
 * Log Options
 *
 *   Logging behavior can be altered by setting properties of the log.options
 *   object, such as the options described earlier to enable or disable logging
 *   for given categories. A few other options are available:
 *
 *     log.options.timestamp: If this property is true, each log message
 *        will have the date and time added to it.
 *
 *     log.options.maxRecursion: An integer that specifies the maximum number
 *        of nested tables to display when logging objects. Set this to 0 if
 *        you never want a table within a table.
 *
 *     log.options.filter: A function that filters properties out when logging
 *        an object. A filter function is passed the name and value of
```

Example 15-9. A logging facility for client-side JavaScript (continued)

```
 *        a property and returns true if the property should appear in the
 *        object table or false otherwise.
 */
function log(category, message, object) {
    // If this category is explicitly disabled, do nothing
    if (log.options[category + "Disabled"]) return;

    // Find the container
    var id = category + "_log";
    var c = document.getElementById(id);

    // If there is no container, but logging in this category is enabled,
    // create the container.
    if (!c && log.options[category + "Enabled"]) {
        c = document.createElement("div");
        c.id = id;
        c.className = "log";
        document.body.appendChild(c);
    }

    // If still no container, we ignore the message
    if (!c) return;

    // If timestamping is enabled, add the timestamp
    if (log.options.timestamp)
        message = new Date() + ": " + (message?message:"");

    // Create a <div> element to hold the log entry
    var entry = document.createElement("div");
    entry.className = category + "_message";

    if (message) {
        // Add the message to it
        entry.appendChild(document.createTextNode(message));
    }

    if (object && typeof object == "object") {
        entry.appendChild(log.makeTable(object, 0));
    }

    // Finally, add the entry to the logging container
    c.appendChild(entry);
}

// Create a table to display the properties of the specified object
log.makeTable = function(object, level) {
    // If we've reached maximum recursion, return a Text node instead.
    if (level > log.options.maxRecursion)
        return document.createTextNode(object.toString());

    // Create the table we'll be returning
    var table = document.createElement("table");
```

Example 15-9. A logging facility for client-side JavaScript (continued)

```
    table.border = 1;

    // Add a Name|Type|Value header to the table
    var header = document.createElement("tr");
    var headerName = document.createElement("th");
    var headerType = document.createElement("th");
    var headerValue = document.createElement("th");
    headerName.appendChild(document.createTextNode("Name"));
    headerType.appendChild(document.createTextNode("Type"));
    headerValue.appendChild(document.createTextNode("Value"));
    header.appendChild(headerName);
    header.appendChild(headerType);
    header.appendChild(headerValue);
    table.appendChild(header);

    // Get property names of the object and sort them alphabetically
    var names = [];
    for(var name in object) names.push(name);
    names.sort();

    // Now loop through those properties
    for(var i = 0; i < names.length; i++) {
        var name, value, type;
        name = names[i];
        try {
            value = object[name];
            type = typeof value;
        }
        catch(e) { // This should not happen, but it can in Firefox
            value = "<unknown value>";
            type = "unknown";
        };

        // Skip this property if it is rejected by a filter
        if (log.options.filter && !log.options.filter(name, value)) continue;

        // Never display function source code: it takes up too much room
        if (type == "function") value = "{/*source code suppressed*/}";

        // Create a table row to display property name, type and value
        var row = document.createElement("tr");
        row.vAlign = "top";
        var rowName = document.createElement("td");
        var rowType = document.createElement("td");
        var rowValue = document.createElement("td");
        rowName.appendChild(document.createTextNode(name));
        rowType.appendChild(document.createTextNode(type));

        // For objects, recurse to display them as tables
        if (type == "object")
            rowValue.appendChild(log.makeTable(value, level+1));
        else
            rowValue.appendChild(document.createTextNode(value));
```

Example 15-9. A logging facility for client-side JavaScript (continued)

```
        // Add the cells to the row, and add the row to the table
        row.appendChild(rowName);
        row.appendChild(rowType);
        row.appendChild(rowValue);

        table.appendChild(row);
    }

    // Finally, return the table.
    return table;
}

// Create an empty options object
log.options = {};

// Utility versions of the function with hardcoded categories
log.debug = function(message, object) { log("debug", message, object); };
log.warn = function(message, object) { log("warning", message, object); };

// Uncomment the following line to convert alert() dialogs to log messages
// function alert(msg) { log("alert", msg); }
```

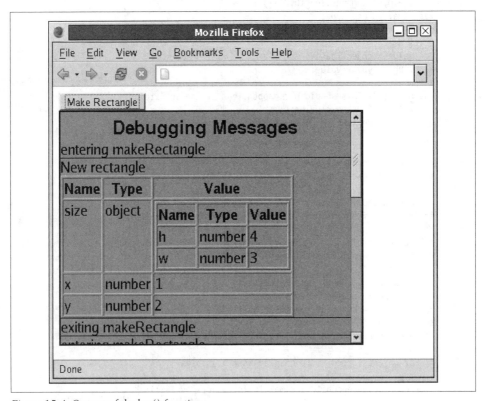

Figure 15-4. Output of the log() function

The debugging messages that appear in Figure 15-4 were created with the following simple code:

```
<head>
<script src="Log.js"></script>                    <!-- include log() -->
<link rel="stylesheet" type="text/css" href="log.css"> <!-- include styles -->
</head>
<body>
<script>
function makeRectangle(x, y, w, h) { // This is the function we want to debug
    log.debug("entering makeRectangle");   // Log a message
    var r = {x:x, y:y, size: { w:w, h:h }};
    log.debug("New rectangle", r);          // Log an object
    log.debug("exiting makeRectangle");     // Log another message
    return r;
}
</script>
<!-- this button invokes the function we want to debug -->
<button onclick="makeRectangle(1,2,3,4);">Make Rectangle</button>
<!-- This is where our logging messages will be placed -->
<!-- We enable logging by putting this <div> in the document -->
<div id="debug_log" class="log"></div>
</body>
```

The appearance of the log messages in Figure 15-4 is created using CSS styles, imported into the code with a <link> tag. The styles used to create the figure are the following:

```
#debug_log { /* Styles for our debug message container */
    background-color: #aaa;    /* gray background */
    border: solid black 2px;   /* black border */
    overflow: auto;            /* scrollbars */
    width: 75%;                /* not as wide as full window */
    height: 300px;             /* don't take up too much vertical space */
}

#debug_log:before { /* Give our logging area a title */
    content: "Debugging Messages";
    display: block;
    text-align: center;
    font: bold 18pt sans-serif ;
}

.debug_message { /* Place a thin black line between debug messages */
    border-bottom: solid black 1px;
}
```

You'll learn more about CSS in Chapter 16. It is not important that you understand the CSS details here. The CSS is included here so you can see how styles are associated with the dynamically generated content created by the log( ) function.

15.8.1 Convenience Methods for Creating Nodes

In reading Example 15-9, you may have noticed that the API creating document content is verbose: first you create an Element, then you set its attributes, and then you create a Text node and add it to the Element. Next, you add the Element to its parent Element. And so on. Simply creating a <table> element, setting one attribute, and adding a header row to it took 13 lines of code in Example 15-9. Example 15-10 defines an Element-creation utility function that simplifies this kind of repetitive DOM programming.

Example 15-10 defines a single function named make( ). make( ) creates an Element with the specified tag name, sets attributes on it, and adds children to it. Attributes are specified as properties of an object, and children are passed in an array. The elements of this array may be strings, which are converted to Text nodes, or they may be other Element objects, which are typically created with nested invocations of make( ).

make( ) has a flexible invocation syntax that allows two shortcuts. First, if no attributes are specified, the attributes argument can be omitted, and the children argument is passed in its place. Second, if there is only a single child, it can be passed directly instead of placing it in a single-element array. The only caveat is that these two shortcuts cannot be combined, unless the single child is a text node passed as a string.

Using make( ), the 13 lines of code for creating a <table> and its header row in Example 15-9 can be shortened to the following:

```
var table = make("table", {border:1}, make("tr", [make("th", "Name"),
                                               make("th", "Type"),
                                               make("th", "Value")]));
```

But you can do even better. Example 15-10 follows the make( ) function with another function called maker( ). Pass a tag name to maker( ), and it returns a nested function that calls make( ) with the tag name you specified hardcoded. If you want to create a lot of tables, you can define creation functions for common table tags like this:

```
var table = maker("table"), tr = maker("tr"), th = maker("th");
```

Then, with these maker functions defined, the table-creation and header-creation code shrinks down to a single line:

```
var mytable = table({border:1}, tr([th("Name"), th("Type"), th("Value")]));
```

Example 15-10. Element-creation utility functions

```
/**
 * make(tagname, attributes, children):
 *   create an HTML element with specified tagname, attributes, and children.
 *
 * The attributes argument is a JavaScript object: the names and values of its
 * properties are taken as the names and values of the attributes to set.
```

Example 15-10. Element-creation utility functions (continued)

```
 * If attributes is null, and children is an array or a string, the attributes
 * can be omitted altogether and the children passed as the second argument.
 *
 * The children argument is normally an array of children to be added to
 * the created element. If there are no children, this argument can be
 * omitted. If there is only a single child, it can be passed directly
 * instead of being enclosed in an array. (But if the child is not a string
 * and no attributes are specified, an array must be used.)
 *
 * Example: make("p", ["This is a ", make("b", "bold"), " word."]);
 *
 * Inspired by the MochiKit library (http://mochikit.com) by Bob Ippolito
 */
function make(tagname, attributes, children) {

    // If we were invoked with two arguments, the attributes argument is
    // an array or string; it should really be the children arguments.
    if (arguments.length == 2 &&
        (attributes instanceof Array || typeof attributes == "string")) {
        children = attributes;
        attributes = null;
    }

    // Create the element
    var e = document.createElement(tagname);

    // Set attributes
    if (attributes) {
        for(var name in attributes) e.setAttribute(name, attributes[name]);
    }

    // Add children, if any were specified.
    if (children != null) {
        if (children instanceof Array) {  // If it really is an array
            for(var i = 0; i < children.length; i++) { // Loop through kids
                var child = children[i];
                if (typeof child == "string")          // Handle text nodes
                    child = document.createTextNode(child);
                e.appendChild(child);  // Assume anything else is a Node
            }
        }
        else if (typeof children == "string") // Handle single text child
            e.appendChild(document.createTextNode(children));
        else e.appendChild(children);          // Handle any other single child
    }

    // Finally, return the element.
    return e;
}

/**
 * maker(tagname): return a function that calls make() for the specified tag.
```

Example 15-10. Element-creation utility functions (continued)

```
 * Example: var table = maker("table"), tr = maker("tr"), td = maker("td");
 */
function maker(tag) {
    return function(attrs, kids) {
        if (arguments.length == 1) return make(tag, attrs);
        else return make(tag, attrs, kids);
    }
}
```

15.8.2 The innerHTML Property

Although it has never been sanctioned by the W3C as an official part of the DOM, the innerHTML property of HTMLElement nodes is an important and powerful property that is supported by all modern browsers. When you query the value of this property for an HTML element, what you get is a string of HTML text that represents the children of the element. If you set this property, the browser invokes its HTML parser to parse your string and replaces the children of the element with whatever the parser returns.

Describing an HTML document as a string of HTML text is usually more convenient and compact than describing it as a sequence of calls to createElement() and appendChild(). Consider again the code from Example 15-9 that created a new <table> element and added a header row to it. You can rewrite that relatively lengthy code using innerHTML as follows:

```
var table = document.createElement("table");  // Create the <table> element
table.border = 1;                              // Set an attribute
// Add a Name|Type|Value header to the table
table.innerHTML = "<tr><th>Name</th><th>Type</th><th>Value</th></tr>";
```

Web browsers are, almost by definition, very good at parsing HTML. It turns out that using innerHTML is a reasonably efficient thing to do, especially when working with large chunks of HTML text to be parsed. Note, however that appending bits of text to the innerHTML property with the += operator is usually not efficient because it requires both a serialization step and a parsing step.

innerHTML was introduced by Microsoft in IE 4. It is the most important and frequently used member of a quartet of related properties. The other three properties, outerHTML, innerText, and outerText are not supported by Firefox and related browsers. They are described at the end of this chapter in Section 15.11.

15.9 Example: A Dynamically Created Table of Contents

The previous sections showed how you can use the Core DOM API to traverse a document, select elements from a document, and alter and add document content.

Example 15-11 brings all these pieces together to automatically create a table of contents (or "TOC") for an HTML document.

The example defines a single function, maketoc( ), and registers an onload event handler so that the function is automatically run when the document finishes loading. When maketoc( ) runs, it traverses the document, looking for <h1>, <h2>, <h3>, <h4>, <h5>, and <h6> tags, which it assumes mark the beginning of important sections within the document. maketoc( ) looks for an element with the ID "toc" and builds a table of contents within that element. As part of this process, maketoc( ) adds section numbers to the title of each section, inserts a named anchor before each section, and then inserts links at the beginning of each section back to the TOC. Figure 15-5 shows what a TOC generated by the maketoc( ) function looks like.

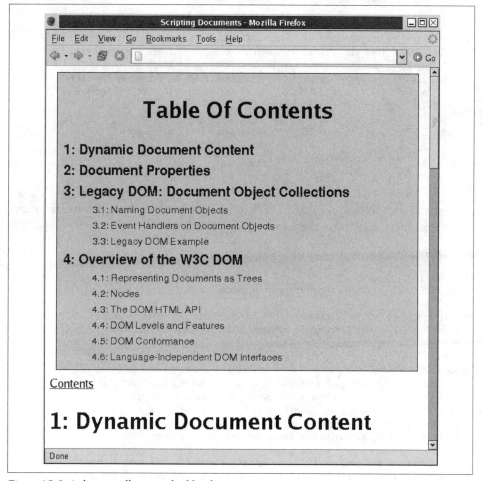

Figure 15-5. A dynamically created table of contents

If you maintain and revise long documents that are broken into sections with <h1>, <h2>, and related tags, the maketoc( ) function may be of interest to you. TOCs are quite useful in long documents, but when you frequently revise a document, it can be difficult to keep the TOC in sync with the document itself. The code in Example 15-11 is written to be unobtrusive: to use it, simply include the module into your HTML document and provide a container element for maketoc( ) to insert the TOC into. Optionally, you can style the TOC with CSS. You might use it like this:

```
<script src="TOC.js"></script>  <!-- Load the maketoc( ) function -->
<style>
#toc { /* these styles apply to the TOC container */
    background: #ddd;               /* light gray background */
    border: solid black 1px;        /* simple border */
    margin: 10px; padding: 10px;    /* indentation */
}
.TOCEntry { font-family: sans-serif; } /* TOC entries in sans-serif */
.TOCEntry a { text-decoration: none; } /* TOC links are not underlined */
.TOCLevel1 { font-size: 16pt; font-weight: bold; } /* level 1 big and bold */
.TOCLevel2 { font-size: 12pt; margin-left: .5in; } /* level 2 indented */
.TOCBackLink { display: block; }        /* back links on a line by themselves */
.TOCSectNum:after { content: ":"; }     /* add colon after section numbers */
</style>
<body>
<div id="toc"><h1>Table Of Contents</h1></div> <!-- the TOC goes here -->
<!--
    ... rest of document goes here ...
-->
```

The code for the *TOC.js* module follows. Example 15-11 is long, but it is well commented and uses techniques that have already been demonstrated. It is worth studying as a practical example of the power of the W3C DOM.

Example 15-11. Automatically generating a table of contents

```
/**
 * TOC.js: create a table of contents for a document.
 *
 * This module defines a single maketoc( ) function and registers an onload
 * event handler so the function is automatically run when the document
 * finishes loading. When it runs, maketoc( ) first looks for a document
 * element with an id of "toc". If there is no such element, maketoc( ) does
 * nothing. If there is such an element, maketoc( ) traverses the document
 * to find all <h1> through <h6> tags and creates a table of contents, which
 * it appends to the "toc" element. maketoc( ) adds section numbers
 * to each section heading and inserts a link back to the table of contents
 * before each heading. maketoc( ) generates links and anchors with names that
 * begin with "TOC", so you should avoid this prefix in your own HTML.
 *
 * The entries in the generated TOC can be styled with CSS. All entries have
 * a class "TOCEntry". Entries also have a class that corresponds to the level
 * of the section heading. <h1> tags generate entries of class "TOCLevel1",
 * <h2> tags generate entries of class "TOCLevel2", and so on. Section numbers
 * inserted into headings have class "TOCSectNum", and the generated links back
```

Example 15-11. Automatically generating a table of contents (continued)

```
 * to the TOC have class "TOCBackLink".
 *
 * By default, the generated links back to the TOC read "Contents".
 * Override this default (for internationalization, e.g.) by setting
 * the maketoc.backlinkText property to the desired text.
 **/
function maketoc() {
    // Find the container. If there isn't one, return silently.
    var container = document.getElementById('toc');
    if (!container) return;

    // Traverse the document, adding all <h1>...<h6> tags to an array
    var sections = [];
    findSections(document, sections);

    // Insert an anchor before the container element so we can link back to it
    var anchor = document.createElement("a");  // Create an <a> node
    anchor.name = "TOCtop";                     // Give it a name
    anchor.id = "TOCtop";                       // And an id (IE needs this)
    container.parentNode.insertBefore(anchor, container); // add before toc

    // Initialize an array that keeps track of section numbers
    var sectionNumbers = [0,0,0,0,0,0];

    // Now loop through the section header elements we found
    for(var s = 0; s < sections.length; s++) {
        var section = sections[s];

        // Figure out what level heading it is
        var level = parseInt(section.tagName.charAt(1));
        if (isNaN(level) || level < 1 || level > 6) continue;

        // Increment the section number for this heading level
        // And reset all lower heading level numbers to zero
        sectionNumbers[level-1]++;
        for(var i = level; i < 6; i++) sectionNumbers[i] = 0;

        // Now combine section numbers for all heading levels
        // to produce a section number like 2.3.1
        var sectionNumber = "";
        for(i = 0; i < level; i++) {
            sectionNumber += sectionNumbers[i];
            if (i < level-1) sectionNumber += ".";
        }

        // Add the section number and a space to the section header title.
        // We place the number in a <span> to make it styleable.
        var frag = document.createDocumentFragment(); // to hold span and space
        var span = document.createElement("span");    // span to hold number
        span.className = "TOCSectNum";                // make it styleable
        span.appendChild(document.createTextNode(sectionNumber)); // add sect#
        frag.appendChild(span);                       // Add span to fragment
```

Example 15-11. Automatically generating a table of contents (continued)

```
        frag.appendChild(document.createTextNode(" ")); // Then add a space
        section.insertBefore(frag, section.firstChild); // Add both to header

        // Create an anchor to mark the beginning of this section.
        var anchor = document.createElement("a");
        anchor.name = "TOC"+sectionNumber;   // Name the anchor so we can link
        anchor.id = "TOC"+sectionNumber;      // In IE, generated anchors need ids

        // Wrap the anchor around a link back to the TOC
        var link = document.createElement("a");
        link.href = "#TOCtop";
        link.className = "TOCBackLink";
        link.appendChild(document.createTextNode(maketoc.backlinkText));
        anchor.appendChild(link);

        // Insert the anchor and link immediately before the section header
        section.parentNode.insertBefore(anchor, section);

        // Now create a link to this section.
        var link = document.createElement("a");
        link.href = "#TOC" + sectionNumber;   // Set link destination
        link.innerHTML = section.innerHTML;   // Make link text same as heading

        // Place the link in a div that is styleable based on the level
        var entry = document.createElement("div");
        entry.className = "TOCEntry TOCLevel" + level; // For CSS styling
        entry.appendChild(link);

        // And add the div to the TOC container
        container.appendChild(entry);
    }

    // This method recursively traverses the tree rooted at node n, looks
    // for <h1> through <h6> tags, and appends them to the sections array.
    function findSections(n, sects) {
        // Loop through all the children of n
        for(var m = n.firstChild; m != null; m = m.nextSibling) {
            // Skip any nodes that are not elements.
            if (m.nodeType != 1 /* Node.Element_NODE */) continue;
            // Skip the container element since it may have its own heading
            if (m == container) continue;
            // As an optimization, skip <p> tags since headings are not
            // supposed to appear inside paragraphs. (We could also skip
            // lists, <pre> tags, etc., but <p> is the most common one.)
            if (m.tagName == "P") continue;  // optimization

            // If we didn't skip the child node, check whether it is a heading.
            // If so, add it to the array. Otherwise, recurse on it.
            // Note that the DOM is interface-based not class-based so we
            // cannot simply test whether (m instanceof HTMLHeadingElement).
            if (m.tagName.length==2 && m.tagName.charAt(0)=="H") sects.push(m);
            else findSections(m, sects);
```

Example 15-11. Automatically generating a table of contents (continued)

```
        }
    }
}

// This is the default text of links back to the TOC
maketoc.backlinkText = "Contents";

// Register maketoc() to run automatically when the document finishes loading
if (window.addEventListener) window.addEventListener("load", maketoc, false);
else if (window.attachEvent) window.attachEvent("onload", maketoc);
```

15.10 Querying Selected Text

It is sometimes useful to be able to determine what text the user has selected within a document. This is an area where little standardization exists, but it is possible to query the selected text in all modern browsers. Example 15-12 shows how.

Example 15-12. Querying the currently selected text

```
function getSelectedText() {
    if (window.getSelection) {
        // This technique is the most likely to be standardized.
        // getSelection() returns a Selection object, which we do not document.
        return window.getSelection().toString();
    }
    else if (document.getSelection) {
        // This is an older, simpler technique that returns a string
        return document.getSelection();
    }
    else if (document.selection) {
        // This is the IE-specific technique.
        // We do not document the IE selection property or TextRange objects.
        return document.selection.createRange().text;
    }
}
```

The code in this example must, to some extent, be taken on faith. The Selection and TextRange objects used in the example are not documented in this book. At the time of this writing, their APIs are simply too complex and nonstandard to cover. Nevertheless, since querying the selected text is a common and relatively simple operation, it is worth illustrating here. You can use it to create bookmarklets (see Section 13.4.1) that operate on the selected text by looking up a word with a search engine or reference site. The following HTML link, for example, looks up the currently selected text in Wikipedia. When bookmarked, this link and the JavaScript URL it contains become a bookmarklet:

```
<a href="javascript:
    var q;
    if (window.getSelection) q = window.getSelection().toString();
```

```
        else if (document.getSelection) q = document.getSelection();
        else if (document.selection) q = document.selection.createRange().text;
        void window.open('http://en.wikipedia.org/wiki/' + q);
    ">
    Look Up Selected Text In Wikipedia
    </a>
```

There is one minor incompatibility in Example 15-12. The getSelection() methods of the Window and Document object do not return selected text if it is within an <input> or <textarea> form element: they only return text selected from the body of the document itself. The IE document.selection property, on the other hand, returns selected text from anywhere in the document.

In Firefox, text input elements define selectionStart and selectionEnd properties that you can use to query (or set) the selected text. For example:

```
function getTextFieldSelection(e) {
    if (e.selectionStart != undefined && e.selectionEnd != undefined) {
        var start = e.selectionStart;
        var end = e.selectionEnd;
        return e.value.substring(start, end);
    }
    else return "";  // Not supported on this browser
}
```

15.11 The IE 4 DOM

Although IE 4 does not implement the W3C DOM, it supports an API with many of the same capabilities as the core W3C DOM. IE 5 and later support the IE 4 DOM, and some other browsers also have at least partial compatibility. At the time of this writing, the IE 4 browser is no longer widely deployed. Newly written JavaScript code does not typically need to be written for compatibility with IE 4, and much of the reference material for the IE 4 DOM has been deleted from Part IV in this edition of the book. Nevertheless, a large body of extant code still uses the IE 4 DOM, and it is valuable to have at least a passing familiarity with this API.

15.11.1 Traversing a Document

The W3C DOM specifies that all Node objects, which includes both the Document object and all Element objects, have a childNodes[] array that contains the children of that node. IE 4 does not support childNodes[], but it provides a similar children[] array on its Document and HTMLElement objects. Thus, it is easy to write a recursive function like that shown in Example 15-2 to traverse the complete set of HTML elements within an IE 4 document.

There is one substantial difference between IE 4's children[] array and the W3C DOM childNodes[] array, however. IE 4 does not have a Text node type and does not consider strings of text to be children. Thus, a `<p>` tag that contains only plain text with no markup has an empty `children[]` array in IE 4. As you'll see shortly, however, the textual content of a `<p>` tag is available through the IE 4 `innerText` property.

15.11.2 Finding Document Elements

IE 4 does not support the `getElementById()` and `getElementsByTagName()` methods of the Document object. Instead, the Document object and all document elements have an array property named `all[]`. As the name suggests, this array represents *all* the elements in a document or all the elements contained within another element. Note that `all[]` does not simply represent the children of the document or the element; it represents all descendants, no matter how deeply nested.

The `all[]` array can be used in several ways. If you index it with an integer *n*, it returns the *n+1*th element of the document or the parent element. For example:

```
var e1 = document.all[0];  // The first element of the document
var e2 = e1.all[4];        // The fifth element of element 1
```

Elements are numbered in the order in which they appear in the document source. Note the one big difference between the IE 4 API and the DOM standard: IE does not have a notion of Text nodes, so the `all[]` array contains only document elements, not the text that appears within and between them.

It is usually much more useful to be able to refer to document elements by name rather than number. The IE 4 equivalent to `getElementbyId()` is to index the `all[]` array with a string rather than a number. When you do this, IE 4 returns the element whose `id` or `name` attribute has the specified value. If there is more than one such element (which can happen, because it is common to have multiple form elements, such as radio buttons, with the same `name` attribute), the result is an array of those elements. For example:

```
var specialParagraph = document.all["special"];
var buttons = form.all["shippingMethod"];  // May return an array
```

JavaScript also allows you to write these expressions by expressing the array index as a property name:

```
var specialParagraph = document.all.special;
var buttons = form.all.shippingMethod;
```

Using the `all[]` array in this way provides the same basic functionality as `getElementById()` and `getElementsByName()`. The main difference is that the `all[]` array combines the features of these two methods, which can cause problems if you inadvertently use the same values for the `id` and `name` attributes of unrelated elements.

The all[] array has an unusual quirk: a tags( ) method that can be used to obtain an array of elements by tag name. For example:

```
var lists = document.all.tags("UL");   // Find all <ul> tags in the document
var items = lists[0].all.tags("LI");   // Find all <li> tags in the first <ul>
```

This IE 4 syntax provides essentially the same functionality as the standard getElementsByTagName( ) method of the Document and Element interfaces. Note, however, that in IE 4, the tag name must be specified using all uppercase letters.

15.11.3 Modifying Documents

Like the W3C DOM, IE 4 exposes the attributes of HTML tags as properties of the corresponding HTMLElement objects. Thus, it is possible to modify a document displayed in IE 4 by dynamically changing its HTML attributes. If an attribute modification changes the size of any element, the document "reflows" to accommodate its new size. The IE 4 HTMLElement object defines setAttribute( ), getAttribute( ), and removeAttribute( ) methods as well. These are similar to the methods of the same name defined by the Element object in the standard DOM API.

The W3C DOM defines an API that makes it possible to create new nodes, insert nodes into the document tree, reparent nodes, and move nodes within the tree. IE 4 cannot do this. Instead, however, all HTMLElement objects in IE 4 define an innerHTML property. Setting this property to a string of HTML text allows you to replace the content of an element with whatever you want. Because this innerHTML property is so powerful, it has been implemented by all modern browsers and seems likely to be incorporated into some future revision of the DOM standard. innerHTML was documented and demonstrated in Section 15.8.2.

IE 4 also defines several related properties and methods. The outerHTML property replaces an element's content and the entire element itself with a specified string of HTML text. The innerText and outerText properties are similar to innerHTML and outerHTML, except that they treat the string as plain text and do not parse it as HTML. Finally, the insertAdjacentHTML( ) and insertAdjacentText( ) methods leave the content of an element alone but insert new HTML or plain-text content near (before or after, inside or outside) it. These properties and functions are not as commonly used as innerHTML and have not been implemented by Firefox.

Cascading Style Sheets and Dynamic HTML

Cascading Style Sheets (CSS) is a standard for specifying the presentation of HTML or XML documents. In theory, you use HTML markup to specify the structure of your document, resisting the temptation to use deprecated HTML tags such as <font> to specify how the document should look. Instead, you use CSS to define a stylesheet that specifies how the structured elements of your document should be displayed. For example, you can use CSS to specify that the level-one headings defined by <h1> tags should be displayed in bold, sans-serif, centered, uppercase, 24-point letters.

CSS is a technology intended for use by graphic designers or anyone concerned with the precise visual display of HTML documents. It is of interest to client-side Java-Script programmers because the Document Object Model allows the styles that are applied to the individual elements of a document to be scripted. Used together, CSS and JavaScript enable a variety of visual effects loosely referred to as Dynamic HTML (DHTML).[*]

The ability to script CSS styles allows you to dynamically change colors, fonts, and so on. More importantly, it allows you to set and change the position of elements and even to hide and show elements. This means that you can use DHTML techniques to create animated transitions where document content "slides in" from the right, for example, or to create an expanding and collapsing outline list in which the user can control the amount of information that is displayed.

This chapter begins with an overview of CSS. It then explains the most important CSS styles for common DHTML effects. Next, the chapter describes various ways of scripting CSS. The most common and important technique is to script the styles that apply to individual document elements using the style property. A related technique indirectly modifies an element's style by altering the set of CSS classes that apply to that element. This is done by setting or modifying the element's className

---

[*] Many advanced DHTML effects also involve the event-handling techniques shown in Chapter 17.

property. It is also possible to script stylesheets directly, and the chapter concludes with a discussion of enabling and disabling stylesheets and querying, adding, and removing rules from stylesheets.

16.1 Overview of CSS

Styles in CSS are specified as a semicolon-separated list of name/value attribute pairs, in which colons separate each name and value. For example, the following style specifies bold, blue, underlined text:

```
font-weight: bold; color: blue; text-decoration: underline;
```

The CSS standard defines quite a few style attributes. Table 16-1 lists most of them, omitting a few poorly supported ones. You are not expected to understand or be familiar with all these attributes, their values, or their meanings. As you become familiar with CSS and use it in your documents and scripts, however, you may find this table a convenient quick reference. For more complete documentation on CSS, consult *Cascading Style Sheets: The Definitive Guide* by Eric Meyer (O'Reilly) or *Dynamic HTML: The Definitive Guide* by Danny Goodman (O'Reilly). Or read the specification itself: you can find it at *http://www.w3c.org/TR/CSS21/*.

The second column of Table 16-1 shows the allowed values for each style attribute. It uses the grammar used by the CSS specification. Items in fixed-width font are keywords and should appear exactly as shown. Items in *italics* specify a datatype such as a string or a length. Note that the *length* type is a number followed by a units specification, such as px (for pixels). See a CSS reference for details on the other types. Items that appear in `italic fixed-width font` represent the set of values allowed by some other CSS attribute. In addition to the values shown in the table, each style attribute may have the value "inherit" to specify that it should inherit the value from its parent.

Values separated by a | are alternatives; you must specify exactly one. Values separated by || are options; you must specify at least one, but you may specify more than one, and they can appear in any order. Square brackets [] group values. An asterisk (*) specifies that the previous value or group may appear zero or more times, a plus sign (+) specifies that the previous value or group may appear one or more times, and a question mark (?) specifies that the previous item is optional and may appear zero or one time. Numbers within curly braces specify a number of repetitions. For example, {2} specifies that the previous item must be repeated twice, and {1,4} specifies that the previous item must appear at least once and no more than four times. (This repetition syntax may seem familiar: it is the same one used by JavaScript regular expressions, discussed in Chapter 11.)

Table 16-1. CSS 2.1 style attributes and their values

Name	Values
background	[*background-color* ‖ *background-image* ‖ *background-repeat* ‖ *background-attachment* ‖ *background-position*]
background-attachment	scroll|fixed
background-color	*color*|transparent
background-image	url(*url*)|none
background-position	[[*percentage*|*length*]{1,2}|[[top|center|bottom]‖[left|center|right]]]
background-repeat	repeat|repeat-x|repeat-y|no-repeat
border	[*border-width* ‖ *border-style* ‖ *color*]
border-collapse	collapse|separate
border-color	*color*{1,4}|transparent
border-spacing	*length length?*
border-style	[none|hidden|dotted|dashed|solid|double|groove|ridge|inset|outset]{1,4}
border-top border-right border-bottom border-left	[*border-top-width* ‖ *border-style* ‖ [*color*|transparent]]
border-top-color border-right-color border-bottom-color border-left-color	*color*|transparent
border-top-style border-right-style border-bottom-style border-left-style	none|hidden|dotted|dashed|solid|double|groove|ridge|inset|outset
border-top-width border-right-width border-bottom-width border-left-width	thin|medium|thick|*length*
border-width	[thin|medium|thick|*length*]{1,4}
bottom	*length*|*percentage*|auto
caption-side	top|bottom
clear	none|left|right|both
clip	[rect([*length*|auto]{4})]|auto
color	*color*
content	[*string*|url(*url*)|*counter*|attr(*attribute-name*)|open-quote|close-quote|no-open-quote|no-close-quote]+|normal
counter-increment	[*identifier integer?*]+|none
counter-reset	[*identifier integer?*]+|none

Table 16-1. CSS 2.1 style attributes and their values (continued)

Name	Values
cursor	[[url(*url*),]*[auto|crosshair|default|pointer|progress|move| e-resize|ne-resize|nw-resize|n-resize|se-resize|sw-resize| s-resize|w-resize|text|wait|help]]
direction	ltr|rtl
display	inline|block|inline-block|list-item|run-in|table|inline-table|table-row-group|table-header-group|table-footer-group |table-row|table-column-group|table-column|table-cell| table-caption|none
empty-cells	show|hide
float	left|right|none
font	[[*font-style* || *font-variant* || *font-weight*]? *font-size* [/*line-height*]? *font-family*]|caption|icon|menu|message-box|small-caption|status-bar
font-family	[[*family-name*|serif|sans-serif|monospace|cursive|fantasy],]+
font-size	xx-small|x-small|small|medium|large|x-large|xx-large| smaller|larger|*length*|*percentage*
font-style	normal|italic|oblique
font-variant	normal|small-caps
font-weight	normal|bold|bolder|lighter|100|200|300|400|500|600|700|800 |900
height	*length*|*percentage*|auto
left	*length*|*percentage*|auto
letter-spacing	normal|*length*
line-height	normal|*number*|*length*|*percentage*
list-style	[*list-style-type* || *list-style-position* || *list-style-image*]
list-style-image	url(*url*)|none
list-style-position	inside|outside
list-style-type	disc|circle|square|decimal|decimal-leading-zero|lower-roman|upper-roman|lower-greek|lower-alpha|lower-latin| upper-alpha|upper-latin|hebrew|armenian|georgian|cjk-ideographic|hiragana|katakana|hiragana-iroha|katakana-iroha|none
margin	[*length*|*percentage*|auto]{1,4}
margin-top margin-right margin-bottom margin-left	*length*|*percentage*|auto
marker-offset	*length*|auto
max-height	*length*|*percentage*|none
max-width	*length*|*percentage*|none
min-height	*length*|*percentage*

Table 16-1. CSS 2.1 style attributes and their values (continued)

Name	Values
min-width	*length* | *percentage*
outline	[*outline-color* || *outline-style* || *outline-width*]
outline-color	*color* | invert
outline-style	none | hidden | dotted | dashed | solid | double | groove | ridge | inset | outset
outline-width	thin | medium | thick | *length*
overflow	visible | hidden | scroll | auto
padding	[*length* | *percentage*]{1,4}
padding-top padding-right padding-bottom padding-left	*length* | *percentage*
page-break-after	auto | always | avoid | left | right
page-break-before	auto | always | avoid | left | right
page-break-inside	avoid | auto
position	static | relative | absolute | fixed
quotes	[*string string*]+ | none
right	*length* | *percentage* | auto
table-layout	auto | fixed
text-align	left | right | center | justify
text-decoration	none | [underline || overline || line-through || blink]
text-indent	*length* | *percentage*
text-transform	capitalize | uppercase | lowercase | none
top	*length* | *percentage* | auto
unicode-bidi	normal | embed | bidi-override
vertical-align	baseline | sub | super | top | text-top | middle | bottom | text-bottom | *percentage* | *length*
visibility	visible | hidden | collapse
white-space	normal | pre | nowrap | pre-wrap | pre-line
width	*length* | *percentage* | auto
word-spacing	normal | *length*
z-index	auto | *integer*

The CSS standard allows certain style attributes that are commonly used together to be combined using special shortcut attributes. For example, the font-family, font-size, font-style, and font-weight attributes can all be set at once using a single font attribute:

```
font: bold italic 24pt helvetica;
```

The `margin` and `padding` attributes are shortcuts for attributes that specify margins, padding, and borders for each of the individual sides of an element. Thus, instead of using the `margin` attribute, you can use `margin-left`, `margin-right`, `margin-top`, and `margin-bottom`, and the same goes for `padding`.

16.1.1 Applying Style Rules to Document Elements

You can apply style attributes to the elements of a document in a number of ways. One way is to use them in the `style` attribute of an HTML tag. For example, to set the margins of an individual paragraph, you can use a tag like this:

```
<p style="margin-left: 1in; margin-right: 1in;">
```

One of the important goals of CSS is to separate document content and structure from document presentation. Specifying styles with the `style` attribute of individual HTML tags does not accomplish this (although it can be a useful technique for DHTML). To achieve the separation of structure from presentation, use *stylesheets*, which group all the style information into a single place. A CSS stylesheet consists of a set of style rules. Each rule begins with a selector that specifies the document element or elements to which it applies, followed by a set of style attributes and their values within curly braces. The simplest kind of rule defines styles for one or more specific tag names. For example, the following rule sets the margins and background color for the `<body>` tag:

```
body { margin-left: 30px; margin-right: 15px; background-color: #ffffff }
```

The following rule specifies that text within `<h1>` and `<h2>` headings should be centered:

```
h1, h2 { text-align: center; }
```

In the previous example, note how a comma is used to separate the tag names to which the styles are to apply. If the comma is omitted, the selector specifies a contextual rule that applies only when one tag is nested within another. For example, the following rules specify that the text inside `<blockquote>` tags is displayed in an italic font, but text inside an `<i>` tag inside a `<blockquote>` is displayed in plain, nonitalic text:

```
blockquote { font-style: italic; }
blockquote i { font-style: normal; }
```

Another kind of stylesheet rule uses a different selector to specify a *class* of elements to which its styles should be applied. The class of an element is defined by the `class` attribute of the HTML tag. For example, the following rule specifies that any tag with the attribute `class="attention"` should be displayed in bold:

```
.attention { font-weight: bold; }
```

Class selectors can be combined with tag name selectors. The following rule specifies that when a `<p>` tag has the `class="attention"` attribute, it should be displayed in red, in addition to being displayed in a bold font (as specified by the previous rule):

```
p.attention { color: red; }
```

Finally, stylesheets can contain rules that apply only to individual elements that have a specified `id` attribute. The following rule specifies that the element with an `id` attribute equal to p1 should not be shown:

```
#p1 { visibility: hidden; }
```

You've seen the `id` attribute before: it is used with the document method `getElementById( )` to return individual elements of a document. As you might imagine, this kind of element-specific stylesheet rule is useful when you want to manipulate the style of an individual element. Given the previous rule, for example, a script might switch the value of the `visibility` attribute from `hidden` to `visible`, causing the element to dynamically appear. You'll see how to do this later in this chapter.

The CSS standard defines a number of other selectors beyond the basic ones shown here, and some are well supported by modern browsers. Consult the CSS spec or a reference book for details.

16.1.2 Associating Stylesheets with Documents

You can incorporate a stylesheet into an HTML document by placing it between `<style>` and `</style>` tags within the `<head>` of the document. For example:

```
<html>
<head><title>Test Document</title>
<style type="text/css">
body { margin-left: 30px; margin-right: 15px; background-color: #ffffff }
p { font-size: 24px; }
</style>
</head>
<body><p>Testing, testing</p></body>
</html>
```

When a stylesheet is to be used by more than one page on a web site, it is usually better to store it in its own file, without any enclosing HTML tags. This CSS file can then be included in the HTML page. Unlike the `<script>` tag, however, the `<style>` tag does not have a `src` attribute. To include a stylesheet into an HTML page, use the `<link>` tag instead:

```
<html>
<head><title>Test Document</title>
<link rel="stylesheet" href="mystyles.css" type="text/css">
</head>
<body><p>Testing, testing</p></body>
</html>
```

You can also use a `<link>` tag to specify an alternate stylesheet. Some browsers (such as Firefox) allow the user to select one of the alternatives you have provided (by choosing **View → Page Style**). You might provide an alternate stylesheet for the benefit of site visitors who prefer large fonts and high-contrast colors, for example:

```
<link rel="alternate stylesheet" href="largetype.css" type="text/css"
      title="Large Type"> <!-- title is displayed in the menu -->
```

If your web page includes a page-specific stylesheet with a `<style>` tag, you can use the CSS @import directive to include a shared CSS file into the page-specific stylesheet:

```
<html>
<head><title>Test Document</title>
<style type="text/css">
@import "mystyles.css"; /* import a common stylesheet */
p { font-size: 48px; }  /* override imported styles */
</style>
</head>
<body><p>Testing, testing</p></body>
</html>
```

16.1.3 The Cascade

Recall that the C in CSS stands for "cascading." This term indicates that the style rules that apply to any given element in a document can come from a cascade of different sources. Each web browser typically has its own default styles for all HTML elements and may allow the user to override these defaults with a user stylesheet. The author of a document can define stylesheets within `<style>` tags or in external files that are linked in or imported into other stylesheets. The author may also define inline styles for individual elements with the HTML `style` attribute.

The CSS specification includes a complete set of rules for determining which rules from the cascade take precedence over the other rules. Briefly, however, what you need to know is that the user stylesheet overrides the default browser stylesheet, author stylesheets override the user stylesheet, and inline styles override everything. The exception to this general rule is that user style attributes whose values include the `!important` modifier override author stylesheets. Within a stylesheet, if more than one rule applies to an element, styles defined by the most specific rule override conflicting styles defined by less specific rules. Rules that specify an element `id` are the most specific. Rules that specify a `class` are next. Rules that specify only tag names are the least specific, but rules that specify multiple nested tag names are more specific than rules that specify only a single tag name.

16.1.4 Versions of CSS

CSS is a relatively old standard. CSS1 was adopted in December 1996 and defines attributes for specifying colors, fonts, margins, borders, and other basic styles. Browsers as old as Netscape 4 and Internet Explorer 4 include substantial support for CSS1. The second edition of the standard, CSS2, was adopted in May 1998; it defines a number of more advanced features, most notably support for absolute positioning of elements. At the time of this writing, CSS2 features are reasonably well supported by current browsers. The crucial positioning features of CSS2 began the standardization process as part of a separate, earlier, CSS-Positioning (CSS-P) effort, and therefore these DHTML-enabling features are available in practically every browser deployed today. (These important positioning-related styles are discussed in detail later in this chapter.)

Work continues on CSS. At the time of this writing, the CSS 2.1 specification is almost complete. It clarifies the CSS 2 specification, fixes errors, and deletes some CSS 2 styles that were never actually implemented by browsers. For version 3, the CSS specification has been broken into various specialized modules that are going through the standardization process separately. Some CSS3 modules are nearing completion, and some browsers are beginning to implement selected CSS3 features, such as the opacity style. You can find the CSS specifications and working drafts at *http://www.w3.org/Style/CSS/*.

16.1.5 CSS Example

Example 16-1 is an HTML file that defines and uses a stylesheet. It demonstrates the previously described tag name, class, and ID-based style rules, and it also has an example of an inline style defined with the `style` attribute. Figure 16-1 shows how this example is rendered in a browser. Remember that this example is meant only as an overview of CSS syntax and capabilities. Full coverage of CSS is beyond the scope of this book.

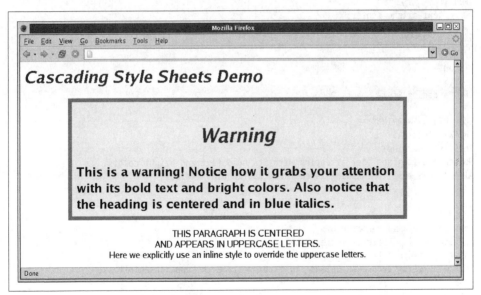

Figure 16-1. A web page styled with CSS

Example 16-1. Defining and using Cascading Style Sheets

```
<head>
<style type="text/css">
/* Specify that headings display in blue italic text. */
h1, h2 { color: blue; font-style: italic }

/*
 * Any element of class="WARNING" displays in big bold text with large margins
 * and a yellow background with a fat red border.
 */
.WARNING {
        font-weight: bold;
        font-size: 150%;
        margin: 0 1in 0 1in; /* top right bottom left */
        background-color: yellow;
        border: solid red 8px;
        padding: 10px;         /* 10 pixels on all 4 sides */
}

/*
 * Text within an h1 or h2 heading within an element with class="WARNING"
 * should be centered, in addition to appearing in blue italics.
 */
.WARNING h1, .WARNING h2 { text-align: center }

/* The single element with id="P23" displays in centered uppercase. */
#P23 {
      text-align: center;
      text-transform: uppercase;
}
</style>
</head>
<body>
<h1>Cascading Style Sheets Demo</h1>

<div class="WARNING">
<h2>Warning</h2>
This is a warning!
Notice how it grabs your attention with its bold text and bright colors.
Also notice that the heading is centered and in blue italics.
</div>

<p id="P23">
This paragraph is centered<br>
and appears in uppercase letters.<br>
<span style="text-transform: none">
Here we explicitly use an inline style to override the uppercase letters.
</span>
</p>
</body>
```

16.2 CSS for DHTML

For DHTML content developers, the most important feature of CSS is the ability to use ordinary CSS style attributes to specify the visibility, size, and precise position of individual elements of a document. Other CSS styles allow you to specify stacking order, transparency, clipping region, margins, padding, borders, and colors. In order to do DHTML programming, it is important to understand how these style attributes work. They are summarized in Table 16-2 and documented in more detail in the sections that follow.

Table 16-2. CSS positioning and visibility attributes

Attribute(s)	Description
position	Specifies the type of positioning applied to an element
top, left	Specify the position of the top and left edges of an element
bottom, right	Specify the position of the bottom and right edges of an element
width, height	Specify the size of an element
z-index	Specifies the "stacking order" of an element relative to any overlapping elements; defines a third dimension of element positioning
display	Specifies how and whether an element is displayed
visibility	Specifies whether an element is visible
clip	Defines a "clipping region" for an element; only portions of the element within this region are displayed
overflow	Specifies what to do if an element is bigger than the space allotted for it
margin, border, padding	Specify spacing and borders for an element.
background	Specifies the background color or image of an element.
opacity	Specifies how opaque (or translucent) and element is. This is a CSS3 attribute, supported by some browsers. A working alternative exists for IE.

16.2.1 The Key to DHTML: Absolute Positioning

The CSS position attribute specifies the type of positioning applied to an element. Here are the four possible values for this attribute:

static

> This is the default value and specifies that the element is positioned according to the normal flow of document content (for most Western languages, this is left to right and top to bottom). Statically positioned elements are not DHTML elements and cannot be positioned with top, left, and other attributes. To use DHTML positioning techniques with a document element, you must first set its position attribute to one of the other three values.

`absolute`

> This value allows you to specify the position of an element relative to its containing element. Absolutely positioned elements are positioned independently of all other elements and are not part of the flow of statically positioned elements. An absolutely positioned element is positioned either relative to the `<body>` of the document or, if it is nested within another positioned element, relative to that element. This is the most commonly used positioning type for DHTML. IE 4 supports only absolute positioning of certain elements. If you want to support this old browser, be sure to wrap your absolutely positioned elements in `<div>` or `<span>` tags.

`fixed`

> This value allows you to specify an element's position with respect to the browser window. Elements with `fixed` positioning are always visible and do not scroll with the rest of the document. Like absolutely positioned elements, fixed-position elements are independent of all others and are not part of the document flow. Fixed positioning is supported in most modern browsers with the notable exception of IE 6.

`relative`

> When the `position` attribute is set to `relative`, an element is laid out according to the normal flow, and its position is then adjusted relative to its position in the normal flow. The space allocated for the element in the normal document flow remains allocated for it, and the elements on either side of it do not close up to fill in that space, nor are they "pushed away" from the new position of the element.

Once you have set the `position` attribute of an element to something other than `static`, you can specify the position of that element with some combination of the `left`, `top`, `right`, and `bottom` attributes. The most common positioning technique is to specify the `left` and `top` attributes, which specify the distance from the left edge of the containing element (usually the document itself) to the left edge of the element and the distance from the top edge of the container to the top edge of the element. For example, to place an element 100 pixels from the left and 100 pixels from the top of the document, you can specify CSS styles in a `style` attribute as follows:

```
<div style="position: absolute; left: 100px; top: 100px;">
```

The containing element relative to which a dynamic element is positioned is not necessarily the same as the containing element within which the element is defined in the document source. Since dynamic elements are not part of normal element flow, their positions are not specified relative to the static container element within which they are defined. Most dynamic elements are positioned relative to the document (the `<body>` tag) itself. The exception is dynamic elements that are defined within other dynamic elements. In this case, the nested dynamic element is positioned relative to its nearest dynamic ancestor. If you wish to position an element relative to a container that is part of the normal document flow, use `position:relative` for the container and specify a `top` and `left` position of `0px`. This makes the container dynamically positioned but leaves it at its normal place in the document flow. Any absolutely positioned children are then positioned relative to the container position.

Although it is most common to specify the position of the upper-left corner of an element with `left` and `top`, you can also use `right` and `bottom` to specify the position of the bottom and right edges of an element relative to the bottom and right edges of the containing element. For example, to position an element so that its bottom-right corner is at the bottom-right of the document (assuming it is not nested within another dynamic element), use the following styles:

```
position: absolute; right: 0px; bottom: 0px;
```

To position an element so that its top edge is 10 pixels from the top of the window and its right edge is 10 pixels from the right of the window, and so that it does not scroll with the document, you might use these styles:

```
position: fixed; right: 10px; top: 10px;
```

In addition to the position of elements, CSS allows you to specify their size. This is most commonly done by providing values for the `width` and `height` style attributes. For example, the following HTML creates an absolutely positioned element with no content. Its `width`, `height`, and `background-color` attributes make it appear as a small blue square.

```
<div style="position: absolute; top: 10px; left: 10px;
            width: 10px; height: 10px; background-color: blue">
</div>
```

Another way to specify the width of an element is to specify a value for both the `left` and `right` attributes. Similarly, you can specify the height of an element by specifying both `top` and `bottom`. If you specify a value for `left`, `right`, and `width`, however, the `width` attribute overrides the `right` attribute; if the height of an element is over-constrained, `height` takes priority over `bottom`.

Bear in mind that it is not necessary to specify the size of every dynamic element. Some elements, such as images, have an intrinsic size. Furthermore, for dynamic elements that contain text or other flowed content, it is often sufficient to specify the desired width of the element and allow the height to be determined automatically by the layout of the element's content.

In the previous positioning examples, values for the position and size attributes were specified with the suffix "px," which stands for pixels. The CSS standard allows measurements to be done in a number of other units, including inches ("in"), centimeters ("cm"), points ("pt"), and ems ("em"—a measure of the line height for the current font). Pixel units are most commonly used with DHTML programming. Note that the CSS standard requires a unit to be specified. Some browsers may assume pixels if you omit the unit specification, but you should not rely on this behavior.

Instead of specifying absolute positions and sizes using the units shown above, CSS also allows you to specify the position and size of an element as a percentage of the size of the containing element. For example, the following HTML creates an empty element with a black border that is half as wide and half as high as the containing element (or the browser window) and centered within that element:

```
<div style="position: absolute; left: 25%; top: 25%; width: 50%; height: 50%;
        border: 2px solid black">
</div>
```

16.2.2 CSS Positioning Example: Shadowed Text

The CSS2 specification included a text-shadow attribute to produce sophisticated drop-shadow effects under text. This attribute was implemented by the Safari browser, but not by any other major browser vendor, and it has been removed from CSS2.1, to be reconsidered for CSS3. You can achieve shadowed text effects even without text-shadow, however. You simply need to use CSS positioning and be willing to repeat desired text: once for the actual text and once (or more than once) for the shadow or shadows. The following code produces the output shown in Figure 16-2:

```
<div style="font: bold 32pt sans-serif;"> <!--shadows look best on big text-->
<!-- Shadowed text must be relatively positioned, so we can offset the -->
<!-- the shadows from its normal position in the flow -->
<span style="position:relative;">
<!-- These are 3 shadows of different colors, using absolute positioning -->
<!-- to offset them different amounts from the regular text -->
<span style="position:absolute; top:5px; left:5px; color: #ccc">Shadow</span>
<span style="position:absolute; top:3px; left:3px; color: #888">Shadow</span>
<span style="position:absolute; top:1px; left:1px; color: #444">Shadow</span>
<!-- And this is the text that casts the shadow.  We use relative -->
<!-- positioning so that it appears on top of its shadows -->
<span style="position:relative">Shadow</span>
</span>
| No Shadow  <!-- For comparison, here is some nonshadowed text -->
</div>
```

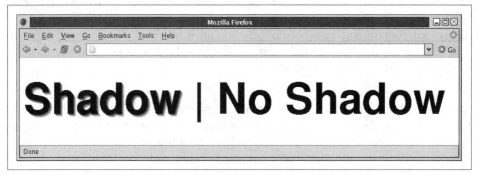

Figure 16-2. Shadowed text with CSS positioning

Adding CSS shadows manually as was done here is cumbersome and violates the principle of separating content from presentation. You can fix this problem with a bit of unobtrusive JavaScript. Example 16-2 is a JavaScript module named *Shadows.js*. It defines a function Shadows.addAll( ) that scans the document (or a portion of the document) for tags that have a shadow attribute. When it finds such a tag, it parses the value of the shadow attribute and uses DOM scripting to add shadows to the text contained within the tag. As an example, you can use this module to produce the output shown in Figure 16-2:

```
<head><script src="Shadows.js"></script></head> <!-- include module -->
<body onload="Shadows.addAll();">              <!-- add shadows on load -->
<div style="font: bold 32pt sans-serif;">      <!-- use big fonts -->
<!-- Note the shadow attribute here -->
<span shadow='5px 5px #ccc 3px 3px #888 1px 1px #444'>Shadow</span> | No Shadow
</div>
</body>
```

The code for the *Shadows.js* module follows. Note that, for the most part, this is a DOM scripting example that happens to use CSS in an interesting way. With the exception of one line, this example does not script CSS itself: it simply sets CSS attributes on the document elements it creates. Later in the chapter I'll detail more techniques for CSS scripting.

Example 16-2. Creating shadowed text with unobtrusive JavaScript

```
/**
 * Shadows.js: shadowed text with CSS.
 *
 * This module defines a single global object named Shadows.
 * The properties of this object are two utility functions.
 *
 * Shadows.add(element, shadows):
 *   Add the specified shadows to the specified element. The first argument
 *   is a document element or element id. This element must have a single
 *   text node as its child. This child is the one that will be shadowed.
 *   Shadows are specified with a string argument whose syntax is explained
 *   below.
 *
 * Shadows.addAll(root, tagname):
 *   Find all descendants of the specified root element that have the
 *   specified tagname. If any of these elements have an attribute named
 *   shadow, then call Shadows.add() for the element and the value of its
 *   shadow attribute. If tagname is not specified, all elements are checked.
 *   If root is not specified, the document object is used. This function is
 *   intended to be called once, when a document is first loaded.
 *
 * Shadow Syntax
 *
 * Shadows are specified by a string of the form [x y color]+. That is, one
 * or more triplets specifying an x offset, a y offset, and a color. Each of
 * these values must be in legal CSS format. If more than one shadow is
 * specified, then the first shadow specified is on the bottom, overlapped
```

Example 16-2. Creating shadowed text with unobtrusive JavaScript (continued)

```
 * by subsequent shadows. For example: "4px 4px #ccc 2px 2px #aaa"
 */
var Shadows = {};

// Add shadows to a single specified element
Shadows.add = function(element, shadows) {
    if (typeof element == "string")
        element = document.getElementById(element);

    // Break the shadows string up at whitespace, first stripping off
    // any leading and trailing spaces.
    shadows = shadows.replace(/^\s+/, "").replace(/\s+$/, "");
    var args = shadows.split(/\s+/);

    // Find the text node that we are going to shadow.
    // This module would be more robust if we shadowed all children.
    // For simplicity, though, we're only going to do one.
    var textnode = element.firstChild;

    // Give the container element relative positioning, so that
    // shadows can be positioned relative to it.
    // We'll learn about scripting the style property in this way later.
    element.style.position = "relative";

    // Create the shadows
    var numshadows = args.length/3;         // how many shadows?
    for(var i = 0; i < numshadows; i++) {   // for each one
        var shadowX = args[i*3];            // get the X offset
        var shadowY = args[i*3 + 1];        // the Y offset
        var shadowColor = args[i*3 + 2];    // and the color arguments

        // Create a new <span> to hold the shadow
        var shadow = document.createElement("span");
        // Use its style attribute to specify offset and color
        shadow.setAttribute("style", "position:absolute; " +
                            "left:" + shadowX + "; " +
                            "top:" + shadowY + "; " +
                            "color:" + shadowColor + ";");

        // Add a copy of the text node to this shadow span
        shadow.appendChild(textnode.cloneNode(false));
        // And add the span to the container
        element.appendChild(shadow);
    }

    // Now we put the text on top of the shadow.  First, create a <span>
    var text = document.createElement("span");
    text.setAttribute("style", "position: relative"); // position it
    text.appendChild(textnode); // Move the original text node to this span
    element.appendChild(text);  // And add this span to the container
};
```

Example 16-2. Creating shadowed text with unobtrusive JavaScript (continued)

```
// Scan the document tree at and beneath the specified root element for
// elements with the specified tagname.  If any have a shadow attribute,
// pass it to the Shadows.add( ) method above to create the shadow.
// If root is omitted, use the document object. If tagname is omitted,
// search all tags.
Shadows.addAll = function(root, tagname) {
    if (!root) root = document;    // Use whole document if no root
    if (!tagname) tagname = '*';   // Use any tag if no tagname specified

    var elements = root.getElementsByTagName(tagname); // Find all tags
    for(var i = 0; i < elements.length; i++) {         // For each tag
        var shadow = elements[i].getAttribute("shadow"); // If it has a shadow
        if (shadow) Shadows.add(elements[i], shadow);    // create the shadow
    }
};
```

16.2.3 Querying Element Position and Size

Now that you know how to set the position and size of HTML elements using CSS, the question naturally arises: how can you query the position and size of an element? You might want to use CSS positioning to center a DHTML pop-up "window" on top of some other HTML element. In order to do this, you need to know the position and size of that element.

In modern browsers, the offsetLeft and offsetTop properties of an element return the X and Y coordinates of the element. Similarly, the offsetWidth and offsetHeight properties return the width and height. These properties are read-only and return pixel values as numbers (not as CSS strings with "px" units appended). They mirror the CSS left, top, width, and height attributes but are not part of the CSS standard. For that matter, they are not part of any standard: they were introduced by Microsoft in IE 4 and have been adopted by other browser vendors.

Unfortunately, the offsetLeft and offsetTop properties are not usually sufficient by themselves. These properties specify the X and Y coordinates of an element relative to some other element. That other element is the value of the offsetParent property. For positioned elements, the offsetParent is typically the <body> tag or the <html> tag (which has an offsetParent of null) or a positioned ancestor of the positioned element. For nonpositioned elements, different browsers handle the offsetParent differently. Table rows are positioned relative to the containing table in IE, for example. In general, therefore, the portable way to determine the position of an element is to loop through the offsetParent references, accumulating offsets. Here is code you might use:

```
// Get the X coordinate of the element e.
function getX(e) {
    var x = 0;              // Start with 0
    while(e) {              // Start at element e
        x += e.offsetLeft;  // Add in the offset
```

```
        e = e.offsetParent;    // And move up to the offsetParent
    }
    return x;                  // Return the total offsetLeft
}
```

A getY( ) function can be written by simply substituting offsetTop for offsetLeft.

Note that in the previous code, the values returned by functions such as getX( ) are in document coordinates. They are compatible with CSS coordinates and are not affected by the position of the browser scrollbars. In Chapter 17 you'll learn that the coordinates associated with mouse events are window coordinates, and must be added to the scrollbar positions to convert to document coordinates.

There is one shortcoming of the getX( ) method shown above. You'll see later that the CSS overflow attribute can be used to create scrolled regions within a document. When an element appears within such a scrolled region, its offset values do not take the scrollbar positions of that region into account. If you use this overflow attribute in your web pages, you may need to use a more sophisticated offset computation function, like this one:

```
function getY(element) {
    var y = 0;
    for(var e = element; e; e = e.offsetParent) // Iterate the offsetParents
        y += e.offsetTop;                       // Add up offsetTop values

    // Now loop up through the ancestors of the element, looking for
    // any that have scrollTop set. Subtract these scrolling values from
    // the total offset. However, we must be sure to stop the loop before
    // we reach document.body, or we'll take document scrolling into account
    // and end up converting our offset to window coordinates.
    for(e = element.parentNode; e && e != document.body; e = e.parentNode)
        if (e.scrollTop) y -= e.scrollTop;  // subtract scrollbar values

    // This is the Y coordinate with document-internal scrolling accounted for.
    return y;
}
```

16.2.4 The Third Dimension: z-index

You've seen that the left, top, right, and bottom attributes can specify the X and Y coordinates of an element within the two-dimensional plane of the containing element. The z-index attribute defines a kind of third dimension: it allows you to specify the stacking order of elements and indicate which of two or more overlapping elements is drawn on top of the others. The z-index attribute is an integer. The default value is zero, but you may specify positive or negative values. When two or more elements overlap, they are drawn in order from lowest to highest z-index; the element with the highest z-index appears on top of all the others. If overlapping elements have the same z-index, they are drawn in the order in which they appear in the document so that the last overlapping element appears on top.

Note that z-index stacking applies only to sibling elements (i.e., elements that are children of the same container). If two elements that are not siblings overlap, setting their individual z-index attributes does not allow you to specify which one is on top. Instead, you must specify the z-index attribute for the two sibling containers of the two overlapping elements.

Nonpositioned elements (i.e., elements with default position:static positioning) are always laid out in a way that prevents overlaps, so the z-index attribute does not apply to them. Nevertheless, they have a default z-index of zero, which means that positioned elements with a positive z-index appear on top of the normal document flow and positioned elements with a negative z-index appear beneath the normal document flow.

Note, finally, that some browsers do not honor the z-index attribute when it is applied to <iframe> tags, and you may find that inline frames float on top of other elements regardless of the specified stacking order. You may have the same problem with other "windowed" elements such as <select> menus. Old browsers may display all form-control elements on top of absolutely positioned elements, regardless of z-index settings.

16.2.5 Element Display and Visibility

Two CSS attributes affect the visibility of a document element: visibility and display. The visibility attribute is simple: when the attribute is set to the value hidden, the element is not shown; when it is set to the value visible, the element is shown. The display attribute is more general and is used to specify the type of display an item receives. It specifies whether an element is a block element, an inline element, a list item, and so on. When display is set to none, however, the affected element is not displayed, or even laid out, at all.

The difference between the visibility and display style attributes has to do with their effect on elements that are not dynamically positioned. For an element that appears in the normal layout flow (with the position attribute set to static or relative), setting visibility to hidden makes the element invisible but reserves space for it in the document layout. Such an element can be repeatedly hidden and shown without changing the document layout. If an element's display attribute is set to none, however, no space is allocated for it in the document layout; elements on either side of it close up as if it were not there. (visibility and display have equivalent effects when used with absolute- or fixed-position elements because these elements are never part of the document layout anyway.) You'll typically use the visibility attribute when you are working with dynamically positioned elements. The display attribute is useful, for example, when creating expanding and collapsing outlines.

Note that it doesn't make much sense to use `visibility` or `display` to make an element invisible unless you are going to use JavaScript to dynamically set these attributes and make the element visible at some point! I'll show you how to do this later in the chapter.

16.2.6 The CSS Box Model and Positioning Details

CSS allows you to specify margins, borders, and padding for any element, and this complicates CSS positioning because you have to know how the `width`, `height`, `top`, and `left` attributes are calculated in the presence of borders and spacing. The CSS *box model* provides a precise specification. It is detailed in the paragraphs that follow and illustrated in Figure 16-3.

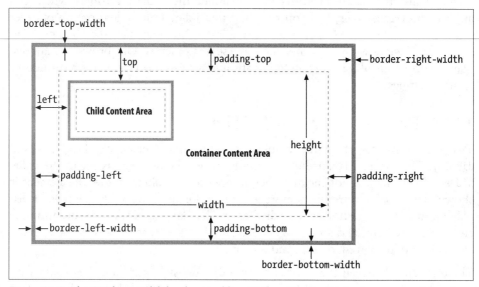

Figure 16-3. The CSS box model: borders, padding, and positioning attributes

Let's begin with a discussion of the `border`, `margin`, and `padding` styles. The border of an element is a rectangle drawn around (or partially around) it. CSS attributes allow you to specify the style, color, and thickness of the border:

```
border: solid black 1px; /* border is drawn with a solid, black 1-pixel line */
border: 3px dotted red;   /* border is drawn in 3-pixel red dots */
```

It is possible to specify the border width, style, and color using individual CSS attributes, and it is also possible to specify the border for individual sides of an element. To draw a line beneath an element, for example, simply specify its `border-bottom` attribute. It is even possible to specify the width, style, or color of a single side of an element. Figure 16-3 illustrates this: it includes border attributes such as `border-top-width` and `border-left-width`.

The `margin` and `padding` attributes both specify blank space around an element. The difference (an important one) is that `margin` specifies space outside the border, between the border and adjacent elements, and `padding` specifies space inside the border, between the border and the element content. A margin provides visual space between a (possibly bordered) element and its neighbors in the normal document flow. Padding keeps element content visually separated from its border. If an element has no border, padding is typically not necessary. If an element is dynamically positioned, it is not part of the normal document flow, and its margins are irrelevant. (This is why no CSS margin attributes are illustrated in Figure 16-3.)

You can specify the margin and padding of an element with the `margin` and `padding` attributes:

```
margin: 5px; padding: 5px;
```

You can also specify margins and paddings for individual sides of an element:

```
margin-left: 25px;
padding-bottom: 5px;
```

Or you can specify margin and padding values for all four edges of an element with the `margin` and `padding` attributes. You specify the top values first and then proceed clockwise: top, right, bottom, and left. For example, the following code shows two equivalent ways to set different padding values for each of the four sides of an element:

```
padding: 1px 2px 3px 4px;
/* The previous line is equivalent to the following lines. */
padding-top: 1px;
padding-right: 2px;
padding-bottom: 3px;
padding-left: 4px;
```

The `margin` attribute works in the same way.

With this understanding of margins, borders, and padding, let's now look at some important details about CSS positioning attributes. First, `width` and `height` specify the size of an element's content area only; they do not include any additional space required for the element's padding, border, or margins. To determine the full on-screen size of an element with a border, you must add the left and right padding and left and right border widths to the element width, and you must add the top and bottom padding and top and bottom border widths to the element's height.

Since `width` and `height` specify the element content area only, you might think that `left` and `top` (and `right` and `bottom`) would be measured relative to the content area of the containing element. This is not the case, though. The CSS standard specifies that these values are measured relative to the outside edge of the containing element's padding (which is the same as the inside edge of the element's border).

This is all illustrated in Figure 16-3, but let's consider an example to make this clearer. Suppose you've created a dynamically positioned container element that has 10 pixels of padding all the way around its content area and a 5-pixel border all the way around the padding. Now suppose you dynamically position a child element inside this container. If you set the left attribute of the child to "0 px", you'll discover that the child is positioned with its left edge right up against the inner edge of the container's border. With this setting, the child overlaps the container's padding, which presumably was supposed to remain empty (since that is the purpose of padding). If you want to position the child element in the upper left corner of the container's content area, you should set both the left and top attributes to "10px".

16.2.6.1 Internet Explorer quirks

Now that you understand that width and height specify the size of an element's content area only and that the left, top, right, and bottom attributes are measured relative to the containing element's padding, there is one more detail you must be aware of: Internet Explorer versions 4 through 5.5 for Windows (but not IE 5 for the Mac) implement the width and height attributes incorrectly and include an element's border and padding (but not its margins). For example, if you set the width of an element to 100 pixels and place a 10-pixel padding and a 5-pixel border on the left and right, the content area of the element ends up being only 70 pixels wide in these buggy versions of Internet Explorer.

In IE 6, the CSS position and size attributes work correctly when the browser is in standards mode and incorrectly (but compatibly with earlier versions) when the browser is in compatibility mode. Standards mode, and hence correct implementation of the CSS box model, is triggered by the presence of a <!DOCTYPE> tag at the start of the document, declaring that the document adheres to the HTML 4.0 (or later) standard or some version of the XHTML standards. For example, any of the following three HTML document type declarations cause IE 6 to display documents in standards mode:

```
<!DOCTYPE HTML PUBLIC "-//W3C//DTD HTML 4.0//EN">
<!DOCTYPE HTML PUBLIC "-//W3C//DTD HTML 4.0 Strict//EN">
<!DOCTYPE HTML PUBLIC "-//W3C//DTD HTML 4.0 Transitional//EN"
    "http://www.w3.org/TR/html4/loose.dtd">
```

This distinction between standards mode and compatibility mode (sometimes called "quirks mode") is not unique to Internet Explorer. Other browsers also rely on <!DOCTYPE> declarations to trigger strict standards compliance and, in the absence of this declaration, default to backward-compatible behavior. Only IE has such an egregious compatibility problem, however.

16.2.7 Color, Transparency, and Translucency

The discussion of borders included examples that specified border colors using the English names of common colors such as "red" and "black." The more general syntax for specifying colors in CSS is to use hexadecimal digits to specify the red, green, and blue components of a color. You can use either one or two digits per component. For example:

```
#000000     /* black */
#fff        /* white */
#f00        /* bright red */
#404080     /* dark unsaturated blue */
#ccc        /* light gray */
```

In addition to specifying border colors using this color notation, you can also specify text color with the CSS color attribute. And you can specify the background color of any element with the background-color attribute. CSS allows you to specify the exact position, size, background color, and border color of elements; this gives you a rudimentary graphics capability for drawing rectangles and (when the height and width are reduced) horizontal and vertical lines. I'll return to this topic in Chapter 22, which covers how to use CSS positioning and DOM scripting to draw bar charts.

In addition to the background-color attribute, you can also specify images to be used as the background of an element. The background-image attribute specifies the image to use, and the background-attachment, background-position, and background-repeat attributes specify further details about how this image is drawn. The shortcut attribute background allows you to specify these attributes together. You can use these background image attributes to create interesting visual effects, but those are beyond the scope of this book.

It is important to understand that if you do not specify a background color or image for an element, that element's background is usually transparent. For example, if you absolutely position a <div> over some existing text in the normal document flow, that text will, by default, show through the <div> element. If the <div> contains its own text, the letters may overlap and become an illegible jumble. Not all elements are transparent by default, however. Form elements don't look right with a transparent background, for example, and tags such as <button> have a default background color. You can override this default with the background-color attribute, and you can even explicitly set it to "transparent" if you desire.

The transparency we've been discussing so far is all-or-none: an element either has a transparent background or an opaque background. It is also possible to specify that an element (both its background and its foreground content) is translucent. (See Figure 16-4 for an example.) You do this with the CSS3 opacity attribute. The value of this attribute is a number between 0 and 1, where 1 means 100% opaque (the default) and 0 means 0% opaque (or 100% transparent). The `opacity` attribute is supported by the `Firefox` browser. Earlier versions of Mozilla support an experimental variant named `-moz-opacity`. IE provides a work-alike alternative through its IE-specific `filter` attribute. To make an element 75 percent opaque, you can use the following CSS styles:

```
opacity: .75;                  /* standard CSS3 style for transparency */
-moz-opacity: .75;             /* transparency for older Mozillas */
filter: alpha(opacity=75);     /* transparency for IE; note no decimal point */
```

16.2.8 Partial Visibility: overflow and clip

The `visibility` attribute allows you to completely hide a document element. The `overflow` and `clip` attributes allow you to display only part of an element. The `overflow` attribute specifies what happens when the content of an element exceeds the size specified (with the width and height style attributes, for example) for the element. The allowed values and their meanings for this attribute are as follows:

visible
> Content may overflow and be drawn outside of the element's box if necessary. This is the default.

hidden
> Content that overflows is clipped and hidden so that no content is ever drawn outside the region defined by the size and positioning attributes.

scroll
> The element's box has permanent horizontal and vertical scrollbars. If the content exceeds the size of the box, the scrollbars allow the user to scroll to view the extra content. This value is honored only when the document is displayed on a computer screen; when the document is printed on paper, for example, scrollbars obviously do not make sense.

auto
> Scrollbars are displayed only when content exceeds the element's size rather than being permanently displayed.

While the `overflow` property allows you to specify what happens when an element's content is bigger than the element's box, the `clip` property allows you to specify exactly which portion of an element should be displayed, whether or not the element overflows. This attribute is especially useful for scripted DHTML effects in which an element is progressively displayed or uncovered.

The value of the `clip` property specifies the clipping region for the element. In CSS2, clipping regions are rectangular, but the syntax of the `clip` attribute leaves open the possibility that future versions of the standard will support clipping shapes other than rectangles. The syntax of the `clip` attribute is:

```
rect(top right bottom left)
```

The *top*, *right*, *bottom*, and *left* values specify the boundaries of the clipping rectangle relative to the upper-left corner of the element's box. For example, to display only a 100×100-pixel portion of an element, you can give that element this style attribute:

```
style="clip: rect(0px 100px 100px 0px);"
```

Note that the four values within the parentheses are length values and must include a unit specification, such as px for pixels. Percentages are not allowed. Values may be negative to specify that the clipping region extends beyond the box specified for the element. You may also use the auto keyword for any of the four values to specify that the edge of the clipping region is the same as the corresponding edge of the element's box. For example, you can display just the leftmost 100 pixels of an element with this style attribute:

```
style="clip: rect(auto 100px auto auto);"
```

Note that there are no commas between the values, and the edges of the clipping region are specified in clockwise order from the top edge.

16.2.9 Example: Overlapping Translucent Windows

This section concludes with an example that demonstrates many of the CSS attributes discussed here. Example 16-3 uses CSS to create the visual effect of scrolling, overlapping, translucent windows within the browser window. Figure 16-4 shows how it looks. The example contains no JavaScript code and no event handlers, so there is no way to interact with the windows (other than to scroll them), but it is a useful demonstration of the powerful effects that can be achieved with CSS.

Example 16-3. Displaying windows with CSS

```
<!DOCTYPE HTML PUBLIC "-//W3C//DTD HTML 4.0//EN">
<head>
<style type="text/css">
/**
 * This is a CSS stylesheet that defines three style rules that we use
 * in the body of the document to create a "window" visual effect.
 * The rules use positioning attributes to set the overall size of the window
 * and the position of its components. Changing the size of the window
 * requires careful changes to positioning attributes in all three rules.
 **/
div.window {  /* Specifies size and border of the window */
    position: absolute;         /* The position is specified elsewhere */
    width: 300px; height: 200px;  /* Window size, not including borders */
    border: 3px outset gray;     /* Note 3D "outset" border effect */
}

div.titlebar {  /* Specifies position, size, and style of the titlebar */
    position: absolute;      /* It's a positioned element */
    top: 0px; height: 18px;  /* Titlebar is 18px + padding and borders */
    width: 290px;            /* 290 + 5px padding on left and right = 300 */
```

Example 16-3. Displaying windows with CSS (continued)

```
        background-color: #aaa;   /* Titlebar color */
        border-bottom: groove gray 2px;   /* Titlebar has border on bottom only */
        padding: 3px 5px 2px 5px;   /* Values clockwise: top, right, bottom, left */
        font: bold 11pt sans-serif;        /* Title font */
}

div.content {  /* Specifies size, position and scrolling for window content */
        position: absolute;        /* It's a positioned element */
        top: 25px;                 /* 18px title+2px border+3px+2px padding */
        height: 165px;             /* 200px total - 25px titlebar - 10px padding*/
        width: 290px;              /* 300px width - 10px of padding */
        padding: 5px;              /* Allow space on all four sides */
        overflow: auto;            /* Give us scrollbars if we need them */
        background-color: #ffffff;  /* White background by default */
}

div.translucent { /* this class makes a window partially transparent */
        opacity: .75;               /* Standard style for transparency */
        -moz-opacity: .75;          /* Transparency for older Mozillas */
        filter: alpha(opacity=75);  /* Transparency for IE */
}
</style>
</head>

<body>
<!-- Here is how we define a window: a "window" div with a titlebar and -->
<!-- content div nested between them. Note how position is specified with -->
<!-- a style attribute that augments the styles from the stylesheet. -->
<div class="window" style="left: 10px; top: 10px; z-index: 10;">
<div class="titlebar">Test Window</div>
<div class="content">
1<br>2<br>3<br>4<br>5<br>6<br>7<br>8<br>9<br>0<br><!-- Lots of lines to -->
1<br>2<br>3<br>4<br>5<br>6<br>7<br>8<br>9<br>0<br><!-- demonstrate scrolling-->
</div>
</div>

<!-- Here's another window with different position, color, and font weight -->
<div class="window" style="left: 75px; top: 110px; z-index: 20;">
<div class="titlebar">Another Window</div>
<div class="content translucent"
     style="background-color:#d0d0d0; font-weight:bold;">
This is another window. Its <tt>z-index</tt> puts it on top of the other one.
CSS styles make its content area translucent, in browsers that support that.
</div>
</div>
</body>
```

The major shortcoming of this example is that the stylesheet specifies a fixed size for all windows. Because the titlebar and content portions of the window must be precisely positioned within the overall window, changing the size of a window requires changing the value of various positioning attributes in all three rules defined by the stylesheet. This is difficult to do in a static HTML document, but it would not be so

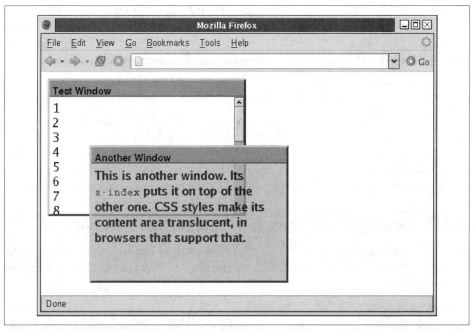

Figure 16-4. Windows created with CSS

difficult if you could use a script to set all the necessary attributes. This topic is explored in the next section.

16.3   Scripting Inline Styles

The crux of DHTML is its ability to use JavaScript to dynamically change the style attributes applied to individual elements within a document. The DOM Level 2 standard defines an API that makes this quite easy to do. In Chapter 15, you saw how to use the DOM API to obtain references to document elements either by tag name or ID, or by recursively traversing the entire document. Once you obtain a reference to the element whose styles you want to manipulate, you use the element's style property to obtain a CSS2Properties object for that document element. This JavaScript object has properties corresponding to each CSS1 and CSS2 style attribute. Setting these properties has the same effect as setting the corresponding styles in a style attribute on the element. Reading these properties returns the CSS attribute value, if any, that was set in the style attribute of the element. The CSS2Properties object is documented in Part IV.

It is important to understand that the CSS2Properties object you obtain with the style property of an element specifies only the inline styles of the element. You cannot use the properties of the CSS2Properties object to obtain information about the stylesheet styles that apply to the element. By setting properties on this object, you are defining inline styles that effectively override stylesheet styles.

Consider the following script, for example. It finds all <img> elements in the document and loops through them looking for ones that appear (based on their size) to be banner advertisements. When it finds an ad, it uses the style.visibility property to set the CSS visibility attribute to hidden, making the ad invisible:

```
var imgs = document.getElementsByTagName("img");   // Find all images
for(var i = 0; i < imgs.length; i++) {             // Loop through them
    var img=imgs[i];
    if (img.width == 468 && img.height == 60)      // If it's a 468x60 banner...
        img.style.visibility = "hidden";           // hide it!
}
```

As an aside, you can transform this simple script into a "bookmarklet" by converting it to a javascript: URL and bookmarking it in your browser (see Section 13.4.1).

16.3.1 Naming Conventions: CSS Attributes in JavaScript

Many CSS style attributes, such as font-family, contain hyphens in their names. In JavaScript, a hyphen is interpreted as a minus sign, so it is not possible to write an expression like:

```
element.style.font-family = "sans-serif";
```

Therefore, the names of the properties of the CSS2Properties object are slightly different from the names of actual CSS attributes. If a CSS attribute name contains one or more hyphens, the CSS2Properties property name is formed by removing the hyphens and capitalizing the letter immediately following each hyphen. Thus, the border-left-width attribute is accessed through the borderLeftWidth property, and you can access the font-family attribute with code like this:

```
element.style.fontFamily = "sans-serif";
```

There is one other naming difference between CSS attributes and the JavaScript properties of CSS2Properties. The word "float" is a keyword in Java and other languages, and although it is not currently used in JavaScript, it is reserved for possible future use. Therefore, the CSS2Properties object cannot have a property named float that corresponds to the CSS float attribute. The solution to this problem is to prefix the float attribute with the string "css" to form the property name cssFloat. Thus, to set or query the value of the float attribute of an element, use the cssFloat property of the CSS2Properties object.

16.3.2 Working with Style Properties

When working with the style properties of the CSS2Properties object, remember that all values must be specified as strings. In a stylesheet or style attribute, you can write:

```
position: absolute; font-family: sans-serif; background-color: #ffffff;
```

To accomplish the same thing for an element e with JavaScript, you have to quote all of the values:

```
e.style.position = "absolute";
e.style.fontFamily = "sans-serif";
e.style.backgroundColor = "#ffffff";
```

Note that the semicolons go outside the strings. These are just normal JavaScript semicolons; the semicolons you use in CSS stylesheets are not required as part of the string values you set with JavaScript.

Furthermore, remember that all the positioning properties require units. Thus, it is not correct to set the left property like this:

```
e.style.left = 300;    // Incorrect: this is a number, not a string
e.style.left = "300";  // Incorrect: the units are missing
```

Units are required when setting style properties in JavaScript, just as they are when setting style attributes in stylesheets. The correct way to set the value of the left property of an element e to 300 pixels is:

```
e.style.left = "300px";
```

If you want to set the left property to a computed value, be sure to append the units at the end of the computation:

```
e.style.left = (x0 + left_margin + left_border + left_padding) + "px";
```

As a side effect of appending the units, the addition of the unit string converts the computed value from a number to a string.

You can also use the CSS2Properties object to query the values of the CSS attributes that were explicitly set in the style attribute of an element, or to read any inline style values previously set by JavaScript code. Once again, however, you must remember that the values returned by these properties are strings, not numbers, so the following code (which assumes that the element e has its margins specified with inline styles) does not do what you might expect it to:

```
var totalMarginWidth = e.style.marginLeft + e.style.marginRight;
```

Instead, you should use code like this:

```
var totalMarginWidth = parseInt(e.style.marginLeft) +
    parseInt(e.style.marginRight);
```

This expression simply discards the unit specifications returned at the ends of both strings. It assumes that both the marginLeft and marginRight properties were specified using the same units. If you exclusively use pixel units in your inline styles, you can usually get away with discarding the units like this.

Recall that some CSS attributes, such as margin, are shortcuts for other properties, such as margin-top, margin-right, margin-bottom, and margin-left. The CSS2Properties object has properties that correspond to these shortcut attributes. For example, you might set the margin property like this:

```
e.style.margin = topMargin + "px " + rightMargin + "px " +
                 bottomMargin + "px " + leftMargin + "px";
```

Arguably, it is easier to set the four margin properties individually:

```
e.style.marginTop = topMargin + "px";
e.style.marginRight = rightMargin + "px";
e.style.marginBottom = bottomMargin + "px";
e.style.marginLeft = leftMargin + "px";
```

You can also query the values of shortcut properties, but this is rarely worthwhile because typically you must then parse the returned value to break it up into its component parts. This is usually difficult to do, and it is much simpler to query the component properties individually.

Finally, let me emphasize again that when you obtain a CSS2Properties object from the style property of an HTMLElement, the properties of this object represent the values of inline style attributes for the element. In other words, setting one of these properties is like setting a CSS attribute in the style attribute of the element: it affects only that one element, and it takes precedence over conflicting style settings from all other sources in the CSS cascade. This precise control over individual elements is exactly what you want when using JavaScript to create DHTML effects.

When you read the values of these CSS2Properties properties, however, they return meaningful values only if they've previously been set by your JavaScript code or if the HTML element with which you are working has an inline style attribute that sets the desired properties. For example, your document may include a stylesheet that sets the left margin for all paragraphs to 30 pixels, but if you read the marginLeft property of one of your paragraph elements, you'll get the empty string unless that paragraph has a style attribute that overrides the stylesheet setting. Thus, although the CSS2Properties object is useful for setting styles that override any other styles, it does not provide a way to query the CSS cascade and determine the complete set of styles that apply to a given element. Section 16.4 briefly considers the getComputedStyle() method and the IE alternative, the currentStyle property, which do provide this ability.

16.3.3 Example: CSS Tool Tips

Example 16-4 is a module of JavaScript code for displaying simple DHTML tool tips, like those pictured in Figure 16-5.

The tool tips are displayed in two nested <div> elements. The outer <div> is absolutely positioned and has a background that serves as the tool tip shadow. The inner <div> is relatively positioned with respect to the shadow and displays the content of the tool tip. The tool tip gets styles from three different places. First, a static

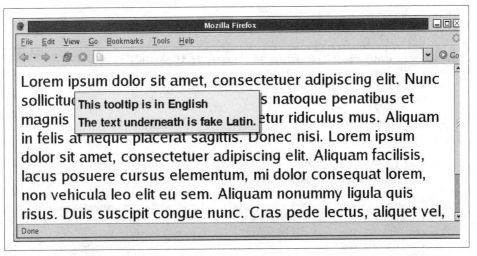

Figure 16-5. A CSS tool tip

stylesheet specifies the shadow, background color, border, and font of the tool tip. Second, inline styles (such as position:absolute) are specified when the tool tip <div> elements are created in the Tooltip( ) constructor. Third, the top, left, and visibility styles are set when the tool tip is displayed with the Tooltip.show( ) method.

Note that Example 16-4 is a simple tool tip module that simply displays and hides tool tips. This example will be extended to be more practical in Example 17-3, which adds support for displaying tool tips in response to mouseover events.

Example 16-4. Tool tips with CSS

```
/**
 * Tooltip.js: simple CSS tool tips with drop shadows.
 *
 * This module defines a Tooltip class. Create a Tooltip object with the
 * Tooltip( ) constructor. Then make it visible with the show( ) method.
 * When done, hide it with the hide( ) method.
 *
 * Note that this module must be used with appropriate CSS class definitions
 * to display correctly. The following are examples:
 *
 *    .tooltipShadow {
 *        background: url(shadow.png);   /* translucent shadow * /
 *    }
 *
 *    .tooltipContent {
 *        left: -4px; top: -4px;        /* how much of the shadow shows * /
 *        background-color: #ff0;       /* yellow background * /
 *        border: solid black 1px;      /* thin black border * /
 *        padding: 5px;                 /* spacing between text and border * /
 *        font: bold 10pt sans-serif;   /* small bold font * /
```

Example 16-4. Tool tips with CSS (continued)

```
*    }
*
* In browsers that support translucent PNG images, it is possible to display
* translucent drop shadows. Other browsers must use a solid color or
* simulate transparency with a dithered GIF image that alternates solid and
* transparent pixels.
*/
function Tooltip() {  // The constructor function for the Tooltip class
    this.tooltip = document.createElement("div"); // create div for shadow
    this.tooltip.style.position = "absolute";    // absolutely positioned
    this.tooltip.style.visibility = "hidden";    // starts off hidden
    this.tooltip.className = "tooltipShadow";     // so we can style it

    this.content = document.createElement("div"); // create div for content
    this.content.style.position = "relative";     // relatively positioned
    this.content.className = "tooltipContent";    // so we can style it

    this.tooltip.appendChild(this.content);       // add content to shadow
}

// Set the content and position of the tool tip and display it
Tooltip.prototype.show = function(text, x, y) {
    this.content.innerHTML = text;              // Set the text of the tool tip.
    this.tooltip.style.left = x + "px";         // Set the position.
    this.tooltip.style.top = y + "px";
    this.tooltip.style.visibility = "visible"; // Make it visible.

    // Add the tool tip to the document if it has not been added before
    if (this.tooltip.parentNode != document.body)
        document.body.appendChild(this.tooltip);
};

// Hide the tool tip
Tooltip.prototype.hide = function() {
    this.tooltip.style.visibility = "hidden";  // Make it invisible.
};
```

16.3.4 DHTML Animations

Some of the most powerful DHTML techniques you can achieve with JavaScript and CSS are animations. There is nothing particularly special about DHTML animations; all you have to do is periodically change one or more style properties of an element or elements. For example, to slide an image into place from the left, you increment the image's style.left property repeatedly until it reaches the desired position. Or you can repeatedly modify the style.clip property to "unveil" the image pixel by pixel.

Example 16-5 contains a simple HTML file that defines a div element to be animated and a short script that changes the border color of the element every 500 milliseconds. Note that the color change is done simply by assigning a value to a CSS style property. What makes it an animation is that the color is changed repeatedly, using the setInterval( ) function of the Window object. (You'll need to use setInterval( ) or setTimeout( ) for all DHTML animations; you may want to refresh your memory by reading about these Window methods in Part IV.) Finally, note the use of the modulo (remainder) operator (%) to cycle through the colors. Consult Chapter 5 if you've forgotten how that operator works.

Example 16-5. A simple color-changing animation

```
<!-- This div is the element we are animating -->
<div id="urgent"><h1>Red Alert!</h1>The Web server is under attack!</div>

<script>
var e = document.getElementById("urgent");      // Get Element object
e.style.border = "solid black 5px";             // Give it a border
e.style.padding = "50px";                       // And some padding
var colors = ["white", "yellow", "orange", "red"]  // Colors to cycle through
var nextColor = 0;                              // Position in the cycle
// Invoke the following function every 500 milliseconds to animate border color
setInterval(function( ) {
            e.style.borderColor=colors[nextColor++%colors.length];
        }, 500);
</script>
```

Example 16-5 produces a very simple animation. In practice, CSS animations typically involve modifications to two or more style properties (such as top, left, and clip) at the same time. Setting up complex animations using a technique like that shown in Example 16-5 can get quite complicated. Furthermore, in order to avoid becoming annoying, animations should typically run for a short while and then stop, unlike the animation in Example 16-5.

Example 16-6 shows a JavaScript file that defines a CSS animation function that makes it much easier to set up animations, even complex ones.

Example 16-6. A framework for CSS-based animations

```
/**
 * AnimateCSS.js:
 * This file defines a function named animateCSS( ), which serves as a framework
 * for creating CSS-based animations. The arguments to this function are:
 *
 *      element: The HTML element to be animated.
 *      numFrames: The total number of frames in the animation.
 *      timePerFrame: The number of milliseconds to display each frame.
 *      animation: An object that defines the animation; described below.
 *      whendone: An optional function to call when the animation finishes.
 *              If specified, this function is passed element as its argument.
 *
 * The animateCSS( ) function simply defines an animation framework. It is
 * the properties of the animation object that specify the animation to be
 * done. Each property should have the same name as a CSS style property. The
```

Example 16-6. A framework for CSS-based animations (continued)

```
 * value of each property must be a function that returns values for that
 * style property. Each function is passed the frame number and the total
 * amount of elapsed time, and it can use these to compute the style value it
 * should return for that frame. For example, to animate an image so that it
 * slides in from the upper left, you might invoke animateCSS as follows:
 *
 *   animateCSS(image, 25, 50,  // Animate image for 25 frames of 50ms each
 *              { // Set top and left attributes for each frame as follows:
 *                  top: function(frame,time) { return frame*8 + "px"; },
 *                  left: function(frame,time) { return frame*8 + "px"; }
 *              });
 *
 **/
function animateCSS(element, numFrames, timePerFrame, animation, whendone) {
    var frame = 0;   // Store current frame number
    var time = 0;    // Store total elapsed time

    // Arrange to call displayNextFrame() every timePerFrame milliseconds.
    // This will display each of the frames of the animation.
    var intervalId = setInterval(displayNextFrame, timePerFrame);

    // The call to animateCSS() returns now, but the previous line ensures that
    // the following nested function will be invoked once for each frame
    // of the animation.
    function displayNextFrame() {
        if (frame >= numFrames) {                 // First, see if we're done
            clearInterval(intervalId);            // If so, stop calling ourselves
            if (whendone) whendone(element);      // Invoke whendone function
            return;                               // And we're finished
        }

        // Now loop through all properties defined in the animation object
        for(var cssprop in animation) {
            // For each property, call its animation function, passing the
            // frame number and the elapsed time. Use the return value of the
            // function as the new value of the corresponding style property
            // of the specified element. Use try/catch to ignore any
            // exceptions caused by bad return values.
            try {
                element.style[cssprop] = animation[cssprop](frame, time);
            } catch(e) {}
        }

        frame++;                  // Increment the frame number
        time += timePerFrame;     // Increment the elapsed time
    }
}
```

The animateCSS( ) function defined in this example is passed five arguments. The first specifies the HTMLElement object to be animated. The second and third arguments specify the number of frames in the animation and the length of time each frame should be displayed. The fourth argument is a JavaScript object that specifies the animation to be performed. The fifth argument is an optional function that should be invoked once when the animation is complete.

The fourth argument to animateCSS( ) is the crucial one. Each property of the JavaScript object must have the same name as a CSS style property, and the value of each property must be a function that returns a legal value for the named style. Every time a new frame of the animation is displayed, each function is called to generate a new value for each style property. Each function is passed the frame number and the total elapsed time and can use these arguments to help it return an appropriate value.

The code in Example 16-6 is fairly straightforward; all the real complexity is embedded in the properties of the animation object that you pass to animateCSS( ), as you'll see shortly. animateCSS( ) defines a nested function called displayNextFrame( ) and does little more than use setInterval( ) to arrange for displayNextFrame( ) to be called repeatedly. displayNextFrame( ) loops through the properties of the animation object and invokes the various functions to compute the new values of the style properties.

Note that because displayNextFrame( ) is defined inside animateCSS( ), it has access to the arguments and local variables of animateCSS( ), even though displayNextFrame( ) is invoked after animateCSS( ) has already returned. (If you don't understand why this works, you may want to review Section 8.8.)

An example should make the use of animateCSS( ) much clearer. The following code moves an element up the screen while gradually uncovering it by enlarging its clipping region:

```
// Animate the element with id "title" for 40 frames of 50 milliseconds each
animateCSS(document.getElementById("title"), 40, 50,
          { // Set top and clip style properties for each frame as follows:
            top:  function(f,t) { return 300-f*5 + "px"; },
            clip: function(f,t) {return "rect(auto "+f*10+"px auto auto)";}
          });
```

The next code fragment uses animateCSS( ) to move a Button object in a circle. It uses the optional fifth argument to animateCSS( ) to change the button text to "Done" when the animation is complete. Note that the element being animated is passed as the argument to the function specified by the fifth argument:

```
// Move a button in a circle, then change the text it displays
animateCSS(document.forms[0].elements[0], 40, 50,  // Button, 40 frames, 50ms
          { // This trigonometry defines a circle of radius 100 at (200,200):
            left: function(f,t){ return 200 + 100*Math.cos(f/8) + "px"},
            top:  function(f,t){ return 200 + 100*Math.sin(f/8) + "px"}
          },
          function(button) { button.value = "Done"; });
```

The Scriptaculous JavaScript library includes a sophisticated animation framework with many powerful predefined animation effects. Visit the cleverly named web site *http://script.aculo.us/* to learn more.

16.4   Scripting Computed Styles

The style property of an HTML element corresponds to the style HTML attribute, and the CSS2Properties object that is the value of the style property includes only inline style information for that one element. It does not include styles from anywhere else in the CSS cascade.

Sometimes you do want to know the exact set of styles that apply to an element, regardless of where in the cascade those styles were specified. What you want is the computed style for the element. The name *computed style* is unfortunately vague; it refers to the computation that is performed before the element is displayed by the web browser: the rules of all stylesheets are tested to see which apply to the element, and the styles of those applicable rules are combined with any inline styles for the element. This aggregate style information can then be used to correctly render the element in the browser window.

The W3C standard API for determining the computed style of an element is the getComputedStyle( ) method of the Window object. The first argument to this method is the element whose computed style is desired. The second argument is any CSS pseudoelement, such as ":before" or ":after" whose style is desired. You probably won't be interested in a pseudoelement, but in the Mozilla and Firefox implementation of this method, the second argument is required and may not be omitted. As a result, you'll usually see getComputedStyle( ) invoked with null as its second argument.

The return value of getComputedStyle( ) is a CSS2Properties object that represents all the styles that apply to the specified element or pseudoelement. Unlike a CSS2Properties object that holds inline style information, the object returned by getComputedStyle( ) is read-only.

IE does not support the getComputedStyle( ) method but provides a simpler alternative: every HTML element has a currentStyle property that holds its computed style. The only shortcoming of the IE API is that it does not provide a way to query the style of pseudoelements.

As an example of computed styles, you could use cross-platform code like the following to determine what typeface an element is displayed in:

```
var p = document.getElementsByTagName("p")[0]; // Get first paragraph of doc
var typeface = "";                             // We want its typeface
if (p.currentStyle)                            // Try simple IE API first
    typeface = p.currentStyle.fontFamily;
else if (window.getComputedStyle)              // Otherwise use W3C API
    typeface = window.getComputedStyle(p, null).fontFamily;
```

Computed styles are quirky, and querying them does not always provide the information you want. Consider the typeface example just shown. The CSS font-family attribute accepts a comma-separated list of desired font families for cross-platform portability. When you query the fontFamily attribute of a computed style, you're simply getting the value of the most specific font-family style that applies to the element. This may return a value such as "arial,helvetica,sans-serif", which does not tell you which typeface is actually in use. Similarly, if an element is not absolutely positioned, attempting to query its position and size through the top and left properties of its computed style often returns the value "auto". This is a perfectly legal CSS value, but it is probably not what you were looking for.

16.5 Scripting CSS Classes

An alternative to scripting individual CSS styles through the style property is to script the value of the HTML class attribute through the className property of any HTML element. Dynamically setting the class of an element can dramatically alter the styles that are applied to the element, assuming that the class you use is appropriately defined in a stylesheet. This technique is used in Example 18-3, a form-validation example that appears later in the book. The JavaScript code in that example sets the className of form elements to "valid" or "invalid" depending on whether the user's input was valid or not. Example 18-2 includes a simple stylesheet that defines the "valid" and "invalid" classes so that they alter the background color of the input elements in a form.

One thing that you must remember about the HTML class attribute and the corresponding className property is that it may list more than one class. In general, then, when scripting the className property, it is not a good idea to simply set and query this value as if it contains a single class name (although, for simplicity, this is what is done in Chapter 18). Instead, you need a function to test whether an element is a member of a class, and functions to add and remove classes from an element's className property. Example 16-7 shows how to define those functions. The code is simple but relies heavily on regular expressions.

Example 16-7. Utility functions for manipulating className

```
/**
 * CSSClass.js: utilities for manipulating the CSS class of an HTML element.
 *
 * This module defines a single global symbol named CSSClass. This object
 * contains utility functions for working with the class attribute (className
 * property) of HTML elements. All functions take two arguments: the element
 * e being tested or manipulated and the CSS class c that is to be tested,
 * added, or removed. If element e is a string, it is taken as an element
 * id and passed to document.getElementById( ).
 */
var CSSClass = {};  // Create our namespace object
```

Example 16-7. Utility functions for manipulating className (continued)

```
// Return true if element e is a member of the class c; false otherwise
CSSClass.is = function(e, c) {
    if (typeof e == "string") e = document.getElementById(e); // element id

    // Before doing a regexp search, optimize for a couple of common cases.
    var classes = e.className;
    if (!classes) return false;      // Not a member of any classes
    if (classes == c) return true; // Member of just this one class

    // Otherwise, use a regular expression to search for c as a word by itself
    // \b in a regular expression requires a match at a word boundary.
    return e.className.search("\\b" + c + "\\b") != -1;
};

// Add class c to the className of element e if it is not already there.
CSSClass.add = function(e, c) {
    if (typeof e == "string") e = document.getElementById(e); // element id
    if (CSSClass.is(e, c)) return; // If already a member, do nothing
    if (e.className) c = " " + c;  // Whitespace separator, if needed
    e.className += c;              // Append the new class to the end
};

// Remove all occurrences (if any) of class c from the className of element e
CSSClass.remove = function(e, c) {
    if (typeof e == "string") e = document.getElementById(e); // element id
    // Search the className for all occurrences of c and replace with "".
    // \s* matches any number of whitespace characters.
    // "g" makes the regular expression match any number of occurrences
    e.className = e.className.replace(new RegExp("\\b"+ c+"\\b\\s*", "g"), "");
};
```

16.6   Scripting Stylesheets

Previous sections have explained two techniques for CSS scripting: altering the inline styles of an element and altering the class of an element. It is also possible to script the stylesheets themselves, as the subsections that follow demonstrate.

16.6.1 Enabling and Disabling Stylesheets

The simplest stylesheet scripting technique is also the most portable and robust. The HTML DOM Level 2 standard defines a disabled property for both <link> and <script> elements. There is no corresponding disabled attribute on the HTML tags, but there is a property that you can query and set in JavaScript. As its name implies, if the disabled property is true, the stylesheet related to the <link> or <style> element is disabled and ignored by the browser.

Example 16-8 demonstrates this. It is an HTML page that includes four stylesheets. It displays four checkboxes that allow the user to enable and disable each of the four stylesheets individually.

Example 16-8. Enabling and disabling stylesheets

```
<head>
<!-- Here we define four stylesheets, using <link> and <style> tags. -->
<!-- Two of the <link>ed sheets are alternate and so disabled by default. -->
<!-- All have id attributes so we can refer to them by name. -->
<link rel="stylesheet" type="text/css" href="ss0.css" id="ss0">
<link rel="alternate stylesheet" type="text/css" href="ss1.css"
      id="ss1" title="Large Type">
<link rel="alternate stylesheet" type="text/css" href="ss2.css"
      id="ss2" title="High Contrast">
<style id="ss3" title="Sans Serif">
body { font-family: sans-serif; }
</style>

<script>
// This function enables or disables a stylesheet specified by id.
// It works for <link> and <style> elements.
function enableSS(sheetid, enabled) {
    document.getElementById(sheetid).disabled = !enabled;
}
</script>
</head>
<body>

<!-- This is a simple HTML form for enabling and disabling stylesheets -->
<!-- It is hardcoded to match the sheets in this document but could be -->
<!-- dynamically generated using stylesheet titles instead. -->
<form>
<input type="checkbox" onclick="enableSS('ss0', this.checked)" checked>Basics
<br><input type="checkbox" onclick="enableSS('ss1', this.checked)">Large Type
<br><input type="checkbox" onclick="enableSS('ss2', this.checked)">Contrast
<br><input type="checkbox" onclick="enableSS('ss3', this.checked)" checked>
Sans Serif
</form>
</body>
```

16.6.2 Stylesheet Objects and Stylesheet Rules

In addition to allowing you to enable and disable the <link> and <style> tags that *refer* to stylesheets, the Level 2 DOM also defines a complete API for querying, traversing, and manipulating stylesheets themselves. At the time of this writing, the only browser to support a substantial portion of this standard stylesheet traversal API is Firefox. IE 5 defines a different API, and other browsers have limited (or no) support for working with stylesheets directly.

In general, manipulating stylesheets directly is not normally a useful thing to do. Instead of adding new rules to a stylesheet, for example, it is typically better to leave your stylesheets static and script the `className` property of your elements instead. On the other hand, if you want to allow the user complete control over the styles used on your pages, you might need to dynamically manipulate a stylesheet (perhaps storing the user's preferred styles in a cookie). If you decide to script stylesheets directly, the code shown in this section works in Firefox and IE, but may not work in other browsers.

The stylesheets that apply to a document are stored in the `styleSheets[]` array of the document object. If a document has only a single stylesheet, you can refer to it as:

```
var ss = document.styleSheets[0]
```

The elements of this array are CSSStyleSheet objects. Note that these objects are *not* the same as the `<link>` or `<style>` tags that refer to or hold the stylesheet. A CSS-StyleSheet object has a `cssRules[]` array that contains the rules of the stylesheet:

```
var firstRule = document.styleSheets[0].cssRules[0];
```

IE does not support the `cssRules` property but does have an equivalent `rules` property.

The elements of the `cssRules[]` or `rules[]` arrays are CSSRule objects. In the W3C standards, a CSSRule object may represent any kind of CSS rule, including *at-rules* such as @import and @page directives. In IE, however, the CSSRule object represents only the actual style rules of the stylesheet.

CSSRule objects have two properties that can be used portably. (In the W3C DOM, a rule that is not a style rule will not have these properties defined, and you probably want to skip over it when traversing the stylesheet.) `selectorText` is the CSS selector for the rule, and `style` refers to a CSS2Properties object that describes the styles associated with that selector. Recall that CSS2Properties is the same interface used to represent the inline styles of an HTML element through the `style` property. You can use this CSS2Properties object to query the style values or to set new styles for the rule. Often, when traversing a stylesheet, you are interested in the text of the rule rather than a parsed representation of the rule. In this case, use the `cssText` property of the CSS2Properties object to obtain the text representation of the rules.

The following code loops through the rules of a stylesheet, demonstrating what you can do with them:

```
// Get the first stylesheet of the document
var ss = document.styleSheets[0];

// Get the rules array using W3C or IE API
var rules = ss.cssRules?ss.cssRules:ss.rules;

// Iterate through those rules
for(var i = 0; i < rules.length; i++) {
    var rule = rules[i];
```

```
    // Skip @import and other nonstyle rules
    if (!rule.selectorText) continue;

    // This is the text form of the rule
    var ruleText = rule.selectorText + " { " + rule.style.cssText + " }";

    // If the rule specifies a margin, assume it is in pixels and double it
    var margin = parseInt(rule.style.margin);
    if (margin) rule.style.margin = (margin*2) + "px";
}
```

In addition to querying and altering the existing rules of a stylesheet, you can also add rules to and remove rules from a stylesheet. The W3C CSSStyleSheet interface defines insertRule( ) and deleteRule( ) methods for adding and removing rules:

```
document.styleSheets[0].insertRule("H1 { text-weight: bold; }", 0);
```

IE does not support insertRule( ) and deleteRule( ) but defines largely equivalent addRule( ) and removeRule( ) functions. The only real difference (aside from the different names) is that addRule( ) expects the selector text and styles text as two separate arguments. Example 16-9 defines a Stylesheet utility class that demonstrates both the W3C and IE APIs for adding and deleting rules.

Example 16-9. Stylesheet utility methods

```
/**
 * Stylesheet.js: utility methods for scripting CSS stylesheets.
 *
 * This module defines a Stylesheet class that is a simple wrapper
 * around an element of the document.styleSheets[] array. It defines useful
 * cross-platform methods for querying and modifying the stylesheet.
 **/

// Construct a new Stylesheet object that wraps the specified CSSStylesheet.
// If ss is a number, look up the stylesheet in the styleSheet[] array.
function Stylesheet(ss) {
    if (typeof ss == "number") ss = document.styleSheets[ss];
    this.ss = ss;
}

// Return the rules array for this stylesheet.
Stylesheet.prototype.getRules = function( ) {
    // Use the W3C property if defined; otherwise use the IE property
    return this.ss.cssRules?this.ss.cssRules:this.ss.rules;
}

// Return a rule of the stylesheet. If s is a number, we return the rule
// at that index.  Otherwise, we assume s is a selector and look for a rule
// that matches that selector.
Stylesheet.prototype.getRule = function(s) {
    var rules = this.getRules( );
    if (!rules) return null;
    if (typeof s == "number") return rules[s];
```

Example 16-9. Stylesheet utility methods (continued)

```
    // Assume s is a selector
    // Loop backward through the rules so that if there is more than one
    // rule that matches s, we find the one with the highest precedence.
    s = s.toLowerCase();
    for(var i = rules.length-1; i >= 0; i--) {
        if (rules[i].selectorText.toLowerCase() == s) return rules[i];
    }
    return null;
};

// Return the CSS2Properties object for the specified rule.
// Rules can be specified by number or by selector.
Stylesheet.prototype.getStyles = function(s) {
    var rule = this.getRule(s);
    if (rule && rule.style) return rule.style;
    else return null;
};

// Return the style text for the specified rule.
Stylesheet.prototype.getStyleText = function(s) {
    var rule = this.getRule(s);
    if (rule && rule.style && rule.style.cssText) return rule.style.cssText;
    else return "";
};

// Insert a rule into the stylesheet.
// The rule consists of the specified selector and style strings.
// It is inserted at index n. If n is omitted, it is appended to the end.
Stylesheet.prototype.insertRule = function(selector, styles, n) {
    if (n == undefined) {
        var rules = this.getRules();
        n = rules.length;
    }
    if (this.ss.insertRule)   // Try the W3C API first
        this.ss.insertRule(selector + "{" + styles + "}", n);
    else if (this.ss.addRule) // Otherwise use the IE API
        this.ss.addRule(selector, styles, n);
};

// Remove the rule from the specified position in the stylesheet.
// If s is a number, delete the rule at that position.
// If s is a string, delete the rule with that selector.
// If n is not specified, delete the last rule in the stylesheet.
Stylesheet.prototype.deleteRule = function(s) {
    // If s is undefined, make it the index of the last rule
    if (s == undefined) {
        var rules = this.getRules();
        s = rules.length-1;
    }

    // If s is not a number, look for a matching rule and get its index.
    if (typeof s != "number") {
```

Example 16-9. Stylesheet utility methods (continued)

```
        s = s.toLowerCase( );       // convert to lowercase
        var rules = this.getRules( );
        for(var i = rules.length-1; i >= 0; i--) {
            if (rules[i].selectorText.toLowerCase( ) == s) {
                s = i;  // Remember the index of the rule to delete
                break;  // And stop searching
            }
        }

        // If we didn't find a match, just give up.
        if (i == -1) return;
    }

    // At this point, s will be a number.
    // Try the W3C API first, then try the IE API
    if (this.ss.deleteRule) this.ss.deleteRule(s);
    else if (this.ss.removeRule) this.ss.removeRule(s);
};
```

CHAPTER 17

Events and Event Handling

As explained in Chapter 13, interactive JavaScript programs use an event-driven programming model. In this style of programming, the web browser generates an *event* whenever something interesting happens to the document or to some element of it. For example, the web browser generates an event when it finishes loading a document, when the user moves the mouse over a hyperlink, or when the user clicks on a button in a form. If a JavaScript application cares about a particular type of event for a particular document element, it can register an *event handler*—a JavaScript function or snippet of code—for that type of event on the element of interest. Then, when that particular event occurs, the browser invokes the handler code. All applications with graphical user interfaces are designed this way: they sit around waiting for the user to do something interesting (i.e., they wait for events to occur), and then they respond.

As an aside, it is worth noting that timers and error handlers (both of which are described in Chapter 14) are related to the event-driven programming model. Like the event handlers described in this chapter, timers and error handlers work by registering a function with the browser and allowing the browser to call that function when the appropriate event occurs. In these cases, however, the event of interest is the passage of a specified amount of time or the occurrence of a JavaScript error. Although timers and error handlers are not discussed in this chapter, it is useful to think of them as related to event handling, and I encourage you to reread Sections 14.1 and 14.7 in the context of this chapter.

Most nontrivial JavaScript programs rely heavily on event handlers. Past chapters have included a number of JavaScript examples that use simple event handlers. This chapter fills in all the missing details about events and event handling. Unfortunately, these details are more complex than they ought to be because three distinct and incompatible event-handling models are in use.[*] These models are:

---

[*] Netscape 4 also had its own distinct and incompatible event model. That browser is no longer widely deployed, however, and documentation of its event model has been removed from this book.

The original event model

> This is the simple event-handling scheme that's been used (but not thoroughly documented) so far in this book. It was codified to a limited extent by the HTML 4 standard and is informally considered part of the DOM Level 0 API. Although its features are limited, it is supported by all JavaScript-enabled web browsers and is therefore portable.

The standard event model

> This powerful and full-featured event model was standardized by DOM Level 2. It is supported by all modern browsers except Internet Explorer.

The Internet Explorer event model

> This event model originated in IE 4 and was extended in IE 5. It has some, but not all, of the advanced features of the standard event model. Although Microsoft participated in the creation of the DOM Level 2 event model and had plenty of time to implement this standard event model in IE 5.5 and IE 6, it has stuck with its proprietary event model instead.[*] This means that JavaScript programmers who want to use advanced event-handling features must write special code for IE browsers.

This chapter documents each of these event models in turn. Coverage of the three event models is followed by three sections that include extended examples of handling mouse, keyboard, and onload events. The chapter concludes with a brief discussion of creating and dispatching synthetic events.

17.1 Basic Event Handling

In the code shown so far in this book, event handlers have been written as strings of JavaScript code that are used as the values of certain HTML attributes, such as onclick. Although this is the key to the original event model, there are a number of additional details, described in the following sections, that you should understand.

17.1.1 Events and Event Types

Different occurrences generate different types of events. When the user moves the mouse over a hyperlink, it causes a different type of event than when the user clicks the mouse on the hyperlink. Even the same occurrence can generate different types of events based on context: when the user clicks the mouse over a **Submit** button, for example, it generates a different event than when the user clicks the mouse over the **Reset** button of a form.

---

[*] At the time of this writing, IE 7 is under development, but there are no indications that it will support the standard event model, either.

In the original event model, an event is an abstraction internal to the web browser, and JavaScript code cannot manipulate an event directly. When we speak of an *event type* in the original event model, what we really mean is the name of the event handler that is invoked in response to the event. In this model, event-handling code is specified using the attributes of HTML elements (and the corresponding properties of the associated JavaScript objects). Thus, if your application needs to know when the user moves the mouse over a specific hyperlink, you use the onmouseover attribute of the <a> tag that defines the hyperlink. If the application needs to know when the user clicks the **Submit** button, you use the onclick attribute of the <input> tag that defines the button or the onsubmit attribute of the <form> element that contains that button.

There are quite a few different event-handler attributes that you can use in the original event model. They are listed in Table 17-1, which also specifies when these event handlers are triggered and which HTML elements support the handler attributes.

As client-side JavaScript programming has evolved, so has the event model it supports. With each new browser version, new event-handler attributes have been added. Finally, the HTML 4 specification codified a standard set of event handler attributes for HTML tags. The third column of Table 17-1 specifies which HTML elements support each event handler attribute. For mouse event handlers, column three specifies that the handler attribute is supported by "most elements." The HTML elements that do not support these event handlers are typically elements that belong in the <head> of a document or do not have a graphical representation of their own. The tags that do not support the nearly universal mouse event handler attributes are <applet>, <bdo>, <br>, <font>, <frame>, <frameset>, <head>, <html>, <iframe>, <isindex>, <meta>, and <style>.

Table 17-1. Event handlers and the HTML elements that support them

Handler	Triggered when	Supported by
onabort	Image loading interrupted.	<img>
onblur	Element loses input focus.	<button>, <input>, <label>, <select>, <textarea>, <body>
onchange	Selection in a <select> element or other form element loses focus, and its value has changed since it gained focus.	<input>, <select>, <textarea>
onclick	Mouse press and release; follows mouseup event. Return false to cancel default action (i.e., follow link, reset, submit).	Most elements
ondblclick	Double-click.	Most elements
onerror	Error when loading image.	<img>
onfocus	Element gains input focus.	<button>, <input>, <label>, <select>, <textarea>, <body>
onkeydown	Key pressed down. Return false to cancel.	Form elements and <body>
onkeypress	Key pressed; follows keydown. Return false to cancel.	Form elements and <body>

Table 17-1. Event handlers and the HTML elements that support them (continued)

Handler	Triggered when	Supported by
onkeyup	Key released; follows keypress.	Form elements and `<body>`
onload	Document load complete.	`<body>`, `<frameset>`, `<img>`
onmousedown	Mouse button pressed.	Most elements
onmousemove	Mouse moved.	Most elements
onmouseout	Mouse moves off element.	Most elements
onmouseover	Mouse moves over element.	Most elements
onmouseup	Mouse button released.	Most elements
onreset	Form reset requested. Return `false` to prevent reset.	`<form>`
onresize	Window size changes.	`<body>`, `<frameset>`
onselect	Text selected.	`<input>`, `<textarea>`
onsubmit	Form submission requested. Return `false` to prevent submission.	`<form>`
onunload	Document or frameset unloaded.	`<body>`, `<frameset>`

17.1.1.1 Device-dependent and device-independent events

If you study the various event handler attributes in Table 17-1 closely, you can discern two broad categories of events. One category is *raw events* or *input events*. These are the events that are generated when the user moves or clicks the mouse or presses a key on the keyboard. These low-level events simply describe a user's gesture and have no other meaning. The second category of events is *semantic events*. These higher-level events have a more complex meaning and can typically occur only in specific contexts: when the browser has finished loading the document or when a form is about to be submitted, for example. A semantic event often occurs as a side effect of a lower-level event. For example, when the user clicks the mouse over a **Submit** button, three of the button's input handlers are triggered: onmousedown, onmouseup, and onclick. Then, as a result of this mouse click, the HTML form that contains the button generates an onsubmit event.

Another important distinction divides events into device-dependent events, which are tied specifically to the mouse or to the keyboard, and device-independent events, which can be triggered in more than one way. This distinction is particularly important for accessibility (see Section 13.7) because some users may be able to use a mouse but not a keyboard, and others may be able to use a keyboard but not a mouse. Semantic events, such as onsubmit and onchange, are almost always device-independent events: all modern browsers allow users to manipulate HTML forms using the mouse or keyboard traversal. The events that have the word "mouse" or "key" in them are clearly device-dependent events. If you use them, you may want to use them in pairs so that you provide handlers for both a mouse gesture and a keyboard alternative. Note that the onclick event can be considered a device-independent event. It is

Client-Side JavaScript

not mouse-dependent because keyboard activation of form controls and hyperlinks also generates this event.

17.1.2 Event Handlers as Attributes

As shown in several examples in earlier chapters, event handlers are specified (in the original event model) as strings of JavaScript code used for the values of HTML attributes. So, for example, to execute JavaScript code when the user clicks a button, specify that code as the value of the onclick attribute of the <input> (or <button>) tag:

```
<input type="button" value="Press Me" onclick="alert('thanks');">
```

The value of an event handler attribute is an arbitrary string of JavaScript code. If the handler consists of multiple JavaScript statements, the statements *must* be separated from each other by semicolons. For example:

```
<input type="button" value="Click Here"
        onclick="if (window.numclicks) numclicks++; else numclicks=1;
              this.value='Click # ' + numclicks;">
```

When an event handler requires multiple statements, it is usually easier to define them in the body of a function and then use the HTML event handler attribute to invoke that function. For example, if you want to validate a user's form input before submitting the form, you can use the onsubmit attribute of the <form> tag.[*] Form validation typically requires several lines of code, at a minimum, so instead of cramming all this code into one long attribute value, it makes more sense to define a form-validation function and simply use the onclick attribute to invoke that function. For example, if you defined a function named validateForm( ) to perform validation, you could invoke it from an event handler like this:

```
<form action="processform.cgi" onsubmit="return validateForm( );">
```

Remember that HTML is case-insensitive, so you can capitalize event-handler attributes any way you choose. One common convention is to use mixed-case capitalization, with the initial "on" prefix in lowercase: onClick, onLoad, onMouseOut, and so on. In this book, I've chosen to use all lowercase for compatibility with XHTML, which is case-sensitive.

The JavaScript code in an event-handler attribute may contain a return statement, and the return value may have special meaning to the browser. This is discussed shortly. Also, note that the JavaScript code of an event handler runs in a different scope (see Chapter 4) than global JavaScript code. This, too, is discussed in more detail later in this section.

---

[*] Chapter 18 covers HTML forms in detail and includes a form-validation example.

17.1.3 Event Handlers as Properties

As shown in Chapter 15, each HTML element in a document has a corresponding DOM element in the document tree, and the properties of this JavaScript object correspond to the attributes of the HTML element. This applies to event-handler attributes as well. So if an `<input>` tag has an onclick attribute, the event handler it contains can be referred to with the onclick property of the form element object. (JavaScript is case-sensitive, so regardless of the capitalization used for the HTML attribute, the JavaScript property must be all lowercase.)

Since the value of an HTML event handler attribute is a string of JavaScript code, you might expect the value of the corresponding JavaScript property to be a string as well. This is not the case: when accessed through JavaScript, event-handler properties are functions. You can verify this with a simple example:

```
<input type="button" value="Click Here" onclick="alert(typeof this.onclick);">
```

If you click the button, it displays a dialog box containing the word "function," not the word "string." (Note that in event handlers, the this keyword refers to the object on which the event occurred. I'll discuss the this keyword shortly.)

To assign an event handler to a document element using JavaScript, simply set the event-handler property to the desired function. For example, consider the following HTML form:

```
<form name="f1">
<input name="b1" type="button" value="Press Me">
</form>
```

The button in this form can be referred to as `document.f1.b1`, which means that an event handler can be assigned with a line of JavaScript like this one:

```
document.f1.b1.onclick=function() { alert('Thanks!'); };
```

An event handler can also be assigned like this:

```
function plead() { document.f1.b1.value += ", please!"; }
document.f1.b1.onmouseover = plead;
```

Pay particular attention to that last line: there are no parentheses after the name of the function. To define an event handler, you assign the function itself—not the result of invoking the function—to the event handler property. This often trips up beginning JavaScript programmers.

There are a couple of advantages to expressing event handlers as JavaScript properties. First, and most importantly, it reduces the intermingling of HTML and JavaScript, promoting modularity and cleaner, more maintainable code. Second, it allows event handler functions to be dynamic. Unlike HTML attributes, which are a static part of the document, JavaScript properties can be changed at any time. In complex interactive programs, it can sometimes be useful to dynamically change the event handlers registered for HTML elements.

One minor disadvantage to defining event handlers in JavaScript is that it separates the handler from the element to which it belongs. If the user interacts with a document element before the document is fully loaded (and before all its scripts have executed), the event handlers for the document element may not yet be defined.

Example 17-1 shows how you can specify a single function to be the event handler for many document elements. The example is a simple function that defines an onclick event handler for every link in a document. The event handler asks for the user's confirmation before allowing the browser to follow the hyperlink on which the user has just clicked. The event-handler function returns false if the user does not confirm, which prevents the browser from following the link. Event-handler return values will be discussed shortly.

Example 17-1. One function, many event handlers

```
// This function is suitable for use as an onclick event handler for <a> and
// <area> elements. It uses the this keyword to refer to the document element
// and may return false to prevent the browser from following the link.
function confirmLink() {
    return confirm("Do you really want to visit " + this.href + "?");
}

// This function loops through all the hyperlinks in a document and assigns
// the confirmLink function to each one as an event handler. Don't call it
// before the document is parsed and the links are all defined. It is best
// to call it from the onload event handler of a <body> tag.
function confirmAllLinks() {
    for(var i = 0; i < document.links.length; i++) {
        document.links[i].onclick = confirmLink;
    }
}
```

17.1.3.1 Explicitly invoking event handlers

Because the values of JavaScript event handler properties are functions, you can use JavaScript to invoke event handler functions directly. For example, if you use the onsubmit attribute of a <form> tag to define a form-validation function and you want to validate the form at some point before the user attempts to submit it, you can use the onsubmit property of the Form object to invoke the event handler function. The code might look like this:

```
document.myform.onsubmit();
```

Note, however, that invoking an event handler is not a way to simulate what happens when the event actually occurs. If you invoke the onclick method of a Link object, for example, it does not make the browser follow the link and load a new document. It merely executes whatever function you've defined as the value of that property. (To make the browser load a new document, set the location property of the Window object, as shown in Chapter 14.) The same is true of the onsubmit method of a Form object or the onclick method of a Submit object: invoking the method runs the event-handler function but does not cause the form to be submitted. (To actually submit the form, call the submit( ) method of the Form object.)

You might want to explicitly invoke an event-handler function if you want to use JavaScript to augment an event handler that is (or may be) already defined by HTML code. Suppose you want to take a special action when the user clicks a button, but you do not want to disrupt any onclick event handler that may have been defined in the HTML document itself. (This is one of the problems with the code in Example 17-1: by adding a handler for each hyperlink, it overwrites any onclick handlers that were already defined for those hyperlinks.) You might accomplish this with code like the following:

```
var b = document.myform.mybutton;  // This is the button we're interested in
var oldHandler = b.onclick;         // Save the HTML event handler
function newHandler() { /* My event-handling code goes here */ }
// Now assign a new event handler that calls both the old and new handlers
b.onclick = function() { oldHandler(); newHandler(); }
```

17.1.4 Event Handler Return Values

In many cases, an event handler (whether specified by HTML attribute or JavaScript property) uses its return value to indicate the disposition of the event. For example, if you use the onsubmit event handler of a Form object to perform form validation and discover that the user has not filled in all the fields, you can return false from the handler to prevent the form from actually being submitted. You can ensure that an empty form is not submitted with code like this:

```
<form action="search.cgi"
      onsubmit="if (this.elements[0].value.length == 0) return false;">
<input type="text">
</form>
```

Generally, if the web browser performs some kind of default action in response to an event, you can return false to prevent the browser from performing that action. In addition to onsubmit, other event handlers from which you can return false to prevent the default action include onclick, onkeydown, onkeypress, onmousedown, onmouseup, and onreset. The second column of Table 17-1 describes what happens when you return false.

There is one exception to the rule about returning false to cancel: when the user moves the mouse over a hyperlink, the browser's default action is to display the link's URL in the status line. To prevent this from happening, you return true from the onmouseover event handler. For example, you can try to display a message other than a URL with code like this:

```
<a href="help.htm" onmouseover="window.status='Help!!'; return true;">Help</a>
```

There is no good reason for this exception: it is this way simply because that is always the way it has been. As noted in Chapter 14, however, most modern browsers consider the ability to hide the destination of a link to be a security hole and have disabled it. Therefore, the single exception to the "return false to cancel" rule has become moot.

Note that event handlers are never required to explicitly return a value. If you don't return a value, the default behavior occurs.

17.1.5 Event Handlers and the this Keyword

Whether you define an event handler with an HTML attribute or with a JavaScript property, you are assigning a function to a property of a document element. In other words, you're defining a new method of the document element. When your event handler is invoked, it is invoked as a method of the element on which the event occurred, so the this keyword refers to that target element. This behavior is useful and unsurprising.

Be sure, however, that you understand the implications. Suppose you have an object o with a method mymethod. You might register an event handler like this:

```
button.onclick= o.mymethod;
```

This statement makes button.onclick refer to the same function that o.mymethod does. This function is now a method of both o and button. When the browser triggers this event handler, it invokes the function as a method of the button object, not as a method of o. The this keyword refers to the Button object, not to your object o. Do not make the mistake of thinking you can trick the browser into invoking an event handler as a method of some other object. If you want to do that, you must do it explicitly, like this:

```
button.onclick = function() { o.mymethod(); }
```

17.1.6 Scope of Event Handlers

As discussed in Section 8.8, functions in JavaScript are lexically scoped. This means that they run in the scope in which they were defined, not in the scope from which they are called. When you define an event handler by setting the value of an HTML attribute to a string of JavaScript code, you are implicitly defining a JavaScript function. It is important to understand that the scope of an event-handler function defined in this way is not the same as the scope of other normally defined global JavaScript functions. This means that event handlers defined as HTML attributes execute in a different scope than other functions.*

Recall from the discussion in Chapter 4 that the scope of a function is defined by a scope chain, or list of objects, that is searched, in turn, for variable definitions. When

---

* It is important to understand this, and while the discussion that follows is interesting, it is also dense. You may want to skip it on your first time through this chapter and come back to it later.

a variable x is looked up or resolved in a normal function, JavaScript first looks for a local variable or argument by checking the call object of the function for a property of that name. If no such property is found, JavaScript proceeds to the next object in the scope chain: the global object. It checks the properties of the global object to see if the variable is a global variable.

Event handlers defined as HTML attributes have a more complex scope chain than this. The head of the scope chain is the call object. Any arguments passed to the event handler are defined here (you'll see later in this chapter that in some advanced event models, event handlers are passed an argument), as are any local variables declared in the body of the event handler. The next object in an event handler's scope chain isn't the global object, however; it is the object that triggered the event handler. So, for example, suppose you use an `<input>` tag to define a Button object in an HTML form and then use the `onclick` attribute to define an event handler. If the code for the event handler uses a variable named `form`, that variable is resolved to the `form` property of the Button object. This can be a useful shortcut when writing event handlers as HTML attributes. For example:

```
<form>
    <!-- In event handlers, "this" refers to the target element of the event -->
    <!-- So we can refer to a sibling element in the form like this -->
    <input id="b1" type="button" value="Button 1"
           onclick="alert(this.form.b2.value);">
    <!-- The target element is also in the scope chain, so we can omit "this" -->
    <input id="b2" type="button" value="Button 2"
           onclick="alert(form.b1.value);">
    <!-- And the <form> is in the scope chain, so we can omit "form". -->
    <input id="b3" type="button" value="Button 3"
           onclick="alert(b4.value);">
    <!-- The Document object is on the scope chain, so we can use its methods -->
    <!-- without prefixing them with "document". This is bad style, though. -->
    <input id="b4" type="button" value="Button 4"
           onclick="alert(getElementById('b3').value);">
</form>
```

As you can see from this sample code, the scope chain of an event handler does not stop with the object that defines the handler: it proceeds up the containment hierarchy and includes, at a minimum, the HTML `<form>` element that contains the button and the Document object that contains the form.[*] The final object in the scope chain is the Window object, because it always is in client-side JavaScript.

Another way to think about the extended scope chain of event handlers is to consider the translation of the JavaScript text of the HTML event handler attribute into a JavaScript function. Consider the following lines from the previous example:

```
<input id="b3" type="button" value="Button 3"
       onclick="alert(b4.value);">
```

---

[*] The precise composition of the scope chain has never been standardized and may be implementation-dependent.

The equivalent JavaScript code would be the following:

```
var b3 = document.getElementById('b3'); // Find the button we're interested in
b3.onclick = function() {
    with (document) {
        with(this.form) {
            with(this) {
                alert(b4.value);
            }
        }
    }
}
```

The repeated with statements create an extended scope chain. See Section 6.18 if you've forgotten about this infrequently used statement.

Having the target object in the scope chain of an event handler can be a useful shortcut. But having an extended scope chain that includes other document elements can be a nuisance. Consider, for example, that both the Window and Document objects define methods named open( ). If you use the identifier open without qualification, you are almost always referring to the window.open( ) method. In an event handler defined as an HTML attribute, however, the Document object is in the scope chain before the Window object, and using open by itself refers to the document.open( ) method. Similarly, consider what would happen if you added a property named window to a Form object (or defined an input field with name="window"). If you then define an event handler within the form that uses the expression window.open( ), the identifier window resolves to the property of the Form object rather than the global Window object, and event handlers within the form have no easy way to refer to the global Window object or to call the window.open( ) method!

The moral is that you must be careful when defining event handlers as HTML attributes. Your safest bet is to keep any such handlers very simple. Ideally, they should just call a global function defined elsewhere and perhaps return the result:

```
<script>function validateForm() { /* Form validation code here */ }</script>
<form onsubmit="return validateForm();">...</form>
```

A simple event handler like this is still executed using an unusual scope chain, but by keeping the code short, you minimize the likelihood that the long scope chain will trip you up. Once again, remember that functions are executed using the scope in which they were defined, not the scope from which they are invoked. So, even though our sample validateForm( ) method is invoked from an unusual scope, it is executed in its own global scope with no possibility for confusion.

Since there is no standard for the precise composition of the scope chain of an event handler, it is safest to assume that it contains only the target element and the global Window object. For example, use this to refer to the target element, and when the target is an <input> element, feel free to use form to refer to the containing Form object instead of this.form. However, don't rely on the Form or Document objects being in the scope chain; for example, don't use `action` instead of `form.action` or `getElementById` instead of `document.getElementById`.

Finally, keep in mind that this entire discussion of event-handler scope applies only to event handlers defined as HTML attributes. If you specify an event handler by assigning a function to an appropriate JavaScript event-handler property, there is no special scope chain involved, and your function executes in the scope in which it was defined. This is almost always the global scope, unless it is a nested function, in which case the scope chain can get interesting again!

17.2   Advanced Event Handling with DOM Level 2

The event-handling techniques presented so far in this chapter are part of DOM Level 0, the de facto standard API that is supported by every JavaScript-enabled browser. DOM Level 2 defines an advanced event-handling API that is significantly different (and quite a bit more powerful) than the Level 0 API. The Level 2 standard does not incorporate the existing API into the standard DOM, but there is no danger of the Level 0 API being dropped. For basic event-handling tasks, you should feel free to continue to use the simple API.

The DOM Level 2 event model is supported by all modern browsers except Internet Explorer.

17.2.1 Event Propagation

In the Level 0 event model, the browser dispatches events to the document elements on which they occur. If that object has an appropriate event handler, that handler is run. There is nothing more to it. The situation is more complex in DOM Level 2. In this advanced event model, when an event occurs on a document element (known as the event *target*), the target's event handler or handlers are triggered, but in addition, each of the target's ancestor elements has one or two opportunities to handle that event. Event propagation proceeds in three phases. First, during the *capturing* phase, events propagate from the Document object down through the document tree to the target node. If any of the ancestors of the target (but not the target itself) has a specially registered capturing event handler, those handlers are run during this phase of event propagation. (You'll see how both regular and capturing event handlers are registered shortly.)

The next phase of event propagation occurs *at the target node itself*: any appropriate event handlers registered directly on the target are run. This is akin to the kind of event handling provided by the Level 0 event model.

The third phase of event propagation is the *bubbling* phase, in which the event propagates or bubbles back up the document hierarchy from the target element up to the Document object. Although all events are subject to the capturing phase of event propagation, not all types of events bubble: for example, it does not make sense for a submit event to propagate up the document beyond the <form> element to which it is directed. On the other hand, generic events such as mousedown events can be of interest to any element in the document, so they do bubble up through the document hierarchy, triggering any appropriate event handlers on each of the ancestors of the target element. In general, raw input events bubble while higher-level semantic events do not. (See Table 17-3 later in this chapter for a definitive list of which events bubble and which do not.)

During event propagation, it is possible for any event handler to stop further propagation of the event by calling the stopPropagation( ) method of the Event object that represents the event. The Event object and its stopPropagation( ) method are discussed further later in this chapter.

Some events cause an associated default action to be performed by the web browser. For example, when a click event occurs on an <a> tag, the browser's default action is to follow the hyperlink. Default actions like these are performed only after all three phases of event propagation complete, and any of the handlers invoked during event propagation can prevent the default action from occurring by calling the preventDefault( ) method of the Event object.

Although this kind of event propagation may seem convoluted, it can help you centralize your event-handling code. DOM Level 1 exposes all document elements and allows events (such as mouseover events) to occur on any of those elements. This means that there are many, many more places for event handlers to be registered than there were with the old Level 0 event model. Suppose you want to trigger an event handler whenever the user moves the mouse over a <p> element in your document. Instead of registering an onmouseover event handler for each <p> tag, you can instead register a single event handler on the Document object and handle these events during either the capturing or bubbling phase of event propagation.

There is one other important detail about event propagation. In the Level 0 model, you can register only a single event handler for a particular type of event for a particular object. In the Level 2 model, however, you can register any number of handler functions for a particular event type on a particular object. This applies also to ancestors of an event target whose handler function or functions are invoked during the capturing or bubbling phases of event propagation.

17.2.2 Event Handler Registration

In the Level 0 API, you register an event handler by setting an attribute in your HTML or an object property in your JavaScript code. In the Level 2 event model, you register an event handler for a particular element by calling the addEventListener( ) method of that object. (The DOM standard uses the term *listener* in its API, but I'll continue to use the synonymous word *handler* in this discussion.) This method takes three arguments. The first is the name of the event type for which the handler is being registered. The event type should be a string that contains the lowercase name of the HTML handler attribute, with the leading "on" removed. Thus, if you use an onmousedown HTML attribute or onmousedown property in the Level 0 model, you'll use the string "mousedown" in the Level 2 event model.

The second argument to addEventListener( ) is the handler (or listener) function that should be invoked when the specified type of event occurs. When your function is invoked, it is passed an Event object as its only argument. This object contains details about the event (such as which mouse button was pressed) and defines methods such as stopPropagation( ). The Event interface and its subinterfaces are discussed further later in this chapter.

The final argument to addEventListener( ) is a boolean value. If true, the specified event handler captures events during the capturing phase of event propagation. If the argument is false, the event handler is a normal event handler and is triggered when the event occurs directly on the object or on a descendant of the element and subsequently bubbles up to the element.

For example, you might use addEventListener( ) as follows to register a handler for submit events on a <form> element:

```
document.myform.addEventListener("submit",
                          function(e) {return validate(e.target); }
                          false);
```

If you wanted to capture all mousedown events that occur within a particular named <div> element, you might use addEventListener( ) like this:

```
var mydiv = document.getElementById("mydiv");
mydiv.addEventListener("mousedown", handleMouseDown, true);
```

Note that these examples assume that you've defined functions named validate( ) and handleMouseDown( ) elsewhere in your JavaScript code.

Event handlers registered with addEventListener( ) are executed in the scope in which they are defined. They are not invoked with the augmented scope chain described in Section 17.1.6.

Because event handlers are registered in the Level 2 model by invoking a method rather than by setting an attribute or property, you can register more than one event handler for a given type of event on a given object. If you call addEventListener( ) multiple times to register more than one handler function for the same event type on the same object, all the functions you've registered are invoked when an event of that type occurs on (or bubbles up to, or is captured by) that object. It is important to understand that the DOM standard makes no guarantees about the order in which the handler functions of a single object are invoked, so you should not rely on them being called in the order in which you registered them. Also note that if you register the same handler function more than once on the same element, all registrations after the first are ignored.

Why would you want to have more than one handler function for the same event on the same object? This can be quite useful for modularizing your software. Suppose, for example, that you've written a reusable module of JavaScript code that uses mouseover events on images to perform image rollovers. Now suppose that you have another module that wants to use the same mouseover events to display additional information about the image in a DHTML pop up or tool tip. With the Level 0 API, you'd have to merge your two modules into one so that they could share the single onmouseover property of the Image object. With the Level 2 API, on the other hand, each module can register the event handler it needs without knowing about or interfering with the other module.

addEventListener( ) is paired with a removeEventListener( ) method that expects the same three arguments but removes an event-handler function from an object rather than adding it. It is often useful to temporarily register an event handler and then remove it soon afterward. For example, when you get a mousedown event, you might register temporary capturing event handlers for mousemove and mouseup events so that you can see if the user drags the mouse. You'd then deregister these handlers when the mouseup event arrives. In such a situation, your event-handler removal code might look as follows:

```
document.removeEventListener("mousemove", handleMouseMove, true);
document.removeEventListener("mouseup", handleMouseUp, true);
```

Both the addEventListener( ) and removeEventListener( ) methods are defined by the EventTarget interface. In web browsers that support the DOM Level 2 Events module, Element and Document nodes implement this interface and provide these event-registration methods.* Part IV documents these methods under Document and Element and does not have an entry for the EventTarget interface itself.

17.2.3 addEventListener( ) and the this Keyword

In the original Level 0 event model, when a function is registered as an event handler for a document element, it becomes a method of that document element (as discussed previously in Section 17.1.5). When the event handler is invoked, it is invoked as a method of the element, and, within the function, the this keyword refers to the element on which the event occurred.

---

* Technically, the DOM says that all nodes in a document (including Text nodes, for example) implement the EventTarget interface. In practice, however, web browsers support event-handler registration only on Element and Document nodes, and also on the Window object, even though this is outside the scope of the DOM.

DOM Level 2 is written in a language-independent fashion and specifies that event listeners are objects rather than simple functions. The JavaScript binding of the DOM makes JavaScript functions event handlers instead of requiring the use of a JavaScript object. Unfortunately, the binding does not actually say how the handler function is invoked and does not specify the value of the this keyword.

Despite the lack of standardization, all known implementations invoke handlers registered with addEventListener( ) as if they were methods of the target element. That is, when the handler is invoked, the this keyword refers to the object on which the handler was registered. If you prefer not to rely on this unspecified behavior, you can use the currentTarget property of the Event object that is passed to your handler functions. As you'll see when the Event object is discussed later in this chapter, the currentTarget property refers to the object on which the event handler was registered.

17.2.4 Registering Objects as Event Handlers

addEventListener( ) allows you to register event-handler functions. For object-oriented programming, you may prefer to define event handlers as methods of a custom object and then have them invoked as methods of that object. For Java programmers, the DOM standard allows exactly this: it specifies that event handlers are objects that implement the EventListener interface and a method named handleEvent( ). In Java, when you register an event handler, you pass an object to addEventListener( ), not a function. For simplicity, the JavaScript binding of the DOM API does not require you to implement an EventListener interface and instead allows you to pass function references directly to addEventListener( ).

However, if you are writing an object-oriented JavaScript program and prefer to use objects as event handlers, you might use a function like this to register them:

```
function registerObjectEventHandler(element, eventtype, listener, captures) {
    element.addEventListener(eventtype,
                        function(event) { listener.handleEvent(event); }
                        captures);
}
```

Any object can be registered as an event listener with this function, as long as it defines a method named handleEvent( ). That method is invoked as a method of the listener object, and the this keyword refers to the listener object, not to the document element that generated the event.

Although it is not part of the DOM specification, Firefox (and other browsers built on the Mozilla codebase) allow event listener objects that define a handleEvent( ) method to be passed directly to addEventListener( ) instead of a function. For these browsers, a special registration function like the one just shown is not necessary.

17.2.5 Event Modules and Event Types

As I've noted before, DOM Level 2 is modularized, so an implementation can support parts of it and omit support for other parts. The Events API is one such module. You can test whether a browser supports this module with code like this:

```
document.implementation.hasFeature("Events", "2.0")
```

The Events module contains only the API for the basic event-handling infrastructure, however. Support for specific types of events is delegated to submodules. Each submodule provides support for a category of related event types and defines an Event type that is passed to event handlers for each of those types. For example, the submodule named MouseEvents provides support for mousedown, mouseup, click, and related event types. It also defines the MouseEvent interface. An object that implements this interface is passed to the handler function for any event type supported by the module.

Table 17-2 lists each event module, the event interface it defines, and the types of events it supports. Note that DOM Level 2 does not standardize any type of keyboard event, so no module of key events is listed here. Current browsers do support key events, however, and you'll learn more about them later in this chapter. Table 17-2, and the rest of this book, omit coverage for the MutationEvents module. Mutation events are triggered when the structure of a document is changed. They are useful for applications such as HTML editors but are not commonly implemented by web browsers or used by web programmers.

Table 17-2. Event modules, interfaces, and types

Module name	Event interface	Event types
HTMLEvents	Event	abort, blur, change, error, focus, load, reset, resize, scroll, select, submit, unload
MouseEvents	MouseEvent	click, mousedown, mousemove, mouseout, mouseover, mouseup
UIEvents	UIEvent	DOMActivate, DOMFocusIn, DOMFocusOut

As you can see from Table 17-2, the HTMLEvents and MouseEvents modules define event types that are familiar from the Level 0 event module. The UIEvents module defines event types that are similar to the focus, blur, and click events supported by HTML form elements but are generalized so that they can be generated by any document element that can receive focus or be activated in some way.

As I noted earlier, when an event occurs, its handler is passed an object that implements the Event interface associated with that type of event. The properties of this object provide details about the event that may be useful to the handler. Table 17-3 lists the standard events again, but this time organizes them by event type rather than by event module. For each event type, this table specifies the kind of event object that is passed to its handler, whether this type of event bubbles up the document hierarchy during event propagation (the "B" column), and whether the event has a default action that can be canceled with the preventDefault( ) method (the "C" column). For events in the HTMLEvents module, the fifth column of the table specifies which HTML elements can generate the event. For all other event types, the fifth column specifies which properties of the event object contain meaningful event details (these properties are documented in the next section). Note that the properties listed in this column do not include the properties that are defined by the basic Event interface, which contain meaningful values for all event types.

It is useful to compare Table 17-3 with Table 17-1, which lists the Level 0 event handlers defined by HTML 4. The event types supported by the two models are largely the same (excluding the UIEvents module). The DOM Level 2 standard adds support for the abort, error, resize, and scroll event types that were not standardized by HTML 4, but it does not support the key events or dblclick event that are part of the HTML 4 standard. (Instead, as you'll see shortly, the detail property of the object passed to a click event handler specifies the number of consecutive clicks that have occurred.)

Table 17-3. Event types

Event type	Interface	B	C	Supported by/detail properties
abort	Event	yes	no	<img>, <object>
blur	Event	no	no	<a>, <area>, <button>, <input>, <label>, <select>, <textarea>
change	Event	yes	no	<input>, <select>, <textarea>
click	MouseEvent	yes	yes	screenX, screenY, clientX, clientY, altKey, ctrlKey, shiftKey, metaKey, button, detail
error	Event	yes	no	<body>, <frameset>, <img>, <object>
focus	Event	no	no	<a>, <area>, <button>, <input>, <label>, <select>, <textarea>
load	Event	no	no	<body>, <frameset>, <iframe>, <img>, <object>
mousedown	MouseEvent	yes	yes	screenX, screenY, clientX, clientY, altKey, ctrlKey, shiftKey, metaKey, button, detail
mousemove	MouseEvent	yes	no	screenX, screenY, clientX, clientY, altKey, ctrlKey, shiftKey, metaKey
mouseout	MouseEvent	yes	yes	screenX, screenY, clientX, clientY, altKey, ctrlKey, shiftKey, metaKey, relatedTarget
mouseover	MouseEvent	yes	yes	screenX, screenY, clientX, clientY, altKey, ctrlKey, shiftKey, metaKey, relatedTarget
mouseup	MouseEvent	yes	yes	screenX, screenY, clientX, clientY, altKey, ctrlKey, shiftKey, metaKey, button, detail
reset	Event	yes	no	<form>
resize	Event	yes	no	<body>, <frameset>, <iframe>
scroll	Event	yes	no	<body>

Table 17-3. Event types (continued)

Event type	Interface	B	C	Supported by/detail properties
select	Event	yes	no	`<input>`,`<textarea>`
submit	Event	yes	yes	`<form>`
unload	Event	no	no	`<body>`,`<frameset>`
DOMActivate	UIEvent	yes	yes	`detail`
DOMFocusIn	UIEvent	yes	no	none
DOMFocusOut	UIEvent	yes	no	none

17.2.6 Event Interfaces and Event Details

When an event occurs, the DOM Level 2 API provides additional details about the event (such as when and where it occurred) as properties of an object that is passed to the event handler. Each event module has an associated event interface that specifies details appropriate to that type of event. Table 17-2 listed three different event modules and three different event interfaces.

These three interfaces are actually related to one another and form a hierarchy. The Event interface is the root of the hierarchy; all event objects implement this most basic event interface. UIEvent is a subinterface of Event: any event object that implements UIEvent also implements all the methods and properties of Event. The Mouse-Event interface is a subinterface of UIEvent. This means, for example, that the event object passed to an event handler for a click event implements all the methods and properties defined by each of the MouseEvent, UIEvent, and Event interfaces.

The following sections introduce each event interface and highlight their most important properties and methods. You will find complete details about each interface in Part IV.

17.2.6.1 Event

The event types defined by the HTMLEvents module use the Event interface. All other event types use subinterfaces of this interface, which means that Event is implemented by all event objects and provides detailed information that applies to all event types. The Event interface defines the following properties (note that these properties, and the properties of all Event subinterfaces, are read-only):

type
> The type of event that occurred. The value of this property is the name of the event type and is the same string value that was used when registering the event handler (e.g., "click" or "mouseover").

target
> The node on which the event occurred, which may not be the same as currentTarget.

currentTarget

> The node at which the event is currently being processed (i.e., the node whose event handler is currently being run). If the event is being processed during the capturing or bubbling phase of propagation, the value of this property is different from the value of the target property. As discussed earlier, you can use this property instead of the this keyword in your event handler functions.

eventPhase

> A number that specifies what phase of event propagation is currently in process. The value is one of the constants Event.CAPTURING_PHASE, Event.AT_TARGET, or Event.BUBBLING_PHASE.

timeStamp

> A Date object that specifies when the event occurred.

bubbles

> A boolean that specifies whether this event (and events of this type) bubbles up the document tree.

cancelable

> A boolean that specifies whether the event has a default action associated with it that can be canceled with the preventDefault( ) method.

In addition to these seven properties, the Event interface defines two methods that are also implemented by all event objects: stopPropagation( ) and preventDefault( ). Any event handler can call stopPropagation( ) to prevent the event from being propagated beyond the node at which it is currently being handled. Any event handler can call preventDefault( ) to prevent the browser from performing a default action associated with the event. Calling preventDefault( ) in the DOM Level 2 API is like returning false in the Level 0 event model.

17.2.6.2 UIEvent

The UIEvent interface is a subinterface of Event. It defines the type of event object passed to events of type DOMFocusIn, DOMFocusOut, and DOMActivate. These event types are not commonly used; what is more important about the UIEvent interface is that it is the parent interface of MouseEvent. UIEvent defines two properties in addition to those defined by Event:

view

> The Window object (known as a *view* in DOM terminology) within which the event occurred.

detail

> A number that may provide additional information about the event. For click, mousedown, and mouseup events, this field is the click count: 1 for a single-click, 2 for a double-click, and 3 for a triple-click. (Note that each click generates an event, but if multiple clicks are close enough together, the detail value

indicates that. That is, a mouse event with a `detail` of 2 is always preceded by a mouse event with a `detail` of 1.) For DOMActivate events, this field is 1 for a normal activation or 2 for a hyperactivation, such as a double-click or **Shift-Enter** combination.

17.2.6.3 MouseEvent

The MouseEvent interface inherits the properties and methods of Event and UIEvent, and defines the following additional properties:

button

A number that specifies which mouse button changed state during a mouse-down, mouseup, or click event. A value of 0 indicates the left button, 1 indicates the middle button, and 2 indicates the right button. This property is used only when a button changes state; it is not used to report whether a button is held down during a mousemove event, for example. Note also that Netscape 6 gets this wrong and uses the values 1, 2, and 3, instead of 0, 1, and 2. This problem is fixed in Netscape 6.1.

altKey , ctrlKey, metaKey, shiftKey

These four boolean fields indicate whether the **Alt**, **Ctrl**, **Meta**, or **Shift** keys were held down when a mouse event occurred. Unlike the button property, these key properties are valid for any type of mouse event.

clientX, clientY

These two properties specify the X and Y coordinates of the mouse pointer, relative to the client area or browser window. Note that these coordinates do not take document scrolling into account: if an event occurs at the very top of the window, clientY is 0, regardless of how far down the document has been scrolled. Unfortunately, DOM Level 2 does not provide a standard way to translate these window coordinates to document coordinates. In browsers other than IE, you can add window.pageXOffset and window.pageYOffset. (See Section 14.3.1 for details.)

screenX, screenY

These two properties specify the X and Y coordinates of the mouse pointer relative to the upper-left corner of the user's monitor. These values are useful if you plan to open a new browser window at or near the location of the mouse event.

relatedTarget

This property refers to a node that is related to the target node of the event. For mouseover events, it is the node that the mouse left when it moved over the target. For mouseout events, it is the node that the mouse entered when leaving the target. It is unused for other event types.

17.2.7 Mixing Event Models

So far, I've discussed the traditional Level 0 event model and the new standard DOM Level 2 model. For backward compatibility, browsers that support the Level 2 model will continue to support the Level 0 event model. This means that you can mix event models within a document.

It is important to understand that web browsers that support the Level 2 event model always pass an event object to event handlers—even handlers registered by setting an HTML attribute or a JavaScript property using the Level 0 model. When an event handler is defined as an HTML attribute, it is implicitly converted to a function that has an argument named event. This means that such an event handler can use the identifier event to refer to the event object. (You'll see later that using the identifier event in an HTML attribute is also compatible with the IE event model.)

The DOM standard recognizes that the Level 0 event model will remain in use and specifies that implementations that support the Level 0 model treat handlers registered with that model as if they were registered using addEventListener( ). That is, if you assign a function f to the onclick property of a document element e (or set the corresponding HTML onclick attribute), it is equivalent to registering that function as follows:

```
e.addEventListener("click", f, false);
```

When f is invoked, it is passed an event object as its argument, even though it was registered using the Level 0 model.

17.3   The Internet Explorer Event Model

The event model supported by Internet Explorer 4, 5, 5.5, and 6 is an intermediate model, halfway between the original Level 0 model and the standard DOM Level 2 model. The IE event model includes an Event object that provides details about events that occur. Instead of being passed to event-handler functions, however, the Event object is made available as a property of the Window object. The IE model supports event propagation by bubbling—but not by capturing, as the DOM model does (although IE 5 and later provide special functionality for capturing mouse events). In IE 4, event handlers are registered in the same way as they are in the original Level 0 model. In IE 5 and later, however, multiple handlers may be registered with special (but nonstandard) registration functions.

The following sections provide more detail about this event model and compare it with the original Level 0 event model and the standard Level 2 event model. You should be sure you understand those two event models before reading about the IE model.

17.3.1 The IE Event Object

Like the standard DOM Level 2 event model, the IE event model provides details about each event in the properties of an Event object. The Event objects defined in the standard model were in fact modeled on the IE Event object, so you'll notice a number of similarities between the properties of the IE Event object and the properties of the DOM Event, UIEvent, and MouseEvent objects.

The most important properties of the IE Event object are:

type

> A string that specifies the type of event that occurred. The value of this property is the name of the event handler with the leading "on" removed (e.g., "click" or "mouseover"). Compatible with the type property of the DOM Event object.

srcElement

> The document element on which the event occurred. Compatible with the target property of the DOM Event object.

button

> An integer that specifies the mouse button that was pressed. A value of 1 indicates the left button, 2 indicates the right button, and 4 indicates the middle button. If multiple buttons are pressed, these values are added together; the left and right buttons together produce a value of 3, for example. Compare this with the button property of the DOM Level 2 MouseEvent object, but note that although the property names are the same, the interpretation of the property values differs.

clientX, clientY

> These integer properties specify the mouse coordinates at the time of the event, relative to the upper-left corner of the containing window. These properties are compatible with the DOM Level 2 MouseEvent properties of the same name. Note that for documents that are larger than the window, these coordinates are not the same as the position within the document. To convert from these window coordinates to document coordinates, you need to add the amount that the document has scrolled. See Section 14.3.1 for information on how to do this.

offsetX, offsetY

> These integer properties specify the position of the mouse pointer relative to the source element. They enable you to determine which pixel of an Image object was clicked on, for example. These properties have no equivalent in the DOM event model.

altKey, ctrlKey, shiftKey

> These boolean properties specify whether the **Alt**, **Ctrl**, and **Shift** keys were held down when the event occurred. These properties are compatible with the properties of the same name in the DOM MouseEvent object. Note, however, that the IE Event object does not have a metaKey property.

keyCode

> This integer property specifies the keycode for keydown and keyup events and the Unicode character code for keypress events. Use String.fromCharCode() to convert character codes to strings. Key events are covered in more detail later in this chapter.

fromElement, toElement

> fromElement specifies the document element that the mouse came from for mouseover events. toElement specifies the document element that the mouse has moved to for mouseout events. Comparable to the relatedTarget property of the DOM MouseEvent object.

cancelBubble

> A boolean property that, when set to true, prevents the current event from bubbling any further up the element containment hierarchy. Comparable to the stopPropagation() method of the DOM Event object.

returnValue

> A boolean property that can be set to false to prevent the browser from performing the default action associated with the event. This is an alternative to the traditional technique of returning false from the event handler. Comparable to the preventDefault() method of the DOM Event object.

You can find complete documentation for the IE Event object in Part IV.

17.3.2 The IE Event Object as a Global Variable

Although the IE event model provides event details in an Event object, it never passes Event objects as arguments to event handlers. Instead, it makes the Event object available as the event property of the global Window object. This means that an event-handling function in IE can refer to the Event object as window.event, or simply as event. Although it seems strange to use a global variable where a function argument would do, the IE scheme works because it is implicit in the event-driven programming model that only one event at a time is being processed. Since two events are never handled concurrently, it is safe to use a global variable to store details on the event that is currently being processed.

The fact that the Event object is a global variable is incompatible with the standard DOM Level 2 event model, but there is a one-line workaround. If you want to write an event-handler function that works with either event model, write the function so that it expects an argument, and then, if no argument is passed, initialize the argument from the global variable. For example:

```
function portableEventHandler(e) {
    if (!e) e = window.event;  // Get event details for IE
    // Body of the event handler goes here
}
```

Another common idiom you may see relies on the || to return its first defined argument:

```
function portableEventHandler(event) {
    var e = event || window.event;
    // Body of the event handler goes here
}
```

17.3.3 IE Event-Handler Registration

In IE 4, event handlers are registered in the same way they are in the original Level 0 event model: by specifying them as HTML attributes or assigning functions to the event handler properties of document elements.

IE 5 and later introduced the attachEvent( ) and detachEvent( ) methods, which provide a way to register more than one handler function for a given event type on a given object. You can use attachEvent( ) to register an event handler as follows:

```
function highlight() { /* Event-handler code goes here */ }
document.getElementById("myelt").attachEvent("onmouseover", highlight);
```

The attachEvent( ) and detachEvent( ) methods work like addEventListener( ) and removeEventListener( ), with the following exceptions:

- Since the IE event model does not support event capturing, attachEvent( ) and detachEvent( ) expect only two arguments: the event type and the handler function.

- The event-handler names passed to the IE methods should include the "on" prefix. For example, use "onclick" with attachEvent( ) instead of "click" with addEventListener( ).

- Functions registered with attachEvent( ) are invoked as global functions, rather than as methods of the document element on which the event occurred. That is, when an event handler registered with attachEvent( ) executes, the this keyword refers to the Window object, not to the event's target element.

- attachEvent( ) allows the same event-handler function to be registered more than once. When an event of the specified type occurs, the registered function will be invoked as many times as it was registered.

17.3.4 Event Bubbling in IE

The IE event model does not have any notion of event capturing, as the DOM Level 2 model does. However, events do bubble up through the containment hierarchy in the IE model, just as they do in the Level 2 model. As with the Level 2 model, event bubbling applies only to raw or input events (primarily mouse and keyboard events), not to higher-level semantic events. The primary difference between event bubbling in the IE and DOM Level 2 event models is the way that you stop bubbling. The IE Event object does not have a stopPropagation( ) method, as the DOM Event object does. To prevent an event from bubbling or stop it from bubbling any further up the containment hierarchy, an IE event handler must set the `cancelBubble` property of the Event object to `true`:

```
window.event.cancelBubble = true;
```

Note that setting `cancelBubble` applies only to the current event. When a new event is generated, a new Event object is assigned to `window.event`, and `cancelBubble` is restored to its default value of `false`.

17.3.5 Capturing Mouse Events

To implement any user interface that involves dragging the mouse (such as pull-down menus or drag-and-drop), it is important to be able to capture mouse events so that the mouse drag can be properly handled regardless of what the user drags over. In the DOM event model, this can be done with capturing event handlers. In IE 5 and later, it is done with the `setCapture()` and `releaseCapture()` methods.

`setCapture()` and `releaseCapture()` are methods of all HTML elements. When you call `setCapture()` on an element, all subsequent mouse events are directed to that element, and that element's handlers can handle the events before they bubble up. Note that this applies only to mouse events and that it includes all mouse-related events: mousedown, mouseup, mousemove, mouseover, mouseout, click, and dblclick.

When you call `setCapture()`, mouse events are dispatched specially until you call `releaseCapture()` or until the capture is interrupted. Mouse capture can be interrupted if your web browser loses focus, an `alert()` dialog appears, a system menu is displayed, or in similar cases. If any of these things happen, the element on which `setCapture()` was called will receive an `onlosecapture` event to notify it of the fact that it is no longer receiving captured mouse events.

In the most common scenario, `setCapture()` is called in response to a mousedown event, ensuring that subsequent mousemove events are received by the same element. The element performs its drag operation in response to mousemove events and calls `releaseCapture()` in response to a (captured) mouseup event.

See Example 17-4 for an example that uses `setCapture()` and `releaseCapture()`.

17.3.6 attachEvent( ) and the this Keyword

As noted earlier, event handlers registered with `attachEvent()` are invoked as global functions instead of as methods of the element on which they are registered. This means that the `this` keyword refers to the global window object. By itself, this is not such a problem. It is compounded, however, by the fact that the IE event object has no equivalent to the DOM `currentTarget` property. `srcElement` specifies the element that generated the event, but if the event has bubbled, this may be different from the element that is handling the event.

If you want to write a generic event handler that can be registered on any element, and if that handler needs to know what element it is registered on, you cannot use attachEvent( ) to register the handler. You must either register the handler using the Level 0 event model or define a wrapper function around the handler and register that wrapper function:

```
// Here are an event handler and an element we want to register it on
function genericHandler() { /* code that uses the this keyword */ }
var element = document.getElementById("myelement");

// We can register this handler with the Level 0 API
element.onmouseover = genericHandler;

// Or we can use a closure
element.attachEvent("onmouseover", function() {
                    // Invoke the handler as a method of element
                    genericHandler.call(element, event);
});
```

The problem with the Level 0 API is that it doesn't allow multiple handler functions to be registered, and the problem with using closures is that they lead to memory leaks in IE. The next section has details.

17.3.7 Event Handlers and Memory Leaks

As discussed in Section 8.8.4.2, Internet Explorer (up to version 6, at least) is vulnerable to a class of memory leaks that can occur when you use nested functions as event handlers. Consider the following code:

```
// Add a validation event handler to a form
function addValidationHandler(form) {
    form.attachEvent("onsubmit", function() { return validate(); });
}
```

When this function is called, it adds an event handler to the specified form element. The handler is defined as a nested function, and although the function itself does not refer to any form elements, its scope, which is captured as part of the closure, does. As a result, a form element refers to a JavaScript Function object, and that object (via its scope chain) refers back to the form object. This is the kind of circular reference that causes memory leaks in IE.

One solution to this problem is to studiously avoid nested functions when programming for IE. Another solution is to carefully remove all your event handlers in response to an onunload( ) event. The code shown in the next section takes this latter approach.

17.3.8 Example: Event Model Compatibility for IE

This section has highlighted a number of incompatibilities between the IE event model and the standard DOM Level 2 model. Example 17-2 is a module of code that addresses many of these incompatibilities. It defines two functions, `Handler.add()` and `Handler.remove()`, to add and remove event handlers from a specified element. On platforms that support `addEventListener()`, these functions are trivial wrappers around these standard methods. On IE 5 and later, however, Example 17-2 defines these methods in such as way as to fix the following incompatibilities:

- Event handlers are invoked as methods of the element on which they are registered.
- Event handlers are passed a simulated event object that matches the DOM standard event object to the extent possible.
- Duplicate registration of event handlers is ignored.
- All handlers are deregistered on document unload to prevent memory leaks in IE.

In order to invoke event handlers with the correct value of the `this` keyword and pass a simulated event object, Example 17-2 must wrap the specified handler function within another function that invokes it correctly. The trickiest part of this example is the code that maps from the handler function passed to `Handler.add()` and the wrapper function that is actually registered with `attachEvent()`. This mapping must be maintained so that `Handler.remove()` can remove the correct wrapper function and so that handlers can be deleted on document unload.

Example 17-2. An event compatibility layer for IE

```
/*
 * Handler.js -- Portable event-handler registration functions
 *
 * This module defines event-handler registration and deregistration functions
 * Handler.add() and Handler.remove(). Both functions take three arguments:
 *
 *   element: the DOM element, document, or window on which the handler
 *       is to be added or removed.
 *
 *   eventType: a string that specifies the type of event for which the
 *       handler is to be invoked. Use DOM-standard type names, which do
 *       not include an "on" prefix. Examples: "click", "load", "mouseover".
 *
 *   handler: The function to be invoked when an event of the specified type
 *       occurs on the specified element. This function will be invoked as
 *       a method of the element on which it is registered, and the "this"
 *       keyword will refer to that element. The handler function will be
 *       passed an event object as its sole argument. This event object will
 *       either be a DOM-standard Event object or a simulated one. If a
 *       simulated event object is passed, it will have the following DOM-
 *       compliant properties: type, target, currentTarget, relatedTarget,
 *       eventPhase, clientX, clientY, screenX, screenY, altKey, ctrlKey,
 *       shiftKey, charCode, stopPropagation(), and preventDefault()
 *
 * Handler.add() and Handler.remove() have no return value.
 *
 * Handler.add() ignores duplicate registrations of the same handler for
```

Example 17-2. An event compatibility layer for IE (continued)

```
 * the same event type and element. Handler.remove( ) does nothing if called
 * to remove a handler that has not been registered.
 *
 * Implementation notes:
 *
 * In browsers that support the DOM standard addEventListener( ) and
 * removeEventListener( ) event-registration functions, Handler.add( ) and
 * Handler.remove( ) simply invoke these functions, passing false as the
 * third argument (meaning that the event handlers are never registered as
 * capturing event handlers).
 *
 * In versions of Internet Explorer that support attachEvent( ), Handler.add( )
 * and Handler.remove() use attachEvent( ) and detachEvent( ). To
 * invoke the handler function with the correct this keyword, a closure is
 * used. Since closures of this sort cause memory leaks in Internet Explorer,
 * Handler.add( ) automatically registers an onunload handler to deregister
 * all event handlers when the page is unloaded. To keep track of
 * registered handlers, Handler.add( ) creates a property named _allHandlers on
 * the window object and creates a property named _handlers on any element on
 * which a handler is registered.
 */
var Handler = {};

// In DOM-compliant browsers, our functions are trivial wrappers around
// addEventListener( ) and removeEventListener( ).
if (document.addEventListener) {
    Handler.add = function(element, eventType, handler) {
        element.addEventListener(eventType, handler, false);
    };

    Handler.remove = function(element, eventType, handler) {
        element.removeEventListener(eventType, handler, false);
    };
}
// In IE 5 and later, we use attachEvent( ) and detachEvent( ), with a number of
// hacks to make them compatible with addEventListener and removeEventListener.
else if (document.attachEvent) {
    Handler.add = function(element, eventType, handler) {
        // Don't allow duplicate handler registrations
        // _find( ) is a private utility function defined below.
        if (Handler._find(element, eventType, handler) != -1) return;

        // To invoke the handler function as a method of the
        // element, we've got to define this nested function and register
        // it instead of the handler function itself.
        var wrappedHandler = function(e) {
            if (!e) e = window.event;

            // Create a synthetic event object with partial compatibility
            // with DOM events.
            var event = {
                _event: e,     // In case we really want the IE event object
```

Example 17-2. An event compatibility layer for IE (continued)

```
            type: e.type,              // Event type
            target: e.srcElement,      // Where the event happened
            currentTarget: element,    // Where we're handling it
            relatedTarget: e.fromElement?e.fromElement:e.toElement,
            eventPhase: (e.srcElement==element)?2:3,

            // Mouse coordinates
            clientX: e.clientX, clientY: e.clientY,
            screenX: e.screenX, screenY: e.screenY,

            // Key state
            altKey: e.altKey, ctrlKey: e.ctrlKey,
            shiftKey: e.shiftKey, charCode: e.keyCode,

            // Event-management functions
            stopPropagation: function() {this._event.cancelBubble = true;},
            preventDefault: function() {this._event.returnValue = false;}
        }

        // Invoke the handler function as a method of the element, passing
        // the synthetic event object as its single argument.
        // Use Function.call() if defined; otherwise do a hack
        if (Function.prototype.call)
            handler.call(element, event);
        else {
            // If we don't have Function.call, fake it like this.
            element._currentHandler = handler;
            element._currentHandler(event);
            element._currentHandler = null;
        }
    };

    // Now register that nested function as our event handler.
    element.attachEvent("on" + eventType, wrappedHandler);

    // Now we must do some record keeping to associate the user-supplied
    // handler function and the nested function that invokes it.
    // We have to do this so that we can deregister the handler with the
    // remove() method and also deregister it automatically on page unload.

    // Store all info about this handler into an object.
    var h = {
        element: element,
        eventType: eventType,
        handler: handler,
        wrappedHandler: wrappedHandler
    };

    // Figure out what document this handler is part of.
    // If the element has no "document" property, it is not
    // a window or a document element, so it must be the document
    // object itself.
```

Example 17-2. An event compatibility layer for IE (continued)

```
        var d = element.document || element;
        // Now get the window associated with that document.
        var w = d.parentWindow;

        // We have to associate this handler with the window,
        // so we can remove it when the window is unloaded.
        var id = Handler._uid();  // Generate a unique property name
        if (!w._allHandlers) w._allHandlers = {};  // Create object if needed
        w._allHandlers[id] = h; // Store the handler info in this object

        // And associate the id of the handler info with this element as well.
        if (!element._handlers) element._handlers = [];
        element._handlers.push(id);

        // If there is not an onunload handler associated with the window,
        // register one now.
        if (!w._onunloadHandlerRegistered) {
            w._onunloadHandlerRegistered = true;
            w.attachEvent("onunload", Handler._removeAllHandlers);
        }
    };

    Handler.remove = function(element, eventType, handler) {
        // Find this handler in the element._handlers[] array.
        var i = Handler._find(element, eventType, handler);
        if (i == -1) return;  // If the handler was not registered, do nothing

        // Get the window of this element.
        var d = element.document || element;
        var w = d.parentWindow;

        // Look up the unique id of this handler.
        var handlerId = element._handlers[i];
        // And use that to look up the handler info.
        var h = w._allHandlers[handlerId];
        // Using that info, we can detach the handler from the element.
        element.detachEvent("on" + eventType, h.wrappedHandler);
        // Remove one element from the element._handlers array.
        element._handlers.splice(i, 1);
        // And delete the handler info from the per-window _allHandlers object.
        delete w._allHandlers[handlerId];
    };

    // A utility function to find a handler in the element._handlers array
    // Returns an array index or -1 if no matching handler is found
    Handler._find = function(element, eventType, handler) {
        var handlers = element._handlers;
        if (!handlers) return -1;  // if no handlers registered, nothing found

        // Get the window of this element
        var d = element.document || element;
        var w = d.parentWindow;
```

Example 17-2. An event compatibility layer for IE (continued)

```
            // Loop through the handlers associated with this element, looking
            // for one with the right type and function.
            // We loop backward because the most recently registered handler
            // is most likely to be the first removed one.
            for(var i = handlers.length-1; i >= 0; i--) {
                var handlerId = handlers[i];        // get handler id
                var h = w._allHandlers[handlerId];  // get handler info
                // If handler info matches type and handler function, we found it.
                if (h.eventType == eventType && h.handler == handler)
                    return i;
            }
            return -1;  // No match found
    };

    Handler._removeAllHandlers = function() {
        // This function is registered as the onunload handler with
        // attachEvent. This means that the this keyword refers to the
        // window in which the event occurred.
        var w = this;

        // Iterate through all registered handlers
        for(id in w._allHandlers) {
            // Get handler info for this handler id
            var h = w._allHandlers[id];
            // Use the info to detach the handler
            h.element.detachEvent("on" + h.eventType, h.wrappedHandler);
            // Delete the handler info from the window
            delete w._allHandlers[id];
        }
    }

    // Private utility to generate unique handler ids
    Handler._counter = 0;
    Handler._uid = function() { return "h" + Handler._counter++; };
}
```

17.4 Mouse Events

Now that we've covered the three event models, let's look at some practical event-handling code. This section discusses mouse events in more detail.

17.4.1 Converting Mouse Coordinates

When a mouse event occurs, the clientX and clientY properties of the event object hold the position of the mouse pointer. This position is in window coordinates: it is relative to the upper-left corner of the browser's "viewport" and does not take document scrolling into account. You may often need to convert these values to document coordinates; for example, to display a tool tip window near the mouse pointer, you need document coordinates in order to position the tool tip. Example 17-3 is a continuation of the tool tip code of Example 16-4. Example 16-4 simply showed how to display a tool tip window at document coordinates that you specify. This example expands upon that one, adding a Tooltip.schedule( ) method that displays a tool tip at coordinates extracted from a mouse event. Since the mouse event specifies the position of the mouse in window coordinates, the schedule( ) method converts these to document coordinates using the Geometry module methods defined in Example 14-2.

Example 17-3. Tool tips positioned via mouse events

```
// The following values are used by the schedule( ) method below.
// They are used like constants but are writable so that you can override
// these default values.
Tooltip.X_OFFSET = 25;  // Pixels to the right of the mouse pointer
Tooltip.Y_OFFSET = 15;  // Pixels below the mouse pointer
Tooltip.DELAY = 500;    // Milliseconds after mouseover

/**
 * This method schedules a tool tip to appear over the specified target
 * element Tooltip.DELAY milliseconds from now. The argument e should
 * be the event object of a mouseover event. This method extracts the
 * mouse coordinates from the event, converts them from window
 * coordinates to document coordinates, and adds the offsets above.
 * It determines the text to display in the tool tip by querying the
 * "tooltip" attribute of the target element. This method
 * automatically registers and unregisters an onmouseout event handler
 * to hide the tool tip or cancel its pending display.
 */
Tooltip.prototype.schedule = function(target, e) {
    // Get the text to display. If none, we don't do anything.
    var text = target.getAttribute("tooltip");
    if (!text) return;

    // The event object holds the mouse position in window coordinates.
    // We convert these to document coordinates using the Geometry module.
    var x = e.clientX + Geometry.getHorizontalScroll( );
    var y = e.clientY + Geometry.getVerticalScroll( );

    // Add the offsets so the tool tip doesn't appear right under the mouse.
    x += Tooltip.X_OFFSET;
    y += Tooltip.Y_OFFSET;

    // Schedule the display of the tool tip.
    var self = this;  // We need this for the nested functions below
    var timer = window.setTimeout(function( ) { self.show(text, x, y); },
                            Tooltip.DELAY);

    // Also, register an onmouseout handler to hide a tool tip or cancel
    // the pending display of a tool tip.
    if (target.addEventListener) target.addEventListener("mouseout", mouseout,
                                                    false);
    else if (target.attachEvent) target.attachEvent("onmouseout", mouseout);
    else target.onmouseout = mouseout;
```

Example 17-3. Tool tips positioned via mouse events (continued)

```
    // Here is the implementation of the event listener
    function mouseout( ) {
        self.hide( );                  // Hide the tool tip if it is displayed,
        window.clearTimeout(timer); // cancel any pending display,
        // and remove ourselves so we're called only once
        if (target.removeEventListener)
            target.removeEventListener("mouseout", mouseout, false);
        else if (target.detachEvent) target.detachEvent("onmouseout",mouseout);
        else target.onmouseout = null;
    }
}

// Define a single global Tooltip object for general use
Tooltip.tooltip = new Tooltip( );

/*
 * This static version of the schedule( ) method uses the global tooltip
 * Use it like this:
 *
 *    <a href="www.davidflanagan.com" tooltip="good Java/JavaScript blog"
 *        onmouseover="Tooltip.schedule(this, event)">David Flanagan's blog</a>
 */
Tooltip.schedule = function(target, e) { Tooltip.tooltip.schedule(target, e); }
```

17.4.2 Example: Dragging Document Elements

Now that event propagation, event-handler registration, and the various event object interfaces for the DOM Level 2 and the IE event models have all been covered, it's time to put them together in a practical example. Example 17-4 shows a JavaScript function, drag( ), that, when invoked from a mousedown event handler, allows an absolutely positioned document element to be dragged by the user. drag( ) works with both the DOM and IE event models.

drag( ) takes two arguments. The first is the element that is to be dragged. This may be the element on which the mousedown event occurred or a containing element (e.g., you might allow the user to drag on the titlebar of a window to move the entire window). In either case, however, it must refer to a document element that is absolutely positioned using the CSS position attribute. The second argument is the event object associated with the triggering mousedown event.

drag( ) records the position of the mousedown event and then registers event handlers for the mousemove and mouseup events that follow the mousedown event. The handler for the mousemove event is responsible for moving the document element, and the handler for the mouseup event is responsible for deregistering itself and the mousemove handler. It is important to note that the mousemove and mouseup handlers are registered as capturing event handlers because the user may move the mouse faster than the document element can follow it, and some of these events occur outside the original target element. Without capturing, the events may not be dispatched to the

Client-Side
JavaScript

correct handlers. Also, note that the moveHandler( ) and upHandler( ) functions that are registered to handle these events are defined as functions nested within drag( ). Because they are defined in this nested scope, they can use the arguments and local variables of drag( ), which considerably simplifies their implementation.

Example 17-4. Dragging document elements

```
/**
 * Drag.js: drag absolutely positioned HTML elements.
 *
 * This module defines a single drag( ) function that is designed to be called
 * from an onmousedown event handler. Subsequent mousemove events will
 * move the specified element. A mouseup event will terminate the drag.
 * If the element is dragged off the screen, the window does not scroll.
 * This implementation works with both the DOM Level 2 event model and the
 * IE event model.
 *
 * Arguments:
 *
 *   elementToDrag: the element that received the mousedown event or
 *      some containing element. It must be absolutely positioned. Its
 *      style.left and style.top values will be changed based on the user's
 *      drag.
 *
 *   event: the Event object for the mousedown event.
 **/
function drag(elementToDrag, event) {
    // The mouse position (in window coordinates)
    // at which the drag begins
    var startX = event.clientX, startY = event.clientY;

    // The original position (in document coordinates) of the
    // element that is going to be dragged. Since elementToDrag is
    // absolutely positioned, we assume that its offsetParent is the
    // document body.
    var origX = elementToDrag.offsetLeft, origY = elementToDrag.offsetTop;

    // Even though the coordinates are computed in different
    // coordinate systems, we can still compute the difference between them
    // and use it in the moveHandler( ) function. This works because
    // the scrollbar position never changes during the drag.
    var deltaX = startX - origX, deltaY = startY - origY;

    // Register the event handlers that will respond to the mousemove events
    // and the mouseup event that follow this mousedown event.
    if (document.addEventListener) {  // DOM Level 2 event model
        // Register capturing event handlers
        document.addEventListener("mousemove", moveHandler, true);
        document.addEventListener("mouseup", upHandler, true);
    }
    else if (document.attachEvent) {  // IE 5+ Event Model
        // In the IE event model, we capture events by calling
        // setCapture( ) on the element to capture them.
```

Example 17-4. Dragging document elements (continued)

```
        elementToDrag.setCapture( );
        elementToDrag.attachEvent("onmousemove", moveHandler);
        elementToDrag.attachEvent("onmouseup", upHandler);
        // Treat loss of mouse capture as a mouseup event.
        elementToDrag.attachEvent("onlosecapture", upHandler);
    }
    else {  // IE 4 Event Model
        // In IE 4 we can't use attachEvent( ) or setCapture( ), so we set
        // event handlers directly on the document object and hope that the
        // mouse events we need will bubble up.
        var oldmovehandler = document.onmousemove; // used by upHandler( )
        var olduphandler = document.onmouseup;
        document.onmousemove = moveHandler;
        document.onmouseup = upHandler;
    }

    // We've handled this event. Don't let anybody else see it.
    if (event.stopPropagation) event.stopPropagation( );  // DOM Level 2
    else event.cancelBubble = true;                        // IE

    // Now prevent any default action.
    if (event.preventDefault) event.preventDefault( );    // DOM Level 2
    else event.returnValue = false;                       // IE

    /**
     * This is the handler that captures mousemove events when an element
     * is being dragged. It is responsible for moving the element.
     **/
    function moveHandler(e) {
        if (!e) e = window.event;  // IE Event Model

        // Move the element to the current mouse position, adjusted as
        // necessary by the offset of the initial mouse-click.
        elementToDrag.style.left = (e.clientX - deltaX) + "px";
        elementToDrag.style.top = (e.clientY - deltaY) + "px";

        // And don't let anyone else see this event.
        if (e.stopPropagation) e.stopPropagation( );  // DOM Level 2
        else e.cancelBubble = true;                    // IE
    }

    /**
     * This is the handler that captures the final mouseup event that
     * occurs at the end of a drag.
     **/
    function upHandler(e) {
        if (!e) e = window.event;  // IE Event Model

        // Unregister the capturing event handlers.
        if (document.removeEventListener) {  // DOM event model
            document.removeEventListener("mouseup", upHandler, true);
            document.removeEventListener("mousemove", moveHandler, true);
```

Example 17-4. Dragging document elements (continued)

```
        }
        else if (document.detachEvent) {  // IE 5+ Event Model
            elementToDrag.detachEvent("onlosecapture", upHandler);
            elementToDrag.detachEvent("onmouseup", upHandler);
            elementToDrag.detachEvent("onmousemove", moveHandler);
            elementToDrag.releaseCapture();
        }
        else {  // IE 4 Event Model
            // Restore the original handlers, if any
            document.onmouseup = olduphandler;
            document.onmousemove = oldmovehandler;
        }

        // And don't let the event propagate any further.
        if (e.stopPropagation) e.stopPropagation();  // DOM Level 2
        else e.cancelBubble = true;                  // IE
    }
}
```

The following code shows how you can use drag( ) in an HTML file (it's a simplified version of Example 16-3, with the addition of dragging):

```
<script src="Drag.js"></script> <!-- Include the Drag.js script -->
<!-- Define the element to be dragged -->
<div style="position:absolute; left:100px; top:100px; width:250px;
            background-color: white; border: solid black;">
<!-- Define the "handle" to drag it with. Note the onmousedown attribute. -->
<div style="background-color: gray; border-bottom: dotted black;
            padding: 3px; font-family: sans-serif; font-weight: bold;"
     onmousedown="drag(this.parentNode, event);">
Drag Me  <!-- The content of the "titlebar" -->
</div>
<!-- Content of the draggable element -->
<p>This is a test. Testing, testing, testing.<p>This is a test.<p>Test.
</div>
```

The key here is the onmousedown attribute of the inner <div> element. Although drag( ) uses the DOM and IE event models internally, it's registered here using the Level 0 model for convenience.

Here's another simple example that uses drag( ); it defines an image that the user can drag if the **Shift** key is held down:

```
<script src="Drag.js"></script>
<img src="draggable.gif" width="20" height="20"
     style="position:absolute; left:0px; top:0px;"
     onmousedown="if (event.shiftKey) drag(this, event);">
```

17.5 Key Events

As you've already learned, events and event handling are subject to many browser incompatibilities. And key events are more incompatible than most: they are not standardized in the DOM Level 2 Events module, and IE and Mozilla-based browsers treat them somewhat differently. Unfortunately, this simply reflects the state of the art in keyboard input handling. The OS and windowing system APIs upon which browsers are built are typically complex and confusing. Text input handling is tricky on many levels, from hardware keyboard layouts to input method processing for ideographic languages.

Despite the difficulties, useful key event-handling scripts can be written to work in at least Firefox and IE. This section demonstrates a couple of simple scripts and then presents a more general Keymap class for mapping keyboard events to JavaScript handler functions.

17.5.1 Types of Key Events

There are three keyboard event types: keydown, keypress, and keyup; they correspond to the onkeydown, onkeypress, and onkeyup event handlers. A typical keystroke generates all three events: keydown, keypress, and then keyup when the key is released. If a key is held down and autorepeats, there may be multiple keypress events between the keydown and keyup, but this is OS- and browser-dependent and cannot be counted on.

Of the three event types, keypress events are the most user-friendly: the event object associated with them contains the encoding of the actual character generated. The keydown and keyup events are lower-level; their key events include a "virtual keycode" that is related to the hardware codes generated by the keyboard. For alphanumeric characters in the ASCII character set, these virtual keycodes match the ASCII codes, but they are not fully processed. If you hold down the **Shift** key and press the key labeled **2**, the keydown event will tell you that the keystroke "shift-2" has occurred. The keypress event will interpret this for you and let you know that that keystroke produced the printable character "@". (This mapping may be different with different keyboard layouts.)

Nonprinting function keys, such as **Backspace**, **Enter**, **Escape**, the arrow keys, **Page Up**, **Page Down**, and **F1** through **F12** generate keydown and keyup events. In some browsers, they also generate keypress events. In IE, however, keypress events occur only when the keystroke has an ASCII code—that is, when it is a printing character or a control character. Nonprinting function keys have virtual keycodes as printing keys do, and these are available through the event object associated with the keydown event. For example, the left arrow key generates a keycode of 37 (at least using a standard U.S. keyboard layout).

As a general rule of thumb, the keydown event is most useful for function keys, and the keypress event is most useful for printing keys.

17.5.2 Key Event Details

The event objects passed to keydown, keypress, and keyup event handlers are the same for each type of event, but the interpretation of certain properties of those objects depends on the event type. The event objects are browser-dependent, of course, with different properties in Firefox and IE.

If the **Alt**, **Ctrl**, or **Shift** keys are held down when a key is pressed, this is indicated by the state of the altKey, ctrlKey, and shiftKey properties of the event object. These properties are actually portable: they work in both Firefox and IE, and for all key event types. (One exception: **Alt** key combinations are considered nonprinting in IE, so they don't generate a keypress event.)

Getting the keycode or character code of a key event is less portable, however. Firefox defines two properties. keyCode holds the low-level virtual keycode of a key and is sent with the keydown event. charCode holds the encoding of the printable character generated by pressing that key and is sent with the keypress event. In Firefox, function keys generate a keypress event; in this case, charCode is zero, and the keyCode contains the virtual keycode.

In IE, there is only the keyCode property, and its interpretation depends on the type of event. For keydown events, keyCode is a virtual keycode; for keypress events, keyCode is a character code.

Character codes can be converted to characters with the static function String.fromCharCode( ). To process keycodes correctly, you must simply know which keys generate which keycodes. Example 17-6 at the end of this section includes a mapping of keycodes to the function keys they represent (on a standard U.S. keyboard layout, at least).

17.5.3 Filtering Keyboard Input

Key event handlers can be used with <input> and <textarea> elements to filter the user's input. For example, suppose you want to force the user's input to uppercase:

```
Surname: <input id="surname" type="text"
                onkeyup="this.value = this.value.toUpperCase( );">
```

An <input> element appends the typed character to its value property after the keypress event occurs. By the time the keyup event arrives, therefore, the value property has been updated, and you can simply convert the entire thing to uppercase. This works no matter where the cursor is positioned within the text field, and you can accomplish it using the DOM Level 0 event model. You do not need to know what key was pressed, and so you do not need to access the event object associated with the event. (Note that the onkeyup event handler is not triggered if the user pastes text into the field using the mouse. To handle that case, you'd probably also want to register an onchange handler. See Chapter 18 for further details about form elements and their event handlers.)

A more complex example of key event filtering uses the onkeypress handler to restrict the user's input to a certain subset of characters. You might want to prevent a user from entering letters into a field intended for numeric data, for example. Example 17-5 is an unobtrusive module of JavaScript code that allows exactly this sort of filtering. It looks for <input type=text> tags that have an additional (non-standard) attribute named allowed. The module registers a keypress event handler on any such text field to restrict input to characters that appear in the value of the allowed attribute. The initial comment at the top of Example 17-5 includes some sample HTML that uses the module.

Example 17-5. Restricting user input to a set of characters

```
/**
 * InputFilter.js: unobtrusive filtering of keystrokes for <input> tags
 *
 * This module finds all <input type="text"> elements in the document that
 * have a nonstandard attribute named "allowed". It registers an onkeypress
 * event handler for any such element to restrict the user's input so that
 * only characters that appear in the value of the allowed attribute may be
 * entered. If the <input> element also has an attribute named "messageid",
 * the value of that attribute is taken to be the id of another document
 * element. If the user types a character that is not allowed, the messageid
 * element is made visible. If the user types a character that is allowed,
 * the messageid element is hidden. This message id element is intended to
 * offer an explanation to the user of why her keystroke was rejected. It
 * should typically be styled with CSS so that it is initially invisible.
 *
 * Here is some sample HTML that uses this module.
 *    Zipcode:
 *    <input id="zip" type="text" allowed="0123456789" messageid="zipwarn">
 *    <span id="zipwarn" style="color:red;visibility:hidden">Digits only</span>
 *
 * In browsers such as IE, which do not support addEventListener(), the
 * keypress handler registered by this module overwrites any keypress handler
 * defined in HTML.
 *
 * This module is purely unobtrusive: it does not define any symbols in
 * the global namespace.
 */
(function() {  // The entire module is within an anonymous function
    // When the document finishes loading, call the init() function below
    if (window.addEventListener) window.addEventListener("load", init, false);
    else if (window.attachEvent) window.attachEvent("onload", init);

    // Find all the <input> tags we need to register an event handler on
    function init() {
```

Example 17-5. Restricting user input to a set of characters (continued)

```
        var inputtags = document.getElementsByTagName("input");
        for(var i = 0 ; i < inputtags.length; i++) { // Loop through all tags
            var tag = inputtags[i];
            if (tag.type != "text") continue; // We only want text fields
            var allowed = tag.getAttribute("allowed");
            if (!allowed) continue;  // And only if they have an allowed attr

            // Register our event handler function on this input tag
            if (tag.addEventListener)
                tag.addEventListener("keypress", filter, false);
            else {
                // We don't use attachEvent because it does not invoke the
                // handler function with the correct value of the this keyword.
                tag.onkeypress = filter;
            }
        }
}

// This is the keypress handler that filters the user's input
function filter(event) {
    // Get the event object and character code in a portable way
    var e = event || window.event;          // Key event object
    var code = e.charCode || e.keyCode;      // What key was pressed

    // If this keystroke is a function key of any kind, do not filter it
    if (e.charCode == 0) return true;        // Function key (Firefox only)
    if (e.ctrlKey || e.altKey) return true; // Ctrl or Alt held down
    if (code < 32) return true;              // ASCII control character

    // Now look up information we need from this input element
    var allowed = this.getAttribute("allowed");      // Legal chars
    var messageElement = null;                        // Message to hide/show
    var messageid = this.getAttribute("messageid"); // Message id, if any
    if (messageid)  // If there is a message id, get the element
        messageElement = document.getElementById(messageid);

    // Convert the character code to a character
    var c = String.fromCharCode(code);

    // See if the character is in the set of allowed characters
    if (allowed.indexOf(c) != -1) {
        // If c is a legal character, hide the message, if any
        if (messageElement) messageElement.style.visibility = "hidden";
        return true; // And accept the character
    }
    else {
        // If c is not in the set of allowed characters, display message
        if (messageElement) messageElement.style.visibility = "visible";
        // And reject this keypress event
        if (e.preventDefault) e.preventDefault();
        if (e.returnValue) e.returnValue = false;
        return false;
```

Example 17-5. Restricting user input to a set of characters (continued)

```
        }
    }
})( ); // Finish anonymous function and invoke it.
```

17.5.4 Keyboard Shortcuts with a Keymap

Graphical programs that run on a user's desktop typically define keyboard shortcuts for commands that are also accessible through pull-down menus, toolbars, and so on. Web browsers (and HTML) are quite mouse-centric, and web applications do not, by default, support keyboard shortcuts. They should, however. If you use DHTML to simulate pull-down menus for your web application, you should also support keyboard shortcuts for those menus. Example 17-6 shows how you might do this. It defines a Keymap class that maps from keystroke identifiers such as "Escape", "Delete", "Alt_Z", and "alt_ctrl_shift_F5" to JavaScript functions that are invoked in response to those keystrokes.

Pass key bindings to the Keymap( ) constructor in the form of a JavaScript object in which property names are keystroke identifiers and property values are handler functions. Add and remove bindings with the bind( ) and unbind( ) methods. Install a Keymap on an HTML element (often the Document object) with the install( ) method. Installing a keymap on an element registers both onkeydown and onkeypress event handlers on that element in order to capture both function keys and printable characters.

Example 17-6 begins with a long comment that explains the module in more detail. See especially the section of this comment titled "Limitations."

Example 17-6. A Keymap class for keyboard shortcuts

```
/*
 * Keymap.js: bind key events to handler functions.
 *
 * This module defines a Keymap class. An instance of this class represents a
 * mapping of key identifiers (defined below) to handler functions. A
 * Keymap can be installed on an HTML element to handle keydown and keypress
 * events. When such an event occurs, the Keymap uses its mapping to invoke
 * the appropriate handler function.
 *
 * When you create a Keymap, pass a JavaScript object that represents the
 * initial set of bindings for the Keymap. The property names of this object
 * are key identifers, and the property values are the handler functions.
 *
 * After a Keymap has been created, you can add new bindings by passing a key
 * identifer and handler function to the bind( ) method. You can remove a
 * binding by passing a key identifier to the unbind( ) method.
 *
 * To make use of a Keymap, call its install( ) method, passing an HTML element,
 * such as the document object. install( ) adds an onkeypress and onkeydown
 * event handler to the specified object, replacing any handlers previously set
```

Example 17-6. A Keymap class for keyboard shortcuts (continued)

```
 * on those properties. When these handlers are invoked, they determine the
 * key identifier from the key event and invoke the handler function, if any,
 * bound to that key identifier. If there is no mapping for the event, it uses
 * the default handler function (see below), if one is defined. A single
 * Keymap may be installed on more than one HTML element.
 *
 * Key Identifiers
 *
 * A key identifier is a case-insensitive string representation of a key plus
 * any modifier keys that are held down at the same time. The key name is the
 * name of the key: this is often the text that appears on the physical key of
 * an English keyboard. Legal key names include "A", "7", "F2", "PageUp",
 * "Left", "Delete", "/", "~". For printable keys, the key name is simply the
 * character that the key generates. For nonprinting keys, the names are
 * derived from the KeyEvent.DOM_VK_ constants defined by Firefox. They are
 * simply the constant name, with the "DOM_VK_" portion and any underscores
 * removed. For example, the KeyEvent constant DOM_VK_BACK_SPACE becomes
 * BACKSPACE. See the Keymap.keyCodeToFunctionKey object in this module for a
 * complete list of names.
 *
 * A key identifier may also include modifier key prefixes. These prefixes are
 * Alt_, Ctrl_, and Shift_. They are case-insensitive, but if there is more
 * than one, they must appear in alphabetical order. Some key identifiers that
 * include modifiers include "Shift_A", "ALT_F2", and "alt_ctrl_delete". Note
 * that "ctrl_alt_delete" is not legal because the modifiers are not in
 * alphabetical order.
 *
 * Shifted punctuation characters are normally returned as the appropriate
 * character. Shift-2 generates a key identifier of "@", for example. But if
 * Alt or Ctrl is also held down, the unshifted symbol is used instead.
 * We get a key identifier of Ctrl_Shift_2 instead of Ctrl_@, for example.
 *
 * Handler Functions
 *
 * When a handler function is invoked, it is passed three arguments:
 *    1) the HTML element on which the key event occurred
 *    2) the key identifier of the key that was pressed
 *    3) the event object for the keydown event
 *
 * Default Handler
 *
 * The reserved key name "default" may be mapped to a handler function. That
 * function will be invoked when no other key-specific binding exists.
 *
 * Limitations
 *
 * It is not possible to bind a handler function to all keys. The operating
 * system traps some key sequences (Alt-F4, for example). And the browser
 * itself may trap others (Ctrl-S, for example). This code is browser, OS,
 * and locale-dependent. Function keys and modified function keys work well,
 * and unmodified printable keys work well. The combination of Ctrl and Alt
 * with printable characters, and particularly with punctuation characters, is
```

Example 17-6. A Keymap class for keyboard shortcuts (continued)

```
  * less robust.
  */

// This is the constructor function
function Keymap(bindings) {
    this.map = {};      // Define the key identifier->handler map
    if (bindings) {     // Copy initial bindings into it, converting to lowercase
        for(name in bindings) this.map[name.toLowerCase()] = bindings[name];
    }
}

// Bind the specified key identifier to the specified handler function
Keymap.prototype.bind = function(key, func) {
    this.map[key.toLowerCase()] = func;
};

// Delete the binding for the specified key identifier
Keymap.prototype.unbind = function(key) {
    delete this.map[key.toLowerCase()];
};

// Install this Keymap on the specified HTML element
Keymap.prototype.install = function(element) {
    // This is the event-handler function
    var keymap = this;
    function handler(event) { return keymap.dispatch(event); }

    // Now install it
    if (element.addEventListener) {
        element.addEventListener("keydown", handler, false);
        element.addEventListener("keypress", handler, false);
    }
    else if (element.attachEvent) {
        element.attachEvent("onkeydown", handler);
        element.attachEvent("onkeypress", handler);
    }
    else {
        element.onkeydown = element.onkeypress = handler;
    }
};

// This object maps keyCode values to key names for common nonprinting
// function keys. IE and Firefox use mostly compatible keycodes for these.
// Note, however that these keycodes may be device-dependent and different
// keyboard layouts may have different values.
Keymap.keyCodeToFunctionKey = {
    8:"backspace", 9:"tab", 13:"return", 19:"pause", 27:"escape", 32:"space",
    33:"pageup", 34:"pagedown", 35:"end", 36:"home", 37:"left", 38:"up",
    39:"right", 40:"down", 44:"printscreen", 45:"insert", 46:"delete",
    112:"f1", 113:"f2", 114:"f3", 115:"f4", 116:"f5", 117:"f6", 118:"f7",
    119:"f8", 120:"f9", 121:"f10", 122:"f11", 123:"f12",
    144:"numlock", 145:"scrolllock"
```

Example 17-6. A Keymap class for keyboard shortcuts (continued)
```
};

// This object maps keydown keycode values to key names for printable
// characters. Alphanumeric characters have their ASCII code, but
// punctuation characters do not. Note that this may be locale-dependent
// and may not work correctly on international keyboards.
Keymap.keyCodeToPrintableChar = {
    48:"0", 49:"1", 50:"2", 51:"3", 52:"4", 53:"5", 54:"6", 55:"7", 56:"8",
    57:"9", 59:";", 61:"=", 65:"a", 66:"b", 67:"c", 68:"d",
    69:"e", 70:"f", 71:"g", 72:"h", 73:"i", 74:"j", 75:"k", 76:"l", 77:"m",
    78:"n", 79:"o", 80:"p", 81:"q", 82:"r", 83:"s", 84:"t", 85:"u", 86:"v",
    87:"w", 88:"x", 89:"y", 90:"z", 107:"+", 109:"-", 110:".", 188:",",
    190:".", 191:"/", 192:"`", 219:"[", 220:"\\", 221:"]", 222:"\""
};

// This method dispatches key events based on the keymap bindings.
Keymap.prototype.dispatch = function(event) {
    var e = event || window.event;  // Handle IE event model

    // We start off with no modifiers and no key name
    var modifiers = ""
    var keyname = null;

    if (e.type == "keydown") {
        var code = e.keyCode;
        // Ignore keydown events for Shift, Ctrl, and Alt
        if (code == 16 || code == 17 || code == 18) return;

        // Get the key name from our mapping
        keyname = Keymap.keyCodeToFunctionKey[code];

        // If this wasn't a function key, but the ctrl or alt modifiers are
        // down, we want to treat it like a function key
        if (!keyname && (e.altKey || e.ctrlKey))
            keyname = Keymap.keyCodeToPrintableChar[code];

        // If we found a name for this key, figure out its modifiers.
        // Otherwise just return and ignore this keydown event.
        if (keyname) {
            if (e.altKey) modifiers += "alt_";
            if (e.ctrlKey) modifiers += "ctrl_";
            if (e.shiftKey) modifiers += "shift_";
        }
        else return;
    }
    else if (e.type == "keypress") {
        // If ctrl or alt are down, we've already handled it.
        if (e.altKey || e.ctrlKey) return;

        // In Firefox we get keypress events even for nonprinting keys.
        // In this case, just return and pretend it didn't happen.
        if (e.charCode != undefined && e.charCode == 0) return;
```

Example 17-6. A Keymap class for keyboard shortcuts (continued)

```
                // Firefox gives us printing keys in e.charCode, IE in e.charCode
                var code = e.charCode || e.keyCode;

                // The code is an ASCII code, so just convert to a string.
                keyname=String.fromCharCode(code);

                // If the key name is uppercase, convert to lower and add shift
                // We do it this way to handle CAPS LOCK; it sends capital letters
                // without having the shift modifier set.
                var lowercase = keyname.toLowerCase();
                if (keyname != lowercase) {
                    keyname = lowercase;      // Use the lowercase form of the name
                    modifiers = "shift_";     // and add the shift modifier.
                }
            }

        // Now that we've determined the modifiers and key name, we look for
        // a handler function for the key and modifier combination
        var func = this.map[modifiers+keyname];

        // If we didn't find one, use the default handler, if it exists
        if (!func) func = this.map["default"];

        if (func) {  // If there is a handler for this key, handle it
            // Figure out what element the event occurred on
            var target = e.target;                    // DOM standard event model
            if (!target) target = e.srcElement; // IE event model

            // Invoke the handler function
            func(target, modifiers+keyname, e);

            // Stop the event from propagating, and prevent the default action for
            // the event. Note that preventDefault doesn't usually prevent
            // top-level browser commands like F1 for help.
            if (e.stopPropagation) e.stopPropagation();  // DOM model
            else e.cancelBubble = true;                  // IE model
            if (e.preventDefault) e.preventDefault();    // DOM
            else e.returnValue = false;                  // IE
            return false;                                // Legacy event model
        }
    }
};
```

17.6   The onload Event

JavaScript code that modifies the document in which it is contained must typically run after the document is fully loaded (this is discussed in further detail in Section 13.5.7). Web browsers fire an onload event on the Window object when document loading is complete, and this event is commonly used to trigger code that needs access to the complete document. When your web page includes multiple independent modules that need to run code in response to the onload event, you may find a cross-platform utility function like the one shown in Example 17-7 to be useful.

Example 17-7. Portable event registration for onload event handlers

```
/*
 * runOnLoad.js: portable registration for onload event handlers.
 *
 * This module defines a single runOnLoad() function for portably registering
 * functions that can be safely invoked only when the document is fully loaded
 * and the DOM is available.
 *
 * Functions registered with runOnLoad() will not be passed any arguments when
 * invoked. They will not be invoked as a method of any meaningful object, and
 * the this keyword should not be used. Functions registered with runOnLoad()
 * will be invoked in the order in which they were registered. There is no
 * way to deregister a function once it has been passed to runOnLoad().
 *
 * In old browsers that do not support addEventListener() or attachEvent(),
 * this function relies on the DOM Level 0 window.onload property and will not
 * work correctly when used in documents that set the onload attribute
 * of their <body> or <frameset> tags.
 */
function runOnLoad(f) {
    if (runOnLoad.loaded) f();     // If already loaded, just invoke f() now.
    else runOnLoad.funcs.push(f); // Otherwise, store it for later
}

runOnLoad.funcs = []; // The array of functions to call when the document loads
runOnLoad.loaded = false; // The functions have not been run yet.

// Run all registered functions in the order in which they were registered.
// It is safe to call runOnLoad.run() more than once: invocations after the
// first do nothing. It is safe for an initialization function to call
// runOnLoad() to register another function.
runOnLoad.run = function() {
    if (runOnLoad.loaded) return;  // If we've already run, do nothing

    for(var i = 0; i < runOnLoad.funcs.length; i++) {
        try { runOnLoad.funcs[i](); }
        catch(e) { /* An exception in one function shouldn't stop the rest */ }
    }

    runOnLoad.loaded = true; // Remember that we've already run once.
    delete runOnLoad.funcs;  // But don't remember the functions themselves.
    delete runOnLoad.run;    // And forget about this function too!
};

// Register runOnLoad.run() as the onload event handler for the window
if (window.addEventListener)
    window.addEventListener("load", runOnLoad.run, false);
else if (window.attachEvent) window.attachEvent("onload", runOnLoad.run);
else window.onload = runOnLoad.run;
```

17.7 Synthetic Events

Both the DOM Level 2 event model and the IE event model allow you to create synthetic event objects and dispatch them to event handlers registered on document elements. In essence, this is a technique for tricking browsers into invoking the event handlers registered on an element (and, in the case of bubbling events, the handlers registered on the ancestors of the element). With the Level 0 event model, synthetic events are not necessary because event handlers are available through the various event handler properties. In the advanced event models, however, there is no way to query the set of handlers registered with `addEventListener` or `attachEvent`, and those handlers can only be invoked using the techniques demonstrated in this section.

In the DOM event model, you create a synthetic event with `Document.createEvent()`, initialize that event with `Event.initEvent()`, `UIEvent.initUIEvent()`, or `MouseEvent.initMouseEvent()` and then dispatch the event with the `dispatchEvent` method of the node to which it is to be dispatched. In IE, you create a new event object with `Document.createEventObject` and then dispatch it with the `fireEvent()` method of the target element. Example 17-8 demonstrates these methods. It defines a cross-platform function for dispatching synthetic dataavailable events and a function for registering event handlers for events of that type.

It is important to understand that synthetic events dispatched with `dispatchEvent()` and `fireEvent()` are not queued and handled asynchronously. Instead, they are dispatched immediately, and their handlers are invoked synchronously before the call to `dispatchEvent()` or `fireEvent()` returns. This means that dispatching a synthetic event is not a technique for deferring execution of code until the browser has handled all pending events. For that, it is necessary to call `setTimeout()` with a timeout value of 0 milliseconds.

It is possible to synthesize and dispatch low-level raw events such as mouse events, but it is not well specified how document elements respond to these events. It is typically more useful to use this functionality for higher-level semantic events to which the browser does not have a default response. This is why Example 17-8 uses the dataavailable event type.

Example 17-8. Dispatching synthetic events

```
/**
 * DataEvent.js: send and receive ondataavailable events.
 *
 * This module defines two functions, DataEvent.send() and DataEvent.receive(),
 * for dispatching synthetic dataavailable events and registering event
 * handlers for those events. The code is written to work in Firefox and other
 * DOM-compliant browsers, and also in IE.
 *
 * The DOM event model allows synthetic events of any type, but the IE model
 * supports only synthetic events of predefined types. dataavailable events
 * are the most generic predefined type supported by IE and are used here.
```

Example 17-8. Dispatching synthetic events (continued)

```
 *
 * Note that events dispatched with DataEvent.send( ) are not queued the way
 * real events would be. Instead, registered handlers are invoked immediately.
 */
var DataEvent = {};

/**
 * Send a synthetic ondataavailable event to the specified target.
 * The event object will include properties named datatype and data
 * that have the specified values. datatype is intended to be a string
 * or other primitive value (or null) identifying the type of this message,
 * and data can be any JavaScript value, including an object or array.
 */
DataEvent.send = function(target, datatype, data) {
    if (typeof target == "string") target = document.getElementById(target);

        // Create an event object. If we can't create one, return silently
    if (document.createEvent) {              // DOM event model
        // Create the event, specifying the name of the event module.
        // For a mouse event, we'd use "MouseEvents".
        var e = document.createEvent("Events");
        // Initialize the event object, using a module-specific init method.
        // Here we specify the event type, bubbling, and noncancelable.
        // See Event.initEvent, MouseEvent.initMouseEvent, and UIEvent.initUIEvent
        e.initEvent("dataavailable", true, false);
    }
    else if (document.createEventObject) { // IE event model
        // In the IE event model, we just call this simple method
        var e = document.createEventObject( );
    }
    else return;  // Do nothing in other browsers

    // Here we add some custom properties to the event object.
    // We could set existing properties as well.
    e.datatype = datatype;
    e.data = data;

    // Dispatch the event to the specified target.
    if (target.dispatchEvent) target.dispatchEvent(e); // DOM
    else if (target.fireEvent) target.fireEvent("ondataavailable", e); // IE
};

/**
 * Register an event handler for an ondataavailable event on the specified
 * target element.
 */
DataEvent.receive = function(target, handler) {
    if (typeof target == "string") target = document.getElementById(target);
    if (target.addEventListener)
        target.addEventListener("dataavailable", handler, false);
    else if (target.attachEvent)
        target.attachEvent("ondataavailable", handler);
};
```

Forms and Form Elements

As shown in examples throughout this book, HTML forms are an important component of many client-side JavaScript programs. This chapter explains the details of programming with forms in JavaScript. It is assumed that you are already somewhat familiar with the creation of HTML forms and with the input elements that they contain. If not, you may want to refer to a good book on HTML.*

If you are already familiar with server-side programming using HTML forms, you may find that things are done differently when forms are used with JavaScript. In the server-side model, a form with the input data it contains is submitted to the web server all at once. The emphasis is on processing a complete batch of input data and dynamically producing a new web page in response. With JavaScript, the programming model is quite different. In JavaScript programs, the emphasis is not on form submission and processing but instead on event handling. A form and all input elements in it have event handlers that JavaScript can use to respond to user interactions within the form. If the user clicks on a checkbox, for example, a JavaScript program can receive notification through an event handler and may respond by changing the value displayed in some other element of the form.

With server-side programs, an HTML form isn't useful unless it has a **Submit** button (or unless it has only a single text input field that allows the user to press the **Enter** key as a shortcut for submission). With JavaScript, on the other hand, a **Submit** button is never necessary (though it may still be useful). With JavaScript event handlers, a form can have any number of push buttons that perform various actions (including form submission) when clicked.

Examples throughout this book have also shown that event handlers are often the central element of a JavaScript program. Some of the most commonly used event handlers are those used with forms or form elements. This chapter introduces the JavaScript Form object and the various JavaScript objects that represent form

---

* Such as *HTML and XHTML: The Definitive Guide* by Chuck Musciano and Bill Kennedy (O'Reilly).

elements. It concludes with an example that illustrates how you can use JavaScript to validate user input on the client before submitting it to a server-side program running on the web server.

18.1 The Form Object

The JavaScript Form object represents an HTML form. As explained in Chapter 15, Form objects are available as elements of the forms[] array, which is a property of the Document object. Forms appear in this array in the order in which they appear within the document. Thus, document.forms[0] refers to the first form in a document. You can refer to the last form in a document with the following:

```
document.forms[document.forms.length-1]
```

The most interesting property of the Form object is the elements[] array, which contains JavaScript objects (of various types) that represent the various input elements of the form. Again, elements appear in this array in the same order they appear in the document. You can refer to the third element of the second form in the document of the current window like this:

```
document.forms[1].elements[2]
```

The remaining properties of the Form object are of less importance. The action, encoding, method, and target properties correspond directly to the action, encoding, method, and target attributes of the <form> tag. These properties and attributes are all used to control how form data is submitted to the web server and where the results are displayed; they are therefore useful only when the form is actually submitted to a server-side program. See a book on HTML or server-side web programming for a thorough discussion of these attributes. What is worth noting here is that these Form properties are all read/write strings, so a JavaScript program can dynamically set their values in order to change the way the form is submitted.

In the days before JavaScript, a form was submitted with a special-purpose **Submit** button, and form elements had their values reset with a special-purpose **Reset** button. The JavaScript Form object supports two methods, submit( ) and reset( ), that serve the same purpose. Invoking the submit( ) method of a Form submits the form, and invoking reset( ) resets the form elements.

To accompany the submit( ) and reset( ) methods, the Form object provides the onsubmit event handler to detect form submission and the onreset event handler to detect form resets. The onsubmit handler is invoked just before the form is submitted; it can cancel the submission by returning false. This provides an opportunity for a JavaScript program to check the user's input for errors in order to avoid submitting incomplete or invalid data over the network to a server-side program. You can find an example of such error checking at the end of this chapter. Note that the onsubmit handler is triggered only by a genuine click on a **Submit** button. Calling the submit( ) method of a form does not trigger the onsubmit handler.

The onreset event handler is similar to the onsubmit handler. It is invoked just before the form is reset, and it can prevent the form elements from being reset by returning false. This allows a JavaScript program to ask for confirmation of the reset, which can be a good idea when the form is long or detailed. You might request this sort of confirmation with an event handler like the following:

```
<form...
    onreset="return confirm('Really erase ALL data and start over?')"
>
```

Like the onsubmit handler, onreset is triggered only by a genuine **Reset** button. Calling the reset( ) method of a form does not trigger onreset.

18.2 Defining Form Elements

HTML form elements allow you to create simple user interfaces for your JavaScript programs. Figure 18-1 shows a complex form that contains at least one of each of the basic form elements. In case you are not already familiar with HTML form elements, the figure includes a numbered key identifying each type of element. This section concludes with an example (Example 18-1) that shows the HTML and JavaScript code used to create the form pictured in Figure 18-1 and to hook up event handlers to each form element.

Table 18-1 lists the types of form elements that are available to HTML designers and JavaScript programmers. The first column of the table names the type of form element, the second column shows the HTML tags that define elements of that type, and the third column lists the value of the type property for each type of element. As shown earlier, each Form object has an elements[ ] array that contains the objects that represent the form's elements. Each element has a type property that can distinguish one type of element from another. By examining the type property of an unknown form element, JavaScript code can determine the type of the element and figure out what it can do with that element. Finally, the fourth column of the table provides a short description of each element and also lists the most important or most commonly used event handler for that element type.

Note that the names Button, Checkbox, and so on from the first column of Table 18-1 may not correspond to an actual client-side JavaScript object. Complete details about the various types of elements are available in Part IV, under the entries Input, Option, Select, and Textarea. These form elements are discussed in more depth later in this chapter.

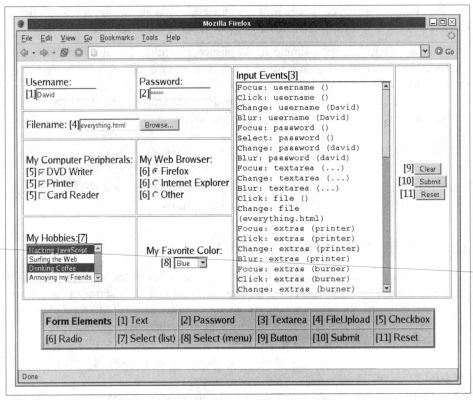

Figure 18-1. HTML form elements

Table 18-1. HTML form elements

Object	HTML tag	type property	Description and events
Button	`<input type="button">` or `<button type="button">`	"button"	A push button; `onclick`.
Checkbox	`<input type="checkbox">`	"checkbox"	A toggle button without radio-button behavior; `onclick`.
File	`<input type="file">`	"file"	An input field for entering the name of a file to upload to the web server; `onchange`.
Hidden	`<input type="hidden">`	"hidden"	Data submitted with the form but not visible to the user; no event handlers.
Option	`<option>`	none	A single item within a Select object; event handlers are on the Select object, not on individual Option objects.
Password	`<input type="password">`	"password"	An input field for password entry—typed characters are not visible; `onchange`.
Radio	`<input type="radio">`	"radio"	A toggle button with radio-button behavior—only one selected at a time; `onclick`.

Table 18-1. HTML form elements (continued)

Object	HTML tag	type property	Description and events
Reset	`<input type="reset">` or `<button type="reset">`	"reset"	A push button that resets a form; onclick.
Select	`<select>`	"select-one"	A list or drop-down menu from which one item may be selected; onchange. (See also Option object.)
Select	`<select multiple>`	"select-multiple"	A list from which multiple items may be selected; onchange. (See also Option object.)
Submit	`<input type="submit">` or `<button type="submit">`	"submit"	A push button that submits a form; onclick.
Text	`<input type="text">`	"text"	A single-line text entry field; onchange.
Textarea	`<textarea>`	"textarea"	A multiline text entry field; onchange.

Now that you've taken a look at the various types of form elements and the HTML tags used to create them, Example 18-1 shows the HTML code used to create the form shown in Figure 18-1. Although the example consists primarily of HTML, it also contains JavaScript code that defines event handlers for each form element. You'll notice that the event handlers are not defined as HTML attributes. Instead, they are JavaScript functions assigned to the properties of the objects in the form's elements[] array. The event handlers all call the function report( ), which contains code that works with the various form elements. The next section of this chapter explains everything you need to know to understand what the report( ) function is doing.

Example 18-1. An HTML form containing all form elements

```
<form name="everything">       <!-- A one-of-everything HTML form... -->
  <table border="border" cellpadding="5">    <!-- in a big HTML table -->
    <tr>
      <td>Username:<br>[1]<input type="text" name="username" size="15"></td>
      <td>Password:<br>[2]<input type="password" name="password" size="15"></td>
      <td rowspan="4">Input Events[3]<br>
        <textarea name="textarea" rows="20" cols="28"></textarea></td>
      <td rowspan="4" align="center" valign="center">
        [9]<input type="button" value="Clear" name="clearbutton"><br>
        [10]<input type="submit" name="submitbutton" value="Submit"><br>
        [11]<input type="reset" name="resetbutton" value="Reset"></td></tr>
    <tr>
      <td colspan="2">
        Filename: [4]<input type="file" name="file" size="15"></td></tr>
    <tr>
      <td>My Computer Peripherals:<br>
        [5]<input type="checkbox" name="extras" value="burner">DVD Writer<br>
        [5]<input type="checkbox" name="extras" value="printer">Printer<br>
        [5]<input type="checkbox" name="extras" value="card">Card Reader</td>
      <td>My Web Browser:<br>
        [6]<input type="radio" name="browser" value="ff">Firefox<br>
```

Example 18-1. An HTML form containing all form elements (continued)

```
     [6]<input type="radio" name="browser" value="ie">Internet Explorer<br>
     [6]<input type="radio" name="browser" value="other">Other</td></tr>
  <tr>
    <td>My Hobbies:[7]<br>
      <select multiple="multiple" name="hobbies" size="4">
        <option value="programming">Hacking JavaScript
        <option value="surfing">Surfing the Web
        <option value="caffeine">Drinking Coffee
        <option value="annoying">Annoying my Friends
      </select></td>
    <td align="center" valign="center">My Favorite Color:<br>[8]
      <select name="color">
        <option value="red">Red          <option value="green">Green
        <option value="blue">Blue         <option value="white">White
        <option value="violet">Violet   <option value="peach">Peach
      </select></td></tr>
  </table>
</form>

<div align="center">         <!-- Another table--the key to the one above -->
  <table border="4" bgcolor="pink" cellspacing="1" cellpadding="4">
    <tr>
      <td align="center"><b>Form Elements</b></td>
      <td>[1] Text</td>  <td>[2] Password</td>  <td>[3] Textarea</td>
      <td>[4] FileU</td> <td>[5] Checkbox</td></tr>
    <tr>
      <td>[6] Radio</td>  <td>[7] Select (list)</td>
      <td>[8] Select (menu)</td>   <td>[9] Button</td>
      <td>[10] Submit</td>   <td>[11] Reset</td></tr>
  </table>
</div>

<script>
// This generic function appends details of an event to the big Textarea
// element in the form above. It is called from various event handlers.
function report(element, event) {
    if ((element.type == "select-one") || (element.type == "select-multiple")){
        value = " ";
        for(var i = 0; i < element.options.length; i++)
            if (element.options[i].selected)
                value += element.options[i].value + " ";
    }
    else if (element.type == "textarea") value = "...";
    else value = element.value;
    var msg = event + ": " + element.name + ' (' + value + ')\n';
    var t = element.form.textarea;
    t.value = t.value + msg;
}

// This function adds a bunch of event handlers to every element in a form.
// It doesn't bother checking to see if the element supports the event handler,
// it just adds them all. Note that the event handlers call report().
```

Example 18-1. An HTML form containing all form elements (continued)

```
// We're defining event handlers by assigning functions to the
// properties of JavaScript objects rather than by assigning strings to
// the attributes of HTML elements.
function addhandlers(f) {
    // Loop through all the elements in the form.
    for(var i = 0; i < f.elements.length; i++) {
        var e = f.elements[i];
        e.onclick = function() { report(this, 'Click'); }
        e.onchange = function() { report(this, 'Change'); }
        e.onfocus = function() { report(this, 'Focus'); }
        e.onblur = function() { report(this, 'Blur'); }
        e.onselect = function() { report(this, 'Select'); }
    }

    // Define some special-case event handlers for the three buttons.
    f.clearbutton.onclick = function() {
        this.form.textarea.value=''; report(this,'Click');
    }
    f.submitbutton.onclick = function () {
        report(this, 'Click'); return false;
    }
    f.resetbutton.onclick = function() {
        this.form.reset(); report(this, 'Click'); return false;
    }
}
// Finally, activate our form by adding all possible event handlers!
addhandlers(document.everything);
</script>
```

18.3   Scripting Form Elements

The previous section listed the form elements provided by HTML and explained how to embed these elements in your HTML documents. This section takes the next step and shows you how you can work with those elements in your JavaScript programs.

18.3.1 Naming Forms and Form Elements

Every form element has a name attribute that must be set in its HTML tag if the form is to be submitted to a server-side program. While form submission is not necessarily of interest to JavaScript programs, there is another useful reason to specify this name attribute, as you'll see shortly.

The <form> tag itself also has a name attribute that you can set. This attribute has nothing to do with form submission. As described in Chapter 15, it exists for the convenience of JavaScript programmers. If the name attribute is defined in a <form> tag, when the Form object is created for that form, it is stored as an element in the forms[] array of the Document object, as usual, and it is also stored in its own personal property of the Document object. The name of this newly defined property is the value of the name attribute. In Example 18-1, for instance, a form is defined with this tag:

```
<form name="everything">
```

This allows you to refer to the Form object as:

```
document.everything
```

Often, you'll find this more convenient than the array notation:

```
document.forms[0]
```

Furthermore, using a form name makes your code position-independent: it works even if the document is rearranged so that forms appear in a different order.

<img> and <applet> tags also have name attributes that work the same as the name attribute of <form>. With forms, however, this style of naming goes a step further because all elements contained within a form also have name attributes. When you give a form element a name, you create a new property of the Form object that refers to that element. The name of this property is the value of the attribute. Thus, you can refer to an element named "zipcode" in a form named "address" as:

```
document.address.zipcode
```

With reasonably chosen names, this syntax is much more elegant than the alternative, which relies on hardcoded (and position-dependent) array indices:

```
document.forms[1].elements[4]
```

In order for a group of radio elements in an HTML form to exhibit mutually exclusive "radio-button" behavior, they must all be given the same name. In Example 18-1, for instance, three radio elements are defined that all have a name attribute of "browser". Although it is not strictly necessary, it is also common practice to define related groups of checkbox elements with the same name attribute. When more than one element in a form has the same name attribute, JavaScript simply places those elements into an array with the specified name. The elements of the array are in the same order as they appear in the document. So, the radio objects in Example 18-1 can be referred to as:

```
document.everything.browser[0]
document.everything.browser[1]
document.everything.browser[2]
```

18.3.2 Form Element Properties

All (or most) form elements have the following properties in common. Some elements have other special-purpose properties that are described later in this chapter, where the various types of form elements are considered individually:

type

A read-only string that identifies the type of the form element. The third column of Table 18-1 lists the value of this property for each form element.

form

A read-only reference to the Form object in which the element is contained.

name

A read-only string specified by the HTML name attribute.

value

A read/write string that specifies the "value" contained or represented by the form element. This is the string that is sent to the web server when the form is submitted, and it is only sometimes of interest to JavaScript programs. For Text and Textarea elements, this property contains the text that the user entered. For button elements, this property specifies the text displayed within the button, which is something that you might occasionally want to change from a script. For radio and checkbox elements, however, the value property is not edited or displayed to the user in any way. It is simply a string set by the HTML value attribute that is passed to the web server when the form is submitted. The value property is discussed further in the sections on the different categories of form elements, later in this chapter.

18.3.3 Form Element Event Handlers

Most form elements support most of the following event handlers:

onclick

Triggered when the user clicks the mouse on the element. This handler is particularly useful for button and related form elements.

onchange

Triggered when the user changes the value represented by the element by entering text or selecting an option, for example. Button and related elements typically do not support this event handler because they do not have an editable value. Note that this handler is not triggered every time the user types a key in a text field, for example. It is triggered only when the user changes the value of an element and then moves the input focus to some other form element. That is, the invocation of this event handler indicates a completed change.

onfocus

Triggered when the form element receives the input focus.

onblur

Triggered when the form element loses the input focus.

Example 18-1 defined event handlers for form elements by setting the event handler property to a JavaScript function. The example is designed to report events as they occur by listing them in a large Textarea element. This makes the example a useful way to experiment with form elements and the event handlers they trigger.

An important thing to know about event handlers is that within the code of an event handler, the this keyword refers to the document element that triggered the event.

Since all form elements have a form property that refers to the containing form, the event handlers of a form element can always refer to the Form object as this.form. Going a step further, this means that an event handler for one form element can refer to a sibling form element named x as this.form.x.

Note that the four form element event handlers listed in this section are the ones that have particular significance for form elements. Form elements also support the various event handlers (such as onmousedown) that are supported by (nearly) all HTML elements. See Chapter 17 for a full discussion of events and event handlers. And see Example 17-5 in that chapter for a demonstration of the use of keyboard event handlers with form elements.

18.3.4 Push Buttons

The button form element is one of the most commonly used because it provides a clear visual way to allow the user to trigger some scripted action. The button element has no default behavior of its own, and it is never useful in a form unless it has an onclick (or other) event handler. The value property of a button element controls the text that appears within the button itself. You can set this property to change the text (plain text only, not HTML) that appears in the button, which can occasionally be a useful thing to do.

Note that hyperlinks provide the same onclick event handler that buttons do, and any button object can be replaced with a link that does the same thing when clicked. Use a button when you want an element that looks like a graphical push button. Use a link when the action to be triggered by the onclick handler can be conceptualized as "following a link."

Submit and reset elements are just like button elements, but they have default actions (submitting and resetting a form) associated with them. Because these elements have default actions, they can be useful even without an onclick event handler. On the other hand, because of their default actions, they are more useful for forms that are submitted to a web server than for pure client-side JavaScript programs. If the onclick event handler returns false, the default action of these buttons is not performed. You can use the onclick handler of a submit element to perform form validation, but it is more common to do this with the onsubmit handler of the Form object itself.

You can also create push buttons, including submit and reset buttons, with the <button> tag instead of the traditional <input> tag. <button> is more flexible because instead of simply displaying the plain text specified by the value attribute, it displays any HTML content (formatted text and/or images) that appears between <button> and </button>. The <button> tag may be used anywhere in an HTML document and need not be placed within a <form>.

The button elements created by a `<button>` tag are technically different from those created by an `<input>` tag, but they have the same value for the type field and otherwise behave quite similarly. The main difference is that because the `<button>` tag doesn't use its value attribute to define the appearance of the button, you can't change that appearance by setting the value property.

Part IV does not include a Button entry. See the Input entry for details on all form element push buttons, including those created with the `<button>` tag.

18.3.5 Toggle Buttons

The checkbox and radio elements are toggle buttons, or buttons that have two visually distinct states: they can be checked or unchecked. The user can change the state of a toggle button by clicking on it. Radio elements are designed to be used in groups of related elements, all of which have the same value for the HTML name attribute. Radio elements created in this way are mutually exclusive: when you check one, the one that was previously checked becomes unchecked. Checkboxes are also often used in groups that share a name attribute, and when you refer to these elements by name, you must remember that the object you refer to by name is an array of same-named elements. In Example 18-1, there are three checkbox elements with the name "extras". In this example, you can refer to an array of these elements as:

```
document.everything.extras
```

To refer to an individual checkbox element, index the array:

```
document.everything.extras[0]  // First form element named "extras"
```

Radio and checkbox elements both define a checked property. This read/write boolean value specifies whether the element is currently checked. The defaultChecked property is a boolean that has the value of the HTML checked attribute; it specifies whether the element is checked when the page is first loaded.

Radio and checkbox elements do not display any text themselves and are typically displayed with adjacent HTML text (or with an associated `<label>` tag.) This means that setting the value property of a checkbox or radio element does not alter the visual appearance of the element, as it does for button elements created with an `<input>` tag. You can set value, but this changes only the string that is sent to the web server when the form is submitted.

When the user clicks on a toggle button, the radio or checkbox element triggers its onclick event handler to notify the JavaScript program of the change of state. Newer web browsers also trigger the onchange handler for these elements. Both event handlers convey the same essential information, but the onclick handler is more portable.

18.3.6 Text Fields

The Text element is probably the most commonly used element in HTML forms and JavaScript programs. It allows the user to enter a short, single-line string of text. The value property represents the text the user has entered. You can set this property to specify explicitly the text that should be displayed in the field. The onchange event handler is triggered when the user enters new text or edits existing text and then indicates that he is finished editing by moving input focus out of the text field.

The Textarea element is like a Text element, except that it allows the user to input (and your JavaScript programs to display) multiline text. Textarea elements are created with a <textarea> tag using a syntax significantly different from the <input> tag that creates a Text element. (See the Textarea entry in Part IV.) Nevertheless, the two types of elements behave quite similarly. You can use the value property and onchange event handler of a Textarea element just as you can for a Text element.

The password element is a modified Text element that displays asterisks as the user types into it. As the name indicates, this is useful to allow the user to enter passwords without worrying about others reading over his shoulder. Note that the Password element protects the user's input from prying eyes, but when the form is submitted, that input is not encrypted in any way (unless it is submitted over a secure HTTPS connection), and it may be visible as it is transmitted over the network.

Finally, the file element allows the user to enter the name of a file to be uploaded to the web server. It is essentially a Text element combined with a built-in button that pops up a file-chooser dialog box. File has an onchange event handler, like the Text element. Unlike text, however, the value property of a file element is read-only. This prevents malicious JavaScript programs from tricking the user into uploading a file that should not be shared.

The W3C has not yet defined standard event handlers or event objects for keyboard input. Nevertheless, modern browsers define onkeypress, onkeydown, and onkeyup event handlers. These handlers can be specified for any Document object, but they are most useful when specified on text and related form elements that actually accept keyboard input. You may return false from the onkeypress or onkeydown event handlers to prevent the user's keystroke from being recorded. This can be useful, for example, if you want to force the user to enter only digits into a particular text input field. See Example 17-5 for a demonstration of this technique.

18.3.7 Select and Option Elements

The Select element represents a set of options (represented by Option elements) from which the user can select. Browsers typically render Select elements in drop-down menus or listboxes. The Select element can operate in two very distinct ways, and the value of the type property depends on how it is configured. If the <select> tag has the multiple attribute, the user is allowed to select multiple options, and the type property of the Select object is "select-multiple". Otherwise, if the `multiple` attribute is not present, only a single item may be selected, and the type property is "select-one".

In some ways, a select-multiple element is like a set of checkbox elements, and a select-one element is like a set of radio elements. The Select element differs from the toggle-button elements in that a single Select element represents an entire set of options. These options are specified in HTML with the `<option>` tag, and they are represented in JavaScript by Option objects stored in the `options[]` array of the Select element. Because a Select element represents a set of choices, it does not have a `value` property, as all other form elements do. Instead, as I'll discuss shortly, each Option object contained by the Select element defines a `value` property.

When the user selects or deselects an option, the Select element triggers its onchange event handler. For select-one Select elements, the read/write `selectedIndex` property specifies by number which one of the options is currently selected. For select-multiple elements, the single `selectedIndex` property is not sufficient to represent the complete set of selected options. In this case, to determine which options are selected, you must loop through the elements of the `options[]` array and check the value of the `selected` property for each Option object.

In addition to its `selected` property, the Option element has a `text` property that specifies the string of plain text that appears in the Select element for that option. You can set this property to change the text that is displayed to the user. The `value` property is also a read/write string that specifies the text to be sent to the web server when the form is submitted. Even if you are writing a pure client-side program and your form never gets submitted, the `value` property (or its corresponding HTML value attribute) can be a useful place to store any data that you'll need if the user selects a particular option. Note that the Option element does not define form-related event handlers; use the onchange handler of the containing Select element instead.

In addition to setting the `text` property of Option objects, you can dynamically change the options displayed in a Select element in other ways. You can truncate the array of Option elements by setting `options.length` to the desired number of options, and you can remove all Option objects by setting `options.length` to 0. Suppose you have a Select object named "country" in a form named "address". You can remove all options from the element like this:

```
document.address.country.options.length = 0;  // Remove all options
```

You can remove an individual Option object from the Select element by setting its spot in the `options[]` array to null. This deletes the Option object, and any higher elements in the `options[]` array automatically get moved down to fill the empty spot:

```
// Remove a single Option object from the Select element
// The Option that was previously at options[11] gets moved to options[10]...
document.address.country.options[10] = null;
```

See the Option entry in Part IV. Also, see `Select.add( )` for a DOM Level 2 alternative for adding new options.

Finally, the Option element defines an `Option( )` constructor you can use to dynamically create new Option elements, and you can append new options to a Select element by assigning them to the end of the `options[ ]` array. For example:

```
// Create a new Option object
var zaire = new Option("Zaire",   // The text property
                       "zaire",   // The value property
                       false,     // The defaultSelected property
                       false);    // The selected property

// Display it in a Select element by appending it to the options array:
var countries = document.address.country;  // Get the Select object
countries.options[countries.options.length] = zaire;
```

You can use the `<optgroup>` tag to group related options within a Select element. The `<optgroup>` tag has a `label` attribute that specifies text to appear in the Select element. Despite its visual presence, however, an `<optgroup>` tag is not selectable by the user, and objects corresponding to the `<optgroup>` tag never appear in the `options[ ]` array.

18.3.8 Hidden Elements

As its name implies, the hidden element has no visual representation in a form. It exists to allow arbitrary text to be transmitted to the server when a form is submitted. Server-side programs use this as a way to save state information that is passed back to them with form submission. Since they have no visual appearance, hidden elements cannot generate events and have no event handlers. The `value` property allows to you read and write the text associated with a hidden element, but, in general, hidden elements are not commonly used in client-side JavaScript programming.

18.3.9 Fieldset Elements

In addition to the active form elements described previously, HTML forms can also include `<fieldset>` and `<label>` tags. These tags can be important for web designers, but they are not scriptable in interesting ways, and client-side JavaScript programmers do not usually work with them. You need to know about `<fieldset>` tags only because placing one in a form causes a corresponding object to be added to the form's `elements[ ]` array. (This does not happen with `<label>` tags, however.) Unlike all other objects in the `elements[ ]` array, the object that represents the `<fieldset>` tag does not have a `type` property, and this can cause problems for code that expects one.

18.4 Form Verification Example

I'll close the discussion of forms with an extended example showing how you can use unobtrusive client-side JavaScript to perform form validation.[*] Example 18-3, which appears later, is a module of unobtrusive JavaScript code that enables automatic client-side form validation. To use it, simply include the module in your HTML page, define a CSS style to highlight form fields that fail validation, and then add additional attributes to your form fields. To make a field required, simply add a required attribute. To make sure that the user's input matches a regular expression, set the pattern attribute to the desired regexp. Example 18-2 shows how you can use this module, and Figure 18-2 shows what happens when you attempt to submit a form containing invalid input.

Example 18-2. Adding form validation to your HTML forms

```
<script src="Validate.js"></script> <!-- include form validation module -->
<style>
/*
 * Validate.js requires us to define styles for the "invalid" class to give
 * invalid fields a distinct visual appearance that the user will recognize.
 * We can optionally define styles for valid fields as well.
 */
input.invalid { background: #faa; } /* Reddish background for invalid fields */
input.valid { background: #afa; }   /* Greenish background for valid fields */
</style>

<!--
  Now to get form fields validated, simply set required or pattern attributes.
-->
<form>
  <!-- A value (anything other than whitespace) is required in this field -->
  Name: <input type="text" name="name" required><br>
  <!-- \s* means optional space. \w+ means one or more alphanumeric chars-->
  email: <input type="text" name="email" pattern="^\s*\w+@\w+\.\w+\s*$"><br>
  <!-- \d{5} means exactly five digits -->
  zipcode: <input type="text" name="zip" pattern="^\s*\d{5}\s*$"><br>
  <!-- no validation on this field -->
  unvalidated: <input type="text"><br>
  <input type="submit">
</form>
```

Example 18-3 is the code for the form-validation module. Note that including this module in an HTML file does not add any symbols to the global namespace and that

---

[*] Note that client-side form validation is merely a convenience for users: it makes it possible to catch input errors before a form is submitted to the server. But client-side validation is never guaranteed to happen because some users will have JavaScript disabled. Furthermore, client-side validation is trivial for a malicious user to subvert. For these reasons, client-side validation can never take the place of robust server-side validation.

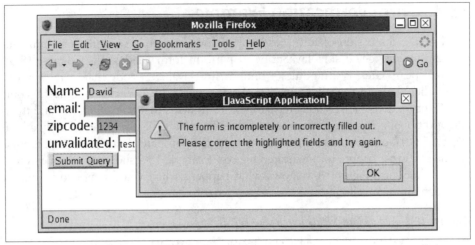

Figure 18-2. A form that failed validation

it automatically registers an onload event handler that traverses all forms in the document, looking for required and pattern attributes and adding onchange and onsubmit handlers as needed. These event handlers set the className property of each form field they validate to "invalid" or "valid", and you should use CSS to provide a distinct visual appearance for at least the "invalid" class.[*]

Example 18-3. Automatic form validation with unobtrusive JavaScript

```
/**
 * Validate.js: unobtrusive HTML form validation.
 *
 * On document load, this module scans the document for HTML forms and
 * textfield form elements. If it finds elements that have a "required" or
 * "pattern" attribute, it adds appropriate event handlers for client-side
 * form validation.
 *
 * If a form element has a "pattern" attribute, the value of that attribute
 * is used as a JavaScript regular expression, and the element is given an
 * onchange event handler that tests the user's input against the pattern.
 * If the input does not match the pattern, the background color of the
 * input element is changed to bring the error to the user's attention.
 * By default, the textfield value must contain some substring that matches
 * the pattern. If you want to require the complete value to match precisely,
 * use the ^ and $ anchors at the beginning and end of the pattern.
 *
 * A form element with a "required" attribute must have a value provided.
 * The presence of "required" is shorthand for pattern="\S". That is, it
```

---

[*] At the time of this writing, the AutoFill feature of the Google Toolbar interferes with the use of CSS styles to set the background of certain text fields. Google's browser extension sets the text field background to light yellow to indicate that it may be possible to automatically enter values into the field.

```
 * simply requires that the value contain a single non-whitespace character
 *
 * If a form element passes validation, its "class" attribute is set to
 * "valid". And if it fails validation, its class is set to "invalid".
 * In order for this module to be useful, you must use it in conjunction with
 * a CSS stylesheet that defines styles for "invalid" class.  For example:
 *
 *     <!-- attention grabbing orange background for invalid form elements -->
 *     <style>input.invalid { background: #fa0; }</style>
 *
 * When a form is submitted, the textfield elements subject to validation are
 * revalidated. If any fail, the submission is blocked and a dialog box
 * is displayed to the user letting him know that the form is incomplete
 * or incorrect.
 *
 * You may not use this module to validate any form fields or forms on which
 * you define your own onchange or onsubmit event handlers, or any fields
 * for which you define a class attribute.
 *
 * This module places all its code within an anonymous function and does
 * not define any symbols in the global namespace.
 */
(function() { // Do everything in this one anonymous function
    // When the document finishes loading, call init()
    if (window.addEventListener) window.addEventListener("load", init, false);
    else if (window.attachEvent) window.attachEvent("onload", init);

    // Define event handlers for any forms and form elements that need them.
    function init() {
        // Loop through all forms in the document
        for(var i = 0; i < document.forms.length; i++) {
            var f = document.forms[i];  // the form we're working on now

            // Assume, for now, that this form does not need any validation
            var needsValidation = false;

            // Now loop through the elements in our form
            for(j = 0; j < f.elements.length; j++) {
                var e = f.elements[j];  // the element we're working on

                // We're only interested in <input type="text"> textfields
                if (e.type != "text") continue;

                // See if it has attributes that require validation
                var pattern = e.getAttribute("pattern");
                // We could use e.hasAttribute(), but IE doesn't support it
                var required = e.getAttribute("required") != null;

                // Required is just a shortcut for a simple pattern
                if (required && !pattern) {
                    pattern = "\\S";
                    e.setAttribute("pattern", pattern);
```

Example 18-3. Automatic form validation with unobtrusive JavaScript (continued)

```
            }

            // If this element requires validation,
            if (pattern) {
                // validate the element each time it changes
                e.onchange = validateOnChange;
                // Remember to add an onsubmit handler to this form
                needsValidation = true;
            }
        }

        // If at least one of the form elements needed validation,
        // we also need an onsubmit event handler for the form
        if (needsValidation) f.onsubmit = validateOnSubmit;
    }
}

// This function is the onchange event handler for textfields that
// require validation. Remember that we converted the required attribute
// to a pattern attribute in init( ).
function validateOnChange( ) {
    var textfield = this;                               // the textfield
    var pattern = textfield.getAttribute("pattern");    // the pattern
    var value = this.value;                             // the user's input

    // If the value does not match the pattern, set the class to "invalid".
    if (value.search(pattern) == -1) textfield.className = "invalid";
    else textfield.className = "valid";
}

// This function is the onsubmit event handler for any form that
// requires validation.
function validateOnSubmit( ) {
    // When the form is submitted, we revalidate all the fields in the
    // form and then check their classNames to see if they are invalid.
    // If any of those fields are invalid, display an alert and prevent
    // form submission.
    var invalid = false;  // Start by assuming everything is valid
    // Loop through all form elements
    for(var i = 0; i < this.elements.length; i++) {
        var e = this.elements[i];
        // If the element is a text field and has our onchange handler
        if (e.type == "text" && e.onchange == validateOnChange) {
            e.onchange( ); // Invoke the handler to re-validate
            // If validation fails for the element, it fails for the form
            if (e.className == "invalid") invalid = true;
        }
    }
```

```
        // If the form is invalid, alert user and block submission
        if (invalid) {
            alert("The form is incompletely or incorrectly filled out.\n" +
                "Please correct the highlighted fields and try again.");
            return false;
        }
    }
})();
```

CHAPTER 19

Cookies and Client-Side Persistence

The Document object has a property named cookie that was not discussed in Chapter 15. On the surface, this property appears to be a simple string value; however, the cookie property is much more than this: it enables JavaScript code to persistently store data to the user's hard disk and to retrieve data that was previously stored in this way. Client-side persistence is an easy way to give web applications a memory: a web site can store user preferences so that they can be used again when the user revisits the page, for example.

Cookies are also used for server-side scripting and are a standard extension to the HTTP protocol. All modern web browsers support them and allow them to be scripted with the Document.cookie property. There are other client-side persistence mechanisms that are more powerful but less standard than cookies, and I discuss them briefly at the end of this chapter.

19.1 An Overview of Cookies

A *cookie* is a small amount of named data stored by the web browser and associated with a particular web page or web site.[*] Cookies serve to give the web browser a memory so that scripts and server-side programs can use data that was input on one page on another page, or so the browser can recall user preferences or other state variables when the user leaves a page and then returns. Cookies were originally designed for server-side programming, and at the lowest level, they are implemented as an extension to the HTTP protocol. Cookie data is automatically transmitted between the web browser and web server, so server-side scripts can read and write

---

[*] The name "cookie" does not have a lot of significance, but it is not used without precedent. In the obscure annals of computing history, the term "cookie" or "magic cookie" has been used to refer to a small chunk of data, particularly a chunk of privileged or secret data, akin to a password, that proves identity or permits access. In JavaScript, cookies are used to save state and can establish a kind of identity for a web browser. Cookies in JavaScript do not use any kind of cryptography, however, and are not secure in any way (although transmitting them across an encrypted https: connection helps).

cookie values that are stored on the client. As you'll see, JavaScript can also manipulate cookies using the cookie property of the Document object.

cookie is a string property that allows you to read, create, modify, and delete the cookie or cookies that apply to the current web page. Although cookie appears at first to be a normal read/write string property, its behavior is actually more complex. When you read the value of cookie, you get a string that contains the names and values of all the cookies that apply to the document. You create, modify, or delete an individual cookie by setting the value of the cookie property using a special syntax. Later sections of this chapter explain in detail how this works. To use the cookie property effectively, however, you need to know more about cookies and how they work.

In addition to a name and a value, each cookie has optional attributes that control its lifetime, visibility, and security. Cookies are transient by default; the values they store last for the duration of the web-browser session but are lost when the user exits the browser. If you want a cookie to last beyond a single browsing session, you must tell the browser how long you would like it to retain the cookie. The original way to do this was by setting the expires attribute to an expiration date in the future. While the expires attribute still works, it has been superseded by the max-age attribute, which specifies the lifetime, in seconds, of the cookie. Setting either of these attributes causes the browser to save the cookie in a local file so that it can read it back in during future browsing sessions if the user revisits the web page. Once the expiration date has passed, or the max-age lifetime has been exceeded, the browser automatically deletes the cookie from its cookie file.

Another important cookie attribute is path, which specifies the web pages with which a cookie is associated. By default, a cookie is associated with, and accessible to, the web page that created it and any other web pages in the same directory or any subdirectories of that directory. If the web page *http://www.example.com/catalog/index.html* creates a cookie, for example, that cookie is also visible to *http://www.example.com/catalog/order.html* and *http://www.example.com/catalog/widgets/index.html*, but it is not visible to *http://www.example.com/about.html*.

This default visibility behavior is often exactly what you want. Sometimes, though, you'll want to use cookie values throughout a web site, regardless of which page creates the cookie. For instance, if the user enters his mailing address in a form on one page, you may want to save that address to use as the default the next time he returns to the page and also as the default in an entirely unrelated form on another page where he is asked to enter a billing address. To allow this usage, you specify a path for the cookie. Then, any web page from the same web server that contains that path in its URL can share the cookie. For example, if a cookie set by *http://www.example.com/catalog/widgets/index.html* has its path set to "/catalog", that cookie is also visible to *http://www.example.com/catalog/order.html*. Or, if the path is set to "/", the cookie is visible to any page on the *www.example.com* web server.

By default, cookies are accessible only to pages on the same web server from which they were set. Large web sites may want cookies to be shared across multiple web servers, however. For example, the server at *order.example.com* may need to read cookie values set from *catalog.example.com*. This is where the next cookie attribute, domain, comes in. If a cookie created by a page on *catalog.example.com* sets its path attribute to "/" and its domain attribute to ".example.com", that cookie is available to all web pages on *catalog.example.com*, *orders.example.com*, and any other server in the *example.com* domain. If the domain attribute is not set for a cookie, the default is the hostname of the web server that serves the page. Note that you cannot set the domain of a cookie to a domain other than the domain of your server.

The final cookie attribute is a boolean attribute named secure that specifies how cookie values are transmitted over the network. By default, cookies are insecure, which means that they are transmitted over a normal, insecure HTTP connection. If a cookie is marked secure, however, it is transmitted only when the browser and server are connected via HTTPS or another secure protocol.

Note that the expires, max-age, path, domain, and secure attributes of a cookie are not JavaScript object properties. Later in the chapter, you'll see how to set these cookie attributes.

Cookies have gotten a bad reputation for many web users because of the unscrupulous use of third-party cookies—cookies associated with the images on a web page rather than the web page itself. Third-party cookies enable an ad-hosting company to track a user from one client site to another client site, for example, and the privacy implications of this practice cause some users to disable cookies in their web browsers. Before using cookies in your JavaScript code, you may want to first check that they are enabled. In most browsers, you can do this by checking the navigator.cookieEnabled property. If true, cookies are enabled, and if false, cookies are disabled (although non-persistent cookies that last for only the current browsing session may still be enabled). This is not a standard property, and if you find that it is undefined in the browser your code is running in, you must test for cookie support by trying to write, read, and delete a test cookie. I'll explain how to do these things later in the chapter, and Example 19-2 includes code for testing for cookie support.

If you are interested in the complete technical details of how cookies work (at the HTTP protocol level), see RFC 2965 at *http://www.ietf.org/rfc/rfc2965.txt*. Cookies were originally created by Netscape, and Netscape's original cookie specification is still of interest. Although parts of it are now obsolete, it is much shorter and easier to read than the formal RFC. Find this old document at *http://wp.netscape.com/newsref/std/cookie_spec.html*.

The sections that follow discuss how you can set and query cookie values in JavaScript and how you can specify the expires, path, domain, and secure attributes of a cookie. These are followed by a section on cookie alternatives.

19.2 Storing Cookies

To associate a transient cookie value with the current document, simply set the cookie property to a string of the form:

name=value

For example:

```
document.cookie = "version=" + encodeURIComponent(document.lastModified);
```

The next time you read the cookie property, the name/value pair you stored is included in the list of cookies for the document. Cookie values may not include semicolons, commas, or whitespace. For this reason, you may want to use the core JavaScript global function encodeURIComponent() to encode the value before storing it in the cookie. If you do this, you'll have to use the corresponding decodeURIComponent() function when you read the cookie value. (It is also common to see code that uses the older escape() and unescape() functions, but these are now deprecated.)

A cookie written with a simple name/value pair lasts for the current web-browsing session but is lost when the user exits the browser. To create a cookie that can last across browser sessions, specify its lifetime (in seconds) with a max-age attribute. You can do this by setting the cookie property to a string of the form:

name=value; max-age=*seconds*

For example, to create a cookie that persists for a year, you can use code like this:

```
document.cookie = "version=" + document.lastModified +
                  "; max-age=" + (60*60*24*365);
```

You can also specify the lifetime of a cookie with the obsolete expires attribute, which should be set to a date in the format written by Date.toGMTString(). For example:

```
var nextyear = new Date();
nextyear.setFullYear(nextyear.getFullYear() + 1);
document.cookie = "version=" + document.lastModified +
                  "; expires=" + nextyear.toGMTString();
```

Similarly, you can set the path, domain, and secure attributes of a cookie by appending strings of the following format to the cookie value before that value is written to the cookie property:

```
; path=path
; domain=domain
; secure
```

To change the value of a cookie, set its value again using the same name, path, and domain along with the new value. You can change the lifetime of a cookie when you change its value by specifying a new max-age or expires attribute.

To delete a cookie, set it again using the same name, path, and domain, specifying an arbitrary (or empty) value, and a max-age attribute of 0 (or use the expires attribute to specify an expiration date that has already passed). Note that the browser is not required to delete expired cookies immediately, so a cookie may remain in the browser's cookie file past its expiration date.

19.2.1 Cookie Limitations

Cookies are intended for infrequent storage of small amounts of data. They are not intended as a general-purpose communication or data-transfer mechanism, so you should use them in moderation. RFC 2965 encourages browser manufacturers to allow unlimited numbers of cookies of unrestricted size. You should know, however, that the standard does not require browsers to retain more than 300 cookies total, 20 cookies per web server (for the entire server, not just for your page or site on the server), or 4 KB of data per cookie (both name and value count toward this 4 KB limit). In practice, modern browsers allow many more than 300 cookies total, but the 4 KB size limit is still enforced by some.

19.3   Reading Cookies

When you use the cookie property in a JavaScript expression, the value it returns is a string that contains all the cookies that apply to the current document. The string is a list of *name=value* pairs separated by semicolons, where *name* is the name of a cookie, and *value* is its string value. This value does not include any of the attributes that may have been set for the cookie. To determine the value of a particular named cookie, you can use the String.indexOf( ) and String.substring( ) methods, or you can use String.split( ) to break the string into individual cookies.

Once you have extracted the value of a cookie from the cookie property, you must interpret that value based on whatever format or encoding was used by the cookie's creator. For example, the cookie might store multiple pieces of information in colon-separated fields. In this case, you would have to use appropriate string methods to extract the various fields of information. Don't forget to use the decodeURIComponent( ) function on the cookie value if it was encoded using the encodeURIComponent( ) function.

The following code shows how to read the cookie property, extract a single cookie from it, and use the value of that cookie:

```
// Read the cookie property. This returns all cookies for this document.
var allcookies = document.cookie;
// Look for the start of the cookie named "version"
var pos = allcookies.indexOf("version=");

// If we find a cookie by that name, extract and use its value
if (pos != -1) {
    var start = pos + 8;                          // Start of cookie value
    var end = allcookies.indexOf(";", start);     // End of cookie value
    if (end == -1) end = allcookies.length;
```

```
            var value = allcookies.substring(start, end);   // Extract the value
            value = decodeURIComponent(value);                 // Decode it

            // Now that we have the cookie value, we can use it.
            // In this case, the cookie was previously set to the modification
            // date of the document, so we can use it to see if the document has
            // changed since the user last visited.
            if (value != document.lastModified)
                alert("This document has changed since you were last here");
    }
```

Note that the string returned when you read the value of the cookie property does not contain any information about the various cookie attributes. The cookie property allows you to set those attributes, but it does not allow you to read them.

19.4 Cookie Example

We end this discussion of cookies with a useful utility for working with cookies, shown a little later in Example 19-2. The Cookie( ) constructor reads the value of a named cookie. The store( ) method of a cookie stores data in that cookie, using the lifetime, path, and domain you specify, and the remove( ) method of a cookie deletes the cookie by setting its max-age attribute to 0.

The Cookie class defined in this example stores the names and values of multiple state variables in a single cookie. To associate data with a cookie, simply set properties of the Cookie object. When you call the store( ) method on the cookie, the names and values of the properties you have added to the object become the cookie value that is saved. Similarly, when you create a new Cookie object, the Cookie( ) constructor looks for an existing cookie with the name you have specified. If it finds it, it parses its value as a set of name/value pairs and sets them as properties of the newly created Cookie object.

To help you understand Example 19-2, Example 19-1 begins with a simple web page that uses the Cookie class.

Example 19-1. Using the Cookie class

```
<script src="Cookie.js"></script><!-- include the cookie class -->
<script>
// Create the cookie we'll use to save state for this web page.
var cookie = new Cookie("vistordata");

// First, try to read data stored in the cookie. If the cookie doesn't
// exist yet (or doesn't have the data we expect), query the user
if (!cookie.name || !cookie.color) {
    cookie.name = prompt("What is your name:", "");
    cookie.color = prompt("What is your favorite color:", "");
}

// Keep track of how many times this user has visited the page
```

Example 19-1. Using the Cookie class (continued)

```
if (!cookie.visits) cookie.visits = 1;
else cookie.visits++;

// Store the cookie data, which includes the updated visit count. We set
// the cookie lifetime to 10 days. Since we don't specify a path, this
// cookie will be accessible to all web pages in the same directory as this
// one or "below" it.  We should be sure, therefore, that the cookie
// name, "visitordata" is unique among these pages.
cookie.store(10);

// Now we can use the data we obtained from the cookie (or from the
// user) to greet a user by name and in her favorite color.
document.write('<h1 style="color:' + cookie.color + '">' +
               'Welcome, ' + cookie.name + '!' + '</h1>' +
               '<p>You have visited ' + cookie.visits + ' times.' +
               '<button onclick="window.cookie.remove();">Forget Me</button>');
</script>
```

The Cookie class itself is listed in Example 19-2.

Example 19-2. A Cookie utility class

```
/**
 * This is the Cookie() constructor function.
 *
 * This constructor looks for a cookie with the specified name for the
 * current document. If one exists, it parses its value into a set of
 * name/value pairs and stores those values as properties of the newly created
 * object.
 *
 * To store new data in the cookie, simply set properties of the Cookie
 * object. Avoid properties named "store" and "remove", since these are
 * reserved as method names.
 *
 * To save cookie data in the web browser's local store, call store().
 * To remove cookie data from the browser's store, call remove().
 *
 * The static method Cookie.enabled() returns true if cookies are
 * enabled and returns false otherwise.
 */
function Cookie(name) {
    this.$name = name;  // Remember the name of this cookie

    // First, get a list of all cookies that pertain to this document.
    // We do this by reading the magic Document.cookie property.
    // If there are no cookies, we don't have anything to do.
    var allcookies = document.cookie;
    if (allcookies == "") return;

    // Break the string of all cookies into individual cookie strings
    // Then loop through the cookie strings, looking for our name
    var cookies = allcookies.split(';');
    var cookie = null;
```

Example 19-2. A Cookie utility class (continued)

```
    for(var i = 0; i < cookies.length; i++) {
        // Does this cookie string begin with the name we want?
        if (cookies[i].substring(0, name.length+1) == (name + "=")) {
            cookie = cookies[i];
            break;
        }
    }

    // If we didn't find a matching cookie, quit now
    if (cookie == null) return;

    // The cookie value is the part after the equals sign
    var cookieval = cookie.substring(name.length+1);

    // Now that we've extracted the value of the named cookie, we
    // must break that value down into individual state variable
    // names and values. The name/value pairs are separated from each
    // other by ampersands, and the individual names and values are
    // separated from each other by colons. We use the split() method
    // to parse everything.
    var a = cookieval.split('&'); // Break it into an array of name/value pairs
    for(var i=0; i < a.length; i++)  // Break each pair into an array
        a[i] = a[i].split(':');

    // Now that we've parsed the cookie value, set all the names and values
    // as properties of this Cookie object. Note that we decode
    // the property value because the store() method encodes it.
    for(var i = 0; i < a.length; i++) {
        this[a[i][0]] = decodeURIComponent(a[i][1]);
    }
}

/**
 * This function is the store() method of the Cookie object.
 *
 * Arguments:
 *
 *    daysToLive: the lifetime of the cookie, in days. If you set this
 *       to zero, the cookie will be deleted. If you set it to null, or
 *       omit this argument, the cookie will be a session cookie and will
 *       not be retained when the browser exits. This argument is used to
 *       set the max-age attribute of the cookie.
 *    path: the value of the path attribute of the cookie
 *    domain: the value of the domain attribute of the cookie
 *    secure: if true, the secure attribute of the cookie will be set
 */
Cookie.prototype.store = function(daysToLive, path, domain, secure) {
    // First, loop through the properties of the Cookie object and
    // put together the value of the cookie. Since cookies use the
    // equals sign and semicolons as separators, we'll use colons
    // and ampersands for the individual state variables we store
    // within a single cookie value. Note that we encode the value
    // of each property in case it contains punctuation or other
```

Example 19-2. A Cookie utility class (continued)

```
        // illegal characters.
        var cookieval = "";
        for(var prop in this) {
            // Ignore properties with names that begin with '$' and also methods
            if ((prop.charAt(0) == '$') || ((typeof this[prop]) == 'function'))
                continue;
            if (cookieval != "") cookieval += '&';
            cookieval += prop + ':' + encodeURIComponent(this[prop]);
        }

        // Now that we have the value of the cookie, put together the
        // complete cookie string, which includes the name and the various
        // attributes specified when the Cookie object was created
        var cookie = this.$name + '=' + cookieval;
        if (daysToLive || daysToLive == 0) {
            cookie += "; max-age=" + (daysToLive*24*60*60);
        }

        if (path) cookie += "; path=" + path;
        if (domain) cookie += "; domain=" + domain;
        if (secure) cookie += "; secure";

        // Now store the cookie by setting the magic Document.cookie property
        document.cookie = cookie;
}

/**
 * This function is the remove( ) method of the Cookie object; it deletes the
 * properties of the object and removes the cookie from the browser's
 * local store.
 *
 * The arguments to this function are all optional, but to remove a cookie
 * you must pass the same values you passed to store( ).
 */
Cookie.prototype.remove = function(path, domain, secure) {
    // Delete the properties of the cookie
    for(var prop in this) {
        if (prop.charAt(0) != '$' && typeof this[prop] != 'function')
            delete this[prop];
    }

    // Then, store the cookie with a lifetime of 0
    this.store(0, path, domain, secure);
}

/**
 * This static method attempts to determine whether cookies are enabled.
 * It returns true if they appear to be enabled and false otherwise.
 * A return value of true does not guarantee that cookies actually persist.
 * Nonpersistent session cookies may still work even if this method
 * returns false.
 */
```

Example 19-2. A Cookie utility class (continued)

```
Cookie.enabled = function( ) {
    // Use navigator.cookieEnabled if this browser defines it
    if (navigator.cookieEnabled != undefined) return navigator.cookieEnabled;

    // If we've already cached a value, use that value
    if (Cookie.enabled.cache != undefined) return Cookie.enabled.cache;

    // Otherwise, create a test cookie with a lifetime
    document.cookie = "testcookie=test; max-age=10000";  // Set cookie

    // Now see if that cookie was saved
    var cookies = document.cookie;
    if (cookies.indexOf("testcookie=test") == -1) {
        // The cookie was not saved
        return Cookie.enabled.cache = false;
    }
    else {
        // Cookie was saved, so we've got to delete it before returning
        document.cookie = "testcookie=test; max-age=0";  // Delete cookie
        return Cookie.enabled.cache = true;
    }
}
```

19.5 Cookie Alternatives

There are a couple of drawbacks to using cookies for client-side persistence:

- They are limited to 4 KB of data.
- Even when cookies are used only for client-side scripting, they are still uploaded to the web server in the request for any web page with which they are associated. When the cookies are not used on the server, it's a waste of bandwidth.

Two cookie alternatives exist. Microsoft Internet Explorer and the Adobe Flash plugin both define proprietary mechanisms for client-side persistence. Although neither is standard, both IE and Flash are widely deployed, which means that at least one of these mechanisms is available in a large majority of browsers. The IE and Flash persistence mechanisms are briefly described in the sections that follow, and the chapter concludes with an advanced example that provides persistent storage with IE, Flash, or cookies.

19.5.1 IE userData Persistence

Internet Explorer enables client-side persistence with a DHTML behavior. To access this mechanism, you apply a special behavior to an element (such as <div>) of your document. One way to do this is with CSS:

```
<!-- This stylesheet defines a class named "persistent" -->
<style>.persistent { behavior:url(#default#userData);}</style>
```

```
<!-- This <div> element is a member of that class -->
<div id="memory" class="persistent"></div>
```

Since the behavior attribute is not standard CSS, other web browsers simply ignore it. You can also set the behavior style attribute on an element with JavaScript:

```
var memory = document.getElementById("memory");
memory.style.behavior = "url('#default#userData')";
```

When an HTML element has this "userData" behavior associated with it, new methods (defined by the behavior) become available for that element.* To store data persistently, set attributes of the element with setAttribute( ) and then save those attributes with save( ):

```
var memory = document.getElementById("memory");        // Get persistent element
memory.setAttribute("username", username);             // Set data as attributes
memory.setAttribute("favoriteColor", favoriteColor);
memory.save("myPersistentData");                       // Save the data
```

Note that the save( ) method takes a string argument: this is the (arbitrary) name under which the data is to be stored. You'll need to use the same name when you retrieve the data.

Data saved using the IE persistence mechanism can be given an expiration date, just as cookie data can. To do this, simply set the expires property before calling the save( ) method. This property should be set to a string in the form returned by Date.toUTCString( ). For example, you might add the following lines to the previous code to specify an expiration date 10 days in the future:

```
var now = (new Date()).getTime();                      // now, in milliseconds
var expires = now + 10 * 24 * 60 * 60 * 1000;          // 10 days from now in ms
memory.expires = (new Date(expires)).toUTCString(); // convert to a string
```

To retrieve persistent data, reverse these steps, calling load( ) to load saved attributes and calling getAttribute( ) to query attribute values:

```
var memory = document.getElementById("memory");        // Get persistent element
memory.load("myPersistentData");                       // Retrieve saved data by name
var user = memory.getAttribute("username");            // Query attributes
var color = memory.getAttribute("favoriteColor");
```

19.5.1.1 Storing hierarchical data

The userData persistence behavior is not limited to storing and retrieving the values of attributes. Any element to which this behavior is applied has a complete XML document associated with it. Applying the behavior to an HTML element creates an XMLDocument property on the element, and the value of this property is a DOM Document object. You can use DOM methods (see Chapter 15) to add content to this

---

* The userData behavior is just one of four persistence-related behaviors available to Internet Explorer. See
  http://msdn.microsoft.com/workshop/author/persistence/overview.asp for further details on persistence in IE.

document before calling save( ) or to extract content after calling load( ). Here's an example:

```
var memory = document.getElementById("memory");     // Get persistent element
var doc = memory.XMLDocument;                         // Get its document
var root = doc.documentElement;                       // Root element of document
root.appendChild(doc.createTextNode("data here"));  // Store text in document
```

The use of an XML document enables the storage of hierarchical data; you might convert a tree of JavaScript objects to a tree of XML elements, for example.

19.5.1.2 Storage limits

The IE persistence mechanism allows much more data to be stored than cookies do. Each page may store up to 64 KB, and each web server is allowed a total of 640 KB. Sites on a trusted intranet are allowed even more storage. There is no documented way for an end user to alter these storage limits or to disable the persistence mechanism altogether.

19.5.1.3 Sharing persistent data

Like cookies, data stored with the IE persistence mechanism is available to all web pages in the same directory. Unlike cookies, however, a web page cannot access persistent data saved by pages in its ancestor directories using IE. Also, the IE persistence mechanism has no equivalent to the path and domain attributes of cookies, so there is no way to share persistent data more widely among pages. Finally, persistent data in IE is shared only between pages in the same directory, loaded via the same protocols. That is, data stored by a page loaded with the https: protocol cannot be accessed by a page loaded with regular http:.

19.5.2 Flash SharedObject Persistence

The Flash plug-in, versions 6 and later, enables client-side persistence with the SharedObject class, which can be scripted with ActionScript code in a Flash movie.* To do this, create a SharedObject with ActionScript code like the following. Note that you must specify a name (like a cookie name) for your persistent data:

```
var so = SharedObject.getLocal("myPersistentData");
```

The SharedObject class does not define a load( ) method as the IE persistence mechanism does. When you create a SharedObject, any data previously saved under the specified name is automatically loaded. Each SharedObject has a data property. This data property refers to a regular ActionScript object, and the persistent data is

---

* For complete details on the SharedObject class and Flash-based persistence, see the Adobe web site at *http:// www.adobe.com/support/flash/action_scripts/local_shared_object/*. I learned about Flash-based persistence from Brad Neuberg, who pioneered its use from client-side JavaScript with his AMASS project (*http:// codinginparadise.org/projects/storage/README.html*). This project is evolving at the time of this writing, and you may find further information on client-side persistence at Brad's blog (*http://codinginparadise.org*).

available as properties of that object. To read or write persistent data, simply read or write the properties of the data object:

```
var name = so.data.username;    // Get some persistent data
so.data.favoriteColor = "red";  // Set a persistent field
```

The properties you set on the data object are not limited to primitive types such as numbers and strings. Arrays, for example, are also allowed.

SharedObject does not have a save( ) method, either. It does have a flush( ) method that immediately stores the current state of the SharedObject. Calling this method is not necessary, however: properties set in the data object of a SharedObject are automatically saved when the Flash movie is unloaded. Note also that SharedObject does not support any way to specify an expiration date or lifetime for the persistent data.

Keep in mind that all the code shown in this section is ActionScript code run by the Flash plug-in, not JavaScript code running in the browser. If you want to use the Flash persistence mechanism in your JavaScript code, you need a way for JavaScript to communicate with Flash. Techniques for doing this are covered in Chapter 23. Example 22-12 demonstrates the use of the ExternalInterface class (available in Flash 8 and later), which makes it trivial to invoke ActionScript methods from JavaScript. Examples 19-3 and 19-4, later in this chapter, use a lower-level communication mechanism to connect JavaScript and ActionScript. The GetVariable( ) and SetVariable( ) methods of the Flash plug-in object enable JavaScript to query and set ActionScript variables, and the ActionScript fscommand( ) function sends data to JavaScript.

19.5.2.1 Storage limits

By default, the Flash player allows up to 100 KB of persistent data per web site. The user can adjust this limit down to 10 KB or up to 10 MB. Alternatively, the user can allow unlimited storage or disallow any persistent storage whatsoever. If a web site attempts to exceed the limit, Flash asks the user to allow or deny more storage for your web site.

19.5.2.2 Persistent data sharing

By default, persistent data in Flash is accessible only to the movie that created it. It is possible, however, to loosen this restriction so that two different movies in the same directory or anywhere on the same server can share access to persistent data. The way this is done is very similar to how it's done in the path attribute of a cookie. When you create a SharedObject with SharedObject.getLocal( ), you can pass a path as the second argument. This path must be a prefix of the actual path in the movie's URL. Any other movie that uses the same path can access the persistent data stored by this movie. For example, the following code creates a SharedObject that can be shared by any Flash movie that originates from the same web server:

```
var so = SharedObject.getLocal("My/Shared/Persistent/Data",  // Object name
                               "/");                          // Path
```

When scripting the SharedObject class from JavaScript, you probably are not interested in sharing persistent data between Flash movies. Instead, you most likely care about sharing data between web pages that script the same movie (see Example 19-3 in the next section).

19.5.3 Example: Persistent Objects

This section concludes with an extended example that defines a unified API for the three persistence mechanisms you've studied in this chapter. Example 19-3 defines a PObject class for persistent objects. The PObject class works much like the Cookie class of Example 19-2. You create a persistent object with the PObject( ) constructor, to which you pass a name, a set of default values, and an onload handler function. The constructor creates a new JavaScript object and attempts to load persistent data previously stored under the name you specify. If it finds this data, it parses it into a set of name/value pairs and sets these pairs as properties of the newly created object. If it does not find any previously stored data, it uses the properties of the defaults object you specify. In either case, the onload handler function you specify is invoked asynchronously when your persistent data is ready for use.

Once your onload handler has been called, you can use the persistent data simply by reading the properties of the PObject as you would do with any regular JavaScript object. To store new persistent data, first set that data as properties (of type boolean, number, or string) of the PObject. Then call the save( ) method of the PObject, optionally specifying a lifetime (in days) for the data. To delete the persistent data, call the forget( ) method of the PObject.

The PObject class defined here uses IE-based persistence if it is running in IE. Otherwise, it checks for a suitable version of the Flash plug-in and uses Flash-based persistence if that is available. If neither of these options are available, it falls back on cookies.[*]

Note that the PObject class allows only primitive values to be saved and converts numbers and booleans to strings when they are retrieved. It is possible to serialize array and object values as strings and parse those strings back into arrays and objects (see *http://www.json.org*, for example), but this example does not do that.

Example 19-3 is long but well commented and should be easy to follow. Be sure to read the long introductory comment that documents the PObject class and its API.

Example 19-3. PObject.js: persistent objects for JavaScript

```
/**
 * PObject.js: JavaScript objects that persist across browser sessions and may
 *   be shared by web pages within the same directory on the same host.
 *
```

___

[*] It is also possible to define a persistence class that uses cookies whenever possible and falls back on IE or Flash-based persistence if cookies have been disabled.

Example 19-3. PObject.js: persistent objects for JavaScript (continued)

```
* This module defines a PObject() constructor to create a persistent object.
* PObject objects have two public methods. save() saves, or "persists," the
* current properties of the object, and forget() deletes the persistent
* properties of the object. To define a persistent property in a PObject,
* simply set the property on the object as if it were a regular JavaScript
* object and then call the save() method to save the current state of
* the object. You may not use "save" or "forget" as a property name, nor
* any property whose name begins with $. PObject is intended for use with
* property values of type string. You may also save properties of type
* boolean and number, but these will be converted to strings when retrieved.
*
* When a PObject is created, the persistent data is read and stored in the
* newly created object as regular JavaScript properties, and you can use the
* PObject just as you would use a regular JavaScript object. Note, however,
* that persistent properties may not be ready when the PObject() constructor
* returns, and you should wait for asynchronous notification using an onload
* handler function that you pass to the constructor.
*
* Constructor:
*    PObject(name, defaults, onload):
*
* Arguments:
*
*    name       A name that identifies this persistent object. A single pages
*               can have more than one PObject, and PObjects are accessible
*               to all pages within the same directory, so this name should
*               be unique within the directory. If this argument is null or
*               is not specified, the filename (but not directory) of the
*               containing web page is used.
*
*    defaults   An optional JavaScript object. When no saved value for the
*               persistent object can be found (which happens when a PObject
*               is created for the first time), the properties of this object
*               are copied into the newly created PObject.
*
*    onload     The function to call (asynchronously) when persistent values
*               have been loaded into the PObject and are ready for use.
*               This function is invoked with two arguments: a reference
*               to the PObject and the PObject name. This function is
*               called *after* the PObject() constructor returns. PObject
*               properties should not be used before this.
*
* Method PObject.save(lifetimeInDays):
*   Persist the properties of a PObject. This method saves the properties of
*   the PObject, ensuring that they persist for at least the specified
*   number of days.
*
* Method PObject.forget():
*   Delete the properties of the PObject. Then save this "empty" PObject to
*   persistent storage and, if possible, cause the persistent store to expire.
*
* Implementation Notes:
*
```

Example 19-3. PObject.js: persistent objects for JavaScript (continued)

```
 * This module defines a single PObject API but provides three distinct
 * implementations of that API. In Internet Explorer, the IE-specific
 * "UserData" persistence mechanism is used. On any other browser that has an
 * Adobe Flash plug-in, the Flash SharedObject persistence mechanism is
 * used. Browsers that are not IE and do not have Flash available fall back on
 * a cookie-based implementation. Note that the Flash implementation does not
 * support expiration dates for saved data, so data stored with that
 * implementation persists until deleted.
 *
 * Sharing of PObjects:
 *
 * Data stored with a PObject on one page is also available to other pages
 * within the same directory of the same web server. When the cookie
 * implementation is used, pages in subdirectories can read (but not write)
 * the properties of PObjects created in parent directories. When the Flash
 * implementation is used, any page on the web server can access the shared
 * data if it cheats and uses a modified version of this module.
 *
 * Distinct web browser applications store their cookies separately and
 * persistent data stored using cookies in one browser is not accessible using
 * a different browser. If two browsers both use the same installation of
 * the Flash plug-in, however, these browsers may share persistent data stored
 * with the Flash implementation.
 *
 * Security Notes:
 *
 * Data saved through a PObject is stored unencrypted on the user's hard disk.
 * Applications running on the computer can access the data, so PObject is
 * not suitable for storing sensitive information such as credit card numbers,
 * passwords, or financial account numbers.
 */


// This is the constructor
function PObject(name, defaults, onload) {
    if (!name) { // If no name was specified, use the last component of the URL
        name = window.location.pathname;
        var pos = name.lastIndexOf("/");
        if (pos != -1) name = name.substring(pos+1);
    }
    this.$name = name;   // Remember our name

    // Just delegate to a private, implementation-defined $init() method.
    this.$init(name, defaults, onload);
}

// Save the current state of this PObject for at least the specified # of days.
PObject.prototype.save = function(lifetimeInDays) {
    // First serialize the properties of the object into a single string
    var s = "";                         // Start with empty string
    for(var name in this) {             // Loop through properties
        if (name.charAt(0) == "$") continue; // Skip private $ properties
        var value = this[name];         // Get property value
```

Example 19-3. PObject.js: persistent objects for JavaScript (continued)

```
        var type = typeof value;              // Get property type
        // Skip properties whose type is object or function
        if (type == "object" || type == "function") continue;
        if (s.length > 0) s += "&";           // Separate properties with &
        // Add property name and encoded value
        s += name + ':' + encodeURIComponent(value);
    }

    // Then delegate to a private implementation-defined method to actually
    // save that serialized string.
    this.$save(s, lifetimeInDays);
};

PObject.prototype.forget = function() {
    // First, delete the serializable properties of this object using the
    // same property-selection criteria as the save() method.
    for(var name in this) {
        if (name.charAt(0) == '$') continue;
        var value = this[name];
        var type = typeof value;
        if (type == "function" || type == "object") continue;
        delete this[name];  // Delete the property
    }

    // Then erase and expire any previously saved data by saving the
    // empty string and setting its lifetime to 0.
    this.$save("", 0);
};

// Parse the string s into name/value pairs and set them as properties of this.
// If the string is null or empty, copy properties from defaults instead.
// This private utility method is used by the implementations of $init() below.
PObject.prototype.$parse = function(s, defaults) {
    if (!s) {  // If there is no string, use default properties instead
        if (defaults) for(var name in defaults) this[name] = defaults[name];
        return;
    }

    // The name/value pairs are separated from each other by ampersands, and
    // the individual names and values are separated from each other by colons.
    // We use the split() method to parse everything.
    var props = s.split('&'); // Break it into an array of name/value pairs
    for(var i = 0; i < props.length; i++) { // Loop through name/value pairs
        var p = props[i];
        var a = p.split(':');       // Break each name/value pair at the colon
        this[a[0]] = decodeURIComponent(a[1]); // Decode and store property
    }
};

/*
 * The implementation-specific portion of the module is below.
 * For each implementation, we define an $init() method that loads
```

Example 19-3. PObject.js: persistent objects for JavaScript (continued)

```
 * persistent data and a $save() method that saves it.
 */

// Determine if we're in IE and, if not, whether we've got a Flash
// plug-in installed and whether it has a high-enough version number
var isIE = navigator.appName == "Microsoft Internet Explorer";
var hasFlash7 = false;
if (!isIE && navigator.plugins) { // If we use the Netscape plug-in architecture
    var flashplayer = navigator.plugins["Shockwave Flash"];
    if (flashplayer) {      // If we've got a Flash plug-in
        // Extract the version number
        var flashversion = flashplayer.description;
        var flashversion = flashversion.substring(flashversion.search("\\d"));
        if (parseInt(flashversion) >= 7) hasFlash7 = true;
    }
}

if (isIE) {  // If we're in IE
    // The PObject() constructor delegates to this initialization function
    PObject.prototype.$init = function(name, defaults, onload) {
        // Create a hidden element with the userData behavior to persist data
        var div = document.createElement("div");  // Create a <div> tag
        this.$div = div;                          // Remember it
        div.id = "PObject" + name;                // Name it
        div.style.display = "none";               // Make it invisible

        // This is the IE-specific magic that makes persistence work.
        // The "userData" behavior adds the getAttribute(), setAttribute(),
        // load(), and save() methods to this <div> element. We use them below.
        div.style.behavior = "url('#default#userData')";

        document.body.appendChild(div);  // Add the element to the document

        // Now we retrieve any previously saved persistent data.
        div.load(name);  // Load data stored under our name
        // The data is a set of attributes. We only care about one of these
        // attributes. We've arbitrarily chosen the name "data" for it.
        var data = div.getAttribute("data");

        // Parse the data we retrieved, breaking it into object properties
        this.$parse(data, defaults);

        // If there is an onload callback, arrange to call it asynchronously
        // once the PObject() constructor has returned.
        if (onload) {
            var pobj = this;  // Can't use "this" in the nested function
            setTimeout(function() { onload(pobj, name);}, 0);
        }
    }

    // Persist the current state of the persistent object
    PObject.prototype.$save = function(s, lifetimeInDays) {
```

Example 19-3. PObject.js: persistent objects for JavaScript (continued)

```
        if (lifetimeInDays) { // If lifetime specified, convert to expiration
            var now = (new Date( )).getTime( );
            var expires = now + lifetimeInDays * 24 * 60 * 60 * 1000;
            // Set the expiration date as a string property of the <div>
            this.$div.expires = (new Date(expires)).toUTCString( );
        }

        // Now save the data persistently
        this.$div.setAttribute("data", s); // Set text as attribute of the <div>
        this.$div.save(this.$name);        // And make that attribute persistent
    };
}
else if (hasFlash7) { // This is the Flash-based implementation
    PObject.prototype.$init = function(name, defaults, onload) {
        var moviename = "PObject_" + name;    // id of the <embed> tag
        var url = "PObject.swf?name=" + name; // URL of the movie file

        // When the Flash player has started up and has our data ready,
        // it notifies us with an FSCommand. We must define a
        // handler that is called when that happens.
        var pobj = this; // for use by the nested function
        // Flash requires that we name our function with this global symbol
        window[moviename + "_DoFSCommand"] = function(command, args) {
            // We know Flash is ready now, so query it for our persistent data
            var data = pobj.$flash.GetVariable("data")
            pobj.$parse(data, defaults);    // Parse data or copy defaults
            if (onload) onload(pobj, name); // Call onload handler, if any
        };

        // Create an <embed> tag to hold our Flash movie. Using an <object>
        // tag is more standards-compliant, but it seems to cause problems
        // receiving the FSCommand. Note that we'll never be using Flash with
        // IE, which simplifies things quite a bit.
        var movie = document.createElement("embed");  // element to hold movie
        movie.setAttribute("id", moviename);          // element id
        movie.setAttribute("name", moviename);        // and name
        movie.setAttribute("type", "application/x-shockwave-flash");
        movie.setAttribute("src", url);  // This is the URL of the movie
        // Make the movie inconspicuous at the upper-right corner
        movie.setAttribute("width", 1);  // If this is 0, it doesn't work
        movie.setAttribute("height", 1);
        movie.setAttribute("style", "position:absolute; left:0px; top:0px;");

        document.body.appendChild(movie);  // Add the movie to the document
        this.$flash = movie;               // And remember it for later
    };

    PObject.prototype.$save = function(s, lifetimeInDays) {
        // To make the data persistent, we simply set it as a variable on
        // the Flash movie. The ActionScript code in the movie persists it.
        // Note that Flash persistence does not support lifetimes.
        this.$flash.SetVariable("data", s); // Ask Flash to save the text
```

Example 19-3. PObject.js: persistent objects for JavaScript (continued)

```
    };
}
else { /* If we're not IE and don't have Flash 7, fall back on cookies */
    PObject.prototype.$init = function(name, defaults, onload) {
        var allcookies = document.cookie;          // Get all cookies
        var data = null;                            // Assume no cookie data
        var start = allcookies.indexOf(name + '='); // Look for cookie start
        if (start != -1) {                          // Found it
            start += name.length + 1;               // Skip cookie name
            var end = allcookies.indexOf(';', start); // Find end of cookie
            if (end == -1) end = allcookies.length;
            data = allcookies.substring(start, end);  // Extract cookie data
        }
        this.$parse(data, defaults);  // Parse the cookie value to properties
        if (onload) {                 // Invoke onload handler asynchronously
            var pobj = this;
            setTimeout(function() { onload(pobj, name); }, 0);
        }
    };

    PObject.prototype.$save = function(s, lifetimeInDays) {
        var cookie = this.$name + '=' + s;          // Cookie name and value
        if (lifetimeInDays != null)                 // Add expiration
            cookie += "; max-age=" + (lifetimeInDays*24*60*60);
        document.cookie = cookie;                   // Save the cookie
    };
}
```

19.5.3.1 ActionScript code for Flash persistence

The code in Example 19-3 is not complete as it stands. The Flash-based persistence implementation relies on a Flash movie named *PObject.swf*. This movie is nothing more than a compiled ActionScript file. Example 19-4 shows the ActionScript code.

Example 19-4. ActionScript code for Flash-based persistence

```
class PObject {
    static function main( ) {
        // SharedObject exists in Flash 6 but isn't protected against
        // cross-domain scripting until Flash 7, so make sure we've got
        // that version of the Flash player.
        var version = getVersion( );
        version = parseInt(version.substring(version.lastIndexOf(" ")));
        if (isNaN(version) || version < 7) return;

        // Create a SharedObject to hold our persistent data.
        // The name of the object is passed in the movie URL like this:
        // PObject.swf?name=name
        _root.so = SharedObject.getLocal(_root.name);

        // Retrieve the initial data and store it on _root.data.
        _root.data = _root.so.data.data;
```

Example 19-4. ActionScript code for Flash-based persistence (continued)

```
        // Watch the data variable. When it changes, persist its new value.
        _root.watch("data", function(propName, oldValue, newValue) {
                    _root.so.data.data = newValue;
                    _root.so.flush( );
            });

        // Notify JavaScript that it can retrieve the persistent data now.
        fscommand("init");
    }
}
```

The ActionScript code is quite simple. It starts by creating a SharedObject, using a name specified (by JavaScript) in the query portion of the URL of the movie object. Creating this SharedObject loads the persistent data, which in this case is simply a single string. This data string is passed back to JavaScript with the fscommand( ) function that invokes the doFSCommand handler defined in JavaScript. The ActionScript code also sets up a handler function to be invoked whenever the data property of the root object changes. The JavaScript code uses SetVariable( ) to set the data property, and this ActionScript handler function is invoked in response, causing the data to be made persistent.

The ActionScript code shown in the *PObject.as* file of Example 19-4 must be compiled into a *PObject.swf* file before it can be used with the Flash player. You can do this with the open source ActionScript compiler *mtasc* (available from *http://www.mtasc.org*). Invoke the compiler like this:

```
    mtasc -swf PObject.swf -main -header 1:1:1 PObject.as
```

mtasc produces a SWF file that invokes the PObject.main( ) method from the first frame of the movie. If you use the Flash IDE instead, you must explicitly call PObject.main( ) from the first frame. Alternatively, you can simply copy code from the main( ) method and insert it into the first frame.

19.6   Persistent Data and Security

The documentation at the beginning of Example 19-3 highlights a security concern that you should keep in mind when using client-side persistence. Remember that any data you store resides on the user's hard disk in unencrypted form. It is therefore accessible to curious users who share access to the computer and to malicious software (such as spyware) that exists on the computer. For this reason, no form of client-side persistence should ever be used for any kind of sensitive information: passwords, financial account numbers, and so on. Remember: just because a user types something into a form field when interacting with your web site doesn't mean that he wants a copy of that value stored on disk. Consider a credit card number as an example. This is sensitive information that people keep hidden in their wallets. If you save this information using client-side persistence, it is almost as if you wrote the credit card number on a sticky note and stuck it to the user's keyboard. Because spyware is pervasive (at least on Windows platforms), it is almost as though you posted it on the Internet.

Also, bear in mind that many web users mistrust web sites that use cookies or other persistence mechanisms to do anything that resembles "tracking." Try to use the persistence mechanisms discussed in this chapter to enhance a user's experience at your site; don't use them as a data-collection mechanism.

CHAPTER 20

Scripting HTTP

The Hypertext Transfer Protocol (HTTP) specifies how web browsers request documents from and post form contents to web servers, and how web servers respond to those requests and posts. Web browsers obviously handle a lot of HTTP. Usually, however, HTTP is not under the control of scripts and instead occurs when the user clicks on a link, submits a form, or types a URL. Usually, but not always: it *is* possible for JavaScript code to script HTTP.

HTTP requests can be initiated when a script sets the `location` property of a window object or calls the `submit()` method of a form object. In both cases, the browser loads a new page into the window, overwriting any script that was running there. This kind of trivial HTTP scripting can be useful in a multiframed web page but is not the subject of this chapter. Here we consider how JavaScript code can communicate with a web server without causing the web browser to reload the currently displayed page.

The `<img>`, `<iframe>`, and `<script>` tags have `src` properties. When a script sets these properties to a URL, an HTTP GET request is initiated to download the content of the URL. A script can therefore pass information to a web server by encoding that information into the query-string portion of the URL of an image and setting the `src` property of an `<img>` element. The web server must actually return some image as the result of this request, but it can be invisible: a transparent 1-pixel-by-1-pixel image, for instance.[*]

`<iframe>` tags are a newer addition to HTML and are more versatile than `<img>` tags because the web server can return a result that can be inspected by the script instead of a binary image file. To do HTTP scripting with an `<iframe>` tag, the script first

---

[*] Images of this sort are sometimes called *web bugs*. They have a bad reputation because privacy concerns arise when web bugs are used to communicate information to a server other than the one from which the web page was loaded. One common, and legitimate, use of this kind of third-party web bug is for hit counting and traffic analysis. When a web page scripts the `src` property of an image to send information back to the server from which the page was originally loaded, there are no third-party privacy issues to worry about.

encodes information for the web server into a URL and then sets the src property of the <iframe> to that URL. The server creates an HTML document containing its response and sends it back to the web browser which displays it in the <iframe>. The <iframe> need not be visible to the user; it can be hidden with CSS, for example. A script can access the server's response by traversing the document object of the <iframe>. Note that this traversal is subject to the constraints of the same-origin policy described in Section 13.8.2.

Even the <script> tag has a src property that can be set to cause a dynamic HTTP request. Doing HTTP scripting with <script> tags is particularly attractive because when the server's response takes the form of JavaScript code, no parsing is required: the JavaScript interpreter executes the server's response.

Although HTTP scripting with <img>, <iframe>, and <script> tags is possible, it is harder than it sounds to do it portably, and this chapter focuses on another, more powerful way to do it. The XMLHttpRequest object is well supported in modern browsers and provides full access to the HTTP protocol, including the ability to make POST and HEAD requests, in addition to regular GET requests. XMLHttp-Request can return the web server's response synchronously or asynchronously, and can return the content as text or as a DOM document. Despite its name, the XML-HttpRequest object is not limited to use with XML documents: it can fetch any kind of text document. The XMLHttpRequest object is the key feature of a web application architecture known as Ajax. I'll discuss Ajax applications after illustrating how XMLHttpRequest works.

At the end of the chapter, I'll return to the topic of scripting HTTP with <script> tags and show how you can do this when an XMLHttpRequest object is not available.

20.1 Using XMLHttpRequest

Scripting HTTP with XMLHttpRequest is a three-part process:

- Creating an XMLHttpRequest object
- Specifying and submitting your HTTP request to a web server
- Synchronously or asynchronously retrieving the server's response

The following subsections include more details on each step.

20.1.1 Obtaining a Request Object

The XMLHttpRequest object has never been standardized, and the process of creating one is different in Internet Explorer than on other platforms. (Fortunately, however, the API for using an XMLHttpRequest object, once created, is the same on all platforms.)

In most browsers, you create an XMLHttpRequest object with a simple constructor call:

```
var request = new XMLHttpRequest();
```

Prior to Internet Explorer 7, IE does not have a native XMLHttpRequest() constructor function. In IE 5 and 6, XMLHttpRequest is an ActiveX object, and you must create it by passing the object name to the ActiveXObject() constructor:

```
var request = new ActiveXObject("Msxml2.XMLHTTP");
```

Unfortunately, the name of the object is different in different releases of Microsoft's XML HTTP library. Depending on the libraries installed on the client, you may sometimes have to use this code instead:

```
var request = new ActiveXObject("Microsoft.XMLHTTP");
```

Example 20-1 is a cross-platform utility function named HTTP.newRequest() for creating XMLHttpRequest objects.

Example 20-1. The HTTP.newRequest() utility

```
// This is a list of XMLHttpRequest-creation factory functions to try
HTTP._factories = [
    function() { return new XMLHttpRequest(); },
    function() { return new ActiveXObject("Msxml2.XMLHTTP"); },
    function() { return new ActiveXObject("Microsoft.XMLHTTP"); }
];

// When we find a factory that works, store it here.
HTTP._factory = null;

// Create and return a new XMLHttpRequest object.
//
// The first time we're called, try the list of factory functions until
// we find one that returns a non-null value and does not throw an
// exception. Once we find a working factory, remember it for later use.
//
HTTP.newRequest = function() {
    if (HTTP._factory != null) return HTTP._factory();

    for(var i = 0; i < HTTP._factories.length; i++) {
        try {
            var factory = HTTP._factories[i];
            var request = factory();
            if (request != null) {
                HTTP._factory = factory;
                return request;
            }
        }
        catch(e) {
            continue;
        }
    }
```

Example 20-1. The HTTP.newRequest() utility (continued)

```
    // If we get here, none of the factory candidates succeeded,
    // so throw an exception now and for all future calls.
    HTTP._factory = function() {
        throw new Error("XMLHttpRequest not supported");
    }
    HTTP._factory(); // Throw an error
}
```

20.1.2 Submitting a Request

Once an XMLHttpRequest object has been created, the next step is to submit a request to a web server. This is itself a multistep process. First, call the open( ) method to specify the URL you are requesting and the HTTP *method* of the request. Most HTTP requests are done with the GET method, which simply downloads the content of the URL. Another useful method is POST, which is what most HTML forms use: it allows the values of named variables to be included as part of the request. HEAD is another useful HTTP method: it asks the server to just return the headers associated with the URL. This allows a script to check the modification date of a document, for example, without downloading the document content itself. Specify the method and URL of your request with the open( ) method:

```
    request.open("GET", url, false);
```

By default, the open( ) method sets up an asynchronous XMLHttpRequest. Passing false as the third argument tells it to get the server's response synchronously instead. Asynchronous responses are generally preferred, but synchronous responses are slightly easier, so we will consider that case first.

In addition to the optional third argument, the open( ) method can also accept a name and password as optional fourth and fifth arguments. These are used when requesting a URL from a server that requires authorization.

The open( ) method does not actually send the request to the web server. It simply stores its arguments to use later when the request is actually sent. Before you send the request, you must set any necessary request headers. Here are some examples:*

```
    request.setRequestHeader("User-Agent", "XMLHttpRequest");
    request.setRequestHeader("Accept-Language", "en");
    request.setRequestHeader("If-Modified-Since", lastRequestTime.toString());
```

Note that the web browser automatically adds relevant cookies to the request you're building. You need to explicitly set a "Cookie" header only if you want to send a fake cookie to the server.

---

* Details of the HTTP protocol are beyond the scope of this book. Refer to an HTTP reference for details on these and other headers that you can set when issuing an HTTP request.

Finally, after creating the request object, calling the open() method, and setting headers, send the request to the server:

```
request.send(null);
```

The argument to the send() function is the body of the request. For HTTP GET requests, this is always null. For POST requests, however, it should contain the form data to be sent to the server (see Example 20-5). For now, simply pass null. (Note that the null argument is required. XMLHttpRequest is a client-side object and—in Firefox, at least—its methods are not forgiving of omitted arguments as core Java-Script functions are.)

20.1.3 Obtaining a Synchronous Response

The XMLHttpRequest object holds not only the details of the HTTP request that is made but also represents the server's response. If you pass false as the third argument to open(), the send() method is synchronous: it blocks and does not return until the server's response has arrived.[*]

send() does not return a status code. Once it returns, you can check the HTTP status code returned from the server with the status property of the request object. The possible values of this code are defined by the HTTP protocol. A status of 200 means that the request was successful and that the response is available. A status of 404, on the other hand, is a "not found" error that occurs when the requested URL does not exist.

The XMLHttpRequest object makes the server's response available as a string through the responseText property of the request object. If the response is an XML document, you can also access the document as a DOM Document object through the responseXML property. Note that the server must identify its XML documents with the MIME type "text/xml" in order for XMLHttpRequest to parse the response into a Document object.

When a request is synchronous, the code that follows send() usually looks something like this:

```
if (request.status == 200) {
    // We got the server's response. Display the response text.
    alert(request.responseText);
}
else {
    // Something went wrong. Display error code and error message.
    alert("Error " + request.status + ": " + request.statusText);
}
```

[*] XMLHttpRequest has wonderfully powerful features, but its API is not particularly well designed. The boolean value that specifies synchronous or asynchronous behavior really ought to be an argument of the send() method, for example.

In addition to the status codes and the response text or document, the XMLHttp-Request object also provides access to the HTTP headers returned by the web server. getAllResponseHeaders( ) returns the response headers as an unparsed block of text, and getResponseHeader( ) returns the value of a named header. For example:

```
if (request.status == 200) {  // Make sure there were no errors
    // Make sure the response is an XML document
    if (request.getResponseHeader("Content-Type") == "text/xml") {
        var doc = request.responseXML;
        // Now do something with the response document
    }
}
```

There is one serious problem with using XMLHttpRequest synchronously: if the web server stops responding, the send( ) method blocks for a long time. JavaScript execution stops, and the web browser may appear to have hung (this is platform-dependent, of course). If a server hangs during a normal page load, the user can simply click the browser's **Stop** button and try another link or another URL. But there is no **Stop** button for XMLHttpRequest. The send( ) method does not offer any way to specify a maximum length of time to wait, and the single-threaded execution model of client-side JavaScript does not allow a script to interrupt a synchronous XMLHttpRequest once the request has been sent.

The solution to these problems is to use XMLHttpRequest asynchronously.

20.1.4 Handling an Asynchronous Response

To use an XMLHttpRequest object in asynchronous mode, pass true as the third argument to the open( ) method (or simply omit the third argument: true is used by default). If you do this, the send( ) method sends the request to the server and then returns immediately. When the server's response arrives, it becomes available through the XMLHttpRequest object via the same properties described earlier for synchronous usage.

An asynchronous response from the server is just like an asynchronous mouse click from a user: you need to be notified when it happens. This is done with an event handler. For XMLHttpRequest, the event handler is set on the onreadystatechange property. As the name of this property implies, the event-handler function is invoked whenever the value of the readyState property changes. readyState is an integer that specifies the status of an HTTP request, and its possible values are enumerated in Table 20-1. The XMLHttpRequest object does not define symbolic constants for the five values listed in the table.

Table 20-1. XMLHttpRequest readyState values

readyState	Meaning
0	open( ) has not been called yet.
1	open( ) has been called, but send( ) has not been called.

Table 20-1. XMLHttpRequest readyState values (continued)

readyState	Meaning
2	send( ) has been called, but the server has not responded yet.
3	Data is being received from the server. readyState 3 differs somewhat in Firefox and Internet Explorer; see Section 20.1.4.1.
4	The server's response is complete.

Since XMLHttpRequest has only this one event handler, it is invoked for all possible events. A typical onreadystatechange handler is invoked once when open( ) is called and again when send( ) is called. It is invoked again when the server's response starts arriving, and one final time when the response is complete. In contrast to most events in client-side JavaScript, no event object is passed to the onreadystatechange handler. You must check the readyState property of the XMLHttpRequest object to determine why your event handler was invoked. Unfortunately, the XMLHttp-Request object is not passed as an argument to the event handler, either, so you'll have to make sure that the event-handler function is defined in a scope from which it can access the request object. A typical event handler for an asynchronous request looks like this:

```
// Create an XMLHttpRequest using the utility defined earlier
var request = HTTP.newRequest( );

// Register an event handler to receive asynchronous notifications.
// This code says what to do with the response, and it appears in a nested
// function here before we have even submitted the request.
request.onreadystatechange = function( ) {
    if (request.readyState == 4) {  // If the request is finished
        if (request.status == 200)  // If it was successful
            alert(request.responseText);  // Display the server's response
    }
}

// Make a GET request for a given URL. We don't pass a third argument,
// so this is an asynchronous request
request.open("GET", url);

// We could set additional request headers here if we needed to.

// Now send the request. Since it is a GET request, we pass null for
// the body. Since it is asynchronous, send( ) does not block but
// returns immediately.
request.send(null);
```

20.1.4.1 Notes on readyState 3

The XMLHttpRequest object has never been standardized, and browsers differ in their handling of readyState 3. For example, during large downloads, Firefox invokes the onreadystatechange handler multiple times in readyState 3, to provide download progress feedback. A script might use these multiple invocations to display a progress indicator to the user. Internet Explorer, on the other hand, interprets the event handler name strictly, and invokes it only when the readyState value actually changes. This means that it is invoked only once for readyState 3, no matter how large the downloaded document is.

Browsers also differ as to what part of the server's response is available in readyState 3. Even though state 3 means that some part of the response has arrived from the server, Microsoft's documentation for XMLHttpRequest explicitly states that it is an error to query responseText in this state. In other browsers, it appears to be an undocumented feature that responseText returns whatever portion of the server's response is available.

Unfortunately, none of the major browser vendors have produced adequate documentation of their XMLHttpRequest objects. Until there is a standard or at least clear documentation, it is safest to ignore any value of readyState other than 4.

20.1.5 XMLHttpRequest Security

As part of the same-origin security policy (see Section 13.8.2), the XMLHttpRequest object can issue HTTP requests only to the server from which the document that uses it was downloaded. This is a reasonable restriction, but you can circumvent it if you need to, by using a server-side script as a proxy to fetch the content of some off-site URL for you.

This XMLHttpRequest security restriction has one very important implication: XMLHttpRequest makes HTTP requests and does not work with other URL schemes. It cannot work with URLs that use the file:// protocol, for example. This means that you cannot test XMLHttpRequest scripts from your local filesystem. You must upload your test scripts to a web server (or run a server on your desktop). Your test scripts must be loaded into your web browser via HTTP in order for them to make HTTP requests of their own.

20.2   XMLHttpRequest Examples and Utilities

At the beginning of this chapter, I presented the HTTP.newRequest( ) utility function, which can obtain an XMLHttpRequest object for any browser. It is also possible to simplify the use of XMLHttpRequest with utility functions. The subsections that follow include sample utilities.

20.2.1 Basic GET Utilities

Example 20-2 is a very simple function that can handle the most common use of XMLHttpRequest: simply pass it the URL you want to fetch and the function that should be passed the text of that URL.

Example 20-2. The HTTP.getText() utility

```
/**
 * Use XMLHttpRequest to fetch the contents of the specified URL using
 * an HTTP GET request. When the response arrives, pass it (as plain
 * text) to the specified callback function.
 *
 * This function does not block and has no return value.
 */
HTTP.getText = function(url, callback) {
    var request = HTTP.newRequest();
    request.onreadystatechange = function() {
        if (request.readyState == 4 && request.status == 200)
            callback(request.responseText);
    }
    request.open("GET", url);
    request.send(null);
};
```

Example 20-3 is a trivial variant used to fetch XML documents and pass their parsed representation to a callback function.

Example 20-3. The HTTP.getXML() utility

```
HTTP.getXML = function(url, callback) {
    var request = HTTP.newRequest();
    request.onreadystatechange = function() {
        if (request.readyState == 4 && request.status == 200)
            callback(request.responseXML);
    }
    request.open("GET", url);
    request.send(null);
};
```

20.2.2 Getting Headers Only

One of the features of XMLHttpRequest is that it allows you to specify the HTTP method to use. The HTTP HEAD request asks the server to return the headers for a given URL without returning the content of that URL. This might be done, for example, to check the modification date of a resource before downloading it.

Example 20-4 shows how you can make a HEAD request. It includes a function for parsing HTTP header name/value pairs and storing them as the names and values of the properties of a JavaScript object. It also introduces an error handler function that is invoked if the server returns a 404 or other error code.

Example 20-4. The HTTP.getHeaders() utility

```
/**
 * Use an HTTP HEAD request to obtain the headers for the specified URL.
 * When the headers arrive, parse them with HTTP.parseHeaders() and pass the
 * resulting object to the specified callback function. If the server returns
```

Example 20-4. The HTTP.getHeaders() utility (continued)

```
 * an error code, invoke the specified errorHandler function instead. If no
 * error handler is specified, pass null to the callback function.
 */
HTTP.getHeaders = function(url, callback, errorHandler) {
    var request = HTTP.newRequest();
    request.onreadystatechange = function() {
        if (request.readyState == 4) {
            if (request.status == 200) {
                callback(HTTP.parseHeaders(request));
            }
            else {
                if (errorHandler) errorHandler(request.status,
                                                request.statusText);
                else callback(null);
            }
        }
    }
    request.open("HEAD", url);
    request.send(null);
};

// Parse the response headers from an XMLHttpRequest object and return
// the header names and values as property names and values of a new object.
HTTP.parseHeaders = function(request) {
    var headerText = request.getAllResponseHeaders();  // Text from the server
    var headers = {}; // This will be our return value
    var ls = /^\s*/;  // Leading space regular expression
    var ts = /\s*$/;  // Trailing space regular expression

    // Break the headers into lines
    var lines = headerText.split("\n");
    // Loop through the lines
    for(var i = 0; i < lines.length; i++) {
        var line = lines[i];
        if (line.length == 0) continue;  // Skip empty lines
        // Split each line at first colon, and trim whitespace away
        var pos = line.indexOf(':');
        var name = line.substring(0, pos).replace(ls, "").replace(ts, "");
        var value = line.substring(pos+1).replace(ls, "").replace(ts, "");
        // Store the header name/value pair in a JavaScript object
        headers[name] = value;
    }
    return headers;
};
```

20.2.3 HTTP POST

HTML forms are (by default) submitted to web servers using the HTTP POST method. With POST requests, data is passed to the server in the body of the request, rather than encoding it into the URL itself. Since request parameters are encoded into the URL of a GET request, the GET method is suitable only when the request has no side effects on the server—that is, when repeated GET requests for the same URL with the same parameters can be expected to return the same result. When there are side effects to a request (such as when the server stores some of the parameters in a database), a POST request should be used instead.

Example 20-5 shows how to make a POST request with an XMLHttpRequest object. The `HTTP.post()` method uses the `HTTP.encodeFormData()` function to convert the properties of an object to a string form that can be used as the body of a POST request. This string is then passed to the `XMLHttpRequest.send()` method and becomes the body of the request. (The string returned by `HTTP.encodeFormData()` can also be appended to a GET URL; just use a question-mark character to separate the URL from the data.) Example 20-5 also uses the `HTTP._getResponse()` method. This method parses the server's response based on its type and is implemented in the next section.

Example 20-5. The HTTP.post() utility

```
/**
 * Send an HTTP POST request to the specified URL, using the names and values
 * of the properties of the values object as the body of the request.
 * Parse the server's response according to its content type and pass
 * the resulting value to the callback function. If an HTTP error occurs,
 * call the specified errorHandler function, or pass null to the callback
 * if no error handler is specified.
 **/
HTTP.post = function(url, values, callback, errorHandler) {
    var request = HTTP.newRequest();
    request.onreadystatechange = function() {
        if (request.readyState == 4) {
            if (request.status == 200) {
                callback(HTTP._getResponse(request));
            }
            else {
                if (errorHandler) errorHandler(request.status,
                                               request.statusText);
                else callback(null);
            }
        }
    }

    request.open("POST", url);
    // This header tells the server how to interpret the body of the request.
    request.setRequestHeader("Content-Type",
                             "application/x-www-form-urlencoded");
    // Encode the properties of the values object and send them as
    // the body of the request.
    request.send(HTTP.encodeFormData(values));
};

/**
 * Encode the property name/value pairs of an object as if they were from
```

Example 20-5. The HTTP.post() utility (continued)

```
 * an HTML form, using application/x-www-form-urlencoded format
 */
HTTP.encodeFormData = function(data) {
    var pairs = [];
    var regexp = /%20/g; // A regular expression to match an encoded space

    for(var name in data) {
        var value = data[name].toString();
        // Create a name/value pair, but encode name and value first
        // The global function encodeURIComponent does almost what we want,
        // but it encodes spaces as %20 instead of as "+". We have to
        // fix that with String.replace()
        var pair = encodeURIComponent(name).replace(regexp,"+") + '=' +
            encodeURIComponent(value).replace(regexp,"+");
        pairs.push(pair);
    }

    // Concatenate all the name/value pairs, separating them with &
    return pairs.join('&');
};
```

Example 21-14 is another example that makes a POST request with an XMLHttp-Request object. That example invokes a web service, and instead of passing form values in the body of the request, it passes the text of an XML document.

20.2.4 HTML, XML, and JSON-Encoded Responses

In most of the examples shown so far, the server's response to an HTTP request has been treated as a plain-text value. This is a perfectly legal thing to do, and there is nothing that says that web servers can't return documents with a content type of "text/plain". Your JavaScript code can parse such a response with the various String methods and do whatever is needed with it.

You can always treat the server's response as plain text, even when it has a different content type. If the server returns an HTML document, for example, you might retrieve the content of that document with the responseText property and then use it to set the innerHTML property of some document element.

There are other ways to handle the server's response, however. As noted at the beginning of this chapter, if the server sends a response with a content type of "text/xml", you can retrieve a parsed representation of the XML document with the responseXML property. The value of this property is a DOM Document object, and you can search and traverse it using DOM methods.

Note, however that using XML as a data format may not always be the best choice. If the server wants to pass data to be manipulated by a JavaScript script, it is inefficient to encode that data into XML form on the server, have the XMLHttpRequest object parse that data to a tree of DOM nodes, and then have your script traverse that tree to extract data. A shorter path is to have the server encode the data using JavaScript object and array literals and pass the JavaScript source text to the web browser. The script then "parses" the response simply by passing it to the JavaScript eval( ) method.

Encoding data in the form of JavaScript object and array literals is known as JSON, or JavaScript Object Notation.* Here are XML and JSON encodings of the same data:

```
<!-- XML encoding -->
<author>
  <name>Wendell Berry</name>
  <books>
    <book>The Unsettling of America</book>
    <book>What are People For?</book>
  </books>
</author>

// JSON Encoding
{
  "name": "Wendell Berry",
  "books": [
    "The Unsettling of America",
    "What are People For?"
  ]
}
```

The HTTP.post( ) function shown in Example 20-5 invokes the HTTP._getResponse( ) function, which looks at the Content-Type header to determine the form of the response. Example 20-6 is a simple implementation of HTTP._getResponse( ) that returns XML documents as Document objects, evaluates JavaScript or JSON documents with eval( ), and returns any other content as plain text.

Example 20-6. HTTP._getResponse()

```
HTTP._getResponse = function(request) {
    // Check the content type returned by the server
    switch(request.getResponseHeader("Content-Type")) {
    case "text/xml":
        // If it is an XML document, use the parsed Document object.
        return request.responseXML;

    case "text/json":
    case "text/javascript":
    case "application/javascript":
    case "application/x-javascript":
        // If the response is JavaScript code, or a JSON-encoded value,
        // call eval() on the text to "parse" it to a JavaScript value.
```

---

* Learn more about JSON at *http://json.org*. The idea was introduced by Douglas Crockford, and this web site includes pointers to JSON encoders and decoders for a variety of programming languages; it can be a useful data encoding even if you are not using JavaScript.

Example 20-6. HTTP._getResponse( ) (continued)

```
        // Note: only do this if the JavaScript code is from a trusted server!
        return eval(request.responseText);

    default:
        // Otherwise, treat the response as plain text and return as a string.
        return request.responseText;
    }
};
```

Do not use the eval( ) method to parse JSON-encoded data, as is done in Example 20-6, unless you are confident that the web server will never send malicious executable JavaScript code in place of properly encoded JSON data. A secure alternative is to use a JSON decoder that parses JavaScript object literals "by hand" without calling eval( ).

20.2.5 Timing Out a Request

A shortcoming of the XMLHttpRequest object is that it provides no way to specify a timeout value for a request. For synchronous requests, this shortcoming is severe. If the server hangs, the web browser remains blocked in the send( ) method and everything freezes up. Asynchronous requests aren't subject to freezing; since the send( ) method does not block, the web browser can keep processing user events. There is still a timeout issue here, however. Suppose your application issues an HTTP request with an XMLHttpRequest object when the user clicks a button. In order to prevent multiple requests, it is a good idea to deactivate the button until the response arrives. But what if the server goes down or somehow fails to respond to the request? The browser does not lock up, but your application is now frozen with a deactivated button.

To prevent this sort of problem, it can be useful to set your own timeouts with the Window.setTimeout( ) function when issuing HTTP requests. Normally, you'll get your response before your timeout handler is triggered; in this case, you simply use the Window.clearTimeout( ) function to cancel the timeout. On the other hand, if your timeout is triggered before the XMLHttpRequest has reached readyState 4, you can cancel that request with the XMLHttpRequest.abort( ) method. After doing this, you typically let the user know that the request failed (perhaps with Window.alert( )). If, as in the hypothetical example, you disabled a button before issuing the request, you would re-enable it after the timeout arrived.

Example 20-7 defines an HTTP.get( ) function that demonstrates this timeout technique. It is a more advanced version of the HTTP.getText( ) method of Example 20-2 and integrates many of the features introduced in earlier examples, including an error handler, request parameters, and the HTTP._getResponse( ) method described earlier. It also allows the caller to specify an optional progress callback function that is invoked any time the onreadystatechange handler is called with a readyState other than 4. In browsers such as Firefox that invoke this handler multiple times in state 3, a progress callback allows a script to display download feedback to the user.

Example 20-7. The HTTP.get() utility

```
/**
 * Send an HTTP GET request for the specified URL. If a successful
 * response is received, it is converted to an object based on the
 * Content-Type header and passed to the specified callback function.
 * Additional arguments may be specified as properties of the options object.
 *
 * If an error response is received (e.g., a 404 Not Found error),
 * the status code and message are passed to the options.errorHandler
 * function. If no error handler is specified, the callback
 * function is called instead with a null argument.
 *
 * If the options.parameters object is specified, its properties are
 * taken as the names and values of request parameters. They are
 * converted to a URL-encoded string with HTTP.encodeFormData() and
 * are appended to the URL following a '?'.
 *
 * If an options.progressHandler function is specified, it is
 * called each time the readyState property is set to some value less
 * than 4. Each call to the progress-handler function is passed an
 * integer that specifies how many times it has been called.
 *
 * If an options.timeout value is specified, the XMLHttpRequest
 * is aborted if it has not completed before the specified number
 * of milliseconds have elapsed. If the timeout elapses and an
 * options.timeoutHandler is specified, that function is called with
 * the requested URL as its argument.
 **/
HTTP.get = function(url, callback, options) {
    var request = HTTP.newRequest();
    var n = 0;
    var timer;
    if (options.timeout)
        timer = setTimeout(function() {
                            request.abort();
                            if (options.timeoutHandler)
                                options.timeoutHandler(url);
                        },
                        options.timeout);

    request.onreadystatechange = function() {
        if (request.readyState == 4) {
            if (timer) clearTimeout(timer);
            if (request.status == 200) {
                callback(HTTP._getResponse(request));
            }
            else {
                if (options.errorHandler)
                    options.errorHandler(request.status,
                                        request.statusText);
```

Example 20-7. The HTTP.get() utility (continued)

```
                else callback(null);
            }
        }
        else if (options.progressHandler) {
            options.progressHandler(++n);
        }
    }

    var target = url;
    if (options.parameters)
        target += "?" + HTTP.encodeFormData(options.parameters)
    request.open("GET", target);
    request.send(null);
};
```

20.3 Ajax and Dynamic Scripting

The term *Ajax* describes an architecture for web applications that prominently features scripted HTTP and the XMLHttpRequest object. (Indeed, for many, the XMLHttpRequest object and Ajax are virtually synonymous.) Ajax is an (uncapitalized) acronym for Asynchronous JavaScript and XML.* The term was coined by Jesse James Garrett and first appeared in his February 2005 essay "Ajax: A New Approach to Web Applications." You can find this seminal essay at *http://www.adaptivepath.com/ publications/essays/archives/000385.php.*

The XMLHttpRequest object upon which Ajax is based was available in web browsers from Microsoft and Netscape/Mozilla for about four years before Garrett's essay was published but had never received much attention.† In 2004, that changed when Google released its Gmail web mail application using XMLHttpRequest. The combination of this high-profile and professionally executed example along with Garrett's early 2005 essay opened the floodgates to a torrent of interest in Ajax.

The key feature of an Ajax application is that it uses scripted HTTP to communicate with a web server without causing pages to reload. Since the amount of data exchanged is often small, and since the browser does not have to parse and render a document (and its associated stylesheets and scripts), response time is greatly

---

* The Ajax architecture is compelling, and having a simple name for it has served to catalyze a revolution in web application design. It turns out, however, that the acronym is not particularly descriptive of the technologies that compose Ajax applications. All client-side JavaScript uses event handlers and is therefore asynchronous. Also, the use of XML in Ajax-style applications is often convenient, but always optional. The defining characteristic of Ajax applications is their use of scripted HTTP, but this characteristic does not appear in the acronym.

† I regret that I did not document XMLHttpRequest in the fourth edition of this book. That edition of the book was heavily standards-based, and XMLHttpRequest was omitted because it has never been endorsed by any standards-setting body. Had I recognized the power of scripting HTTP at the time, I would have broken my rules and included it anyway.

improved, and the result is web applications that feel more like traditional desktop applications.

An optional feature of Ajax applications is the use of XML as the encoding for data interchange between client and server. Chapter 21 shows how to use client-side JavaScript to manipulate XML data, including doing XPath queries and XSL transformations of XML into HTML. Some Ajax applications use XSLT to separate content (XML data) from presentation (HTML formatting, captured as an XSL stylesheet). This approach has the additional benefits of reducing the amount of data to transfer from server to client and of offloading the transformation from the server to the client.

It is possible to formalize Ajax into an RPC mechanism.[*] In this formulation, web developers use low-level Ajax libraries on both the client and server side to facilitate higher-level communication between client and server. This chapter does not describe any such RPC-over-Ajax libraries because it focuses instead on the lower-level technology that makes Ajax work.

Ajax is a young application architecture, and Garrett's essay describing it concludes with a call to action that is worth reproducing here:

> The biggest challenges in creating Ajax applications are not technical. The core Ajax technologies are mature, stable, and well understood. Instead, the challenges are for the designers of these applications: to forget what we think we know about the limitations of the Web, and begin to imagine a wider, richer range of possibilities.
>
> It's going to be fun.

20.3.1 Ajax Example

The XMLHttpRequest examples that have appeared so far in this chapter have been utility functions that demonstrate how to use the XMLHttpRequest object. They have not demonstrated *why* you might want to use the object or illustrated *what* you can accomplish with it. As the quote from Garrett illustrates, the Ajax architecture opens up many possibilities that have only begun to be explored. The next example is a simple one, but it captures some of the flavor and utility of the Ajax architecture.

Example 20-8 is an unobtrusive script that registers event handlers on links in the document so that they display tool tips when the user hovers the mouse over them. For links that refer back to the same server from which the document was loaded, the script uses XMLHttpRequest to issue an HTTP HEAD request. From the returned headers, it extracts the content type, size, and modification date of the linked document and displays this information in the tool tip (see Figure 20-1). Thus, the tool tip provides a kind of a preview of the link's destination and can help a user decide whether to click on it or not.

---

[*] RPC stands for Remote Procedure Call and describes a strategy used in distributed computing to simplify client/server communication.

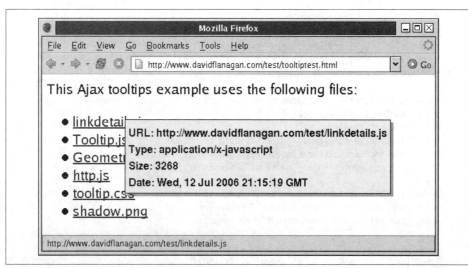

Figure 20-1. An Ajax tool tip

The code relies on the Tooltip class developed in Example 16-4 (however, it does not require the extension to that class developed in Example 17-3). It also uses the Geometry module of Example 14-2 and the HTTP.getHeaders( ) utility function developed in Example 20-4. The code involves several layers of asynchronicity, in the form of an onload event handler, an onmouseover event handler, a timer, and a callback function for the XMLHttpRequest object. Therefore, it ends up with deeply nested functions.

Example 20-8. Ajax tool tips

```
/**
 * linkdetails.js
 *
 * This unobtrusive JavaScript module adds event handlers to links in a
 * document so that they display tool tips when the mouse hovers over them for
 * half a second. If the link points to a document on the same server as
 * the source document, the tool tip includes type, size, and date
 * information obtained with an XMLHttpRequest HEAD request.
 *
 * This module requires the Tooltip.js, HTTP.js, and Geometry.js modules
 */
(function( ) {  // Anonymous function to hold all our symbols
    // Create the tool tip object we'll use
    var tooltip = new Tooltip( );

    // Arrange to have the init() function called on document load
    if (window.addEventListener) window.addEventListener("load", init, false);
    else if (window.attachEvent) window.attachEvent("onload", init);

    // To be called when the document loads
    function init( ) {
        var links = document.getElementsByTagName('a');
```

Example 20-8. Ajax tool tips (continued)

```
        // Loop through all the links, adding event handlers to them
        for(var i = 0; i < links.length; i++)
            if (links[i].href) addTooltipToLink(links[i]);
}

// This is the function that adds event handlers
function addTooltipToLink(link) {
    // Add event handlers
    if (link.addEventListener) {  // Standard technique
        link.addEventListener("mouseover", mouseover, false);
        link.addEventListener("mouseout", mouseout, false);
    }
    else if (link.attachEvent) {  // IE-specific technique
        link.attachEvent("onmouseover", mouseover);
        link.attachEvent("onmouseout", mouseout);
    }
}

var timer; // Used with setTimeout/clearTimeout

function mouseover(event) {
    var e = event || window.event;
    // Get mouse position, convert to document coordinates, add offset
    var x = e.clientX + Geometry.getHorizontalScroll() + 25;
    var y = e.clientY + Geometry.getVerticalScroll() + 15;

    // If a tool tip is pending, cancel it
    if (timer) window.clearTimeout(timer);

    // Schedule a tool tip to appear in half a second
    timer = window.setTimeout(showTooltip, 500);

    function showTooltip() {
        // If it is an HTTP link, and if it is from the same host
        // as this script is, we can use XMLHttpRequest
        // to get more information about it.
        if (link.protocol == "http:" && link.host == location.host) {
            // Make an XMLHttpRequest for the headers of the link
            HTTP.getHeaders(link.href, function(headers) {
                // Use the headers to build a string of text
                var tip = "URL: " + link.href + "<br>" +
                    "Type: " + headers["Content-Type"] + "<br>" +
                    "Size: " + headers["Content-Length"] + "<br>" +
                    "Date: " + headers["Last-Modified"];
                // And display it as a tool tip
                tooltip.show(tip, x, y);
            });

        }
        else {
            // Otherwise, if it is an off-site link, the
            // tool tip is just the URL of the link
            tooltip.show("URL: " + link.href, x, y);
```

Example 20-8. Ajax tool tips (continued)

```
                }
            }
        }

        function mouseout(e) {
            // When the mouse leaves a link, clear any
            // pending tool tips or hide it if it is shown
            if (timer) window.clearTimeout(timer);
            timer = null;
            tooltip.hide( );
        }
    }
})( );
```

20.3.2 Single-Page Applications

A *single-page application* is exactly what its name implies: a JavaScript-driven web application that requires only a single page load. Some single-page applications never need to talk to the server after loading. Examples are DHTML games in which all interaction with the user simply results in scripted modifications to the loaded document.

The XMLHttpRequest object and Ajax architecture open up many possibilities, however. Web applications can use these techniques to exchange data with the server and still be single-page applications. A web application designed along these lines might consist a small amount of JavaScript bootstrapping code and a simple HTML "splash screen" to be displayed while the application was initializing. Once the splash screen was displayed, the bootstrap code could use an XMLHttpRequest object to download the actual JavaScript code for the application, which would then be executed with the eval( ) method. The JavaScript code would then take charge, loading data as needed with XMLHttpRequest and using the DOM to render that data as DHTML to be displayed to the user.

20.3.3 Remote Scripting

The term *remote scripting* predates the term *Ajax* by more than four years and is simply a less catchy name for the same basic idea: using scripted HTTP to create a tighter integration (and improved response time) between client and server. One widely read 2002 article from Apple, for example, explains how to use an <iframe> tag to make scripted HTTP requests to a web server (see *http://developer.apple.com/internet/webcontent/iframe.html*). This article goes on to point out that if the web server sends back an HTML file with <script> tags in it, the JavaScript code those tags contain is executed by the browser and can invoke methods defined in the window that contains that <iframe>. In this way, the server can send very direct commands to its client in the form of JavaScript statements.

20.3.4 Ajax Cautions

Like any architecture, Ajax has some pitfalls. This section describes three issues to be aware of when designing Ajax applications.

First is the issue of visual feedback. When a user clicks on a traditional hyperlink, the web browser provides feedback to indicate that the content of the link is being fetched. This feedback appears even before that content is available for display so that the user knows the browser is working on her request. However, when an HTTP request is issued via XMLHttpRequest, the browser does not provide any feedback. Even on a broadband connection, network latencies often cause noticeable delays between issuing an HTTP request and receiving the response. It is valuable, therefore, for Ajax-based applications to provide some kind of visual feedback (such as a simple DHTML animation: see Chapter 16) while waiting for a response to an XMLHttpRequest.

Note that Example 20-8 does not heed this advice to provide visual feedback. This is because in this example, the user does not take any active action to initiate the HTTP request. Instead, the request is initiated whenever the user (passively) hovers the mouse over a link. The user does not explicitly ask the application to perform an action and therefore does not expect feedback.

The second issue has to do with URLs. Traditional web applications transition from one state to the next by loading new pages, and each page has a unique URL. The same is not true with Ajax applications: when an Ajax application uses HTTP scripting to download and display new content, the URL in the location bar does not change. Users may want to bookmark a particular state within the application and will find that they cannot do this with the browser's bookmarking facility. They can't even cut and paste a URL from the browser's location bar.

This issue, and its solution, are well illustrated by the Google Maps application (*http://local.google.com*). As you zoom and scroll the map, lots of data is transferred back and forth between client and server, but the URL displayed in the browser does not change at all. Google solves the bookmarking problem by including a "link to this page" link on every page. Clicking the link generates a URL for the currently displayed map and reloads the page using that URL. Once this reload is done, the current state of the map can be bookmarked, the link emailed to a friend, and so on. The lesson for Ajax application developers is that it remains important to be able to encapsulate application state in a URL and that these URLs should be available to users when necessary.

A third issue that is often mentioned in discussions of Ajax has to do with the **Back** button. By taking control of HTTP away from the browser itself, scripts that use XMLHttpRequest bypass the browser history mechanism. Users are accustomed to navigating the web with **Back** and **Forward** buttons. If an Ajax application uses HTTP scripting to display substantial chunks of new content, users may to try to use these buttons to navigate within the application. When they do, they'll be frustrated to find that the **Back** button backs their browser all the way out of the application rather than just reverting to the most recently displayed "chunk."

Attempts have been made to solve the **Back** button problem by tricking the browser into inserting URLs into its history. These techniques are typically mired in browser-specific code, however, and are not really satisfactory. And even when they can be made to work, they subvert the Ajax paradigm and encourage the user to navigate with page reloads instead of scripted HTTP.

In my opinion, the **Back** button problem is not as serious a problem as it is made out to be, and it can be minimized with thoughtful web design. Application elements that look like hyperlinks should behave like hyperlinks and should do real page reloads. This makes them subject to the browser's history mechanism, as the user expects. Conversely, application elements that perform scripted HTTP, which is not subject to the browser's history mechanism, should not look like hyperlinks. Consider the Google Maps application again. When the user clicks and drags to scroll a map, he does not expect the **Back** button to undo his scrolling action, any more than he expects the **Back** button to undo the effect of using the browser's scrollbar to scroll within a web page.

Ajax applications should be careful not to use words like "forward" and "back" in their own intra-application navigation controls. If an application uses a wizard-style interface with **Next** and **Previous** buttons, for example, it should use traditional page loads (instead of XMLHttpRequest) to display the next screen or the previous screen because this is a situation in which the user expects the browser's **Back** button to work the same way as the application's **Previous** button.

More generally, the browser's **Back** button should not be confused with an application's **Undo** feature. Ajax applications may implement their own undo/redo options, if this is useful to their users, but it should be clear that this is different from what is provided by the **Back** and **Forward** buttons.

20.4 Scripting HTTP with <script> Tags

In Internet Explorer 5 and 6, the XMLHttpRequest object is an ActiveX object. Users sometimes disable all ActiveX scripting in Internet Explorer for security reasons, and in this case, scripts are unable to create an XMLHttpRequest object. If necessary, it is possible to issue basic HTTP GET requests using <script> and <iframe> tags. While it is not possible to reimplement all the functionality of XMLHttpRequest in this way,* you can at least create a version of the HTTP.getText( ) utility function that works without ActiveX scripting.

---

* A complete substitute for XMLHttpRequest probably requires using a Java applet.

It is relatively easy to generate HTTP requests by setting the src property of a <script> or <iframe> tag. What is more tricky is extracting the data you want from those elements without having that data modified by the browser. An <iframe> tag expects an HTML document to be loaded into it. If you try to download the content of a plain-text file into an iframe, you'll find that your text gets converted to HTML. Furthermore, some versions of Internet Explorer do not properly implement an onload or onreadystatechange handler for <iframe> tags, which makes the job harder.

The approach taken here uses a <script> tag and a server-side script. You tell the server-side script the URL whose content you want and what client-side function that content should be passed to. The server-side script gets the contents of the desired URL, encodes it as a (possibly quite long) JavaScript string, and returns a client-side script that passes that string to the function you specify. Since this client-side script is being loaded into a <script> tag, the specified function is automatically invoked on the URL contents when the download completes.

Example 20-9 is an implementation of a suitable server-side script in the PHP scripting language.

Example 20-9. jsquoter.php

```php
<?php
// Tell the browser that we're sending a script
header("Content-Type: text/javascript");
// Get arguments from the URL
$func = $_GET["func"];        // The function to invoke in our js code
$filename = $_GET["url"];     // The file or URL to pass to the func
$lines = file($filename);     // Get the lines of the file
$text = implode("", $lines);  // Concatenate into a string
// Escape quotes and newlines
$escaped = str_replace(array("'", "\"", "\n", "\r"),
                       array("\\'", "\\\"", "\\n", "\\r"),
                       $text);
// Output everything as a single JavaScript function call
echo "$func('$escaped');"
?>
```

The client-side function in Example 20-10 uses the *jsquoter.php* server-side script of Example 20-9 and works like the HTTP.getText( ) function shown in Example 20-2.

Example 20-10. The HTTP.getTextWithScript() utility

```
HTTP.getTextWithScript = function(url, callback) {
    // Create a new script element and add it to the document.
    var script = document.createElement("script");
    document.body.appendChild(script);

    // Get a unique function name.
    var funcname = "func" + HTTP.getTextWithScript.counter++;

    // Define a function with that name, using this function as a
```

Example 20-10. The HTTP.getTextWithScript( ) utility (continued)

```
    // convenient namespace. The script generated on the server
    // invokes this function.
    HTTP.getTextWithScript[funcname] = function(text) {
        // Pass the text to the callback function
        callback(text);

        // Clean up the script tag and the generated function.
        document.body.removeChild(script);
        delete HTTP.getTextWithScript[funcname];
    }

    // Encode the URL we want to fetch and the name of the function
    // as arguments to the jsquoter.php server-side script. Set the src
    // property of the script tag to fetch the URL.
    script.src = "jsquoter.php" +
                 "?url=" + encodeURIComponent(url) + "&func=" +
                 encodeURIComponent("HTTP.getTextWithScript." + funcname);
}

// We use this to generate unique function callback names in case there
// is more than one request pending at a time.
HTTP.getTextWithScript.counter = 0;
```

CHAPTER 21

JavaScript and XML

The most important feature of the Ajax web application architecture is its ability to script HTTP with the XMLHttpRequest object, which was covered in Chapter 20. The X in "Ajax" stands for XML, however, and for many web applications, Ajax's use of XML-formatted data is its second most important feature.

This chapter explains how to use JavaScript to work with XML data. It starts by demonstrating techniques for obtaining XML data: loading it from the network, parsing it from a string, and obtaining it from XML *data islands* within an HTML document. After this discussion of obtaining XML data, the chapter explains basic techniques for working with this data. It covers use of the W3C DOM API, transforming XML data with XSL stylesheets, querying XML data with XPath expressions, and serializing XML data back to string form.

This coverage of basic XML techniques is followed by two sections that demonstrate applications of those techniques. First, you'll see how it is possible to define HTML templates and automatically expand them, using the DOM and XPath, with data from an XML document. Second, you'll see how to write a web services client in JavaScript using the XML techniques from this chapter.

Finally, the chapter concludes with a brief introduction to E4X, which is a powerful extension to the core JavaScript language for working with XML.

21.1 Obtaining XML Documents

Chapter 20 showed how to use the XMLHttpRequest object to obtain an XML document from a web server. When the request is complete, the responseXML property of the XMLHttpRequest object refers to a Document object that is the parsed representation of the XML document. This is not the only way to obtain an XML Document object, however. The subsections that follow show how you can create an empty XML document, load an XML document from a URL without using XMLHttp-Request, parse an XML document from a string, and obtain an XML document from an XML data island.

As with many advanced client-side JavaScript features, the techniques for obtaining XML data are usually browser-specific. The following subsections define utility functions that work in both Internet Explorer (IE) and Firefox.

21.1.1 Creating a New Document

You can create an empty (except for an optional root element) XML Document in Firefox and related browsers with the DOM Level 2 method document.implementation. createDocument(). You can accomplish a similar thing in IE with the ActiveX object named MSXML2.DOMDocument. Example 21-1 defines an XML.newDocument() utility function that hides the differences between these two approaches. An empty XML document isn't useful by itself, but creating one is the first step of the document loading and parsing techniques that are shown in the examples that follow this one.

Example 21-1. Creating an empty XML document

```
/**
 * Create a new Document object. If no arguments are specified,
 * the document will be empty. If a root tag is specified, the document
 * will contain that single root tag. If the root tag has a namespace
 * prefix, the second argument must specify the URL that identifies the
 * namespace.
 */
XML.newDocument = function(rootTagName, namespaceURL) {
    if (!rootTagName) rootTagName = "";
    if (!namespaceURL) namespaceURL = "";

    if (document.implementation && document.implementation.createDocument) {
        // This is the W3C standard way to do it
        return document.implementation.createDocument(namespaceURL,
                                        rootTagName, null);
    }
    else { // This is the IE way to do it
        // Create an empty document as an ActiveX object
        // If there is no root element, this is all we have to do
        var doc = new ActiveXObject("MSXML2.DOMDocument");

        // If there is a root tag, initialize the document
        if (rootTagName) {
            // Look for a namespace prefix
            var prefix = "";
            var tagname = rootTagName;
            var p = rootTagName.indexOf(':');
            if (p != -1) {
                prefix = rootTagName.substring(0, p);
                tagname = rootTagName.substring(p+1);
            }

            // If we have a namespace, we must have a namespace prefix
            // If we don't have a namespace, we discard any prefix
            if (namespaceURL) {
```

Example 21-1. Creating an empty XML document (continued)

```
            if (!prefix) prefix = "a0"; // What Firefox uses
        }
        else prefix = "";

        // Create the root element (with optional namespace) as a
        // string of text
        var text = "<" + (prefix?(prefix+":"):"") +  tagname +
            (namespaceURL
             ?(" xmlns:" + prefix + '="' + namespaceURL +'"')
             :"") +
            "/>";
        // And parse that text into the empty document
        doc.loadXML(text);
    }
    return doc;
  }
};
```

21.1.2 Loading a Document from the Network

Chapter 20 showed how to use the XMLHttpRequest object to dynamically issue HTTP requests for text-based documents. When used with XML documents, the responseXML property refers to the parsed representation as a DOM Document object. XMLHttpRequest is nonstandard but widely available and well understood, and is usually the best technique for loading XML documents.

There *is* another way, however. An XML Document object created using the techniques shown in Example 21-1 can load and parse an XML document using a less well-known technique. Example 21-2 shows how it is done. Amazingly, the code is the same in both Mozilla-based browsers and in IE.

Example 21-2. Loading an XML document synchronously

```
/**
 * Synchronously load the XML document at the specified URL and
 * return it as a Document object
 */
XML.load = function(url) {
    // Create a new document with the previously defined function
    var xmldoc = XML.newDocument();
    xmldoc.async = false;   // We want to load synchronously
    xmldoc.load(url);       // Load and parse
    return xmldoc;          // Return the document
};
```

Like XMLHttpRequest, this load() method is nonstandard. It differs from XML-HttpRequest in several important ways. First, it works only with XML documents; XMLHttpRequest can be used to download any kind of text document. Second, it is not restricted to the HTTP protocol. In particular, it can be used to read files from the local filesystem, which is helpful during the testing and development phase of a web application. Third, when used with HTTP, it generates only GET requests and cannot be used to POST data to a web server.

Like XMLHttpRequest, the load( ) method can be used asynchronously. In fact, this is the default method of operation unless async property is set to false. Example 21-3 shows an asynchronous version of the XML.load( ) method.

Example 21-3. Loading an XML document asynchronously

```
/**
 * Asynchronously load and parse an XML document from the specified URL.
 * When the document is ready, pass it to the specified callback function.
 * This function returns immediately with no return value.
 */
XML.loadAsync = function(url, callback) {
    var xmldoc = XML.newDocument();

    // If we created the XML document using createDocument, use
    // onload to determine when it is loaded
    if (document.implementation && document.implementation.createDocument) {
        xmldoc.onload = function( ) { callback(xmldoc); };
    }
    // Otherwise, use onreadystatechange as with XMLHttpRequest
    else {
        xmldoc.onreadystatechange = function( ) {
            if (xmldoc.readyState == 4) callback(xmldoc);
        };
    }

    // Now go start the download and parsing
    xmldoc.load(url);
};
```

21.1.3 Parsing XML Text

Sometimes, instead of parsing an XML document loaded from the network, you simply want to parse an XML document from a JavaScript string. In Mozilla-based browsers, a DOMParser object is used; in IE, the loadXML( ) method of the Document object is used. (If you paid attention to the XML.newDocument( ) code in Example 21-1, you've already seen this method used once.)

Example 21-4 shows a cross-platform XML parsing function that works in Mozilla and IE. For platforms other than these two, it attempts to parse the text by loading it with an XMLHttpRequest from a data: URL.

Example 21-4. Parsing an XML document

```
/**
 * Parse the XML document contained in the string argument and return
 * a Document object that represents it.
```

Example 21-4. Parsing an XML document (continued)

```
 */
XML.parse = function(text) {
    if (typeof DOMParser != "undefined") {
        // Mozilla, Firefox, and related browsers
        return (new DOMParser()).parseFromString(text, "application/xml");
    }
    else if (typeof ActiveXObject != "undefined") {
        // Internet Explorer.
        var doc = XML.newDocument();  // Create an empty document
        doc.loadXML(text);            // Parse text into it
        return doc;                   // Return it
    }
    else {
        // As a last resort, try loading the document from a data: URL
        // This is supposed to work in Safari. Thanks to Manos Batsis and
        // his Sarissa library (sarissa.sourceforge.net) for this technique.
        var url = "data:text/xml;charset=utf-8," + encodeURIComponent(text);
        var request = new XMLHttpRequest();
        request.open("GET", url, false);
        request.send(null);
        return request.responseXML;
    }
};
```

21.1.4 XML Documents from Data Islands

Microsoft has extended HTML with an <xml> tag that creates an XML data island within the surrounding "sea" of HTML markup. When IE encounters this <xml> tag, it treats its contents as a separate XML document, which you can retrieve using document.getElementById() or other HTML DOM methods. If the <xml> tag has a src attribute, the XML document is loaded from the URL specified by that attribute instead of being parsed from the content of the <xml> tag.

If a web application requires XML data, and the data is known when the application is first loaded, there is an advantage to including that data directly within the HTML page: the data is already available, and the web application does not have to establish another network connection to download the data. XML data islands can be a useful way to accomplish this. It is possible to approximate IE data islands in other browsers using code like that shown in Example 21-5.

Example 21-5. Getting an XML document from a data island

```
/**
 * Return a Document object that holds the contents of the <xml> tag
 * with the specified id. If the <xml> tag has a src attribute, an XML
 * document is loaded from that URL and returned instead.
 *
 * Since data islands are often looked up more than once, this function caches
 * the documents it returns.
 */
```

Example 21-5. Getting an XML document from a data island (continued)

```
XML.getDataIsland = function(id) {
    var doc;

    // Check the cache first
    doc = XML.getDataIsland.cache[id];
    if (doc) return doc;

    // Look up the specified element
    doc = document.getElementById(id);

    // If there is a "src" attribute, fetch the Document from that URL
    var url = doc.getAttribute('src');
    if (url) {
        doc = XML.load(url);
    }
    // Otherwise, if there was no src attribute, the content of the <xml>
    // tag is the document we want to return. In Internet Explorer, doc is
    // already the document object we want. In other browsers, doc refers to
    // an HTML element, and we've got to copy the content of that element
    // into a new document object
    else if (!doc.documentElement) {// If this is not already a document...

        // First, find the document element within the <xml> tag. This is
        // the first child of the <xml> tag that is an element, rather
        // than text, comment, or processing instruction
        var docelt = doc.firstChild;
        while(docelt != null) {
            if (docelt.nodeType == 1 /*Node.ELEMENT_NODE*/) break;
            docelt = docelt.nextSibling;
        }

        // Create an empty document
        doc = XML.newDocument();

        // If the <xml> node had some content, import it into the new document
        if (docelt) doc.appendChild(doc.importNode(docelt, true));
    }

    // Now cache and return the document
    XML.getDataIsland.cache[id] = doc;
    return doc;
};
XML.getDataIsland.cache = {}; // Initialize the cache
```

This code does not perfectly simulate XML data islands in non-IE browsers. The HTML standard requires browsers to parse (but ignore) tags such as <xml> that they don't know about. This means that browsers don't discard XML data within an <xml> tag. It also means that any text within the data island is displayed by default. An easy way to prevent this is with the following CSS stylesheet:

```
<style type="text/css">xml { display: none; }</style>
```

Another incompatibility is that non-IE browsers treat the content of XML data islands as HTML rather than XML content. If you use the code in Example 21-5 in Firefox, for example, and then serialize the resulting document (you'll see how to do this later in the chapter), you'll find that the tag names are all converted to uppercase because Firefox thinks they are HTML tags. In some cases, this may be problematic; in many other cases, it is not. Finally, notice that XML namespaces break if the browser treats the XML tags as HTML tags. This means that inline XML data islands are not suitable for things like XSL stylesheets (XSL is covered in more detail later in this chapter) because those stylesheets always use namespaces.

If you want the network benefits of including XML data directly in an HTML page, but don't want the browser incompatibilities that come with using XML data islands and the <xml> tag, consider encoding your XML document text as a JavaScript string and then parsing the document using code like that shown in Example 21-4.

21.2 Manipulating XML with the DOM API

The previous section showed a number of ways to obtain parsed XML data in the form of a Document object. The Document object is defined by the W3C DOM API and is much like the HTMLDocument object that is referred to by the document property of the web browser.

The following subsections explain some important differences between the HTML DOM and the XML DOM and then demonstrate how you can use the DOM API to extract data from an XML document and display that data to a user by dynamically creating nodes in the browser's HTML document.

21.2.1 XML Versus HTML DOM

Chapter 15 explained the W3C DOM but focused on its application in client-side JavaScript to HTML documents. In fact, the W3C designed the DOM API to be language-neutral and focused primarily on XML documents; its use with HTML documents is through an optional extension module. In Part IV, notice that there are separate entries for Document and HTMLDocument, and for Element and HTMLElement. HTMLDocument and HTMLElement are extensions of the core XML Document and Element objects. If you are used to manipulating HTML documents with the DOM, you must be careful not to use HTML-specific API features when working with XML documents.

Probably the most important difference between the HTML and XML DOMs is that the getElementById( ) method is not typically useful with XML documents. In DOM Level 1, the method is actually HTML-specific, defined only by the HTML-Document interface. In DOM Level 2, the method is moved up a level to the Document interface, but there is a catch. In XML documents, getElementById( ) searches for elements with the specified value of an attribute whose *type* is "id". It is not sufficient to define an attribute *named* "id" on an element: the name of the attribute does not matter—only the type of the attribute. Attribute types are declared in the DTD of a document, and a document's DTD is specified in the DOCTYPE declaration. XML documents used by web applications often have no DOCTYPE declaration specifying a DTD, and a call to getElementById( ) on such a document always returns null. Note that the getElementsByTagName( ) method of the Document and Element interfaces works fine for XML documents. (Later in the chapter, I'll show you how to query an XML document using powerful XPath expressions; XPath can be used to retrieve elements based on the value of any attribute.)

Another difference between HTML and XML Document objects is that HTML documents have a body property that refers to the <body> tag within the document. For XML documents, only the documentElement property refers to the top-level element of the document. Note that this top-level element is also available through the childNodes[ ] property of the document, but it may not be the first or only element of that array because an XML document may also contain a DOCTYPE declaration, comments, and processing instructions at the top level.

There is also an important difference between the XML Element interface and the HTMLElement interface that extends it. In the HTML DOM, standard HTML attributes of an element are made available as properties of the HTMLElement interface. The src attribute of an <img> tag, for example, is available through the src property of the HTMLImageElement object that represents the <img> tag. This is not the case in the XML DOM: the Element interface has only a single tagName property. The attributes of an XML element must be explicitly queried and set with getAttribute( ), setAttribute( ), and related methods.

As a corollary, note that special attributes that are meaningful on any HTML element are meaningless on all XML elements. Recall that setting an attribute named "id" on an XML element does not mean that that element can be found with getElementById( ). Similarly, you cannot style an XML element by setting its style attribute. Nor can you associate a CSS class with an XML element by setting its class attribute. All these attributes are HTML-specific.

21.2.2 Example: Creating an HTML Table from XML Data

Example 21-7 defines a function named makeTable( ) that uses both the XML and HTML DOMs to extract data from an XML document and insert that data into an HTML document in the form of a table. The function expects a JavaScript object literal argument that specifies which elements of the XML document contain table data and how that data should be arranged in the table.

Before looking at the code for makeTable( ), let's first consider a usage example. Example 21-6 shows a sample XML document that's used here (and elsewhere throughout this chapter).

Example 21-6. An XML datafile

```xml
<?xml version="1.0"?>
<contacts>
  <contact name="Able Baker"><email>able@example.com</email></contact>
  <contact name="Careful Dodger"><email>dodger@example.com</email></contact>
  <contact name="Eager Framer" personal="true"><email>framer@example.com</email></contact>
</contacts>
```

The following HTML fragment shows how the makeTable( ) function might be used with that XML data. Note that the schema object refers to tag and attribute names from this sample datafile:

```javascript
<script>
// This function uses makeTable( )
function displayAddressBook( ) {
    var schema = {
        rowtag: "contact",
        columns: [
            { tagname: "@name", label: "Name" },
            { tagname: "email", label: "Address" }
        ]
    };

    var xmldoc = XML.load("addresses.xml");  // Read the XML data
    makeTable(xmldoc, schema, "addresses");  // Convert to an HTML table
}
</script>

<button onclick="displayAddressBook( )">Display Address Book</button>
<div id="addresses"><!--table will be inserted here --></div>
```

The implementation of makeTable( ) is shown in Example 21-7.

Example 21-7. Building an HTML table from XML data

```
/**
 * Extract data from the specified XML document and format it as an HTML table.
 * Append the table to the specified HTML element. (If element is a string,
 * it is taken as an element ID, and the named element is looked up.)
 *
 * The schema argument is a JavaScript object that specifies what data is to
 * be extracted and how it is to be displayed. The schema object must have a
 * property named "rowtag" that specifies the tag name of the XML elements that
 * contain the data for one row of the table. The schema object must also have
 * a property named "columns" that refers to an array. The elements of this
 * array specify the order and content of the columns of the table. Each
 * array element may be a string or a JavaScript object. If an element is a
 * string, that string is used as the tag name of the XML element that contains
 * table data for the column, and also as the column header for the column.
 * If an element of the columns[] array is an object, it must have one property
 * named "tagname" and one named "label". The tagname property is used to
 * extract data from the XML document and the label property is used as the
 * column header text. If the tagname begins with an @ character, it is
 * an attribute of the row element rather than a child of the row.
```

Example 21-7. Building an HTML table from XML data (continued)
```
*/
function makeTable(xmldoc, schema, element) {
    // Create the <table> element
    var table = document.createElement("table");

    // Create the header row of <th> elements in a <tr> in a <thead>
    var thead = document.createElement("thead");
    var header = document.createElement("tr");
    for(var i = 0; i < schema.columns.length; i++) {
        var c = schema.columns[i];
        var label = (typeof c == "string")?c:c.label;
        var cell = document.createElement("th");
        cell.appendChild(document.createTextNode(label));
        header.appendChild(cell);
    }
    // Put the header into the table
    thead.appendChild(header);
    table.appendChild(thead);

    // The remaining rows of the table go in a <tbody>
    var tbody = document.createElement("tbody");
    table.appendChild(tbody);

    // Now get the elements that contain our data from the xml document
    var xmlrows = xmldoc.getElementsByTagName(schema.rowtag);

    // Loop through these elements. Each one contains a row of the table.
    for(var r=0; r < xmlrows.length; r++) {
        // This is the XML element that holds the data for the row
        var xmlrow = xmlrows[r];
        // Create an HTML element to display the data in the row
        var row = document.createElement("tr");

        // Loop through the columns specified by the schema object
        for(var c = 0; c < schema.columns.length; c++) {
            var sc = schema.columns[c];
            var tagname = (typeof sc == "string")?sc:sc.tagname;
            var celltext;
            if (tagname.charAt(0) == '@') {
                // If the tagname begins with '@', it is an attribute name
                celltext = xmlrow.getAttribute(tagname.substring(1));
            }
            else {
                // Find the XML element that holds the data for this column
                var xmlcell = xmlrow.getElementsByTagName(tagname)[0];
                // Assume that element has a text node as its first child
                var celltext = xmlcell.firstChild.data;
            }
            // Create the HTML element for this cell
            var cell = document.createElement("td");
            // Put the text data into the HTML cell
            cell.appendChild(document.createTextNode(celltext));
```

Example 21-7. Building an HTML table from XML data (continued)

```
            // Add the cell to the row
            row.appendChild(cell);
        }

        // And add the row to the tbody of the table
        tbody.appendChild(row);
    }

    // Set an HTML attribute on the table element by setting a property.
    // Note that in XML we must use setAttribute( ) instead.
    table.frame = "border";

    // Now that we've created the HTML table, add it to the specified element.
    // If that element is a string, assume it is an element ID.
    if (typeof element == "string") element = document.getElementById(element);
    element.appendChild(table);
}
```

21.3   Transforming XML with XSLT

Once you've loaded, parsed, or otherwise obtained a Document object representing an XML document, one of the most powerful things you can do with it is transform it using an XSLT stylesheet. XSLT stands for XSL Transformations, and XSL stands for Extensible Stylesheet Language. XSL stylesheets are XML documents and can be loaded and parsed in the same way that any XML document can. A tutorial on XSL is well beyond the scope of this book, but Example 21-8 shows a sample stylesheet that can transform an XML document like the one shown in Example 21-6 into an HTML table.

Example 21-8. A simple XSL stylesheet

```
<?xml version="1.0"?><!-- this is an xml document -->
<!-- declare the xsl namespace to distinguish xsl tags from html tags -->
<xsl:stylesheet version="1.0"
                xmlns:xsl="http://www.w3.org/1999/XSL/Transform">
  <xsl:output method="html"/>

  <!-- When we see the root element, output the HTML framework of a table -->
  <xsl:template match="/">
    <table>
      <tr><th>Name</th><th>E-mail Address</th></tr>
      <xsl:apply-templates/>  <!-- and recurse for other templates -->
    </table>
  </xsl:template>

  <!-- When we see a <contact> element... -->
  <xsl:template match="contact">
    <tr> <!-- Begin a new row of the table -->
      <!-- Use the name attribute of the contact as the first column -->
      <td><xsl:value-of select="@name"/></td>
```

Example 21-8. A simple XSL stylesheet (continued)

```
      <xsl:apply-templates/>  <!-- and recurse for other templates -->
    </tr>
  </xsl:template>

  <!-- When we see an <email> element, output its content in another cell -->
  <xsl:template match="email">
    <td><xsl:value-of select="."/></td>
  </xsl:template>
</xsl:stylesheet>
```

XSLT transforms the content of an XML document using the rules in an XSL stylesheet. In the context of client-side JavaScript, this is usually done to transform the XML document into HTML. Many web application architectures use XSLT on the server side, but Mozilla-based browsers and IE support XSLT on the client side, and pushing the transform off the server and onto the client can save server resources and network bandwidth (because XML data is usually more compact than the HTML presentation of that data).

Many modern browsers can style XML using either CSS or XSL stylesheets. If you specify a stylesheet in an xml-stylesheet processing instruction, you can load an XML document directly into the browser, and the browser styles and displays it. The requisite processing instruction might look like this:

```
    <?xml-stylesheet href="dataToTable.xml" type="text/xsl"?>
```

Note that the browser performs this kind of XSLT transformation automatically when an XML document containing an appropriate processing instruction is loaded into the browser display window. This is important and useful, but it is not the subject matter of this section. What I explain here is how to use JavaScript to dynamically perform XSL transformations.

The W3C has not defined a standard API for performing XSL transformations on DOM Document and Element objects. In Mozilla-based browsers, the XSLTProcessor object provides a JavaScript XSLT API. And in IE, XML Document and Element objects have a transformNode( ) method for performing transformations. Example 21-9 shows both APIs. It defines an XML.Transformer class that encapsulates an XSL stylesheet and allows it to be used to transform more than one XML document. The transform( ) method of an XML.Transformer object uses the encapsulated stylesheet to transform a specified XML document and then replaces the content of a specified DOM element with the results of the transformation.

Example 21-9. XSLT in Mozilla and Internet Explorer

```
/**
 * This XML.Transformer class encapsulates an XSL stylesheet.
 * If the stylesheet parameter is a URL, we load it.
 * Otherwise, we assume it is an appropriate DOM Document.
 */
```

Example 21-9. XSLT in Mozilla and Internet Explorer (continued)

```
XML.Transformer = function(stylesheet) {
    // Load the stylesheet if necessary.
    if (typeof stylesheet == "string") stylesheet = XML.load(stylesheet);
    this.stylesheet = stylesheet;

    // In Mozilla-based browsers, create an XSLTProcessor object and
    // tell it about the stylesheet.
    if (typeof XSLTProcessor != "undefined") {
        this.processor = new XSLTProcessor( );
        this.processor.importStylesheet(this.stylesheet);
    }
};

/**
 * This is the transform( ) method of the XML.Transformer class.
 * It transforms the specified xml node using the encapsulated stylesheet.
 * The results of the transformation are assumed to be HTML and are used to
 * replace the content of the specified element.
 */
XML.Transformer.prototype.transform = function(node, element) {
    // If element is specified by id, look it up.
    if (typeof element == "string") element = document.getElementById(element);

    if (this.processor) {
        // If we've created an XSLTProcessor (i.e., we're in Mozilla) use it.
        // Transform the node into a DOM DocumentFragment.
        var fragment = this.processor.transformToFragment(node, document);
        // Erase the existing content of element.
        element.innerHTML = "";
        // And insert the transformed nodes.
        element.appendChild(fragment);
    }
    else if ("transformNode" in node) {
        // If the node has a transformNode( ) function (in IE), use that.
        // Note that transformNode( ) returns a string.
        element.innerHTML = node.transformNode(this.stylesheet);
    }
    else {
        // Otherwise, we're out of luck.
        throw "XSLT is not supported in this browser";
    }
};

/**
 * This is an XSLT utility function that is useful when a stylesheet is
 * used only once.
 */
XML.transform = function(xmldoc, stylesheet, element) {
    var transformer = new XML.Transformer(stylesheet);
    transformer.transform(xmldoc, element);
}
```

At the time of this writing, IE and Mozilla-based browsers are the only major ones that provide a JavaScript API to XSLT. If support for other browsers is important to you, you might be interested in the AJAXSLT open-source JavaScript XSLT implementation. AJAXSLT originated at Google and is under development at *http://goog-ajaxslt. sourceforge.net*.

21.4 Querying XML with XPath

XPath is a simple language that refers to elements, attributes, and text within an XML document. An XPath expression can refer to an XML element by its position in the document hierarchy or can select an element based on the value of (or simple presence of) an attribute. A full discussion of XPath is beyond the scope of this chapter, but Section 21.4.1 presents a simple XPath tutorial that explains common XPath expressions by example.

The W3C has drafted an API for selecting nodes in a DOM document tree using an XPath expression. Firefox and related browsers implement this W3C API using the evaluate( ) method of the Document object (for both HTML and XML documents). Mozilla-based browsers also implement Document.createExpression( ), which compiles an XPath expression so that it can be efficiently evaluated multiple times.

IE provides XPath expression evaluation with the selectSingleNode( ) and selectNodes( ) methods of XML (but not HTML) Document and Element objects. Later in this section, you'll find example code that uses both the W3C and IE APIs.

If you wish to use XPath with other browsers, consider the open-source AJAXSLT project at *http://goog-ajaxslt.sourceforge.net*.

21.4.1 XPath Examples

If you understand the tree structure of a DOM document, it is easy to learn simple XPath expressions by example. In order to understand these examples, though, you must know that an XPath expression is evaluated in relation to some *context* node within the document. The simplest XPath expressions simply refer to children of the context node:

```
contact            // The set of all <contact> tags beneath the context node
contact[1]         // The first <contact> tag beneath the context
contact[last()]    // The last <contact> child of the context node
contact[last()-1]  // The penultimate <contact> child of the context node
```

Note that XPath array syntax uses 1-based arrays instead of JavaScript-style 0-based arrays.

The "path" in the name XPath refers to the fact that the language treats levels in the XML element hierarchy like directories in a filesystem and uses the "/" character to separate levels of the hierarchy. Thus:

```
contact/email      // All <email> children of <contact> children of context
/contacts          // The <contacts> child of the document root (leading /)
contact[1]/email   // The <email> children of the first <contact> child
contact/email[2]   // The 2nd <email> child of any <contact> child of context
```

Note that contact/email[2] evaluates to the set of <email> elements that are the second <email> child of any <contact> child of the context node. This is not the same as contact[2]/email or (contact/email)[2].

A dot (.) in an XPath expression refers to the context element. And a double-slash (//) elides levels of the hierarchy, referring to any descendant instead of an immediate child. For example:

```
.//email           // All <email> descendants of the context
//email            // All <email> tags in the document (note leading slash)
```

XPath expressions can refer to XML attributes as well as elements. The @ character is used as a prefix to identify an attribute name:

```
@id                // The value of the id attribute of the context node
contact/@name      // The values of the name attributes of <contact> children
```

The value of an XML attribute can filter the set of elements returned by an XPath expression. For example:

```
contact[@personal="true"]  // All <contact> tags with attribute personal="true"
```

To select the textual content of XML elements, use the text( ) method:

```
contact/email/text()  // The text nodes within <email> tags
//text()              // All text nodes in the document
```

XPath is namespace-aware, and you can include namespace prefixes in your expressions:

```
//xsl:template       // Select all <xsl:template> elements
```

When you evaluate an XPath expression that uses namespaces, you must, of course, provide a mapping of namespace prefixes to namespace URLs.

These examples are just a survey of common XPath usage patterns. XPath has other syntax and features not described here. One example is the count( ) function, which returns the number of nodes in a set rather than returning the set itself:

```
count(//email)       // The number of <email> elements in the document
```

21.4.2 Evaluating XPath Expressions

Example 21-10 shows an XML.XPathExpression class that works in IE and in standards-compliant browsers such as Firefox.

Example 21-10. Evaluating XPath expressions

```
/**
 * XML.XPathExpression is a class that encapsulates an XPath query and its
 * associated namespace prefix-to-URL mapping. Once an XML.XPathExpression
 * object has been created, it can be evaluated one or more times (in one
 * or more contexts) using the getNode() or getNodes() methods.
 *
 * The first argument to this constructor is the text of the XPath expression.
 *
 * If the expression includes any XML namespaces, the second argument must
 * be a JavaScript object that maps namespace prefixes to the URLs that define
 * those namespaces. The properties of this object are the prefixes, and
 * the values of those properties are the URLs.
 */
XML.XPathExpression = function(xpathText, namespaces) {
    this.xpathText = xpathText;    // Save the text of the expression
    this.namespaces = namespaces;  // And the namespace mapping

    if (document.createExpression) {
        // If we're in a W3C-compliant browser, use the W3C API
        // to compile the text of the XPath query
        this.xpathExpr =
            document.createExpression(xpathText,
                                  // This function is passed a
                                  // namespace prefix and returns the URL.
                                  function(prefix) {
                                      return namespaces[prefix];
                                  });
    }
    else {
        // Otherwise, we assume for now that we're in IE and convert the
        // namespaces object into the textual form that IE requires.
        this.namespaceString = "";
        if (namespaces != null) {
            for(var prefix in namespaces) {
                // Add a space if there is already something there
                if (this.namespaceString) this.namespaceString += ' ';
                // And add the namespace
                this.namespaceString += 'xmlns:' + prefix + '="' +
                    namespaces[prefix] + '"';
            }
        }
    }
};

/**
 * This is the getNodes() method of XML.XPathExpression. It evaluates the
 * XPath expression in the specified context. The context argument should
 * be a Document or Element object. The return value is an array
 * or array-like object containing the nodes that match the expression.
 */
XML.XPathExpression.prototype.getNodes = function(context) {
    if (this.xpathExpr) {
```

Example 21-10. Evaluating XPath expressions (continued)

```
        // If we are in a W3C-compliant browser, we compiled the
        // expression in the constructor. We now evaluate that compiled
        // expression in the specified context.
        var result =
            this.xpathExpr.evaluate(context,
                                    // This is the result type we want
                                    XPathResult.ORDERED_NODE_SNAPSHOT_TYPE,
                                    null);

        // Copy the results we get into an array.
        var a = new Array(result.snapshotLength);
        for(var i = 0; i < result.snapshotLength; i++) {
            a[i] = result.snapshotItem(i);
        }
        return a;
    }
    else {
        // If we are not in a W3C-compliant browser, attempt to evaluate
        // the expression using the IE API.
        try {
            // We need the Document object to specify namespaces
            var doc = context.ownerDocument;
            // If the context doesn't have ownerDocument, it is the Document
            if (doc == null) doc = context;
            // This is IE-specific magic to specify prefix-to-URL mapping
            doc.setProperty("SelectionLanguage", "XPath");
            doc.setProperty("SelectionNamespaces", this.namespaceString);

            // In IE, the context must be an Element not a Document,
            // so if context is a document, use documentElement instead
            if (context == doc) context = doc.documentElement;
            // Now use the IE method selectNodes() to evaluate the expression
            return context.selectNodes(this.xpathText);
        }
        catch(e) {
            // If the IE API doesn't work, we just give up
            throw "XPath not supported by this browser.";
        }
    }
}


/**
 * This is the getNode() method of XML.XPathExpression. It evaluates the
 * XPath expression in the specified context and returns a single matching
 * node (or null if no node matches). If more than one node matches,
 * this method returns the first one in the document.
 * The implementation differs from getNodes() only in the return type.
 */
XML.XPathExpression.prototype.getNode = function(context) {
    if (this.xpathExpr) {
        var result =
```

Example 21-10. Evaluating XPath expressions (continued)

```
                this.xpathExpr.evaluate(context,
                                        // We just want the first match
                                        XPathResult.FIRST_ORDERED_NODE_TYPE,
                                        null);
        return result.singleNodeValue;
    }
    else {
        try {
            var doc = context.ownerDocument;
            if (doc == null) doc = context;
            doc.setProperty("SelectionLanguage", "XPath");
            doc.setProperty("SelectionNamespaces", this.namespaceString);
            if (context == doc) context = doc.documentElement;
            // In IE call selectSingleNode instead of selectNodes
            return context.selectSingleNode(this.xpathText);
        }
        catch(e) {
            throw "XPath not supported by this browser.";
        }
    }
};

// A utility to create an XML.XPathExpression and call getNodes() on it
XML.getNodes = function(context, xpathExpr, namespaces) {
    return (new XML.XPathExpression(xpathExpr, namespaces)).getNodes(context);
};

// A utility to create an XML.XPathExpression and call getNode() on it
XML.getNode  = function(context, xpathExpr, namespaces) {
    return (new XML.XPathExpression(xpathExpr, namespaces)).getNode(context);
};
```

21.4.3 More on the W3C XPath API

Because of the limitations in the IE XPath API, the code in Example 21-10 handles only queries that evaluate to a document node or set of nodes. It is not possible in IE to evaluate an XPath expression that returns a string of text or a number. This is possible with the W3C standard API, however, using code that looks like this:

```
// How many <p> tags in the document?
var n = document.evaluate("count(//p)", document, null,
                          XPathResult.NUMBER_TYPE, null).numberValue;
// What is the text of the 2nd paragraph?
var text = document.evaluate("//p[2]/text()", document, null,
                             XPathResult.STRING_TYPE, null).stringValue;
```

There are two things to note about these simple examples. First, they use the document.evaluate() method to evaluate an XPath expression directly without compiling it first. The code in Example 21-10 instead used document.createExpression() to compile an XPath expression into a form that could be reused. Second, notice that these examples are working with HTML <p> tags in the document object. In Firefox, XPath queries can be used on HTML documents as well as XML documents.

See Document, XPathExpression, and XPathResult in Part IV for complete details on the W3C XPath API.

21.5 Serializing XML

It is sometimes useful to *serialize* an XML document (or some subelement of the document) by converting it to a string. One reason you might do this is to send an XML document as the body of an HTTP POST request generated with the XMLHttpRequest object. Another common reason to serialize XML documents and elements is for use in debugging messages!

In Mozilla-based browsers, serialization is done with an XMLSerializer object. In IE, it is even easier: the xml property of an XML Document or Element object returns the serialized form of the document or element.

Example 21-11 shows serialization code that works in Mozilla and IE.

Example 21-11. Serializing XML

```
/**
 * Serialize an XML Document or Element and return it as a string.
 */
XML.serialize = function(node) {
    if (typeof XMLSerializer != "undefined")
        return (new XMLSerializer( )).serializeToString(node);
    else if (node.xml) return node.xml;
    else throw "XML.serialize is not supported or can't serialize " + node;
};
```

21.6 Expanding HTML Templates with XML Data

One key feature of IE's XML data islands is that they can be used with an automatic templating facility in which data from a data island is automatically inserted into HTML elements. These HTML templates are defined in IE by adding datasrc and datafld ("fld" is short for "field") attributes to the elements.

This section applies the XML techniques seen earlier in the chapter and uses XPath and the DOM to create an improved templating facility that works in IE and Firefox. A template is any HTML element with a datasource attribute. The value of this attribute should be the ID of an XML data island or the URL of an external XML document. The template element should also have a foreach attribute. The value of this attribute is an XPath expression that evaluates to the list of nodes from which XML data will be extracted. For each XML node returned by the foreach expression, an expanded copy of the template is inserted into the HTML document. The template is expanded by finding all elements within it that have a data attribute. This attribute is another XPath expression to be evaluated in the context of a node returned by the foreach expression. This data expression is evaluated with XML.getNode( ), and the text contained by the returned node is used as the content of the HTML element on which the data attribute was defined.

This description becomes much clearer with a concrete example. Example 21-12 is a simple HTML document that includes an XML data island and a template that uses it. It has an onload( ) event handler that expands the template.

Example 21-12. An XML data island and HTML template

```
<html>
<!-- Load our XML utilities for data islands and templates -->
<head><script src="xml.js"></script></head>
<!-- Expand all templates on document load -->
<body onload="XML.expandTemplates( )">

<!-- This is an XML data island with our data -->
<xml id="data" style="display:none"> <!-- hidden with CSS -->
  <contacts>
    <contact name="Able Baker"><email>able@example.com</email></contact>
    <contact name="Careful Dodger"><email>dodger@example.com</email></contact>
    <contact name="Eager Framer"><email>framer@example.com</email></contact>
  </contacts>
</xml>

<!-- These are just regular HTML elements -->
<table>
<tr><th>Name</th><th>Address</th></tr>
<!-- This is a template. Data comes from the data island with id "data". -->
<!-- The template will be expanded and copied once for each <contact> tag -->
<tr datasource="#data" foreach="//contact">
<!-- The "name" attribute of the <contact> is inserted into this element -->
<td data="@name"></td>
<!-- The content of the <email> child of the <contact> goes in here -->
<td data="email"></td>
</tr> <!-- end of the template -->
</table>
</body>
</html>
```

A critical piece of Example 21-12 is the onload event handler, which calls a function named XML.expandTemplates( ). Example 21-13 shows the implementation of this function. The code is fairly platform-independent, relying on basic Level 1 DOM functionality and on the XPath utility functions XML.getNode( ) and XML.getNodes( ) defined in Example 21-10.

Example 21-13. Expanding HTML templates

```
/*
 * Expand any templates at or beneath element e.
 * If any of the templates use XPath expressions with namespaces, pass
```

Example 21-13. Expanding HTML templates (continued)

```
 * a prefix-to-URL mapping as the second argument as with XML.XPathExpression( )
 *
 * If e is not supplied, document.body is used instead. A common
 * use case is to call this function with no arguments in response to an
 * onload event handler. This automatically expands all templates.
 */
XML.expandTemplates = function(e, namespaces) {
    // Fix up arguments a bit.
    if (!e) e = document.body;
    else if (typeof e == "string") e = document.getElementById(e);
    if (!namespaces) namespaces = null; // undefined does not work

    // An HTML element is a template if it has a "datasource" attribute.
    // Recursively find and expand all templates. Note that we don't
    // allow templates within templates.
    if (e.getAttribute("datasource")) {
        // If it is a template, expand it.
        XML.expandTemplate(e, namespaces);
    }
    else {
        // Otherwise, recurse on each of the children. We make a static
        // copy of the children first so that expanding a template doesn't
        // mess up our iteration.
        var kids = []; // To hold copy of child elements
        for(var i = 0; i < e.childNodes.length; i++) {
            var c = e.childNodes[i];
            if (c.nodeType == 1) kids.push(e.childNodes[i]);
        }

        // Now recurse on each child element
        for(var i = 0; i < kids.length; i++)
            XML.expandTemplates(kids[i], namespaces);
    }
};

/**
 * Expand a single specified template.
 * If the XPath expressions in the template use namespaces, the second
 * argument must specify a prefix-to-URL mapping
 */
XML.expandTemplate = function(template, namespaces) {
    if (typeof template=="string") template=document.getElementById(template);
    if (!namespaces) namespaces = null; // Undefined does not work

    // The first thing we need to know about a template is where the
    // data comes from.
    var datasource = template.getAttribute("datasource");

    // If the datasource attribute begins with '#', it is the name of
    // an XML data island. Otherwise, it is the URL of an external XML file.
    var datadoc;
    if (datasource.charAt(0) == '#')    // Get data island
```

Example 21-13. Expanding HTML templates (continued)

```
        datadoc = XML.getDataIsland(datasource.substring(1));
    else                                    // Or load external document
        datadoc = XML.load(datasource);


    // Now figure out which nodes in the datasource will be used to
    // provide the data. If the template has a foreach attribute,
    // we use it as an XPath expression to get a list of nodes. Otherwise,
    // we use all child elements of the document element.
    var datanodes;
    var foreach = template.getAttribute("foreach");
    if (foreach) datanodes = XML.getNodes(datadoc, foreach, namespaces);
    else {
        // If there is no "foreach" attribute, use the element
        // children of the documentElement
        datanodes = [];
        for(var c=datadoc.documentElement.firstChild; c!=null; c=c.nextSibling)
            if (c.nodeType == 1) datanodes.push(c);
    }


    // Remove the template element from its parent,
    // but remember the parent, and also the nextSibling of the template.
    var container = template.parentNode;
    var insertionPoint = template.nextSibling;
    template = container.removeChild(template);


    // For each element of the datanodes array, we'll insert a copy of
    // the template back into the container. Before doing this, though, we
    // expand any child in the copy that has a "data" attribute.
    for(var i = 0; i < datanodes.length; i++) {
        var copy = template.cloneNode(true);          // Copy template
        expand(copy, datanodes[i], namespaces);       // Expand copy
        container.insertBefore(copy, insertionPoint); // Insert copy
    }


    // This nested function finds any child elements of e that have a data
    // attribute. It treats that attribute as an XPath expression and
    // evaluates it in the context of datanode. It takes the text value of
    // the XPath result and makes it the content of the HTML node being
    // expanded. All other content is deleted.
    function expand(e, datanode, namespaces) {
        for(var c = e.firstChild; c != null; c = c.nextSibling) {
            if (c.nodeType != 1) continue;  // elements only
            var dataexpr = c.getAttribute("data");
            if (dataexpr) {
                // Evaluate XPath expression in context.
                var n = XML.getNode(datanode, dataexpr, namespaces);
                // Delete any content of the element
                c.innerHTML = "";
                // And insert the text content of the XPath result
                c.appendChild(document.createTextNode(getText(n)));
            }
            // If we don't expand the element, recurse on it.
```

Example 21-13. Expanding HTML templates (continued)

```
        else expand(c, datanode, namespaces);
      }
    }

    // This nested function extracts the text from a DOM node, recursing
    // if necessary.
    function getText(n) {
        switch(n.nodeType) {
        case 1: /* element */
            var s = "";
            for(var c = n.firstChild; c != null; c = c.nextSibling)
                s += getText(c);
            return s;
        case 2: /* attribute*/
        case 3: /* text */
        case 4: /* cdata */
            return n.nodeValue;
        default:
            return "";
        }
    }
};
```

21.7   XML and Web Services

Web services represent an important use for XML, and SOAP is a popular web service protocol that is entirely XML-based. In this section, I'll show you how to use the
XMLHttpRequest object and XPath queries to make a simple SOAP request to a web
service.

Example 21-14 is JavaScript code that constructs an XML document representing a
SOAP request and uses XMLHttpRequest to send it to a web service. (The web service
returns the conversion rate between the currencies of two countries.) The code then
uses an XPath query to extract the result from the SOAP response returned by the
server.

Before considering the code, here are some caveats. First, details on the SOAP protocol are beyond the scope of this chapter, and this example demonstrates a simple
SOAP request and SOAP response without any attempt to explain the protocol or
the XML format. Second, the example does not use Web Services Definition Language (WSDL) files to look up web service details. The server URL, method, and
parameter name are all hardcoded into the sample code.

The third caveat is a big one. The use of web services from client-side JavaScript is
severely constrained by the same-origin security policy (see Section 13.8.2). Recall that
the same-origin policy prevents client-side scripts from connecting to, or accessing

data from, any host other than the one from which the document that contains the script was loaded. This means that JavaScript code for accessing a web service is typically useful only if it is hosted on the same server as the web service itself. Web service implementors may want to use JavaScript to provide a simple HTML-based interface to their services, but the same-origin policy precludes the widespread use of client-side JavaScript to aggregate the results of web services from across the Internet onto a single web page.

In order to run Example 21-14 in IE, you can relax the same-origin security policy. Select **Tools** → **Internet Options** → **Security** and then click on the **Internet** tab in the resulting dialog. Scroll through the list of security options to find one named **Access data sources across domains**. This option is usually (and should be) set to **disabled**. In order to run this example, change it to **prompt**.

To allow Example 21-14 to run in Firefox, the example includes a call to the Firefox-specific enablePrivilege( ) method. This call prompts the user to grant enhanced privileges to the script so that it can override the same-origin policy. This works when the example is run from a file: URL in the local filesystem but does not work if the example is downloaded from a web server (unless the script has been digitally signed, which is beyond the scope of this book).

With those caveats out of the way, let's move on to the code.

Example 21-14. Querying a web service with SOAP

```
/**
 * This function returns the exchange rate between the currencies of two
 * countries. It determines the exchange rate by making a SOAP request to a
 * demonstration web service hosted by XMethods (http://www.xmethods.net).
 * The service is for demonstration only and is not guaranteed to be
 * responsive, available, or to return accurate data. Please do not
 * overload XMethod's servers by running this example too often.
 * See http://www.xmethods.net/v2/demoguidelines.html
 */
function getExchangeRate(country1, country2) {
    // In Firefox, we must ask the user to grant the privileges we need to run.
    // We need special privileges because we're talking to a web server other
    // than the one that served the document that contains this script. UniversalXPConnect
    // allows us to make an XMLHttpRequest to the server, and
    // UniversalBrowserRead allows us to look at its response.
    // In IE, the user must instead enable "Access data sources across domains"
    // in the Tools->Internet Options->Security dialog.
    if (typeof netscape != "undefined") {
        netscape.security.PrivilegeManager.
                enablePrivilege("UniversalXPConnect UniversalBrowserRead");
    }

    // Create an XMLHttpRequest to issue the SOAP request. This is a utility
    // function defined in the last chapter.
```

Example 21-14. Querying a web service with SOAP (continued)

```
    var request = HTTP.newRequest( );

    // We're going to be POSTing to this URL and want a synchronous response
    request.open("POST", "http://services.xmethods.net/soap", false);

    // Set some headers: the body of this POST request is XML
    request.setRequestHeader("Content-Type", "text/xml");

    // This header is a required part of the SOAP protocol
    request.setRequestHeader("SOAPAction", '""');

    // Now send an XML-formatted SOAP request to the server
    request.send(
        '<?xml version="1.0" encoding="UTF-8"?>' +
        '<soap:Envelope' +
        '   xmlns:ex="urn:xmethods-CurrencyExchange"' +
        '   xmlns:soap="http://schemas.xmlsoap.org/soap/envelope/"' +
        '   xmlns:soapenc="http://schemas.xmlsoap.org/soap/encoding/"' +
        '   xmlns:xs="http://www.w3.org/2001/XMLSchema"' +
        '   xmlns:xsi="http://www.w3.org/2001/XMLSchema-instance">' +
        '   <soap:Body ' +
        '     soap:encodingStyle="http://schemas.xmlsoap.org/soap/encoding/">'+
        '       <ex:getRate>' +
        '           <country1 xsi:type="xs:string">' + country1 + '</country1>' +
        '           <country2 xsi:type="xs:string">' + country2 + '</country2>' +
        '       </ex:getRate>' +
        '   </soap:Body>' +
        '</soap:Envelope>'
    );

    // If we got an HTTP error, throw an exception
    if (request.status != 200) throw request.statusText;

    // This XPath query gets us the <getRateResponse> element from the document
    var query = "/s:Envelope/s:Body/ex:getRateResponse";

    // This object defines the namespaces used in the query
    var namespaceMapping = {
        s:  "http://schemas.xmlsoap.org/soap/envelope/",  // SOAP namespace
        ex: "urn:xmethods-CurrencyExchange" // the service-specific namespace
    };

    // Extract the <getRateResponse> element from the response document
    var responseNode=XML.getNode(request.responseXML, query, namespaceMapping);

    // The actual result is contained in a text node within a <Result> node
    // within the <getRateReponse>
    return responseNode.firstChild.firstChild.nodeValue;
}
```

21.8 E4X: ECMAScript for XML

ECMAScript for XML, better known as E4X, is a standard extension[*] to JavaScript that defines a number of powerful features for processing XML documents. At the time of this writing, E4X is not widely available. Firefox 1.5 supports it, and it is also available in version 1.6 of Rhino, the Java-based JavaScript interpreter. Microsoft does not plan to support it in IE 7, and it is not clear when or whether other browsers will add support.

Although it is an official standard, E4X is not yet widely enough deployed to warrant full coverage in this book. Despite its limited availability, though, the powerful and unique features of E4X deserve some coverage. This section presents an overview-by-example of E4X. Future editions of this book may expand the coverage.

The most striking thing about E4X is that XML syntax becomes part of the JavaScript language, and you can include XML literals like these directly in your JavaScript code:

```
// Create an XML object
var pt =
    <periodictable>
      <element id="1"><name>Hydrogen</name></element>
      <element id="2"><name>Helium</name></element>
      <element id="3"><name>Lithium</name></element>
    </periodictable>;

// Add a new element to the table
pt.element += <element id="4"><name>Beryllium</name></element>;
```

The XML literal syntax of E4X uses curly braces as escape characters that allow you to place JavaScript expressions within XML. This, for example, is another way to create the XML element just shown:

```
pt = <periodictable></periodictable>;             // Start with empty table
var elements = ["Hydrogen", "Helium", "Lithium"]; // Elements to add
// Create XML tags using array contents
for(var n = 0; n < elements.length; n++) {
    pt.element += <element id={n+1}><name>{elements[n]}</name></element>;
}
```

In addition to this literal syntax, you can also work with XML parsed from strings. The following code adds another element to your periodic table:

```
pt.element += new XML('<element id="5"><name>Boron</name></element>');
```

When working with XML fragments, use XMLList( ) instead of XML( ):

```
pt.element += new XMLList('<element id="6"><name>Carbon</name></element>' +
                          '<element id="7"><name>Nitrogen</name></element>');
```

---

[*] E4X is defined by the ECMA-357 standard. You can find the official specification at *http://www.ecma-international.org/publications/standards/Ecma-357.htm*.

Once you have an XML document defined, E4X defines an intuitive syntax for accessing its content:

```
var elements = pt.element;     // Evaluates to a list of all <element> tags
var names = pt.element.name;   // A list of all <name> tags
var n = names[0];              // "Hydrogen": content of <name> tag 0.
```

E4X also adds new syntax for working with XML objects. The `..` operator is the descendant operator; you can use it in place of the normal `.` member-access operator:

```
// Here is another way to get a list of all <name> tags
var names2 = pt..name;
```

E4X even has a wildcard operator:

```
// Get all descendants of all <element> tags.
// This is yet another way to get a list of all <name> tags.
var names3 = pt.element.*;
```

Attribute names are distinguished from tag names in E4X using the @ character (a syntax borrowed from XPath). For example, you can query the value of an attribute like this:

```
// What is the atomic number of Helium?
var atomicNumber = pt.element[1].@id;
```

The wildcard operator for attribute names is `@*`:

```
// A list of all attributes of all <element> tags
var atomicNums = pt.element.@*;
```

E4X even includes a powerful and remarkably concise syntax for filtering a list using an arbitrary predicate:

```
// Start with a list of all elements and filter it so
// it includes only those whose id attribute is < 3
var lightElements = pt.element.(@id < 3);

// Start with a list of all <element> tags and filter so it includes only
// those whose names begin with "B". Then make a list of the <name> tags
// of each of those remaining <element> tags.
var bElementNames = pt.element.(name.charAt(0) == 'B').name;
```

E4X defines a new looping statement for iterating through lists of XML tags and attributes. The for/each/in loop is like the for/in loop, except that instead of iterating through the properties of an object, it iterates through the values of the properties of an object:

```
// Print the names of each element in the periodic table
// (Assuming you have a print() function defined.)
for each (var e in pt.element) {
    print(e.name);
}

// Print the atomic numbers of the elements
for each (var n in pt.element.@*) print(n);
```

In E4X-enabled browsers, this for/each/in loop is also useful for iterating through arrays.

E4X expressions can appear on the left side of an assignment. This allows existing tags and attributes to be changed and new tags and attributes to be added:

```
// Modify the <element> tag for Hydrogen to add a new attribute
// and a new child element so that it looks like this:
//
// <element id="1" symbol="H">
//   <name>Hydrogen</name>
//   <weight>1.00794</weight>
// </element>
//
pt.element[0].@symbol = "H";
pt.element[0].weight = 1.00794;
```

Removing attributes and tags is also easy with the standard delete operator:

```
delete pt.element[0].@symbol; // delete an attribute
delete pt..weight;            // delete all <weight> tags
```

E4X is designed so that you can perform most common XML manipulations using language syntax. E4X also defines methods you can invoke on XML objects. Here, for example, is the insertChildBefore( ) method:

```
pt.insertChildBefore(pt.element[1],
            <element id="1"><name>Deuterium</name></element>);
```

Note that the objects created and manipulated by E4X expressions are XML objects. They are not DOM Node or Element objects and do not interoperate with the DOM API. The E4X standard defines an optional XML method domNode( ) that returns a DOM Node equivalent to the XML object, but this method is not implemented in Firefox 1.5. Similarly, the E4X standard says a DOM Node can be passed to the XML( ) constructor to obtain the E4X equivalent of the DOM tree. This feature is also unimplemented in Firefox 1.5, which restricts the utility of E4X for client-side JavaScript.

E4X is fully namespace-aware and includes language syntax and APIs for working with XML namespaces. For simplicity, though, the examples shown here have not illustrated this syntax.

CHAPTER 22
Scripted Client-Side Graphics

This chapter describes how to use JavaScript to manipulate graphics. It begins by explaining traditional JavaScript techniques for visual effects such as image rollovers (in which one static image is replaced by another when the mouse pointer moves over it). It then moves on to describe how to use JavaScript to draw your own graphics. Combining JavaScript with CSS allows you to draw horizontal and vertical lines and rectangles, which is sufficient for many kinds of "boxes and arrows" drawings, as well more complex graphics such as bar charts.

Next, the chapter covers vector-graphics technologies, which provide a far more powerful client-side drawing capability. The ability to dynamically generate sophisticated graphics on the client-side is important for several reasons:

- The code used to produce graphics on the client side is typically much smaller than the images themselves, creating a substantial bandwidth savings.

- Dynamically generating graphics from real-time data uses a lot of CPU cycles. Offloading this task to the client (which usually has CPU power to spare) reduces the load on the server, potentially saving on hardware costs.

- Generating graphics on the client is consistent with the Ajax application architecture in which servers provide data and clients manage the presentation of that data.

This chapter includes examples of five vector-graphics technologies that can be harnessed with client-side JavaScript:

- Scalable Vector Graphics, or SVG, is a W3C standard XML-based language for describing drawings. SVG is supported natively by Firefox 1.5 and is available in other browsers via plug-ins. Because SVG drawings are XML documents, they can be dynamically created in JavaScript.

- Vector Markup Language, or VML, is a Microsoft-only SVG alternative. It is not well known but has been available since Internet Explorer 5.5. Like SVG, VML is XML-based, and VML drawings can be dynamically created on the client.

- The HTML <canvas> tag provides an explicit JavaScript-based drawing API. It was introduced in Safari 1.3 and adopted by Firefox 1.5 and Opera 9.
- The Flash player is available as a plug-in in a large majority of web browsers. Flash 6 introduced a drawing API, and Flash 8 makes it very easy to use that API from client-side JavaScript.
- Finally, Java supports a powerful drawing API and is available in many web browsers through a plug-in from Sun Microsystems. As described in Chapters 12 and 23, JavaScript code can invoke methods of Java applets and, in Mozilla-based browsers, can even call Java methods in the absence of an applet. This ability to script Java allows client-side JavaScript code to use Java's sophisticated vector drawing API.

Before tackling these advanced drawing techniques, however, let's begin with the basics.

22.1 Scripting Images

Web pages include images that use the HTML <img> tag. Like all HTML elements, an <img> tag is part of the DOM and can therefore be scripted like any other element in a document. This section illustrates common techniques.

22.1.1 Images and the Level 0 DOM

Images were one of the first scriptable HTML elements, and the Level 0 DOM allows you to access them through the images[] array of the Document object. Each element of this array is an Image object that represents one <img> tag in the document. You can find complete documentation of the Image object in Part IV. Image objects can also be accessed with Level 1 DOM methods such as getElementById() and getElementsByTagName() (see Chapter 15).

The document.images[] array lists Image objects in the order in which they appear in the document. More usefully, however, it provides access to named images. If an <img> tag has a name attribute, the image can be retrieved using the name specified by that attribute. Consider this <img> tag, for example:

```
<img name="nextpage" src="nextpage.gif">
```

Assuming that no other <img> tag has the same value for its name attribute, the corresponding Image object is available as:

```
document.images.nextpage
```

or as:

```
document.images["nextpage"]
```

If no other tag (of any type) in the document shares the same `name` attribute, the Image object can even be accessed through a property of the document object itself:

```
document.nextpage
```

22.1.2 Traditional Image Rollovers

The main feature of the Image object is that its `src` property is read/write. You can read this property to obtain the URL from which an image was loaded, and, more importantly, you can set the `src` property to make the browser load and display a new image in the same space.

The ability to dynamically replace one image with another in an HTML document opens the door to any number of special effects, from animation to digital clocks that update themselves in real time. In practice, the most common use for image replacement is to implement image rollovers, in which an image changes when the mouse pointer moves over it. (To prevent jarring visual effects, the new image should be the same size as the original.) When you make images clickable by placing them inside your hyperlinks, rollover effects are a powerful way to invite the user to click on the image.* This simple HTML fragment displays an image within an `<a>` tag and uses JavaScript code in the `onmouseover` and `onmouseout` event handlers to create a rollover effect:

```
<a href="help.html"
    onmouseover="document.helpimage.src='images/help_rollover.gif';"
    onmouseout="document.helpimage.src='images/help.gif';">
<img name="helpimage" src="images/help.gif" border="0">
</a>
```

Note that in this code fragment, the `<img>` tag has a `name` attribute that makes it easy to refer to the corresponding Image object in the event handlers of the `<a>` tag. The `border` attribute prevents the browser from displaying a blue hyperlink border around the image. The event handlers of the `<a>` tag do all the work: they change the image that is displayed simply by setting the `src` property of the image to the URLs of the desired images. These event handers are placed on the `<a>` tag for the benefit of very old browsers that support those handlers only on specific tags, such as `<a>`. In virtually every browser deployed today, you can also put the event handlers on the `<img>` tag itself, which simplifies the image lookup. The event-handler code can then refer to the Image object with the `this` keyword:

```
<img src="images/help.gif"
    onmouseover="this.src='images/help_rollover.gif'"
    onmouseout="this.src='images/help.gif'">
```

---

* No discussion of image rollovers is complete without pointing out that they can also be implemented using the CSS `:hover` pseudoclass to apply different CSS background images to elements when the mouse "hovers" over them. Unfortunately, making CSS image rollovers work portably is difficult. In practice, `:hover` is more useful when applied to hyperlinks containing text, rather than images.

Image rollovers are strongly associated with clickability, so this `<img>` tag should still be enclosed in an `<a>` tag or given an `onclick` event handler.

22.1.3 Offscreen Images and Caching

In order to be viable, image rollovers and related effects need to be responsive. This means that you need some way to ensure that the necessary images are "prefetched" into the browser's cache. To force an image to be cached, you first create an Image object using the `Image( )` constructor. Next, load an image into it by setting the `src` property of this object to the desired URL. This image is not added to the document, so it does not become visible, but the browser nevertheless loads and caches the image data. Later, when the same URL is used for an onscreen image, it can be quickly loaded from the browser's cache, rather than slowly loaded over the network.

The image-rollover code fragment shown in the previous section did not prefetch the rollover image it used, so the user might notice a delay in the rollover effect the first time she moves the mouse over the image. To fix this problem, modify the code as follows:

```
<script>(new Image( )).src = "images/help_rollover.gif";</script>
<img src="images/help.gif"
    onmouseover="this.src='images/help_rollover.gif'"
    onmouseout="this.src='images/help.gif'">
```

22.1.4 Unobtrusive Image Rollovers

The image rollover code just shown requires one `<script>` tag and two JavaScript event-handler attributes to implement a single rollover effect. This is a perfect example of *obtrusive* JavaScript. Although it is common to see code that mixes presentation (HTML) with behavior (JavaScript) like this, it is better to avoid it when you can. Especially when, as in this case, the amount of JavaScript code is so large that it effectively obscures the HTML. As a start, Example 22-1 shows a function that adds a rollover effect to a specified `<img>` element.

Example 22-1. Adding a rollover effect to an image

```
/**
 * Add a rollover effect to the specified image, by adding event
 * handlers to switch the image to the specified URL while the
 * mouse is over the image.
 *
 * If the image is specified as a string, search for an image with that
 * string as its id or name attribute.
 *
 * This method sets the onmouseover and onmouseout event-handler properties
 * of the specified image, overwriting and discarding any handlers previously
 * set on those properties.
```

Example 22-1. Adding a rollover effect to an image (continued)

```
 */
function addRollover(img, rolloverURL) {
    if (typeof img == "string") {  // If img is a string,
        var id = img;               // it is an id, not an image
        img = null;                 // and we don't have an image yet.

        // First try looking the image up by id
        if (document.getElementById) img = document.getElementById(id);
        else if (document.all) img = document.all[id];

        // If not found by id, try looking the image up by name.
        if (!img) img = document.images[id];

        // If we couldn't find the image, do nothing and fail silently
        if (!img) return;
    }

    // If we found an element but it is not an <img> tag, we also fail
    if (img.tagName.toLowerCase() != "img") return;

    // Remember the original URL of the image
    var baseURL = img.src;

    // Preload the rollover image into the browser's cache
    (new Image()).src = rolloverURL;

    img.onmouseover = function() { img.src = rolloverURL; }
    img.onmouseout = function() { img.src = baseURL; }
}
```

The addRollover() function defined in Example 22-1 is not completely unobtrusive because in order to use it, you must still include a script in your HTML files that invokes the function. To achieve the goal of truly unobtrusive image rollovers, you need a way to indicate which images have rollovers and what the URL of the rollover image is, without resorting to JavaScript. One simple way to do so is to include a fake HTML attribute on the <img> tags. For example, you might code images that have rollover effects like this:

```
<img src="normalImage.gif" rollover="rolloverImage.gif">
```

With an HTML coding convention like this, you can easily locate all images that require rollover effects and set up those effects with the initRollovers() function defined in Example 22-2.

Example 22-2. Adding rollover effects unobtrusively

```
/**
 * Find all <img> tags in the document that have a "rollover"
 * attribute on them.  Use the value of this attribute as the URL of an
 * image to be displayed when the mouse passes over the image and set
 * appropriate event handlers to create the rollover effect.
```

Example 22-2. Adding rollover effects unobtrusively (continued)
```
 */
function initRollovers() {
    var images = document.getElementsByTagName("img");
    for(var i = 0; i < images.length; i++) {
        var image = images[i];
        var rolloverURL = image.getAttribute("rollover");
        if (rolloverURL) addRollover(image, rolloverURL);
    }
}
```

All that remains is to ensure that this `initRollovers()` method is invoked when the document has loaded. Code like the following should work in current browsers:

```
if (window.addEventListener)
    window.addEventListener("load", initRollovers, false);
else if (window.attachEvent)
    window.attachEvent("onload", initRollovers);
```

See Chapter 17 for a more complete discussion of `onload` handling.

Note that if you place the `addRollover()` function and the `initRollovers()` function in the same file as the event-handler registration code, you have a completely unobtrusive solution for image rollovers. Simply include the file of code with a `<script src=>` tag, and place rollover attributes on any `<img>` tags that need rollover effects.

If you don't want your HTML files to fail validation because you've added a nonstandard rollover attribute to your `<img>` tags, you can switch to XHTML and use XML namespaces for the new attribute. Example 22-3 shows a namespace-aware version of the `initRollovers()` function. Note, however, that this version of the function does not work in Internet Explorer 6 because that browser does not support the DOM methods that support namespaces.

Example 22-3. Initializing rollovers with XHTML and namespaces
```
/**
 * Find all <img> tags in the document that have a "ro:src"
 * attribute on them.  Use the value of this attribute as the URL of an
 * image to be displayed when the mouse passes over the image, and set
 * appropriate event handlers to create the rollover effect.
 * The ro: namespace prefix should be mapped to the URI
 * "http://www.davidflanagan.com/rollover"
 */
function initRollovers() {
    var images = document.getElementsByTagName("img");
    for(var i = 0; i < images.length; i++) {
        var image = images[i];
        var rolloverURL = image.getAttributeNS(initRollovers.xmlns, "src");
        if (rolloverURL) addRollover(image, rolloverURL);
    }
}
// This is a made-up namespace URI for our "ro:" namespace
initRollovers.xmlns = "http://www.davidflanagan.com/rollover";
```

22.1.5 Image Animations

Another reason to script the src property of an <img> tag is to perform an image animation in which an image is changed frequently enough that it approximates smooth motion. A typical application for this technique might be to display a series of weather maps that show the historical or forecast evolution of a storm system at hourly intervals over a two-day period.

Example 22-4 shows a JavaScript ImageLoop class for creating this kind of image animation. It demonstrates the same scripting of the src property and image prefetching techniques shown in Example 22-1. It also introduces the onload event handler of the Image object, which can determine when an image (or, in this case, a series of images) has finished loading. The animation code itself is driven by Window.setInterval() and is quite simple: simply increment the frame number and set the src property of the specified <img> tag to the URL of the next frame.

Here is a simple HTML file that uses this ImageLoop class:

```
<head>
<script src="ImageLoop.js"></script>
<script>
var animation =
    new ImageLoop("loop", 5,["images/0.gif", "images/1.gif", "images/2.gif",
                             "images/3.gif", "images/4.gif", "images/5.gif",
                             "images/6.gif", "images/7.gif", "images/8.gif"]);
</script>
</head>
<body>
<img id="loop" src="images/loading.gif">
<button onclick="animation.start()">Start</button>
<button onclick="animation.stop()">Stop</button>
</body>
```

The code in Example 22-4 is somewhat more complicated than you might expect because both the Image.onload event handler and the Window.setInterval() timer function invoke functions as functions rather than as methods. For this reason, the ImageLoop() constructor must define nested functions that know how to operate on the newly constructed ImageLoop.

Example 22-4. Image animations

```
/**
 * ImageLoop.js: An ImageLoop class for performing image animations
 *
 * Constructor Arguments:
 *   imageId:   the id of the <img> tag that will be animated
 *   fps:       the number of frames to display per second
 *   frameURLs: an array of URLs, one for each frame of the animation
 *
 * Public Methods:
 *   start():   start the animation (but wait for all frames to load first)
```

Example 22-4. Image animations (continued)

```
 *    stop( ):     stop the animation
 *
 * Public Properties:
 *    loaded:      true if all frames of the animation have loaded,
 *                 false otherwise
 */
function ImageLoop(imageId, fps, frameURLs) {
    // Remember the image id. Don't look it up yet since this constructor
    // may be called before the document is loaded.
    this.imageId = imageId;
    // Compute the time to wait between frames of the animation
    this.frameInterval = 1000/fps;
    // An array for holding Image objects for each frame
    this.frames = new Array(frameURLs.length);

    this.image = null;          // The <img> element, looked up by id
    this.loaded = false;        // Whether all frames have loaded
    this.loadedFrames = 0;      // How many frames have loaded
    this.startOnLoad = false;   // Start animating when done loading?
    this.frameNumber = -1;      // What frame is currently displayed
    this.timer = null;          // The return value of setInterval( )

    // Initialize the frames[] array and preload the images
    for(var i = 0; i < frameURLs.length; i++) {
        this.frames[i] = new Image( );      // Create Image object
        // Register an event handler so we know when the frame is loaded
        this.frames[i].onload = countLoadedFrames; // defined later
        this.frames[i].src = frameURLs[i]; // Preload the frame's image
    }

    // This nested function is an event handler that counts how many
    // frames have finished loading. When all are loaded, it sets a flag,
    // and starts the animation if it has been requested to do so.
    var loop = this;
    function countLoadedFrames( ) {
        loop.loadedFrames++;
        if (loop.loadedFrames == loop.frames.length) {
            loop.loaded = true;
            if (loop.startOnLoad) loop.start( );
        }
    }

    // Here we define a function that displays the next frame of the
    // animation. This function can't be an ordinary instance method because
    // setInterval( ) can only invoke functions, not methods. So we make
    // it a closure that includes a reference to the ImageLoop object.
    this._displayNextFrame = function( ) {
        // First, increment the frame number. The modulo operator (%) means
        // that we loop from the last to the first frame
        loop.frameNumber = (loop.frameNumber+1)%loop.frames.length;
        // Update the src property of the image to the URL of the new frame
        loop.image.src = loop.frames[loop.frameNumber].src;
```

Example 22-4. Image animations (continued)

```
    };
}

/**
 * This method starts an ImageLoop animation. If the frame images have not
 * finished loading, it instead sets a flag so that the animation will
 * automatically be started when loading completes
 */
ImageLoop.prototype.start = function( ) {
    if (this.timer != null) return;    // Already started
    // If loading is not complete, set a flag to start when it is
    if (!this.loaded) this.startOnLoad = true;
    else {
        // If we haven't looked up the image by id yet, do so now
        if (!this.image) this.image = document.getElementById(this.imageId);
        // Display the first frame immediately
        this._displayNextFrame( );
        // And set a timer to display subsequent frames
        this.timer = setInterval(this._displayNextFrame, this.frameInterval);
    }
};

/** Stop an ImageLoop animation */
ImageLoop.prototype.stop = function( ) {
    if (this.timer) clearInterval(this.timer);
    this.timer = null;
};
```

22.1.6 Other Image Properties

In addition to the onload event handler demonstrated in Example 22-4, the Image object supports two others. The onerror event handler is invoked when an error occurs during image loading, such as when the specified URL refers to corrupt image data. The onabort handler is invoked if the user cancels the image load (for example, by clicking the **Stop** button in the browser) before it has finished. For any image, one (and only one) of these handlers is called.

Each Image object also has a complete property. This property is false while the image is loading; it is changed to true once the image has loaded or once the browser has stopped trying to load it. In other words, the complete property becomes true after one of the three possible event handlers is invoked.

The other properties of the Image object simply mirror the attributes of the HTML <img> tag. In modern browsers, these properties are read/write, and you can use Java-Script to dynamically change the size of an image, causing the browser to stretch or shrink it.

22.2 Graphics with CSS

Cascading Style Sheets (CSS) is described in Chapter 16, where you learned how to script CSS styles to produce DHTML effects. CSS can also produce simple graphics: the background-color property "fills" a rectangle with a solid color, and the border property outlines a rectangle. Furthermore, more specific border properties such as border-left and border-top can be used to draw just a border on one side of a rectangle, which produces horizontal and vertical lines. On browsers that support the styles, these lines can even be dotted or dashed!

It's not much, but when combined with absolute positioning, these simple CSS rectangle and line primitives can produce diagrams such as those shown in Figures 22-1 and 22-2. The subsections that follow demonstrate how these figures were generated.

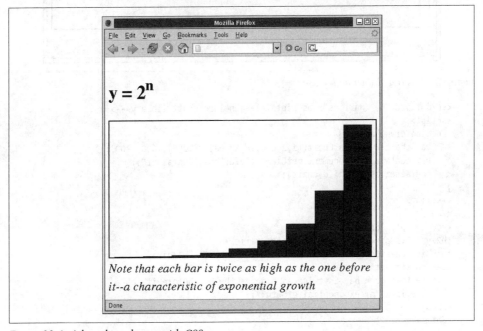

Figure 22-1. A bar chart drawn with CSS

22.2.1 Bar Charts with CSS

The bar chart in Figure 22-1 was created with the following HTML file:

```
<!DOCTYPE HTML PUBLIC "-//W3C//DTD HTML 4.01 Transitional//EN"
                "http://www.w3.org/TR/html4/loose.dtd">
<!-- The drawing won't look right in IE without a doctype like this -->
<html>
<head>
```

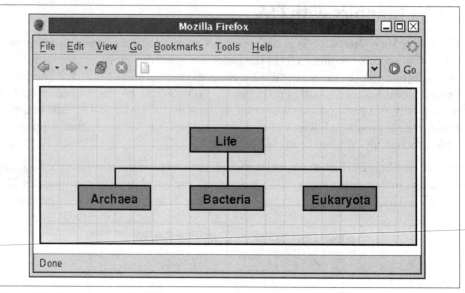

Figure 22-2. A tree drawn with CSS

```html
<script src="BarChart.js"></script> <!-- Include chart library -->
<script>
function drawChart() {
    var chart = makeBarChart([1,2,4,8,16,32,64,128,256], 600, 300);
    var container = document.getElementById("chartContainer");
    container.appendChild(chart);
}
</script>
</head>
<body onload="drawChart()">
<h2>y = 2<sup>n</sup></h2><!-- Chart title -->
<div id="chartContainer"><!-- Chart will go here --></div>
<!-- chart caption -->
<i>Note that each bar is twice as high as the one before it--a
characteristic of exponential growth</i>
</body>
</html>
```

Obviously, the interesting code is the makeBarChart( ) function, defined in the
BarChart.js file listed in Example 22-5.

Example 22-5. Drawing bar charts with CSS

```
/**
 * BarChart.js:
 * This file defines makeBarChart(), a function that creates a bar chart to
 * display the numbers from the data[] array. The overall size of the chart
 * is specified by the optional width and height arguments, which include the
 * space required for the chart borders and internal padding. The optional
 * barcolor argument specifies the color of the bars. The function returns the
```

Example 22-5. Drawing bar charts with CSS (continued)

```
 * <div> element it creates, so the caller can further manipulate it by
 * setting a margin size, for example. The caller must insert the returned
 * element into the document in order to make the chart visible.
 **/
function makeBarChart(data, width, height, barcolor) {
    // Provide default values for the optional arguments
    if (!width) width = 500;
    if (!height) height = 350;
    if (!barcolor) barcolor = "blue";

    // The width and height arguments specify the overall size of the
    // generated chart. We have to subtract the border and padding
    // sizes from this to get the size of the element we create.
    width -= 24;  // Subtract 10px padding and 2px border left and right
    height -= 14; // Subtract 10px top padding and 2px top and bottom border

    // Now create an element to hold the chart. Note that we make the chart
    // relatively positioned so that it can have absolutely positioned children
    // but still appear in the normal element flow.
    var chart = document.createElement("div");
    chart.style.position = "relative";        // Set relative positioning
    chart.style.width = width + "px";          // Set the chart width
    chart.style.height = height + "px";        // Set the chart height
    chart.style.border = "solid black 2px";    // Give it a border
    chart.style.paddingLeft = "10px";          // Add padding on the left
    chart.style.paddingRight = "10px";         // and on the right
    chart.style.paddingTop = "10px";           // and on the top
    chart.style.paddingBottom = "0px";         // but not on the bottom
    chart.style.backgroundColor = "white";     // Make chart background white

    // Compute the width of each bar
    var barwidth = Math.floor(width/data.length);
    // Find largest number in data[]. Note clever use of Function.apply().
    var maxdata = Math.max.apply(this, data);
    // The scaling factor for the chart: scale*data[i] gives height of a bar
    var scale = height/maxdata;

    // Now loop through the data array and create a bar for each datum
    for(var i = 0; i < data.length; i++) {
        var bar = document.createElement("div"); // Create div for bar
        var barheight = data[i] * scale;          // Compute height of bar
        bar.style.position = "absolute";          // Set bar position and size
        bar.style.left = (barwidth*i+1+10)+"px";  // Add bar border and chart pad
        bar.style.top = height-barheight+10+"px"; // Add chart padding
        bar.style.width = (barwidth-2) + "px";    // -2 for the bar border
        bar.style.height = (barheight-1) + "px";  // -1 for the bar top border
        bar.style.border = "solid black 1px";     // Bar border style
        bar.style.backgroundColor = barcolor;     // Bar color
        bar.style.fontSize = "0px";               // IE workaround
        chart.appendChild(bar);                    // Add bar to chart
    }
```

Example 22-5. Drawing bar charts with CSS (continued)

```
    // Finally, return the chart element so the caller can manipulate it
    return chart;
}
```

The code for Example 22-5 is straightforward and fairly simple to understand. It uses the techniques shown in Chapter 15 to create new <div> elements and add them to the document. In addition, it uses the techniques shown in Chapter 16 to set CSS style properties on the elements it creates. No text or other content is involved; the bar chart is simply a bunch of rectangles carefully sized and positioned within another rectangle. CSS border and background-color attributes make the rectangles visible. One critical piece of the code sets the style position:relative on the bar chart itself without setting the top or left styles. This setting allows the chart to remain in the normal document flow but also have children that are absolutely positioned relative to the upper-left corner of the chart. If the chart is not set to relative (or absolute) positioning, none of its bars will be positioned correctly.

Example 22-5 includes some simple math that computes the height in pixels of each bar based on the values of the data to be charted. The code that sets the position and size of the chart and of its bars also includes some simple arithmetic to account for the presence of borders and padding.

22.2.2 A CSSDrawing Class

The code in Example 22-5 is quite task-specific: it draws bar charts and nothing else. It is also quite possible to use CSS to draw more general diagrams, such as the tree shown in Figure 22-2, as long as they consist of boxes, horizontal lines, and vertical lines.

Example 22-6 is a CSSDrawing class that defines a simple API for drawing boxes and lines, and Example 22-7 is code that uses the CSSDrawing class to produce the figure shown in Figure 22-2.

Example 22-6. The CSSDrawing class

```
/**
 * This constructor function creates a div element into which a
 * CSS-based figure can be drawn. Instance methods are defined to draw
 * lines and boxes and to insert the figure into the document.
 *
 * The constructor may be invoked using two different signatures:
 *
 *    new CSSDrawing(x, y, width, height, classname, id)
 *
 * In this case a <div> is created using position:absolute at the
 * specified position and size.
 *
 * The constructor may also be invoked with only a width and height:
 *
```

Example 22-6. The CSSDrawing class (continued)

```
 *     new CSSDrawing(width, height, classname, id)
 *
 * In this case, the created <div> has the specified width and height
 * and uses position:relative (which is required so that the child
 * elements used to draw lines and boxes can use absolute positioning).
 *
 * In both cases, the classname and id arguments are optional. If specified,
 * they are used as the value of the class and id attributes of the created
 * <div> and can be used to associate CSS styles, such as borders with
 * the figure.
 */
function CSSDrawing(/* variable arguments, see above */) {
    // Create and remember the <div> element for the drawing
    var d = this.div = document.createElement("div");
    var next;

    // Figure out whether we have four numbers or two numbers, sizing and
    // positioning the div appropriately
    if (arguments.length >= 4 && typeof arguments[3] == "number") {
        d.style.position = "absolute";
        d.style.left = arguments[0] + "px";
        d.style.top = arguments[1] + "px";
        d.style.width = arguments[2] + "px";
        d.style.height = arguments[3] + "px";
        next = 4;
    }
    else {
        d.style.position = "relative"; // This is important
        d.style.width = arguments[0] + "px";
        d.style.height = arguments[1] + "px";
        next = 2;
    }

    // Set class and id attributes if they were specified.
    if (arguments[next]) d.className = arguments[next];
    if (arguments[next+1]) d.id = arguments[next+1];
}

/**
 * Add a box to the drawing.
 *
 * x, y, w, h:    specify the position and size of the box.
 * content:       a string of text or HTML that will appear in the box
 * classname, id: optional class and id values for the box. Useful to
 *                associate styles with the box for color, border, etc.
 * Returns: The <div> element created to display the box
 */
CSSDrawing.prototype.box = function(x, y, w, h, content, classname, id) {
    var d = document.createElement("div");
    if (classname) d.className = classname;
    if (id) d.id = id;
    d.style.position = "absolute";
```

Client-Side
JavaScript

Example 22-6. The CSSDrawing class (continued)

```
        d.style.left = x + "px";
        d.style.top = y + "px";
        d.style.width = w + "px";
        d.style.height = h + "px";
        d.innerHTML = content;
        this.div.appendChild(d);
        return d;
};

/**
 * Add a horizontal line to the drawing.
 *
 * x, y, width:    specify start position and width of the line
 * classname, id: optional class and id values for the box. At least one
 *                 must be present and must specify a border style which
 *                 will be used for the line style, color, and thickness.
 * Returns: The <div> element created to display the line
 */
CSSDrawing.prototype.horizontal = function(x, y, width, classname, id) {
        var d = document.createElement("div");
        if (classname) d.className = classname;
        if (id) d.id = id;
        d.style.position = "absolute";
        d.style.left = x + "px";
        d.style.top = y + "px";
        d.style.width = width + "px";
        d.style.height = 1 + "px";
        d.style.borderLeftWidth = d.style.borderRightWidth =
            d.style.borderBottomWidth = "0px";
        this.div.appendChild(d);
        return d;
};

/**
 * Add a vertical line to the drawing.
 * See horizontal() for details.
 */
CSSDrawing.prototype.vertical = function(x, y, height, classname, id) {
        var d = document.createElement("div");
        if (classname) d.className = classname;
        if (id) d.id = id;
        d.style.position = "absolute";
        d.style.left = x + "px";
        d.style.top = y + "px";
        d.style.width = 1 + "px";
        d.style.height = height + "px";
        d.style.borderRightWidth = d.style.borderBottomWidth =
            d.style.borderTopWidth = "0px";
        this.div.appendChild(d);
        return d;
};
```

Example 22-6. The CSSDrawing class (continued)

```
/** Add the drawing to the document as a child of the specified container */
CSSDrawing.prototype.insert = function(container) {
    if (typeof container == "string")
        container = document.getElementById(container);
    container.appendChild(this.div);
}

/** Add the drawing to the document by replacing the specified element */
CSSDrawing.prototype.replace = function(elt) {
    if (typeof elt == "string") elt = document.getElementById(elt);
    elt.parentNode.replaceChild(this.div, elt);
}
```

The CSSDrawing( ) constructor creates a new CSSDrawing object, which is nothing more than a wrapper around a <div> element. The box( ), vertical( ), and horizontal( ) instance methods use CSS to draw boxes, vertical lines, and horizontal lines, respectively. Each method allows you to specify the position and size of the box or line to draw and a class and/or an ID for the box or line element that is created. The class or ID allows you to associate CSS styles with the element to specify colors, line thicknesses, and so on. Creating a CSSDrawing object is not enough to make it visible. Use the insert( ) or replace( ) methods to add it to the document.

Example 22-7 shows how the CSSDrawing class might be used. Both the JavaScript code in the drawFigure( ) method and the CSS stylesheet are critical to the figure. The code defines the positions and sizes of the boxes and lines, and the stylesheet defines colors and line thicknesses. Notice that the JavaScript and CSS get entangled, and code in the drawFigure( ) method has to take border widths and padding sizes specified in the stylesheet into account. This is a shortcoming of the drawing API defined by the CSSDrawing class.

Example 22-7. Drawing a figure with the CSSDrawing class

```
<!DOCTYPE HTML PUBLIC "-//W3C//DTD HTML 4.01 Transitional//EN"
                    "http://www.w3.org/TR/html4/loose.dtd">
<!-- The drawing won't look right in IE without a doctype like this -->
<html>
<head>
<script src="CSSDrawing.js"></script> <!-- Include our drawing class -->
<style>
/* Styles for the figure box itself */
.figure { border: solid black 2px; background-color: #eee;}
/* Styles for grid lines */
.grid { border: dotted black 1px; opacity: .1; }
/* Styles for boxes in the figure */
.boxstyle {
    border: solid black 2px;
    background: #aaa;
    padding: 2px 10px 2px 10px;
    font: bold 12pt sans-serif;
```

Example 22-7. Drawing a figure with the CSSDrawing class (continued)

```
      text-align: center;
}
/* styles for line connecting the boxes */
.boldline { border: solid black 2px; }
</style>

<script>
// Draw a grid in the specfied rectangle with dx,dy line spacing
function drawGrid(drawing, x, y, w, h, dx, dy) {
    for(var x0 = x; x0 < x +w; x0 += dx)
        drawing.vertical(x0, y, h, "grid");
    for(var y0 = y; y0 < y + h; y0 += dy)
        drawing.horizontal(x, y0, w, "grid");
}

function drawFigure( ) {
    // Create a new figure
    var figure = new CSSDrawing(500, 200, "figure");

    // Add a grid to the drawing
    drawGrid(figure, 0, 0, 500, 200, 25, 25);

    // Draw four boxes in the figure
    figure.box(200, 50, 75, 25, "Life", "boxstyle");        // top box
    figure.box(50, 125, 75, 25, "Archaea", "boxstyle");     // line of 3
    figure.box(200, 125, 75, 25, "Bacteria", "boxstyle");   // ..boxes below
    figure.box(350, 125, 75, 25, "Eukaryota", "boxstyle");  // ..the top one

    // This line is drawn down from the bottom center of the top "Life" box.
    // The starting y position of this line is 50+25+2+2+2 or
    // y + height + top border + top padding + bottom padding + bottom border
    // Note that this computation requires knowledge of both the code and
    // the stylesheet, which is is not ideal.
    figure.vertical(250, 83, 20, "boldline");

    figure.horizontal(100, 103, 300, "boldline");  // line above 3 lower boxes
    figure.vertical(100, 103, 22, "boldline");      // connect to "archaea"
    figure.vertical(250, 103, 22, "boldline");      // connect to "bacteria"
    figure.vertical(400, 103, 22, "boldline");      // connect to "eukaryota"

    // Now insert the figure into the document, replacing the placeholder
    figure.replace("placeholder");
}
</script>
</head>
<body onload="drawFigure( )">
<div id="placeholder"></div>
</body>
</html>
```

22.3 SVG: Scalable Vector Graphics

SVG is an XML grammar for graphics. The word "vector" in its name indicates that it is fundamentally different from raster image formats such as GIF, JPEG, and PNG that specify a matrix of pixel values. Instead, an SVG "image" is a precise, resolution-independent (hence "scalable") description of the steps necessary to draw the desired graphic. Here is what a simple SVG image looks like in text format:

```
        <!-- Begin an SVG figure and declare our namespace -->
<svg xmlns="http://www.w3.org/2000/svg"
     viewBox="0 0 1000 1000">  <!-- Coordinate system for figure -->
    <defs>                <!-- Set up some definitions we'll use -->
      <linearGradient id="fade"> <!-- a color gradient named "fade" -->
        <stop offset="0%" stop-color="#008"/>    <!-- Start a dark blue -->
        <stop offset="100%" stop-color="#ccf"/> <!-- Fade to light blue -->
      </linearGradient>
    </defs>
    <!-- Draw a rectangle with a thick black border and fill it with the fade -->
    <rect x="100" y="200" width="800" height="600"
       stroke="black" stroke-width="25" fill="url(#fade)"/>
</svg>
```

Figure 22-3 shows what this SVG file looks like when rendered graphically.

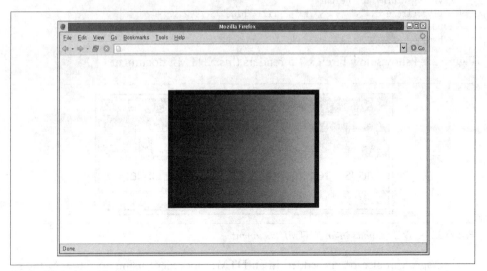

Figure 22-3. A simple SVG graphic

SVG is a large and moderately complex grammar. In addition to simple shape-drawing primitives, it includes support for arbitrary curves, text, and animation. SVG graphics can even incorporate JavaScript scripts and CSS stylesheets to add behavior and presentation information. This section shows how client-side JavaScript code (embedded in HTML, not in SVG) can dynamically draw graphics using SVG. It includes examples of SVG drawing but can only scratch the surface of what is possible with SVG. Full details about SVG are available in the comprehensive, but quite readable, specification. The specification is maintained by the W3C at *http://www. w3.org/TR/SVG/*. Note that this specification includes a complete Document Object Model for SVG documents. This section manipulates SVG graphics using the standard XML DOM and does not use the SVG DOM at all.

At the time of this writing, the only mainstream web browser to support SVG graphics natively is Firefox 1.5. In this browser, you can display an SVG graphic simply by typing the URL of the image you want to display. More usefully, SVG graphics can be embedded directly into an XHTML file, like this simple one:

```
<?xml version="1.0"?>
<!-- declare HTML as default namespace and SVG with "svg:" prefix -->
<html xmlns="http://www.w3.org/1999/xhtml"
      xmlns:svg="http://www.w3.org/2000/svg">
<body>
This is a red square: <!-- This is HTML text -->
<svg:svg width="10" height="10"> <!-- This is an SVG image -->
  <svg:rect x="0" y="0" width="10" height="10" fill="red"/></svg:svg>
This is a blue circle:
<svg:svg width="10" height="10">
  <svg:circle cx="5" cy="5" r="5" fill="blue"/></svg:svg>
</body>
</html>
```

Figure 22-4 shows how Firefox 1.5 renders this XHTML document.

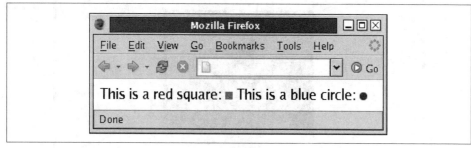

Figure 22-4. SVG graphics in an XHTML document

SVG images can also be embedded in an HTML document using an <object> tag so that they can be displayed using a plug-in. Adobe has a free (but not open source) SVG viewer plug-in that works with common browsers and operating systems. You can find it by following links from *http://www.adobe.com/svg*.

Since SVG is an XML grammar, drawing SVG graphics is simply a matter of using the DOM to create appropriate XML elements. Example 22-8 is a listing of a pieChart( ) function that creates the SVG elements to produce a pie chart like that shown in Figure 22-5. (The other vector-graphics technologies explored in this chapter will also be used to draw pie charts very similar to this one.)

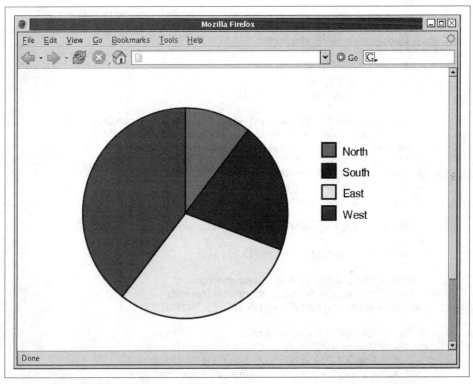

Figure 22-5. An SVG pie chart built with JavaScript

Example 22-8. Drawing a pie chart with JavaScript and SVG

```
/**
 * Draw a pie chart into an <svg> element.
 * Arguments:
 *   canvas: the SVG element (or the id of that element) to draw into
 *   data: an array of numbers to chart, one for each wedge of the pie
 *   cx, cy, r: the center and radius of the pie
 *   colors: an array of HTML color strings, one for each wedge
 *   labels: an array of labels to appear in the legend, one for each wedge
 *   lx, ly: the upper-left corner of the chart legend
 */
function pieChart(canvas, data, cx, cy, r, colors, labels, lx, ly) {
    // Locate canvas if specified by id instead of element
    if (typeof canvas == "string") canvas = document.getElementById(canvas);

    // Add up the data values so we know how big the pie is
    var total = 0;
    for(var i = 0; i < data.length; i++) total += data[i];
```

Example 22-8. Drawing a pie chart with JavaScript and SVG (continued)

```
    // Now figure out how big each slice of pie is. Angles in radians.
    var angles = []
    for(var i = 0; i < data.length; i++) angles[i] = data[i]/total*Math.PI*2;

    // Loop through each slice of pie.
    startangle = 0;
    for(var i = 0; i < data.length; i++) {
        // This is where the wedge ends
        var endangle = startangle + angles[i];

        // Compute the two points where our wedge intersects the circle.
        // These formulas are chosen so that an angle of 0 is at 12 o'clock
        // and positive angles increase clockwise.
        var x1 = cx + r * Math.sin(startangle);
        var y1 = cy - r * Math.cos(startangle);
        var x2 = cx + r * Math.sin(endangle);
        var y2 = cy - r * Math.cos(endangle);

        // This is a flag for angles larger than than a half-circle
        var big = 0;
        if (endangle - startangle > Math.PI) big = 1;

        // We describe a wedge with an <svg:path> element
        // Notice that we create this with createElementNS( )
        var path = document.createElementNS(SVG.ns, "path");

        // This string holds the path details
        var d = "M " + cx + "," + cy +    // Start at circle center
            " L " + x1 + "," + y1 +       // Draw line to (x1,y1)
            " A " + r + "," + r +         // Draw an arc of radius r
            " 0 " + big + " 1 " +         // Arc details...
            x2 + "," + y2 +               // Arc goes to to (x2,y2)
            " Z";                         // Close path back to (cx,cy)
        // This is an XML element, so all attributes must be set
        // with setAttribute( ). We can't just use JavaScript properties
        path.setAttribute("d", d);                  // Set this path
        path.setAttribute("fill", colors[i]);       // Set wedge color
        path.setAttribute("stroke", "black");       // Outline wedge in black
        path.setAttribute("stroke-width", "2");     // 2 units thick
        canvas.appendChild(path);                   // Add wedge to canvas

        // The next wedge begins where this one ends
        startangle = endangle;

        // Now draw a little matching square for the key
        var icon = document.createElementNS(SVG.ns, "rect");
        icon.setAttribute("x", lx);                 // Position the square
        icon.setAttribute("y", ly + 30*i);
        icon.setAttribute("width", 20);             // Size the square
        icon.setAttribute("height", 20);
        icon.setAttribute("fill", colors[i]);       // Same fill color as wedge
        icon.setAttribute("stroke", "black");       // Same outline, too.
```

Example 22-8. Drawing a pie chart with JavaScript and SVG (continued)

```
        icon.setAttribute("stroke-width", "2");
        canvas.appendChild(icon);              // Add to the canvas

        // And add a label to the right of the rectangle
        var label = document.createElementNS(SVG.ns, "text");
        label.setAttribute("x", lx + 30);       // Position the text
        label.setAttribute("y", ly + 30*i + 18);
        // Text style attributes could also be set via CSS
        label.setAttribute("font-family", "sans-serif");
        label.setAttribute("font-size", "16");
        // Add a DOM text node to the <svg:text> element
        label.appendChild(document.createTextNode(labels[i]));
        canvas.appendChild(label);              // Add text to the canvas
    }
```

The code in Example 22-8 is relatively straightforward. There is a little math to convert the data being charted into pie-wedge angles. The bulk of the example, however, is DOM code that creates SVG elements and sets attributes on those elements. Note that since SVG uses a namespace, createElementNS( ) is used instead of createElement( ). The namespace constant SVG.ns is defined later in Example 22-9.

The most opaque part of this example is the code that draws the actual pie wedges. The tag used to display each wedge is <svg:path>. This SVG element describes arbitrary shapes comprised of lines and curves. The shape description is specified by the d attribute of the <svg:path> tag. The value of this attribute uses a compact grammar of letter codes and numbers that specify coordinates, angles, and other values. The letter M, for example, means "move to" and is followed by X and Y coordinates. The letter L means "line to" and draws a line from the current point to the coordinates that follow it. This example also uses the letter A to draw an arc. This letter is followed by seven numbers describing the arc. The precise details are not important here, but you can look them up in the specification at *http://www.w3.org/TR/SVG/*.

The code in Example 22-8 uses the constant SVG.ns to describe the SVG namespace. This constant and several SVG utility functions are defined in a separate *SVG.js* file, shown in Example 22-9.

Example 22-9. SVG utility code

```
// Create a namespace for our SVG-related utilities
var SVG = {};

// These are SVG-related namespace URLs
SVG.ns = "http://www.w3.org/2000/svg";
SVG.xlinkns = "http://www.w3.org/1999/xlink";

// Create and return an empty <svg> element.
// Note that the element is not added to the document.
// Note that we can specify the pixel size of the image as well as
// its internal coordinate system.
```

Example 22-9. SVG utility code (continued)

```
SVG.makeCanvas = function(id, pixelWidth, pixelHeight, userWidth, userHeight) {
    var svg = document.createElementNS(SVG.ns, "svg:svg");
    svg.setAttribute("id", id);
    // How big is the canvas in pixels
    svg.setAttribute("width", pixelWidth);
    svg.setAttribute("height", pixelHeight);
    // Set the coordinates used by drawings in the canvas
    svg.setAttribute("viewBox", "0 0 " + userWidth + " " + userHeight);
    // Define the XLink namespace that SVG uses
    svg.setAttributeNS("http://www.w3.org/2000/xmlns/", "xmlns:xlink",
                       SVG.xlinkns);
    return svg;
};


// Serialize the canvas element to a string and use this string
// in a data: URL for display in an <object> tag. This allows SVG
// to work in browsers that support the data: URL scheme and have an SVG
// plug-in installed.
SVG.makeDataURL = function(canvas) {
    // We don't bother with the IE serialization technique since it
    // doesn't support data: URLs
    var text = (new XMLSerializer()).serializeToString(canvas);
    var encodedText = encodeURIComponent(text);
    return "data:image/svg+xml," + encodedText;
};


// Create an <object> to display an SVG drawing using a data: URL
SVG.makeObjectTag = function(canvas, width, height) {
    var object = document.createElement("object"); // Create HTML <object> tag
    object.width = width;                          // Set size of object
    object.height = height;
    object.data = SVG.makeDataURL(canvas);         // SVG image as data: URL
    object.type = "image/svg+xml"                  // SVG MIME type
    return object;
}
```

The most important of the utility functions in the example is SVG.makeCanvas(). It uses DOM methods to create a new <svg> element that you can then use to draw SVG graphics. makeCanvas() allows you to specify both the size (in pixels) at which the SVG graphic is rendered and also the size of the internal coordinate system (or "user space") the drawing uses. (For example: when a drawing that is 1000×1000 in user space is rendered into a square that is 250×250 pixels, each unit in user space equals one quarter pixel.) makeCanvas() creates and returns an <svg> tag, but it does not insert it into the document. The calling code must do that.

The other two utility methods in Example 22-9 are used in browsers that display SVG graphics through a plug-in. SVG.makeDataURL() serializes the XML text of an <svg> tag and encodes it into a data: URL. SVG.makeObjectTag() goes one step further, creating an HTML <object> tag to embed an SVG graphic and then calling SVG.makeDataURL()

to set the data attribute of that tag. Like SVG.makeCanvas( ), the SVG.makeObjectTag( ) method returns the <object> tag but does not insert it into the document.

The SVG.makeObjectTag( ) works in browsers such as Firefox 1.0 that support the data: URL scheme, support namespace-aware DOM methods like document. createElementNS( ), and have an SVG plug-in installed. Note that they do not work in IE because that browser does not support data: URLs or createElementNS( ). In IE, an alternative approach to SVG drawing would be to build the SVG document through string manipulation rather than DOM method calls. The graphic can then be encoded using a javascript: URL instead of a data: URL.

I'll conclude this discussion of scripted SVG graphics with the HTML file that ties together the pieChart( ) function of Example 22-8 and the SVG utility methods of Example 22-9. The following code creates an SVG canvas, draws into it, and then inserts it into the document twice: once natively and once via an <object> tag:

```
<script src="SVG.js"></script>          <!-- Utility methods -->
<script src="svgpiechart.js"></script>   <!-- Pie chart drawing method -->
<script>
function init( ) {
    // Create an <svg> tag to draw into 600x400 resolution, rendered
    // at 300x200 pixels
    var canvas = SVG.makeCanvas("canvas", 300, 200, 600, 400);
    pieChart(canvas, [12, 23, 34, 45], 200, 200, 150,    // Canvas, data, size
             ["red", "blue", "yellow", "green"],          // Wedge colors
             ["North","South","East","West"], 400, 100);  // Legend info

    // Add the graphic directly to the document:
    document.body.appendChild(canvas);

    // Embed it with an <object> tag
    var object = SVG.makeObjectTag(canvas, 300, 200);
    document.body.appendChild(object);
}
// Run this function when the document finishes loading
window.onload = init;
</script>
```

22.4 VML: Vector Markup Language

VML is Microsoft's answer to SVG. Like SVG, VML is an XML grammar for describing drawings. VML is similar to SVG in many ways. Though not quite as extensive, VML provides a full set of drawing capabilities and is available natively in IE 5.5 and later. Microsoft (and several partner companies) submitted VML to the W3C for consideration as a standard, but this effort never went anywhere. The best documentation for VML is Microsoft's submission, still available at the W3C web site at *http://www.w3.org/TR/NOTE-VML*. Note that despite the presence of this document on the W3C site, it has never been standardized, and the implementation in IE is proprietary to Microsoft.

VML is a powerful technology that never really caught on. Because it is not widely used,* it has apparently never been carefully documented. Microsoft's own web sites typically point to their W3C submission as the authoritative source of documentation. Unfortunately, since this document was a preliminary submission, it never went through the careful review of the standardization process and remains incomplete in some parts and confusing in others. When working with VML, you may need to experiment with the IE implementation in order to create the drawings you want. That is a relatively minor caveat when you consider that VML is a powerful client-side vector-drawing engine, embedded in the web browser that still dominates the market.

VML is an XML dialect, distinct from HTML, but IE does not support true XHTML documents, and its DOM implementation does not support namespace-aware functions such as `document.createElementNS()`. IE makes VML work by using an HTML "behavior" (another IE-specific extension) to handle tags in the VML namespace. All HTML files that contain VML must first declare the namespace like this:

```
<html xmlns:v="urn:schemas-microsoft-com:vml">
```

Alternatively, this namespace declaration can be achieved in an IE-specific (and nonstandard) way like this:

```
<xml:namespace ns="urn:schemas-microsoft-com:vml" prefix="v"/>
```

Then you must specify how tags in that namespace are handled with this nonstandard bit of CSS:

```
<style>v\:* { behavior: url(#default#VML); }</style>
```

Once these pieces are in place, VML drawings can be freely intermixed with HTML, as in the following code that produces results much like the SVG figure of Figure 22-4:

```
<html xmlns:v="urn:schemas-microsoft-com:vml">
<head><style>v\:* { behavior: url(#default#VML); }</style></head>
<body>
This is a red square:<v:rect style="width:10px;height:10px;" fillcolor="red"/>
This is a blue circle:<v:oval style="width:10px;height:10px;" fillcolor="blue"/>
</body>
</html>
```

However, this chapter focuses on using client-side JavaScript to draw graphics dynamically. Example 22-10 shows how to create a pie chart using VML. The example is much like the SVG pie chart example, with the substitution of VML drawing primitives for SVG primitives. For simplicity, this example combines a `makeVMLCanvas()` function and `pieChart()` function with the code that invokes those functions to produce the chart. The output of this code is not shown here: it looks quite a bit like the SVG pie chart of Figure 22-5.

* Google Maps (*http://local.google.com*) is the only high-profile site I know of that uses VML.

Example 22-10. Drawing a pie chart with JavaScript and VML

```
<!-- HTML documents that use VML must declare a namespace for it -->
<html xmlns:v="urn:schemas-microsoft-com:vml">
<head>
<!-- This is how we associate VML behavior with the VML namespace -->
<style>v\:* { behavior: url(#default#VML); }</style>
<script>
/*
 * Create and return a VML <v:group> element in which VML drawing can be done.
 * Note that the returned element has not yet been added to the document.
 */
function makeVMLCanvas(id, pixelWidth, pixelHeight) {
    var vml = document.createElement("v:group");
    vml.setAttribute("id", id);
    vml.style.width = pixelWidth + "px";
    vml.style.height = pixelHeight + "px";
    vml.setAttribute("coordsize", pixelWidth + " " + pixelHeight);

    // Start with a white rectangle with a thin black outline.
    var rect = document.createElement("v:rect");
    rect.style.width = pixelWidth + "px";
    rect.style.height = pixelHeight + "px";
    vml.appendChild(rect);

    return vml;
}

/* Draw a pie chart in a VML canvas */
function pieChart(canvas, data, cx, cy, r, colors, labels, lx, ly) {
    // Get the canvas element if specified by id
    if (typeof canvas == "string") canvas = document.getElementById(canvas);

    // Add up the data values
    var total = 0;
    for(var i = 0; i < data.length; i++) total += data[i];

    // Figure out the size (in degrees) of each wedge
    var angles = []
    for(var i = 0; i < data.length; i++) angles[i] = data[i]/total*360;

    // Now loop through all the wedges
    // VML measures angles in degrees/65535 and goes
    // counterclockwise from 3 o'clock
    startangle = 90;   // Start at 12 o'clock.
    for(var i = 0; i < data.length; i++) {
        // Tweak the angles so that our pie goes clockwise from 12 o'clock.
        var sa = Math.round(startangle * 65535);
        var a = -Math.round(angles[i] * 65536);

        // Create a VML shape element
        var wedge = document.createElement("v:shape");
        // VML describes the shape of a path in a similar way to SVG
        var path = "M " + cx + " " + cy +     // Move to (cx,cy)
            " AE " + cx + " " + cy + " " +     // Arc with center at (cx,cy)
```

Example 22-10. Drawing a pie chart with JavaScript and VML (continued)

```
                r + " " + r + " " +                 // Horiz and vertical radii
                sa + " " + a +                       // Start angle and total angle
                " X E";                              // Close path to center and end
        wedge.setAttribute("path", path);            // Set wedge shape
        wedge.setAttribute("fillcolor", colors[i]);  // Set wedge color
        wedge.setAttribute("strokeweight", "2px");   // Outline width
        // Position the wedge using CSS styles. The coordinates of the
        // path are interpreted relative to this size, so we give each
        // shape the same size as the canvas itself.
        wedge.style.position = "absolute";
        wedge.style.width = canvas.style.width;
        wedge.style.height = canvas.style.height;

        // Add the wedge to the canvas
        canvas.appendChild(wedge);

        // Next wedge begins where this one ends
        startangle -= angles[i];

        // Create a VML <rect> element for the legend
        var icon = document.createElement("v:rect");
        icon.style.left = lx + "px";                 // CSS positioning
        icon.style.top = (ly+i*30) + "px";
        icon.style.width = "20px";                   // CSS size
        icon.style.height = "20px";
        icon.setAttribute("fillcolor", colors[i]);   // Same color as wedge
        icon.setAttribute("stroke", "black");        // Outline color
        icon.setAttribute("strokeweight", "2");      // Outline width
        canvas.appendChild(icon);                    // Add to canvas

        // VML has advanced text capabilities, but most text is simple
        // HTML and is added directly to the VML canvas, using
        // canvas coordinates
        var label = document.createElement("div");   // <div> to hold the text
        label.appendChild(document.createTextNode(labels[i]));  // the text
        label.style.position = "absolute";           // Position with CSS
        label.style.left = (lx + 30) + "px";
        label.style.top = (ly + 30*i + 5) + "px";
        label.style.fontFamily = "sans-serif";       // Text styles
        label.style.fontSize = "16px";
        canvas.appendChild(label);                   // Add text to canvas
    }
}

function init() {
    var canvas = makeVMLCanvas("canvas", 600, 400);
    document.body.appendChild(canvas);
    pieChart(canvas, [12, 23, 34, 45], 200, 200, 150,
            ["red", "blue", "yellow", "green"],
            ["North", "South", "East", "West"],
            400, 100);
}
</script>
```

Example 22-10. Drawing a pie chart with JavaScript and VML (continued)

```
</head>
<body onload="init( )">
</body>
</html>
```

22.5 Graphics in a <canvas>

The next stop in our tour of client-side vector-graphics technologies is the <canvas> tag. This nonstandard HTML element is explicitly designed for client-side vector graphics. It has no appearance of its own but exposes a drawing API to client-side JavaScript so that scripts can draw anything they want into a canvas. The <canvas> tag was introduced by Apple in the Safari 1.3 web browser. (The reason for this radical extension to HTML is that the HTML rendering capability of Safari is also used by the Dashboard component of the Mac OS X desktop, and Apple wanted a way to support scripted graphics in Dashboard.)

Firefox 1.5 and Opera 9 have followed Safari's lead. Both browsers also support the <canvas> tag. You can even use the <canvas> tag in IE, with open source JavaScript code (initially from Google) that builds canvas compatibility on top of IE's VML support. (see *http://excanvas.sourceforge.net*). Standardization efforts for the <canvas> tag are underway by an informal consortium of web browser manufacturers, and a preliminary specification can be found at *http://www.whatwg.org/specs/web-apps/current-work*.

An important difference between the <canvas> tag and SVG and VML is that <canvas> has a JavaScript-based drawing API while SVG and VML describe a drawing with an XML document. These two approaches are functionally equivalent: either one can be simulated with the other. On the surface, they are quite different, however, and each has its strengths and weaknesses. An SVG drawing, for example, is easily edited by removing elements from its description. To remove an element from the same graphic in a <canvas> tag, it is often necessary to erase the drawing and redraw it from scratch. Since the Canvas drawing API is JavaScript-based and relatively compact (unlike the SVG and VML grammars), it is documented in this book. See Canvas, CanvasRenderingContext2D, and related entries in Part IV.

Most of the Canvas drawing API is defined not on the <canvas> element itself but instead on a "drawing context" object obtained with the getContext( ) method of the canvas.* This script draws a small red square and blue circle and is typical for drawing to a canvas:

```
<head>
<script>
window.onload = function( ) {  // Do the drawing when the document loads
```

---

* This method requires a single argument that must be the string "2d" and returns a drawing context that implements a two-dimensional API. In the future, if the <canvas> tag is extended to support 3D drawing, the getContext( ) method will presumably allow you to pass the string "3d".

```
    var canvas = document.getElementById("square");   // Get canvas element
    var context = canvas.getContext("2d");            // Get 2D drawing context
    context.fillStyle = "#f00";                       // Set fill color to red
    context.fillRect(0,0,10,10);                      // Fill a square

    canvas = document.getElementById("circle");       // New canvas element
    context = canvas.getContext("2d");                // Get its context
    context.fillStyle = "#00f";                       // Set blue fill color
    context.beginPath();                              // Begin a shape
    // Add a complete circle of radius 5 centered at (5,5) to the shape
    context.arc(5, 5, 5, 0, 2*Math.PI, true);
    context.fill();                                   // Fill the shape
}
</script>
</head>
<body>
This is a red square: <canvas id="square" width=10 height=10></canvas>.
This is a blue circle: <canvas id="circle" width=10 height=10></canvas>.
</body>
```

In previous sections, you've seen that SVG and VML describe complex shapes as a "path" of lines and curves that can be drawn or filled. The Canvas API also uses the notion of a path. But instead of describing a path as a string of letters and numbers, a path is defined by a series of method calls, such as the beginPath( ) and arc( ) invocations in the example. Once a path is defined, other methods, such as fill( ), operate on that path. Various properties of the drawing context, such as fillStyle, specify how these operations are performed.

One reason the Canvas API can be so compact is that it does not provide any support for drawing text. To incorporate text into a <canvas> graphic, you must either draw it yourself, incorporate it with bitmap images, or overlay HTML text on top of the <canvas> with CSS positioning.

Example 22-11 shows how to draw pie charts using a canvas. Much of the code in this example will be familiar from the SVG and VML examples. The new code in the example is the Canvas API, and you can look up those methods in Part IV.

Example 22-11. Drawing a pie chart in a <canvas> tag

```
<html>
<head>
<script>
// Create and return a new canvas tag with the specified id and size.
// Note that this method does not add the canvas to the document
function makeCanvas(id, width, height) {
    var canvas = document.createElement("canvas");
    canvas.id = id;
    canvas.width = width;
    canvas.height = height;
    return canvas;
}
```

Example 22-11. Drawing a pie chart in a <canvas> tag (continued)

```
/**
 * Draw a pie chart in the canvas specified by element or id.
 * Data is an array of numbers: each number represents a wedge of the chart.
 * The pie chart is centered at (cx, cy) and has radius r.
 * The colors of the wedges are HTML color strings in the colors[] array.
 * A legend appears at (lx,ly) to associate the labels in the labels[]
 * array with each of the colors.
 */
function pieChart(canvas, data, cx, cy, r, colors, labels, lx, ly) {
    // Get the canvas if specified by id
    if (typeof canvas == "string") canvas = document.getElementById(canvas);

    // We draw with the canvas's drawing context
    var g = canvas.getContext("2d");

    // All the lines we draw are 2-pixel-wide black lines
    g.lineWidth = 2;
    g.strokeStyle = "black";

    // Total the data values
    var total = 0;
    for(var i = 0; i < data.length; i++) total += data[i];

    // And compute the angle (in radians) for each one
    var angles = []
    for(var i = 0; i < data.length; i++) angles[i] = data[i]/total*Math.PI*2;

    // Now, loop through the wedges of the pie
    startangle = -Math.PI/2;  // Start at 12 o'clock instead of 3 o'clock
    for(var i = 0; i < data.length; i++) {
        // This is the angle where the wedge ends
        var endangle = startangle + angles[i];

        // Draw a wedge
        g.beginPath();              // Start a new shape
        g.moveTo(cx,cy);            // Move to center
        // Line to startangle point and arc to endangle
        g.arc(cx,cy,r,startangle, endangle, false);
        g.closePath();              // Back to center and end shape
        g.fillStyle = colors[i];    // Set wedge color
        g.fill();                   // Fill the wedge
        g.stroke();                 // Outline ("stroke") the wedge

        // The next wedge starts where this one ends.
        startangle = endangle;

        // Draw the rectangle in the legend for this wedge
        g.fillRect(lx, ly+30*i, 20, 20);
        g.strokeRect(lx, ly+30*i, 20, 20);

        // And put a label next to the rectangle.
        // The Canvas API does not support text, so we just do
        // ordinary html text here. We use CSS positioning to put the text
```

Example 22-11. Drawing a pie chart in a <canvas> tag (continued)

```
            // in the right spot on top of the Canvas element. This would be
            // a little cleaner if the canvas tag itself were absolutely positioned
            var label = document.createElement("div");
            label.style.position = "absolute";
            label.style.left = (canvas.offsetLeft + lx+30)+"px";
            label.style.top = (canvas.offsetTop+ly+30*i-4) + "px";
            label.style.fontFamily = "sans-serif";
            label.style.fontSize = "16px";
            label.appendChild(document.createTextNode(labels[i]));
            document.body.appendChild(label);
        }
    }

function init() {
    // Create a canvas element
    var canvas = makeCanvas("canvas", 600, 400);
    // Add it to the document
    document.body.appendChild(canvas);
    // And draw a pie chart in it
    pieChart("canvas", [12, 23, 34, 45], 200, 200, 150,
            ["red", "blue", "yellow", "green"],
            ["North", "South", "East", "West"],
            400, 100);
}
</script>
</head>
<body onload="init()"></body>
</html>
```

22.6   Graphics with Flash

Each vector-graphics technology discussed so far in this chapter has limited availability: the <canvas> tag is only in Safari 1.3, Firefox 1.5, and Opera 9, VML is (and will always be) IE-only, and SVG is supported natively only in Firefox 1.5. Plug-in support for SVG is available, but the plug-in is not widely installed.

One powerful vector-graphics plug-in *is* widely (almost universally) installed, however: the Flash player from Adobe (formerly Macromedia). The Flash player has its own scripting language, called ActionScript (actually a dialect of JavaScript). Since Flash 6, the player has exposed a simple but powerful drawing API to ActionScript code. Flash 6 and 7 also provide limited communication channels between client-side JavaScript and ActionScript, making it possible for client-side JavaScript to send drawing commands to the Flash plug-in to be executed by the plug-in's ActionScript interpreter.

This chapter relies on Flash 8, which is brand new at the time of this writing. Flash 8 includes an ExternalInterface API that makes it trivial to export ActionScript methods so that they can be transparently invoked by client-side JavaScript. Chapter 23 illustrates how Flash drawing methods can be invoked in Flash 6 and 7.

To create a Flash-based drawing canvas, you need a *.swf* file that does no drawing of its own but just exports a drawing API to client-side JavaScript.[*] Let's begin with the ActionScript file shown in Example 22-12.

Example 22-12. Canvas.as

```
import flash.external.ExternalInterface;

class Canvas {
    // The open source mtasc ActionScript compiler automatically invokes
    // this main() method in the compiled .swf file it produces. If you use
    // the Flash IDE to create a Canvas.swf file, you'll need to call
    // Canvas.main() from the first frame of the movie instead.
    static function main() { var canvas = new Canvas(); }

    // This constructor contains initialization code for our Flash Canvas
    function Canvas() {
        // Specify resize behavior for the canvas
        Stage.scaleMode = "noScale";
        Stage.align = "TL";

        // Now simply export the functions of the Flash drawing API
        ExternalInterface.addCallback("beginFill", _root, _root.beginFill);
        ExternalInterface.addCallback("beginGradientFill", _root,
                                      _root.beginGradientFill);
        ExternalInterface.addCallback("clear", _root, _root.clear);
        ExternalInterface.addCallback("curveTo", _root, _root.curveTo);
        ExternalInterface.addCallback("endFill", _root, _root.endFill);
        ExternalInterface.addCallback("lineTo", _root, _root.lineTo);
        ExternalInterface.addCallback("lineStyle", _root, _root.lineStyle);
        ExternalInterface.addCallback("moveTo", _root, _root.moveTo);

        // Also export the addText() function below
        ExternalInterface.addCallback("addText", null, addText);
    }

    static function addText(text, x, y, w, h, depth, font, size) {
        // Create a TextField object to display text at the specified location
        var tf = _root.createTextField("tf", depth, x, y, w, h);
        // Tell it what text to display
        tf.text = text;
        // Set the font family and point size for the text
        var format = new TextFormat();
        format.font = font;
        format.size = size;
        tf.setTextFormat(format);
    }
}
```

[*] The Flash-based pie chart code in Example 22-13 uses this Flash drawing API, but I don't document it here. You can find documentation at the Adobe web site.

The ActionScript code shown in the *Canvas.as* file of Example 22-12 must be compiled into a *Canvas.swf* file before it can be used with the Flash player. Details on doing this are beyond the scope of this book, but you can use a commercial Flash IDE from Adobe or an open source ActionScript compiler.*

Unfortunately, Flash offers only a low-level API. In particular, the only function for drawing curves is curveTo( ), which draws a quadratic Bezier curve. All circles, ellipses, and cubic Bezier curves must be approximated with simpler quadratic curves. This low-level API is well-suited to the compiled SWF Flash format: all the computation required for more complex curves can be done at compilation time, and the Flash player need only know how to draw simpler curves. A higher-level drawing API can be built on top of the primitives provided by the Flash player, and it's possible to do this in ActionScript or in JavaScript (Example 22-13 is in JavaScript).

Example 22-13 begins with a utility function for embedding the *Canvas.swf* file into the HTML document. This is done differently in different browsers, and the insertCanvas( ) utility simplifies things. Next comes a wedge( ) function, which uses the simple Flash drawing API to draw a wedge of the pie chart. The pieChart( ) function follows and calls wedge( ) to draw its slices of pie. Finally, the example defines an onload handler to insert the Flash canvas into the document and draw into it.

Example 22-13. Drawing a pie chart with JavaScript and Flash

```
<html>
<head>
<script>
// Embed a Flash canvas of the specified size, inserting it as the sole
// child of the specified container element. For portability, this function
// uses an <embed> tag in Netscape-style browsers and an <object> tag in others
// Inspired by FlashObject from Geoff Stearns.
// See http://blog.deconcept.com/flashobject/
function insertCanvas(containerid, canvasid, width, height) {
    var container = document.getElementById(containerid);
    if (navigator.plugins && navigator.mimeTypes&&navigator.mimeTypes.length){
        container.innerHTML =
            "<embed src='Canvas.swf' type='application/x-shockwave-flash' " +
            "width='" + width +
            "' height='" + height +
            "' bgcolor='#ffffff' " +
            "id='" + canvasid +
            "' name='" + canvasid +
            "'>";
    }
    else {
        container.innerHTML =
```

---

* I used the open source *mtasc* compiler (*http://www.mtasc.org*) and compiled the code with this command:

    mtasc -swf Canvas.swf -main -version 8 -header 500:500:1 Canvas.as

After compilation, the resulting *Canvas.swf* file is a mere 578 bytes long—smaller than most bitmap images.

Example 22-13. Drawing a pie chart with JavaScript and Flash (continued)

```
                "<object classid='clsid:D27CDB6E-AE6D-11cf-96B8-444553540000' "+
                "width='" + width +
                "' height='" + height +
                "' id='"+ canvasid + "'>" +
                "  <param name='movie' value='Canvas.swf'>" +
                "  <param name='bgcolor' value='#ffffff'>" +
                "</object>";
    }
}

// The Flash drawing API is lower-level than others, with only a simple
// bezier-curve primitive. This method draws a pie wedge using that API.
// Note that angles must be specified in radians.
function wedge(canvas, cx, cy, r, startangle, endangle, color) {
    // Figure out the starting point of the wedge
    var x1 = cx + r*Math.sin(startangle);
    var y1 = cy - r*Math.cos(startangle);

    canvas.beginFill(color, 100); // Fill with specified color, fully opaque
    canvas.moveTo(cx, cy);        // Move to center of circle
    canvas.lineTo(x1, y1);        // Draw a line to the edge of the circle

    // Now break the arc into pieces < 45 degrees and draw each
    // with a separate call to the nested arc() method
    while(startangle < endangle) {
        var theta;
        if (endangle-startangle > Math.PI/4) theta = startangle+Math.PI/4;
        else theta = endangle;
        arc(canvas,cx,cy,r,startangle,theta);
        startangle += Math.PI/4;
    }

    canvas.lineTo(cx, cy);        // Finish with a line back to the center
    canvas.endFill();             // Fill the wedge we've outlined

    // This nested function draws a portion of a circle using a Bezier curve.
    // endangle-startangle must be <= 45 degrees.
    // The current point must already be at the startangle point.
    // You can take this on faith if you don't understand the math.
    function arc(canvas, cx, cy, r, startangle, endangle) {
        // Compute end point of the curve
        var x2 = cx + r*Math.sin(endangle);
        var y2 = cy - r*Math.cos(endangle);

        var theta = (endangle - startangle)/2;
        // This is the distance from the center to the control point
        var l = r/Math.cos(theta);
        // angle from center to control point is:
        var alpha = (startangle + endangle)/2;

        // Compute the control point for the curve
        var controlX = cx + l * Math.sin(alpha);
```

Example 22-13. Drawing a pie chart with JavaScript and Flash (continued)

```
        var controlY = cy - l * Math.cos(alpha);

        // Now call the Flash drawing API to draw the arc as a Bezier curve.
        canvas.curveTo(controlX, controlY, x2, y2);
    }
}

/**
 * Draw a pie chart in the Flash canvas specified by element or id.
 * data is an array of numbers: each number corresponds to a wedge of the chart.
 * The pie chart is centered at (cx, cy) and has radius r.
 * The colors of the wedges are Flash color values in the colors[] array.
 * A legend appears at (lx,ly) to associate the labels in the labels[]
 * array with each of the colors.
 */
function pieChart(canvas, data, cx, cy, r, colors, labels, lx, ly) {
    // Get the canvas if specified by id
    if (typeof canvas == "string")
        canvas = document.getElementById(canvas);

    // All the lines we draw are 2 pixels wide, black, and 100% opaque.
    canvas.lineStyle(2, 0x000000, 100);

    // Figure out the total of the data values
    var total = 0;
    for(var i = 0; i < data.length; i++) total += data[i];

    // And compute the angle (in radians) for each one.
    var angles = []
    for(var i = 0; i < data.length; i++) angles[i] = data[i]/total*Math.PI*2;

    // Now, loop through the wedges of the pie
    startangle = 0;
    for(var i = 0; i < data.length; i++) {
        // This is the angle where the wedge ends
        var endangle = startangle + angles[i];

        // Draw a wedge: this function is defined earlier
        wedge(canvas, cx, cy, r, startangle, endangle, colors[i]);

        // The next wedge starts where this one ends.
        startangle = endangle;

        // Draw a box for the legend
        canvas.beginFill(colors[i], 100);
        canvas.moveTo(lx, ly+30*i);
        canvas.lineTo(lx+20, ly+30*i);
        canvas.lineTo(lx+20, ly+30*i+20);
        canvas.lineTo(lx, ly+30*i+20);
        canvas.lineTo(lx, ly+30*i);
        canvas.endFill();
```

Example 22-13. Drawing a pie chart with JavaScript and Flash (continued)

```
        // Add text next to the box
        canvas.addText(labels[i], lx+30, ly+i*30, 100, 20, // Text and position
                       i, // each text field must have a different depth
                       "Helvetica", 16);                    // Font info
    }
}

// When the document loads, insert a Flash canvas and draw on it
// Note that colors in Flash are integers instead of strings
window.onload = function( ) {
    insertCanvas("placeholder", "canvas", 600, 400);
    pieChart("canvas", [12, 23, 34, 45], 200, 200, 150,
             [0xff0000, 0x0000ff, 0xffff00, 0x00ff00],
             ["North", "South", "East", "West"],
             400, 100);
}
</script>
</head>
<body>
<div id="placeholder"></div>
</body>
</html>
```

22.7 Graphics with Java

The Java plug-in from Sun Microsystems is not as widely deployed as the Flash plug-in is, but it is becoming more and more common, and some computer manufacturers are preinstalling it on their hardware. The Java2D API is a powerful vector-drawing API. It has been around since Java 1.2, is higher-level and easier to use than the Flash drawing API, and is more extensive (supporting text, for example) than the <canvas> API. In terms of features, Java2D is most similar to SVG. This section demonstrates two useful ways to use the Java2D API from client-side JavaScript.

22.7.1 Pie Charts with Java

You can take the same approach with Java as with Flash: create a "Canvas" applet that has no behavior of its own but exists simply to export the Java2D API so that it can be invoked by client-side JavaScript. (See Chapter 23 for more on scripting Java from JavaScript.) Such an applet might look like the one shown in Example 22-14. Note that this applet only scratches the surface of the Java2D API and exposes a bare-minimum number of methods. The Flash drawing API consisted of eight simple methods, and it was easy to export them all. Java2D has many more methods, and while it is not technically difficult to make them all available through a Canvas applet, such an applet would be too long to list here. The code in Example 22-14 shows a basic approach and provides a rich-enough API for the pie chart in Figure 22-5.

Example 22-14. A Java canvas applet for client-side drawing

```java
import java.applet.*;
import java.awt.*;
import java.awt.geom.*;
import java.awt.image.*;

/**
 * This simple applet does nothing by itself: it simply exports an API
 * for the use of client-side JavaScript code.
 */
public class Canvas extends Applet {
    BufferedImage image;  // We draw into this offscreen image
    Graphics2D g;         // using this graphics context

    // The browser calls this method to initialize the applet
    public void init() {
        // Find out how big the applet is and create an offscreen image
        // that size.
        int w = getWidth();
        int h = getHeight();
        image = new BufferedImage(w, h, BufferedImage.TYPE_INT_RGB);
        // Get a graphics context for drawing into the image
        g = image.createGraphics();
        // Start with a pure white background
        g.setPaint(Color.WHITE);
        g.fillRect(0, 0, w, h);
        // Turn on antialiasing
        g.setRenderingHint(RenderingHints.KEY_ANTIALIASING,
                           RenderingHints.VALUE_ANTIALIAS_ON);
    }

    // The browser automatically calls this method when the applet needs
    // to be redrawn. We copy the offscreen image onscreen.
    // JavaScript code drawing to this applet must call the inherited
    // repaint() method to request a redraw.
    public void paint(Graphics g) { g.drawImage(image, 0, 0, this); }

    // These methods set basic drawing parameters
    // This is just a subset: the Java2D API supports many others
    public void setLineWidth(float w) { g.setStroke(new BasicStroke(w)); }
    public void setColor(int color) { g.setPaint(new Color(color)); }
    public void setFont(String fontfamily, int pointsize) {
        g.setFont(new Font(fontfamily, Font.PLAIN, pointsize));
    }

    // These are simple drawing primitives
    public void fillRect(int x, int y, int w, int h) { g.fillRect(x,y,w,h); }
    public void drawRect(int x, int y, int w, int h) { g.drawRect(x,y,w,h); }
    public void drawString(String s, int x, int y) { g.drawString(s, x, y); }

    // These methods fill and draw arbitrary shapes
    public void fill(Shape shape) { g.fill(shape); }
    public void draw(Shape shape) { g.draw(shape); }
```

Example 22-14. A Java canvas applet for client-side drawing (continued)

```java
    // These methods return simple Shape objects
    // This is just a sampler. The Java2D API supports many others.
    public Shape createRectangle(double x, double y, double w, double h) {
        return new Rectangle2D.Double(x, y, w, h);
    }
    public Shape createEllipse(double x, double y, double w, double h) {
        return new Ellipse2D.Double(x, y, w, h);
    }
    public Shape createWedge(double x, double y, double w, double h,
                             double start, double extent) {
        return new Arc2D.Double(x, y, w, h, start, extent, Arc2D.PIE);
    }
}
```

This applet is compiled with the *javac* compiler to produce a file named *Canvas.class*:

```
% javac Canvas.java
```

The compiled *Canvas.class* can then be embedded in an HTML file and scripted like this:

```html
<head>
<script>
window.onload = function( ) {
    var canvas = document.getElementById('square');
    canvas.setColor(0x0000ff);  // Note integer color
    canvas.fillRect(0,0,10,10);
    canvas.repaint( );

    canvas = document.getElementById('circle');
    canvas.setColor(0xff0000);
    canvas.fill(canvas.createEllipse(0,0,10,10));
    canvas.repaint( );
};
</script>
</head>
<body>
This is a blue square:
<applet id="square" code="Canvas.class" width=10 height=10></applet>
This is a red circle:
<applet id="circle" code="Canvas.class" width=10 height=10></applet>
</body>
```

This code relies on the onload event handler not being called until the applet is fully loaded and ready. With older browsers and versions of the Java plug-in prior to Java 5, the onload handler is often called before applets are initialized, which causes code like this to fail. If you do your drawing in response to user events instead of the onload event, this is typically not a problem.

Example 22-15 is the JavaScript code for drawing a pie chart using the Java canvas applet. This example omits the makeCanvas( ) function defined in other examples. Because of the onload problem described earlier, this example also draws the chart in response to a button click instead of doing so automatically when the document loads.

Example 22-15. Drawing a pie chart with JavaScript and Java

```
<head>
<script>
// Draw a pie chart using the Java Canvas applet
function pieChart(canvas, data, cx, cy, r, colors, labels, lx, ly) {
    // Locate canvas by name if needed
    if (typeof canvas == "string") canvas = document.getElementById(canvas);

    // All lines are 2 units thick. All text is 16pt bold sans-serif.
    canvas.setLineWidth(2);
    canvas.setFont("SansSerif", 16);

    // Add up the data
    var total = 0;
    for(var i = 0; i < data.length; i++) total += data[i];

    // Compute wedge angles in degrees
    var angles = []
    for(var i = 0; i < data.length; i++) angles[i] = data[i]/total*360;

    startangle = 90;   // Start at 12 o'clock instead of 3 o'clock
    // Loop through the wedges
    for(var i = 0; i < data.length; i++) {
        // This object describes one wedge of the pie
        var arc = canvas.createWedge(cx-r, cy-r, r*2, r*2,
                                     startangle, -angles[i]);
        canvas.setColor(colors[i]);         // Set this color
        canvas.fill(arc);                   // Fill the wedge
        canvas.setColor(0x000000);          // Switch to black
        canvas.draw(arc);                   // Outline the wedge

        startangle -= angles[i]; // for next time

        // Now draw the box in the legend
        canvas.setColor(colors[i]);              // Back to wedge color
        canvas.fillRect(lx, ly+30*i, 20, 20);    // Fill the box
        canvas.setColor(0x000000);               // Back to black again
        canvas.drawRect(lx, ly+30*i, 20, 20);    // Outline the box

        // And draw the label for each wedge
        // Remember that we set the font earlier
        canvas.drawString(labels[i], lx+30, ly+30*i+18);
    }
    // Tell the applet to display itself
    canvas.repaint();  // Don't forget to call this
}

// This function is invoked when the Draw! button is clicked
function draw() {
    pieChart("canvas", [12, 23, 34, 45], 200, 200, 150,
```

Example 22-15. Drawing a pie chart with JavaScript and Java (continued)

```
            [0xff0000, 0x0000ff, 0xffff00, 0x00ff00], // Colors are integers
            ["North", "South", "East", "West"],
            400, 100);
}
</script>
</head>
<body>
<applet id="canvas" code="Canvas.class" width=600 height=400></applet>
<button onclick="draw( )">Draw!</button>
</body>
```

22.7.2 Client-Side Sparkline Images with Java

This section uses the Java2D API to draw graphics, but instead of displaying those graphics directly in an applet, the rendered graphic is written as a PNG byte stream and then that byte stream is encoded as a data: URL. In this way, client-side Java-Script can create its own inline images. Although this can be done using an applet, the approach used here scripts Java directly using LiveConnect (see Chapter 12), which is possible in Firefox and related browsers.

The application for this image-generation technique is the display of sparklines. A *sparkline* is a small data-display graphic that's included within the flow of text. Here is an example: **Server load:** ⌇⌇⌇16

The term *sparkline* was coined by author Edward Tufte who describes them as "small, high-resolution graphics embedded in a context of words, numbers, images. Sparklines are data-intense, design-simple, word-sized graphics." (Learn more about sparklines in Tufte's book *Beautiful Evidence* [Graphics Press].)

Example 22-16 shows the code used to produce the server-load sparkline shown earlier. The JavaScript function makeSparkline( ) uses LiveConnect extensively to script the Java2D API without relying on an applet.

Example 22-16. Creating a sparkline image with Javascript and Java

```
<head>
<script>
/**
 * data is an array of numbers to be plotted as a time-series
 * dx is the number of x pixels between data points
 * config is an object that holds values that are likely to
 * be the same for multiple invocations:
 *    height: the height, in pixels of the generated image
 *    ymin, ymax: the range, or Y axis bounds in user-space
 *    backgroundColor: the background color as a numeric HTML color.
 *    lineWidth: the width of the line to draw
 *    lineColor: the color of the line to draw as an HTML # color spec
 *    dotColor: if specified, a dot of this color will be placed on
 *              the last data point
 *    bandColor: if specified, a band of this color will be drawn between
```

Example 22-16. Creating a sparkline image with Javascript and Java (continued)

```
 *         the bandMin and bandMax values to represent a "normal" range of
 *         data values, and emphasize the values that exceed that range
 */
function makeSparkline(data, dx, config) {
    var width = data.length * dx + 1; // overall image width
    var yscale = config.height/(config.ymax - config.ymin); // For scaling data

    // Convert data point number to a pixel value
    function x(i) { return i * dx; }
    // Convert a Y coordinate from user space to pixel space
    function y(y) { return config.height - (y - config.ymin)*yscale; }
    // Convert an HTML color spec to a java.awt.Color object
    function color(c) {
        c = c.substring(1);   // Remove leading #
        if (c.length == (3)) {  // convert to 6-char rep, if needed
            c = c.charAt(0) + c.charAt(0) + c.charAt(1) + c.charAt(1) +
                c.charAt(2) + c.charAt(2);
        }
        var red   = parseInt(c.substring(0,2), 16);
        var green = parseInt(c.substring(2,4), 16);
        var blue  = parseInt(c.substring(4,6), 16);
        return new java.awt.Color(red/255, green/255, blue/255);
    }

    // Create an offscreen image for the sparkline
    var image = new java.awt.image.BufferedImage(width, config.height,
                              java.awt.image.BufferedImage.TYPE_INT_RGB);

    // Get a Graphics object that lets us draw into that image
    var g = image.createGraphics();

    // Antialias everything. Tradeoff: makes the line smoother but fuzzier
    g.setRenderingHint(java.awt.RenderingHints.KEY_ANTIALIASING,
                       java.awt.RenderingHints.VALUE_ANTIALIAS_ON);

    // Fill the image with the background color
    g.setPaint(color(config.backgroundColor));
    g.fillRect(0, 0, width, config.height);

    // If a bandColor was specified, draw the band
    if (config.bandColor) {
        g.setPaint(color(config.bandColor));
        g.fillRect(0, y(config.bandMax),
                   width, y(config.bandMin)-y(config.bandMax));
    }


    // Now build the line
    var line = new java.awt.geom.GeneralPath();
    line.moveTo(x(0), y(data[0]));
    for(var i = 1; i < data.length; i++) line.lineTo(x(i), y(data[i]));
```

```
    // Set the line color and width, then draw the line
    g.setPaint(color(config.lineColor));            // Set line color
    g.setStroke(new java.awt.BasicStroke(config.lineWidth)); // Set width
    g.draw(line);                                   // Draw!

    // If the dotColor was set, draw the dot
    if (config.dotColor) {
        g.setPaint(color(config.dotColor));
        var dot=new java.awt.geom.Ellipse2D$Double(x(data.length-1)-.75,
                                                    y(data[data.length-1])-.75,
                                                    1.5, 1.5)

        g.draw(dot);
    }

    // Write the image out as a byte array in PNG format
    var stream = new java.io.ByteArrayOutputStream();
    Packages.javax.imageio.ImageIO.write(image, "png", stream);
    var imageData = stream.toByteArray();

    // Convert the data to a URL-encoded string
    var rawString = new java.lang.String(imageData, "iso8859-1");
    var encodedString = java.net.URLEncoder.encode(rawString, "iso8859-1");
    encodedString = encodedString.replaceAll("\\+", "%20");

    // And return it all as a data: URL
    return "data:image/png," + encodedString;
}

// Here is an example that uses the makeSparkline() function
window.onload = function() {
    // Create the img tag for the sparkline
    var img = document.createElement("img");
    img.align = "center";
    img.hspace = 1;

    // Set its src attribute to the data: URL of the sparkline
    img.src = makeSparkline([3, 4, 5, 6, 7, 8, 8, 9, 10, 10, 12,
                             16, 11, 10, 11, 10, 10, 10, 11, 12,
                             16, 11, 10, 11, 10, 10, 10, 11, 12,
                             14, 16, 18, 18, 19, 18, 17, 17, 16,
                             14, 16, 18, 18, 19, 18, 17, 17, 16],
                        2, { height: 20, ymin: 0, ymax: 20,
                            backgroundColor: "#fff",
                            lineWidth: 1, lineColor: "#000",
                            dotColor: "#f00", bandColor: "#ddd",
                            bandMin: 6, bandMax: 14
                        });

    // Find the placeholder element for the sparkline
    var placeholder = document.getElementById("placeholder");
```

```
    // And replace it with the image.
    placeholder.parentNode.replaceChild(img, placeholder);
}
</script>
</head>
<body>
Server load: <span id="placeholder"></span><span style="color:#f00">16</span>
</body>
```

CHAPTER 23

Scripting Java Applets and Flash Movies

A *plug-in* is a software module that can be "plugged in" to a web browser to extend its functionality in some way. Two of the most widely deployed (and, not coincidentally, the most powerful) plug-ins are the Java plug-in from Sun Microsystems and the Flash Player from Adobe (which acquired Macromedia). The Java plug-in enables a browser to run applications known as *applets* written in the Java programming language. The Java security system prevents untrusted applets from reading or writing files on the local system or doing anything else that could alter data or compromise privacy. Despite the security restrictions that are imposed on applets, the Java plug-in ships with a huge library of predefined classes that applets can take advantage of. This library includes graphics and GUI packages, powerful networking capabilities, XML parsing and manipulation packages, and cryptographic algorithms. Java 6, in prerelease at the time of this writing, will include a complete suite of packages for web services.

The Flash Player is extraordinarily popular and almost universally deployed. It is a virtual machine that interprets "movies," which may include true streaming video but typically consist of animations and rich GUIs. Flash movies may include scripts written in a language known as ActionScript. ActionScript is a variant of JavaScript, with the addition of object-oriented programming constructs such as classes, static methods, and optional variable typing. ActionScript code in a Flash movie has access to a powerful (though not as extensive as Java) library of code that includes graphics, networking, and XML manipulation capabilities.

The term *plug-in* doesn't really do justice to Java and Flash. These are not simple add-ons to the browser; they are both suitable for application development in their own right, and both can provide a richer user experience than DHTML-based web applications do. Once you realize how much power these plug-ins bring to the web browser environment, it is only natural to want to tap that power with JavaScript. Fortunately, you can do exactly that. JavaScript can be used to script both Java applets and Flash movies. Furthermore you can even do the reverse: Java applets and Flash movies can call JavaScript functions. This chapter explains how to make it work. Be prepared, however: the interfaces between JavaScript, Java, and Action-Script are awkward, and if you do any serious scripting of Java and Flash, you will encounter incompatibilities, bugs, and frustration.

This chapter begins by explaining how you can use client-side JavaScript to script Java applets. (You may remember that Example 22-14 scripted a Java applet to create client-side graphics.) Next, it explains how, in Firefox and related browsers, JavaScript code can script the Java plug-in itself, even when no applet is present. (This technique was shown in Example 22-16.)

After explaining how to script Java with JavaScript, this chapter goes on to explain how to create applets that read and write JavaScript properties and invoke JavaScript methods, including applets that use the Java version of the DOM API to interact with the document displayed by the web browser.

Java and JavaScript are also covered in Chapter 12. That chapter was very different, however. It described how to embed a JavaScript interpreter in a Java application and how to allow scripts run by that interpreter to interact with a Java program. Chapter 12 did not cover client-side JavaScript nor did it cover applets. It did cover LiveConnect, a technology that enables JavaScript to communicate with Java, and the material on LiveConnect from that chapter is relevant to this chapter. Note, however, that the features described in Chapter 12 as being specific to the "Rhino version of LiveConnect" do not work with client-side JavaScript and applets.

The Java sections of this chapter assume you have at least a basic familiarity with Java programming. If you do not use applets in your web pages, you can skip them.

After covering Java, I turn to the topic of scripting Flash: allowing JavaScript code to invoke ActionScript methods defined within a Flash movie and allowing the Action-Script code in a movie to call JavaScript code. I discuss this material twice, first covering techniques that work in all recent versions of Flash and then covering a much simpler new technique that works only in Flash version 8 and later.

Because Flash is so powerful, it was used in earlier chapters of this book. In Chapter 22, the Flash Player displayed dynamic client-side graphics with the help of some simple ActionScript code (Example 22-12) in a Flash movie. And in Chapter 19, Example 19-4 took advantage of the Flash Player's client-side persistence mechanism.

23.1 Scripting Applets

In order to script an applet, you must first be able to refer to the HTML element that represents the applet. As discussed in Chapter 15, all Java applets embedded in a web page become part of the `Document.applets[]` array. Also, if given a name or id, an applet can be accessed directly as a property of the Document object. For example, the applet created with an `<applet name="chart">` tag can be referred to as `document.chart`.

And if you specify an `id` attribute for your applet, you can, of course, look up the applet with `Document.getElementById( )`.

Once you have the applet object, the public fields and methods defined by the applet are accessible to JavaScript as if they were the properties and methods of the HTML `<applet>` element itself. As an example, consider the Canvas applet defined in Example 22-14. If an instance of this applet is embedded in an HTML page with the id "canvas", the following code can be used to invoke methods of the applet:

```
var canvas = document.getElementById('canvas');
canvas.setColor(0x0000ff);
canvas.fillRect(0,0,10,10);
canvas.repaint( );
```

JavaScript can query and set the values of public fields of an applet, even fields that are arrays. Suppose that an applet with `name="chart"` defines two fields declared as follows (Java code):

```
public int numPoints;
public double[] points;
```

A JavaScript program might use these fields with code like this:

```
for(var i = 0; i < document.chart.numPoints; i++)
    document.chart.points[i] = i*i;
```

This code snippet illustrates the tricky thing about connecting JavaScript and Java: *type conversion*. Java is a strongly typed language with a number of distinct primitive types; JavaScript is loosely typed and has only a single numeric type. In the previous example, a Java integer is converted to a JavaScript number, and various JavaScript numbers are converted to Java double values. There is a lot of work going on behind the scenes to ensure that these values are properly converted as needed. The topic of data conversion when JavaScript is used to script Java is covered in Chapter 12, and you may want to refer back to that chapter now. Part III also has useful entries for JavaObject, JavaArray, JavaClass, and JavaPackage. Note that Chapter 12 documents LiveConnect, a technology that originated with Netscape. Not all browsers use LiveConnect. IE, for example, uses its own ActiveX technology as the bridge between JavaScript and Java. Regardless of the technology underneath, the basic rules for converting values between Java and JavaScript are more or less the same in all browsers.

Finally, it is also important to note that Java methods can return Java objects, and JavaScript can read and write the public fields and invoke the public methods of those objects just as it can do with the applet object. JavaScript can also use Java objects as arguments to Java methods. Consider the Canvas applet of Example 22-14 again. It defines methods that return Shape objects. JavaScript code can invoke methods of these Shape objects, and it can pass them to other applet methods that expect Shape arguments.

Example 23-1 is a sample Java applet that does nothing but define a useful method for JavaScript to invoke. This getText( ) method reads a URL (which must come from the same server as the applet did) and returns its content as a Java string. Here's an example that uses this applet in a simple self-listing HTML file:

```
<!-- Self-listing HTML file using an applet to fetch a URL -->
<body onload="alert(document.http.getText('GetText.html'));">
<applet name="http" code="GetTextApplet.class" width="1" height="1"></applet>
</body>
```

Example 23-1 uses basic Java networking, I/O, and text manipulation classes, but doesn't do anything particularly tricky. It simply defines a useful method and declares it public so that JavaScript can script it.

Example 23-1. An applet suitable for scripting

```
import java.applet.Applet;
import java.net.URL;
import java.io.*;

public class GetTextApplet extends Applet {
    public String getText(String url)
        throws java.net.MalformedURLException, java.io.IOException
    {
        URL resource = new URL(this.getDocumentBase( ), url);
        InputStream is = resource.openStream( );
        BufferedReader in = new BufferedReader(new InputStreamReader(is));
        StringBuilder text = new StringBuilder( );
        String line;
        while((line = in.readLine( )) != null) {
            text.append(line);
            text.append("\n");
        }
        in.close( );
        return text.toString( );
    }
}
```

23.2   Scripting the Java Plug-in

In addition to scripting applets, Firefox and related browsers can script the Java plug-in directly without the need for an applet. LiveConnect technology allows Java-Script code running in these browsers to instantiate Java objects and use them, even in the absence of an applet. This technique is not portable, however, and does not work in browsers such as Internet Explorer.

In browsers that support this plug-in scripting capability, the Packages object provides access to all Java packages the browser knows about. The expression Packages.java. lang refers to the *java.lang* package, and the expression Packages.java.lang.System refers to the *java.lang.System* class. For convenience, java is a shortcut for Packages.java (see the Packages and java entries in Part III). So JavaScript code might invoke a static method of this *java.lang.System* class as follows:

```
// Invoke the static Java method System.getProperty( )
var javaVersion = java.lang.System.getProperty("java.version");
```

However, you're not limited to using static methods and predefined objects: Live-Connect allows you to use the JavaScript new operator to create new instances of Java classes. Example 23-2 shows JavaScript code that creates a new Java window and displays a message in it. Note that this JavaScript code looks almost like Java code. This code first appeared in Chapter 12, but here it is embedded in a <script> tag in an HTML file. Figure 23-1 shows the Java window created when this script is run in Firefox.

Example 23-2. Scripting the Java plug-in

```
<script>
// Define a shortcut to the javax.* package hierarchy
var javax = Packages.javax;

// Create some Java objects
var frame = new javax.swing.JFrame("Hello World");
var button = new javax.swing.JButton("Hello World");
var font = new java.awt.Font("SansSerif", java.awt.Font.BOLD, 24);

// Invoke methods on the new objects
frame.add(button);
button.setFont(font);
frame.setSize(300, 200);
frame.setVisible(true);
</script>
```

Figure 23-1. A Java window created from JavaScript

When you script the Java plug-in, your scripts are subject to the same security restrictions that untrusted applets are. A JavaScript program cannot use the *java.io.File* class, for example, because that would give it the power to read, write, and delete files on the client system.

23.3 Scripting with Java

Having explored how to control Java from JavaScript code, let's now turn to the opposite problem: how to control JavaScript from a Java applet. All Java interactions with JavaScript are handled through an instance of the netscape.javascript. JSObject class. (Complete documentation for JSObject is in Part IV.) An instance of this class is a wrapper around a single JavaScript object. The class defines methods that allow you to read and write property values and array elements of the JavaScript object and to invoke methods of the object. Here is a synopsis of this class:

```
public final class JSObject extends Object {
    // This static method returns an initial JSObject for the browser window
    public static JSObject getWindow(java.applet.Applet applet);

    // These instance methods manipulate the object
    public Object getMember(String name);                   // Read object property
    public Object getSlot(int index);                       // Read array element
    public void setMember(String name, Object value);       // Set object property
    public void setSlot(int index, Object value);           // Set array element
    public void removeMember(String name);                  // Delete property
    public Object call(String name, Object args[]);         // Invoke method
    public Object eval(String s);                           // Evaluate string
    public String toString();                               // Convert to string
    protected void finalize();
}
```

The JSObject class does not have a constructor. A Java applet obtains its first JSObject with the static getWindow() method. When passed a reference to an applet, this method returns a JSObject that represents the browser window in which the applet appears. Thus, every applet that interacts with JavaScript includes a line that looks something like this:

```
JSObject win = JSObject.getWindow(this);   // "this" is the applet itself
```

Having obtained a JSObject that refers to the Window object, you can use instance methods of this initial JSObject to obtain other JSObjects representing other JavaScript objects:

```
import netscape.javascript.JSObject;  // This must be at the top of the file
...
// Get the initial JSObject representing the Window
JSObject win = JSObject.getWindow(this);              // window
// Use getMember() to get a JSObject representing the Document object
JSObject doc = (JSObject)win.getMember("document");   // .document
// Use call() to get a JSObject representing an element of the document
JSObject div = (JSObject)doc.call("getElementById",   // .getElementById('test')
                         new Object[] { "test" });
```

Note that getMember() and call() both return a value of type Object, which generally must be cast to some more specific type, such as JSObject. Also note that when you invoke a JavaScript method with call(), you pass arguments as an array of Java

Object values. This array is required even if the method you are invoking expects one argument or none at all.

The JSObject class has one more important method: eval( ). This Java method works like the JavaScript function of the same name: it executes a string that contains JavaScript code. You'll find that using eval( ) is often much easier than using the other methods of the JSObject class. For example, consider the following use of eval( ) to set a CSS style on a document element:

```
JSObject win = JSObject.getWindow(this);
win.eval("document.getElementById('test').style.backgroundColor = 'gray';");
```

Doing the same thing without the eval( ) method takes more code:

```
JSObject win = JSObject.getWindow(this);              // window
JSObject doc = (JSObject)win.getMember("document");   // .document
JSObject div = (JSObject)doc.call("getElementById",   // .getElementById('test')
                        new Object[] { "test" });
JSObject style = (JSObject)div.getMember("style");    // .style
style.setMember("backgroundColor", "gray");           // .backgroundColor="gray"
```

23.3.1 Compiling and Deploying Applets That Use JSObject

In order to deploy any applet, you must compile it and then embed it in an HTML file. When an applet uses the JSObject class, special care is required for both of these steps.

To compile an applet that interacts with JavaScript, you must tell the compiler where to find the netscape.javascript.JSObject class. When browsers shipped with their own integrated Java interpreter, this was a complicated matter. However, now that all browsers use Sun's Java plug-in, it is much simpler. The JSObject class is in the *jre/lib/plugin.jar* file of the Java distribution. So, to compile an applet that uses JSObject, use a command like this, substituting the Java installation directory used on your system:

```
% javac -cp /usr/local/java/jre/lib/plugin.jar ScriptedApplet.java
```

There is an additional requirement for running an applet that interacts with Java-Script. As a security precaution, an applet is not allowed to use JavaScript unless the web page author (who may not be the applet author) explicitly gives the applet permission to do so. To give this permission, you include the mayscript attribute in the applet's <applet> (or <object> or <embed>) tag. For example:

```
<applet code="ScriptingApplet.class" mayscript width="300" height="300">
</applet>
```

If you forget the mayscript attribute, the applet is not allowed to use the JSObject class.

23.3.2 Java-to-JavaScript Data Conversion

The JSObject class must convert Java values to JavaScript values when it invokes a method or sets a field, and convert JavaScript values back to Java values when it returns from a method or reads a field. The conversions performed by JSObject are different from the LiveConnect conversions documented in Chapter 12. Unfortunately, the conversions performed by JSObject are also more platform-dependent than the conversions performed when JavaScript scripts Java.

When Java reads a JavaScript value, the conversions are straightforward:

- JavaScript numbers convert to `java.lang.Double`.
- JavaScript strings convert to `java.lang.String`.
- JavaScript boolean values convert to `java.lang.Boolean`.
- The JavaScript `null` value converts to the Java `null` value.
- The JavaScript `undefined` value converts in a platform-dependent way: with the Java 5 plug-in, `undefined` converts to `null` in Internet Explorer but to the string "undefined" with Firefox.

When Java sets a JavaScript property or passes an argument to a JavaScript method, the conversions ought to be similarly straightforward. Unfortunately, they are platform-dependent. Using Firefox 1.0 and the Java 5 plug-in, Java values are not converted, and JavaScript sees them as JavaObject objects (which it can interact with using LiveConnect):

Using IE 6 and the Java 5 plug-in, the conversion is more sensible:

- Java numbers and characters convert to JavaScript numbers.
- Java String objects convert to JavaScript strings.
- Java boolean values convert to JavaScript boolean values.
- The Java null value converts to the JavaScript `null` value.
- Any other Java values convert to JavaObjects.

Because of this discrepancy between Firefox and IE, you should should take care to convert values as necessary in your JavaScript code. When writing a JavaScript function that will be invoked by an applet, for example, you should explicitly convert the arguments, using the `Number( )`, `String( )`, and `Boolean( )` conversion functions before using them.

One way to avoid the whole issue of data conversion is to use the `JSObject.eval( )` method whenever your Java code wants to communicate with JavaScript.

23.3.3 The Common DOM API

In Java version 1.4 and later, the Java plug-in includes the Common DOM API, which is a Java implementation of DOM Level 2 that is layered on top of the netscape.javascript.JSObject class. It allows Java applets to interact with the document in which they are embedded using the Java binding of the DOM.

This is an exciting idea, but, unfortunately, its implementation leaves much to be desired. One serious problem is that the implementation (in both IE and Firefox) seems to be incapable of creating a new Text node or obtaining an existing Text node, making the Common DOM API useless for querying or modifying the content of a document. Some DOM manipulations are supported, however, and Example 23-3 demonstrates how an applet can use the Common DOM API to set a CSS style on an HTML element.

Client-Side
JavaScript

There are a few points to note about this example. First, the API for manipulating the DOM is somewhat unusual. You place your DOM code in the run( ) method of a DOMAction object. You then pass this DOMAction object to a method of a DOMService object. When your run( ) method is invoked, it is passed a DOMAccessor object you can use to obtain the Document object, which is the root of the DOM object hierarchy.

The second thing you'll notice about Example 23-3 is that the Java binding of the DOM API is significantly more verbose and awkward than the JavaScript binding of the same API. Finally, note that the task accomplished by this example would be more easily accomplished by passing a line of JavaScript code to the JSObject.eval( ) method!

The code in Example 23-3 does not make explicit use of the JSObject class, and it compiles without any additions to the classpath.

Example 23-3. An applet using the Common DOM API

```
import java.applet.Applet;          // The Applet class itself
import com.sun.java.browser.dom.*;  // The Common DOM API
import org.w3c.dom.*;               // The W3C core DOM API
import org.w3c.dom.css.*;           // The W3C CSS DOM API

// This applet does nothing on its own. It simply defines a method for
// JavaScript code to call. That method then uses the Common DOM API to
// manipulate the document in which the applet is embedded.
public class DOMApplet extends Applet {
    // Set the background of the element with the specified id to the
    // specified color.
    public void setBackgroundColor(final String id, final String color)
        throws DOMUnsupportedException, DOMAccessException
    {
        // We start with a DOMService object, which we obtain like this
        DOMService service = DOMService.getService(this);

        // Then we call invokeAndWait() on the DOMService, passing a DOMAction
        service.invokeAndWait(new DOMAction() {
            // The DOM code we want to execute is in the run() method
            public Object run(DOMAccessor accessor) {
                // We use the DOMAccessor to get the Document object
```

Example 23-3. An applet using the Common DOM API (continued)

```
            // Note that we pass the applet object as an argument
            Document d = accessor.getDocument(DOMApplet.this);

            // Get the element we want to manipulate
            Element e = d.getElementById(id);

            // Cast the element to an ElementCSSInlineStyle so we can
            // call its getStyle() method. Then cast the return value
            // of that method to a CSS2Properties object.
            CSS2Properties style =
                (CSS2Properties) ((ElementCSSInlineStyle)e).getStyle();

            // Finally, we can set the backgroundColor property
            style.setBackgroundColor(color);

            // A DOMAction can return a value, but this one doesn't
            return null;
        }
    });
  }
}
```

23.4 Scripting Flash

Having explained how JavaScript can script Java and vice versa, let's now turn to the Flash Player and the scripting of Flash movies. The subsections that follow explain several different levels of Flash scripting. First, you can use JavaScript to control the Flash Player itself: starting and stopping the movies, jumping to specified frames, and so forth. A more interesting kind of scripting actually invokes ActionScript functions defined within a Flash movie. This section shows the tricks required (prior to Flash 8) to accomplish this.

Next, the roles are reversed, and you'll see how ActionScript code can communicate with JavaScript. Then Section 23.4.5 provides an example in two parts (the Java-Script code and the ActionScript code) that demonstrates bidirectional communication between JavaScript and ActionScript. Section 23.5 shows the same basic example again, rewritten and simplified using the facilities of Flash 8.

There is more to Flash than ActionScript, and most Flash content developers use a commercial Flash development environment from Adobe. All Flash examples in this chapter contain only ActionScript code that can be converted to SWF files (i.e., Flash movies) using a tool such as the open source ActionScript compiler *mtasc* (see *http://www.mtasc.org*). The sample movies don't include embedded media, but they can be compiled for use without an expensive development environment.

This chapter does not attempt to teach the ActionScript programming language or the API of the libraries available to the Flash Player. Many resources online can help you learn ActionScript and the Flash API. One you may find particularly useful is the ActionScript Dictionary.*

23.4.1 Embedding and Accessing Flash Movies

Before a Flash movie can be scripted, it must first be embedded in an HTML page so that your JavaScript code can refer to it. This is tricky only because of browser incompatibilities: IE requires an <object> tag with certain attributes, and other browsers want an <object> tag with different attributes or an <embed> tag. <object> is the standard HTML tag, but the Flash-to-JavaScript scripting technique described here seems to expect the use of <embed>.

The solution in this case relies on IE-specific HTML conditional comments to hide the <object> tag from all browsers except IE and to hide the <embed> tag from IE. Here's how to embed the Flash movie *mymovie.swf* and give it the name "movie":

```
<!--[if IE]>
<object id="movie" type="application/x-shockwave-flash"
        width="300" height="300">
  <param name="movie" value="mymovie.swf">
</object>
<![endif]--><!--[if !IE]> <-->
<embed name="movie" type="application/x-shockwave-flash"
       src="mymovie.swf" width="300" height="300">
</embed>
<!--> <![endif]-->
```

The <object> tag has an id attribute, and the <embed> tag has a name attribute. This is a common practice and means that you can refer to the embedding element with the following cross-browser snippet of code:

```
// Get the Flash movie from Window in IE and Document in others
var flash = window.movie || document.movie; // Get Flash object
```

The <embed> tag must have a name attribute if Flash-to-JavaScript scripting is to work correctly. You can also give it an id, if you wish, and if you do this, you can portably use getElementById( ) to locate the <object> or the <embed> tag.

23.4.2 Controlling the Flash Player

Once you have embedded the Flash movie in your HTML page and used JavaScript to obtain a reference to the HTML element that embeds the movie, you can script

---

* At the time of this writing, the Dictionary is located at *http://www.macromedia.com/support/flash/action_scripts/actionscript_dictionary/*. Since Macromedia was acquired by Adobe, however, this URL may change by the time you read this book.

the Flash Player simply by calling methods of that element. Here are some of the things you might do with these methods:

```
var flash = window.movie || document.movie;  // Get the movie object
if (flash.IsPlaying()) {                      // If it is playing,
    flash.StopPlay();                         // stop it
    flash.Rewind();                           // and rewind it
}
if (flash.PercentLoaded() == 100)             // If it is fully loaded,
    flash.Play();                             // start it.
flash.Zoom(50);                               // Zoom in 50%
flash.Pan(25, 25, 1);                         // Pan 25% right and down
flash.Pan(100, 0, 0);                         // Pan 100 pixels right
```

These Flash Player methods are documented in Part IV under FlashPlayer, and some are demonstrated in Example 23-5.

23.4.3 Scripting Flash Movies

More interesting than controlling the Flash Player is invoking ActionScript methods defined in the movie itself. With Java applets, this is easy to do: simply call the desired methods as if they were methods of the HTML <applet> tag. It is also this easy in Flash 8. But if you want to target users who may not yet have upgraded to that version of the player, you'll have to jump through some more hoops.

One of the basic methods for controlling the Flash Player is called SetVariable(). Another is GetVariable(). You can use these to set and retrieve the values of Action-Script variables. There is no InvokeFunction() method, but you can take advantage of an ActionScript extension to JavaScript to use SetVariable() to trigger a function invocation. In ActionScript, every object has a watch() method that can set a debugger-style *watch point*: whenever the value of a specified property of the object changes, a specified function is invoked. Consider the following ActionScript code:

```
/* ActionScript */
// Define some variables to hold function arguments and the return value
// _root refers to the root timeline of the movie. SetVariable() and
// GetVariable() can set and get properties of this object.
_root.arg1 = 0;
_root.arg2 = 0;
_root.result = 0;
// This variable is defined to trigger a function invocation
_root.multiply = 0;
// Now use Object.watch() to invoke a function when the value of
// the "multiply" property changes.  Note that we handle type conversion
// of the arguments explicitly
_root.watch("multiply", function() {
            _root.result = Number(_root.arg1) * Number(_root.arg2);
            // This return value becomes the new value of the property.
            return 0;
        });
```

For the sake of example, let's assume that the Flash Player plug-in is much better at multiplication than the JavaScript interpreter. Here's how to invoke this Action-Script multiplication code from JavaScript:

```
/* JavaScript */
// Ask the Flash movie to multiply two numbers for us
function multiply(x, y) {
    var flash = window.movie || document.movie; // Get the Flash object
    flash.SetVariable("arg1", x);               // Set first argument
    flash.SetVariable("arg2", y);               // Set second argument
    flash.SetVariable("multiply", 1);           // Trigger multiplication code
    var result = flash.GetVariable("result");   // Retrieve the result
    return Number(result);                      // Convert and return it.
}
```

23.4.4 Calling JavaScript from Flash

ActionScript can communicate with JavaScript using a function named fscommand( ), to which it passes two strings:

```
fscommand("eval", "alert('hi from flash')");
```

The arguments to fscommand( ) are called *command* and *args*, but they don't have to represent a command and a set of arguments: they can be any two strings.

When ActionScript code calls fscommand( ), the two strings are passed to a specific JavaScript function, which can take any action it desires in response to the *command*. Note that the JavaScript return value is not passed back to ActionScript. The name of the JavaScript function that fscommand( ) invokes depends on the id or the name used with the <object> or <embed> tag when the movie was embedded. If your movie is named "movie", you must define a JavaScript function named movie_DoFSCommand. Here is an example that can handle the fscommand( ) invocation:

```
function movie_DoFSCommand(command, args) {
    if (command == "eval") eval(args);
}
```

This is straightforward enough, but it does not work in Internet Explorer. For some reason, when Flash is embedded in the IE browser, it cannot communicate directly with JavaScript; however, it can communicate with Microsoft's proprietary scripting language, VBScript. And VBScript can communicate with JavaScript. So to make fscommand( ) work with IE, you must also include the following snippet of code (which also assumes that the movie is named "movie") in your HTML file:

```
<script language="VBScript">
sub movie_FSCommand(byval command, byval args)
  call movie_DoFSCommand(command, args) ' Just call the JavaScript version
end sub
</script>
```

You aren't expected to understand this code; just put it your HTML file. Browsers that don't understand VBScript will simply ignore this <script> tag and its contents.

23.4.5 Example: Flash to JavaScript, and Back to Flash

Now let's put all these pieces together into a two-part example that consists of a file of ActionScript code (Example 23-4) and a file of HTML and JavaScript code (Example 23-5). When the Flash movie loads, it uses fscommand( ) to notify Java-Script, which enables a form button in response. When you click this form button, JavaScript uses the SetVariable( ) technique to get the Flash movie to draw a rectangle. In addition, when the user clicks the mouse within the Flash movie, it uses an fscommand( ) to report the mouse position to JavaScript. Both examples are well commented and should be easy to understand.

Example 23-4. ActionScript code that works with JavaScript

```
/**
 * Box.as: ActionScript code to demonstrate JavaScript <-> Flash communication
 *
 * This file is written in ActionScript 2.0, a language that is based on
 * JavaScript, but extended for stronger object-oriented programming.
 * All we're doing here is defining a single static function named main( )
 * in a class named Box.
 *
 * You can compile this code with the open source ActionScript compiler mtasc
 * using a command like this:
 *
 *   mtasc -header 300:300:1 -main -swf Box1.swf Box1.as
 *
 * mtasc produces a SWF file that invokes the main( ) method from the first
 * frame of the movie. If you use the Flash IDE, you must insert your own
 * call to Box.main( ) in the first frame.
 */
class Box {
    static function main( ) {
        // This is an ActionScript function we want to use from JavaScript.
        // It draws a box and returns the area of the box.
        var drawBox = function(x,y,w,h) {
            _root.beginFill(0xaaaaaa, 100);
            _root.lineStyle(5, 0x000000, 100);
            _root.moveTo(x,y);
            _root.lineTo(x+w, y);
            _root.lineTo(x+w, y+h);
            _root.lineTo(x, y+h);
            _root.lineTo(x,y);
            _root.endFill( );
            return w*h;
        }

        // Here's how we can allow the function to be invoked from JavaScript
        // prior to Flash 8. First, we define properties in our root timeline
        // to hold the function arguments and return value.
        _root.arg1 = 0;
        _root.arg2 = 0;
        _root.arg3 = 0;
```

Example 23-4. ActionScript code that works with JavaScript (continued)

```
        _root.arg4 = 0;
        _root.result = 0;

        // Then we define another property with the same name as the function.
        _root.drawBox = 0;

        // Now we use the Object.watch( ) method to "watch" this property.
        // Whenever it is set, the function we specify will be called.
        // This means that JavaScript code can use SetVariable to trigger
        // a function invocation.
        _root.watch("drawBox",      // The name of the property to watch
                    function() {  // The function to invoke when it changes
                        // Call the drawBox( ) function, converting the
                        // arguments from strings to numbers and storing
                        // the return value.
                        _root.result = drawBox(Number(_root.arg1),
                                               Number(_root.arg2),
                                               Number(_root.arg3),
                                               Number(_root.arg4));

                        // Return 0 so that the value of the property we
                        // are watching does not change.
                        return 0;
                    });


    // This is an ActionScript event handler.
    // It calls the global fscommand( ) function to pass the
    // coordinates of a mouse click to JavaScript.
    _root.onMouseDown = function() {
        fscommand("mousedown", _root._xmouse + "," + _root._ymouse);
    }

    // Here we use fscommand( ) again to tell JavaScript that the
    // Flash movie has loaded and is ready to go.
    fscommand("loaded", "");
    }
}
```

Example 23-5. Scripting a Flash movie

```
<!--
  This is a Flash movie, embedded in our web page.
  Following standard practice, we use <object id=""> for IE and
  <embed name=""> for other browsers.
  Note the IE-specific conditional comments.
-->
<!--[if IE]>
<object id="movie" type="application/x-shockwave-flash"
        width="300" height="300">
  <param name="movie" value="Box1.swf">
</object>
<![endif]--><!--[if !IE]> <-->
```

Example 23-5. Scripting a Flash movie (continued)

```html
<embed name="movie" type="application/x-shockwave-flash"
       src="Box1.swf" width="300" height="300">
</embed>
<!--> <![endif]-->

<!--
   This HTML form has buttons that script the movie or the player.
   Note that the Draw button starts off disabled. The Flash movie
   sends a command to JavaScript when it is loaded, and JavaScript
   then enables the button.
-->
<form name="f" onsubmit="return false;">
<button name="button" onclick="draw( )" disabled>Draw</button>
<button onclick="zoom( )">Zoom</button>
<button onclick="pan( )">Pan</button>
</form>
```

```javascript
<script>
// This function demonstrates how to call Flash the hard way.
function draw( ) {
    // First we get the Flash object. Since we used "movie" as the id
    // and name of the <object> and <embed> tags, the object is
    // in a property named "movie". In IE, it is a window property,
    // and in other browsers, it is a document property.
    var flash = window.movie || document.movie; // Get Flash object.

    // Make sure the movie is fully loaded before we try to script it.
    // This is for demonstration only: it is redundant since we disable
    // the button that invokes this method until Flash tells us it is loaded
    if (flash.PercentLoaded( ) != 100) return;

    // Next we "pass" the function arguments by setting them, one at a time.
    flash.SetVariable("arg1", 10);
    flash.SetVariable("arg2", 10);
    flash.SetVariable("arg3", 50);
    flash.SetVariable("arg4", 50);

    // Now we trigger the function by setting one more property.
    flash.SetVariable("drawBox", 1);

    // Finally, we ask for the function's return value.
    return flash.GetVariable("result");
}

function zoom( ) {
    var flash = window.movie || document.movie; // Get Flash object.
    flash.Zoom(50);
}

function pan( ) {
    var flash = window.movie || document.movie; // Get Flash object.
    flash.Pan(-50, -50, 1);
```

Example 23-5. Scripting a Flash movie (continued)

```
}

// This is the function that is called when Flash calls fscommand( ).
// The two arguments are strings supplied by Flash.
// This function must have this exact name, or it will not be invoked.
// The function name begins with "movie" because that is the id/name of
// the <object> and <embed> tags used earlier.
function movie_DoFSCommand(command, args) {
    if (command=="loaded") {
        // When Flash tells us it is loaded, we can enable the form button.
        document.f.button.disabled = false;
    }
    else if (command == "mousedown") {
        // Flash tells us when the user clicks the mouse.
        // Flash can only send us strings. We've got to parse them
        // as necessary to get the data that Flash is sending us.
        var coords = args.split(",");
        alert("Mousedown: (" + coords[0] + ", " + coords[1] + ")");
    }
    // These are some other useful commands.
    else if (command == "debug") alert("Flash debug: " + args);
    else if (command == "eval") eval(args);
}
</script>

<script language="VBScript">
' This script is not written in JavaScript, but Microsoft's
' Visual Basic Scripting Edition.  This script is required for Internet
' Explorer to receive fscommand( ) notifications from Flash. It will be
' ignored by all other browsers since they do not support VBScript.
' The name of this VBScript subroutine must be exactly as shown.
sub movie_FSCommand(byval command, byval args)
  call movie_DoFSCommand(command, args) ' Just call the JavaScript version
end sub
</script>
```

23.5   Scripting Flash 8

Version 8 of the Flash Player includes a class named ExternalInterface that revolutionizes Flash scripting by greatly simplifying JavaScript-to-Flash communication and Flash-to-JavaScript communication. ExternalInterface defines a static call( ) function for calling named JavaScript functions and obtaining their return values. It also defines a static addCallback( ) method for exporting ActionScript functions for use by JavaScript. ExternalInterface is documented in Part IV.

To demonstrate the ease of scripting with ExternalInterface, let's convert Examples 23-4 and 23-5 to use it. Example 23-6 lists the converted ActionScript code, and Example 23-7 shows the converted JavaScript code (the <object>, <embed>, and <form> tags are not altered from Example 23-5 and are omitted here).

The comments in these examples should tell you everything you need to know about using ExternalInterface. The `ExternalInterface.addCallback( )` method is also demonstrated in Example 22-12.

Example 23-6. ActionScript using ExternalInterface

```
/**
 * Box2.as: ActionScript code to demonstrate JavaScript <-> Flash communication
 *          using the ExternalInterface class of Flash 8.
 *
 * Compile this code using mtasc with a command like this:
 *
 *   mtasc -version 8 -header 300:300:1 -main -swf Box2.swf Box2.as
 *
 * If you use the Flash IDE instead, insert a call to Box.main( ) in the
 * first frame of your movie.
 */
import flash.external.ExternalInterface;

class Box {
    static function main( ) {
        // Use the new External Interface to export our ActionScript function.
        // This makes it very easy to invoke the function from JavaScript,
        // but it is only supported by Flash 8 and later.
        // The first argument of addCallback is the name by which the function
        // will be known in JavaScript. The second argument is the
        // ActionScript object on which the function will be invoked. It
        // will be the value of the 'this' keyword. And the third argument
        // is the function that will be called.
        ExternalInterface.addCallback("drawBox", null, function(x,y,w,h) {
                                    _root.beginFill(0xaaaaaa, 100);
                                    _root.lineStyle(5, 0x000000, 100);
                                    _root.moveTo(x,y);
                                    _root.lineTo(x+w, y);
                                    _root.lineTo(x+w, y+h);
                                    _root.lineTo(x, y+h);
                                    _root.lineTo(x,y);
                                    _root.endFill( );
                                    return w*h;
                            });

        // This is an ActionScript event handler.
        // Tell JavaScript about mouse clicks using ExternalInterface.call( ).
        _root.onMouseDown = function( ) {
            ExternalInterface.call("reportMouseClick",
                            _root._xmouse, _root._ymouse);
        }

        // Tell JavaScript that we're fully loaded and ready to be scripted.
        ExternalInterface.call("flashReady");
    }
}
```

Example 23-7. Simplified Flash scripting with ExternalInterface

```
<script>
// When an ActionScript function is exported with ExternalInterface.addCallback,
// we can just call it as a method of the Flash object.
function draw() {
    var flash = window.movie || document.movie; // Get Flash object
    return flash.drawBox(100, 100, 100, 50);     // Just invoke a function on it
}

// These are functions Flash will call with ExternalInterface.call().
function flashReady() { document.f.button.disabled = false; }
function reportMouseClick(x, y) { alert("click: " + x + ", " + y); }
</script>
```

PART III

Core JavaScript Reference

This part of the book is a complete reference to all of the classes, properties, functions and methods in the core JavaScript API. The first few pages of this part explain how to use this reference material and are worth reading carefully.

Classes and objects documented in this part include:

Arguments	Global	Number
Array	JavaArray	Object
Boolean	JavaClass	RegExp
Date	JavaObject	String
Error	JavaPackage	
Function	Math	

Core JavaScript Reference

This part of the book is a reference that documents the classes, methods, and properties defined by the core JavaScript language. This introduction and the sample reference page that follows explain how to use and get the most out of this section. Take the time to read this material carefully, and you will find it easier to locate and use the information you need!

This reference is arranged alphabetically. The reference pages for the methods and properties of classes are alphabetized by their full names, which include the names of the classes that define them. For example, if you want to read about the `replace()` method of the String class, you would look under `String.replace()`, not just `replace`.

Core JavaScript defines some global functions and properties, such as `eval()` and `NaN`. Technically, these are properties of the global object. Since the global object has no name, however, they are listed in this reference section under their own unqualified names. For convenience, the full set of global functions and properties in core JavaScript is summarized in a special reference page named "Global" (even though there is no object or class by that name).

Once you've found the page you're looking for, you shouldn't have much difficulty finding the information you need. Still, you'll be able to make better use of this reference if you understand how the reference pages are written and organized. What follows is a sample reference page titled Sample Entry that demonstrates the structure of each reference page and tells you where to find various types of information within the pages. Take the time to read this page before diving into the rest of the reference material.

Sample Entry

Availability

how to read these reference pages

Inherits from

Title and Short Description

Every reference entry begins with a four-part title block like that above. The entries are alphabetized by title. The short description, shown below the title, gives you a quick summary of the item documented in the entry; it can help you quickly decide if you're interested in reading the rest of the page.

Availability

The availability information is shown in the upper-right corner of the title block. In earlier versions of this book, this information told you what version of what web browsers supported the item being documented. Today, most browsers support most of the items documented in this book, and this availability section is more likely to tell you what standard provides the formal specification for the item. You might see "ECMAScript v1" or "DOM Level 2 HTML" here, for example. If the item has been deprecated, that is noted here, as well.

Browser names and version numbers do sometimes appear here, typically when the item being documented is a cutting-edge feature that is not universally adopted or when the item is an Internet Explorer-specific feature.

If an item, such as the History object, has never been standardized but is well supported in browsers that support a particular version of JavaScript, then this section may list that JavaScript version number. The History object, for example, has an availability of "JavaScript 1.0".

If the entry for a method does not include any availability information, that means that it has the same availability as the class that defines the method.

Inherits from

If a class inherits from a superclass or a method overrides a method in a superclass, that information is shown in the lower-right corner of the title block.

As described in Chapter 9, JavaScript classes can inherit properties and methods from other classes. For example, the String class inherits from Object, and HTMLDocument inherits from Document, which inherits from Node. The entry for String summarizes this inheritance as "Object → String", and the entry for HTMLDocument says "Node → Document → HTMLDocument". When you see this inheritance information, you may also want to look up the listed superclasses.

When a method has the same name as a method in a superclass, the method overrides the superclass's method. See `Array.toString()` for an example.

Constructor

If the reference page documents a class, and the class has a constructor, this section shows you how to use the constructor method to create instances of the class. Since constructors are a type of method, the Constructor section looks a lot like the Synopsis section of a method's reference page.

Synopsis

Reference pages for functions, methods, and properties have a Synopsis section that shows how you might use the function, method, or property in your code. The reference entries in this book use two different styles of synopses. The entries in the core JavaScript reference and the client-side entries that document methods (such as Window methods) that are not related to the DOM use untyped synopses. For example, the synopsis for the `Array.concat()` method is:

```
array.concat(value, ...)
```

The *italic* font indicates text that is to be replaced with something else. *array* should be replaced with a variable or JavaScript expression that holds or evaluates to an array. And *value* is simply a name for an argument to be passed to the method. This named argument is decribed later in the synopsis, and that description contains information about the type and purpose of the argument. The ellipsis (...) indicates that this method can take any number of *value* arguments. Because the terms concat and the open and close parentheses are not in *italics*, you must include them exactly as shown in your JavaScript code.

Many of the methods documented in the client-side JavaScript section have been standardized by the W3C, and their specifications include definitive type information for method arguments and method return values. These entries include this type information in the synopsis. The synopsis for the `Document.getElementById()` method, for example is:

```
Element getElementById(String elementId);
```

This synopsis uses Java-style syntax to indicate that the `getElementById()` method returns an Element object and expects one string argument named *elementId*. Because this is a method of Document, it is implicit that it is invoked on a document, and no `document` prefix is included.

Arguments

If a reference page documents a function, a method, or a class with a constructor method, the Constructor or Synopsis section is followed by an Arguments subsection that describes the arguments to the method, function, or constructor. If there are no arguments, this subsection is simply omitted:

arg1
> The arguments are described in a list here. This is the description for argument *arg1*, for example.

arg2
> And this is the description for argument *arg2*.

Returns

If a function or method has a return value, this subsection explains that value.

Throws

If a constructor, function, or method can throw an exception, this subsection lists the types of exceptions that may be thrown and explains the circumstances under which this can occur.

Constants

Some classes define a set of constants that serve as the values for a property or as the arguments to a method. The Node interface, for example, defines important constants to serve as the set of legal values for its nodeType property. When an interface defines constants, they are listed and documented in this section. Note that constants are static properties of the class itself, not of instances of that class

Properties

If the reference page documents a class, the Properties section lists the properties defined by the class and provides short explanations of each. In Part III, each property also has a complete reference page of its own. In Part IV, most properties are fully described in this properties list. The most important or complex client-side properties do have a page of their own, and this is noted here. In Part IV, the properties of DOM-related classes include type information. Properties of other classes and all properties in Part III are untyped. The property listing looks like this:

prop1

> This is a summary of untyped property prop1. Only the property name is listed above, but this description will tell you the property's type, its purpose or meaning, and whether it is read-only or read/write.

readonly integer prop2

> This is a summary for a typed property prop2. The property name is included along with its type. This descriptive paragraph explains the purpose of the property.

Methods

The reference page for a class that defines methods includes a Methods section. It is just like the Properties section, except that it summarizes methods instead of properties. All methods also have reference pages of their own. This summary section lists only method names. Argument type and return type information can be found on the method's reference page.

Description

Most reference pages contain a Description section, which is the basic description of the class, method, function, or property that is being documented. This is the heart of the reference page. If you are learning about a class, method, or property for the first time, you may want to skip directly to this section and then go back and look at previous sections, such as Arguments, Properties, and Methods. If you are already familiar with a class, method, or property, you probably won't need to read this section and instead will just want to quickly look up some specific bit of information (for example, from the Arguments or Properties sections).

In some entries, this section is no more than a short paragraph. In others, it may occupy a page or more. For some simple methods, the Arguments and Returns sections document the method sufficiently by themselves, so the Description section is omitted.

Example

Some pages include an example that shows typical usage. Most pages do not contain examples, however; you'll find those in first half of this book.

Bugs

When an item doesn't work quite right, this section describes the bugs. Note, however, that this book does not attempt to catalog every bug.

See Also

Many reference pages conclude with cross-references to related reference pages that may be of interest. Sometimes reference pages also refer back to one of the main chapters of the book.

arguments[ ]   ECMAScript v1

an array of function arguments

Synopsis

```
arguments
```

Description

The arguments[ ] array is defined only within a function body. Within the body of a function, arguments refers to the Arguments object for the function. This object has numbered properties and serves as an array containing all arguments passed to the function. The arguments identifier is essentially a local variable automatically declared and initialized within every function. It refers to an Arguments object only within the body of a function and is undefined in global code.

See Also

Arguments; Chapter 8

Arguments   ECMAScript v1

arguments and other properties of a function   Object → Arguments

Synopsis

```
arguments
arguments[n]
```

Elements

The Arguments object is defined only within a function body. Although it is not technically an array, the Arguments object has numbered properties that function as array elements and a `length` property that specifies the number of array elements. Its elements are the values that are passed as arguments to the function. Element 0 is the first argument, element 1 is the second argument, and so on. All values passed as arguments become array elements of the Arguments object, whether or not those arguments are given names in the function declaration.

Properties

`callee`
> A reference to the function that is currently executing.

`length`
> The number of arguments passed to the function and the number of array elements in the Arguments object.

Description

When a function is invoked, an Arguments object is created for it, and the local variable `arguments` is automatically initialized to refer to that Arguments object. The main purpose of the Arguments object is to provide a way to determine how many arguments are passed to the function and to refer to unnamed arguments. In addition to the array elements and `length` property, however, the `callee` property allows an unnamed function to refer to itself.

For most purposes, the Arguments object can be thought of as an array with the addition of the `callee` property. However, it is not an instance of Array, and the `Arguments.length` property does not have any of the special behaviors of the `Array.length` property and cannot be used to change the size of the array.

The Arguments object has one *very* unusual feature. When a function has named arguments, the array elements of the Arguments object are synonyms for the local variables that hold the function arguments. The Arguments object and the argument names provide two different ways of referring to the same variable. Changing the value of an argument with an argument name changes the value that is retrieved through the Arguments object, and changing the value of an argument through the Arguments object changes the value that is retrieved by the argument name.

See Also

Function; Chapter 8

Arguments.callee   ECMAScript v1

the function that is currently running

Synopsis

`arguments.callee`

Description

arguments.callee refers to the function that is currently running. It provides a way for an unnamed function to refer to itself. This property is defined only within a function body.

Example

```
// An unnamed function literal uses the callee property to refer
// to itself so that it can be recursive
var factorial = function(x) {
    if (x < 2) return 1;
    else return x * arguments.callee(x-1);
}
var y = factorial(5);   // Returns 120
```

Arguments.length   ECMAScript v1

the number of arguments passed to a function

Synopsis

arguments.length

Description

The length property of the Arguments object specifies the number of arguments passed to the current function. This property is defined only within a function body.

Note that this property specifies the number of arguments actually passed, not the number expected. See Function.length for the number of declared arguments. Note also that this property does not have any of the special behavior of the Array.length property.

Example

```
// Use an Arguments object to check that correct # of args were passed
function check(args) {
    var actual = args.length;           // The actual number of arguments
    var expected = args.callee.length;  // The expected number of arguments
    if (actual != expected) {           // Throw exception if they don't match
        throw new Error("Wrong number of arguments: expected: " +
                        expected + "; actually passed " + actual);
    }
}
// A function that demonstrates how to use the function above
function f(x, y, z) {
    check(arguments);  // Check for correct number of arguments
    return x + y + z;  // Now do the rest of the function normally
}
```

See Also

Array.length, Function.length

Array

ECMAScript v1

built-in support for arrays

Object → Array

Constructor

```
new Array( )
new Array(size)
new Array(element0, element1, ..., elementn)
```

Arguments

size

The desired number of elements in the array. The returned array has its length field set to *size*.

element0, ... elementn

An argument list of two or more arbitrary values. When the Array( ) constructor is invoked with these arguments, the newly created array is initialized with the specified argument values as its elements and its length field set to the number of arguments.

Returns

The newly created and initialized array. When Array( ) is invoked with no arguments, the returned array is empty and has a length field of 0. When invoked with a single numeric argument, the constructor returns an array with the specified number of undefined elements. When invoked with any other arguments, the constructor initializes the array with the values specified by the arguments. When the Array( ) constructor is called as a function, without the new operator, it behaves exactly as it does when called with the new operator.

Throws

RangeError

When a single integer *size* argument is passed to the Array( ) constructor, a RangeError exception is thrown if *size* is negative or is larger than $2^{32}-1$.

Literal Syntax

ECMAScript v3 specifies an array literal syntax. You may also create and initialize an array by placing a comma-separated list of expressions within square brackets. The values of these expressions become the elements of the array. For example:

```
var a = [1, true, 'abc'];
var b = [a[0], a[0]*2, f(x)];
```

Properties

length

A read/write integer specifying the number of elements in the array or, when the array does not have contiguous elements, a number one larger than the index of the last element in the array. Changing the value of this property truncates or extends the array.

Methods

concat( )
> Concatenates elements to an array.

join( )
> Converts all array elements to strings and concatenates them.

pop( )
> Removes an item from the end of an array.

push( )
> Pushes an item to the end of an array.

reverse( )
> Reverses, in place, the order of the elements of an array.

shift( )
> Shifts an element off the beginning of an array.

slice( )
> Returns a subarray slice of an array.

sort( )
> Sorts, in place, the elements of an array.

splice( )
> Inserts, deletes, or replaces array elements.

toLocaleString( )
> Converts an array to a localized string.

toString( )
> Converts an array to a string.

unshift( )
> Inserts elements at the beginning of an array.

Description

Arrays are a basic feature of JavaScript and are documented in detail in Chapter 7.

See Also

Chapter 7

Array.concat( )

ECMAScript v3

concatenate arrays

Synopsis

array.concat(*value, ...*)

Arguments

value, ...
> Any number of values to be concatenated with *array*.

Returns

A new array, which is formed by concatenating each of the specified arguments to *array*.

Description

concat( ) creates and returns a new array that is the result of concatenating each of its arguments to *array*. It does not modify *array*. If any of the arguments to concat( ) is itself an array, the elements of that array are concatenated, rather than the array itself.

Example

```
var a = [1,2,3];
a.concat(4, 5)          // Returns [1,2,3,4,5]
a.concat([4,5]);        // Returns [1,2,3,4,5]
a.concat([4,5],[6,7])   // Returns [1,2,3,4,5,6,7]
a.concat(4, [5,[6,7]])  // Returns [1,2,3,4,5,[6,7]]
```

See Also

Array.join( ), Array.push( ), Array.splice( )

Array.join( ) ECMAScript v1

concatenate array elements to form a string

Synopsis

array.join( )
array.join(*separator*)

Arguments

separator

An optional character or string used to separate one element of the array from the next in the returned string. If this argument is omitted, a comma is used.

Returns

The string that results from converting each element of *array* to a string and then concatenating them together, with the *separator* string between elements.

Description

join( ) converts each element of an array to a string and then concatenates those strings, inserting the specified *separator* string between the elements. It returns the resulting string.

You can perform a conversion in the opposite direction—splitting a string into array elements—with the split( ) method of the String object. See String.split( ) for details.

Example

```
a = new Array(1, 2, 3, "testing");
s = a.join("+");  // s is the string "1+2+3+testing"
```

See Also

String.split( )

Array.length

the size of an array

Synopsis

array.length

Description

The length property of an array is always one larger than the index of the highest element defined in the array. For traditional "dense" arrays that have contiguous elements and begin with element 0, the length property specifies the number of elements in the array.

The length property of an array is initialized when the array is created with the Array( ) constructor method. Adding new elements to an array updates the length, if necessary:

```
a = new Array( );                     // a.length initialized to 0
b = new Array(10);                    // b.length initialized to 10
c = new Array("one", "two", "three"); // c.length initialized to 3
c[3] = "four";                        // c.length updated to 4
c[10] = "blastoff";                   // c.length becomes 11
```

You can set the value of the length property to change the size of an array. If you set length to be smaller than its previous value, the array is truncated, and elements at the end are lost. If you set length to be larger than its previous value, the array becomes bigger, and the new elements added at the end of the array have the undefined value.

Array.pop( )

remove and return the last element of an array

Synopsis

array.pop( )

Returns

The last element of *array*.

Description

pop( ) deletes the last element of *array*, decrements the array length, and returns the value of the element that it deleted. If the array is already empty, pop( ) does not change the array and returns the undefined value.

Example

pop( ), and its companion method push( ), provide the functionality of a first-in, last-out stack. For example:

```
var stack = [];       // stack: []
stack.push(1, 2);     // stack: [1,2]      Returns 2
stack.pop( );         // stack: [1]        Returns 2
stack.push([4,5]);    // stack: [1,[4,5]]  Returns 2
stack.pop( )          // stack: [1]        Returns [4,5]
stack.pop( );         // stack: []         Returns 1
```

Core JavaScript
Reference

See Also

Array.push( )

Array.push( )   ECMAScript v3

append elements to an array

Synopsis

array.push(*value*, ...)

Arguments

value, ...
> One or more values to be appended to the end of *array*.

Returns

The new length of the array, after the specified values are appended to it.

Description

push( ) appends its arguments, in order, to the end of *array*. It modifies *array* directly, rather than creating a new array. push( ), and its companion method pop( ), use arrays to provide the functionality of a first in, last out stack. See Array.pop( ) for an example.

See Also

Array.pop( )

Array.reverse( )   ECMAScript v1

reverse the elements of an array

Synopsis

array.reverse( )

Description

The reverse( ) method of an Array object reverses the order of the elements of an array. It does this *in place*: it rearranges the elements of the specified *array* without creating a new array. If there are multiple references to *array*, the new order of the array elements is visible through all references.

Example

```
a = new Array(1, 2, 3);    // a[0] == 1, a[2] == 3;
a.reverse();               // Now a[0] == 3, a[2] == 1;
```

Array.shift( )

shift array elements down

Synopsis

array.shift( )

Returns

The former first element of the array.

Description

shift( ) removes and returns the first element of *array*, shifting all subsequent elements down one place to occupy the newly vacant space at the start of the array. If the array is empty, shift( ) does nothing and returns the undefined value. Note that shift( ) does not create a new array; instead, it modifies *array* directly.

shift( ) is similar to Array.pop( ), except it operates on the beginning of an array rather than the end. shift( ) is often used in conjunction with unshift( ).

Example

```
var a = [1, [2,3], 4]
a.shift();  // Returns 1; a = [[2,3], 4]
a.shift();  // Returns [2,3]; a = [4]
```

See Also

Array.pop( ), Array.unshift( )

Array.slice( )

return a portion of an array

Synopsis

array.slice(*start, end*)

Arguments

start

> The array index at which the slice is to begin. If negative, this argument specifies a position measured from the end of the array. That is, –1 indicates the last element, –2 indicates the next from the last element, and so on.

end

> The array index immediately after the end of the slice. If not specified, the slice includes all array elements from the *start* to the end of the array. If this argument is negative, it specifies an array element measured from the end of the array.

Returns

A new array that contains the elements of *array* from the element specified by *start*, up to, but not including, the element specified by *end*.

Description

slice( ) returns a slice, or subarray, of *array*. The returned array contains the element specified by *start* and all subsequent elements up to, but not including, the element specified by *end*. If *end* is not specified, the returned array contains all elements from the *start* to the end of *array*.

Note that slice( ) does not modify the array. If you want to actually remove a slice of an array, use Array.splice( ).

Example

```
var a = [1,2,3,4,5];
a.slice(0,3);     // Returns [1,2,3]
a.slice(3);       // Returns [4,5]
a.slice(1,-1);    // Returns [2,3,4]
a.slice(-3,-2);   // Returns [3]; buggy in IE 4: returns [1,2,3]
```

Bugs

start can't be a negative number in Internet Explorer 4. This is fixed in later versions of IE.

See Also

Array.splice( )

Array.sort( ) ECMAScript v1

sort the elements of an array

Synopsis

array.sort( )
array.sort(*orderfunc*)

Arguments

orderfunc
> An optional function used to specify the sorting order.

Returns

A reference to the array. Note that the array is sorted in place, and no copy is made.

Description

The sort( ) method sorts the elements of *array* in place: no copy of the array is made. If sort( ) is called with no arguments, the elements of the array are arranged in alphabetical order (more precisely, the order determined by the character encoding). To do this, elements are first converted to strings, if necessary, so that they can be compared.

If you want to sort the array elements in some other order, you must supply a comparison function that compares two values and returns a number indicating their relative order. The comparison function should take two arguments, *a* and *b*, and should return one of the following:

- A value less than zero, if, according to your sort criteria, *a* is less than *b* and should appear before *b* in the sorted array.
- Zero, if *a* and *b* are equivalent for the purposes of this sort.
- A value greater than zero, if *a* is greater than *b* for the purposes of the sort.

Note that undefined elements of an array are always sorted to the end of the array. This is true even if you provide a custom ordering function: undefined values are never passed to the *orderfunc* you supply.

Example

The following code shows how you might write a comparison function to sort an array of numbers in numerical, rather than alphabetical order:

```
// An ordering function for a numerical sort
function numberorder(a, b) { return a - b; }
a = new Array(33, 4, 1111, 222);
a.sort();              // Alphabetical sort: 1111, 222, 33, 4
a.sort(numberorder);   // Numerical sort: 4, 33, 222, 1111
```

Array.splice( )   ECMAScript v3

insert, remove, or replace array elements

Synopsis

array.splice(*start, deleteCount, value, ...*)

Arguments

start
   The array element at which the insertion and/or deletion is to begin.

deleteCount
   The number of elements, starting with and including *start*, to be deleted from *array*. This argument is optional; if not specified, splice( ) deletes all elements from *start* to the end of the array.

value, ...
   Zero or more values to be inserted into *array*, beginning at the index specified by *start*.

Returns

An array containing the elements, if any, deleted from *array*.

Description

splice( ) deletes zero or more array elements starting with and including the element *start* and replaces them with zero or more values specified in the argument list. Array elements that appear after the insertion or deletion are moved as necessary so that they remain contiguous with the rest of the array. Note that, unlike the similarly named slice( ), splice( ) modifies *array* directly.

Example

The operation of splice( ) is most easily understood through an example:

```
var a = [1,2,3,4,5,6,7,8]
a.splice(4);        // Returns [5,6,7,8]; a is [1,2,3,4]
a.splice(1,2);      // Returns [2,3]; a is [1,4]
a.splice(1,1);      // Returns [4]; a is [1]
a.splice(1,0,2,3);  // Returns []; a is [1 2 3]
```

See Also

Array.slice( )

Array.toLocaleString( )   ECMAScript v1

convert an array to a localized string   Overrides Object.toLocaleString( )

Synopsis

array.toLocaleString( )

Returns

A localized string representation of *array*.

Throws

TypeError
> If this method is invoked on an object that is not an Array.

Description

The toLocaleString( ) method of an array returns a localized string representation of an array. It does this by calling the toLocaleString( ) method of all of the array elements, then concatenating the resulting strings using a locale-specific separator character.

See Also

Array.toString( ), Object.toLocaleString( )

Array.toString( )   ECMAScript v1

convert an array to a string   Overrides Object.toString( )

Synopsis

array.toString( )

Returns

A string representation of *array*.

Throws

TypeError
> If this method is invoked on an object that is not an Array.

Description

The toString( ) method of an array converts an array to a string and returns the string. When an array is used in a string context, JavaScript automatically converts it to a string by calling this method. On some occasions, however, you may want to call toString( ) explicitly.

toString( ) converts an array to a string by first converting each array element to strings (by calling its toString( ) method). Once each element is converted to a string, toString( ) outputs them in a comma-separated list. This return value is the same string that would be returned by the join( ) method with no arguments.

See Also

Array.toLocaleString( ), Object.toString( )

Array.unshift( )   ECMAScript v3

insert elements at the beginning of an array

Synopsis

array.unshift(*value*, ...)

Arguments

value, ...
 One or more values that are inserted at the start of *array*.

Returns

The new length of the array.

Description

unshift( ) inserts its arguments at the beginning of *array*, shifting the existing elements to higher indexes to make room. The first argument to shift( ) becomes the new element 0 of the array; the second argument, if any, becomes the new element 1; and so on. Note that unshift( ) does not create a new array; it modifies *array* directly.

Example

unshift( ) is often used in conjunction with shift( ). For example:

```
var a = [];              // a:[]
a.unshift(1);            // a:[1]           Returns: 1
a.unshift(22);           // a:[22,1]        Returns: 2
a.shift( );              // a:[1]           Returns: 22
a.unshift(33,[4,5]);     // a:[33,[4,5],1]  Returns: 3
```

See Also

Array.shift( )

Core JavaScript Reference

Boolean

ECMAScript v1

support for boolean values

Object → Boolean

Constructor

```
new Boolean(value) // Constructor function
Boolean(value)     // Conversion function
```

Arguments

value

    The value to be held by the Boolean object or to be converted to a boolean value.

Returns

When invoked as a constructor with the new operator, Boolean( ) converts its argument to a boolean value and returns a Boolean object that contains that value. When invoked as a function, without the new operator, Boolean( ) simply converts its argument to a primitive boolean value and returns that value.

The values 0, NaN, null, the empty string "", and the undefined value are all converted to false. All other primitive values, except false (but including the string "false"), and all objects and arrays are converted to true.

Methods

toString( )

    Returns "true" or "false", depending on the boolean value represented by the Boolean object.

valueOf( )

    Returns the primitive boolean value contained in the Boolean object.

Description

Boolean values are a fundamental datatype in JavaScript. The Boolean object is an object wrapper around the boolean value. This Boolean object type exists primarily to provide a toString( ) method to convert boolean values to strings. When the toString( ) method is invoked to convert a boolean value to a string (and it is often invoked implicitly by Java-Script), JavaScript internally converts the boolean value to a transient Boolean object, on which the method can be invoked.

See Also

Object

Boolean.toString( )

ECMAScript v1

convert a boolean value to a string

Overrides Object.toString( )

Synopsis

b.toString( )

Returns

The string "true" or "false", depending on the value of the primitive boolean value or Boolean object *b*.

Throws

TypeError

    If this method is invoked on an object that is not a Boolean.

Boolean.valueOf( )

the boolean value of a Boolean object   Overrides Object.valueOf( )

Synopsis

b.valueOf( )

Returns

The primitive boolean value held by the Boolean object *b*.

Throws

TypeError

    If this method is invoked on an object that is not a Boolean.

Date

manipulate dates and times   Object → Date

Constructor

```
new Date( )
new Date(milliseconds)
new Date(datestring)
new Date(year, month, day, hours, minutes, seconds, ms)
```

With no arguments, the Date( ) constructor creates a Date object set to the current date and time. When one numeric argument is passed, it is taken as the internal numeric representation of the date in milliseconds, as returned by the getTime( ) method. When one string argument is passed, it is a string representation of a date, in the format accepted by the Date.parse( ) method. Otherwise, the constructor is passed between two and seven numeric arguments that specify the individual fields of the date and time. All but the first two arguments—the year and month fields—are optional. Note that these date and time fields are specified using local time, not Coordinated Universal Time (UTC) (which is similar to Greenwich Mean Time [GMT]). See the static Date.UTC( ) method for an alternative.

Date( ) may also be called as a function, without the new operator. When invoked in this way, Date( ) ignores any arguments passed to it and returns a string representation of the current date and time.

Arguments

milliseconds

The number of milliseconds between the desired date and midnight on January 1, 1970 (UTC). For example, passing the argument 5000 creates a date that represents five seconds past midnight on 1/1/70.

datestring

A single argument that specifies the date and, optionally, the time as a string. The string should be in a format accepted by Date.parse( ).

year

The year, in four-digit format. For example, specify 2001 for the year 2001. For compatibility with early implementations of JavaScript, if this argument is between 0 and 99, 1900 is added to it.

month

The month, specified as an integer from 0 (January) to 11 (December).

day

The day of the month, specified as an integer from 1 to 31. Note that this argument uses 1 as its lowest value, while other arguments use 0 as their lowest value. Optional.

hours

The hour, specified as an integer from 0 (midnight) to 23 (11 p.m.). Optional.

minutes

The minutes in the hour, specified as an integer from 0 to 59. Optional.

seconds

The seconds in the minute, specified as an integer from 0 to 59. Optional.

ms

The milliseconds in the second, specified as an integer from 0 to 999. Optional.

Methods

The Date object has no properties that can be read and written directly; instead, all access to date and time values is done through methods. Most methods of the Date object come in two forms: one that operates using local time and one that operates using universal (UTC or GMT) time. If a method has "UTC" in its name, it operates using universal time. These pairs of methods are listed together below. For example, the listing for get[UTC]Day( ) refers to both the methods getDay( ) and getUTCDay( ).

Date methods may be invoked only on Date objects, and they throw a TypeError exception if you attempt to invoke them on any other type of object:

get[UTC]Date( )

Returns the day of the month of a Date object, in local or universal time.

get[UTC]Day( )

Returns the day of the week of a Date object, in local or universal time.

get[UTC]FullYear( )

Returns the year of the date in full four-digit form, in local or universal time.

get[UTC]Hours( )

Returns the hours field of a Date object, in local or universal time.

get[UTC]Milliseconds( )
> Returns the milliseconds field of a Date object, in local or universal time.

get[UTC]Minutes( )
> Returns the minutes field of a Date object, in local or universal time.

get[UTC]Month( )
> Returns the month field of a Date object, in local or universal time.

get[UTC]Seconds( )
> Returns the seconds field of a Date object, in local or universal time.

getTime( )
> Returns the internal, millisecond representation of a Date object. Note that this value is independent of time zone, and therefore, there is not a separate getUTCTime( ) method.

getTimezoneOffset( )
> Returns the difference, in minutes, between the local and UTC representations of this date. Note that the value returned depends on whether daylight saving time is or would be in effect at the specified date.

getYear( )
> Returns the year field of a Date object. Deprecated in favor of getFullYear( ).

set[UTC]Date( )
> Sets the day of the month field of the date, using local or universal time.

set[UTC]FullYear( )
> Sets the year (and optionally month and day) field of the date, using local or universal time.

set[UTC]Hours( )
> Sets the hour field (and optionally the minutes, seconds, and milliseconds fields) of the date, using local or universal time.

set[UTC]Milliseconds( )
> Sets the milliseconds field of a date, using local or universal time.

set[UTC]Minutes( )
> Sets the minutes field (and optionally the seconds and milliseconds fields) of a date, using local or universal time.

set[UTC]Month( )
> Sets the month field (and optionally the day of the month) of a date, using local or universal time.

set[UTC]Seconds( )
> Sets the seconds field (and optionally the milliseconds field) of a date, using local or universal time.

setTime( )
> Sets the fields of a Date object using the millisecond format.

setYear( )
> Sets the year field of a Date object. Deprecated in favor of setFullYear( ).

toDateString( )
> Returns a string that represents the date portion of the date, expressed in the local time zone.

Core JavaScript Reference

toGMTString( )

> Converts a Date to a string, using the GMT time zone. Deprecated in favor of toUTCString( ).

toLocaleDateString( )

> Returns a string that represents the date portion of the date, expressed in the local time zone, using the local date formatting conventions.

toLocaleString( )

> Converts a Date to a string, using the local time zone and the local date formatting conventions.

toLocaleTimeString( )

> Returns a string that represents the time portion of the date, expressed in the local time zone, using the local time formatting conventions.

toString( )

> Converts a Date to a string using the local time zone.

toTimeString( )

> Returns a string that represents the time portion of the date, expressed in the local time zone.

toUTCString( )

> Converts a Date to a string, using universal time.

valueOf( )

> Converts a Date to its internal millisecond format.

Static Methods

In addition to the many instance methods listed previously, the Date object also defines two static methods. These methods are invoked through the Date( ) constructor itself, not through individual Date objects:

Date.parse( )

> Parses a string representation of a date and time and returns the internal millisecond representation of that date.

Date.UTC( )

> Returns the millisecond representation of the specified UTC date and time.

Description

The Date object is a datatype built into the JavaScript language. Date objects are created with the new Date( ) syntax shown earlier.

Once a Date object is created, a number of methods allow you to operate on it. Most methods simply allow you to get and set the year, month, day, hour, minute, second, and millisecond fields of the object, using either local time or UTC (universal, or GMT) time. The toString( ) method and its variants convert dates to human-readable strings. getTime( ) and setTime( ) convert to and from the internal representation of the Date object—the number of milliseconds since midnight (GMT) on January 1, 1970. In this standard millisecond format, a date and time are represented by a single integer, which makes date arithmetic particularly easy. The ECMAScript standard requires the Date object to be able to represent any date and time, to millisecond precision, within 100 million days before or after 1/1/1970. This is a range of plus or minus 273,785 years, so the JavaScript clock will not "roll over" until the year 275755.

Examples

Once you create a Date object, there are a variety of methods you can use to operate on it:

```
d = new Date( );  // Get the current date and time
document.write('Today is: " + d.toLocaleDateString( ) + '. ');  // Display date
document.write('The time is: ' + d.toLocaleTimeString( ));      // Display time
var dayOfWeek = d.getDay( );                                    // What weekday is it?
var weekend = (dayOfWeek == 0) || (dayOfWeek == 6);             // Is it a weekend?
```

Another common use of the Date object is to subtract the millisecond representations of the current time from some other time to determine the difference between the two times. The following client-side example shows two such uses:

```
<script language="JavaScript">
today = new Date( );          // Make a note of today's date
christmas = new Date( );      // Get a date with the current year
christmas.setMonth(11);       // Set the month to December...
christmas.setDate(25);        // and the day to the 25th
// If Christmas hasn't already passed, compute the number of
// milliseconds between now and Christmas, convert this
// to a number of days and print a message
if (today.getTime( ) < christmas.getTime( )) {
    difference = christmas.getTime( ) - today.getTime( );
    difference = Math.floor(difference / (1000 * 60 * 60 * 24));
    document.write('Only ' + difference + ' days until Christmas!<p>');
}
</script>
// ... rest of HTML document here ...
<script language="JavaScript">
// Here we use Date objects for timing
// We divide by 1000 to convert milliseconds to seconds
now = new Date( );
document.write('<p>It took ' +
    (now.getTime( )-today.getTime( ))/1000 +
    'seconds to load this page.');
</script>
```

See Also

Date.parse( ), Date.UTC( )

Date.getDate( ) ECMAScript v1

return the day-of-the-month field of a Date

Synopsis

date.getDate( )

Returns

The day of the month of the specified Date object *date*, using local time. Return values are between 1 and 31.

Date.getDay( ) ECMAScript v1

return the day-of-the-week field of a Date

Synopsis

date.getDay( )

Returns

The day of the week of the specified Date object *date*, using local time. Return values are between 0 (Sunday) and 6 (Saturday).

Date.getFullYear( ) ECMAScript v1

return the year field of a Date

Synopsis

date.getFullYear( )

Returns

The year that results when *date* is expressed in local time. The return value is a full four-digit year, including the century, not a two-digit abbreviation.

Date.getHours( ) ECMAScript v1

return the hours field of a Date

Synopsis

date.getHours( )

Returns

The hours field, expressed in local time, of the specified Date object *date*. Return values are between 0 (midnight) and 23 (11 p.m.).

Date.getMilliseconds( )

return the milliseconds field of a Date

Synopsis

date.getMilliseconds( )

Returns

The milliseconds field, expressed in local time, of *date*.

Date.getMinutes( )

return the minutes field of a Date

Synopsis

date.getMinutes( )

Returns

The minutes field, expressed in local time, of the specified Date object *date*. Return values are between 0 and 59.

Date.getMonth( )

return the month field of a Date

Synopsis

date.getMonth( )

Returns

The month field, expressed in local time, of the specified Date object *date*. Return values are between 0 (January) and 11 (December).

Date.getSeconds( )

return the seconds field of a Date

Synopsis

date.getSeconds( )

Returns

The seconds field, expressed in local time, of the specified Date object *date*. Return values are between 0 and 59.

Date.getTime( )   ECMAScript v1

return a Date in milliseconds

Synopsis

date.getTime( )

Returns

The millisecond representation of the specified Date object *date*—that is, the number of milliseconds between midnight (GMT) on 1/1/1970 and the date and time specified by *date*.

Description

getTime( ) converts a date and time to a single integer. This is useful when you want to compare two Date objects or to determine the time elapsed between two dates. Note that the millisecond representation of a date is independent of the time zone, so there is no getUTCTime( ) method in addition to this one. Don't confuse this getTime( ) method with the getDay( ) and getDate( ) methods, which return the day of the week and the day of the month, respectively.

Date.parse( ) and Date.UTC( ) allow you to convert a date and time specification to a millisecond representation without going through the overhead of first creating a Date object.

See Also

Date, Date.parse( ), Date.setTime( ), Date.UTC( )

Date.getTimezoneOffset( )   ECMAScript v1

determine the offset from GMT

Synopsis

date.getTimezoneOffset( )

Returns

The difference, in minutes, between GMT and local time.

Description

getTimezoneOffset( ) returns the number of minutes difference between the GMT or UTC time and the local time. In effect, this function tells you what time zone the JavaScript code is running in and whether or not daylight saving time is (or would be) in effect at the specified *date*.

The return value is measured in minutes, rather than hours, because some countries have time zones that are not at even one-hour intervals.

Date.getUTCDate( )   ECMAScript v1

return the day-of-the-month field of a Date (universal time)

Synopsis

date.getUTCDate( )

Returns

The day of the month (a value between 1 and 31) that results when *date* is expressed in universal time.

Date.getUTCDay( )   ECMAScript v1

return the day-of-the-week field of a Date (universal time)

Synopsis

date.getUTCDay( )

Returns

The day of the week that results when *date* is expressed in universal time. Return values are between 0 (Sunday) and 6 (Saturday).

Date.getUTCFullYear( )   ECMAScript v1

return the year field of a Date (universal time)

Synopsis

date.getUTCFullYear( )

Returns

The year that results when *date* is expressed in universal time. The return value is a full four-digit year, not a two-digit abbreviation.

Date.getUTCHours( )   ECMAScript v1

return the hours field of a Date (universal time)

Synopsis

date.getUTCHours( )

Returns

The hours field, expressed in universal time, of *date*. The return value is an integer between 0 (midnight) and 23 (11 p.m.).

Date.getUTCMilliseconds( )   ECMAScript v1

return the milliseconds field of a Date (universal time)

Synopsis

date.getUTCMilliseconds( )

Returns

The milliseconds field, expressed in universal time, of *date*.

Date.getUTCMinutes( )   ECMAScript v1

return the minutes field of a Date (universal time)

Synopsis

date.getUTCMinutes( )

Returns

The minutes field, expressed in universal time, of *date*. The return value is an integer between 0 and 59.

Date.getUTCMonth( )   ECMAScript v1

return the month-of-the-year field of a Date (universal time)

Synopsis

date.getUTCMonth( )

Returns

The month of the year that results when *date* is expressed in universal time. The return value is an integer between 0 (January) and 11 (December). Note that the Date object represents the first day of the month as 1 but represents the first month of the year as 0.

Date.getUTCSeconds( )   ECMAScript v1

return the seconds field of a Date (universal time)

Synopsis

date.getUTCSeconds( )

Returns

The seconds field, expressed in universal time, of *date*. The return value is an integer between 0 and 59.

Date.getYear( )

return the year field of a Date

Synopsis

date.getYear( )

Returns

The year field of the specified Date object *date* minus 1900.

Description

getYear( ) returns the year field of a specified Date object minus 1900. As of ECMAScript v3, it is not required in conforming JavaScript implementations; use getFullYear( ) instead.

Date.parse( )

parse a date/time string

Synopsis

Date.parse(*date*)

Arguments

date
> A string containing the date and time to be parsed.

Returns

The number of milliseconds between the specified date and time and midnight GMT on January 1, 1970.

Description

Date.parse( ) is a static method of Date. It is always invoked through the Date constructor as Date.parse( ), not through a Date object as *date*.parse( ). Date.parse( ) takes a single string argument. It parses the date contained in this string and returns it in millisecond format, which can be used directly, used to create a new Date object, or used to set the date in an existing Date object with Date.setTime( ).

The ECMAScript standard does not specify the format of the strings that can be parsed by Date.parse( ) except to say that this method can parse the strings returned by the Date.toString( ) and Date.toUTCString( ) methods. Unfortunately, these functions format dates in an implementation-dependent way, so it is not, in general, possible to write dates in a way that is guaranteed to be understood by all JavaScript implementations.

See Also

Date, Date.setTime( ), Date.toGMTString( ), Date.UTC( )

Date.setDate( )   ECMAScript v1

set the day-of-the-month field of a Date

Synopsis

date.setDate(*day_of_month*)

Arguments

day_of_month

> An integer between 1 and 31 that is used as the new value (in local time) of the day-of-the-month field of *date*.

Returns

The millisecond representation of the adjusted date. Prior to ECMAScript standardization, this method returns nothing.

Date.setFullYear( )   ECMAScript v1

set the year and, optionally, the month and date fields of a Date

Synopsis

date.setFullYear(*year*)
date.setFullYear(*year*, *month*)
date.setFullYear(*year*, *month*, *day*)

Arguments

year

> The year, expressed in local time, to be set in *date*. This argument should be an integer that includes the century, such as 1999; it should not be an abbreviation, such as 99.

month

> An optional integer between 0 and 11 that is used as the new value (in local time) of the month field of *date*.

day

> An optional integer between 1 and 31 that is used as the new value (in local time) of the day-of-the-month field of *date*.

Returns

The internal millisecond representation of the adjusted date.

Date.setHours( )   ECMAScript v1

set the hours, minutes, seconds, and milliseconds fields of a Date

Synopsis

date.setHours(*hours*)
date.setHours(*hours*, *minutes*)
date.setHours(*hours*, *minutes*, *seconds*)
date.setHours(*hours*, *minutes*, *seconds*, *millis*)

Arguments

hours

An integer between 0 (midnight) and 23 (11 p.m.) local time that is set as the new hours value of *date*.

minutes

An optional integer, between 0 and 59, that is used as the new value (in local time) of the minutes field of *date*. This argument is not supported prior to ECMAScript standardization.

seconds

An optional integer, between 0 and 59, that is used as the new value (in local time) of the seconds field of *date*. This argument is not supported prior to ECMAScript standardization.

millis

An optional integer, between 0 and 999, that is used as the new value (in local time) of the milliseconds field of *date*. This argument is not supported prior to ECMAScript standardization.

Returns

The millisecond representation of the adjusted date. Prior to ECMAScript standardization, this method returns nothing.

Date.setMilliseconds( )   ECMAScript v1

set the milliseconds field of a Date

Synopsis

date.setMilliseconds(*millis*)

Arguments

millis

The milliseconds field, expressed in local time, to be set in *date*. This argument should be an integer between 0 and 999.

Returns

The millisecond representation of the adjusted date.

Date.setMinutes( )   ECMAScript v1

set the minutes, seconds, and milliseconds fields of a Date

Synopsis

date.setMinutes(*minutes*)
date.setMinutes(*minutes, seconds*)
date.setMinutes(*minutes, seconds, millis*)

Arguments

minutes

An integer between 0 and 59 that is set as the minutes value (in local time) of the Date object *date*.

seconds

An optional integer, between 0 and 59, that is used as the new value (in local time) of the seconds field of *date*. This argument is not supported prior to ECMAScript standardization.

millis

An optional integer, between 0 and 999, that is used as the new value (in local time) of the milliseconds field of *date*. This argument is not supported prior to ECMAScript standardization.

Returns

The millisecond representation of the adjusted date. Prior to ECMAScript standardization, this method returns nothing.

Date.setMonth( )   ECMAScript v1

set the month and day fields of a Date

Synopsis

```
date.setMonth(month)
date.setMonth(month, day)
```

Arguments

month

An integer between 0 (January) and 11 (December) that is set as the month value (in local time) for the Date object *date*. Note that months are numbered beginning with 0, while days within the month are numbered beginning with 1.

day

An optional integer between 1 and 31 that is used as the new value (in local time) of the day-of-the-month field of *date*. This argument is not supported prior to ECMA-Script standardization.

Returns

The millisecond representation of the adjusted date. Prior to ECMAScript standardization, this method returns nothing.

Date.setSeconds( )   ECMAScript v1

set the seconds and milliseconds fields of a Date

Synopsis

```
date.setSeconds(seconds)
date.setSeconds(seconds, millis)
```

Arguments

seconds
> An integer between 0 and 59 that is set as the seconds value for the Date object *date*.

millis
> An optional integer, between 0 and 999, that is used as the new value (in local time) of the milliseconds field of *date*. This argument is not supported prior to ECMAScript standardization.

Returns

The millisecond representation of the adjusted date. Prior to ECMAScript standardization, this method returns nothing.

Date.setTime( ) ECMAScript v1

set a Date in milliseconds

Synopsis

date.setTime(*milliseconds*)

Arguments

milliseconds
> The number of milliseconds between the desired date and time and midnight GMT on January 1, 1970. A millisecond value of this type may also be passed to the Date( ) constructor and may be obtained by calling the Date.UTC( ) and Date.parse( ) methods. Representing a date in this millisecond format makes it independent of time zone.

Returns

The *milliseconds* argument. Prior to ECMAScript standardization, this method returns nothing.

Date.setUTCDate( ) ECMAScript v1

set the day-of-the-month field of a Date (universal time)

Synopsis

date.setUTCDate(*day_of_month*)

Arguments

day_of_month
> The day of the month, expressed in universal time, to be set in *date*. This argument should be an integer between 1 and 31.

Returns

The internal millisecond representation of the adjusted date.

Date.setUTCFullYear( )   ECMAScript v1

set the year, month, and day fields of a Date (universal time)

Synopsis

```
date.setUTCFullYear(year)
date.setUTCFullYear(year, month)
date.setUTCFullYear(year, month, day)
```

Arguments

year

> The year, expressed in universal time, to be set in *date*. This argument should be an integer that includes the century, such as 1999, not an abbreviation, such as 99.

month

> An optional integer between 0 and 11 that is used as the new value (in universal time) of the month field of *date*. Note that months are numbered beginning with 0, while days within the month are numbered beginning with 1.

day

> An optional integer between 1 and 31 that is used as the new value (in universal time) of the day-of-the-month field of *date*.

Returns

The internal millisecond representation of the adjusted date.

Date.setUTCHours( )   ECMAScript v1

set the hours, minutes, seconds, and milliseconds fields of a Date (universal time)

Synopsis

```
date.setUTCHours(hours)
date.setUTCHours(hours, minutes)
date.setUTCHours(hours, minutes, seconds)
date.setUTCHours(hours, minutes, seconds, millis)
```

Arguments

hours

> The hours field, expressed in universal time, to be set in *date*. This argument should be an integer between 0 (midnight) and 23 (11 p.m.).

minutes

> An optional integer, between 0 and 59, that is used as the new value (in universal time) of the minutes field of *date*.

seconds

> An optional integer, between 0 and 59, that is used as the new value (in universal time) of the seconds field of *date*.

millis

> An optional integer, between 0 and 999, that is used as the new value (in universal time) of the milliseconds field of *date*.

Returns

The millisecond representation of the adjusted date.

Date.setUTCMilliseconds( )

set the milliseconds field of a Date (universal time)

Synopsis

date.setUTCMilliseconds(*millis*)

Arguments

millis
> The milliseconds field, expressed in universal time, to be set in *date*. This argument should be an integer between 0 and 999.

Returns

The millisecond representation of the adjusted date.

Date.setUTCMinutes( )

set the minutes, seconds, and milliseconds fields of a Date (universal time)

Synopsis

date.setUTCMinutes(*minutes*)
date.setUTCMinutes(*minutes, seconds*)
date.setUTCMinutes(*minutes, seconds, millis*)

Arguments

minutes
> The minutes field, expressed in universal time, to be set in *date*. This argument should be an integer between 0 and 59.

seconds
> An optional integer between 0 and 59 that is used as the new value (in universal time) of the seconds field of *date*.

millis
> An optional integer between 0 and 999 that is used as the new value (in universal time) of the milliseconds field of *date*.

Returns

The millisecond representation of the adjusted date.

Date.setUTCMonth( )

set the month and day fields of a Date (universal time)

Synopsis

date.setUTCMonth(*month*)
date.setUTCMonth(*month, day*)

Arguments

month

The month, expressed in universal time, to be set in *date*. This argument should be an integer between 0 (January) and 11 (December). Note that months are numbered beginning with 0, while days within the month are numbered beginning with 1.

day

An optional integer between 1 and 31 that is used as the new value (in universal time) of the day-of-the-month field of *date*.

Returns

The millisecond representation of the adjusted date.

Date.setUTCSeconds( )   ECMAScript v1

set the seconds and milliseconds fields of a Date (universal time)

Synopsis

date.setUTCSeconds(*seconds*)
date.setUTCSeconds(*seconds, millis*)

Arguments

seconds

The seconds field, expressed in universal time, to be set in *date*. This argument should be an integer between 0 and 59.

millis

An optional integer between 0 and 999 that is used as the new value (in universal time) of the milliseconds field of *date*.

Returns

The millisecond representation of the adjusted date.

Date.setYear( )   ECMAScript v1; deprecated by ECMAScript v3

set the year field of a Date

Synopsis

date.setYear(*year*)

Arguments

year

An integer that is set as the year value (in local time) for the Date object *date*. If this value is between 0 and 99, inclusive, 1900 is added to it and it is treated as a year between 1900 and 1999.

Returns

The millisecond representation of the adjusted date. Prior to ECMAScript standardization, this method returns nothing.

Description

setYear( ) sets the year field of a specified Date object, with special behavior for years between 1900 and 1999.

As of ECMAScript v3, this function is no longer required in conforming JavaScript implementations; use setFullYear( ) instead.

Date.toDateString( ) ECMAScript v3

return the date portion of a Date as a string

Synopsis

date.toDateString( )

Returns

An implementation-dependent, human-readable string representation of the date portion of *date*, expressed in the local time zone.

See Also

```
Date.toLocaleDateString( )
Date.toLocaleString( )
Date.toLocaleTimeString( )
Date.toString( )
Date.toTimeString( )
```

Date.toGMTString( ) ECMAScript v1; deprecated by ECMAScript v3

convert a Date to a universal time string

Synopsis

date.toGMTString( )

Returns

A string representation of the date and time specified by the Date object *date*. The date is converted from the local time zone to the GMT time zone before being converted to a string.

Description

toGMTString( ) is deprecated in favor of the identical method Date.toUTCString( ).

As of ECMAScript v3, conforming implementations of JavaScript are no longer required to provide this method; use toUTCString( ) instead.

See Also

Date.toUTCString( )

Core JavaScript Reference

Date.toLocaleDateString( )   ECMAScript v3

return the date portion of a Date as a locally formatted string

Synopsis

date.toLocaleDateString( )

Returns

An implementation-dependent, human-readable string representation of the date portion of *date*, expressed in the local time zone and formatted according to local conventions.

See Also

Date.toDateString( ), Date.toLocaleString( ), Date.toLocaleTimeString( ), Date.toString( ), Date.toTimeString( )

Date.toLocaleString( )   ECMAScript v1

convert a Date to a locally formatted string

Synopsis

date.toLocaleString( )

Returns

A string representation of the date and time specified by *date*. The date and time are represented in the local time zone and formatted using locally appropriate conventions.

Usage

toLocaleString( ) converts a date to a string, using the local time zone. This method also uses local conventions for date and time formatting, so the format may vary from platform to platform and from country to country. toLocaleString( ) returns a string formatted in what is likely the user's preferred date and time format.

See Also

Date.toLocaleDateString( ), Date.toLocaleTimeString( ), Date.toString( ), Date.toUTCString( )

Date.toLocaleTimeString( )   ECMAScript v3

return the time portion of a Date as a locally formatted string

Synopsis

date.toLocaleTimeString( )

Returns

An implementation-dependent, human-readable string representation of the time portion of *date*, expressed in the local time zone and formatted according to local conventions.

See Also

Date.toDateString( ), Date.toLocaleDateString( ), Date.toLocaleString( ), Date.toString( ),
Date.toTimeString( )

Date.toString( )   ECMAScript v1
convert a Date to a string   Overrides Object.toString( )

Synopsis

date.toString( )

Returns

A human-readable string representation of *date*, expressed in the local time zone.

Description

toString( ) returns a human-readable, implementation-dependent string representation of
date. Unlike toUTCString( ), toString( ) expresses the date in the local time zone. Unlike
toLocaleString( ), toString( ) may not represent the date and time using locale-specific
formatting.

See Also

Date.parse( )
Date.toDateString( )
Date.toLocaleString( )
Date.toTimeString( )
Date.toUTCString( )

Date.toTimeString( )   ECMAScript v3
return the time portion of a Date as a string

Synopsis

date.toTimeString( )

Returns

A implementation-dependent, human-readable string representation of the time portion of
date, expressed in the local time zone.

See Also

Date.toString( ), Date.toDateString( ), Date.toLocaleDateString( ), Date.toLocaleString( ),
Date.toLocaleTimeString( )

Core JavaScript Reference

Date.toUTCString( )   ECMAScript v1

convert a Date to a string (universal time)

Synopsis

date.toUTCString( )

Returns

A human-readable string representation, expressed in universal time, of *date*.

Description

toUTCString( ) returns an implementation-dependent string that represents *date* in universal time.

See Also

Date.toLocaleString( ), Date.toString( )

Date.UTC( )   ECMAScript v1

convert a Date specification to milliseconds

Synopsis

Date.UTC(*year, month, day, hours, minutes, seconds, ms*)

Arguments

year

> The year in four-digit format. If this argument is between 0 and 99, inclusive, 1900 is added to it and it is treated as a year between 1900 and 1999.

month

> The month, specified as an integer from 0 (January) to 11 (December).

day

> The day of the month, specified as an integer from 1 to 31. Note that this argument uses 1 as its lowest value, while other arguments use 0 as their lowest value. This argument is optional.

hours

> The hour, specified as an integer from 0 (midnight) to 23 (11 p.m.). This argument is optional.

minutes

> The minutes in the hour, specified as an integer from 0 to 59. This argument is optional.

seconds

> The seconds in the minute, specified as an integer from 0 to 59. This argument is optional.

ms

> The number of milliseconds, specified as an integer from 0 to 999. This argument is optional and is ignored prior to ECMAScript standardization.

Returns

The millisecond representation of the specified universal time. That is, this method returns the number of milliseconds between midnight GMT on January 1, 1970 and the specified time.

Description

Date.UTC( ) is a static method; it is invoked through the Date( ) constructor, not through an individual Date object.

The arguments to Date.UTC( ) specify a date and time and are understood to be in UTC; they are in the GMT time zone. The specified UTC time is converted to the millisecond format, which can be used by the Date( ) constructor method and by the Date.setTime( ) method.

The Date( ) constructor method can accept date and time arguments identical to those that Date.UTC( ) accepts. The difference is that the Date( ) constructor assumes local time, while Date.UTC( ) assumes universal time (GMT). To create a Date object using a UTC time specification, you can use code like this:

```
d = new Date(Date.UTC(1996, 4, 8, 16, 30));
```

See Also

Date, Date.parse( ), Date.setTime( )

Date.valueOf( )   ECMAScript v1

convert a Date to millisecond representation   Overrides Object.valueOf( )

Synopsis

date.valueOf( )

Returns

The millisecond representation of *date*. The value returned is the same as that returned by Date.getTime( ).

decodeURI( )   ECMAScript v3

unescape characters in a URI

Synopsis

decodeURI(*uri*)

Arguments

uri

    A string that contains an encoded URI or other text to be decoded.

Returns

A copy of *uri*, with any hexadecimal escape sequences replaced with the characters they represent.

Throws

URIError

> Indicates that one or more of the escape sequences in *uri* is malformed and cannot be correctly decoded.

Description

decodeURI( ) is a global function that returns a decoded copy of its *uri* argument. It reverses the encoding performed by encodeURI( ); see that function's reference page for details.

See Also

decodeURIComponent( ), encodeURI( ), encodeURIComponent( ), escape( ), unescape( )

decodeURIComponent( )   ECMAScript v3

unescape characters in a URI component

Synopsis

decodeURI(*s*)

Arguments

s   A string that contains an encoded URI component or other text to be decoded.

Returns

A copy of *s*, with any hexadecimal escape sequences replaced with the characters they represent.

Throws

URIError

> Indicates that one or more of the escape sequences in *s* is malformed and cannot be correctly decoded.

Description

decodeURIComponent( ) is a global function that returns a decoded copy of its *s* argument. It reverses the encoding performed by encodeURIComponent( ). See that function's reference page for details.

See Also

decodeURI( ), encodeURI( ), encodeURIComponent( ), escape( ), unescape( )

encodeURI( )   ECMAScript v3

escape characters in a URI

Synopsis

encodeURI(*uri*)

Arguments

uri

> A string that contains the URI or other text to be encoded.

Returns

A copy of *uri*, with certain characters replaced by hexadecimal escape sequences.

Throws

URIError

> Indicates that *uri* contains malformed Unicode surrogate pairs and cannot be encoded.

Description

encodeURI( ) is a global function that returns an encoded copy of its *uri* argument. ASCII letters and digits are not encoded, nor are the following ASCII punctuation characters:

```
- _ . ! ~ * ' ( )
```

Because encodeURI( ) is intended to encode complete URIs, the following ASCII punctuation characters, which have special meaning in URIs, are not escaped either:

```
; / ? : @ & = + $ , #
```

Any other characters in *uri* are replaced by converting each character to its UTF-8 encoding and then encoding each of the resulting one, two, or three bytes with a hexadecimal escape sequence of the form %xx. In this encoding scheme, ASCII characters are replaced with a single %xx escape, characters with encodings between \u0080 and \u07ff are replaced with two escape sequences, and all other 16-bit Unicode characters are replaced with three escape sequences.

If you use this method to encode a URI, you should be certain that none of the components of the URI (such as the query string) contain URI separator characters such as ? and #. If the components have to contain these characters, you should encode each component separately with encodeURIComponent( ).

Use decodeURI( ) to reverse the encoding applied by this method. Prior to ECMAScript v3, you can use escape( ) and unescape( ) methods (which are now deprecated) to perform a similar kind of encoding and decoding.

Example

```
// Returns http://www.isp.com/app.cgi?arg1=1&arg2=hello%20world
encodeURI("http://www.isp.com/app.cgi?arg1=1&arg2=hello world");
encodeURI("\u00a9");  // The copyright character encodes to %C2%A9
```

See Also

decodeURI( ), decodeURIComponent( ), encodeURIComponent( ), escape( ), unescape( )

encodeURIComponent( ) ECMAScript v3

escape characters in a URI component

Synopsis

encodeURIComponent(s)

Arguments

s   A string that contains a portion of a URI or other text to be encoded.

Returns

A copy of s, with certain characters replaced by hexadecimal escape sequences.

Throws

URIError
  Indicates that s contains malformed Unicode surrogate pairs and cannot be encoded.

Description

encodeURIComponent( ) is a global function that returns an encoded copy of its s argument. ASCII letters and digits are not encoded, nor are the following ASCII punctuation characters:

  - _ . ! ~ * ' ( )

All other characters, including punctuation characters such as /, :, and # that serve to separate the various components of a URI, are replaced with one or more hexadecimal escape sequences. See encodeURI( ) for a description of the encoding scheme used.

Note the difference between encodeURIComponent( ) and encodeURI( ): encodeURIComponent( ) assumes that its argument is a portion (such as the protocol, hostname, path, or query string) of a URI. Therefore it escapes the punctuation characters that are used to separate the portions of a URI.

Example

```
encodeURIComponent("hello world?");   // Returns hello%20world%3F
```

See Also

decodeURI( ), decodeURIComponent( ), encodeURI( ), escape( ), unescape( )

Error ECMAScript v3

a generic exception Object → Error

Constructor

```
new Error( )
new Error(message)
```

Arguments

message
> An optional error message that provides details about the exception.

Returns

A newly constructed Error object. If the *message* argument is specified, the Error object uses it as the value of its `message` property; otherwise, it uses an implementation-defined default string as the value of that property. When the `Error()` constructor is called as a function, without the `new` operator, it behaves just as it does when called with the `new` operator.

Properties

`message`
> An error message that provides details about the exception. This property holds the string passed to the constructor or an implementation-defined default string.

`name`
> A string that specifies the type of the exception. For instances of the Error class and all of its subclasses, this property specifies the name of the constructor used to create the instance.

Methods

`toString( )`
> Returns an implementation-defined string that represents this Error object.

Description

Instances of the Error class represent errors or exceptions and are typically used with the `throw` and `try/catch` statements. The `name` property specifies the type of the exception, and the `message` property can provide human-readable details about the exception.

The JavaScript interpreter never throws Error objects directly; instead, it throws instances of one of the Error subclasses, such as SyntaxError or RangeError. In your own code, you may find it convenient to throw Error objects to signal exceptions, or you may prefer to simply throw an error message or error code as a primitive string or number value.

Note that the ECMAScript specification defines a `toString( )` method for the Error class (it is inherited by each of the subclasses of Error) but that it does not require this `toString( )` method to return a string that contains the contents of the `message` property. Therefore, you should not expect the `toString( )` method to convert an Error object to a meaningful, human-readable string. To display an error message to a user, you should explicitly use the `name` and `message` properties of the Error object.

Examples

You might signal an exception with code like the following:

```
function factorial(x) {
    if (x < 0) throw new Error("factorial: x must be >= 0");
    if (x <= 1) return 1; else return x * factorial(x-1);
}
```

And if you catch an exception, you might display its to the user with code like the following (which uses the client-side `Window.alert( )` method):

```
try { &*(&/* an error is thrown here */ }
catch(e) {
    if (e instanceof Error) {  // Is it an instance of Error or a subclass?
        alert(e.name + ": " + e.message);
    }
}
```

See Also

`EvalError`, `RangeError`, `ReferenceError`, `SyntaxError`, `TypeError`, `URIError`

Error.message   ECMAScript v3

a human-readable error message

Synopsis

error.message

Description

The `message` property of an Error object (or of an instance of any subclass of Error) is intended to contain a human-readable string that provides details about the error or exception that occurred. If a *message* argument is passed to the `Error( )` constructor, this message becomes the value of the `message` property. If no *message* argument is passed, an Error object inherits an implementation-defined default value (which may be the empty string) for this property.

Error.name   ECMAScript v3

the type of an error

Synopsis

error.name

Description

The `name` property of an Error object (or of an instance of any subclass of Error) specifies the type of error or exception that occurred. All Error objects inherit this property from their constructor. The value of the property is the same as the name of the constructor. Thus SyntaxError objects have a `name` property of "SyntaxError", and EvalError objects have a `name` of "EvalError".

Error.toString( )   ECMAScript v3

convert an Error object to a string   Overrides Object.toString( )

Synopsis

error.toString( )

Returns

An implementation-defined string. The ECMAScript standard does not specify anything about the return value of this method, except that it is a string. Notably, it does not require the returned string to contain the error name or the error message.

escape( )

encode a string

Synopsis

escape(s)

Arguments

s   The string that is to be "escaped" or encoded.

Returns

An encoded copy of s in which certain characters have been replaced by hexadecimal escape sequences.

Description

escape( ) is a global function. It returns a new string that contains an encoded version of s. The string s itself is not modified.

escape( ) returns a string in which all characters of s other than ASCII letters, digits, and the punctuation characters @, *, _, +, -, ., and / have been replaced by escape sequences of the form %xx or %uxxxx (where x represents a hexadecimal digit). Unicode characters \u0000 to \u00ff are replaced with the %xx escape sequence, and all other Unicode characters are replaced with the %uxxxx sequence.

Use the unescape( ) function to decode a string encoded with escape( ).

Although the escape( ) function was standardized in the first version of ECMAScript, it was deprecated and removed from the standard by ECMAScript v3. Implementations of ECMAScript are likely to implement this function, but they are not required to. You should use encodeURI( ) and encodeURIComponent( ) instead of escape( ).

Example

```
escape("Hello World!");  // Returns "Hello%20World%21"
```

See Also

encodeURI( ), encodeURIComponent( )

eval( )

execute JavaScript code from a string

Synopsis

eval(code)

Arguments

code

> A string that contains the JavaScript expression to be evaluated or the statements to be executed.

Returns

The value of the evaluated *code*, if any.

Throws

SyntaxError

> Indicates that *code* does not contain legal JavaScript.

EvalError

> Indicates that eval( ) was called illegally, through an identifier other than "eval", for example. See the restrictions on this function described in the next section.

Other exception

> If the JavaScript code passed to eval( ) generates an exception, eval( ) passes that exception on to the caller.

Description

eval( ) is a global method that evaluates a string of JavaScript code in the current lexical scope. If *code* contains an expression, eval evaluates the expression and returns its value. If *code* contains a JavaScript statement or statements, eval( ) executes those statements and returns the value, if any, returned by the last statement. If *code* does not return any value, eval( ) returns undefined. Finally, if *code* throws an exception, eval( ) passes that exception on to the caller.

eval( ) provides a very powerful capability to the JavaScript language, but its use is infrequent in real-world programs. Obvious uses are to write programs that act as recursive JavaScript interpreters and to write programs that dynamically generate and evaluate JavaScript code.

Most JavaScript functions and methods that expect string arguments accept arguments of other types as well and simply convert those argument values to strings before proceeding. eval( ) does not behave like this. If the *code* argument is not a primitive string, it is simply returned unchanged. Be careful, therefore, that you do not inadvertently pass a String object to eval( ) when you intended to pass a primitive string value.

For purposes of implementation efficiency, the ECMAScript v3 standard places an unusual restriction on the use of eval( ). An ECMAScript implementation is allowed to throw an EvalError exception if you attempt to overwrite the eval property or if you assign the eval( ) method to another property and attempt to invoke it through that property.

Example

```
eval("1+2");        // Returns 3
// This code uses client-side JavaScript methods to prompt the user to
// enter an expression and to display the results of evaluating it.
// See the client-side methods Window.alert() and Window.prompt() for details.
try {
    alert("Result: " + eval(prompt("Enter an expression:","")));
```

```
    }
    catch(exception) {
        alert(exception);
    }
    var myeval = eval;  // May throw an EvalError
    myeval("1+2");      // May throw an EvalError
```

EvalError

thrown when eval( ) is used improperly

Constructor

```
new EvalError( )
new EvalError(message)
```

Arguments

message
> An optional error message that provides details about the exception. If specified, this argument is used as the value for the message property of the EvalError object.

Returns

A newly constructed EvalError object. If the *message* argument is specified, the Error object uses it as the value of its message property; otherwise, it uses an implementation-defined default string as the value of that property. When the EvalError( ) constructor is called as a function without the new operator, it behaves just as it does when called with the new operator.

Properties

message
> An error message that provides details about the exception. This property holds the string passed to the constructor or an implementation-defined default string. See Error.message for details.

name
> A string that specifies the type of the exception. All EvalError objects inherit the value "EvalError" for this property.

Description

An instance of the EvalError class may be thrown when the global function eval( ) is invoked under any other name. See eval( ) for an explanation of the restrictions on how this function may be invoked. See Error for details about throwing and catching exceptions.

See Also

Error, Error.message, Error.name

Function

ECMAScript v1

a JavaScript function

Object → Function

Synopsis

```
function functionname(argument_name_list) // Function definition statement
{
    body
}
function (argument_name_list) {body}        // Unnamed function literal
functionname(argument_value_list)          // Function invocation
```

Constructor

```
new Function(argument_names..., body)
```

Arguments

argument_names...

>   Any number of string arguments, each naming one or more arguments of the Function object being created.

body

>   A string that specifies the body of the function. It may contain any number of Java-Script statements, separated with semicolons, and may refer to any of the argument names specified by previous arguments to the constructor.

Returns

A newly created Function object. Invoking the function executes the JavaScript code specified by *body*.

Throws

SyntaxError

>   Indicates that there was a JavaScript syntax error in the *body* argument or in one of the *argument_names* arguments.

Properties

`arguments[]`

>   An array of arguments that were passed to the function. Deprecated.

`caller`

>   A reference to the Function object that invoked this one, or `null` if the function was invoked from top-level code. Deprecated.

`length`

>   The number of named arguments specified when the function was declared.

`prototype`

>   An object which, for a constructor function, defines properties and methods shared by all objects created with that constructor function.

Methods

apply( )

Invokes a function as a method of a specified object, passing a specified array of arguments.

call( )

Invokes a function as a method of a specified object, passing the specified arguments.

toString( )

Returns a string representation of the function.

Description

A function is a fundamental datatype in JavaScript. Chapter 8 explains how to define and use functions, and Chapter 9 covers the related topics of methods, constructors, and the prototype property of functions. See those chapters for complete details. Note that although function objects may be created with the Function( ) constructor described here, this is not efficient, and the preferred way to define functions, in most cases, is with a function definition statement or a function literal.

In JavaScript 1.1 and later, the body of a function is automatically given a local variable, named arguments, that refers to an Arguments object. This object is an array of the values passed as arguments to the function. Don't confuse this with the deprecated arguments[ ] property listed earlier. See the Arguments reference page for details.

See Also

Arguments; Chapter 8, Chapter 9

Function.apply( ) ECMAScript v3

invoke a function as a method of an object

Synopsis

function.apply(*thisobj, args*)

Arguments

thisobj

The object to which *function* is to be applied. In the body of the function, *thisobj* becomes the value of the this keyword. If this argument is null, the global object is used.

args

An array of values to be passed as arguments to *function*.

Returns

Whatever value is returned by the invocation of *function*.

Throws

TypeError

> If this method is invoked on an object that is not a function or if this method is invoked with an *args* argument that is not an array or an Arguments object.

Description

apply( ) invokes the specified *function* as if it were a method of *thisobj*, passing it the arguments contained in the *args* array. It returns the value returned by the function invocation. Within the body of the function, the this keyword refers to the *thisobj* object.

The *args* argument must be an array or an Arguments object. Use Function.call( ) instead if you want to specify the arguments to pass to the function individually instead of as array elements.

Example

```
// Apply the default Object.toString( ) method to an object that
// overrides it with its own version of the method. Note no arguments.
Object.prototype.toString.apply(o);
// Invoke the Math.max( ) method with apply to find the largest
// element in an array. Note that first argument doesn't matter
// in this case.
var data = [1,2,3,4,5,6,7,8];
Math.max.apply(null, data);
```

See Also

Function.call( )

Function.arguments[]   ECMAScript v1; deprecated by ECMAScript v3

arguments passed to a function

Synopsis

function.arguments[*i*]
function.arguments.length

Description

The arguments property of a Function object is an array of the arguments that are passed to a function. It is defined only while the function is executing. arguments.length specifies the number of elements in the array.

This property is deprecated in favor of the Arguments object. Although ECMAScript v1 supports the Function.arguments property, it has been removed from ECMAScript v3 and conforming implementations may no longer support this property. Therefore, it should never be used in new JavaScript code.

See Also

Arguments

Function.call( )

invoke a function as a method of an object

Synopsis

function.call(*thisobj, args...*)

Arguments

thisobj
> The object on which *function* is to be invoked. In the body of the function, *thisobj* becomes the value of the this keyword. If this argument is null, the global object is used.

args...
> Any number of arguments, which will be passed as arguments to *function*.

Returns

Whatever value is returned by the invocation of *function*.

Throws

TypeError
> If this method is invoked on an object that is not a function.

Description

call( ) invokes the specified *function* as if it were a method of *thisobj*, passing it any arguments that follow *thisobj* in the argument list. The return value of call( ) is the value returned by the function invocation. Within the body of the function, the this keyword refers to the *thisobj* object, or to the global object if *thisobj* is null.

Use Function.apply( ) instead if you want to specify the arguments to pass to the function in an array.

Example

```
// Call the default Object.toString( ) method on an object that
// overrides it with its own version of the method. Note no arguments.
Object.prototype.toString.call(o);
```

See Also

Function.apply( )

Function.caller

the function that called this one

Synopsis

function.caller

Description

In early versions of JavaScript, the `caller` property of a Function object is a reference to the function that invoked the current one. If the function is invoked from the top level of a JavaScript program, `caller` is `null`. This property may be used only from within the function (i.e., the `caller` property is only defined for a function while that function is executing).

`Function.caller` is not part of the ECMAScript standard and is not required in conforming implementations. It should not be used.

Function.length   ECMAScript v1

the number of declared arguments

Synopsis

function.length

Description

The `length` property of a function specifies the number of named arguments declared when the function was defined. The function may actually be invoked with more than or fewer than this number of arguments. Don't confuse this property of a Function object with the `length` property of the Arguments object, which specifies the number of arguments actually passed to the function. See `Arguments.length` for an example.

See Also

`Arguments.length`

Function.prototype   ECMAScript v1

the prototype for a class of objects

Synopsis

function.prototype

Description

The prototype property is used when a function is used as a constructor. It refers to an object that serves as the prototype for an entire class of objects. Any object created by the constructor inherits all properties of the object referred to by the prototype property.

See Chapter 9 for a full discussion of constructor functions, the prototype property, and the definition of classes in JavaScript.

See Also

Chapter 9

Function.toString( )

convert a function to a string

Synopsis

function.toString( )

Returns

A string that represents the function.

Throws

TypeError
> If this method is invoked on an object that is not a Function.

Description

The toString( ) method of the Function object converts a function to a string in an implementation-dependent way. In most implementations, such as the implementations in
Firefox and IE, this method returns a string of valid JavaScript code—code that includes
the function keyword, argument list, the complete body of the function, and so on. In
these implementations, the output of this toString( ) method is valid input for the global
eval( ) function. This behavior is not required by the specification, however, and should
not be relied upon.

getClass( )   LiveConnect

return the JavaClass of a JavaObject

Synopsis

getClass(*javaobj*)

Arguments

javaobj
> A JavaObject object.

Returns

The JavaClass object of *javaobj*.

Description

getClass( ) is a function that takes a JavaObject object (*javaobj*) as an argument. It returns
the JavaClass object of that JavaObject. That is, it returns the JavaClass object that represents the Java class of the Java object represented by the specified JavaObject.

Usage

Don't confuse the JavaScript getClass( ) function with the *getClass* method of all Java
objects. Similarly, don't confuse the JavaScript JavaClass object with the Java *java.lang.Class*
class.

Consider the Java Rectangle object created with the following line:

```
var r = new java.awt.Rectangle( );
```

r is a JavaScript variable that holds a JavaObject object. Calling the JavaScript function getClass( ) returns a JavaClass object that represents the *java.awt.Rectangle* class:

```
var c = getClass(r);
```

You can see this by comparing this JavaClass object to java.awt.Rectangle:

```
if (c == java.awt.Rectangle) ...
```

The Java getClass( ) method is invoked differently and performs an entirely different function:

```
c = r.getClass( );
```

After executing this line of code, c is a JavaObject that represents a java.lang.Class object. This java.lang.Class object is a Java object that is a Java representation of the *java.awt. Rectangle* class. See your Java documentation for details on what you can do with the *java. lang.Class* class.

To summarize, you can see that the following expression always evaluates to true for any JavaObject o:

```
(getClass(o.getClass( )) == java.lang.Class)
```

See Also

JavaArray, JavaClass, JavaObject, JavaPackage; Chapter 12, Chapter 23

Global

the global object

ECMAScript v1

Object → Global

Synopsis

```
this
```

Global Properties

The global object is not a class, so the following global properties have individual reference entries under their own names. That is, you can find details on the undefined property listed under the name undefined, not under Global.undefined. Note that all top-level variables are also properties of the global object:

Infinity
  A numeric value that represents positive infinity.

java
  A JavaPackage that represents the *java.** package hierarchy

NaN
  The not-a-number value.

Packages
  The root JavaPackage object.

undefined
  The undefined value.

Global Functions

The global object is an object, not a class. The global functions listed here are not methods of any object, and their reference entries appear under the function name. For example, you'll find details on the parseInt( ) function under parseInt( ), not Global.parseInt( ):

decodeURI( )
: Decodes a string escaped with encodeURI( ).

decodeURIComponent( )
: Decodes a string escaped with encodeURIComponent( ).

encodeURI
: Encodes a URI by escaping certain characters.

encodeURIComponent
: Encodes a URI component by escaping certain characters.

escape( )
: Encodes a string by replacing certain characters with escape sequences.

eval( )
: Evaluates a string of JavaScript code and returns the result.

getClass( )
: Returns the JavaClass of a JavaObject

isFinite( )
: Tests whether a value is a finite number.

isNaN( )
: Tests whether a value is the not-a-number value.

parseFloat( )
: Parses a number from a string.

parseInt( )
: Parses an integer from a string.

unescape( )
: Decodes a string encoded with escape( ).

Global Objects

In addition to the global properties and functions listed earlier, the global object also defines properties that refer to all the other predefined JavaScript objects. All these properties are constructor functions that define classes except for Math, which is a reference to an object that is not a constructor:

Array
: The Array( ) constructor.

Boolean
: The Boolean( ) constructor.

Date
: The Date( ) constructor.

Error
: The Error( ) constructor.

EvalError
> The EvalError( ) constructor.

Function
> The Function( ) constructor.

Math
> A reference to an object that defines mathematical functions.

Number
> The Number( ) constructor.

Object
> The Object( ) constructor.

RangeError
> The RangeError( ) constructor.

ReferenceError
> The ReferenceError( ) constructor.

RegExp
> The RegExp( ) constructor.

String
> The String( ) constructor.

SyntaxError
> The SyntaxError( ) constructor.

TypeError
> The TypeError( ) constructor.

URIError
> The URIError( ) constructor.

Description

The global object is a predefined object that serves as a placeholder for the global properties and functions of JavaScript. All other predefined objects, functions, and properties are accessible through the global object. The global object is not a property of any other object, so it does not have a name. (The title of this reference page was chosen simply for organizational convenience and does not indicate that the global object is named "Global"). In top-level JavaScript code, you can refer to the global object with the keyword this. It is rarely necessary to refer to the global object in this way, however, because the global object serves as the top of the scope chain, which means that unqualified variable and function names are looked up as properties of the object. When JavaScript code refers to the parseInt( ) function, for example, it is referring to the parseInt property of the global object. The fact that the global object is the top of the scope chain also means that all variables declared in top-level JavaScript code become properties of the global object.

The global object is simply an object, not a class. There is no Global( ) constructor, and there is no way to instantiate a new global object.

When JavaScript is embedded in a particular environment, the global object is usually given additional properties that are specific to that environment. In fact, the type of the global object is not specified by the ECMAScript standard, and an implementation or embedding of JavaScript may use an object of any type as the global object, as long as the object defines the basic properties and functions listed here. For example, in JavaScript implementations that allow the scripting of Java via LiveConnect or related technologies, the global object is given the java and Packages properties and the getClass( ) method listed here. And in client-side JavaScript, the global object is a Window object and represents the web browser window within which the JavaScript code is running.

Example

In core JavaScript, none of the predefined properties of the global object are enumerable, so you can list all implicitly and explicitly declared global variables with a for/in loop like this:

```
var variables = ""
for(var name in this)
    variables += name + "\n";
```

See Also

Window in Part IV; Chapter 4

Infinity

a numeric property that represents infinity

Synopsis

Infinity

Description

Infinity is a global property that contains the special numeric value representing positive infinity. The Infinity property is not enumerated by for/in loops and cannot be deleted with the delete operator. Note that Infinity is not a constant and can be set to any other value, something that you should take care not to do. (Number.POSITIVE_INFINITY is a constant, however.)

See Also

isFinite( ), NaN, Number.POSITIVE_INFINITY

isFinite( )

determine whether a number is finite

Synopsis

isFinite(n)

Arguments

n   The number to be tested.

Returns

true if *n* is (or can be converted to) a finite number, or false if *n* is NaN (not a number) or positive or negative infinity.

See Also

Infinity, isNaN( ), NaN, Number.NaN, Number.NEGATIVE_INFINITY, Number.POSITIVE_INFINITY

isNaN( )   ECMAScript v1

check for not-a-number

Synopsis

isNaN(*x*)

Arguments

x   The value to be tested.

Returns

true if *x* is (or can be converted to) the special not-a-number value; false if *x* is any other value.

Description

isNaN( ) tests its argument to determine whether it is the value NaN, which represents an illegal number (such as the result of division by zero). This function is required because comparing a NaN with any value, including itself, always returns false, so it is not possible to test for NaN with the == or === operators.

A common use of isNaN( ) is to test the results of parseFloat( ) and parseInt( ) to determine if they represent legal numbers. You can also use isNaN( ) to check for arithmetic errors, such as division by zero.

Example

```
isNaN(0);                 // Returns false
isNaN(0/0);               // Returns true
isNaN(parseInt("3"));     // Returns false
isNaN(parseInt("hello")); // Returns true
isNaN("3");               // Returns false
isNaN("hello");           // Returns true
isNaN(true);              // Returns false
isNaN(undefined);         // Returns true
```

See Also

isFinite( ), NaN, Number.NaN, parseFloat( ), parseInt( )

java

the JavaPackage for the java.* package hierarchy

Synopsis

java

Description

In JavaScript implementations that include LiveConnect or other technology for scripting Java, the global java property is a JavaPackage object that represents the *java.** package hierarchy. The existence of this property means that a JavaScript expression such as java.util refers to the Java package *java.util*. For Java packages that do not fall in the *java.** hierarchy, see the global Packages property.

See Also

JavaPackage, Packages; Chapter 12

JavaArray

JavaScript representation of a Java array

Synopsis

```
javaarray.length // The length of the array
javaarray[index] // Read or write an array element
```

Properties

length
  A read-only integer that specifies the number of elements in the Java array represented by the JavaArray object.

Description

The JavaArray object is a JavaScript representation of a Java array that allows JavaScript code to read and write the elements of the array using familiar JavaScript array syntax. In addition, the JavaArray object has a length field that specifies the number of elements in the Java array.

When reading and writing values from array elements, data conversion between JavaScript and Java representations is automatically handled by the system. See Chapter 12 for full details.

Usage

Note that Java arrays differ from JavaScript arrays in a couple of important aspects. First, Java arrays have a fixed length that is specified when they are created. For this reason, the JavaArray length field is read-only. The second difference is that Java arrays are *typed* (i.e., their elements must all be of the same type of data). Attempting to set an array element to a value of the wrong type results in a JavaScript error or exception.

Example

java.awt.Polygon is a JavaClass object. You can create a JavaObject representing an instance of the class like this:

```
p = new java.awt.Polygon( );
```

The object p has properties xpoints and ypoints, which are JavaArray objects representing Java arrays of integers. You can initialize the contents of these arrays with JavaScript code like the following:

```
for(var i = 0; i < p.xpoints.length; i++)
    p.xpoints[i] = Math.round(Math.random( )*100);
for(var i = 0; i < p.ypoints.length; i++)
    p.ypoints[i] = Math.round(Math.random( )*100);
```

See Also

getClass( ), JavaClass, JavaObject, JavaPackage; Chapter 12

JavaClass LiveConnect

JavaScript representation of a Java class

Synopsis

```
javaclass.static_member    // Read or write a static Java field or method
new javaclass(...)         // Create a new Java object
```

Properties

Each JavaClass object contains properties that have the same names as the public static fields and methods of the Java class it represents. These properties allow you to read and write the static fields of the class and invoke the static methods of the class. Each JavaClass object has different properties; you can use a for/in loop to enumerate them for any given JavaClass object.

Description

The JavaClass object is a JavaScript representation of a Java class. The properties of a Java-Class object represent the public static fields and methods (sometimes called class fields and class methods) of the represented class. Note that the JavaClass object does not have properties representing the *instance* fields of a Java class; individual instances of a Java class are represented by the JavaObject object.

The JavaClass object implements the LiveConnect functionality that allows JavaScript programs to read and write the static variables of Java classes using normal JavaScript syntax. It also provides the functionality that allows JavaScript to invoke the static methods of a Java class.

In addition to allowing JavaScript to read and write Java variable and method values, the JavaClass object allows JavaScript programs to create Java objects (represented by a JavaObject object) by using the new keyword and invoking the constructor method of a JavaClass.

The data conversion required for communication between JavaScript and Java through the JavaClass object is handled automatically by LiveConnect. See Chapter 12 for full details.

Usage

Bear in mind that Java is a *typed* language. This means that each of the fields of an object has a specific datatype that is set to values of only that type. Attempting to set a field to a value that is not of the correct type results in a JavaScript error or exception. Attempting to invoke a method with arguments of the wrong type also causes an error or exception.

Example

java.lang.System is a JavaClass object that represents the *java.lang.System* class in Java. You can read a static field of this class with code like the following:

```
var java_console = java.lang.System.out;
```

You can invoke a static method of this class with a line like this one:

```
var version = java.lang.System.getProperty("java.version");
```

Finally, the JavaClass object also allows you to create new Java objects:

```
var java_date = new java.lang.Date();
```

See Also

getClass( ), JavaArray, JavaObject, JavaPackage; Chapter 12

JavaObject   LiveConnect

JavaScript representation of a Java object

Synopsis

javaobject.member // Read or write an instance field or method

Properties

Each JavaObject object contains properties that have the same names as the public instance fields and methods (but not the static or class fields and methods) of the Java object it represents. These properties allow you to read and write the value of public fields and invoke the public methods. The properties of a given JavaObject object obviously depend on the type of Java object it represents. You can use the for/in loop to enumerate the properties of any given JavaObject.

Description

The JavaObject object is a JavaScript representation of a Java object. The properties of a JavaObject object represent the public instance fields and public instance methods defined for the Java object. (The class or static fields and methods of the object are represented by the JavaClass object.)

The JavaObject object implements the LiveConnect functionality that allows JavaScript programs to read and write the public instance fields of a Java object using normal Java-Script syntax. It also provides the functionality that allows JavaScript to invoke the

Core JavaScript Reference

methods of a Java object. Data conversion between JavaScript and Java representations is handled automatically by LiveConnect. See Chapter 12 for full details.

Usage

Bear in mind that Java is a *typed* language. This means that each field of an object has a specific datatype, and you can set it only to values of that type. For example, the width field of a java.awt.Rectangle object is an integer field, and attempting to set it to a string causes a JavaScript error or exception.

Example

java.awt.Rectangle is a JavaClass that represents the *java.awt.Rectangle* class. You can create a JavaObject that represents an instance of this class like this:

```
var r = new java.awt.Rectangle(0,0,4,5);
```

You can then read the public instance variables of this JavaObject r with code like this:

```
var perimeter = 2*r.width + 2*r.height;
```

You can also set the value of public instance variables of r using JavaScript syntax:

```
r.width = perimeter/4;
r.height = perimeter/4;
```

See Also

getClass( ), JavaArray, JavaClass, JavaPackage; Chapter 12

JavaPackage   LiveConnect

JavaScript representation of a Java package

Synopsis

```
package.package_name  // Refers to another JavaPackage
package.class_name     // Refers to a JavaClass object
```

Properties

The properties of a JavaPackage object are the names of the JavaPackage objects and Java-Class objects that it contains. These properties are different for each individual JavaPackage. Note that it is not possible to use the JavaScript for/in loop to iterate over the list of property names of a Package object. Consult a Java reference manual to determine the packages and classes contained within any given package.

Description

The JavaPackage object is a JavaScript representation of a Java package. A package in Java is a collection of related classes. In JavaScript, a JavaPackage can contain classes (represented by the JavaClass object) and other JavaPackage objects.

The global object has a JavaPackage property named java that represents the *java.** package hierarchy. This JavaPackage object defines properties that refer to other JavaPackage objects. For example, java.lang and java.net refer to the *java.lang* and *java.net* packages.

The java.awt JavaPackage contains properties named Frame and Button, which are references to JavaClass objects and represent the classes *java.awt.Frame* and *java.awt.Button*.

The global object also defines a property named Packages, which is the root JavaPackage whose properties refer to the roots of all known package hierarchies. For example, the expression Packages.javax.swing refers to the Java package *javax.swing*.

It is not possible to use the for/in loop to determine the names of the packages and classes contained within a JavaPackage. You must have this information in advance. You can find it in any Java reference manual or by examining the Java class hierarchy.

See Chapter 12 for further details on working with Java packages, classes, and objects.

See Also

java, JavaArray, JavaClass, JavaObject, Packages; Chapter 12

JSObject

see JSObject in Part IV

Math   ECMAScript v1

mathematical functions and constants

Synopsis

Math.*constant*
Math.*function*( )

Constants

Math.E
> The constant *e*, the base of the natural logarithm.

Math.LN10
> The natural logarithm of 10.

Math.LN2
> The natural logarithm of 2.

Math.LOG10E
> The base-10 logarithm of *e*.

Math.LOG2E
> The base-2 logarithm of *e*.

Math.PI
> The constant π.

Math.SQRT1_2
> The number 1 divided by the square root of 2.

Math.SQRT2
> The square root of 2.

Core JavaScript Reference

Static Functions

`Math.abs( )`
> Computes an absolute value.

`Math.acos( )`
> Computes an arccosine.

`Math.asin( )`
> Computes an arcsine.

`Math.atan( )`
> Computes an arctangent.

`Math.atan2( )`
> Computes the angle from the X axis to a point.

`Math.ceil( )`
> Rounds a number up.

`Math.cos( )`
> Computes a cosine.

`Math.exp( )`
> Computes a power of e.

`Math.floor( )`
> Rounds a number down.

`Math.log( )`
> Computes a natural logarithm.

`Math.max( )`
> Returns the larger of two numbers.

`Math.min( )`
> Returns the smaller of two numbers.

`Math.pow( )`
> Computes x^y.

`Math.random( )`
> Computes a random number.

`Math.round( )`
> Rounds to the nearest integer.

`Math.sin( )`
> Computes a sine.

`Math.sqrt( )`
> Computes a square root.

`Math.tan( )`
> Computes a tangent.

Description

Math is an object that defines properties that refer to useful mathematical functions and constants. These functions and constants are invoked with syntax like this:

```
y = Math.sin(x);
area = radius * radius * Math.PI;
```

Math is not a class of objects as Date and String are. There is no Math( ) constructor, and functions like Math.sin( ) are simply functions, not methods that operate on an object.

See Also

Number

Math.abs( )

compute an absolute value

Synopsis

Math.abs(x)

Arguments

x   Any number.

Returns

The absolute value of x.

Math.acos( )

compute an arccosine

Synopsis

Math.acos(x)

Arguments

x   A number between −1.0 and 1.0.

Returns

The arccosine, or inverse cosine, of the specified value x. This return value is between 0 and π radians.

Math.asin( )

compute an arcsine

Synopsis

Math.asin(x)

Arguments

x   A number between −1.0 and 1.0.

Returns

The arcsine of the specified value x. This return value is between $-\pi/2$ and $\pi/2$ radians.

Math.atan( )
ECMAScript v1

compute an arctangent

Synopsis

```
Math.atan(x)
```

Arguments

x   Any number.

Returns

The arc tangent of the specified value *x*. This return value is between -$\pi/2$ and $\pi/2$ radians.

Math.atan2( )
ECMAScript v1

compute the angle from the X axis to a point

Synopsis

```
Math.atan2(y, x)
```

Arguments

y   The Y coordinate of the point.

x   The X coordinate of the point.

Returns

A value between -π and π radians that specifies the counterclockwise angle between the positive X axis and the point (*x*, *y*).

Description

The Math.atan2( ) function computes the arc tangent of the ratio *y*/*x*. The *y* argument can be considered the Y coordinate (or "rise") of a point, and the *x* argument can be considered the X coordinate (or "run") of the point. Note the unusual order of the arguments to this function: the Y coordinate is passed before the X coordinate.

Math.ceil( )
ECMAScript v1

round a number up

Synopsis

```
Math.ceil(x)
```

Arguments

x   Any numeric value or expression.

Returns

The closest integer greater than or equal to *x*.

Description

`Math.ceil( )` computes the ceiling function—i.e., it returns the closest integer value that is greater than or equal to the function argument. `Math.ceil( )` differs from `Math.round( )` in that it always rounds up, rather than rounding up or down to the closest integer. Also note that `Math.ceil( )` does not round negative numbers to larger negative numbers; it rounds them up toward zero.

Example

```
a = Math.ceil(1.99);    // Result is 2.0
b = Math.ceil(1.01);    // Result is 2.0
c = Math.ceil(1.0);     // Result is 1.0
d = Math.ceil(-1.99);   // Result is -1.0
```

Math.cos( )   ECMAScript v1

compute a cosine

Synopsis

`Math.cos(x)`

Arguments

x   An angle, measured in radians. To convert degrees to radians, multiply the degree value by 0.017453293 ($2\pi/360$).

Returns

The cosine of the specified value x. This return value is between −1.0 and 1.0.

Math.E   ECMAScript v1

the mathematical constant e

Synopsis

`Math.E`

Description

`Math.E` is the mathematical constant e, the base of the natural logarithm, with a value of approximately 2.71828.

Math.exp( )   ECMAScript v1

compute e^x

Synopsis

`Math.exp(x)`

Arguments

x   A numeric value or expression to be used as the exponent.

Returns

e^x, *e* raised to the power of the specified exponent *x*, where *e* is the base of the natural logarithm, with a value of approximately 2.71828.

Math.floor( )   ECMAScript v1

round a number down

Synopsis

`Math.floor(x)`

Arguments

x   Any numeric value or expression.

Returns

The closest integer less than or equal to *x*.

Description

`Math.floor( )` computes the floor function; in other words, it returns the nearest integer value that is less than or equal to the function argument.

`Math.floor( )` rounds a floating-point value down to the closest integer. This behavior differs from that of `Math.round( )`, which rounds up or down to the nearest integer. Also note that `Math.floor( )` rounds negative numbers down (i.e., to be more negative), not up (i.e., closer to zero).

Example

```
a = Math.floor(1.99);    // Result is 1.0
b = Math.floor(1.01);    // Result is 1.0
c = Math.floor(1.0);     // Result is 1.0
d = Math.floor(-1.01);   // Result is -2.0
```

Math.LN10   ECMAScript v1

the mathematical constant $\log_e 10$

Synopsis

`Math.LN10`

Description

`Math.LN10` is $\log_e 10$, the natural logarithm of 10. This constant has a value of approximately 2.3025850929940459011.

Math.LN2 ECMAScript v1

the mathematical constant $\log_e 2$

Synopsis

```
Math.LN2
```

Description

Math.LN2 is $\log_e 2$, the natural logarithm of 2. This constant has a value of approximately 0.69314718055994528623.

Math.log( ) ECMAScript v1

compute a natural logarithm

Synopsis

```
Math.log(x)
```

Arguments

x   Any numeric value or expression greater than zero.

Returns

The natural logarithm of *x*.

Description

Math.log( ) computes $\log_e x$, the natural logarithm of its argument. The argument must be greater than zero.

You can compute the base-10 and base-2 logarithms of a number with these formulas:

$$\log_{10} x = \log_{10} e \cdot \log_e x$$

$$\log_2 x = \log_2 e \cdot \log_e x$$

These formulas translate into the following JavaScript functions:

```
function log10(x) { return Math.LOG10E * Math.log(x); }
function log2(x) { return  Math.LOG2E * Math.log(x); }
```

Math.LOG10E ECMAScript v1

the mathematical constant $\log_{10} e$

Synopsis

```
Math.LOG10E
```

Description

Math.LOG10E is $\log_{10} e$, the base-10 logarithm of the constant *e*. It has a value of approximately 0.43429448190325181667.

Math.LOG2E

ECMAScript v1

the mathematical constant $\log_2 e$

Synopsis

```
Math.LOG2E
```

Description

Math.LOG2E is $\log_2 e$, the base-2 logarithm of the constant e. It has a value of approximately 1.442695040888963387.

Math.max( )

ECMAScript v1; enhanced in ECMAScript v3

return the largest argument

Synopsis

```
Math.max(args...)
```

Arguments

args...

Zero or more values. Prior to ECMAScript v3, this method expects exactly two arguments.

Returns

The largest of the arguments. Returns -Infinity if there are no arguments. Returns NaN if any of the arguments is NaN or is a nonnumeric value that cannot be converted to a number.

Math.min( )

ECMAScript v1; enhanced in ECMAScript v3

return the smallest argument

Synopsis

```
Math.min(args...)
```

Arguments

args...

Any number of arguments. Prior to ECMAScript v3, this function expects exactly two arguments.

Returns

The smallest of the specified arguments. Returns Infinity if there are no arguments. Returns NaN if any argument is NaN or is a nonnumeric value that cannot be converted to a number.

Math.PI
ECMAScript v1

the mathematical constant π

Synopsis

```
Math.PI
```

Description

`Math.PI` is the constant π or pi, the ratio of the circumference of a circle to its diameter. It has a value of approximately 3.14159265358979.

Math.pow( )
ECMAScript v1

compute x^y

Synopsis

```
Math.pow(x, y)
```

Arguments

x The number to be raised to a power.

y The power that *x* is to be raised to.

Returns

x to the power of *y*, x^y.

Description

`Math.pow( )` computes *x* to the power of *y*. Any values of *x* and *y* may be passed to `Math.pow( )`. However, if the result is an imaginary or complex number, `Math.pow( )` returns NaN. In practice, this means that if *x* is negative, *y* should be a positive or negative integer. Also, bear in mind that large exponents can easily cause floating-point overflow and return a value of Infinity.

Math.random( )
ECMAScript v1

return a pseudorandom number

Synopsis

```
Math.random( )
```

Returns

A pseudorandom number between 0.0 and 1.0.

Math.round( )   ECMAScript v1

round to the nearest integer

Synopsis

`Math.round(x)`

Arguments

x   Any number.

Returns

The integer closest to *x*.

Description

`Math.round( )` rounds its argument up or down to the nearest integer. It rounds .5 up. For example, it rounds 2.5 to 3 and rounds -2.5 to -2.

Math.sin( )   ECMAScript v1

compute a sine

Synopsis

`Math.sin(x)`

Arguments

x   An angle, in radians. To convert degrees to radians, multiply by 0.017453293 ($2\pi/360$).

Returns

The sine of *x*. This return value is between -1.0 and 1.0.

Math.sqrt( )   ECMAScript v1

compute a square root

Synopsis

`Math.sqrt(x)`

Arguments

x   A numeric value greater than or equal to zero.

Returns

The square root of *x*. Returns NaN if *x* is less than zero.

Description

`Math.sqrt( )` computes the square root of a number. Note, however, that you can compute arbitrary roots of a number with `Math.pow( )`. For example:

```
Math.cuberoot = function(x){ return Math.pow(x,1/3); }
Math.cuberoot(8);  // Returns 2
```

Math.SQRT1_2

the mathematical constant $1/\sqrt{2}$

Synopsis

```
Math.SQRT1_2
```

Description

`Math.SQRT1_2` is $1/\sqrt{2}$, the reciprocal of the square root of 2. This constant has a value of approximately 0.7071067811865476.

Math.SQRT2

the mathematical constant $\sqrt{2}$

Synopsis

```
Math.SQRT2
```

Description

`Math.SQRT2` is the constant $\sqrt{2}$, the square root of 2. This constant has a value of approximately 1.414213562373095.

Math.tan( )

compute a tangent

Synopsis

```
Math.tan(x)
```

Arguments

x   An angle, measured in radians. To convert degrees to radians, multiply the degree value by 0.017453293 ($2\pi/360$).

Returns

The tangent of the specified angle *x*.

NaN

the not-a-number property

Synopsis

```
NaN
```

Description

`NaN` is a global property that refers to the special numeric not-a-number value. The `NaN` property is not enumerated by `for/in` loops and cannot be deleted with the `delete` operator. Note that NaN is not a constant and can be set to any other value, something that you should take care not to do.

To determine if a value is not a number, use isNaN( ), because NaN always compares as nonequal to any other value, including itself!

See Also

Infinity, isNaN( ), Number.NaN

Number

ECMAScript v1

support for numbers

Object → Number

Constructor

```
new Number(value)
Number(value)
```

Arguments

value

> The numeric value of the Number object being created or a value to be converted to a number.

Returns

When Number( ) is used with the new operator as a constructor, it returns a newly constructed Number object. When Number( ) is invoked as a function without the new operator, it converts its argument to a primitive numeric value and returns that value (or NaN if the conversion failed).

Constants

Number.MAX_VALUE

> The largest representable number.

Number.MIN_VALUE

> The smallest representable number.

Number.NaN

> Not-a-number value.

Number.NEGATIVE_INFINITY

> Negative infinite value; returned on overflow.

Number.POSITIVE_INFINITY

> Infinite value; returned on overflow.

Methods

toString( )

> Converts a number to a string using a specified radix (base).

toLocaleString( )

> Converts a number to a string using local number-formatting conventions.

toFixed( )
> Converts a number to a string that contains a specified number of digits after the decimal place.

toExponential( )
> Converts a number to a string using exponential notation with the specified number of digits after the decimal place.

toPrecision( )
> Converts a number to a string using the specified number of significant digits. Uses exponential or fixed-point notation depending on the size of the number and the number of significant digits specified.

valueOf( )
> Returns the primitive numeric value of a Number object.

Description

Numbers are a basic, primitive datatype in JavaScript. JavaScript also supports the Number object, which is a wrapper object around a primitive numeric value. JavaScript automatically converts between the primitive and object forms as necessary. You can explicitly create a Number object with the Number( ) constructor, although there is rarely any need to do so.

The Number( ) constructor can also be used without the new operator, as a conversion function. When invoked in this way, it attempts to convert its argument to a number and returns the primitive numeric value (or NaN) that results from the conversion.

The Number( ) constructor is also used as a placeholder for five useful numeric constants: the largest and smallest representable numbers, positive and negative infinity, and the special NaN value. Note that these values are properties of the Number( ) constructor function itself, not of individual number objects. For example, you can use the MAX_VALUE property as follows:

```
var biggest = Number.MAX_VALUE
```

but *not* like this:

```
var n = new Number(2);
var biggest = n.MAX_VALUE
```

By contrast, the toString( ) and other methods of the Number object are methods of each Number object, not of the Number( ) constructor function. As noted earlier, JavaScript automatically converts from primitive numeric values to Number objects whenever necessary. This means that you can use the Number methods with primitive numeric values as well as with Number objects.

```
var value = 1234;
var binary_value = n.toString(2);
```

See Also

Infinity, Math, NaN

Number.MAX_VALUE ECMAScript v1

the maximum numeric value

Synopsis

Number.MAX_VALUE

Description

Number.MAX_VALUE is the largest number representable in JavaScript. Its value is approximately 1.79E+308.

Number.MIN_VALUE ECMAScript v1

the minimum numeric value

Synopsis

Number.MIN_VALUE

Description

Number.MIN_VALUE is the smallest (closest to zero, not most negative) number representable in JavaScript. Its value is approximately 5E-324.

Number.NaN ECMAScript v1

the special not-a-number value

Synopsis

Number.NaN

Description

Number.NaN is a special value that indicates that the result of some mathematical operation (such as taking the square root of a negative number) is not a number. parseInt( ) and parseFloat( ) return this value when they cannot parse the specified string, and you might use Number.NaN in a similar way to indicate an error condition for some function that normally returns a valid number.

JavaScript prints the Number.NaN value as NaN. Note that the NaN value always compares as unequal to any other number, including NaN itself. Thus, you cannot check for the not-a-number value by comparing to Number.NaN; use the isNaN( ) function instead. In ECMA-Script v1 and later, you can also use the predefined global property NaN instead of Number.NaN.

See Also

isNaN( ), NaN

Number.NEGATIVE_INFINITY

negative infinity

Synopsis

```
Number.NEGATIVE_INFINITY
```

Description

`Number.NEGATIVE_INFINITY` is a special numeric value that is returned when an arithmetic operation or mathematical function generates a negative value greater than the largest representable number in JavaScript (i.e., more negative than `-Number.MAX_VALUE`).

JavaScript displays the `NEGATIVE_INFINITY` value as `-Infinity`. This value behaves mathematically like infinity; for example, anything multiplied by infinity is infinity, and anything divided by infinity is zero. In ECMAScript v1 and later, you can also use `-Infinity` instead of `Number.NEGATIVE_INFINITY`.

See Also

`Infinity`, `isFinite()`

Number.POSITIVE_INFINITY

infinity

Synopsis

```
Number.POSITIVE_INFINITY
```

Description

`Number.POSITIVE_INFINITY` is a special numeric value returned when an arithmetic operation or mathematical function overflows or generates a value greater than the largest representable number in JavaScript (i.e., greater than `Number.MAX_VALUE`). Note that when numbers "underflow," or become less than `Number.MIN_VALUE`, JavaScript converts them to zero.

JavaScript displays the `POSITIVE_INFINITY` value as `Infinity`. This value behaves mathematically like infinity; for example, anything multiplied by infinity is infinity, and anything divided by infinity is zero. In ECMAScript v1 and later, you can also use the predefined global property `Infinity` instead of `Number.POSITIVE_INFINITY`.

See Also

`Infinity`, `isFinite()`

Core JavaScript Reference

Number.toExponential( )   *ECMAScript v3*

format a number using exponential notation

Synopsis

number.toExponential(*digits*)

Arguments

digits

> The number of digits that appears after the decimal point. This may be a value between 0 and 20, inclusive, and implementations may optionally support a larger range of values. If this argument is omitted, as many digits as necessary are used.

Returns

A string representation of *number*, in exponential notation, with one digit before the decimal place and *digits* digits after the decimal place. The fractional part of the number is rounded, or padded with zeros, as necessary, so that it has the specified length.

Throws

RangeError

> If *digits* is too small or too large. Values between 0 and 20, inclusive, will not cause a RangeError. Implementations are allowed to support larger and smaller values as well.

TypeError

> If this method is invoked on an object that is not a Number.

Example

```
var n = 12345.6789;
n.toExponential(1);    // Returns 1.2e+4
n.toExponential(5);    // Returns 1.23457e+4
n.toExponential(10);   // Returns 1.2345678900e+4
n.toExponential( );    // Returns 1.23456789e+4
```

See Also

Number.toFixed( ), Number.toLocaleString( ), Number.toPrecision( ), Number.toString( )

Number.toFixed( )   *ECMAScript v3*

format a number using fixed-point notation

Synopsis

number.toFixed(*digits*)

Arguments

digits

> The number of digits to appear after the decimal point; this may be a value between 0 and 20, inclusive, and implementations may optionally support a larger range of values. If this argument is omitted, it is treated as 0.

Returns

A string representation of *number* that does not use exponential notation and has exactly *digits* digits after the decimal place. The number is rounded if necessary, and the fractional part is padded with zeros if necessary so that it has the specified length. If *number* is greater than 1e+21, this method simply calls `Number.toString( )` and returns a string in exponential notation.

Throws

RangeError

    If *digits* is too small or too large. Values between 0 and 20, inclusive, will not cause a RangeError. Implementations are allowed to support larger and smaller values as well.

TypeError

    If this method is invoked on an object that is not a Number.

Example

```
var n = 12345.6789;
n.toFixed( );           // Returns 12346: note rounding, no fractional part
n.toFixed(1);           // Returns 12345.7: note rounding
n.toFixed(6);           // Returns 12345.678900: note added zeros
(1.23e+20).toFixed(2);  // Returns 123000000000000000000.00
(1.23e-10).toFixed(2)   // Returns 0.00
```

See Also

`Number.toExponential( )`, `Number.toLocaleString( )`, `Number.toPrecision( )`, `Number.toString( )`

Number.toLocaleString( )   ECMAScript v3

convert a number to a locally formatted string

Synopsis

number`.toLocaleString( )`

Returns

An implementation-dependent string representation of the number, formatted according to local conventions, which may affect such things as the punctuation characters used for the decimal point and the thousands separator.

Throws

TypeError

    If this method is invoked on an object that is not a Number.

See Also

`Number.toExponential( )`, `Number.toFixed( )`, `Number.toPrecision( )`, `Number.toString( )`

Core JavaScript Reference

Number.toPrecision( )

ECMAScript v3

format the significant digits of a number

Synopsis

number.toPrecision(*precision*)

Arguments

precision

>The number of significant digits to appear in the returned string. This may be a value between 1 and 21, inclusive. Implementations are allowed to optionally support larger and smaller values of *precision*. If this argument is omitted, the toString( ) method is used instead to convert the number to a base-10 value.

Returns

A string representation of *number* that contains *precision* significant digits. If *precision* is large enough to include all the digits of the integer part of *number*, the returned string uses fixed-point notation. Otherwise, exponential notation is used with one digit before the decimal place and *precision*–1 digits after the decimal place. The number is rounded or padded with zeros as necessary.

Throws

RangeError

>If *digits* is too small or too large. Values between 1 and 21, inclusive, will not cause a RangeError. Implementations are allowed to support larger and smaller values as well.

TypeError

>If this method is invoked on an object that is not a Number.

Example

```
var n = 12345.6789;
n.toPrecision(1);    // Returns 1e+4
n.toPrecision(3);    // Returns 1.23e+4
n.toPrecision(5);    // Returns 12346: note rounding
n.toPrecision(10);   // Returns 12345.67890: note added zero
```

See Also

Number.toExponential( ), Number.toFixed( ), Number.toLocaleString( ), Number.toString( )

Number.toString( )

ECMAScript v1

convert a number to a string

Overrides Object.toString( )

Synopsis

number.toString(*radix*)

Arguments

radix

An optional argument that specifies the radix, or base, between 2 and 36, in which the number should be represented. If omitted, base 10 is used. Note, however, that the ECMAScript specification allows an implementation to return any value if this argument is specified as any value other than 10.

Returns

A string representation of the number, in the specified base.

Throws

TypeError

If this method is invoked on an object that is not a Number.

Description

The toString( ) method of the Number object converts a number to a string. When the *radix* argument is omitted or is specified as 10, the number is converted to a base-10 string. Although the ECMAScript specification does not require implementations to honor any other values for radix, all implementations in common use accept values between 2 and 36.

See Also

Number.toExponential( ),   Number.toFixed( ),   Number.toLocaleString( ),   Number.toPrecision( )

Number.valueOf( )   ECMAScript v1

return the primitive number value   Overrides Object.valueOf( )

Synopsis

number.valueOf( )

Returns

The primitive number value of this Number object. It is rarely necessary to call this method explicitly.

Throws

TypeError

If this method is invoked on an object that is not a Number.

See Also

Object.valueOf( )

Object

a superclass that contains features of all JavaScript objects

Constructor

```
new Object( )
new Object(value)
```

Arguments

value

> This optional argument specifies a primitive JavaScript value—a number, boolean, or string—that is to be converted to a Number, Boolean, or String object.

Returns

If no *value* argument is passed, this constructor returns a newly created Object instance. If a primitive *value* argument is specified, the constructor creates and returns a Number, Boolean, or String object wrapper for the primitive value. When the Object( ) constructor is called as a function, without the new operator, it behaves just as it does when used with the new operator.

Properties

constructor

> A reference to the JavaScript function that was the constructor for the object.

Methods

hasOwnProperty( )

> Checks whether an object has a locally defined (noninherited) property with a specified name.

isPrototypeOf( )

> Checks whether this object is the prototype object of a specified object.

propertyIsEnumerable( )

> Checks whether a named property exists and would be enumerated by a for/in loop.

toLocaleString( )

> Returns a localized string representation of the object. The default implementation of this method simply calls toString( ), but subclasses may override it to provide localization.

toString( )

> Returns a string representation of the object. The implementation of this method provided by the Object class is quite generic and does not provide much useful information. Subclasses of Object typically override this method by defining their own toString( ) method, which produces more useful output.

valueOf( )

> Returns the primitive value of the object, if any. For objects of type Object, this method simply returns the object itself. Subclasses of Object, such as Number and Boolean, override this method to return the primitive value associated with the object.

Description

The Object class is a built-in datatype of the JavaScript language. It serves as the superclass for all other JavaScript objects; therefore, methods and behavior of the Object class are inherited by all other objects. The basic behavior of objects in JavaScript is explained in Chapter 7.

In addition to the Object( ) constructor shown above, objects can also be created and initialized using the Object literal syntax described in Chapter 7.

See Also

Array, Boolean, Function, Function.prototype, Number, String; Chapter 7

Object.constructor   ECMAScript v1

an object's constructor function

Synopsis

object.constructor

Description

The constructor property of any object is a reference to the function that was used as the constructor for that object. For example, if you create an array a with the Array( ) constructor, a.constructor is an Array:

```
a = new Array(1,2,3);   // Create an object
a.constructor == Array  // Evaluates to true
```

One common use of the constructor property is to determine the type of unknown objects. Given an unknown value, you can use the typeof operator to determine whether it is a primitive value or an object. If it is an object, you can use the constructor property to determine what type of object it is. For example, the following function determines whether a given value is an array:

```
function isArray(x) {
    return ((typeof x == "object") && (x.constructor == Array));
}
```

Note, however, that while this technique works for the objects built into core JavaScript, it is not guaranteed to work with host objects such as the Window object of client-side Java-Script. The default implementation of the Object.toString( ) method provides another way to determine the type of an unknown object.

See Also

Object.toString( )

Object.hasOwnProperty( )   ECMAScript v3

check whether a property is inherited

Synopsis

object.hasOwnProperty(*propname*)

Arguments

propname

A string that contains the name of a property of *object*.

Returns

true if *object* has a noninherited property with the name specified by *propname*; false if *object* does not have a property with the specified name or if it inherits that property from its prototype object.

Description

As explained in Chapter 9, JavaScript objects may have properties of their own, and they may also inherit properties from their prototype object. The hasOwnProperty( ) method provides a way to distinguish between inherited properties and noninherited local properties.

Example

```
var o = new Object();           // Create an object
o.x = 3.14;                     // Define a noninherited local property
o.hasOwnProperty("x");          // Returns true: x is a local property of o
o.hasOwnProperty("y");          // Returns false: o doesn't have a property y
o.hasOwnProperty("toString");   // Returns false: toString property is inherited
```

See Also

Function.prototype, Object.propertyIsEnumerable( ); Chapter 9

Object.isPrototypeOf( )   ECMAScript v3

is one object the prototype of another?

Synopsis

object.isPrototypeOf(*o*)

Arguments

o   Any object.

Returns

true if *object* is the prototype of *o*; false if *o* is not an object or if *object* is not the prototype of *o*.

Description

As explained in Chapter 9, JavaScript objects inherit properties from their prototype object. The prototype of an object is referred to by the prototype property of the constructor function that creates and initializes the object. The isPrototypeOf( ) method provides a way to determine if one object is the prototype of another. This technique can be used to determine the class of an object.

Example

```
var o = new Object();                       // Create an object
Object.prototype.isPrototypeOf(o)           // true: o is an object
Function.prototype.isPrototypeOf(o.toString);  // true: toString is a function
Array.prototype.isPrototypeOf([1,2,3]);     // true: [1,2,3] is an array
// Here is a way to perform a similar test
(o.constructor == Object);  // true: o was created with Object() constructor
(o.toString.constructor == Function);       // true: o.toString is a function
// Prototype objects themselves have prototypes. The following call
// returns true, showing that function objects inherit properties
// from Function.prototype and also from Object.prototype.
Object.prototype.isPrototypeOf(Function.prototype);
```

See Also

Function.prototype, Object.constructor; Chapter 9

Object.propertyIsEnumerable( ) ECMAScript v3

will property be seen by a for/in loop?

Synopsis

object.propertyIsEnumerable(*propname*)

Arguments

propname
    A string that contains the name of a property of *object*.

Returns

true if *object* has a noninherited property with the name specified by *propname* and if that property is *enumerable*, which means that it would be enumerated by a for/in loop on *object*.

Description

The for/in statement loops through the enumerable properties of an object. Not all properties of an object are enumerable, however: properties added to an object by JavaScript code are enumerable, but the predefined properties (such as methods) of built-in objects are not usually enumerable. The propertyIsEnumerable( ) method provides a way to distinguish between enumerable and nonenumerable properties. Note, however, that the ECMAScript specification states that propertyIsEnumerable( ) does not examine the prototype chain, which means it works only for local properties of an object and does not provide any way to test the enumerability of inherited properties.

Core JavaScript Reference

Example

```
var o = new Object();           // Create an object
o.x = 3.14;                     // Define a property
o.propertyIsEnumerable("x");    // true: property x is local and enumerable
o.propertyIsEnumerable("y");    // false: o doesn't have a property y
o.propertyIsEnumerable("toString"); // false: toString property is inherited
Object.prototype.propertyIsEnumerable("toString");  // false: nonenumerable
```

See Also

Function.prototype, Object.hasOwnProperty( ); Chapter 7

Object.toLocaleString( )   ECMAScript v3

return an object's localized string representation

Synopsis

object.toString( )

Returns

A string representing the object.

Description

This method is intended to return a string representation of the object, localized as appropriate for the current locale. The default toLocaleString( ) method provided by the Object class simply calls the toString( ) method and returns the nonlocalized string that it returns. Note, however, that other classes, including Array, Date, and Number, define their own versions of this method to perform localized string conversions. When defining your own classes, you may want to override this method as well.

See Also

Array.toLocaleString( ), Date.toLocaleString( ), Number.toLocaleString( ), Object.toString( )

Object.toString( )   ECMAScript v1

define an object's string representation

Synopsis

object.toString( )

Returns

A string representing the object.

Description

The toString( ) method is not one you often call explicitly in your JavaScript programs. Instead, you define this method in your objects, and the system calls it whenever it needs to convert your object to a string.

The JavaScript system invokes the toString() method to convert an object to a string whenever the object is used in a string context. For example, an object is converted to a string when it is passed to a function that expects a string argument:

```
alert(my_object);
```

Similarly, objects are converted to strings when they are concatenated to strings with the + operator:

```
var msg = 'My object is: ' + my_object;
```

The toString() method is invoked without arguments and should return a string. To be useful, the string you return should be based, in some way, on the value of the object for which the method was invoked.

When you define a custom class in JavaScript, it is good practice to define a toString() method for the class. If you do not, the object inherits the default toString() method from the Object class. This default method returns a string of the form:

```
[object class]
```

where *class* is the class of the object: a value such as "Object", "String", "Number", "Function", "Window", "Document", and so on. This behavior of the default toString() method is occasionally useful to determine the type or class of an unknown object. Because most objects have a custom version of toString(), however, you must explicitly invoke the Object.toString() method on an object o with code like this:

```
Object.prototype.toString.apply(o);
```

Note that this technique for identifying unknown objects works only for built-in objects. If you define your own object class, it will have a *class* of "Object". In this case, you can use the Object.constructor property to obtain more information about the object.

The toString() method can be quite useful when you are debugging JavaScript programs; it allows you to print objects and see their value. For this reason alone, it is a good idea to define a toString() method for every object class you create.

Although the toString() method is usually invoked automatically by the system, there are times when you may invoke it yourself. For example, you might want to do an explicit conversion of an object to a string in a situation where JavaScript does not do it automatically for you:

```
y = Math.sqrt(x);       // Compute a number
ystr = y.toString();    // Convert it to a string
```

Note in this example that numbers have a built-in toString() method you can use to force a conversion.

In other circumstances, you can choose to use a toString() call even in a context where JavaScript does the conversion automatically. Using toString() explicitly can help to make your code clearer:

```
alert(my_obj.toString());
```

See Also

Object.constructor, Object.toLocaleString(), Object.valueOf()

Core JavaScript Reference

Object.valueOf( )

the primitive value of the specified object

Synopsis

object.valueOf( )

Returns

The primitive value associated with the *object*, if any. If there is no value associated with *object*, returns the object itself.

Description

The valueOf( ) method of an object returns the primitive value associated with that object, if there is one. For objects of type Object, there is no primitive value, and this method simply returns the object itself.

For objects of type Number, however, valueOf( ) returns the primitive numeric value represented by the object. Similarly, it returns the primitive boolean value associated with a Boolean object and the string associated with a String object.

It is rarely necessary to invoke the valueOf( ) method yourself. JavaScript does this automatically whenever an object is used where a primitive value is expected. In fact, because of this automatic invocation of the valueOf( ) method, it is difficult to even distinguish between primitive values and their corresponding objects. The typeof operator shows you the difference between strings and String objects for example, but in practical terms, you can use them equivalently in your JavaScript code.

The valueOf( ) methods of the Number, Boolean, and String objects convert these wrapper objects to the primitive values they represent. The Object( ) constructor performs the opposite operation when invoked with a number, boolean, or string argument: it wraps the primitive value in an appropriate object wrapper. JavaScript performs this primitive-to-object conversion for you in almost all circumstances, so it is rarely necessary to invoke the Object( ) constructor in this way.

In some circumstances, you may want to define a custom valueOf( ) method for your own objects. For example, you might define a JavaScript object type to represent complex numbers (a real number plus an imaginary number). As part of this object type, you would probably define methods for performing complex addition, multiplication, and so on (see Example 9-2). But you might also want to treat your complex numbers like ordinary real numbers by discarding the imaginary part. To achieve this, you might do something like the following:

```
Complex.prototype.valueOf = new Function("return this.real");
```

With this valueOf( ) method defined for your Complex object type, you can, for example, pass one of your complex number objects to Math.sqrt( ), which computes the square root of the real portion of the complex number.

See Also

Object.toString( )

Packages

the root JavaPackage

Synopsis

Packages

Description

In JavaScript implementations that include LiveConnect or other technology for scripting Java, the global Packages property is a JavaPackage object whose properties are all the package roots known to the Java interpreter. For example, Packages.javax.swing refers to the Java package *javax.swing*. The global property java is a shortcut for Packages.java.

See Also

java, JavaPackage; Chapter 12

parseFloat( )

convert a string to a number

Synopsis

parseFloat(s)

Arguments

s   The string to be parsed and converted to a number.

Returns

The parsed number, or NaN if s does not begin with a valid number. In JavaScript 1.0, parseFloat( ) returns 0 instead of NaN when s cannot be parsed as a number.

Description

parseFloat( ) parses and returns the first number that occurs in s. Parsing stops, and the value is returned, when parseFloat( ) encounters a character in s that is not a valid part of the number. If s does not begin with a number that parseFloat( ) can parse, the function returns the not-a-number value NaN. Test for this return value with the isNaN( ) function. If you want to parse only the integer portion of a number, use parseInt( ) instead of parseFloat( ).

See Also

isNaN( ), parseInt( )

parseInt( ) ECMAScript v1

convert a string to an integer

Synopsis

```
parseInt(s)
parseInt(s, radix)
```

Arguments

s   The string to be parsed.

radix

An optional integer argument that represents the radix (i.e., base) of the number to be parsed. If this argument is omitted or is 0, the number is parsed in base 10—or in base 16 if it begins with 0x or 0X. If this argument is less than 2 or greater than 36, parseInt( ) returns NaN.

Returns

The parsed number, or NaN if s does not begin with a valid integer. In JavaScript 1.0, parseInt( ) returns 0 instead of NaN when it cannot parse s.

Description

parseInt( ) parses and returns the first number (with an optional leading minus sign) that occurs in s. Parsing stops, and the value is returned, when parseInt( ) encounters a character in s that is not a valid digit for the specified radix. If s does not begin with a number that parseInt( ) can parse, the function returns the not-a-number value NaN. Use the isNaN( ) function to test for this return value.

The radix argument specifies the base of the number to be parsed. Specifying 10 makes parseInt( ) parse a decimal number. The value 8 specifies that an octal number (using digits 0 through 7) is to be parsed. The value 16 specifies a hexadecimal value, using digits 0 through 9 and letters A through F. radix can be any value between 2 and 36.

If radix is 0 or is not specified, parseInt( ) tries to determine the radix of the number from s. If s begins (after an optional minus sign) with 0x, parseInt( ) parses the remainder of s as a hexadecimal number. If s begins with a 0, the ECMAScript v3 standard allows an implementation of parseInt( ) to interpret the following characters as an octal number or as a decimal number. Otherwise, if s begins with a digit from 1 through 9, parseInt( ) parses it as a decimal number.

Example

```
parseInt("19", 10);  // Returns 19  (10 + 9)
parseInt("11", 2);   // Returns 3   (2 + 1)
parseInt("17", 8);   // Returns 15  (8 + 7)
parseInt("1f", 16);  // Returns 31  (16 + 15)
parseInt("10");      // Returns 10
parseInt("0x10");    // Returns 16
parseInt("010");     // Ambiguous: returns 10 or 8
```

Bugs

When no *radix* is specified, ECMAScript v3 allows an implementation to parse a string that begins with 0 (but not 0x or 0X) as an octal or as a decimal number. To avoid this ambiguity, you should explicitly specify a radix or leave the radix unspecified only when you are sure that all numbers to be parsed will be decimal numbers, or hexadecimal numbers with the 0x or 0X prefix.

See Also

isNaN( ), parseFloat( )

RangeError   ECMAScript v3

thrown when a number is out of its legal range   Object → Error → RangeError

Constructor

```
new RangeError( )
new RangeError(message)
```

Arguments

message
> An optional error message that provides details about the exception. If specified, this argument is used as the value for the message property of the RangeError object.

Returns

A newly constructed RangeError object. If the *message* argument is specified, the Error object uses it as the value of its message property; otherwise, it uses an implementation-defined default string as the value of that property. When the RangeError( ) constructor is called as a function, without the new operator, it behaves just as it would when called with the new operator.

Properties

message
> An error message that provides details about the exception. This property holds the string passed to the constructor or an implementation-defined default string. See Error.message for details.

name
> A string that specifies the type of the exception. All RangeError objects inherit the value "RangeError" for this property.

Description

An instance of the RangeError class is thrown when a numeric value is not in its legal range. For example, setting the length of an array to a negative number causes a RangeError to be thrown. See Error for details about throwing and catching exceptions.

See Also

Error, Error.message, Error.name

ReferenceError

ECMAScript v3

thrown when reading a variable that does not exist

Object → Error → ReferenceError

Constructor

```
new ReferenceError( )
new ReferenceError(message)
```

Arguments

message

> An optional error message that provides details about the exception. If specified, this argument is used as the value for the message property of the ReferenceError object.

Returns

A newly constructed ReferenceError object. If the *message* argument is specified, the Error object uses it as the value of its message property; otherwise, it uses an implementation-defined default string as the value of that property. When the ReferenceError( ) constructor is called as a function, without the new operator, it behaves just as it would with the new operator.

Properties

message

> An error message that provides details about the exception. This property holds the string passed to the constructor or an implementation-defined default string. See Error.message for details.

name

> A string that specifies the type of the exception. All ReferenceError objects inherit the value "ReferenceError" for this property.

Description

An instance of the ReferenceError class is thrown when you attempt to read the value of a variable that does not exist. See Error for details about throwing and catching exceptions.

See Also

Error, Error.message, Error.name

RegExp

ECMAScript v3

regular expressions for pattern matching

Object → RegExp

Literal Syntax

/pattern/attributes

Constructor

new RegExp(*pattern, attributes*)

Arguments

pattern

A string that specifies the pattern of the regular expression or another regular expression.

attributes

An optional string containing any of the "g", "i", and "m" attributes that specify global, case-insensitive, and multiline matches, respectively. The "m" attribute is not available prior to ECMAScript standardization. If the *pattern* argument is a regular expression instead of a string, this argument must be omitted.

Returns

A new RegExp object, with the specified pattern and flags. If the *pattern* argument is a regular expression rather than a string, the RegExp( ) constructor creates a new RegExp object using the same pattern and flags as the specified RegExp. If RegExp( ) is called as a function without the new operator, it behaves just as it would with the new operator, except when *pattern* is a regular expression; in that case, it simply returns *pattern* instead of creating a new RegExp object.

Throws

SyntaxError

If *pattern* is not a legal regular expression, or if *attributes* contains characters other than "g", "i", and "m".

TypeError

If *pattern* is a RegExp object, and the *attributes* argument is not omitted.

Instance Properties

global

Whether the RegExp has the "g" attribute.

ignoreCase

Whether the RegExp has the "i" attribute.

lastIndex

The character position of the last match; used for finding multiple matches in a string.

multiline

Whether the RegExp has the "m" attribute.

source

The source text of the regular expression.

Methods

exec( )

Performs powerful, general-purpose pattern matching.

test( )

Tests whether a string contains a pattern.

Description

The RegExp object represents a regular expression, a powerful tool for performing pattern matching on strings. See Chapter 11 for complete details on regular-expression syntax and use.

See Also

Chapter 11

RegExp.exec( )

general-purpose pattern matching

Synopsis

regexp.exec(*string*)

Arguments

string

> The string to be searched.

Returns

An array containing the results of the match or null if no match was found. The format of the returned array is described below.

Throws

TypeError

> If this method is invoked on an object that is not a RegExp.

Description

exec( ) is the most powerful of all the RegExp and String pattern-matching methods. It is a general-purpose method that is somewhat more complex to use than RegExp.test( ), String.search( ), String.replace( ), and String.match( ).

exec( ) searches *string* for text that matches *regexp*. If it finds a match, it returns an array of results; otherwise, it returns null. Element 0 of the returned array is the matched text. Element 1 is the text that matched the first parenthesized subexpression, if any, within *regexp*. Element 2 contains the text that matched the second subexpression, and so on. The array length property specifies the number of elements in the array, as usual. In addition to the array elements and the length property, the value returned by exec( ) also has two other properties. The index property specifies the character position of the first character of the matched text. The input property refers to *string*. This returned array is the same as the array that is returned by the String.match( ) method, when invoked on a nonglobal RegExp object.

When exec( ) is invoked on a nonglobal pattern, it performs the search and returns the result described earlier. When *regexp* is a global regular expression, however, exec( ) behaves in a slightly more complex way. It begins searching *string* at the character position specified by the lastIndex property of *regexp*. When it finds a match, it sets lastIndex to the position of the first character after the match. This means that you can invoke exec( ) repeatedly in order to loop through all matches in a string. When exec( ) cannot find any more matches, it returns null and resets lastIndex to zero. If you begin searching a new string immediately after successfully finding a match in another string, you must be careful to manually reset lastIndex to zero.

Note that exec( ) always includes full details of every match in the array it returns, whether or not *regexp* is a global pattern. This is where exec( ) differs from String.match( ), which returns much less information when used with global patterns. Calling the exec( ) method repeatedly in a loop is the only way to obtain complete pattern-matching information for a global pattern.

Example

You can use exec( ) in a loop to find all matches within a string. For example:

```
var pattern = /\bJava\w*\b/g;
var text = "JavaScript is more fun than Java or JavaBeans!";
var result;
while((result = pattern.exec(text)) != null) {
    alert("Matched `" + result[0] +
          "' at position " + result.index +
          " next search begins at position " + pattern.lastIndex);
}
```

See Also

RegExp.lastIndex, RegExp.test( ), String.match( ), String.replace( ), String.search( ); Chapter 11

RegExp.global   ECMAScript v3

whether a regular expression matches globally

Synopsis

regexp.global

Description

global is a read-only boolean property of RegExp objects. It specifies whether a particular regular expression performs global matching—i.e., whether it was created with the "g" attribute.

RegExp.ignoreCase   ECMAScript v3

whether a regular expression is case-insensitive

Synopsis

regexp.ignoreCase

Description

ignoreCase is a read-only boolean property of RegExp objects. It specifies whether a particular regular expression performs case-insensitive matching—i.e., whether it was created with the "i" attribute.

RegExp.lastIndex   ECMAScript v3

the starting position of the next match

Synopsis

regexp.lastIndex

Description

lastIndex is a read/write property of RegExp objects. For regular expressions with the "g" attribute set, it contains an integer that specifies the character position immediately following the last match found by the RegExp.exec( ) and RegExp.test( ) methods. These methods use this property as the starting point for the next search they conduct. This allows you to call those methods repeatedly, to loop through all matches in a string. Note that lastIndex is not used by RegExp objects that do not have the "g" attribute set and do not represent global patterns.

This property is read/write, so you can set it at any time to specify where in the target string the next search should begin. exec( ) and test( ) automatically reset lastIndex to 0 when they fail to find a match (or another match). If you begin to search a new string after a successful match of some other string, you have to explicitly set this property to 0.

See Also

RegExp.exec( ), RegExp.test( )

RegExp.source   ECMAScript v3

the text of the regular expression

Synopsis

regexp.source

Description

source is a read-only string property of RegExp objects. It contains the text of the RegExp pattern. This text does not include the delimiting slashes used in regular-expression literals, and it does not include the "g", "i", and "m" attributes.

RegExp.test( )   ECMAScript v3

test whether a string matches a pattern

Synopsis

regexp.test(*string*)

Arguments

string
> The string to be tested.

Returns

true if *string* contains text that matches *regexp*; false otherwise.

Throws

TypeError
> If this method is invoked on an object that is not a RegExp.

Description

test( ) tests *string* to see if it contains text that matches *regexp*. If so, it returns true; otherwise, it returns false. Calling the test( ) method of a RegExp r and passing it the string s is equivalent to the following expression:

```
(r.exec(s) != null)
```

Example

```
var pattern = /java/i;
pattern.test("JavaScript");   // Returns true
pattern.test("ECMAScript");   // Returns false
```

See Also

RegExp.exec( ), RegExp.lastIndex, String.match( ), String.replace( ), String.substring( );
Chapter 11

RegExp.toString( )   ECMAScript v3

convert a regular expression to a string   Overrides Object.toString( )

Synopsis

regexp.toString( )

Returns

A string representation of *regexp*.

Throws

TypeError
> If this method is invoked on an object that is not a RegExp.

Description

The RegExp.toString( ) method returns a string representation of a regular expression in the form of a regular-expression literal.

Note that implementations are not required to add escape sequences to ensure that the returned string is a legal regular-expression literal. Consider the regular expression created by the expression new RegExp("/","g"). An implementation of RegExp.toString() could return ///g for this regular expression; it could also add an escape sequence and return /\//g.

String

support for strings

Constructor

```
new String(s) // Constructor function
String(s)     // Conversion function
```

Arguments

s   The value to be stored in a String object or converted to a primitive string.

Returns

When String() is used as a constructor with the new operator, it returns a String object, which holds the string s or the string representation of s. When the String() constructor is used without the new operator, it simply converts s to a primitive string and returns the converted value.

Properties

length
    The number of characters in the string.

Methods

charAt( )
    Extracts the character at a given position from a string.
charCodeAt( )
    Returns the encoding of the character at a given position in a string.
concat( )
    Concatenates one or more values to a string.
indexOf( )
    Searches the string for a character or substring.
lastIndexOf( )
    Searches the string backward for a character or substring.
localeCompare( )
    Compares strings using locale-specific ordering.
match( )
    Performs pattern matching with a regular expression.
replace( )
    Performs a search-and-replace operation with a regular expression.
search( )
    Searches a string for a substring that matches a regular expression.

slice( )
> Returns a slice or substring of a string.

split( )
> Splits a string into an array of strings, breaking at a specified delimiter string or regular expression.

substr( )
> Extracts a substring of a string; a variant of substring( ).

substring( )
> Extracts a substring of a string.

toLowerCase( )
> Returns a copy of the string, with all characters converted to lowercase.

toString( )
> Returns the primitive string value.

toUpperCase( )
> Returns a copy of the string, with all characters converted to uppercase.

valueOf( )
> Returns the primitive string value.

Static Methods

String.fromCharCode( )
> Creates a new string using the character codes passed as arguments.

HTML Methods

Since the earliest days of JavaScript, the String class has defined a number of methods that return a string modified by placing it within HTML tags. These methods have never been standardized by ECMAScript but can be useful in both client- and server-side JavaScript code that dynamically generates HTML. If you are willing to use nonstandard methods, you might create the HTML source for a bold, red hyperlink with code like this:

```
var s = "click here!";
var html = s.bold( ).link("javascript:alert('hello')").fontcolor("red");
```

Because these methods are not standardized, they do not have individual reference entries in the pages that follow:

anchor(*name*)
> Returns a copy of the string, in an <a name=> environment.

big( )
> Returns a copy of the string, in a <big> environment.

blink( )
> Returns a copy of the string, in a <blink> environment.

bold( )
> Returns a copy of the string, in a <b> environment.

fixed( )
> Returns a copy of the string, in a <tt> environment.

fontcolor(*color*)
> Returns a copy of the string, in a <font color=> environment.

```
fontsize(size)
```
　　　Returns a copy of the string, in a <font size=> environment.
```
italics( )
```
　　　Returns a copy of the string, in an <i> environment.
```
link(url)
```
　　　Returns a copy of the string, in an <a href=> environment.
```
small( )
```
　　　Returns a copy of the string, in a <small> environment.
```
strike( )
```
　　　Returns a copy of the string, in a <strike> environment.
```
sub( )
```
　　　Returns a copy of the string, in a <sub> environment.
```
sup( )
```
　　　Returns a copy of the string, in a <sup> environment.

Description

Strings are a primitive datatype in JavaScript. The String class type exists to provide methods for operating on primitive string values. The length property of a String object specifies the number of characters in the string. The String class defines a number of methods for operating on strings; for example, there are methods for extracting a character or a substring from the string or searching for a character or a substring. Note that JavaScript strings are *immutable*: none of the methods defined by the String class allows you to change the contents of a string. Instead, methods such as String.toUpperCase( ) return an entirely new string, without modifying the original.

In implementations of JavaScript derived from the original Netscape code base (such as the implementation in Firefox), strings behave like read-only arrays of characters. For example, to extract the third character from a string s, you can write s[2] instead of the more standard s.charAt(2). In addition, when the for/in statement is applied to a string, it enumerates these array indexes for each character in the string. (Note, however, that the length property is not enumerated, as per the ECMAScript specification.) Because this string-as-array behavior is not standard, you should avoid using it.

See Also

Chapter 3

String.charAt( )   ECMAScript v1

get the *n*th character from a string

Synopsis

string.charAt(*n*)

Arguments

n　　　The index of the character that should be returned from *string*.

Returns

The *n*th character of *string*.

Description

`String.charAt( )` returns the *n*th character of the string *string*. The first character of the string is numbered 0. If *n* is not between 0 and *string.length*–1, this method returns an empty string. Note that JavaScript does not have a character data type that is distinct from the string type, so the returned character is a string of length 1.

See Also

`String.charCodeAt( )`, `String.indexOf( )`, `String.lastIndexOf( )`

String.charCodeAt( )   ECMAScript v1

get the *n*th character code from a string

Synopsis

string.charCodeAt(*n*)

Arguments

n   The index of the character whose encoding is to be returned.

Returns

The Unicode encoding of the *n*th character within *string*. This return value is a 16-bit integer between 0 and 65535.

Description

`charCodeAt( )` is like `charAt( )`, except that it returns the character encoding at a specific location, rather than returning a substring that contains the character itself. If *n* is negative or greater than or equal to the string length, `charCodeAt( )` returns `NaN`.

See `String.fromCharCode( )` for a way to create a string from Unicode encodings.

See Also

`String.charAt( )`, `String.fromCharCode( )`

String.concat( )   ECMAScript v3

concatenate strings

Synopsis

string.concat(*value*, ...)

Arguments

value, ...
    One or more values to be concatenated to *string*.

Returns

A new string that results from concatenating each of the arguments to *string*.

Description

concat( ) converts each of its arguments to a string (if necessary) and appends them, in order, to the end of *string*. It returns the resulting concatenation. Note that *string* itself is not modified.

String.concat( ) is an analog to Array.concat( ). Note that it is often easier to use the + operator to perform string concatenation.

See Also

Array.concat( )

String.fromCharCode( )   ECMAScript v1

create a string from character encodings

Synopsis

String.fromCharCode(*c1, c2, ...*)

Arguments

c1, c2, ...

Zero or more integers that specify the Unicode encodings of the characters in the string to be created.

Returns

A new string containing characters with the specified encodings.

Description

This static method provides a way to create a string by specifying the individual numeric Unicode encodings of its characters. Note that as a static method, fromCharCode( ) is a property of the String( ) constructor and is not actually a method of strings or String objects.

String.charCodeAt( ) is a companion instance method that provides a way to obtain the encodings of the individual characters of a string.

Example

```
// Create the string "hello"
var s = String.fromCharCode(104, 101, 108, 108, 111);
```

See Also

String.charCodeAt( )

String.indexOf( ) ECMAScript v1

search a string

Synopsis

```
string.indexOf(substring)
string.indexOf(substring, start)
```

Arguments

substring
> The substring that is to be searched for within *string*.

start
> An optional integer argument that specifies the position within *string* at which the search is to start. Legal values are 0 (the position of the first character in the string) to `string.length–1` (the position of the last character in the string). If this argument is omitted, the search begins at the first character of the string.

Returns

The position of the first occurrence of *substring* within *string* that appears after the *start* position, if any, or –1 if no such occurrence is found.

Description

`String.indexOf( )` searches the string *string* from beginning to end to see if it contains an occurrence of *substring*. The search begins at position *start* within *string*, or at the beginning of *string* if *start* is not specified. If an occurrence of *substring* is found, `String.indexOf( )` returns the position of the first character of the first occurrence of *substring* within *string*. Character positions within *string* are numbered starting with zero.

If no occurrence of *substring* is found within *string*, `String.indexOf( )` returns –1.

See Also

`String.charAt( )`, `String.lastIndexOf( )`, `String.substring( )`

String.lastIndexOf( ) ECMAScript v1

search a string backward

Synopsis

```
string.lastIndexOf(substring)
string.lastIndexOf(substring, start)
```

Arguments

substring
> The substring to be searched for within *string*.

start
> An optional integer argument that specifies the position within *string* where the search is to start. Legal values are from 0 (the position of the first character in the string) to *string*.length–1 (the position of the last character in the string). If this argument is omitted, the search begins with the last character of the string.

Returns

The position of the last occurrence of *substring* within *string* that appears before the *start* position, if any, or –1 if no such occurrence is found within *string*.

Description

String.lastIndexOf( ) searches the string from end to beginning to see if it contains an occurrence of *substring*. The search begins at position *start* within *string*, or at the end of *string* if *start* is not specified. If an occurrence of *substring* is found, String.lastIndexOf( ) returns the position of the first character of that occurrence. Since this method searches from end to beginning of the string, the first occurrence found is the last one in the string that occurs before the *start* position.

If no occurrence of *substring* is found, String.lastIndexOf( ) returns –1.

Note that although String.lastIndexOf( ) searches *string* from end to beginning, it still numbers character positions within *string* from the beginning. The first character of the string has position 0, and the last has position *string*.length–1.

See Also

String.charAt( ), String.indexOf( ), String.substring( )

String.length   ECMAScript v1

the length of a string

Synopsis

string.length

Description

The String.length property is a read-only integer that indicates the number of characters in the specified *string*. For any string *s*, the index of the last character is *s*.length–1. The length property of a string is not enumerated by a for/in loop and may not be deleted with the delete operator.

String.localeCompare( )   ECMAScript v3

compare one string to another, using locale-specific ordering

Synopsis

string.localeCompare(*target*)

Arguments

target
> A string to be compared, in a locale-sensitive fashion, with *string*.

Returns

A number that indicates the result of the comparison. If *string* is "less than" *target*, localeCompare( ) returns a number less than zero. If *string* is "greater than" *target*, the method returns a number greater than zero. And if the strings are identical or indistinguishable according to the locale ordering conventions, the method returns 0.

Description

When the < and > operators are applied to strings, they compare those strings using only the Unicode encodings of those characters and do not consider the collation order of the current locale. The ordering produced in this way is not always correct. Consider Spanish, for example, in which the letters "ch" are traditionally sorted as if they were a single letter that appeared between the letters "c" and "d".

localeCompare( ) provides a way to compare strings that does take the collation order of the default locale into account. The ECMAScript standard does not specify how the locale-specific comparison is done; it merely specifies that this function utilize the collation order provided by the underlying operating system.

Example

You can use code like the following to sort an array of strings into a locale-specific ordering:

```
var strings;  // The array of strings to sort; initialized elsewhere
strings.sort(function(a,b) { return a.localeCompare(b) });
```

String.match( ) ECMAScript v3

find one or more regular-expression matches

Synopsis

string.match(*regexp*)

Arguments

regexp
> A RegExp object that specifies the pattern to be matched. If this argument is not a RegExp, it is first converted to one by passing it to the RegExp( ) constructor.

Returns

An array containing the results of the match. The contents of the array depend on whether *regexp* has the global "g" attribute set. Details on this return value are given in the Description.

Description

match( ) searches *string* for one or more matches of *regexp*. The behavior of this method depends significantly on whether *regexp* has the "g" attribute or not (see Chapter 11 for full details on regular expressions).

If *regexp* does not have the "g" attribute, match( ) searches *string* for a single match. If no match is found, match( ) returns null. Otherwise, it returns an array containing information about the match that it found. Element 0 of the array contains the matched text. The remaining elements contain the text that matches any parenthesized subexpressions within the regular expression. In addition to these normal array elements, the returned array also has two object properties. The index property of the array specifies the character position within *string* of the start of the matched text. Also, the input property of the returned array is a reference to *string* itself.

If *regexp* has the "g" flag, match( ) does a global search, searching *string* for all matching substrings. It returns null if no match is found, and it returns an array if one or more matches are found. The contents of this returned array are quite different for global matches, however. In this case, the array elements contain each of the matched substrings within *string*. The returned array does not have index or input properties in this case. Note that for global matches, match( ) does not provide information about parenthesized subexpressions, nor does it specify where within *string* each match occurred. If you need to obtain this information for a global search, you can use RegExp.exec( ).

Example

The following global match finds all numbers within a string:

```
"1 plus 2 equals 3".match(/\d+/g)  // Returns ["1", "2", "3"]
```

The following nonglobal match uses a more complex regular expression with several parenthesized subexpressions. It matches a URL, and its subexpressions match the protocol, host, and path portions of the URL:

```
var url = /(\w+):\/\/([\w.]+)\/(\S*)/;
var text = "Visit my home page at http://www.isp.com/~david";
var result = text.match(url);
if (result != null) {
    var fullurl = result[0];   // Contains "http://www.isp.com/~david"
    var protocol = result[1];  // Contains "http"
    var host = result[2];      // Contains "www.isp.com"
    var path = result[3];      // Contains "~david"
}
```

See Also

RegExp, RegExp.exec( ), RegExp.test( ), String.replace( ), String.search( ); Chapter 11

String.replace( )   ECMAScript v3

replace substring(s) matching a regular expression

Synopsis

string.replace(*regexp, replacement*)

Arguments

regexp

    The RegExp object that specifies the pattern to be replaced. If this argument is a string, it is used as a literal text pattern to be searched for; it is not first converted to a RegExp object.

replacement

    A string that specifies the replacement text, or a function that is invoked to generate the replacement text. See the Description section for details.

Returns

A new string, with the first match, or all matches, of *regexp* replaced with *replacement*.

Description

replace( ) performs a search-and-replace operation on *string*. It searches *string* for one or more substrings that match *regexp* and replaces them with *replacement*. If *regexp* has the global "g" attribute specified, replace( ) replaces all matching substrings. Otherwise, it replaces only the first matching substring.

replacement may be a string or a function. If it is a string, each match is replaced by the string. Note that the $ character has special meaning within the *replacement* string. As shown in the following table, it indicates that a string derived from the pattern match is used in the replacement.

Characters	Replacement
$1, $2, ..., $99	The text that matched the 1st through 99th parenthesized subexpression within *regexp*
$&	The substring that matched *regexp*
$`	The text to the left of the matched substring
$'	The text to the right of the matched substring
$$	A literal dollar sign

ECMAScript v3 specifies that the *replacement* argument to replace( ) may be a function instead of a string. In this case, the function is invoked for each match, and the string it returns is used as the replacement text. The first argument to the function is the string that matches the pattern. The next arguments are the strings that match any parenthesized subexpressions within the pattern; there may be zero or more of these arguments. The next argument is an integer that specifies the position within *string* at which the match occurred, and the final argument to the *replacement* function is *string* itself.

Example

To ensure that the capitalization of the word "JavaScript" is correct:

```
text.replace(/javascript/i, "JavaScript");
```

To convert a single name from "Doe, John" format to "John Doe" format:

```
name.replace(/(\w+)\s*,\s*(\w+)/, "$2 $1");
```

To replace all double quotes with double back and forward single quotes:

```
text.replace(/"([^"]*)"/g, "``$1''");
```

To capitalize the first letter of all words in a string:

```
text.replace(/\b\w+\b/g, function(word) {
                    return word.substring(0,1).toUpperCase() +
                        word.substring(1);
        });
```

See Also

RegExp, RegExp.exec( ), RegExp.test( ), String.match( ), String.search( ); Chapter 11

String.search( )   ECMAScript v3

search for a regular expression

Synopsis

string.search(*regexp*)

Arguments

regexp

> A RegExp object that specifies the pattern to be searched for in *string*. If this argument is not a RegExp, it is first converted to one by passing it to the RegExp( ) constructor.

Returns

The position of the start of the first substring of *string* that matches *regexp*, or −1 if no match is found.

Description

search( ) looks for a substring matching *regexp* within *string* and returns the position of the first character of the matching substring, or −1 if no match was found.

search( ) does not do global matches; it ignores the g flag. It also ignores the lastIndex property of *regexp* and always searches from the beginning of the string, which means that it always returns the position of the first match in *string*.

Example

```
var s = "JavaScript is fun";
s.search(/script/i)  // Returns 4
s.search(/a(.)a/)    // Returns 1
```

See Also

RegExp, RegExp.exec( ), RegExp.test( ), String.match( ), String.replace( ); Chapter 11

String.slice( )

extract a substring

Synopsis

string.slice(*start, end*)

Arguments

start
> The string index where the slice is to begin. If negative, this argument specifies a position measured from the end of the string. That is, −1 indicates the last character, −2 indicates the second from last character, and so on.

end
> The string index immediately after the end of the slice. If not specified, the slice includes all characters from *start* to the end of the string. If this argument is negative, it specifies a position measured from the end of the string.

Returns

A new string that contains all the characters of *string* from and including *start*, and up to but not including *end*.

Description

slice( ) returns a string containing a slice, or substring, of *string*. It does not modify *string*.

The String methods slice( ), substring( ), and the deprecated substr( ) all return specified portions of a string. slice( ) is more flexible than substring( ) because it allows negative argument values. slice( ) differs from substr( ) in that it specifies a substring with two character positions, while substr( ) uses one position and a length. Note also that String.slice( ) is an analog of Array.slice( ).

Example

```
var s = "abcdefg";
s.slice(0,4)    // Returns "abcd"
s.slice(2,4)    // Returns "cd"
s.slice(4)      // Returns "efg"
s.slice(3,-1)   // Returns "def"
s.slice(3,-2)   // Returns "de"
s.slice(-3,-1)  // Should return "ef"; returns "abcdef" in IE 4
```

Bugs

Negative values for *start* do not work in Internet Explorer 4 (but they do in later versions of IE). Instead of specifying a character position measured from the end of the string, they specify character position 0.

See Also

Array.slice( ), String.substring( )

String.split( )

break a string into an array of strings

Synopsis

string.split(*delimiter, limit*)

Arguments

delimiter
> The string or regular expression at which the *string* splits.

limit
> This optional integer specifies the maximum length of the returned array. If specified, no more than this number of substrings will be returned. If not specified, the entire string will be split, regardless of its length.

Returns

An array of strings, created by splitting *string* into substrings at the boundaries specified by *delimiter*. The substrings in the returned array do not include *delimiter* itself, except in the case noted in the Description.

Description

The split( ) method creates and returns an array of as many as *limit* substrings of the specified string. These substrings are created by searching the string from start to end for text that matches *delimiter* and breaking the string before and after that matching text. The delimiting text is not included in any of the returned substrings, except as noted at the end of this section. Note that if the delimiter matches the beginning of the string, the first element of the returned array will be an empty string—the text that appears before the delimiter. Similarly, if the delimiter matches the end of the string, the last element of the array (assuming no conflicting *limit*) will be the empty string.

If no *delimiter* is specified, the string is not split at all, and the returned array contains only a single, unbroken string element. If *delimiter* is the empty string or a regular expression that matches the empty string, the string is broken between each character, and the returned array has the same length as the string does, assuming no smaller *limit* is specified. (Note that this is a special case because the empty strings before the first character and after the last character are not matched.)

As noted earlier, the substrings in the array returned by this method do not contain the delimiting text used to split the string. However, if *delimiter* is a regular expression that contains parenthesized subexpressions, the substrings that match those parenthesized subexpressions (but not the text that matches the regular expression as a whole) are included in the returned array.

Note that the String.split( ) method is the inverse of the Array.join( ) method.

Example

The split( ) method is most useful when you are working with highly structured strings. For example:

```
"1:2:3:4:5".split(":");  // Returns ["1","2","3","4","5"]
"|a|b|c|".split("|");    // Returns ["", "a", "b", "c", ""]
```

Another common use of the split( ) method is to parse commands and similar strings by breaking them down into words delimited by spaces:

```
var words = sentence.split(' ');
```

It is easier to split a string into words using a regular expression as a delimiter:

```
var words = sentence.split(/\s+/);
```

To split a string into an array of characters, use the empty string as the delimiter. Use the *limit* argument if you only want to split a prefix of the string into an array of characters:

```
"hello".split("");      // Returns ["h","e","l","l","o"]
"hello".split("", 3);   // Returns ["h","e","l"]
```

If you want the delimiters or one or more portions of the delimiter included in the returned array, use a regular expression with parenthesized subexpressions. For example, the following code breaks a string at HTML tags and includes those tags in the returned array:

```
var text = "hello <b>world</b>";
text.split(/(<[^>]*>)/);  // Returns ["hello ","<b>","world","</b>",""]
```

See Also

Array.join( ), RegExp; Chapter 11

String.substr( ) JavaScript 1.2; deprecated

extract a substring

Synopsis

string.substr(*start*, *length*)

Arguments

start
> The start position of the substring. If this argument is negative, it specifies a position measured from the end of the string: −1 specifies the last character, −2 specifies the second-to-last character, and so on.

length
> The number of characters in the substring. If this argument is omitted, the returned substring includes all characters from the starting position to the end of the string.

Returns

A copy of the portion of *string* starting at and including the character specified by *start* and continuing for *length* characters, or to the end of the string if *length* is not specified.

Description

substr( ) extracts and returns a substring of *string*. It does not modify *string*.

Note that substr( ) specifies the desired substring with a character position and a length. This provides a useful alternative to String.substring( ) and String.splice( ), which specify a substring with two character positions. Note, however, that this method has not been standardized by ECMAScript and is therefore deprecated.

Example

```
var s = "abcdefg";
s.substr(2,2);    // Returns "cd"
s.substr(3);      // Returns "defg"
s.substr(-3,2);   // Should return "ef"; returns "ab" in IE 4
```

Bugs

Negative values for *start* do not work in IE 4 (this is fixed in later versions of IE). Instead of specifying a character position measured from the end of the string, they specify character position 0.

See Also

String.slice( ), String.substring( )

String.substring( )

return a substring of a string

Synopsis

```
string.substring(from, to)
```

Arguments

from

> A nonnegative integer that specifies the position within *string* of the first character of the desired substring.

to

> A nonnegative optional integer that is one greater than the position of the last character of the desired substring. If this argument is omitted, the returned substring runs to the end of the string.

Returns

A new string, of length *to–from*, which contains a substring of *string*. The new string contains characters copied from positions *from* to *to–1* of *string*.

Description

String.substring( ) returns a substring of *string* consisting of the characters between positions *from* and *to*. The character at position *from* is included, but the character at position *to* is not included.

If *from* equals *to*, this method returns an empty (length 0) string. If *from* is greater than *to*, this method first swaps the two arguments and then returns the substring between them.

It is important to remember that the character at position *from* is included in the substring but that the character at position *to* is not included in the substring. While this may seem arbitrary or counterintuitive, a notable feature of this system is that the length of the returned substring is always equal to *to–from*.

Note that String.slice( ) and the nonstandard String.substr( ) can also extract substrings from a string. Unlike those methods, String.substring( ) does not accept negative arguments.

See Also

String.charAt( ), String.indexOf( ), String.lastIndexOf( ), String.slice( ), String. substr( )

String.toLocaleLowerCase( )   ECMAScript v3

convert a string to lowercase

Synopsis

string.toLocaleLowerCase( )

Returns

A copy of *string*, converted to lowercase letters in a locale-specific way. Only a few languages, such as Turkish, have locale-specific case mappings, so this method usually returns the same value as toLowerCase( ).

See Also

String.toLocaleUpperCase( ), String.toLowerCase( ), String.toUpperCase( )

String.toLocaleUpperCase( )   ECMAScript v3

convert a string to uppercase

Synopsis

string.toLocaleUpperCase( )

Returns

A copy of *string*, converted to uppercase letters in a locale-specific way. Only a few languages, such as Turkish, have locale-specific case mappings, so this method usually returns the same value as toUpperCase( ).

See Also

String.toLocaleLowerCase( ), String.toLowerCase( ), String.toUpperCase( )

String.toLowerCase( )   ECMAScript v1

convert a string to lowercase

Synopsis

string.toLowerCase( )

Returns

A copy of *string*, with each uppercase letter converted to its lowercase equivalent, if it has one.

String.toString( )

ECMAScript v1

return the string

Overrides Object.toString( )

Synopsis

string.toString( )

Returns

The primitive string value of *string*. It is rarely necessary to call this method.

Throws

TypeError

    If this method is invoked on an object that is not a String.

See Also

String.valueOf( )

String.toUpperCase( )

ECMAScript v1

convert a string to uppercase

Synopsis

string.toUpperCase( )

Returns

A copy of *string*, with each lowercase letter converted to its uppercase equivalent, if it has one.

String.valueOf( )

ECMAScript v1

return the string

Overrides Object.valueOf( )

Synopsis

string.valueOf( )

Returns

The primitive string value of *string*.

Throws

TypeError

    If this method is invoked on an object that is not a String.

See Also

String.toString( )

SyntaxError

thrown to signal a syntax error

Constructor

```
new SyntaxError( )
new SyntaxError(message)
```

Arguments

message

> An optional error message that provides details about the exception. If specified, this argument is used as the value for the message property of the SyntaxError object.

Returns

A newly constructed SyntaxError object. If the *message* argument is specified, the Error object uses it as the value of its message property; otherwise, it uses an implementation-defined default string as the value of that property. When the SyntaxError( ) constructor is called as a function, without the new operator, it behaves just as it does when called with the new operator.

Properties

message

> An error message that provides details about the exception. This property holds the string passed to the constructor, or an implementation-defined default string. See Error.message for details.

name

> A string that specifies the type of the exception. All SyntaxError objects inherit the value "SyntaxError" for this property.

Description

An instance of the SyntaxError class is thrown to signal a syntax error in JavaScript code. The eval( ) method, the Function( ) constructor, and the RegExp( ) constructor may all throw exceptions of this type. See Error for details about throwing and catching exceptions.

See Also

Error, Error.message, Error.name

TypeError

thrown when a value is of the wrong type

Constructor

```
new TypeError( )
new TypeError(message)
```

Arguments

message

> An optional error message that provides details about the exception. If specified, this argument is used as the value for the message property of the TypeError object.

Returns

A newly constructed TypeError object. If the *message* argument is specified, the Error object uses it as the value of its message property; otherwise, it uses an implementation-defined default string as the value of that property. When the TypeError( ) constructor is called as a function, without the new operator, it behaves just as it does when called with the new operator.

Properties

message

> An error message that provides details about the exception. This property holds the string passed to the constructor, or an implementation-defined default string. See Error.message for details.

name

> A string that specifies the type of the exception. All TypeError objects inherit the value "TypeError" for this property.

Description

An instance of the TypeError class is thrown when a value is not of the type expected. This happens most often when you attempt to access a property of a null or undefined value. It can also occur if you invoke a method defined by one class on an object that is an instance of some other class, or if you use the new operator with a value that is not a constructor function, for example. JavaScript implementations are also permitted to throw TypeError objects when a built-in function or method is called with more arguments than expected. See Error for details about throwing and catching exceptions.

See Also

Error, Error.message, Error.name

undefined

ECMAScript v3

the undefined value

Synopsis

undefined

Description

undefined is a global property that holds the JavaScript undefined value. This is the same value that is returned when you attempt to read the value of a nonexistent object property. The undefined property is not enumerated by for/in loops and cannot be deleted with the delete operator. Note that undefined is not a constant and can be set to any other value, something that you should take care not to do.

When testing a value to see whether it is undefined, use the === operator, because the == operator treats the undefined value as equal to null.

unescape( ) ECMAScript v1; deprecated in ECMAScript v3

decode an escaped string

Synopsis

unescape(s)

Arguments

s   The string that is to be decoded or "unescaped."

Returns

A decoded copy of s.

Description

unescape( ) is a global function that decodes a string encoded with escape( ). It decodes s by finding and replacing character sequences of the form %xx and %uxxxx (where x represents a hexadecimal digit) with the Unicode characters \u00xx and \uxxxx.

Although unescape( ) was standardized in the first version of ECMAScript, it has been deprecated and removed from the standard by ECMAScript v3. Implementations of ECMAScript are likely to implement this function, but they are not required to. You should use decodeURI( ) and decodeURIComponent( ) instead of unescape( ). See escape( ) for more details and an example.

See Also

decodeURI( ), decodeURIComponent( ), escape( ), String

URIError ECMAScript v3

thrown by URI encoding and decoding methods   Object → Error → URIError

Constructor

new URIError( )
new URIError(message)

Arguments

message
    An optional error message that provides details about the exception. If specified, this argument is used as the value for the message property of the URIError object.

Returns

A newly constructed URIError object. If the *message* argument is specified, the Error object uses it as the value of its message property; otherwise, it uses an implementation-defined default string as the value of that property. When the URIError( ) constructor is called as a function without the new operator, it behaves just as it does when called with the new operator.

Properties

message

> An error message that provides details about the exception. This property holds the string passed to the constructor, or an implementation-defined default string. See Error.message for details.

name

> A string that specifies the type of the exception. All URIError objects inherit the value "URIError" for this property.

Description

An instance of the URIError class is thrown by decodeURI( ) and decodeURIComponent( ) if the specified string contains illegal hexadecimal escapes. It can also be thrown by encodeURI( ) and encodeURIComponent( ) if the specified string contains illegal Unicode surrogate pairs. See Error for details about throwing and catching exceptions.

See Also

Error, Error.message, Error.name

PART IV

Client-Side JavaScript Reference

This part of the book is a complete reference to all of the objects, properties, functions, methods, and event handlers in client-side JavaScript. See the sample entry at the beginning of Part III for an explanation of how to use this reference.

Classes and objects documented in this part include:

Anchor	DOMException	JSObject	Table
Applet	DOMImplementation	KeyEvent	TableCell
Attr	DOMParser	Link	TableRow
Canvas	Element	Location	TableSection
CanvasGradient	Event	MimeType	Text
CanvasPattern	ExternalInterface	MouseEvent	Textarea
CanvasRenderingContext2D	FlashPlayer	Navigator	UIEvent
CDATASection	Form	Node	Window
CharacterData	Frame	NodeList	XMLHttpRequest
Comment	History	Option	XMLSerializer
CSS2Properties	HTMLCollection	Plugin	XPathExpression
CSSRule	HTMLDocument	ProcessingInstruction	XPathResult
CSSStyleSheet	HTMLElement	Range	XSLTProcessor
Document	IFrame	RangeException	
DocumentFragment	Image	Screen	
DocumentType	Input	Select	

Client-Side JavaScript Reference

This part of the book is a reference section that documents the classes, methods, properties, and event handlers defined in client-side JavaScript. This introduction and the sample reference page found at the beginning of Part III explain how to use and get the most out of this reference section. Take the time to read this material carefully, and you will find it easier to locate and use the information you need!

This reference section is arranged alphabetically. The reference pages for the methods and properties of classes are alphabetized by their full names, which include the names of the classes that define them. For example, if you want to read about the submit( ) method of the Form class, you would look under "Form.submit," not just "submit."

Most client-side JavaScript properties do not have reference pages of their own (all methods and event handlers do have their own reference pages, however). Instead, simple properties are completely documented in the reference page for the class that defines them. For example, you can read about the images[ ] property of the HTML-Document class in the HTMLDocument reference page. Nontrivial properties that require substantial explanation do have reference pages of their own, and you'll find a cross-reference to these pages within the reference page of the class or interface that defines the properties. For example, when you look up the cookie property in the HTMLDocument reference page, you'll find a short description of the property and a reference to more information under HTMLDocument.cookie.

Client-side JavaScript has a number of global properties and functions, such as window, history, and alert( ). In client-side JavaScript, a Window object serves as the global object, and the "global" properties and functions of client-side JavaScript are actually properties of the Window class. Therefore, global properties and functions are documented in the Window reference page or under names such as Window.alert( ).

Once you've found the reference page you're looking for, you shouldn't have much difficulty finding the information you need. Still, you'll be able to make better use of this reference section if you understand how the reference pages are written and organized. Part III begins with an a sample reference page titled "Sample Entry." That entry explains the structure of each reference page and tells how to find the information you need within a reference page.

Anchor

the target of a hypertext link

DOM Level 0

Node → Element → HTMLElement → Anchor

Properties

String name

Contains the name of an Anchor object. The value of this property is set by the name attribute of the `<a>` tag.

Methods

focus( )

Scrolls the document so the location of the anchor is visible.

HTML Syntax

An Anchor object is created by any standard HTML `<a>` tag that contains a name attribute:

```
<a name="name">  // Links may refer to this anchor by this name
    ...
</a>
```

Description

An anchor is a named location within an HTML document. Anchors are created with an `<a>` tag that has a name attribute specified. The Document object has an anchors[] array property that contains Anchor objects that represent each of the anchors in the document. Anchor objects can be referenced by index or by name within this array.

You can make a browser display the location of an anchor by setting the hash property of the Location object to a # character followed by the name of the anchor or by simply calling the focus( ) method of the Anchor object itself.

Note that the `<a>` tag used to create anchors is also used to create hypertext links. Although hypertext links are often called anchors in HTML parlance, they are represented in Java-Script with the Link object, not with the Anchor object.

Example

```
// Scroll the document so the anchor named "_bottom_" is visible
document.anchors['_bottom_'].focus();
```

See Also

Document, Link, Location

Anchor.focus( )

scroll to make the anchor location visible

Synopsis

```
void focus( );
```

Description

This method scrolls the document so the location of the Anchor object is visible.

Applet

an applet embedded in a web page

Synopsis

```
document.applets[i]
document.appletName
```

Properties

The Applet object has properties that mirror the HTML attributes of the `<applet>` tag (see `HTMLElement` for details). It also has properties corresponding to the public fields of the Java applet it represents.

Methods

The methods of an Applet object are the same as the public methods of the Java applet it represents.

Description

The Applet object represents a Java applet embedded in an HTML document. The Applet objects of a document may be obtained through the `applets[]` collection of the Document object.

The properties of the Applet object represent the public fields of the applet, and the methods of the Applet object represent the public methods of the applet. Remember that Java is a strongly typed language. This means that each field of an applet has been declared to have a specific data type, and setting it to a value of some other type causes a runtime error. The same is true of applet methods: each argument has a specific type, and arguments cannot be omitted as they can be in JavaScript. See Chapter 23 for further details.

See Also

`JSObject`; `JavaObject` in Part III; Chapter 12, Chapter 23

Attr

an attribute of a document element

Properties

readonly String name
> The name of the attribute.

readonly Element ownerElement [DOM Level 2]
> The Element object that contains this attribute, or null if the Attr object is not currently associated with any Element.

readonly boolean specified
> true if the attribute is explicitly specified in the document source or set by a script; false if the attribute is not explicitly specified but a default value is specified in the document's DTD.

String value
> The value of the attribute. When reading this property, the attribute value is returned as a string. When you set this property to a string, it automatically creates a Text node that contains the same text and makes that Text node the sole child of the Attr object.

Description

An Attr object represents an attribute of an Element node. Attr objects are associated with Element nodes but are not directly part of the document tree (and have a null parentNode property). You can obtain an Attr object through the attributes property of the Node interface or by calling the getAttributeNode() or getAttributeNodeNS() methods of the Element interface.

The value of an attribute is represented by the descendant nodes of an Attr node. In HTML documents, an Attr node always has a single Text node child, and the value property provides a shortcut for reading and writing the value of this child node.

The XML grammar allows XML documents to have attributes that consist of Text nodes and EntityReference nodes, which is why an attribute value cannot be fully represented by a string. In practice, however, web browsers expand any entity references in XML attribute values and do not implement the EntityReference interface (which is not documented in this book). Therefore, in client-side JavaScript, the value property is all that is needed to read and write attribute values.

Since attribute values can be completely represented by strings, it is not usually necessary to use the Attr interface at all. In most cases, the easiest way to work with attributes is with the Element.getAttribute() and Element.setAttribute() methods. These methods use strings for attribute values and avoid the use of Attr nodes altogether.

See Also

Element

Button

see Input

Canvas

an HTML element for scripted drawing

Properties

`String height`
> The height of the canvas. As with an image, this may be specified as an integer pixel value or percentage of the window height. When this value is changed, any drawing that has been done in the canvas is erased. The default value is 300.

`String width`
> The width of the canvas. As with an image, this may be specified as an integer pixel value or percentage of the window width. When this value is changed, any drawing that has been done in the canvas is erased. The default value is 300.

Methods

`getContext( )`
> Returns a CanvasRenderingContext2D object with which to draw on the canvas. You must pass the string "2d" to this method to specify that you want to do two-dimensional drawing.

Description

The Canvas object represents an HTML canvas element. It has no behavior of its own but defines an API that supports scripted client-side drawing operations. You may specify the width and height directly on this object, but most of its functionality is available via the CanvasRenderingContext2D object. This is obtained by calling the `getContext( )` method of the Canvas object and passing the literal string "2d" as the sole argument.

The <canvas> tag was introduced in Safari 1.3 and, at this writing, is also supported in Firefox 1.5 and Opera 9. The <canvas> tag, and its API, can be simulated in IE with the ExplorerCanvas open source project at *http://excanvas.sourceforge.net/*.

See Also

CanvasRenderingContext2D; Chapter 22

Canvas.getContext( )

return a context for drawing on the canvas

Synopsis

`CanvasRenderingContext2D getContext(String `*`contextID`*`)`

Arguments

contextID
> This argument specifies the type of drawing you want to do with the canvas. Currently the only valid value is "2d", which specifies two-dimensional drawing and causes this method to return a context object that exports a 2-D drawing API.

Returns

A CanvasRenderingContext2D object with which you can draw into the Canvas element.

Description

Returns a context representing the type of context to use in drawing. The intent is to provide different contexts for different drawing types (2-D, 3-D). Currently, the only one supported is "2d", which returns a CanvasRenderingContext2D object that implements most of the methods used by a canvas.

See Also

CanvasRenderingContext2D

CanvasGradient

a color gradient for use in a canvas

Firefox 1.5, Safari 1.3, Opera 9

Object → CanvasGradient

Methods

addColorStop( )
> Specifies a color and position for the gradient.

Description

A CanvasGradient object represents a color gradient that may be assigned to both the strokeStyle and fillStyle properties of a CanvasRenderingContext2D object. The createLinearGradient( ) and createRadialGradient( ) methods of CanvasRenderingContext2D both return CanvasGradient objects.

Once you have created a CanvasGradient object, use addColorStop( ) to specify what colors should appear at what positions within the gradient. Between the positions you specify, colors are interpolated to create a smooth gradient or fade. Transparent black stops are created implicitly at the start and end points of the gradient.

See Also

CanvasRenderingContext2D.createLinearGradient( )
CanvasRenderingContext2D.createRadialGradient( )

CanvasGradient.addColorStop( )

add a change of color at some point in the gradient

Synopsis

void addColorStop(float *offset*, String *color*)

Arguments

offset
> A floating-point value in the range 0.0 to 1.0 that represents a fraction between the start and end points of the gradient. An offset of 0 corresponds to the start point, and an offset of 1 corresponds to the end point.

color
> Specifies the color to be displayed at the specified offset, as a CSS color string. Colors at other points along the gradient are interpolated based on this and any other color stops.

Description

addColorStop( ) provides the mechanism for describing color changes in a gradient. This method may be called one or more times to change the color at particular percentages between the gradient's start and end points.

If this method is never called on a gradient, the gradient is transparent. At least one color stop must be specified to produce a visible color gradient.

CanvasPattern
Firefox 1.5, Safari 1.3, Opera 9

an image-based pattern for use in a Canvas
Object → CanvasPattern

Description

A CanvasPattern object is returned by the createPattern( ) method of a Canvas-RenderingContext2D object. A CanvasPattern object may be used as the value of the strokeStyle and fillStyle properties of a CanvasRenderingContext2D object.

A CanvasPattern object has no properties or methods of its own. See CanvasRenderingContext2D.createPattern( ) for details on how to create one.

See Also

CanvasRenderingContext2D.createPattern( )

CanvasRenderingContext2D
Firefox 1.5, Safari 1.3, Opera 9

the object used for drawing on a canvas
Object → CanvasRenderingContext2D

Properties

readonly Canvas canvas
> The Canvas element upon which this context will draw.

Object fillStyle
> The current color, pattern, or gradient used for filling paths. This property may be set to a string or to a CanvasGradient or CanvasPattern object. When set to a string, it is parsed as a CSS color value and used for solid fills. When set to a Canvas-Gradient or CanvasPattern object, fills are done using the specified gradient or pattern. See CanvasRenderingContext2D.createLinearGradient( ), CanvasRenderingContext2D.createRadialGradient( ), and CanvasRenderingContext2D.createPattern( ).

float globalAlpha
> Specifies the opacity of content drawn on the canvas. The range of values is between 0.0 (fully transparent) and 1.0 (no additional transparency). The default value for this property is 1.0.

Client-Side
JavaScript
Reference

`String globalCompositeOperation`

Specifies how colors being drawn are combined (or "composited") with colors already on the canvas. See the individual reference entry for this property for possible values.

`String lineCap`

Specifies how the ends of lines are rendered. Legal values are "butt", "round", and "square". The default is "butt". See the individual reference page for this property for further details.

`String lineJoin`

Specifies how two lines are joined. Legal values are "round", "bevel", and "miter". The default is "miter". See the individual reference page for this property for further details.

`float lineWidth`

Specifies the line width for stroking (line drawing) operations. The default is 1.0, and this property must be greater than 0.0. Wide lines are centered over the path, with half of the line width on each side.

`float miterLimit`

When the `lineJoin` property is "miter", this property specifies the maximum ratio of miter length to line width. See the individual reference page for this property for further details.

`float shadowBlur`

Specifies how much feathering shadows should have. The default is 0. Shadows are supported by Safari but not by Firefox 1.5 or Opera 9.

`String shadowColor`

Specifies the color of shadows as a CSS or web style string and may include an alpha component for transparency. The default is black. Shadows are supported by Safari but not by Firefox 1.5 or Opera 9.

`float shadowOffsetX, shadowOffsetY`

Specify the horizontal and vertical offset of the shadows. Larger values make the shadowed object appear to float higher above the background. The default is 0. Shadows are supported by Safari, but not by Firefox 1.5 or Opera 9.

`Object strokeStyle`

Specifies the color, pattern, or gradient used for stroking (drawing) paths. This property may be a string, or a CanvasGradient or a CanvasPattern object. If it is a string, it is parsed as a CSS color value and the stroking is done with the resulting solid color. If the value of this property is a CanvasGradient or a CanvasPattern object, stroking is done with a gradient or pattern. See CanvasRenderingContext2D.createLinearGradient( ), CanvasRenderingContext2D.createRadialGradient( ), and CanvasRenderingContext2D. createPattern( ).

Methods

`arc( )`

Adds an arc to the current subpath of a canvas, using a center point and radius.

`arcTo( )`

Adds an arc to the current subpath, using tangent points and a radius.

`beginPath( )`

Starts a new path (or a collection of subpaths) in a canvas.

bezierCurveTo( )
> Adds a cubic Bézier curve to the current subpath.

clearRect( )
> Erases the pixels in a rectangular area of a canvas.

clip( )
> Uses the current path as the clipping region for subsequent drawing operations.

closePath( )
> Closes the current subpath if it's open.

createLinearGradient( )
> Returns a CanvasGradient object that represents a linear color gradient.

createPattern( )
> Returns a CanvasPattern object that represents a tiled image.

createRadialGradient( )
> Returns a CanvasGradient object that represents a radial color gradient.

drawImage( )
> Draws an image.

fill( )
> Paints or fills the interior of the current path with the color, gradient, or pattern specified by the fillStyle property.

fillRect( )
> Paints or fills a rectangle.

lineTo( )
> Adds a straight line segment to the current subpath.

moveTo( )
> Sets the current position and begins a new subpath.

quadraticCurveTo( )
> Adds a quadratic Bézier curve to the current subpath.

rect( )
> Add a rectangle subpath to the current path.

restore( )
> Resets the canvas to the graphics state most recently saved.

rotate( )
> Rotates the canvas.

save( )
> Saves the properties, clipping region, and transformation matrix of the CanvasRenderingContext2D object.

scale( )
> Scales the user coordinate system of the canvas.

stroke( )
> Draws, or strokes, a line following the current path. The line is drawn according to the lineWidth, lineJoin, lineCap, and strokeStyle properties, among others.

strokeRect( )
> Draws (but does not fill) a rectangle.

translate( )
> Translates the user coordinate system of the canvas.

Description

The CanvasRenderingContext2D object provides a set of graphics functions to draw on a canvas. While text support is unfortunately omitted, the functions available are quite rich. They fall into a number of categories.

Drawing rectangles

You can outline and fill rectangles with strokeRect( ) and fillRect( ). In addition, you can clear the area defined by a rectangle with clearRect( ).

Drawing images

In the Canvas API, images are specified using Image objects that represent HTML <img> elements or offscreen images created with the Image( ) constructor. (See the Image reference page for details.) A canvas object can also be used as an image source.

You can draw an image into a canvas with the drawImage( ) method, which, in its most general form, allows an arbitrary rectangular region of the source image to be scaled and rendered into the canvas.

Creating and rendering paths

A powerful feature of the canvas is its ability to build shapes up from basic drawing operations, then either draw their outlines (*stroke* them) or paint their contents (*fill* them). The operations accumulated are collectively referred to as the *current path*. A canvas maintains a single current path.

In order to build a connected shape out of multiple segments, a joining point is needed between drawing operations. For this purpose, the canvas maintains a *current position*. The canvas drawing operations implicitly use this as their start point and update it to what is typically their end point. You can think of this like drawing with a pen on paper: when finishing a particular line or curve, the current position is where the pen rested after completing the operation.

You can create a sequence of disconnected shapes in the current path that will be rendered together with the same drawing parameters. To separate shapes, use the moveTo( ) method; this moves the current position to a new location without adding a connecting line. When you do this, you create a new *subpath*, which is the canvas term used for a collection of operations that are connected.

Once the path is formed to your liking, you can draw its outline with stroke( ), paint its contents with fill( ), or do both.

The available shape operations are lineTo( ) for drawing straight lines, rect( ) for drawing rectangles, arc( ) or arcTo( ) for drawing partial circles, and bezierCurveTo( ) or quadraticCurveTo( ) for drawing curves.

In addition to stroking and filling, you can also use the current path to specify the *clipping region* the canvas uses when rendering. Pixels inside this region are displayed; those outside are not. The clipping region is cumulative; calling clip( ) intersects the current path with the current clipping region to yield a new region. Unfortunately, there is no direct method for resetting the clipping region to the extent of the canvas; to do so, you must save and restore the entire graphics state of the canvas (described later in this entry).

If the segments in any of the subpaths do not form a closed shape, fill( ) and clip( ) operations implicitly close them for you by adding a virtual (not visible with a stroke) line segment from the start to the end of the subpath. Optionally, you can call closePath( ) to explicitly add this line segment.

Colors, gradients, and patterns

When filling or stroking paths, you can specify how the lines or painted area are rendered using the fillStyle and strokeStyle properties. Both accept CSS-style color strings, as well as CanvasGradient and CanvasPattern objects that describe gradients and patterns. To create a gradient, use the createLinearGradient( ) or createRadialGradient( ) methods. To create a pattern, use createPattern( ).

To specify an opaque color using CSS notation, use a string of the form "#RRGGBB", where RR, GG, and BB are hexadecimal digits that specify the red, green, and blue components of the color as values between 00 and FF. For example, bright red is "#FF0000". To specify a partially transparent color, use a string of the form "rgba(R,G,B,A)". In this form, R, G, and B specify the red, green, and blue components of the color as decimal integers between 0 and 255, and A specifies the alpha (opacity) component as a floating-point value between 0.0 (fully transparent) and 1.0 (fully opaque). For example, half-transparent bright red is "rgba(255,0,0,0.5)".

Line width, line caps and line joins

Canvas offers several options for tailoring how lines appear. You can specify the width of the line with the lineWidth property, how the end points of lines are drawn with the lineCap property, and how lines are joined using the lineJoin property.

Coordinate space and transformations

By default, the coordinate space for a canvas has its origin at (0,0) in the upper-left corner of the canvas, with *x* values increasing to the right and *y* values increasing down. A single unit in this coordinate space normally translates to a single pixel.

You can, however, *transform* the coordinate space, causing any coordinates or extents you specify in drawing operations to be shifted, scaled, or rotated. This is done with the translate( ), scale( ), and rotate( ) methods, which affect the *transformation matrix* of the canvas. Because the coordinate space can be transformed like this, the coordinates you pass to methods such as lineTo( ) may not be measured in pixels. For this reason, the Canvas API uses floating-point numbers instead of integers.

Transformations are processed in reverse of the order in which they are specified. So, for example, a call to scale( ) followed by a call to translate( ) causes the coordinate system first to be translated, then scaled.

Compositing

Commonly, shapes are drawn on top of one another, with the new shape obscuring any shapes that were previously drawn below it. This is the default behavior in a canvas. However, you can perform many interesting operations by specifying different values for the globalCompositeOperation property. These range from XORing to lightening or darkening shaped regions; see CanvasRenderingContext2D.globalCompositeOperation for all the possible options.

Shadows

The Canvas API includes properties that can automatically add a drop shadow to any shape you draw. At the time of this writing, Safari is the only browser that implements this API, however. The color of the shadow may be specified with shadowColor, and its offset changed using shadowOffsetX and shadowOffsetY. In addition, the amount of feathering applied to the shadow's edge may be set with shadowBlur.

Saving graphics state

The save( ) and restore( ) methods allow you to save and restore the state of a CanvasRenderingContext2D object. save( ) pushes the current state onto a stack, and restore( ) pops the most recently saved state off the top of the stack and sets the current drawing state based on those stored values.

All properties of the CanvasRenderingContext2D object (except for the canvas property, which is a constant) are part of the saved state. The transformation matrix and clipping region are also part of the state, but the current path and current point are not.

See Also

Canvas

CanvasRenderingContext2D.arc( )

add an arc to the current subpath of a canvas, using a center point and radius

Synopsis

```
void arc(float x, float y, float radius,
         float startAngle, endAngle,
         boolean counterclockwise)
```

Arguments

x, y
> The coordinates of the center of the circle describing the arc.

radius
> The radius of the circle describing the arc.

startAngle, endAngle
> The angles that specify the start and end points of the arc along the circle. These angles are measured in radians. The three o'clock position along the positive X axis is an angle of 0, and angles increase in the clockwise direction.

counterclockwise
> Whether the arc is traversed counterclockwise (true) or clockwise (false) along the circle's circumference.

Description

The first five arguments to this method describe specify a start point and an end point on the circumference of a circle. Invoking this method adds a straight line between the current point and the start point to the current subpath. Next it adds the arc along the circumference of the circle between the start and end points to the subpath. The final argument specifies the direction in which the circle should be traversed to connect the start and end points. This method leaves the current point set to the end point of the arc.

See Also

CanvasRenderingContext2D.arcTo()
CanvasRenderingContext2D.beginPath()
CanvasRenderingContext2D.closePath()

CanvasRenderingContext2D.arcTo()

add an arc of a circle to the current subpath, using tangent points and a radius

Synopsis

```
void arcTo(float x1, float y1,
           float x2, float y2,
           float radius)
```

Arguments

x1, y1
> The coordinates of point P1.

x2, y2
> The coordinates of point P2.

radius
> The radius of the circle that defines the arc.

Description

This method adds an arc to the current subpath but describes that arc much differently than the arc() method does. The arc that is added to the path is a portion of a circle with the specified *radius*. The arc has one point tangent to the line from the current position to P1 and one point that is tangent to the line from P1 to P2. The arc begins and ends at these two tangent points and is drawn in the direction that connects those two points with the shortest arc.

In many common uses, the arc begins at the current position and ends at P2, but this is not always the case. If the current position is not the same as the starting point of the arc, this method adds a straight line from the current position to the start position of the arc. This method always leaves the current position set to the end point of the arc.

Example

You could draw the upper-right corner of a rectangle, giving it a rounded corner with code like the following:

```
c.moveTo(10,10);              // start at upper left
c.lineTo(90, 10)              // horizontal line to start of round corner
c.arcTo(100, 10, 100, 20, 10); // rounded corner
c.lineTo(100, 100);           // vertical line down to lower right
```

Bugs

This method is not implemented in Firefox 1.5.

See Also

CanvasRenderingContext2D.arc( )

CanvasRenderingContext2D.beginPath( )

start a new collection of subpaths in a canvas

Synopsis

void beginPath( )

Description

beginPath( ) discards any currently defined path and begins a new one. It sets the current point to (0,0).

When the context for a canvas is first created, beginPath( ) is implicitly called.

See Also

CanvasRenderingContext2D.closePath( )
CanvasRenderingContext2D.fill( )
CanvasRenderingContext2D.stroke( )
Chapter 22

CanvasRenderingContext2D.bezierCurveTo( )

add a cubic Bézier curve to the current subpath

Synopsis

void bezierCurveTo(float cpX1, float cpY1,
                   float cpX2, float cpY2,
                   float x, float y)

Arguments

cpX1, cpX2
> The coordinates of the control point associated with the curve's start point (the current position).

cpX2, cpY2
> The coordinates of the control point associated with the curve's end point.

x, y
> The coordinates of the curve's end point.

Description

bezierCurveTo( ) adds a cubic Bézier curve to the current subpath of a canvas. The start point of the curve is the current point of the canvas, and the end point is (x,y). The two

Bezier control points (cpX1, cpY1) and (cpX2, cpY2) define the shape of the curve. When this method returns, the current position is (x,y).

See Also

CanvasRenderingContext2D.quadraticCurveTo( )

CanvasRenderingContext2D.clearRect( )

erase a rectangular area of a canvas

Synopsis

```
void clearRect(float x, float y,
               float width, float height)
```

Arguments

x, y
   The coordinates of the upper-left corner of the rectangle.

width, height
   The dimensions of the rectangle.

Description

clearRect( ) erases the specified rectangle, filling it with a transparent color.

CanvasRenderingContext2D.clip( )

set the clipping path of a canvas

Synopsis

```
void clip( )
```

Description

This method clips the current path using the current clipping path and then uses the clipped path as the new clipping path. Note that there is no way to enlarge the clipping path. If you want a temporary clipping path, you should first call save( ) in order to use restore( ) to restore the original clipping path. The default clipping path for a canvas is the canvas rectangle itself.

This method resets the current path so that it is empty.

CanvasRenderingContext2D.closePath( )

closes an open subpath

Synopsis

```
void closePath( )
```

Description

If the current subpath of the canvas is open, closePath( ) closes it by adding a line connecting the current point to the subpath's starting point. If the subpath is already closed, this method does nothing. Once a subpath is closed, no more lines or curves can be added to it. To continue adding to the path, you must begin a new subpath with a call to moveTo( ).

You do not need to call closePath( ) before stroking or filling a path. Paths are implicitly closed when filled (and also when you call clip( )).

See Also

CanvasRenderingContext2D.beginPath( )
CanvasRenderingContext2D.moveTo( )
CanvasRenderingContext2D.stroke( )
CanvasRenderingContext2D.fill( )

CanvasRenderingContext2D.createLinearGradient( )

create a linear color gradient

Synopsis

```
CanvasGradient createLinearGradient(float xStart, float yStart,
                                    float xEnd, float yEnd)
```

Arguments

xStart, yStart
> The coordinates of the gradient's start point.

xEnd, yEnd
> The coordinates of the gradient's end point.

Returns

A CanvasGradient object representing a linear color gradient.

Description

This method creates and returns a new CanvasGradient object that linearly interpolates colors between the specified start point and end point. Note that this method does not specify any colors for the gradient. Use the addColorStop( ) method of the returned object to do that. To stroke lines or fill areas using a gradient, assign a CanvasGradient object to the strokeStyle or fillStyle properties.

See Also

CanvasGradient.addColorStop( ), CanvasRenderingContext2D.createRadialGradient( )

CanvasRenderingContext2D.createPattern( )

create a pattern of tiled images

Synopsis

```
CanvasPattern createPattern(Image image,
                            String repetitionStyle)
```

Arguments

image
> The image to be tiled. This argument is typically an Image object, but you may also use a Canvas element.

repetitionStyle
> Specifies how the image is tiled. The possible values are the following:

Value	Meaning
"repeat"	Tile the image in both directions. This is the default.
"repeat-x"	Tile the image in the X dimension only.
"repeat-y"	Tile the image in the Y dimension only.
"no-repeat"	Do not tile the image; use it a single time only.

Returns

A CanvasPattern object representing the pattern.

Description

This method creates and returns a CanvasPattern object that represents the pattern defined by a tiled image. To use a pattern for stroking lines or filling areas, use a CanvasPattern object as the value of the strokeStyle or fillStyle properties.

Bugs

Firefox 1.5 supports only the "repeat" style. Others are ignored.

See Also

CanvasPattern

CanvasRenderingContext2D.createRadialGradient( )

create a radial color gradient

Synopsis

```
CanvasGradient createRadialGradient(float xStart, float yStart, float radiusStart,
                                    float xEnd, float yEnd, float radiusEnd)
```

Arguments

xStart, yStart
> The coordinates of the center of the starting circle.

radiusStart
> The radius of the starting circle.

xEnd, yEnd
> The coordinates of the center of the ending circle.

radiusEnd
> The radius of the ending circle.

Returns

A CanvasGradient object representing a radial color gradient.

Description

This method creates and returns a new CanvasGradient object that radially interpolates colors between the circumferences of the two specified circles. Note that this method does not specify any colors for the gradient. Use the `addColorStop()` method of the returned object to do that. To stroke lines or fill areas using a gradient, assign a CanvasGradient object to the `strokeStyle` or `fillStyle` properties.

Radial gradients are rendered by using the color at offset 0 for the circumference of the first circle, the color at offset 1 for the second circle, and interpolated color values (red, green, blue, and alpha) at circles between the two.

See Also

`CanvasGradient.addColorStop()`, `CanvasRenderingContext2D.createLinearGradient()`

CanvasRenderingContext2D.drawImage()

draw an image

Synopsis

```
void drawImage(Image image, float x, float y)

void drawImage(Image image, float x, float y,
          float width, float height)

void drawImage(Image image, integer sourceX, integer sourceY,
          integer sourceWidth, integer sourceHeight,
          float destX, float destY,
          float destWidth, float destHeight)
```

Arguments

image
> The image to be drawn. This must be an Image object representing an `<img>` tag, or an offscreen image or a Canvas object.

x, y
> The point at which the upper-left corner of the image is drawn.

width, height
> The size at which the image should be drawn. Specifying these arguments causes the image to be scaled.

sourceX, sourceY
> The upper-left corner of the region of the image that is to be drawn. These integer arguments are measured in image pixels.

sourceWidth, sourceHeight
> The dimensions, in image pixels, of the region of the image that is to be drawn.

destX, destY
> The canvas coordinates at which the upper-left corner of the image region is to be drawn

destWidth, destHeight
> The canvas dimensions at which the image region should be drawn.

Description

There are three variants of this method. The first copies the entire image to the canvas, placing its upper-left corner at the specified point and mapping each image pixel to one unit in the canvas coordinate system. The second variant also copies the entire image to the canvas but allows you to specify the desired width and height of the image in canvas units. The third variant is fully general: it allows you to specify any rectangular region of the image and copy it, with arbitrary scaling to any position within the canvas.

The images passed to this method must be Image or Canvas objects. An Image object may represent an <img> tag in the document or an offscreen image created with the Image( ) constructor.

See Also

Image

CanvasRenderingContext2D.fill( )

fill the path

Synopsis

void fill( )

Description

fill( ) fills the current path with the color, gradient, or pattern specified by the fillStyle property. Each subpath of the path is filled independently. Any subpaths that are not closed are filled as if the closePath( ) method had been called on them. (Note, however, that this does not actually cause those subpaths to become closed.)

The canvas uses the "non-zero winding rule" to determine which points are inside the path and which are outside. The details of this rule are beyond the scope of this book, but they typically matter only for complex paths that intersect themselves.

Client-Side
JavaScript
Reference

Filling a path does not clear the path. You may call stroke( ) after calling fill( ) without redefining the path.

See Also

CanvasRenderingContext2D.fillRect( )

CanvasRenderingContext2D.fillRect( )

fill a rectangle

Synopsis

```
void fillRect(float x, float y,
              float width, float height)
```

Arguments

x, y

  The coordinates of the upper-left corner of rectangle.

width, height

  The dimensions of the rectangle.

Description

fillRect( ) fills the specified rectangle with the color, gradient, or pattern specified by the fillStyle property.

Current implementations of fillRect( ) also clear the path as if beginPath( ) had been called. This surprising behavior may not be standardized and should not be relied upon.

See Also

CanvasRenderingContext2D.fill( )
CanvasRenderingContext2D.rect( )
CanvasRenderingContext2D.strokeRect( )

CanvasRenderingContext2D.globalCompositeOperation

specifies how colors are combined on the canvas

Synopsis

String globalCompositeOperation

Description

This property specifies how colors being rendered onto the canvas are combined (or "composited") with the colors that already exist in the canvas. The following table lists the possible values and their meanings. The word *source* in the these values refers to the colors being drawn onto the canvas, and the word *destination* refers to the existing colors on the canvas. The default is "source-over".

Value	Meaning
"copy"	Draws only the new shape, removing everything else.
"darker"	Where both shapes overlap, the color is determined by subtracting color values.
"destination-atop"	Existing content is kept only where it overlaps the new shape. The new shape is drawn behind the content.
"destination-in"	Existing content is kept where both the new shape and existing canvas content overlap. Everything else is made transparent.
"destination-out"	Existing content is kept where it doesn't overlap the new shape. Everything else is made transparent.
"destination-over"	The new shape is drawn behind existing content.
"lighter"	Where both shapes overlap, the color is determined by adding the two color values.
"source-atop"	The new shape is drawn only where it overlaps existing content.
"source-in"	The new shape is drawn only where both the new shape and existing content overlap. Everything else is made transparent.
"source-out"	The new shape is drawn where it doesn't overlap existing content.
"source-over"	The new shape is drawn on top of existing content. This is the default behavior.
"xor"	Shapes are made transparent where both overlap and drawn normal everywhere else.

Bugs

Firefox 1.5 does not support the values "copy" or "darker".

CanvasRenderingContext2D.lineCap

specifies how the ends of lines are rendered

Synopsis

```
String lineCap
```

Description

The lineCap property specifies how lines should be terminated. It matters only when drawing wide lines. Legal values for this property are listed in the following table. The default value is "butt".

Value	Meaning
"butt"	This default value specifies that the line should have no cap. The end of the line is straight and is perpendicular to the direction of the line. The line is not extended beyond its endpoint.
"round"	This value specifies that lines should be capped with a semicircle whose diameter is equal to the width of the line and which extends beyond the end of the line by one half the width of the line.
"square"	This value specifies that lines should be capped with a rectangle. This value is like "butt", but the line is extended by half of its width.

Bugs

Firefox 1.5 does not properly implement the "butt" cap style. Butt caps are rendered as if they were "square" line caps.

See Also

CanvasRenderingContext2D.lineJoin

CanvasRenderingContext2D.lineJoin

specifies how vertices are rendered

Synopsis

```
String lineJoin
```

Description

When a path includes vertices where line segments and/or curves meet, the lineJoin property specifies how those vertices are drawn. The effect of this property is apparent only when drawing with wide lines.

The default value of the property is "miter", which specifies that the outside edges of the two line segments are extended until they intersect. When two lines meet at an acute angle, mitered joins can become quite long. The miterLimit property places an upper bound on the length of a miter. Beyond this limit, the miter is beveled off.

The value "round" specifies that the outside edges of the vertex should be joined with a filled arc whose diameter is equal to the width of the line.

The value "bevel" specifies that the outside edges of the vertex should be joined with a filled triangle.

Bugs

Firefox 1.5 does not correctly implement beveled joins and renders them as rounded joins. Also, mitered joins are not displayed correctly when stroked in a partially transparent color.

See Also

CanvasRenderingContext2D.lineCap, CanvasRenderingContext2D.miterLimit

CanvasRenderingContext2D.lineTo( )

add a straight line to the current subpath

Synopsis

```
void lineTo(float x, float y)
```

Arguments

x, y
> The coordinates of the end point of the line.

Description

lineTo( ) adds a straight line to the current subpath. The line begins at the current point and ends at (x,y). When this method returns, the current position is (x,y).

See Also

CanvasRenderingContext2D.beginPath( ), CanvasRenderingContext2D.moveTo( )

CanvasRenderingContext2D.miterLimit

maximum-miter-length-to-line-width ratio

Synopsis

float miterLimit

Description

When wide lines are drawn with the lineJoin property set to "miter" and two lines meet at an acute angle, the resulting miter can be quite long. When miters are too long, they become visually jarring. This miterLimit property places an upper bound on the length of the miter. This property expresses a ratio of the miter length to the line width. The default value is 10, which means that a miter should never be longer than 10 times the line width. If a miter reaches this length, it is beveled off. This property has no effect when lineJoin is "round" or "bevel".

Bugs

Firefox 1.5 does not correctly implement this property. When a mitered join exceeds the miterLimit, the join is converted to a rounded join instead.

See Also

CanvasRenderingContext2D.lineJoin

CanvasRenderingContext2D.moveTo( )

sets the current position and begins a new subpath

Synopsis

void moveTo(float *x*, float *y*)

Arguments

x, y
    The coordinates of the new current point.

Description

moveTo( ) sets the current position to (*x,y*) and creates a new subpath with this as its first point. If there was a previous subpath and it consisted of just one point, that subpath is removed from the path.

See Also

CanvasRenderingContext2D.beginPath( )

CanvasRenderingContext2D.quadraticCurveTo( )
add a quadratic Bezier curve to the current subpath

Synopsis

```
void quadraticCurveTo(float cpX, float cpY,
                      float x, float y)
```

Arguments

cpX, cpY
> The coordinates of the control point.

x, y
> The coordinates of the end point of the curve.

Description

This method adds a quadratic Bézier curve segment to the current subpath. The curve starts at the current point and ends at (*x,y*). The control point (*cpX, cpY*) specifies the shape of the curve between these two points. (The mathematics of Bezier curves is beyond the scope of this book, however.) When this method returns, the current position is (*x,y*).

Bugs

Firefox 1.5 implements this method incorrectly.

See Also

CanvasRenderingContext2D.bezierCurveTo( )

CanvasRenderingContext2D.rect( )
add a rectangle subpath to the path

Synopsis

```
void rect(float x, float y,
          float width, float height)
```

Arguments

x, y
> The coordinates of the upper-left corner of the rectangle.

width, height
> The dimensions of the rectangle.

Description

This method adds a rectangle to the path. This rectangle is in a subpath of its own and is not connected to any other subpaths in the path. When this method returns, the current position is (0,0).

See Also

CanvasRenderingContext2D.fillRect( ), CanvasRenderingContext2D.strokeRect( )

CanvasRenderingContext2D.restore( )

reset drawing state to saved values

Synopsis

void restore( )

Description

This method pops the stack of saved graphics states and restores the values of the CanvasRenderingContext2D properties, the clipping path, and the transformation matrix. See the save( ) method for further information.

Bugs

Firefox 1.5 does not correctly save and restore the strokeStyle property.

See Also

CanvasRenderingContext2D.save( )

CanvasRenderingContext2D.rotate( )

rotate the coordinate system of the canvas

Synopsis

void rotate(float *angle*)

Arguments

angle
> The amount of rotation, in radians. Positive values result in clockwise rotation, and negative values result in counterclockwise rotation.

Description

This method alters the mapping between canvas coordinates and the pixels of the <canvas> element in the web browser so that any subsequent drawing appears rotated within the canvas by the specified angle. It does not rotate the <canvas> element itself. Note that the angle is specified in radians. To convert degrees to radians, multiply by Math.PI and divide by 180.

See Also

CanvasRenderingContext2D.scale( ), CanvasRenderingContext2D.translate( )

CanvasRenderingContext2D.save( )

save a copy of the current graphics state

Synopsis

void save( )

Description

save( ) pushes a copy of the current graphics state onto a stack of saved graphics states. This allows you to temporarily change the graphics state, and then restore the previous values with a call to restore( ).

The graphics state of a canvas includes all the properties of the CanvasRenderingContext2D object (except for the read-only canvas property). It also includes the transformation matrix that is the result of calls to rotate( ), scale( ), and translate( ). Additionally, it includes the clipping path, which is specified with the clip( ) method. Note, however, that the current path and current position are not part of the graphics state and are not saved by this method.

Bugs

Firefox 1.5 does not save and restore the strokeStyle property.

See Also

CanvasRenderingContext2D.restore( )

CanvasRenderingContext2D.scale( )

scale the user coordinate system of the canvas

Synopsis

void scale(float *sx*, float *sy*)

Arguments

sx, sy
> The horizontal and vertical scaling factors.

Description

scale( ) adds a scale transformation to the current transformation matrix of the canvas. Scaling is done with independent horizontal and vertical scaling factors. For example, passing the values 2.0 and 0.5 causes subsequently drawn paths to be twice as wide and half as high as they would otherwise have been. Specifying a negative value for *sx* causes X coordinates to be flipped across the Y axis, and a negative value of *sy* causes Y coordinates to be flipped across the X axis.

See Also

CanvasRenderingContext2D.rotate( ), CanvasRenderingContext2D.translate( )

CanvasRenderingContext2D.stroke( )

draw the current path

Synopsis

void stroke( )

Description

The stroke( ) method draws the outline of the current path. The path defines the geometry of the line that is produced, but the visual appearance of that line depends on the strokeStyle, lineWidth, lineCap, lineJoin, and miterLimit properties.

The term *stroke* refers to a pen or brush stroke. It means "draw the outline of." Contrast this stroke( ) method with fill( ), which fills the interior of a path rather than stroking the outline of the path.

See Also

CanvasRenderingContext2D.fill( )
CanvasRenderingContext2D.lineCap
CanvasRenderingContext2D.lineJoin
CanvasRenderingContext2D.strokeRect( )

CanvasRenderingContext2D.strokeRect( )

draw a rectangle

Synopsis

```
void strokeRect(float x, float y,
                float width, float height)
```

Arguments

x, y
> The coordinates of the upper-left corner of the rectangle.

width, height
> The dimensions of the rectangle.

Description

This method draws the outline (but does not fill the interior) of a rectangle with the specified position and size. Line color and line width are specified by the strokeStyle and lineWidth properties. The appearance of the rectangle corners are specified by the lineJoin property.

Current implementations of strokeRect( ) clear the path as if beginPath( ) had been called. This surprising behavior may not be standardized and should not be relied upon.

Client-Side
JavaScript
Reference

See Also

```
CanvasRenderingContext2D.fillRect( )
CanvasRenderingContext2D.lineJoin
CanvasRenderingContext2D.rect( )
CanvasRenderingContext2D.stroke( )
```

CanvasRenderingContext2D.translate( )

translate the user coordinate system of the canvas

Synopsis

```
void translate(float dx, float dy)
```

Arguments

dx, dy

> The amounts to translate in the X and Y dimensions.

Description

`translate( )` adds horizontal and vertical offsets to the transformation matrix of the canvas. The arguments *dx* and *dy* are added to all points in any subsequently defined paths.

See Also

`CanvasRenderingContext2D.rotate( )`, `CanvasRenderingContext2D.scale( )`

CDATASection   DOM Level 1 XML

a CDATA node in an XML document   Node → CharacterData → Text → CDATASection

Description

This infrequently used interface represents a CDATA section in an XML document. Programmers working with HTML documents never encounter nodes of this type and do not need to use this interface.

CDATASection is a subinterface of Text and does not define any properties or methods of its own. The textual content of the CDATA section is available through the `nodeValue` property inherited from Node or through the data property inherited from CharacterData. Although CDATASection nodes can often be treated in the same way as Text nodes, note that the `Node.normalize( )` method does not merge adjacent CDATA sections. Create a CDATASection with `Document.createCDATASection( )`.

See Also

`CharacterData`, `Text`

CharacterData

common functionality for Text and Comment nodes

Subinterfaces

Comment, Text

Properties

String data
> The text contained by this node.

readonly unsigned long length
> The number of characters contained by this node.

Methods

appendData( )
> Appends the specified string to the text contained by this node.

deleteData( )
> Deletes text from this node, starting with the character at the specified offset and continuing for the specified number of characters.

insertData( )
> Inserts the specified string into the text of this node at the specified character offset.

replaceData( )
> Replaces the characters starting at the specified character offset and continuing for the specified number of characters with the specified string.

substringData( )
> Returns a copy of the text starting at the specified character offset and continuing for the specified number of characters.

Description

CharacterData is the superinterface for Text and Comment nodes. Documents never contain CharacterData nodes; they contain only Text and Comment nodes. Since both of these node types have similar functionality, however, that functionality has been defined here so that both Text and Comment can inherit it.

Note that it is not necessary to use the string-manipulation methods defined by this interface. The data property is an ordinary JavaScript string, and you can manipulate it with the + operator for string concatenation and with various String and RegExp methods.

See Also

Comment, Text

CharacterData.appendData( )

append a string to a Text or Comment node

Synopsis

```
void appendData(String arg)
    throws DOMException;
```

Arguments

arg

> The string to be appended to the Text or Comment node.

Throws

This method throws a DOMException with a code of NO_MODIFICATION_ALLOWED_ERR if called on a node that is read-only.

Description

This method appends the string *arg* to the end of the data property for this node.

CharacterData.deleteData( )

delete characters from a Text or Comment node

Synopsis

```
void deleteData(unsigned long offset,
                unsigned long count)
    throws DOMException;
```

Arguments

offset

> The position of the first character to be deleted.

count

> The number of characters to be deleted.

Throws

This method may throw a DOMException with one of the following code values:

INDEX_SIZE_ERR

> The *offset* or *count* argument is negative, or *offset* is greater than the length of the Text or Comment node.

NO_MODIFICATION_ALLOWED_ERR

> The node is read-only and may not be modified.

Description

This method deletes characters from this Text or Comment node, starting with the character at the position *offset* and continuing for *count* characters. If *offset* plus *count* is greater than the number of characters in the Text or Comment node, all characters from *offset* to the end of the string are deleted.

CharacterData.insertData( ) DOM Level 1 Core

insert a string into a Text or Comment node

Synopsis

```
void insertData(unsigned long offset,
                String arg)
    throws DOMException;
```

Arguments

offset
> The character position within the Text or Comment node at which the string is to be inserted.

arg
> The string to insert.

Throws

This method may throw a DOMException with one of the following code values in the following circumstances:

INDEX_SIZE_ERR
> *offset* is negative or greater than the length of the Text or Comment node.

NO_MODIFICATION_ALLOWED_ERR
> The node is read-only and may not be modified.

Description

This method inserts the specified string *arg* into the text of a Text or Comment node at the specified position *offset*.

CharacterData.replaceData( ) DOM Level 1 Core

replace characters of a Text or Comment node with a string

Synopsis

```
void replaceData(unsigned long offset,
                 unsigned long count,
                 String arg)
    throws DOMException;
```

Arguments

offset
> The character position within the Text or Comment node at which the replacement is to begin.

count
> The number of characters to be replaced.

arg
> The string that replaces the characters specified by *offset* and *count*.

Throws

This method may throw a DOMException with one of the following code values in the following circumstances:

INDEX_SIZE_ERR

> *offset* is negative or greater than the length of the Text or Comment node, or *count* is negative.

NO_MODIFICATION_ALLOWED_ERR

> The node is read-only and may not be modified.

Description

This method replaces *count* characters starting at position *offset* with the contents of the string *arg*. If the sum of *offset* and *count* is greater than the length of the Text or Comment node, all characters from *offset* on are replaced.

Notice that the insertData( ) and deleteData( ) methods are both special cases of this one.

CharacterData.substringData( )   DOM Level 1 Core

extract a substring from a Text or Comment node

Synopsis

```
String substringData(unsigned long offset,
                     unsigned long count)
    throws DOMException;
```

Arguments

offset

> The position of the first character to be returned.

count

> The number of characters in the substring to be returned.

Returns

A string that consists of *count* characters of the Text or Comment node starting with the character at position *offset*.

Throws

This method may throw a DOMException with one of the following code values:

INDEX_SIZE_ERR

> *offset* is negative or greater than the length of the Text or Comment node, or *count* is negative.

DOMSTRING_SIZE_ERR

> The specified range of text is too long to fit into a string in the browser's JavaScript implementation.

Description

This method extracts the substring that starts at position *offset* and continues for *count* characters from the text of a Text or Comment node. This method is useful only when the amount of text contained by the node is larger than the maximum number of characters that can fit in a string in a browser's JavaScript implementation. In this case, a JavaScript program cannot use the data property of the Text or Comment node directly and must instead work with shorter substrings of the node's text. This situation is unlikely to arise in practice.

Checkbox

see Input

Comment   DOM Level 1 Core

an HTML or XML comment   Node → CharacterData → Comment

Description

A Comment node represents a comment in an HTML or XML document. The content of the comment (i.e., the text between `<!--` and `-->`) is available through the data property inherited from the CharacterData interface or through the nodeValue property inherited from the Node interface. This content may be manipulated using the various methods inherited from CharacterData. Create a comment object with Document.createComment().

See Also

CharacterData

CSS2Properties   DOM Level 2 CSS2

a set of CSS attributes and their values   Object → CSS2Properties

Properties

String cssText
> The textual representation of a set of style attributes and their values. The text is formated as in a CSS stylesheet, minus the element selector and the curly braces that surround the attributes and values. Setting this property to an illegal value throws a DOMException with a code of SYNTAX_ERR. Attempting to set this property when the CSS2Properties object is read-only throws a DOMException with a code of NO_MODIFICATION_ALLOWED_ERR.

In addition to the cssText property, a CSS2Properties object also has a property corresponding to each CSS attribute that the browser supports. These property names correspond closely to the CSS attribute names, with minor changes required to avoid syntax errors in JavaScript. Multiword attributes that contain hyphens, such as "font-family", are written without hyphens in JavaScript, and each word after the first is capitalized: fontFamily. Also, the "float" attribute conflicts with the reserved word float, so it translates to the property cssFloat.

Client-Side
JavaScript
Reference

The CSS2Properties property names corresponding to each attribute defined by the CSS2 specification are listed in the following table. Note, however, that some browsers do not support all CSS attributes and may not implement all of the listed properties. Since the properties correspond directly to CSS attributes, no individual documentation is given for each property. See a CSS reference, such as *Cascading Style Sheets: The Definitive Guide* by Eric A. Meyer (O'Reilly), for the meaning and legal values of each. All of the properties are strings. Setting any of these properties may throw the same exceptions as setting the cssText property:

azimuth	background	backgroundAttachment	backgroundColor
backgroundImage	backgroundPosition	backgroundRepeat	border
borderBottom	borderBottomColor	borderBottomStyle	borderBottomWidth
borderCollapse	borderColor	borderLeft	borderLeftColor
borderLeftStyle	borderLeftWidth	borderRight	borderRightColor
borderRightStyle	borderRightWidth	borderSpacing	borderStyle
borderTop	borderTopColor	borderTopStyle	borderTopWidth
borderWidth	bottom	captionSide	clear
clip	color	content	counterIncrement
counterReset	cssFloat	cue	cueAfter
cueBefore	cursor	direction	display
elevation	emptyCells	font	fontFamily
fontSize	fontSizeAdjust	fontStretch	fontStyle
fontVariant	fontWeight	height	left
letterSpacing	lineHeight	listStyle	listStyleImage
listStylePosition	listStyleType	margin	marginBottom
marginLeft	marginRight	marginTop	markerOffset
marks	maxHeight	maxWidth	minHeight
minWidth	orphans	outline	outlineColor
outlineStyle	outlineWidth	overflow	padding
paddingBottom	paddingLeft	paddingRight	paddingTop
page	pageBreakAfter	pageBreakBefore	pageBreakInside
pause	pauseAfter	pauseBefore	pitch
pitchRange	playDuring	position	quotes
richness	right	size	speak
speakHeader	speakNumeral	speakPunctuation	speechRate
stress	tableLayout	textAlign	textDecoration
textIndent	textShadow	textTransform	top
unicodeBidi	verticalAlign	visibility	voiceFamily
volume	whiteSpace	widows	width
wordSpacing	zIndex		

Description

A CSS2Properties object represents a set of CSS style attributes and their values. It defines one JavaScript property for each CSS attribute defined by the CSS2 specification. The `style` property of an HTMLElement is a read/write CSS2Properties object, as is the `style` property of a CSSRule object. The return value of `Window.getComputedStyle()`, however, is a CSS2Properties object whose properties are read-only.

See Also

`CSSRule`, `HTMLElement`, `Window.getComputedStyle()`; Chapter 16

CSSRule   DOM Level 2 CSS, IE 5

a rule in a CSS stylesheet   Object → CSSRule

Properties

`String selectorText`

The selector text that specifies the document elements this style rule applies to. Setting this property raises a DOMException with a `code` of `NO_MODIFICATION_ALLOWED_ERR` if the rule is read-only or a `code` of `SYNTAX_ERR` if the new value does not follow CSS syntax rules.

`readonly CSS2Properties style`

The style values that should be applied to elements specified by `selectorText`. Note that while the `style` property itself is read-only, the properties of the CSS2Properties object to which it refers are read/write.

Description

A CSSRule object represents a rule in a CSS stylesheet: it represents style information to be applied to a specific set of document elements. `selectorText` is the string representation of the element selector for this rule, and `style` is a CSS2Properties object that represents the set of style attributes and values to apply to the selected elements.

The DOM Level 2 CSS specification actually defines a somewhat complex hierarchy of CSSRule interfaces to represent different types of rules that can appear in a CSSStyleSheet. The properties listed here are actually defined by the DOM CSSStyleRule interface. Style rules are the most common and most important types of rules in a stylesheet, and the properties listed here are the only ones that can be used portably across browsers. IE does not support the DOM Level 2 specification very well (at least not through IE 7) but does implement a CSSRule object that supports the two properties listed here.

See Also

`CSS2Properties`, `CSSStyleSheet`

CSSStyleSheet

a CSS stylesheet

Properties

readonly CSSRule[] cssRules
>   A read-only, array-like object holding the CSSRule objects that compose the stylesheet. In IE, use the rules property instead. In DOM-compliant implementations, this array includes objects that represent all rules in a stylesheet, including at-rules such as @import directives. Rules of these sorts implement a different interface than that described for CSSRule. These other type of rule objects are not well supported across browsers and are not documented in this book. Be aware, therefore, that you must test any entries in this array to ensure that they define CSSRule properties before you attempt to use those properties.

boolean disabled
>   If true, the stylesheet is disabled and is not applied to the document. If false, the stylesheet is enabled and is applied to the document.

readonly String href
>   The URL of a stylesheet that is linked to the document or null for inline stylesheets.

readonly StyleSheet parentStyleSheet
>   The stylesheet that included this one or null if this stylesheet was included directly in the document.

readonly CSSRule[] rules
>   The IE equivalent of the DOM-standard cssRules[] array.

readonly String title
>   The title of the stylesheet, if specified. A title may be specified by the title attribute of a <style> or <link> element that refers to this stylesheet.

readonly String type
>   The type of this stylesheet, as a MIME type. CSS stylesheets have a type of "text/css".

Methods

addRule( )
>   IE-specific method to add a CSS rule to a stylesheet.

deleteRule( )
>   DOM-standard method to delete the rule at the specified position.

insertRule( )
>   DOM-standard method to insert a new rule into the stylesheet.

removeRule( )
>   IE-specific method to delete a rule.

Description

This interface represents a CSS stylesheet. It has properties and methods for disabling the stylesheet, and for querying, inserting, and removing style rules. IE implements a slightly different API than the DOM standard. In IE, use the rules[] array instead of cssRules[], and use addRule( ) and removeRule( ) instead of the DOM standard insertRule( ) and deleteRule( ).

The CSSStyleSheet objects that apply to a document are members of the styleSheets[] array of the Document object. The DOM standard also requires (although this is not widely implemented at the time of this writing) that any <style> or <link> element or ProcessingInstruction node that defines or links to a stylesheet should make the CSSStyleSheet object available through a sheet property.

See Also

CSSRule, the styleSheets[] property of the Document object; Chapter 16

CSSStyleSheet.addRule( )   IE 4

IE-specific method to insert a rule into a stylesheet

Synopsis

```
void addRule(String selector,
             String style,
             integer index)
```

Arguments

selector
   The CSS selector for the rule.

style
   The styles to be applied to elements that match the *selector*. This style string is a semicolon-delimited list of attribute:value pairs. It does *not* begin and end with curly braces.

index
   The position in the rules array at which the rule is to be inserted or appended. If this optional argument is omitted, the new rule is appended to the array of rules.

Description

This method inserts (or appends) a new CSS style rule at the specified *index* of the rules array of this stylesheet. This is an IE-specific alternative to the standard insertRule( ) method. Note that the arguments to this method are different from those to insertRule( ).

CSSStyleSheet.deleteRule( )   DOM Level 2 CSS

delete a rule from a stylesheet

Synopsis

```
void deleteRule(unsigned long index)
    throws DOMException;
```

Arguments

index

    The index within the `cssRules` array of the rule to be deleted.

Throws

This method throws a DOMException with a code of `INDEX_SIZE_ERR` if *index* is negative or greater than or equal to `cssRules.length`. It throws a DOMException with a code of `NO_MODIFICATION_ALLOWED_ERR` if this stylesheet is read-only.

Description

This method deletes the rule at the specified *index* from the `cssRules` array. This is a DOM-standard method; see `CSSStyleSheet.removeRule( )` for an IE-specific alternative.

CSSStyleSheet.insertRule( )   DOM Level 2 CSS

insert a rule into a stylesheet

Synopsis

```
unsigned long insertRule(String rule,
                         unsigned long index)
    throws DOMException;
```

Arguments

rule

    The complete, parseable text representation of the rule to be added to the stylesheet. For style rules, this includes both the element selector and the style information.

index

    The position in the `cssRules` array at which the rule is to be inserted or appended.

Returns

The value of the *index* argument.

Throws

This method throws a DOMException with one of the following code values in the following circumstances:

`HIERARCHY_REQUEST_ERR`

    CSS syntax does not allow the specified rule at the specified location.

`INDEX_SIZE_ERR`

    index is negative or greater then `cssRules.length`.

`NO_MODIFICATION_ALLOWED_ERR`

    The stylesheet is read-only.

`SYNTAX_ERR`

    The specified *rule* text contains a syntax error.

Description

This method inserts (or appends) a new CSS *rule* at the specified *index* of the cssRules array of this stylesheet. This is a DOM-standard method; see `CSSStyleSheet.addRule()` for an IE-specific alternative.

CSSStyleSheet.removeRule( ) IE 4

IE-specific method to remove a rule from a stylesheet

Synopsis

```
void removeRule(integer index)
```

Arguments

index
> The index in the rules[] array of the rule to be removed. If this optional argument is omitted, the first rule in the array is removed.

Description

This method removes the CSS style rule at the specified *index* of the rules array of this stylesheet. This is an IE-specific alternative to the standard `deleteRule()` method.

Document DOM Level 1 Core

an HTML or XML document   Node → Document

Subinterfaces

HTMLDocument

Properties

readonly Window defaultView
> The web browser Window object (the "view" in DOM terminology) in which this document is displayed.

readonly DocumentType doctype
> For XML documents with a <!DOCTYPE> declaration, specifies a DocumentType node that represents the document's DTD. For HTML documents and for XML documents with no <!DOCTYPE>, this property is null.

readonly Element documentElement
> A reference to the root element of the document. For HTML documents, this property is always the Element object representing the <html> tag. This root element is also available through the childNodes[] array inherited from Node. See also the body property of HTMLDocument.

readonly DOMImplementation implementation
> The DOMImplementation object that represents the implementation that created this document.

`readonly CSSStyleSheet[] styleSheets`

> A collection of objects representing all stylesheets embedded in or linked into a document. In HTML documents, this includes stylesheets defined with `<link>` and `<style>` tags.

Methods

`addEventListener( )`

> Adds an event-handler function to the set of event handlers for this document. This is a DOM-standard method supported by all modern browsers except IE.

`attachEvent( )`

> Adds an event-handler function to the set of handlers for this document. This is the IE-specific alternative to `addEventListener( )`.

`createAttribute( )`

> Creates a new Attr node with the specified name.

`createAttributeNS( )`

> Creates a new Attr node with the specified name and namespace.

`createCDATASection( )`

> Creates a new CDATASection node containing the specified text.

`createComment( )`

> Creates a new Comment node containing the specified string.

`createDocumentFragment( )`

> Creates a new, empty DocumentFragment node.

`createElement( )`

> Creates a new Element node with the specified tag name.

`createElementNS( )`

> Creates a new Element node with the specified tag name and namespace.

`createEvent( )`

> Creates a new synthetic Event object of the named type.

`createExpression( )`

> Creates a new XPathExpression object that represents a compiled XPath query. For an IE-specific alternative, see `Node.selectNodes( )`.

`createProcessingInstruction( )`

> Creates a new ProcessingInstruction node with the specified target and data string.

`createRange( )`

> Creates a new Range object. This method is technically part of the DocumentRange interface; it is implemented by the Document object only in implementations that support the Range module.

`createTextNode( )`

> Creates a new Text node to represent the specified text.

`detachEvent( )`

> Removes an event-handler function from this document. This is the IE-specific alternative to the standard `removeEventListener( )` method.

`dispatchEvent( )`

> Dispatches a synthetic event to this document.

evaluate( )
> Evaluates an XPath query against this document. See Node.selectNodes( ) for an IE-specific alternative.

getElementById( )
> Returns a descendant Element of this document that has the specified value for its id attribute, or null if no such Element exists in the document.

getElementsByTagName( )
> Returns an array (technically a NodeList) of all Element nodes in this document that have the specified tag name. The Element nodes appear in the returned array in the order in which they appear in the document source.

getElementsByTagNameNS( )
> Returns an array of all Element nodes that have the specified tag name and namespace.

importNode( )
> Makes a copy of a node from some other document that is suitable for insertion into this document.

loadXML( ) *[IE only]*
> Parses a string of XML markup and stores the result in this document object.

removeEventListener( )
> Removes an event handler function from the set of handlers for this document. This is a standard DOM method implemented by all modern browsers except IE.

Description

The Document interface is the root node of a document tree. A Document node may have multiple children, but only one of those children may be an Element node: it is the root element of the document. The root element is most easily accessed through the documentElement property. The doctype and implementation properties provide access to the DocumentType object (if any) and the DOMImplementation object for this document.

Most of the methods defined by the Document interface are "factory methods" that create various types of nodes that can be inserted into this document. The notable exceptions are getElementById( ) and getElementsByTagName( ), which are quite useful for finding a specific Element or a set of related Element nodes within the document tree. Other exceptions are event-handler registration methods such as addEventHandler( ). These event-related methods are also defined by the Element interface and are documented in complete detail there.

You most commonly obtain a Document object via the document property of a Window. Document objects are also available through the contentDocument property of Frame and IFrame, and the ownerDocument property of any Node that has been added to a document.

If you are working with XML (including XHTML), you can create new Document objects with the createDocument( ) method of the DOMImplementation:

```
document.implementation.createDocument(namespaceURL, rootTagName, null);
```

In IE, you would use code like this instead:

```
new ActiveXObject("MSXML2.DOMDocument");
```

See Example 21-1 for a cross-platform utility function that creates a new Document object.

It is also possible to load an XML file from the network and parse it into a Document object. See the responseXML property of the XMLHttpRequest object. You can also parse a string of XML markup into a Document object: see DOMParser.parseFromString( ) and the IE-specific Document.loadXML( ). (Example 21-4 is a cross-platform utility function that uses these methods to parse XML markup.)

See HTMLDocument for additional properties and methods that are specific to HTML documents.

See Also

DOMImplementation, DOMParser, HTMLDocument, Window, XMLHttpRequest; Chapter 15

Document.addEventListener( )

see Element.addEventListener( )

Document.attachEvent( )

see Element.attachEvent( )

Document.createAttribute( )   DOM Level 1 Core

create a new Attr node

Synopsis

```
Attr createAttribute(String name)
    throws DOMException;
```

Arguments

name
> The name for the newly created attribute.

Returns

A newly created Attr node with its nodeName property set to *name*.

Throws

This method throws a DOMException with a code of INVALID_CHARACTER_ERR if *name* contains an illegal character.

See Also

Attr, Element.setAttribute( ), Element.setAttributeNode( )

Document.createAttributeNS( ) — DOM Level 2 Core

create an Attr with a name and namespace

Synopsis

```
Attr createAttributeNS(String namespaceURI,
                       String qualifiedName)
    throws DOMException;
```

Arguments

namespaceURI
> The unique identifier of the namespace for the Attr or null for no namespace.

qualifiedName
> The qualified name of the attribute, which should include a namespace prefix, a colon, and a local name.

Returns

A newly created Attr node with the specified name and namespace.

Throws

This method may throw a DOMException with one of the following code values in the following circumstances:

INVALID_CHARACTER_ERR
> *qualifiedName* contains an illegal character.

NAMESPACE_ERR
> *qualifiedName* is malformed or there is a mismatch between *qualifiedName* and *namespaceURI*.

NOT_SUPPORTED_ERR
> The implementation does not support XML documents and therefore does not implement this method.

Description

createAttributeNS( ) is just like createAttribute( ), except that the created Attr node has a name and namespace instead of just a name. This method is useful only with XML documents that use namespaces.

Document.createCDATASection( ) — DOM Level 1 Core

create a new CDATASection node

Synopsis

```
CDATASection createCDATASection(String data)
    throws DOMException;
```

Arguments

data

> The text of the CDATASection to create.

Returns

A newly created CDATASection node, with the specified *data* as its contents.

Throws

If the document is an HTML document, this method throws a DOMException with a code of NOT_SUPPORTED_ERR because HTML documents do not allow CDATASection nodes.

Document.createComment( )   DOM Level 1 Core

create a new Comment node

Synopsis

```
Comment createComment(String data);
```

Arguments

data

> The text of the Comment node to create.

Returns

A newly created Comment node, with the specified *data* as its text.

Document.createDocumentFragment( )   DOM Level 1 Core

create a new, empty DocumentFragment node

Synopsis

```
DocumentFragment createDocumentFragment( );
```

Returns

A newly created DocumentFragment node with no children.

Document.createElement( )   DOM Level 1 Core

create a new Element node

Synopsis

```
Element createElement(String tagName)
    throws DOMException;
```

Arguments

tagName

> The tag name of the Element to be created. Since HTML tags are case-insensitive, you may use any capitalization for HTML tag names. XML tag names are case-sensitive.

Returns

A newly created Element node with the specified tag name.

Throws

This method throws a DOMException with a code of INVALID_CHARACTER_ERR if *tagName* contains an illegal character.

Document.createElementNS( )   DOM Level 2 Core

create a new Element node using a namespace

Synopsis

```
Element createElementNS(String namespaceURI,
                        String qualifiedName)
    throws DOMException;
```

Arguments

namespaceURI
> The unique identifier for the namespace of the new Element or null for no namespace.

qualifiedName
> The qualified name of the new Element. This should include a namespace prefix, a colon, and a local name.

Returns

A newly created Element node, with the specified tag name and namespace.

Throws

This method may throw a DOMException with one of the following code values in the following circumstances:

INVALID_CHARACTER_ERR
> *qualifiedName* contains an illegal character.

NAMESPACE_ERR
> *qualifiedName* is malformed or there is a mismatch between *qualifiedName* and *namespaceURI*.

NOT_SUPPORTED_ERR
> The implementation does not support XML documents and therefore does not implement this method.

Description

createElementNS( ) is just like createElement( ), except that the created Element node has a name and namespace instead of just a name. This method is useful only with XML documents that use namespaces.

Document.createEvent( )

create an Event object

Synopsis

```
Event createEvent(String eventType)
    throws DOMException
```

Arguments

eventType

> The name of the event module for which an Event object is desired. Valid event types are listed in the Description.

Returns

A newly created Event object of the specified type.

Throws

This method throws a DOMException with a code of NOT_SUPPORTED_ERR if the implementation does not support events of the requested type.

Description

This method creates a new event object of the type specified by the *eventType* argument. Note that the value of this argument should not be the (singular) name of the event interface to be created but instead should be the (plural) name of the DOM module that defines that interface. The following table shows the legal values for *eventType* and the event interface each value creates:

eventType argument	Event interface	Initialization method
HTMLEvents	Event	initEvent( )
MouseEvents	MouseEvent	initMouseEvent( )
UIEvents	UIEvent	initUIEvent( )

After creating an Event object with this method, you must initialize the object with the initialization method shown in the table. See the appropriate Event interface reference page for details about the initialization method.

This method is actually defined not by the Document interface but by the DOM DocumentEvent interface. If an implementation supports the Events module, the Document object always implements the DocumentEvent interface and supports this method. Note that Internet Explorer does not support the DOM Events module.

See Also

Event, MouseEvent, UIEvent

Document.createExpression( )   Firefox 1.0, Safari 2.01, Opera 9

create an XPath expression for later evaluation

Synopsis

```
XPathExpression createExpression(String xpathText,
                                 Function namespaceURLMapper)
    throws XPathException
```

Arguments

xpathText
    The string representing the XPath expression to compile.

namespaceURLMapper
    A function that will map from a namespace prefix to a full namespace URL, or null if
    no such mapping is required.

Returns

An XPathExpression object.

Throws

This method throws an exception if the *xpathText* contains a syntax error or if it uses a
namespace prefix that cannot be resolved by *namespaceURLMapper*.

Description

This method takes a string representation of an XPath expression and converts it to a
compiled representation, an XPathExpression. In addition to the expression, this method
takes a function of the form function(prefix) that resolves a namespace prefix string and
returns it as a full namespace URL string.

Internet Explorer does not support this API. See Node.selectNodes( ) for an IE-specific
alternative.

See Also

Document.evaluate( ), Node.selectNodes( ), XPathExpression, XPathResult

Document.createProcessingInstruction( )   DOM Level 1 Core

create a ProcessingInstruction node

Synopsis

```
ProcessingInstruction createProcessingInstruction(String target,
                                                  String data)
    throws DOMException;
```

Arguments

target
    The target of the processing instruction.

data
    The content text of the processing instruction.

Returns

A newly created ProcessingInstruction node.

Throws

This method may throw a DOMException with one of the following code values in the following circumstances:

INVALID_CHARACTER_ERR
> The specified *target* contains an illegal character.

NOT_SUPPORTED_ERR
> This is an HTML document and does not support processing instructions.

Document.createRange( ) DOM Level 2 Range

create a Range object

Synopsis

Range createRange( );

Returns

A newly created Range object with both boundary points set to the beginning of the document.

Description

This method creates a Range object that can be used to represent a region of this document or of a DocumentFragment associated with this document.

Note that this method is actually defined not by the Document interface but by the DocumentRange interface. If an implementation supports the Range module, the Document object always implements DocumentRange and defines this method. Internet Explorer 6 does not support this module.

See Also

Range

Document.createTextNode( ) DOM Level 1 Core

create a new Text node

Synopsis

Text createTextNode(String *data*);

Arguments

data
> The content of the Text node.

Returns

A newly created Text node that represents the specified *data* string.

Document.detachEvent( )

see Element.detachEvent( )

Document.dispatchEvent( )

see Element.dispatchEvent( )

Document.evaluate( )

evaluate an XPath expression

Synopsis

```
XPathResult evaluate(String xpathText,
                     Node contextNode,
                     Function namespaceURLMapper,
                     short resultType,
                     XPathResult result)
    throws DOMException, XPathException
```

Arguments

xpathText

The string representing the XPath expression to evaluate.

contextNode

The node in this document against which the expression is to be evaluated.

namespaceURLMapper

A function that will map from a namespace prefix to a full namespace URL or null if no such mapping is required.

resultType

Specifies the type of object expected as a result, using XPath conversions to coerce the result. Possible values for type are the constants defined by the XPathResult object.

result

An XPathResult object to be reused or null if you want a new XPathResult object to be created.

Returns

A XPathResult object representing the evaluation of the expression against the given context node.

Throws

This method may throw an exception if the *xpathText* contains a syntax error, if the result of the expression cannot be converted to the desired *resultType*, if the expression contains namespaces that *namespaceURLMapper* cannot resolve, or if *contextNode* is of the wrong type or is not associated with this document.

Description

This method evaluates the specified XPath expression against the given context node and returns an XPathResult object, using type to determine what the result type should be. If you want to evaluate an expression more than once, use `Document.createExpression( )` to compile the expression to an XPathExpression object and then use the `evaluate( )` method of XPathExpression.

Internet Explorer does not support this API. See `Node.selectNodes( )` and `Node.selectSingleNode( )` for an IE-specific alternative.

See Also

```
Document.createExpression( )
Node.selectNodes( )
Node.selectSingleNode( )
XPathExpression
XPathResult
```

Document.getElementById( )   DOM Level 2 Core

find an element with the specified unique ID

Synopsis

```
Element getElementById(String elementId);
```

Arguments

elementId
> The value of the id attribute of the desired element.

Returns

The Element node that represents the document element with the specified id attribute or null if no such element is found.

Description

This method searches the document for an Element node with an id attribute whose value is *elementId* and returns that Element. If no such Element is found, it returns null. The value of the id attribute is intended to be unique within a document, and if this method finds more than one Element with the specified *elementId*, it may return one at random, or it may return null. This is an important and commonly used method because it provides a simple way to obtain the Element object that represents a specific document element. Note that the name of this method ends with "Id", not with "ID"; be careful not to misspell it.

In HTML documents, this method searches for an element based on the value of its id attribute. Use `HTMLDocument.getElementsByName( )` to search for HTML elements based on the value of their name attributes.

In XML documents, this method performs its search using any attribute whose type is id, regardless of what the name of that attribute is. If XML attribute types are not known (because, for example, the XML parser ignored or could not locate the document's DTD), this method always returns null. In client-side JavaScript, this method is not usually useful with XML documents. In fact, getElementById( ) was originally defined as a member of the HTMLDocument interface but was then moved to the Document interface in DOM Level 2.

See Also

```
Document.getElementsByTagName( )
Element.getElementsByTagName( )
HTMLDocument.getElementsByName( )
```

Document.getElementsByTagName( )   DOM Level 1 Core

return all Element nodes with the specified name

Synopsis

```
Element[] getElementsByTagName(String tagname);
```

Arguments

tagname

> The tag name of the Element nodes to be returned, or the wildcard string "*" to return all Element nodes in the document regardless of tag name. For HTML documents, tag names are compared in a case-insensitive fashion. (Prior to version 6, IE does not support this wildcard syntax.)

Returns

A read-only array (technically, a NodeList) of all Element nodes in the document tree with the specified tag name. The returned Element nodes are in the same order in which they appear in the document source.

Description

This method returns a NodeList (which you can treat as a read-only array) that contains all Element nodes from the document that have the specified tag name, in the order in which they appear in the document source. The NodeList is "live"—i.e., its contents are automatically updated as necessary if elements with the specified tag name are added to or removed from the document.

HTML documents are case-insensitive, and you can specify *tagname* using any capitalization; it matches all tags with the same name in the document, regardless of how those tags are capitalized in the document source. XML documents, on the other hand, are case-sensitive, and *tagname* matches only tags with the same name and exactly the same capitalization in the document source.

Note that the Element interface defines a method by the same name that searches only a subtree of the document. Also, the HTMLDocument interface defines getElementsByName( ), which searches for elements based on the value of their name attributes rather than their tag names.

Example

You can find and iterate through all <h1> tags in a document with code like the following:

```
var headings = document.getElementsByTagName("h1");
for(var i = 0; i < headings.length; i++) {  // Loop through the returned tags
    var h = headings[i];
    // Now do something with the <h1> element in the h variable
}
```

See Also

```
Document.getElementById( )
Element.getElementsByTagName( )
HTMLDocument.getElementsByName( )
```

Document.getElementsByTagNameNS( )   DOM Level 2 Core

return all Element nodes with a specified name and namespace

Synopsis

```
Node[] getElementsByTagNameNS(String namespaceURI,
                              String localName);
```

Arguments

namespaceURI

The unique identifier of the namespace of the desired elements, or "*" to match all namespaces.

localName

The local name of the desired elements, or "*" to match any local name.

Returns

A read-only array (technically, a NodeList) of all Element nodes in the document tree that have the specified namespace and local name.

Description

This method works just like getElementsByTagName( ), except that it searches for elements by namespace and name. It is useful only with XML documents that use namespaces.

Document.importNode( )   DOM Level 2 Core

copy a node from another document for use in this document

Synopsis

```
Node importNode(Node importedNode,
                boolean deep)
    throws DOMException;
```

Arguments

importedNode
> The node to be imported.

deep
> If true, recursively copy all descendants of *importedNode* as well.

Returns

A copy of *importedNode* (and possibly all of its descendants) with its ownerDocument set to this document.

Throws

This method throws a DOMException with a code of NOT_SUPPORTED_ERR if *importedNode* is a Document or DocumentType node, because those types of nodes cannot be imported.

Description

This method is passed a node defined in another document and returns a copy of the node that is suitable for insertion into this document. If *deep* is true, all descendants of the node are also copied. The original node and its descendants are not modified in any way. The returned copy has its ownerDocument property set to this document but has a parentNode of null because it has not yet been inserted into the document. Event-listener functions registered on the original node or tree are not copied.

When an Element node is imported, only the attributes that are explicitly specified in the source document are imported with it. When an Attr node is imported, its specified property is automatically set to true.

See Also

Node.cloneNode( )

Document.loadXML( )   Internet Explorer

populate this Document by parsing a string of XML markup

Synopsis

void loadXML(String *text*)

Arguments

text
> The XML markup to parse.

Description

This IE-specific method parses the specified string of XML text and builds a tree of DOM nodes in the current Document object, discarding any nodes that previously existed in the Document.

Client-Side
JavaScript
Reference

This method does not exist on Document objects that represent HTML documents. Before calling loadXML( ), you typically create a new, empty Document to hold the parsed content:

```
var doc = new ActiveXObject("MSXML2.DOMDocument");
doc.loadXML(markup);
```

See DOMParser.parseFromString( ) for a non-IE alternative.

See Also

DOMParser.parseFromString( )

Document.removeEventListener( )

see Element.removeEventListener( )

DocumentFragment   DOM Level 1 Core

adjacent nodes and their subtrees   Node → DocumentFragment

Description

The DocumentFragment interface represents a portion—or fragment—of a document. More specifically, it is a list of adjacent nodes and all descendants of each, but without any common parent node. DocumentFragment nodes are never part of a document tree, and the inherited parentNode property is always null. DocumentFragment nodes exhibit a special behavior that makes them quite useful, however: when a request is made to insert a DocumentFragment into a document tree, it is not the DocumentFragment node itself that is inserted but it is instead each child of the DocumentFragment. This makes Document-Fragment useful as a temporary placeholder for nodes that you wish to insert, all at once, into a document. DocumentFragment is also particularly useful for implementing document cut, copy, and paste operations, particularly when combined with the Range interface.

You can create a new, empty DocumentFragment with Document.createDocumentFragment( ), or you can use Range.extractContents( ) or Range.cloneContents( ) to obtain a Document-Fragment that contains a fragment of an existing document.

See Also

Range

DocumentType   DOM Level 1 XML

the DTD of an XML document   Node → DocumentType

Properties

readonly String internalSubset *[DOM Level 2]*
> The unparsed text of the internal subset of the DTD (i.e., the portion of the DTD that appears in the document itself rather than in an external file). The delimiting square brackets of the internal subset are not part of the returned value. If there is no internal subset, this property is null.

readonly String `name`
> The name of the document type. This is the identifier that immediately follows `<!DOCTYPE>` at the start of an XML document, and it is the same as the tag name of the document's root element.

readonly String `publicId` *[DOM Level 2]*
> The public identifier of the external subset of the DTD, or `null` if none is specified.

readonly String `systemId` *[DOM Level 2]*
> The system identifier of the external subset of the DTD, or `null` if none is specified.

Description

This infrequently used interface represents the DTD of an XML document. Programmers working exclusively with HTML documents never need to use this interface.

Because a DTD is not part of a document's content, DocumentType nodes never appear in the document tree. If an XML document has a DTD, the DocumentType node for that DTD is available through the doctype property of the Document node.

Although the W3C DOM includes an API for accessing the XML entities and notations defined in a DTD, that API is not documented here. Typical web browsers do not parse the DTDs for the documents they load, and client-side JavaScript can not access those entities and notations. For client-side JavaScript programming, this interface represents only the contents of the `<!DOCTYPE>` tag, not the contents of the DTD file it references.

DocumentType nodes are immutable and may not be modified in any way.

See Also

Document, DOMImplementation.createDocument( ), DOMImplementation.createDocumentType( )

DOMException   DOM Level 1 Core

signal exceptions or errors for core DOM objects   Object → DOMException

Constants

The following constants define the legal values for the code property of a DOMException object. Note that these constants are static properties of DOMException, not properties of individual exception objects:

unsigned short `INDEX_SIZE_ERR = 1`
> Indicates an out-of-bounds error for an array or string index.

unsigned short `DOMSTRING_SIZE_ERR = 2`
> Indicates that a requested text is too big to fit into a string in the current JavaScript implementation.

unsigned short `HIERARCHY_REQUEST_ERR = 3`
> Indicates that an attempt was made to place a node somewhere illegal in the document-tree hierarchy.

unsigned short `WRONG_DOCUMENT_ERR = 4`
> Indicates an attempt to use a node with a document that is different from the document that created the node.

unsigned short `INVALID_CHARACTER_ERR` = 5

Indicates that an illegal character is used (in an element name, for example).

unsigned short `NO_DATA_ALLOWED_ERR` = 6

Not currently used.

unsigned short `NO_MODIFICATION_ALLOWED_ERR` = 7

Indicates that an attempt was made to modify a node that is read-only and does not allow modifications.

unsigned short `NOT_FOUND_ERR` = 8

Indicates that a node was not found where it was expected.

unsigned short `NOT_SUPPORTED_ERR` = 9

Indicates that a method or property is not supported in the current DOM implementation.

unsigned short `INUSE_ATTRIBUTE_ERR` = 10

Indicates that an attempt was made to associate an Attr with an Element when that Attr node was already associated with a different Element node.

unsigned short `INVALID_STATE_ERR` = 11 *[DOM Level 2]*

Indicates an attempt to use an object that is not yet, or is no longer, in a state that allows such use.

unsigned short `SYNTAX_ERR` = 12 *[DOM Level 2]*

Indicates that a specified string contains a syntax error. Commonly used with CSS property specifications.

unsigned short `INVALID_MODIFICATION_ERR` = 13 *[DOM Level 2]*

Indicates an attempt to modify the type of a CSSRule or CSSValue object.

unsigned short `NAMESPACE_ERR` = 14 *[DOM Level 2]*

Indicates an error involving element or attribute namespaces.

unsigned short `INVALID_ACCESS_ERR` = 15 *[DOM Level 2]*

Indicates an attempt to access an object in a way that is not supported by the implementation.

Properties

unsigned short `code`

An error code that provides some detail about what caused the exception. The legal values (and their meanings) for this property are defined by the constants just listed.

Description

A DOMException object is thrown when a DOM method or property is used incorrectly or in an inappropriate context. The value of the code property indicates the general type of exception that occurred. Note that a DOMException may be thrown when reading or writing a property of an object as well as when calling a method of an object.

The descriptions of object properties and methods in this reference include a list of exception types they may throw. Note, however, that certain commonly thrown exceptions are omitted from these lists. A DOMException with a code of `NO_MODIFICATION_ALLOWED_ERR` is thrown any time an attempt is made to modify a read-only node. Thus, most methods and read/write properties of the Node interface (and of its subinterfaces) may throw this exception. Because read-only nodes appear only in XML documents and not in HTML documents, and because it applies so universally to the methods and writable properties of Node objects, the NO_MODIFICATION_ALLOWED_ERR exception is omitted from the descriptions of those methods and properties.

Similarly, many DOM methods and properties that return strings may throw a DOMException with a code of DOMSTRING_SIZE_ERR, which indicates that the text to be returned is too long to be represented as a string value in the underlying JavaScript implementation. Although this type of exception may theoretically be thrown by many properties and methods, it is very rare in practice and is omitted from the descriptions of those methods and properties.

Note that not all exceptions in the DOM are signaled with a DOMException: exceptions involving the DOM Range module cause a RangeException to be thrown.

See Also

RangeException

DOMImplementation   DOM Level 1 Core

methods independent of any particular document   Object → DOMImplementation

Methods

createDocument( )
> Creates a new Document object with a root element (the documentElement property of the returned Document object) of the specified type.

createDocumentType( )
> Creates a new DocumentType node.

hasFeature( )
> Checks whether the current implementation supports a specified version of a named feature.

Description

The DOMImplementation interface is a placeholder for methods that are not specific to any particular Document object but rather are "global" to an implementation of the DOM. You can obtain a reference to the DOMImplementation object through the implementation property of any Document object.

DOMImplementation.createDocument( )   DOM Level 2 Core

create a new Document and the specified root element

Synopsis

```
Document createDocument(String namespaceURI,
                        String qualifiedName,
                        DocumentType doctype)
    throws DOMException;
```

Arguments

namespaceURI

> The unique identifier of the namespace of the root element to be created for the document, or null for no namespace.

qualifiedName

> The name of the root element to be created for this document. If *namespaceURI* is not null, this name should include a namespace prefix and a colon.

doctype

> The DocumentType object for the newly created Document, or null if none is desired.

Returns

A Document object with its documentElement property set to a root Element node of the specified type.

Throws

This method may throw a DOMException with the following code values in the following circumstances:

INVALID_CHARACTER_ERR

> *qualifiedName* contains an illegal character.

NAMESPACE_ERR

> *qualifiedName* is malformed or there is a mismatch between *qualifiedName* and *namespaceURI*.

NOT_SUPPORTED_ERR

> The current implementation does not support XML documents and has not implemented this method.

WRONG_DOCUMENT_ERR

> *doctype* is already in use for another document or was created by a different DOMImplementation object.

Description

This method creates a new XML Document object and the specified root documentElement object for that document. If the *doctype* argument is non-null, the ownerDocument property of this DocumentType object is set to the newly created document.

This method is used to create XML documents and may not be supported by HTML-only implementations.

See Also

DOMImplementation.createDocumentType( )

DOMImplementation.createDocumentType( )   DOM Level 2 Core

create a DocumentType node

Synopsis

```
DocumentType createDocumentType(String qualifiedName,
                                String publicId,
                                String systemId)
    throws DOMException;
```

Arguments

qualifiedName
> The name of the document type. If you are using XML namespaces, this may be a qualified name that specifies a namespace prefix and a local name separated by a colon.

publicId
> The public identifier of the document type, or null.

systemId
> The system identifier of the document type, or null. This argument typically specifies the local filename of a DTD file.

Returns

A new DocumentType object with an ownerDocument property of null.

Throws

This method may throw a DOMException with one of the following code values:

INVALID_CHARACTER_ERR
> *qualifiedName* contains an illegal character.

NAMESPACE_ERR
> *qualifiedName* is malformed.

NOT_SUPPORTED_ERR
> The current implementation does not support XML documents and has not implemented this method.

Description

This method creates a new DocumentType node. This method specifies only an external subset of the document type. As of Level 2, the DOM standard does not provide any way to specify an internal subset, and the returned DocumentType does not define any Entity or Notation nodes. This method is useful only with XML documents.

DOMImplementation.hasFeature( ) DOM Level 1 Core

determine whether the implementation supports a feature

Synopsis

```
boolean hasFeature(String feature,
                   String version);
```

Arguments

feature

> The name of the feature for which support is being tested. The set of valid feature names for the DOM Level 2 standard is listed in the table in the Description. Feature names are case-insensitive.

version

> The feature version number for which support is being tested, or null or the empty string "" if support for any version of the feature is sufficient. In the Level 2 DOM specification, supported version numbers are 1.0 and 2.0.

Returns

true if the implementation completely supports the specified version of the specified feature; false otherwise. If no version number is specified, the method returns true if the implementation completely supports any version of the specified feature.

Description

The W3C DOM standard is modular, and implementations are not required to implement all modules or features of the standard. This method tests whether a DOM implementation supports a named module of the DOM specification. The availability information for each entry in this DOM reference includes the name of the module. Note that although Internet Explorer 5 and 5.5 include partial support for the DOM Level 1 specification, this important method is not supported before IE 6.

The complete set of module names that may be used as the *feature* argument are shown in the following table:

Feature	Description
Core	Node, Element, Document, Text, and the other fundamental interfaces required by all DOM implementations are implemented. All conforming implementations must support this module.
HTML	HTMLElement, HTMLDocument, and the other HTML-specific interfaces are implemented.
XML	Entity, EntityReference, ProcessingInstruction, Notation, and the other node types that are useful only with XML documents are implemented.
StyleSheets	Simple interfaces describing generic stylesheets are implemented.
CSS	Interfaces that are specific to CSS stylesheets are implemented.
CSS2	The CSS2Properties interface is implemented.
Events	The basic event-handling interfaces are implemented.
UIEvents	The interfaces for user-interface events are implemented.
MouseEvents	The interfaces for mouse events are implemented.

Feature	Description
HTMLEvents	The interfaces for HTML events are implemented.
MutationEvents	The interfaces for document mutation events are implemented.
Range	The interfaces for manipulating ranges of a document are implemented.
Traversal	The interfaces for advanced document traversal are implemented.
Views	The interfaces for document views are implemented.

Example

You might use this method in code like the following:

```
// Check whether the browser supports the DOM Level 2 Range API
if (document.implementation &&
    document.implementation.hasFeature &&
    document.implementation.hasFeature("Range", "2.0")) {
  // If so, use it here...
}
else {
  // If not, fall back on code that doesn't require Range objects
}
```

See Also

Node.isSupported( )

DOMParser   Firefox 1.0, Safari 2.01, Opera 7.60

parses XML markup to create a Document   Object → DOMParser

Constructor

new DOMParser( )

Methods

parseFromString( )
   Parses XML markup and returns a Document.

Description

A DOMParser object parses XML text and returns an XML Document object. To use a DOMParser, instantiate one with the no-argument constructor and then call its parseFromString( ) method:

```
var doc = (new DOMParser( )).parseFromString(text);
```

Internet Explorer does not support the DOMParser object. Instead, it supports XML parsing with Document.loadXML( ). Note that the XMLHttpRequest object can also parse XML documents. See the responseXML property of XMLHttpRequest.

See Also

Document.loadXML( ), XMLHttpRequest; Chapter 21

Client-Side JavaScript Reference

DOMParser.parseFromString( )

parse XML markup

Synopsis

```
Document parseFromString(String text,
                         String contentType)
```

Arguments

text

    The XML markup to parse.

contentType

    The content type of the text. This may be one of "text/xml", "application/xml", or "application/xhtml+xml". Note that "text/html" is not supported.

Returns

A Document object that holds the parsed representation of *text*. See Document.loadXML( ) for an IE-specific alternative to this method.

Element

DOM Level 1 Core

an HTML or XML element

Node → Element

Subinterfaces

HTMLElement

Properties

readonly String tagName

    The tag name of the element. This is the string "P" for an HTML <p> element, for example. For HTML documents, the tag name is returned in uppercase, regardless of its capitalization in the document source. XML documents are case-sensitive, and the tag name is returned exactly as it is written in the document source. This property has the same value as the inherited nodeName property of the Node interface.

Methods

addEventListener( )

    Adds an event-handler function to the set of event handlers for this element. This is a DOM-standard method supported by all modern browsers except IE.

attachEvent( )

    Adds an event-handler function to the set of handlers for this element. This is the IE-specific alternative to addEventListener( ).

detachEvent( )

    Removes an event-handler function from this element. This is the IE-specific alternative to the standard removeEventListener( ) method.

dispatchEvent( )

    Dispatches a synthetic event to this node.

getAttribute( )

> Returns the value of a named attribute as a string.

getAttributeNS( )

> Returns the string value of an attribute specified by local name and namespace URI. Useful only with XML documents that use namespaces.

getAttributeNode( )

> Returns the value of a named attribute as an Attr node.

getAttributeNodeNS( )

> Returns the Attr value of an attribute specified by local name and namespace URI. Useful only with XML documents that use namespaces.

getElementsByTagName( )

> Returns an array (technically, a NodeList) of all descendant Element nodes of this element that have the specified tag name, in the order in which they appear in the document.

getElementsByTagNameNS( )

> Like getElementsByTagName( ), except that the element tag name is specified by local name and namespace URI. Useful only with XML documents that use namespaces.

hasAttribute( )

> Returns true if this element has an attribute with the specified name, or false otherwise. Note that this method returns true if the named attribute is explicitly specified in the document source or if the document's DTD specifies a default value for the named attribute.

hasAttributeNS( )

> Like hasAttribute( ), except that the attribute is specified by a combination of local name and namespace URI. This method is useful only with XML documents that use namespaces.

removeAttribute( )

> Deletes the named attribute from this element. Note, however, that this method deletes only attributes that are explicitly specified in the document source for this element. If the DTD specifies a default value for this attribute, that default becomes the new value of the attribute.

removeAttributeNode( )

> Removes the specified Attr node from the list of attributes for this element. Note that this works only to remove attributes that are explicitly specified in the document source for this attribute. If the DTD specifies a default value for the removed attribute, a new Attr node is created to represent the default value of the attribute.

removeAttributeNS( )

> Like removeAttribute( ), except that the attribute to be removed is specified by a combination of local name and namespace URI. Useful only for XML documents that use namespaces.

removeEventListener( )

> Removes an event-handler function from the set of handlers for this element. This is a standard DOM method implemented by all modern browsers except IE, which uses detachEvent( ).

setAttribute( )

> Sets the named attribute to the specified string value. If an attribute with that name does not already exist, a new attribute is added to the element.

setAttributeNode( )

> Adds the specified Attr node to the list of attributes for this element. If an attribute with the same name already exists, its value is replaced.

setAttributeNodeNS( )

> Like setAttributeNode( ), but this method is suitable for use with nodes returned by Document.createAttributeNS( ). Useful only with XML documents that use namespaces.

setAttributeNS( )

> Like setAttribute( ), except that the attribute to be set is specified by the combination of a local name and a namespace URI. Useful only with XML documents that use namespaces.

Description

The Element interface represents HTML or XML elements or tags. The tagName property specifies the name of the element. The documentElement property of a Document refers to the root Element object for that document. The body property of the HTMLDocument object is similar: it refers to the <body> element of the document. To locate a specific named element in an HTML document, use Document.getElementById( ) (and give the element a unique name with the id attribute). To locate elements by tag name, use getElementsByTagName( ), which is a method of both Element and Document. In HTML documents, you can also use similar HTMLDocument.getElementsByName( ) to look up elements based on the value of their name attribute. Finally, you can create new Element objects for insertion into a document with Document.createElement( ).

The addEventListener( ) method (and its IE-specific alternative attachEvent( )) provide a way to register event-handler functions for specific types of events on the element. See Chapter 17 for complete details. Technically, addEventListener( ), removeEventListener( ), and dispatchEvent( ) are defined by the EventTarget interface of the DOM Level 2 Events specification. Since all Element objects implement EventTarget, the methods are listed here instead.

The various other methods of this interface provide access to the attributes of the element. In HTML documents (and many XML documents), all attributes have simple string values, and you can use the simple methods getAttribute( ) and setAttribute( ) for any attribute manipulation you need to do.

If you are working with XML documents that may contain entity references as part of attribute values, you will have to work with Attr objects and their subtree of nodes. You can get and set the Attr object for an attribute with getAttributeNode( ) and setAttributeNode( ), or you can iterate through the Attr nodes in the attributes[] array of the Node interface. If you are working with an XML document that uses XML namespaces, you need to use the various methods whose names end with "NS".

In the DOM Level 1 specification, the normalize( ) method was part of the Element interface. In the Level 2 specification, normalize( ) is instead part of the Node interface. All Element nodes inherit this method and can still use it.

See Also

HTMLElement, Node; Chapter 15, Chapter 17

Element.addEventListener( ) DOM Level 2 Events

register an event handler

Synopsis

```
void addEventListener(String type,
                      Function listener,
                      boolean useCapture);
```

Arguments

type
> The type of event for which the event listener is to be invoked. For example, "load", "click", or "mousedown".

listener
> The event-listener function that is invoked when an event of the specified type is dispatched to this element. When invoked, this listener function is passed an Event object and is invoked as a method of the element on which it is registered.

useCapture
> If true, the specified *listener* is to be invoked only during the capturing phase of event propagation. The more common value of false means that the *listener* is not invoked during the capturing phase but instead is invoked when this node is the actual event target or when the event bubbles up to this node from its original target.

Description

This method adds the specified event-listener function to the set of listeners registered on this node to handle events of the specified *type*. If *useCapture* is true, the listener is registered as a capturing event listener. If *useCapture* is false, it is registered as a normal event listener.

addEventListener( ) may be called multiple times to register multiple event handlers for the same type of event on the same node. Note, however, that the DOM makes no guarantees about the order in which multiple event handlers are invoked.

If the same event-listener function is registered twice on the same node with the same *type* and *useCapture* arguments, the second registration is simply ignored. If a new event listener is registered on this node while an event is being handled at this node, the new event listener is not invoked for that event.

When a node is duplicated with Node.cloneNode( ) or Document.importNode( ), the event listeners registered for the original node are not copied.

This method is also defined by, and works analogously on, the Document and Window objects.

See Also

Event; Chapter 17

Client-Side
JavaScript
Reference

Element.attachEvent( )

register an event handler

Synopsis

```
void attachEvent(String type,
                 Function listener);
```

Arguments

type

> The type of event for which the event listener is to be invoked, with a leading "on" prefix. For example, "onload", "onclick", or "onmousedown".

listener

> The event listener function that is invoked when an event of the specified type is dispatched to this element. This function is not passed any arguments but can obtain the Event object from the event property of the Window object.

Description

This method is an IE-specific event registration method. It serves the same purpose as the standard addEventListener( ) method (which IE does not support) but is different from that function in several important ways:

- Since the IE event model does not support event capturing, attachEvent( ) and detachEvent( ) expect only two arguments: the event type and the handler function.
- The event-handler names passed to the IE methods should include the "on" prefix. For example, use "onclick" with attachEvent( ) instead of "click" for addEventListener( ).
- Functions registered with attachEvent( ) are invoked with no Event object argument. Instead, they must read the event property of the Window object.
- Functions registered with attachEvent( ) are invoked as global functions, rather than as methods of the document element on which the event occurred. That is, when an event handler registered with attachEvent( ) executes, the this keyword refers to the Window object, not to the event's target element.
- attachEvent( ) allows the same event-handler function to be registered more than once. When an event of the specified type occurs, the registered function is invoked as many times as it is registered.

This method is also defined by, and works analogously on, the Document and Window objects.

See Also

Element.addEventListener( ), Event; Chapter 17

Element.detachEvent( )

delete an event listener

Synopsis

```
void detachEvent(String type,
                 Function listener)
```

Arguments

type

> The type of event for which the event listener is to be deleted, with an "on" prefix. For example: "onclick".

listener

> The event-listener function that is to be removed.

Description

This method undoes the event-handler function registration performed by the attachEvent( ) method. It is the IE-specific analog to removeEventListener( ). To remove an event handler function for an element, simply invoke detachEvent with the same arguments you originally passed to attachEvent( ).

This method is also defined by, and works analogously on, the Document and Window objects.

Element.dispatchEvent( )   DOM Level 2 Events

dispatch a synthetic event to this node

Synopsis

```
boolean dispatchEvent(Event evt)
    throws EventException;
```

Arguments

evt

> The Event object to be dispatched.

Returns

false if the preventDefault( ) method of *evt* is called at any time during the propagation of the event, or true otherwise.

Throws

This method throws an exception if the Event object *evt* is not initialized, or if its type property is null or the empty string.

Description

This method dispatches a synthetic event created with Document.createEvent( ) and initialized with the initialization method defined by the Event interface or one of its subinterfaces. The node on which this method is called becomes the target of the event, but the event first propagates down the document tree during the capturing phase, and then, if the bubbles property of the event is true, it bubbles up the document tree after being handled at the event target itself.

See Also

Document.createEvent( ), Event.initEvent( ), MouseEvent.initMouseEvent( )

Element.getAttribute( )

return the string value of a named attribute

Synopsis

```
String getAttribute(String name);
```

Arguments

name

> The name of the attribute whose value is to be returned.

Returns

The value of the named attribute as a string. If the attribute is not defined, this method is supposed to return an empty string. Some implementations return null in this case, however.

Description

getAttribute( ) returns the value of a named attribute of an element. Note that the HTMLElement object defines JavaScript properties that match each of the standard HTML attributes, so you need to use this method with HTML documents only if you are querying the value of nonstandard attributes.

In XML documents, attribute values are not available directly as element properties and must be looked up by calling this method. For XML documents that use namespaces, use getAttributeNS( ).

Example

The following code illustrates two different ways of obtaining an attribute value for an HTML <img> element:

```
// Get all images in the document
var images = document.body.getElementsByTagName("img");
// Get the src attribute of the first one
var src0 = images[0].getAttribute("src");
// Get the src attribute of the second simply by reading the property
var src1 = images[1].src;
```

See Also

Element.getAttributeNode( ), Element.getAttributeNS( ), Node

Element.getAttributeNode( )

return the Attr node for the named attribute

Synopsis

```
Attr getAttributeNode(String name);
```

Arguments

name
> The name of the desired attribute.

Returns

An Attr node that represents the value of the named attribute, or null if this element has no such attribute.

Description

getAttributeNode( ) returns an Attr node that represents the value of a named attribute. Note that this Attr node can also be obtained through the attributes property inherited from the Node interface.

See Also

Element.getAttribute( ), Element.getAttributeNodeNS( )

Element.getAttributeNodeNS( )   DOM Level 2 Core

return the Attr node for an attribute with a namespace

Synopsis

```
Attr getAttributeNodeNS(String namespaceURI,
                        String localName);
```

Arguments

namespaceURI
> The URI that uniquely identifies the namespace of this attribute, or null for no namespace.

localName
> The identifier that specifies the name of the attribute within its namespace.

Returns

The Attr node that represents the value of the specified attribute, or null if this element has no such attribute.

Description

This method works like getAttributeNode( ), except that the attribute is specified by the combination of a namespace URI and a local name defined within that namespace. This method is useful only with XML documents that use namespaces.

See Also

Element.getAttributeNode( ), Element.getAttributeNS( )

Element.getAttributeNS( ) DOM Level 2 Core

get the value of an attribute that uses namespaces

Synopsis

```
String getAttributeNS(String namespaceURI,
                      String localName);
```

Arguments

namespaceURI
> The URI that uniquely identifies the namespace of this attribute or null for no namespace.

localName
> The identifier that specifies the name of the attribute within its namespace.

Returns

The value of the named attribute, as a string. If the attribute is not defined, this method is supposed to return an empty string, but some implementations return null instead.

Description

This method works just like the getAttribute( ) method, except that the attribute is specified by a combination of namespace URI and local name within that namespace. This method is useful only with XML documents that use namespaces.

See Also

Element.getAttribute( ), Element.getAttributeNodeNS( )

Element.getElementsByTagName( ) DOM Level 1 Core

find descendant elements with a specified tag name

Synopsis

```
Element[] getElementsByTagName(String name);
```

Arguments

name
> The tag name of the desired elements, or the value "*" to specify that all descendant elements should be returned, regardless of their tag names.

Returns

A read-only array (technically, a NodeList) of Element objects that are descendants of this element and have the specified tag name.

Description

This method traverses all descendants of this element and returns an array (really a NodeList object) of Element nodes representing all document elements with the specified tag name. The elements in the returned array appear in the same order in which they appear in the source document.

Note that the Document interface also has a getElementsByTagName( ) method that works just like this one but that traverses the entire document, rather than just the descendants of a single element. Do not confuse this method with HTMLDocument.getElementsByName( ), which searches for elements based on the value of their name attributes rather than by their tag names.

Example

You can find all <div> tags in a document with code like the following:

```
var divisions = document.body.getElementsByTagName("div");
```

And you can find all <p> tags within the first <div> tag with code like this:

```
var paragraphs = divisions[0].getElementsByTagname("p");
```

See Also

```
Document.getElementById( )
Document.getElementsByTagName( )
HTMLDocument.getElementsByName( )
```

Element.getElementsByTagNameNS( )   DOM Level 2 Core

return descendant elements with the specified name and namespace

Synopsis

```
Node[] getElementsByTagNameNS(String namespaceURI,
                              String localName);
```

Arguments

namespaceURI
> The URI that uniquely identifies the namespace of the element.

localName
> The identifier that specifies the name of the element within its namespace.

Returns

A read-only array (technically, a NodeList) of Element objects that are descendants of this element and have the specified name and namespace.

Description

This method works like getElementsByTagName( ), except that the tag name of the desired elements is specified as a combination of a namespace URI and a local name defined within that namespace. This method is useful only with XML documents that use namespaces.

See Also

```
Document.getElementsByTagNameNS( ), Element.getElementsByTagName( )
```

Element.hasAttribute( )   DOM Level 2 Core

determine whether this element has a specified attribute

Synopsis

```
boolean hasAttribute(String name);
```

Arguments

name
> The name of the desired attribute.

Returns

true if this element has a specified or default value for the named attribute, and false otherwise.

Description

This method determines whether an element has an attribute with the specified name but does not return the value of that attribute. Note that hasAttribute( ) returns true if the named attribute is explicitly specified in the document and also if the named attribute has a default value specified by the internal subset of the document type.

See Also

Element.getAttribute( ), Element.setAttribute( )

Element.hasAttributeNS( )   DOM Level 2 Core

determine whether this element has a specified attribute

Synopsis

```
boolean hasAttributeNS(String namespaceURI,
                       String localName);
```

Arguments

namespaceURI
> The unique namespace identifier for the attribute, or null for no namespace.

localName
> The name of the attribute within the specified namespace.

Returns

true if this element has an explicitly specified value or a default value for the specified attribute; false otherwise.

Description

This method works like hasAttribute( ), except that the attribute to be checked for is specified by namespace and name. This method is useful only with XML documents that use namespaces.

See Also

Element.getAttributeNS( ), Element.hasAttribute( ), Element.setAttributeNS( )

Element.removeAttribute( ) DOM Level 1 Core

delete a named attribute of an element

Synopsis

void removeAttribute(String *name*);

Arguments

name
> The name of the attribute to be deleted.

Throws

This method may throw a DOMException with a code of NO_MODIFICATION_ALLOWED_ERR if this element is read-only and does not allow its attributes to be removed.

Description

removeAttribute( ) deletes a named attribute from this element. If the named attribute has a default value specified by the document type, subsequent calls to getAttribute( ) return that default value. Attempts to remove nonexistent attributes or attributes that are not specified but have a default value are silently ignored.

See Also

Element.getAttribute( ), Element.setAttribute( ), Node

Element.removeAttributeNode( ) DOM Level 1 Core

remove an Attr node from an element

Synopsis

Attr removeAttributeNode(Attr *oldAttr*)
    throws DOMException;

Arguments

oldAttr
> The Attr node to be removed from the element.

Returns

The Attr node that was removed.

Throws

This method may throw a DOMException with the following code values:

NO_MODIFICATION_ALLOWED_ERR
> This element is read-only and does not allow attributes to be removed.

NOT_FOUND_ERR
>   *oldAttr* is not an attribute of this element.

Description

This method removes (and returns) an Attr node from the set of attributes of an element. If the removed attribute has a default value specified by the DTD, a new Attr is added representing this default value. If is often simpler to use removeAttribute( ) instead of this method.

See Also

Attr, Element.removeAttribute( )

Element.removeAttributeNS( )   DOM Level 2 Core

delete an attribute specified by name and namespace

Synopsis

```
void removeAttributeNS(String namespaceURI,
                       String localName);
```

Arguments

namespaceURI
>   The unique identifier of the namespace of the attribute, or null for no namespace.

localName
>   The name of the attribute within the specified namespace.

Throws

This method may throw a DOMException with a code of NO_MODIFICATION_ALLOWED_ERR if this element is read-only and does not allow its attributes to be removed.

Description

removeAttributeNS( ) works just like removeAttribute( ), except that the attribute to be removed is specified by name and namespace instead of simply by name. This method is useful only with XML documents that use namespaces.

See Also

Element.getAttributeNS( ), Element.removeAttribute( ), Element.setAttributeNS( )

Element.removeEventListener( )   DOM Level 2 Events

delete an event listener

Synopsis

```
void removeEventListener(String type,
                         Function listener,
                         boolean useCapture);
```

Arguments

type
> The type of event for which the event listener is to be deleted.

listener
> The event-listener function that is to be removed.

useCapture
> `true` if a capturing event listener is to be removed; `false` if a normal event listener is to be removed.

Description

This method removes the specified event-listener function. The *type* and *useCapture* arguments must be the same as they are in the corresponding call to `addEventListener( )`. If no event listener is found that matches the specified arguments, this method does nothing.

Once an event-listener function has been removed by this method, it will no longer be invoked for the specified *type* of event on this node. This is true even if the event listener is removed by another event listener registered for the same type of event on the same node.

This method is also defined by, and works analogously on, the Document and Window objects.

Element.setAttribute( )   DOM Level 1 Core

create or change an attribute of an element

Synopsis

```
void setAttribute(String name,
                  String value)
    throws DOMException;
```

Arguments

name
> The name of the attribute to be created or modified.

value
> The string value of the attribute.

Throws

This method may throw a DOMException with the following code values:

`INVALID_CHARACTER_ERR`
> The *name* argument contains a character that is not allowed in HTML or XML attribute names.

`NO_MODIFICATION_ALLOWED_ERR`
> This element is read-only and does not allow modifications to its attributes.

Description

This method sets the specified attribute to the specified value. If no attribute by that name already exists, a new one is created.

Note that HTMLElement objects of an HTML document define JavaScript properties that correspond to all standard HTML attributes. Thus, you need to use this method only if you want to set a nonstandard attribute.

Example

```
// Set the TARGET attribute of all links in a document
var links = document.body.getElementsByTagName("a");
for(var i = 0; i < links.length; i++) {
    links[i].setAttribute("target", "newwindow");
    // Or more easily: links[i].target = "newwindow"
}
```

See Also

Element.getAttribute( ), Element.removeAttribute( ), Element.setAttributeNode( )

Element.setAttributeNode( )   DOM Level 1 Core

add a new Attr node to an Element

Synopsis

```
Attr setAttributeNode(Attr newAttr)
    throws DOMException;
```

Arguments

newAttr

The Attr node that represents the attribute to be added or whose value is to be modified.

Returns

The Attr node that was replaced by *newAttr*, or null if no attribute was replaced.

Throws

This method may throw a DOMException with a code of the following values:

INUSE_ATTRIBUTE_ERR

newAttr is already a member of the attribute set of some other Element node.

NO_MODIFICATION_ALLOWED_ERR

The Element node is read-only and does not allow modifications to its attributes.

WRONG_DOCUMENT_ERR

newAttr has a different ownerDocument property than the Element on which it is being set.

Description

This method adds a new Attr node to the set of attributes of an Element node. If an attribute with the same name already exists for the Element, *newAttr* replaces that attribute, and the replaced Attr node is returned. If no such attribute already exists, this method defines a new attribute for the Element.

It is usually easier to use setAttribute( ) instead of setAttributeNode( ).

See Also

Attr, Document.createAttribute( ), Element.setAttribute( )

Element.setAttributeNodeNS( )

add a namespace Attr node to an Element

Synopsis

```
Attr setAttributeNodeNS(Attr newAttr)
    throws DOMException;
```

Arguments

newAttr

The Attr node that represents the attribute to be added or whose value is to be modified.

Returns

The Attr node that was replaced by *newAttr*, or null if no attribute was replaced.

Throws

This method throws exceptions for the same reasons as setAttributeNode( ). It may also throw a DOMException with a code of NOT_SUPPORTED_ERR to signal that the method is not implemented because the current implementation does not support XML documents and namespaces.

Description

This method works just like setAttributeNode( ), except that it is designed for use with Attr nodes that represent attributes specified by namespace and name.

This method is useful only with XML documents that use namespaces. It may be unimplemented (i.e., throw a NOT_SUPPORTED_ERR) on browsers that do not support XML documents.

See Also

Attr, Document.createAttributeNS( ), Element.setAttributeNS( ), Element.setAttributeNode( )

Element.setAttributeNS( )

create or change an attribute with a namespace

Synopsis

```
void setAttributeNS(String namespaceURI,
                    String qualifiedName,
                    String value)
    throws DOMException;
```

Arguments

namespaceURI

The URI that uniquely identifies the namespace of the attribute to be set or created, or `null` for no namespace.

qualifiedName

The name of the attribute, specified as an optional namespace prefix and colon followed by the local name within the namespace.

value

The new value of the attribute.

Throws

This method may throw a DOMException with the following code values:

`INVALID_CHARACTER_ERR`

The *qualifiedName* argument contains a character that is not allowed in HTML or XML attribute names.

`NAMESPACE_ERR`

qualifiedName is malformed, or there is a mismatch between the namespace prefix of *qualifiedName* and the *namespaceURI* argument.

`NO_MODIFICATION_ALLOWED_ERR`

This element is read-only and does not allow modifications to its attributes.

`NOT_SUPPORTED_ERR`

The DOM implementation does not support XML documents.

Description

This method is like `setAttribute( )`, except that the attribute to be created or set is specified by a namespace URI and a qualified name that consists of a namespace prefix, a colon, and a local name within the namespace.

This method is useful only with XML documents that use namespaces. It may be unimplemented (i.e., throw a `NOT_SUPPORTED_ERR`) on browsers that do not support XML documents.

See Also

`Element.setAttribute( )`, `Element.setAttributeNode( )`

Event

DOM Level 2 Events, IE

information about an event

Object → Event

Subinterfaces

UIEvent

Standard Properties

The following properties are defined by the DOM Level 2 Events standard. See also `KeyEvent`, `MouseEvent`, and `UIEvent` for additional type-specific event properties:

readonly boolean bubbles
> true if the event is of a type that bubbles (unless stopPropagation( ) is called); false otherwise.

readonly boolean cancelable
> true if the default action associated with the event can be canceled with preventDefault( ); false otherwise.

readonly Object currentTarget
> The Element, Document, or Window that is currently handling this event. During capturing and bubbling, this is different from target.

readonly unsigned short eventPhase
> The current phase of event propagation. The value is one of the following three constants, which represent the capturing phase, normal event dispatch, and the bubbling phase:

eventPhase Constant	Value
Event.CAPTURING_PHASE	1
Event.AT_TARGET	2
Event.BUBBLING_PHASE	3

readonly Object target
> The target node for this event—i.e., the Element, Document, or Window that generated the event.

readonly Date timeStamp
> The date and time at which the event occurred (or, technically, at which the Event object was created). Implementations are not required to provide valid time data in this field, and if they do not, the getTime( ) method of this Date object should return 0. See Date in Part III of this book.

readonly String type
> The name of the event that this Event object represents. This is the name under which the event handler was registered, or the name of the event-handler property with the leading "on" removed—for example, "click", "load", or "submit".

IE Properties

Internet Explorer does not (at least as of IE 7) support the standard DOM event model, and IE's Event object defines a completely different set of properties. The IE event model does not define an inheritance hierarchy for different types of events, so all properties relevant to any type of event are listed here:

boolean altKey
> Whether the **Alt** key was held down when the event occurred.

integer button
> For mouse events, button specifies which mouse button or buttons were pressed. This value is a bit mask: the 1 bit is set if the left button was pressed, the 2 bit is set if the right button was pressed, and the 4 bit is set if the middle button (of a three-button mouse) was pressed.

boolean `cancelBubble`

> If an event handler wants to stop an event from being propagated up to containing objects, it must set this property to true.

integer `clientX, clientY`

> The coordinates, relative to the web browser page, at which the event occurred.

boolean `ctrlKey`

> Whether the **Ctrl** key was held down when the event occurred.

Element `fromElement`

> For mouseover and mouseout events, `fromElement` refers to the object from which the mouse pointer is moving.

integer `keyCode`

> For keypress events, this property specifies the Unicode character code generated by the key that was struck. For keydown and keyup events, it specifies the virtual keycode of the key that was struck. Virtual keycodes may be dependent on the keyboard layout in use.

integer `offsetX, offsetY`

> The coordinates at which the event occurred within the coordinate system of the event's source element (see `srcElement`).

boolean `returnValue`

> If this property is set, its value takes precedence over the value actually returned by an event handler. Set this property to `false` to cancel the default action of the source element on which the event occurred.

integer `screenX, screenY`

> Specify the coordinates, relative to the screen, at which the event occurred.

boolean `shiftKey`

> Whether the **Shift** key was held down when the event occurred.

Object `srcElement`

> A reference to the Window, Document, or Element object that generated the event.

Element `toElement`

> For mouseover and mouseout events, `toElement` refers to the object into which the mouse pointer is moving.

String `type`

> The type of the event. Its value is the name of the event handler minus the "on" prefix. So when the `onclick()` event handler is invoked, the type property of the Event object is "click".

integer `x, y`

> Specify the X and Y coordinates at which the event occurred relative to the document or the innermost containing element that is dynamically positioned using CSS.

Standard Methods

The following methods are defined by the DOM Level 2 Events specification. In the IE event model, the Event object has no methods:

`initEvent()`

> Initializes the properties of a newly created Event object.

---

preventDefault( )
> Tells the web browser not to perform the default action associated with this event, if there is one. If the event is not of a type that is cancelable, this method has no effect.

stopPropagation( )
> Stops the event from propagating any further through the capturing, target, or bubbling phases of event propagation. After this method is called, any other event handlers for the same event on the same node are called, but the event is not dispatched to any other nodes.

Description

The properties of an Event object provide details about an event, such as the element on which the event occurred. The methods of an Event object can control the propagation of the event. The DOM Level 2 Events standard defines a standard event model, which is implemented by all modern browsers except Internet Explorer, which defines its own, incompatible model. This reference page lists the properties of both the standard Event object and also of the IE Event object. See Chapter 17 for further details about the two event models. In particular, however, note that an Event object is passed to event-handler functions in the standard event model but is stored in the event property of the Window object in the IE event model.

In the standard event model, various subinterfaces of Event define additional properties that provide details pertinent to specific types of events. In the IE event model, there is only this one type of Event object, and it is used for events of all types.

See Also

KeyEvent, MouseEvent, UIEvent; Chapter 17

Event.initEvent( )   DOM Level 2 Events

initialize the properties of a new event

Synopsis

```
void initEvent(String eventTypeArg,
               boolean canBubbleArg,
               boolean cancelableArg);
```

Arguments

eventTypeArg
> The type of event. This may be one of the predefined event types, such as "load" or "submit", or it may be a custom type of your own choosing. Names that begin with "DOM" are reserved, however.

canBubbleArg
> Whether the event will bubble.

cancelableArg
> Whether the event can be canceled with preventDefault( ).

Description

This method initializes the type, bubbles, and cancelable properties of a synthetic Event object created by Document.createEvent( ). This method may be called on newly created Event objects only before they have been dispatched with the dispatchEvent( ) method of the Document or Element objects.

See Also

Document.createEvent( ), MouseEvent.initMouseEvent( ), UIEvent.initUIEvent( )

Event.preventDefault( )   DOM Level 2 Events

cancel default action of an event

Synopsis

```
void preventDefault( );
```

Description

This method tells the web browser not to perform the default action (if any) associated with this event. For example, if the type property is "submit", any event handler called during any phase of event propagation can prevent form submission by calling this method. Note that if the cancelable property of an Event object is false, either there is no default action or there is a default action that cannot be prevented. In either case, calling this method has no effect.

Event.stopPropagation( )   DOM Level 2 Events

do not dispatch an event any further

Synopsis

```
void stopPropagation( );
```

Description

This method stops the propagation of an event and prevents it from being dispatched to any other Document nodes. It may be called during any phase of event propagation. Note that this method does not prevent other event handlers on the same Document node from being called, but it does prevent the event from being dispatched to any other nodes.

ExternalInterface   ActionScript Object in Flash 8

a bidirectional interface to Flash

Static Properties

available
> Indicates whether Flash may communicate with JavaScript. This will be false if the security policy for the browser prevents communication.

Static Functions

addCallback( )
> Exports an ActionScript method so it can be invoked from JavaScript.

call( )
> Invokes a JavaScript function from ActionScript.

Description

ExternalInterface is an ActionScript object defined by the Adobe Flash plug-in in version 8 and later. It defines two static functions for use by ActionScript code in Flash movies. These functions enable communication between JavaScript code in a web browser and ActionScript code in a Flash movie.

See Also

FlashPlayer; Chapter 23

ExternalInterface.addCallback( )   ActionScript function in Flash 8

expose an ActionScript method for execution from JavaScript

Synopsis

```
boolean ExternalInterface.addCallback(String name,
                                      Object instance,
                                      Function func)
```

Arguments

name
> The name of the JavaScript function to be defined. Invoking a JavaScript function with this name causes the Flash player to invoke the ActionScript function *func* as a method of the *instance* object.

instance
> The ActionScript object on which *func* is to be invoked or null. This argument becomes the value of the this keyword when *func* is invoked.

func
> The ActionScript function that is invoked when the JavaScript function named *name* is invoked.

Returns

true on success or false on failure.

Description

This static function is used by ActionScript code in a Flash movie to enable JavaScript code in a web browser to invoke ActionScript code. When addCallback( ) is invoked, it defines a top-level JavaScript function called *name* which, when invoked, calls the ActionScript function *func* as a method of the ActionScript object *instance*.

The arguments to the JavaScript function are converted and passed to *func*, and the return value of *func* is converted and becomes the return value of the JavaScript function. Arguments and return values can be primitive numbers, strings, boolean values, and objects and arrays that contain primitive values. However, it is not possible, for example, to pass a client-side JavaScript object such as a Window or Document to an ActionScript function. It is also not possible to return a Flash-specific ActionScript object such as a MovieClip to JavaScript.

See Also

FlashPlayer; Chapter 23

ExternalInterface.call( )   ActionScript function in Flash 8

call a JavaScript function from ActionScript

Synopsis

```
Object ExternalInterface.call(String name,
                             Object args...)
```

Arguments

name
> The name of the JavaScript function to invoke.

args...
> Zero or more arguments to convert and pass to the JavaScript function.

Returns

The return value of the JavaScript function, converted to an ActionScript value.

Description

This static function is used by ActionScript code in a Flash movie to invoke a JavaScript function defined in the web browser in which the Flash movie is embedded. See `ExternalInterface.addCallback( )` for a discussion about the conversion of function arguments and return values between ActionScript and JavaScript.

FileUpload

see Input

FlashPlayer   Flash 2.0

plug-in for Flash movies

Methods

`GetVariable( )`
> Returns the value of a variable defined by a Flash movie.

`GotoFrame( )`
> Jumps to the specified frame number in the movie.

IsPlaying( )
> Checks whether the movie is playing.

LoadMovie( )
> Loads an auxiliary Flash movie and displays it at a specified layer or level of the current movie.

Pan( )
> Moves the viewport of the movie.

PercentLoaded( )
> Determines how much of the movie has loaded.

Play( )
> Begins playing the movie.

Rewind( )
> Rewinds the movie to its first frame.

SetVariable( )
> Sets a variable defined by a Flash movie.

SetZoomRect( )
> Sets the area of the movie displayed by the Flash player.

StopPlay( )
> Stops the movie.

TotalFrames( )
> Returns the length of the movie, as a number of frames.

Zoom( )
> Changes the size of the movie's viewport.

Description

A FlashPlayer object represents a Flash movie embedded in a web page and the instance of the Flash plug-in that is playing that movie. You can obtain a FlashPlayer object using Document.getElementById( ), for example, to get the <embed> or <object> tag that embeds the movie in the web page.

Once you have obtained a FlashPlayer object, you can use the various JavaScript methods it defines to control playback of the movie and to interact with it by setting and querying variables. Note that FlashPlayer methods all begin with a capital letter, which is not a common naming convention in client-side JavaScript.

See Also

Chapter 23

FlashPlayer.GetVariable( )   Flash 4

return a value defined in a Flash movie

Synopsis

String GetVariable(String *variableName*)

Arguments

variableName
> The name of the variable defined in the Flash movie.

Returns

The value of the named variable as a string, or null if no such variable exists.

FlashPlayer.GotoFrame( )   Flash 2

skip to the specified frame of a movie

Synopsis

```
void GotoFrame(integer frameNumber)
```

Arguments

frameNumber
> The frame number to skip to.

Description

This function skips to the specified frame of the movie, or skips to the last available frame, if the specified frame has not been loaded yet. To avoid this indeterminate behavior, use PercentLoaded( ) to determine how much of the movie is available.

FlashPlayer.IsPlaying( )   Flash 2

check whether a movie is playing

Synopsis

```
boolean IsPlaying( )
```

Returns

true if the movie is playing; false otherwise.

FlashPlayer.LoadMovie( )   Flash 3

load an auxiliary movie

Synopsis

```
void LoadMovie(integer layer,
              String url)
```

Arguments

layer
> The level or layer within the current movie on which the newly loaded movie is to be displayed.

url
> The URL of the movie to load.

Description

This method loads an auxiliary movie from the specified *url* and displays it at the specified *layer* within the current movie.

FlashPlayer.Pan( )

move the viewport of the movie

Synopsis

```
void Pan(integer dx, integer dy,
        integer mode)
```

Arguments

dx, dy
> The horizontal and vertical amounts to pan.

mode
> This argument specifies how to interpret the *dx* and *dy* values. If this argument is 0, the other arguments are taken as pixels. If this argument is 1, the others are percentages.

Description

The Flash player defines a viewport through which Flash movies are visible. Typically, the size of the viewport and the size of the movie are the same, but this may not be not the case when `SetZoomRect( )` or `Zoom( )` have been called: those methods can alter the viewport so that only a portion of the movie shows through.

When the viewport is showing only a portion of the movie, this `Pan( )` method moves (or "pans") the viewport so that a different portion of the movie shows. This method doesn't allow you to pan beyond the edges of a movie, however.

See Also

`FlashPlayer.SetZoomRect( )`, `FlashPlayer.Zoom( )`

FlashPlayer.PercentLoaded( )

determine how much of the movie has loaded

Synopsis

```
integer PercentLoaded( )
```

Returns

An integer between 0 and 100 representing the approximate percentage of the movie that has been loaded into the player.

FlashPlayer.Play( )   Flash 2

play a movie

Synopsis

```
void Play( )
```

Description

Begins playing the movie.

FlashPlayer.Rewind( )   Flash 2

rewind the movie to its first frame

Synopsis

```
void Rewind( )
```

Description

This method rewinds the movie to its first frame.

FlashPlayer.SetVariable( )   Flash 4

set a variable defined by a Flash movie

Synopsis

```
void SetVariable(String name, String value)
```

Arguments

name
> The name of the variable to set.

value
> The new value for the named variable. This value must be a string.

Description

This method specifies a value for a named variable defined by the Flash movie.

FlashPlayer.SetZoomRect( )   Flash 2

set the viewport of a movie

Synopsis

```
void SetZoomRect(integer left, integer top,
                 integer right, integer bottom)
```

Arguments

left, top
> The coordinates, in twips, of the upper-left corner of the viewport.

right, bottom
> The coordinates, in twips, of the lower-right corner of the viewport.

Description

This method defines the movie's viewport—that is, it specifies a subrectangle of the movie to appear in the Flash player. Flash movies are measured in a unit known as the *twip*. There are 20 twips to a point and 1,440 twips to an inch.

See Also

FlashPlayer.Pan( ), FlashPlayer.Zoom( )

FlashPlayer.StopPlay( )   Flash 2

stop the movie

Synopsis

void StopPlay( )

Description

Stop the movie.

FlashPlayer.TotalFrames( )   Flash 2

return the length of the movie, in frames

Synopsis

integer TotalFrames( )

Description

This method returns the length of the movie in frames.

FlashPlayer.Zoom( )   Flash 2

zoom in or out

Synopsis

void Zoom(integer *percentage*)

Arguments

percentage
> The percentage by which to scale the viewport, or 0 to restore the viewport to its full size.

Description

This method scales the viewport by a specified percentage. Arguments between 1 and 99 reduce the size of the viewport, which makes objects in the movie appear larger. Arguments greater than 100 enlarge the viewport (but never beyond the size of the movie) and make objects in the movie appear smaller. As a special case, the argument 0 restores the viewport to full size, so that the entire movie is visible.

Form   DOM Level 2 HTML

a <form> in an HTML document   Node → Element → HTMLElement → Form

Properties

`readonly HTMLCollection elements`
> An array (HTMLCollection) of all elements in the form. See `Form.elements[]`.

`readonly long length`
> The number of form elements in the form. This is the same value as `elements.length`.

In addition to these properties, Form also defines the properties in the following table, which correspond directly to HTML attributes:

Property	Attribute	Description
String acceptCharset	acceptcharset	Character sets the server can accept
String action	action	URL of the form handler
String enctype	enctype	Encoding of the form
String method	method	HTTP method used for form submission
String name	name	Name of the form
String target	target	Frame or window name for form submission results

Methods

`reset( )`
> Resets all form elements to their default values.

`submit( )`
> Submits the form to a web server.

Event Handlers

`onreset`
> Invoked just before the elements of the form are reset.

`onsubmit`
> Invoked just before the form is submitted. This event handler allows form entries to be validated before being submitted.

HTML Syntax

A Form object is created with a standard HTML <form> tag. The form contains input elements created with <input>, <select>, <textarea>, and other tags:

```
<form
    [ name="form_name" ]                // Used to name the form in JavaScript
    [ target="window_name" ]            // The name of the window for responses
    [ action="url" ]                    // The URL to which the form is submitted
    [ method=("get"|"post") ]           // The method of form submission
    [ enctype="encoding" ]              // How the form data is encoded
    [ onreset="handler" ]               // A handler invoked when form is reset
    [ onsubmit="handler" ]              // A handler invoked when form is submitted
>
    // Form text and input elements go here
</form>
```

Description

The Form object represents a <form> element in an HTML document. The elements property is an HTMLCollection that provides convenient access to all elements of the form. The submit() and reset() methods allow a form to be submitted or reset under program control.

Each form in a document is represented as an element of the Document.forms[] array. Named forms are also represented by the *form_name* property of their document, where *form_name* is the name specified by the name attribute of the <form> tag.

The elements of a form (buttons, input fields, checkboxes, and so on) are collected in the Form.elements[] array. Named elements, like named forms, can also be referenced directly by name: the element name is used as a property name of the Form object. Thus, to refer to an Input element named phone within a form named questionnaire, you might use the JavaScript expression:

```
document.questionnaire.phone
```

See Also

Input, Select, Textarea; Chapter 18

Form.elements[]   DOM Level 2 HTML

the input elements of a form

Synopsis

```
readonly HTMLCollection elements
```

Description

elements[] is an array-like HTMLCollection of the form elements (such as Input, Select, and Textarea objects) that appear in an HTML form. The elements of the array are in the same order they appear in the HTML source code for the form. Each element has a type property whose string value identifies its type.

Usage

If an item in the elements[] array has been given a name with the name="*name*" attribute of its HTML <input> tag, that item's name becomes a property of *form*, and this property refers to the item. Thus, it is possible to refer to input elements by name instead of by number:

> *form.name*

See Also

Input, HTMLCollection, Select, Textarea

Form.onreset DOM Level 0

event handler invoked when a form is reset

Synopsis

Function onreset

Description

The onreset property of a Form object specifies an event-handler function that is invoked when the user clicks on a **Reset** button in the form. Note that this handler is not invoked in response to the Form.reset( ) method. If the onreset handler returns false, the elements of the form are not reset. See Element.addEventListener( ) for another way to register event handlers.

See Also

Element.addEventListener( ), Form.onsubmit, Form.reset( ); Chapter 17

Form.onsubmit DOM Level 0

event handler invoked when a form is submitted

Synopsis

Function onsubmit

Description

The onsubmit property of a Form object specifies an event-handler function that is invoked when the user submits a form by clicking on its **Submit** button. Note that this event handler is not invoked when the Form.submit( ) method is called.

If the onsubmit handler returns false, the elements of the form are not submitted. If the handler returns any other value or returns nothing, the form is submitted normally. Because the onsubmit handler can cancel form submission, it is ideal for performing form data validation.

See Element.addEventListener( ) for another way to register event handlers.

See Also

Element.addEventListener( ), Form.onreset, Form.submit( ); Chapter 17

Form.reset( )

reset the elements of a form to their default values

Synopsis

```
void reset( );
```

Description

This method resets each element of a form to its default value. The results of calling this method are like the results of a user clicking on a **Reset** button, except that the onreset event handler of the form is not invoked.

See Also

Form.onreset, Form.submit( )

Form.submit( )

submit form data to a web server

Synopsis

```
void submit( );
```

Description

This method submits the values of the form elements to the server specified by the form's action property. It submits a form in the same way that a user's clicking on a **Submit** button does, except that the onsubmit event handler of the form is not triggered.

See Also

Form.onsubmit, Form.reset( )

Frame

a <frame> in an HTML document   Node → Element → HTMLElement → Frame

Properties

As explained in the Description, HTML frames can be accessed as Frame objects or as Window objects. When accessed as Frame objects, they inherit properties from HTML-Element and define these additional properties:

Document contentDocument
    The document that holds the content of the frame.

String src
    The URL from which the frame's content was loaded. Setting this property causes the frame to load a new document. This property simply mirrors the src attribute of the HTML <frame> tag: it is not a Location object like Window.location.

In addition to these properties, the Frame object also defines the following properties, which correspond directly to HTML attributes:

Property	Attribute	Description
String frameBorder	frameborder	Set to "0" for borderless frames
String longDesc	longdesc	The URL of a frame description
String marginHeight	marginheight	Top and bottom frame margin, in pixels
String marginWidth	marginwidth	Left and right frame margin, in pixels
String name	name	The name of the frame, for DOM Level 0 lookup and form and link targets
boolean noResize	noresize	If true, user cannot resize frame
String scrolling	scrolling	Frame scroll policy: "auto", "yes", or "no"

Description

Frames have a dual nature and may be represented in client-side JavaScript by either Window or Frame objects. In the traditional Level 0 DOM, each <frame> is treated as an independent window and is represented by a Window object, referenced by name, or as an element of the frames[] array of the containing Window:

```
// Get a frame as a Window object
var win1 = top.frames[0];      // Index frames[] array by number
var win2 = top.frames['f1'];   // Index frames[] array by name
var win3 = top.f1;             // Get frame as a property of its parent
```

When frames are looked up this way, the returned object is a Window, and the properties listed in the previous section are not available. Instead, use Window properties, such as document to access the frame's document and location to access the URL of that document.

In the Level 2 DOM, <frame> elements can be looked up by ID or tag name, just as any other document element can be:

```
// Get a frame as a Frame object
var frame1 = top.document.getElementById('f1');            // by id
var frame2 = top.document.getElementsByTagName('frame')[1];  // by tag name
```

When frames are looked up using DOM methods like these, the result is a Frame object rather than a Window object, and the properties listed previously are available. Use contentDocument to access the frame's document, and use the src property to query the URL of that document or to make the frame load a new document. To obtain the Window object of a Frame object f, use f.contentDocument.defaultView.

<iframe> elements are very similar to <frame> elements. See the IFrame reference page.

Note that the same-origin policy (see Section 13.8.2) applies to multiframed documents. Browsers do not allow you to access the content of frames loaded from a different origin than that of the content that includes the script. This is true whether the frame is represented by a Window or a Frame object.

See Also

IFrame, Window; Chapter 14

Hidden

see Input

History
JavaScript 1.0

the URL history of the browser
Object → History

Synopsis

```
window.history
history
```

Properties

`length`
> This numeric property specifies the number of URLs in the browser's history list. Since there is no way to determine the index of the currently displayed document within this list, knowing the size of this list is not particularly helpful.

Methods

`back( )`
> Goes backward to a previously visited URL.

`forward( )`
> Goes forward to a previously visited URL.

`go( )`
> Goes to a previously visited URL.

Description

The History object was originally designed to represent the browsing history of a window. For privacy reasons, however, the History object no longer allows scripted access to the actual URLs that have been visited. The only functionality that remains is in the use of the `back( )`, `forward( )`, and `go( )` methods.

Example

The following line performs the same action as clicking a browser's **Back** button:

```
history.back( );
```

The following line performs the same action as clicking the **Back** button twice:

```
history.go(-2);
```

See Also

The `history` property of the `Window` object, `Location`

History.back( )
JavaScript 1.0

return to the previous URL

Synopsis

```
history.back( )
```

Description

back( ) causes the window or frame to which the History object belongs to revisit the URL (if any) that was visited immediately before the current one. Calling this method has the same effect as clicking on the browser's **Back** button. It is also equivalent to:

```
history.go(-1);
```

History.forward( )
JavaScript 1.0

visit the next URL

Synopsis

```
history.forward( )
```

Description

forward( ) causes the window or frame to which the History object belongs to revisit the URL (if any) that was visited immediately after the current one. Calling this method has the same effect as clicking on the browser's **Forward** button. It is also equivalent to:

```
history.go(1);
```

Note that if the user has not used the **Back** button or the **Go** menu to move backward through the history, and if JavaScript has not invoked the History.back( ) or History.go( ) methods, the forward( ) method has no effect because the browser is already at the end of its list of URLs, and there is no URL to go forward to.

History.go( )
JavaScript 1.0

revisit a URL

Synopsis

```
history.go(relative_position)
history.go(target_string)
```

Arguments

relative_position
> The relative position in the history list of the URL to be visited.

target_string
> A URL (or URL fragment) to be visited, if a matching URL exists in the history list.

Description

The first form of the History.go( ) method takes an integer argument and causes the browser to visit the URL that is the specified number of positions away in the history list maintained by the History object. Positive arguments move the browser forward through the list, and negative arguments move it backward. Thus, calling history.go(-1) is equivalent to calling history.back( ) and produces the same effect as clicking on the **Back** button. Similarly, history.go(3) revisits the same URL that would be visited by calling history.forward( ) three times.

The second form of the History.go( ) takes a string argument and causes the browser to revisit the first (i.e., most recently visited) URL that contains the specified string. This form of the method is not well specified and may work differently on different browsers. For example, Microsoft's documentation specifies that the argument must match the URL of a previously specified site exactly, while old Netscape documentation (Netscape created the History object) says that the argument may be a substring of a previously visited URL.

HTMLCollection   DOM Level 2 HTML

array of HTML elements accessible by position or name   Object → HTMLCollection

Properties

readonly unsigned long length
    The number of elements in the collection.

Methods

item( )
    Returns the element at the specified position in the collection. You can also simply specify the position within array brackets instead of calling this method explicitly.
namedItem( )
    Returns the element from the collection that has the specified value for its id or name attribute, or null if there is no such element. You can also place the element name within array brackets instead of calling this method explicitly.

Description

An HTMLCollection is a collection of HTML elements with methods that allow you to retrieve an element by its position in the collection or by its id or name attribute. In Java-Script, HTMLCollection objects behave like read-only arrays, and you can use JavaScript square-bracket notation to index an HTMLCollection by number or by name instead of calling the item( ) and namedItem( ) methods.

A number of the properties of the HTMLDocument object are HTMLCollection objects and provide convenient access to document elements such as forms, images, and links. The Form.elements property and Select.options property are HTMLCollection objects. The HTMLCollection object also provides a convenient way to traverse the rows of a Table and the cells of a TableRow.

HTMLCollection objects are read-only: you cannot assign new elements to them, even when using JavaScript array notation. They are "live," meaning that if the underlying document changes, those changes are immediately visible through all HTMLCollection objects.

HTMLCollection objects are similar to NodeList objects but may be indexed by name as well as by number.

Example

```
var c = document.forms;       // This is an HTMLCollection of form elements
var firstform = c[0];         // It can be used like a numeric array
var lastform = c[c.length-1]; // The length property gives the number of elements
var address = c["address"];   // It can be used like an associative array
var address = c.address;      // JavaScript allows this notation, too
```

See Also

HTMLDocument, NodeList

HTMLCollection.item( )   DOM Level 2 HTML

get an element by position

Synopsis

```
Node item(unsigned long index);
```

Arguments

index

> The position of the element to be returned. Elements appear in an HTMLCollection in the same order in which they appear in the document source.

Returns

The element at the specified *index*, or null if *index* is less than zero or greater than or equal to the length property.

Description

The item( ) method returns a numbered element from an HTMLCollection. In JavaScript, it is easier to treat the HTMLCollection as an array and to index it using array notation.

Example

```
var c = document.images;  // This is an HTMLCollection
var img0 = c.item(0);     // You can use the item( ) method this way
var img1 = c[1];          // But this notation is easier and more common
```

See Also

NodeList.item( )

HTMLCollection.namedItem( )

get an element by name

Synopsis

```
Node namedItem(String name);
```

Arguments

name
> The name of the element to be returned.

Returns

The element in the collection that has the specified value for its id or name attribute, or null if no elements in the HTMLCollection have that name.

Description

This method finds and returns an element from the HTMLCollection that has the specified name. If any element has an id attribute whose value is the specified name, that element is returned. If no such element is found, an element whose name attribute has the specified value is returned. If no such element exists, namedItem( ) returns null.

Note that any HTML element may be given an id attribute, but only certain HTML elements—such as forms, form elements, images, and anchors—may have a name attribute.

In JavaScript, it is easier to treat the HTMLCollection as an associative array and to specify *name* between square brackets using array notation.

Example

```
var forms = document.forms;              // An HTMLCollection of forms
var address = forms.namedItem("address"); // Finds <form name="address">
var payment = forms["payment"]  // Simpler syntax: finds <form name="payment">
var login = forms.login;        // Also works: finds <form name="login">
```

HTMLDocument

the root of an HTML document tree   Node → Document → HTMLDocument

Properties

Element[] all *[IE 4]*
> This nonstandard property is an array-like object that provides access to all HTML-Elements in the document. The all[] array originated in IE4, and although it has been superseded by methods such as Document.getElementById( ) and Document. getElementsByTagName( ), it is still used in deployed code. See HTMLDocument.all[] for further details.

readonly HTMLCollection anchors
> An array (HTMLCollection) of all Anchor objects in the document.

readonly HTMLCollection applets
> An array (HTMLCollection) of all Applet objects in a document.

HTMLElement body

A convenience property that refers to the HTMLElement that represents the <body> tag of this document. For documents that define framesets, this property refers to the outermost <frameset> tag instead.

String cookie

Allows cookies to be queried and set for this document. See HTMLDocument.cookie for details.

String domain

The domain name of the server from which the document was loaded, or null if there is none. This property can also be used to ease the same-origin security policy in specific circumstances. See HTMLDocument.domain for details.

readonly HTMLCollection forms

An array (HTMLCollection) of all Form objects in the document.

readonly HTMLCollection images

An array (HTMLCollection) of Image objects in the document. Note that for compatibility with the Level 0 DOM, images defined with an <object> tag instead of the <img> tag are not included in this collection.

readonly String lastModified

Specifies the date and time of the most recent modification to the document. This value comes from the Last-Modified HTTP header that is optionally sent by the web server.

readonly HTMLCollection links

An array (HTMLCollection) of all Link objects in the document.

readonly String referrer

The URL of the document that linked to this document, or null if this document was not accessed through a hyperlink. This property allows client-side JavaScript to access the HTTP referer header. Note the spelling difference, however: the HTTP header has three r's, and the JavaScript property has four r's.

String title

The contents of the <title> tag for this document.

readonly String URL

The URL of the document. This value is often the same as the location.href property of the Window that contains the document. When URL redirection occurs, however, this URL property holds the actual URL of the document, and location.href holds the URL that was requested.

Methods

close( )

Closes a document stream opened with the open( ) method, forcing any buffered output to be displayed.

getElementsByName( )

Returns an array of nodes (a NodeList) of all elements in the document that have a specified value for their name attribute.

open( )
> Opens a stream to which new document contents may be written. Note that this method erases any current document content.

write( )
> Appends a string of HTML text to an open document.

writeln( )
> Appends a string of HTML text followed by a newline character to an open document.

Description

This interface extends Document and defines HTML-specific properties and methods. A number of the properties are HTMLCollection objects (essentially read-only arrays that can be indexed by number or name) that hold references to anchors, forms, links, and other important scriptable elements of the document. These collection properties originated with the Level 0 DOM. They have been superseded by Document.getElementsByTagName( ) but remain in common use because they are so convenient.

The write( ) method is notable: it allows a script to insert dynamically generated content into a document while the document is being loaded and parsed.

Note that in the Level 1 DOM, HTMLDocument defined a very useful method named getElementById( ). In the Level 2 DOM, this method has been moved to the Document interface, and it is now inherited by HTMLDocument rather than defined by it. See Document.getElementById( ) for details.

See Also

Document, Document.getElementById( ), Document.getElementsByTagName( )

HTMLDocument.all[]   IE 4

all HTML elements in a document

Synopsis

document.all[*i*]
document.all[*name*]
document.all.tags(*tagname*)

Description

all[ ] is a versatile array-like object that provides access to all the HTML elements in a document. The all[ ] array originated in IE 4 and has been adopted by a number of other browsers. It has been superseded by the standard getElementById( ) and getElementsByTagName( ) methods of the Document interface, and the standard getElementsByName( ) method of the HTMLDocument interface. Despite this, the all[ ] array is still used in existing code.

all[ ] contains the elements in source order, and you can extract them directly from the array if you know their exact numeric position within the array. It is more common, however, to use the all[ ] array to retrieve elements by the value of their name or id HTML attributes. If more than one element has the specified name, using that name as an index into all[ ] returns an array of elements that share the name.

all.tags( ) is passed a tag name and returns an array of HTML elements of the specified type.

See Also

Document.getElementById( ), Document.getElementsByTagName( ), HTMLElement

HTMLDocument.close( )   DOM Level 0

close an open document and display it

Synopsis

```
void close( );
```

Description

This method closes a document stream that was opened with the open( ) method and forces any buffered output to be displayed. If you use the write( ) method to dynamically output a document, you must remember to call this method when you are done to ensure that all your document content is displayed. Once you have called close( ), you should not call write( ) again, as this implicitly calls open( ) to erase the current document and begin a new one.

See Also

HTMLDocument.open( ), HTMLDocument.write( )

HTMLDocument.cookie   DOM Level 0

the cookie(s) of the document

Synopsis

```
String cookie
```

Description

cookie is a string property that allows you to read, create, modify, and delete the cookie or cookies that apply to the current document. A *cookie* is a small amount of named data stored by the web browser. It gives web browsers a "memory" so they can use data input on one page in another page or recall user preferences across web browsing sessions. Cookie data is automatically transmitted between web browser and web server when appropriate so server-side scripts can read and write cookie values. Client-side JavaScript code can also read and write cookies with this property.

The HTMLDocument.cookie property does not behave like a normal read/write property. You may both read and write the value of HTMLDocument.cookie, but the value you read from this property is, in general, not the same as the value you write. For details on the use of this particularly complex property, see Chapter 19.

Usage

Cookies are intended for infrequent storage of small amounts of data. They are not intended as a general-purpose communication or programming mechanism, so use them in moderation. Note that web browsers are not required to retain the value of more than 20 cookies per web server, nor to retain a cookie *name/value* pair of more than 4 KB in length.

See Also

Chapter 19

HTMLDocument.domain   DOM Level 0

the security domain of a document

Synopsis

```
String domain
```

Description

According to the DOM Level 2 HTML standard, the domain property is simply a read-only string that contains the hostname of the web server from which the document was loaded.

This property has another important use (although this use has not been standardized). The same-origin security policy (described in Section 13.8.2) prevents a script in one document from reading the content of another document (such as a document displayed in an <iframe>) unless the two documents have the same origin (i.e., were retrieved from the same web server). This can cause problems for large web sites that use multiple servers. For example, a script on the host *www.oreilly.com* might want to read the content of documents from the host *search.oreilly.com*.

The domain property helps to address this problem. You can set this property but only in a very restricted way: it can be set only to a domain suffix of itself. For example, a script loaded from *search.oreilly.com* could set its own domain property to "oreilly.com". If a script from *www.oreilly.com* is running in another window, and it also sets its domain property to "oreilly.com", then each script can read content from the other script's document, even though they did not originate on the same server. Note, that a script from *search.oreilly.com* cannot set its domain property to "search.oreilly" or to ".com".

See Also

Section 13.8.2, "The Same-Origin Policy"

HTMLDocument.getElementsByName( )   DOM Level 2 HTML

find elements with the specified name attribute

Synopsis

```
Element[] getElementsByName(String elementName);
```

Client-Side
JavaScript
Reference

Arguments

elementName
> The desired value for the name attribute.

Returns

A read-only array (technically a NodeList) of Element objects that have a name attribute with the specified value. If no such elements are found, the returned array is empty and has a length of 0.

Description

This method searches an HTML document tree for Element nodes that have a name attribute of the specified value and returns a NodeList (which you can treat as a read-only array) containing all matching elements. If there are no matching elements, a NodeList with length 0 is returned.

Do not confuse this method with the Document.getElementById( ) method, which finds a single Element based on the unique value of an id attribute, or with the Document.getElementsByTagName( ) method, which returns a NodeList of elements with the specified tag name.

See Also

Document.getElementById( ), Document.getElementsByTagName( )

HTMLDocument.open( )   DOM Level 0

begin a new document, erasing the current one

Synopsis

```
void open( );
```

Description

This method erases the current HTML document and begins a new one, which may be written to with the write( ) and writeln( ) methods. After calling open( ) to begin a new document and write( ) to specify document content, you must always remember to call close( ) to end the document and force its content to be displayed.

This method should not be called by a script or event handler that is part of the document being overwritten, because the script or handler will itself be overwritten.

Example

```
var w = window.open("");              // Open a new window
var d = w.document;                   // Get its HTMLDocument object
d.open( );                            // Open the document for writing
d.write("<h1>Hello world</h1>");      // Output some HTML to the document
d.close( );                           // End the document and display it
```

See Also

HTMLDocument.close( ), HTMLDocument.write( )

HTMLDocument.write( )   DOM Level 0

append HTML text to an open document

Synopsis

void write(String *text*);

Arguments

text
> The HTML text to be appended to the document.

Description

This method appends the specified HTML text to the document. According to the DOM standard, this method takes a single string argument. According to common practice, however, the write( ) method may be passed any number of arguments. These arguments are converted to strings and appended, in order, to the document.

Document.write( ) is normally used in one of two ways. First, it can be invoked on the current document within a <script> tag or within a function that is executed while the document is being parsed. In this case, the write( ) method writes its HTML output as if that output appeared literally in the file at the location of the code that invoked the method.

Second, you can use Document.write( ) to dynamically generate new documents in a window, frame, or iframe other than the one in which the calling script is running. If the target document is open, write( ) appends to that document. If the document is not open, write( ) discards the existing document and opens a new (empty) one to which it appends its arguments.

Once a document is open, Document.write( ) can append any amount of output to the end of the document. When a new document has been completely generated by this technique, the document must be closed by calling Document.close( ). Note that although the call to open( ) is optional, the call to close( ) is never optional.

The results of calling Document.write( ) may not be immediately visible in the target document. This is because a web browser may buffer up text to parse and display in larger chunks. Calling Document.close( ) is the only way to explicitly force all buffered output to be "flushed" and displayed.

See Also

HTMLDocument.close( ), HTMLDocument.open( )

HTMLDocument.writeln( )   DOM Level 0

append HTML text and a newline to an open document

Synopsis

void writeln(String *text*);

Arguments

text
> The HTML text to be appended to the document.

Description

This method is like `HTMLDocument.write()`, except that it follows the appended text with a newline character, which may be useful when writing the content of a `<pre>` tag, for example.

See Also

`HTMLDocument.write()`

HTMLElement

DOM Level 2 HTML

an element in an HTML document

Node → Element → HTMLElement

Properties

Each element of an HTML document has properties that correspond to the HTML attributes of the element. The properties supported by all HTML tags are listed here. Other properties, specific to certain kinds of HTML tags, are listed in the long table in the following Description section. HTMLElement objects inherit a number of useful standard properties from Node and Element, and also implement several nonstandard properties described here:

String className
> The value of the class attribute of the element, which specifies zero or more space-separated CSS class names. Note that this property is not named "class" because that name is a reserved word in JavaScript.

CSS2Properties currentStyle
> This IE-specific property represents the cascaded set of all CSS properties that apply to the element. It is an IE-only alternative to `Window.getComputedStyle()`.

String dir
> The value of the dir attribute of the element, which specifies the text direction for the document.

String id
> The value of the id attribute. No two elements within the same document should have the same value for id.

String innerHTML
> A read/write string that specifies the HTML text that is contained within the element, not including the opening and closing tags of the element itself. Querying this property returns the content of the element as a string of HTML text. Setting this property to a string of HTML text replaces the content of the element with the parsed representation of the HTML. You cannot set this property while the document is loading (for this ability, see `HTMLDocument.write()`). This is a nonstandard property that originated in IE 4. It has been implemented by all modern browsers.

String lang

The value of the lang attribute, which specifies the language code for the element's content.

int offsetHeight, offsetWidth

The height and width, in pixels, of the element and all its content, including the element's CSS padding and border, but not its margin. These are nonstandard but well-supported properties.

int offsetLeft, offsetTop

The X and Y coordinates of the upper-left corner of the CSS border of the element relative to the offsetParent container element. These are nonstandard but well-supported properties.

Element offsetParent

Specifies the container element that defines the coordinate system in which offsetLeft and offsetTop are measured. For most elements, offsetParent is the Document object that contains them. However, if an element has a dynamically positioned container, the dynamically positioned element is the offsetParent. In some browsers, table cells are positioned relative to the row in which they are contained, rather than relative to the containing document. See Chapter 16 for an example that uses this property portably. This is a nonstandard but well-supported property.

int scrollHeight, scrollWidth

The overall height and width, in pixels, of an element. When an element has scrollbars (because of the CSS overflow attribute, for example) these properties differ from offsetHeight and offsetWidth, which simply report the size of the visible portion of the element. These are non-standard but well-supported properties.

int scrollLeft, scrollTop

The number of pixels that have scrolled off the left edge of the element or off the top edge of the element. These properties are useful only for elements with scrollbars, such as elements with the CSS overflow attribute set to auto. These properties are also defined on the <body> or <html> tag of the document (this is browser-dependent) and specify the amount of scrolling for the document as a whole. Note that these properties do not specify the amount of scrolling in an <iframe> tag. These are non-standard but well-supported properties.

CSS2Properties style

The value of the style attribute that specifies inline CSS styles for this element. Note that the value of this property is not a string. See CSS2Properties for details.

String title

The value of the title attribute of the element. Many browsers display the value of this attribute in a tool tip when the mouse hovers over the element.

Methods

HTMLElement objects inherit the standard methods of Node and Element. Certain types of elements implement tag-specific methods, which are listed in the long table in the Description section and documented in other reference pages such as Form, Input, and Table. Most modern browsers also implement the following nonstandard method as well:

scrollIntoView( )

Scrolls the document so the element is visible at the top or bottom of the window.

Event Handlers

All HTML elements respond to raw mouse and key events and can trigger the event handlers listed here. Some elements, such as links and buttons, perform default actions when these events occur. For elements like these, further details are available on the element-specific reference page; see Input and Link, for example:

onclick
> Invoked when the user clicks on the element.

ondblclick
> Invoked when the user double-clicks on the element.

onkeydown
> Invoked when the user presses a key.

onkeypress
> Invoked when the user presses and releases a key.

onkeyup
> Invoked when the user releases a key.

onmousedown
> Invoked when the user presses a mouse button.

onmousemove
> Invoked when the user moves the mouse.

onmouseout
> Invoked when the user moves the mouse off the element.

onmouseover
> Invoked when the user moves the mouse over an element.

onmouseup
> Invoked when the user releases a mouse button.

Description

Each tag in an HTML document is represented by an HTMLElement object. HTML-Element defines properties that represent the attributes shared by all HTML elements. The following HTML tags do not have any properties other than those listed previously and are fully described by the HTMLElement interface:

<abbr>	<acronym>	<address>	<b>
<bdo>	<big>	<center>	<cite>
<code>	<dd>	<dfn>	<dt>
<em>	<i>	<kbd>	<noframes>
<noscript>	<s>	<samp>	<small>
<span>	<strike>	<strong>	<sub>
<sup>	<tt>	<u>	<var>

Most HTML tags define properties other than those explicitly listed previously. The DOM Level 2 HTML specification defines tag-specific interfaces for these tags, so that all standard HTML attributes have a corresponding standard JavaScript property. Typically, a tag named *T* has a tag-specific interface named HTML*T*Element. For example, the `<head>` tag is represented by the HTMLHeadElement interface. In a few cases, two or more related tags share a single interface, as in the case of the `<h1>` through `<h6>` tags, which are all represented by the HTMLHeadingElement interface.

Most of these tag-specific interfaces do nothing more than define a JavaScript property for each attribute of the HTML tag. The JavaScript properties have the same names as the attributes and use lowercase (e.g., `id`) or, when the attribute name consists of multiple words, mixed case (e.g., `longDesc`). When an HTML attribute name is a reserved word in Java or JavaScript, the property name is changed slightly. For example, the `for` attribute of `<label>` and `<script>` tags becomes the `htmlFor` property of the HTMLLabelElement and HTMLScriptElement interfaces because `for` is a reserved word. The meanings of those properties that correspond directly to HTML attributes are defined by the HTML specification, and documenting each one is beyond the scope of this book.

The following table lists all the HTML tags that have a corresponding subinterface of HTMLElement. For each tag, the table lists the DOM interface name and the names of the properties and methods it defines. All properties are read/write strings unless otherwise specified. For properties that are not read/write strings, the property type is specified in square brackets before the property name. Quite a few tags and attributes are deprecated in HTML 4 and are marked with an * in this table.

Because these interfaces and their properties map so directly to HTML elements and attributes, most interfaces do not have reference pages of their own in this book, and you should consult an HTML reference for details. The exceptions are interfaces that represent tags that are particularly important to client-side JavaScript programmers, such as the `<form>` and `<input>` tags. Those tags are documented in this book, under names that do not include the "HTML" prefix or the "Element" suffix. See, for example, the entries for Anchor, Applet, Canvas, Form, Image, Input, Link, Option, Select, Table, and Textarea:

HTML tag	DOM interface, properties, and methods
all tags	HTMLElement: id, title, lang, dir, className
`<a>`	HTMLAnchorElement: accessKey, charset, coords, href, hreflang, name, rel, rev, shape, [long] tabIndex, target, type, blur( ), focus( )
`<applet>`	HTMLAppletElement*: align*, alt*, archive*, code*, codeBase*, height*, hspace*, name*, object*, vspace*, width*
`<area>`	HTMLAreaElement: accessKey, alt, coords, href, [boolean] noHref, shape, [long] tabIndex, target
`<base>`	HTMLBaseElement: href, target
`<basefont>`	HTMLBaseFontElement*: color*, face*, size*
`<blockquote>`, `<q>`	HTMLQuoteElement: cite
`<body>`	HTMLBodyElement: aLink*, background*, bgColor*, link*, text*, vLink*
` `	HTMLBRElement: clear*
`<button>`	HTMLButtonElement: [readonly HTMLFormElement] form, accessKey, [boolean] disabled, name, [long] tabIndex, [readonly] type, value
`<caption>`	HTMLTableCaptionElement: align*

HTML tag	DOM interface, properties, and methods
`<col>`, `<colgroup>`	HTMLTableColElement: `align, ch, chOff, [long] span, vAlign, width`
`<del>, <ins>`	HTMLModElement: `cite, dateTime`
`<dir>`	HTMLDirectoryElement*: `[boolean] compact*`
`<div>`	HTMLDivElement: `align*`
`<dl>`	HTMLDListElement: `[boolean] compact*`
`<fieldset>`	HTMLFieldSetElement: `[readonly HTMLFormElement] form`
`<font>`	HTMLFontElement*: `color*, face*, size*`
`<form>`	HTMLFormElement: `[readonly HTMLCollection] elements, [readonly long] length, name, acceptCharset, action, enctype, method, target, submit( ), reset( )`
`<frame>`	HTMLFrameElement: `frameBorder, longDesc, marginHeight, marginWidth, name, [boolean] noResize, scrolling, src, [readonly Document] contentDocument`
`<frameset>`	HTMLFrameSetElement: `cols, rows`
`<h1>, <h2>, <h3>, <h4>, <h5>, <h6>`	HTMLHeadingElement: `align*`
`<head>`	HTMLHeadElement: `profile`
`<hr>`	HTMLHRElement: `align*, [boolean] noShade*, size*, width*`
`<html>`	HTMLHtmlElement: `version*`
`<iframe>`	HTMLIFrameElement: `align*, frameBorder, height, longDesc, marginHeight, marginWidth, name, scrolling, src, width, [readonly Document] contentDocument`
`<img>`	HTMLImageElement: `align*, alt, [long] border*, [long] height, [long] hspace*, [boolean] isMap, longDesc, name, src, useMap, [long] vspace*, [long] width`
`<input>`	HTMLInputElement: `defaultValue, [boolean] defaultChecked, [readonly HTMLFormElement] form, accept, accessKey, align*, alt, [boolean] checked, [boolean] disabled, [long] maxLength, name, [boolean] readOnly, size, src, [long] tabIndex, type, useMap, value, blur( ), focus( ), select( ), click( )`
`<ins>`	See `<del>`
`<isindex>`	HTMLIsIndexElement*: `[readonly HTMLFormElement] form, prompt*`
`<label>`	HTMLLabelElement: `[readonly HTMLFormElement] form, accessKey, htmlFor`
`<legend>`	HTMLLegendElement: `[readonly HTMLFormElement] form, accessKey, align*`
`<li>`	HTMLLIElement: `type*, [long] value*`
`<link>`	HTMLLinkElement: `[boolean] disabled, charset, href, hreflang, media, rel, rev, target, type`
`<map>`	HTMLMapElement: `[readonly HTMLCollection of HTMLAreaElement] areas, name`
`<menu>`	HTMLMenuElement*: `[boolean] compact*`
`<meta>`	HTMLMetaElement: `content, httpEquiv, name, scheme`
`<object>`	HTMLObjectElement: `code, align*, archive, border*, codeBase, codeType, data, [boolean] declare, height, hspace*, name, standby, [long] tabIndex, type, useMap, vspace*, width, [readonly Document] contentDocument`
`<ol>`	HTMLOListElement: `[boolean] compact*, [long] start*, type*`

HTML tag	DOM interface, properties, and methods
`<optgroup>`	HTMLOptGroupElement: [boolean] disabled, label
`<option>`	HTMLOptionElement: [readonly HTMLFormElement] form, [boolean] defaultSelected, [readonly] text, [readonly long] index, [boolean] disabled, label, [boolean] selected, value
`<p>`	HTMLParagraphElement: align*
`<param>`	HTMLParamElement: name, type, value, valueType
`<pre>`	HTMLPreElement: [long] width*
`<q>`	See `<blockquote>`
`<script>`	HTMLScriptElement: text, html For, event, charset, [boolean] defer, src, type
`<select>`	HTMLSelectElement: [readonly] type, [long] selectedIndex, value, [readonly long] length, [readonly HTMLFormElement] form, [readonly HTMLCollection of HTMLOptionElement] options, [boolean] disabled, [boolean] multiple, name, [long] size, [long] tabIndex, add( ), remove( ), blur( ), focus( )
`<style>`	HTMLStyleElement: [boolean] disabled, media, type
`<table>`	HTMLTableElement: [HTMLTableCaptionElement] caption, [HTMLTableSectionElement] tHead, [HTMLTableSectionElement] tFoot, [readonly HTMLCollection of HTMLTableRowElement] rows, [readonly HTMLCollection of HTMLTableSectionElement] tBodies, align*, bgColor*, border, cellPadding, cellSpacing, frame, rules, summary, width, createTHead( ), deleteTHead( ), createTFoot( ), deleteTFoot( ), createCaption( ), deleteCaption( ), insertRow( ), deleteRow( )
`<tbody>`, `<tfoot>`, `<thead>`	HTMLTableSectionElement: align, ch, chOff, vAlign, [readonly HTMLCollection of HTMLTableRowElement] rows, insertRow( ), deleteRow( )
`<td>`, `<th>`	HTMLTableCellElement: [readonly long] cellIndex, abbr, align, axis, bgColor*, ch, chOff, [long] colSpan, headers, height*, [boolean] noWrap*, [long] rowSpan, scope, vAlign, width*
`<textarea>`	HTMLTextAreaElement: defaultValue, [readonly HTMLFormElement] form, accessKey, [long] cols, [boolean] disabled, name, [boolean] readOnly, [long] rows, [long] tabIndex, [readonly] type, value, blur( ), focus( ), select( )
`<tfoot>`	See `<tbody>`
`<th>`	See `<td>`
`<thead>`	See `<tbody>`
`<title>`	HTMLTitleElement: text
`<tr>`	HTMLTableRowElement: [readonly long] rowIndex, [readonly long] sectionRowIndex, [readonly HTMLCollection of HTMLTableCellElement] cells, align, bgColor*, ch, chOff, vAlign, insertCell( ), deleteCell( )
`<ul>`	HTMLUListElement: [boolean] compact*, type*

* Indicates deprecated elements and attributes.

See Also

Anchor, Element, Form, HTMLDocument, Image, Input, Link, Node, Option, Select, Table, TableCell, TableRow, TableSection, Textarea; Chapter 15

HTMLElement.onclick   DOM Level 0

event handler invoked when the user clicks on an element

Synopsis

```
Function onclick
```

Description

The onclick property of an HTMLElement object specifies an event-handler function that is invoked when the user clicks on the element. Note that onclick is different from onmousedown. A click event does not occur unless a mousedown event and the subsequent mouseup event both occur over the same element.

See Also

Element.addEventListener( ), Event, MouseEvent; Chapter 17

HTMLElement.ondblclick   DOM Level 0

event handler invoked when the user double-clicks on an element

Synopsis

```
Function ondblclick
```

Description

The ondblclick property of an HTMLElement object specifies an event-handler function that is invoked when the user double-clicks on the element.

See Also

Element.addEventListener( ), Event, MouseEvent; Chapter 17

HTMLElement.onkeydown   DOM Level 0

event handler invoked when the user presses a key

Synopsis

```
Function onkeydown
```

Description

The onkeydown property of an HTMLElement object specifies an event-handler function that is invoked when the user presses a key while the element has keyboard focus. Determing which key or keys were pressed is somewhat browser-dependent. See Chapter 17 for details.

The onkeydown handler is usually the prefered handler for function keys, but use onkeypress to respond to regular alphanumeric key presses.

See Also

HTMLElement.onkeypress; Chapter 17

HTMLElement.onkeypress   DOM Level 0

event handler invoked when the user presses a key

Synopsis

Function onkeypress

Description

The onkeypress property of an HTMLElement object specifies an event-handler function that is invoked when the user presses and releases a key while the element has the keyboard focus. A keypress event is generated after a keydown event and before the corresponding keyup event. The keypress and keydown events are similar, although a keypress event is often more useful for alphanumeric keys, and a keydown handler can be more useful for function keys.

Determining which key was pressed and what modifier keys were in effect at the time is somewhat complex and browser-dependent. See Chapter 17 for details.

See Also

HTMLElement.onkeydown; Chapter 17

HTMLElement.onkeyup   DOM Level 0

event handler invoked when the user releases a key

Synopsis

Function onkeyup

Description

The onkeyup property of an HTMLElement object specifies an event-handler function that is invoked when the user releases a key while the element has the keyboard focus.

See Also

HTMLElement.onkeydown; Chapter 17

HTMLElement.onmousedown   DOM Level 0

event handler invoked when the user presses a mouse button

Synopsis

Function onmousedown

Description

The onmousedown property of an HTMLElement object specifies an event-handler function that is invoked when the user presses a mouse button over the element.

See Also

Element.addEventListener( ), Event, MouseEvent; Chapter 17

HTMLElement.onmousemove DOM Level 0

event handler invoked when the mouse moves within an element

Synopsis

Function onmousemove

Description

The onmousemove property of an HTMLElement object specifies an event-handler function that is invoked when the user moves the mouse pointer within the element.

If you define an onmousemove event handler, mouse motion events are generated and reported in huge quantities when the mouse is moved within *element*. Keep this in mind when writing the function to be invoked by the event handler. If you are interested in tracking mouse drags, register a handler of this type in response to a mousedown event and then deregister it when the mouseup event arrives.

See Also

Element.addEventListener( ), Event, MouseEvent; Chapter 17

HTMLElement.onmouseout DOM Level 0

event handler invoked when mouse moves out of an element

Synopsis

Function onmouseout

Description

The onmouseout property of an HTMLElement object specifies an event-handler function that is invoked when the user moves the mouse pointer out of the element.

See Also

Element.addEventListener( ), Event, MouseEvent; Chapter 17

HTMLElement.onmouseover

DOM Level 0

event handler invoked when the mouse moves over an element

Synopsis

Function onmouseover

Description

The onmouseover property of an HTMLElement object specifies an event-handler function that is invoked when the user moves the mouse pointer over the element.

See Also

Element.addEventListener( ), Event, MouseEvent; Chapter 17

HTMLElement.onmouseup

DOM Level 0

event handler invoked when the user releases a mouse button

Synopsis

Function onmouseup

Description

The onmouseup property of an HTMLElement object specifies an event-handler function that is invoked when the user releases a mouse button over the element.

See Also

Element.addEventListener( ), Event, MouseEvent; Chapter 17

HTMLElement.scrollIntoView( )

Firefox 1.0, IE 4, Safari 2.02, Opera 8.5

make an element visible

Synopsis

element.scrollIntoView(*top*)

Arguments

top

An optional boolean argument that specifies whether the element should be scrolled to the top (true) or bottom (false) of the screen. This argument is not supported by all browsers, and elements near the top or bottom of a document cannot usually be scrolled to the opposite edge of the window, so this argument should be considered only a hint.

Description

If an HTML element is not currently visible in the window, this method scrolls the document so that it becomes visible. The *top* argument is an optional hint about whether the element should be scrolled to the top or bottom of the window. For elements that accept the keyboard focus, such as the Link and Input elements, the focus() method implicitly performs this same scroll-into-view operation.

See Also

Anchor.focus( ), Input.focus( ), Link.focus( ), Window.scrollTo( )

IFrame
DOM Level 2 HTML

an <iframe> in an HTML document   Node → Element → HTMLElement → IFrame

Properties

As explained in the following Description, iframe elements can be accessed as IFrame objects or as Window objects. When accessed as IFrame objects, they inherit properties from HTMLElement and define the additional properties below:

Document contentDocument
> The document that holds the content of the <iframe>.

String src
> The URL from which the iframe's content was loaded. Setting this property causes the iframe to load a new document. This property simply mirrors the src attribute of the HTML <iframe> tag.

In addition to these properties, the IFrame object also defines the following properties, which correspond directly to HTML attributes of the <iframe> tag:

Property	Attribute	Description
deprecated String align	align	Alignment with respect to inline content
String frameBorder	frameborder	Set to "0" for borderless frames
String height	height	Height of the viewport in pixels or percent
String longDesc	longdesc	The URL of a frame description
String marginHeight	marginheight	Top and bottom frame margin, in pixels
String marginWidth	marginwidth	Left and right frame margin, in pixels
String name	name	The name of the frame, for DOM Level 0 lookup and form and link targets
String scrolling	scrolling	Frame scroll policy: "auto", "yes", or "no"
String width	width	Width of the viewport in pixels or percent

Description

Except for small differences in their HTML attributes, <iframe> elements behave very much like <frame> elements in client-side JavaScript. <iframe> elements become part of the frames[] array of the containing window. When accessed through that array, they are represented by Window objects, and the properties listed earlier do not apply.

When an <iframe> element is accessed as a document element by ID or tag name, it is represented by an IFrame object, with the properties shown previously. Use src to query or set the URL of the <iframe>, and use contentDocument to access the contents of the iframe. Be aware, however, that the same-origin policy (see Section 13.8.2) may prevent access to the contentDocument.

See Also

Frame, Window; Chapter 14

Image

an image in an HTML document

DOM Level 2 HTML

Node → Element → HTMLElement → Input

Constructor

new Image(integer *width*, integer *height*)

Arguments

width, height
> An optionally specified width and height for the image.

Properties

String name
> This property specifies the name for the image object. If an <img> tag has a name attribute, you can access the corresponding Image object as a named property of the Document object.

String src
> A read/write string that specifies the URL of the image to be displayed by the browser. The initial value of this property is specified by the src attribute of the <img> tag. When you set this property to the URL of a new image, the browser loads and displays that new image. This is useful for updating the graphical appearance of your web pages in response to user actions and can also be used to perform simple animation.

In addition to these properties, Image objects also support the following properties, which simply mirror HTML attributes:

Property	Attribute	Description
deprecated String align	align	Alignment with respect to inline content
String alt	alt	Alternate text when image can't be displayed
deprecated String border	border	Size of image border
long height	height	Image height, in pixels
deprecated long hspace	hspace	Left and right margins, in pixels
boolean isMap	ismap	Whether to use a server-side image map
String longDesc	longdesc	The URI of a long image description

Client-Side JavaScript Reference

Property	Attribute	Description
String useMap	usemap	Specifies a client-side image map for the image
deprecated long vspace	vspace	Top and bottom margin, in pixels
long width	width	Image width, in pixels.

Event Handlers

Image inherits event handlers from HTMLElement and defines the following:

onabort

> Invoked if page loading is stopped before the image is fully downloaded.

onerror

> Invoked if an error occurs while downloading the image.

onload

> Invoked when the image successfully finishes loading.

HTML Syntax

The Image object is created with a standard HTML <img> tag. Some <img> attributes have been omitted from the following syntax because they are not commonly used in JavaScript:

```
<img src="url"              // The image to display
     width="pixels"         // The width of the image
     height="pixels"        // The height of the image
     alt="description"      // Short description of image
     [ onload="handler" ]   // Invoked when image is fully loaded
     [ onerror="handler" ]  // Invoked if error in loading
     [ onabort="handler" ]  // Invoked if user aborts load
>
```

Description

An Image object represents an image embedded in an HTML document with an <img> tag. The images that appear in a document are collected in the document.images[] array. Images that have name attributes can also be accessed through named properties of the Document object. For example:

```
document.images[0]    // The first image in the document
document.banner       // An image with name="banner"
```

The src property of the Image object is the most interesting one. When you set this property, the browser loads and displays the image specified by the new value. This allows visual effects such as image rollovers and animations. See Chapter 22 for examples.

You can create offscreen Image objects dynamically in your JavaScript code using the Image() constructor function. Note that this constructor method does not have an argument to specify the image to be loaded. As with images created from HTML, you tell the browser to load an image by setting the src property of any images you create explicitly. There is no way to display an Image object created in this way; all you can do is force the Image object to download an image by setting the src property. This is useful, however, because it loads an image into the browser's cache; if that same image URL is used later with an actual <img> tag, it will display quickly since it has already been loaded.

See Also

Chapter 22

Image.onabort

event handler invoked when the user aborts image loading

Synopsis

```
Function onabort
```

Description

The onabort property of an Image object specifies an event-handler function that is invoked when the user aborts the loading of a page (for example, by clicking the **Stop** button) before the image has finished loading.

Image.onerror

event handler invoked when an error occurs during image loading

Synopsis

```
Function onerror
```

Description

The onerror property of an Image object specifies an event-handler function that is invoked when an error occurs during the loading of an image. See also `Window.onerror`.

Image.onload

event handler invoked when an image finishes loading

Synopsis

```
Function onload
```

Description

The onload property of an Image object specifies an event-handler function that is invoked when an image loads successfully. See also `Window.onload`.

Input

an input element in an HTML form   Node → Element → HTMLElement → Input

Properties

```
String accept
```
When type is "file", this property is a comma-separated list of MIME types that specify the types of files that may be uploaded. Mirrors the accept attribute.

String accessKey

> The keyboard shortcut (which must be a single character) a browser can use to transfer keyboard focus to this input element. Mirrors the accesskey attribute.

deprecated String align

> The vertical alignment of this element with respect to the surrounding text, or the left or right float for the element. Mirrors the align attribute.

String alt

> Alternate text to be displayed by browsers that cannot render this input element. Particularly useful when type is "image". Mirrors the alt attribute.

boolean checked

> When type is "radio" or "checkbox", this property specifies whether the element is "checked" or not. Setting this property changes the visual appearance of the input element. Mirrors the checked attribute.

boolean defaultChecked

> When type is "radio" or "checkbox", this property holds the initial value of the checked attribute as it appears in the document source. When the form is reset, the checked property is restored to the value of this property. Changing the value of this property changes the value of the checked property and the current checked state of the element.

String defaultValue

> When type is "text", "password", or "file", this property holds the initial value displayed by the element. When the form is reset, the element is restored to this value. Changing the value of this property also changes the value property and the currently displayed value.

boolean disabled

> If true, the input element is disabled and is unavailable for user input. Mirrors the disabled attribute.

readonly HTMLFormElement form

> The Form object representing the <form> element that contains this input element, or null if the input element is not within a form.

long maxLength

> If type is "text" or "password", this property specifies the maximum number of characters that the user is allowed to enter. Note that this is not the same as the size property. Mirrors the maxlength attribute.

String name

> The name of the input element, as specified by the name attribute. See the following Description section for further details on form element names.

boolean readOnly

> If true and type is "text" or "password", the user is not allowed to enter text into the element. Mirrors the readonly attribute.

unsigned long size

> If type is "text" or "password", this property specifies the width of the element in characters. Mirrors the size attribute. See also maxLength.

String src

> For input elements with a type of "image", specifies the URL of the image to be displayed. Mirrors the src attribute.

long tabIndex
> The position of this input element in the tabbing order. Mirrors the tabindex attribute.

String type
> The type of the input element. Mirrors the type attribute. See the Description section for further details on form element types.

String useMap
> For elements with a type of "image", this property specifies the name of a <map> element that provides a client-side image map for the element.

String value
> The value that is passed to the web server when the form is submitted. For elements with a type of "text", "password", or "file", this property is the editable text contained by the input element. For elements with a type of "button", "submit", or "reset", this is the (noneditable) label that appears in the button. For security reasons, the value property of FileUpload elements may be read-only. Similarly, the value returned by this property for Password elements may not contain the user's actual input.

Methods

blur( )
> Takes keyboard focus away from the element.

click( )
> If type is "button", "checkbox", "radio", "reset", or "submit", this method simulates a mouse-click on the element.

focus( )
> Transfers keyboard focus to this input element.

select( )
> If type is "file", "password", or "text", this method selects the text displayed by the element. In many browsers, this means that when the user next enters a character, the selected text is deleted and replaced with the newly typed character.

Event Handlers

onblur
> Invoked when the user takes keyboard focus away from the element.

onchange
> For text-entry elements, this event handler is invoked when the user changes the displayed text and then "commits" those changes by tabbing or clicking to transfer keyboard focus to another element. This handler does not report keystroke-by-keystroke edits. Toggle button elements of type "checkbox" and "radio" may also fire this event (in addition to the onclick event) when the user toggles them.

onclick
> For push button and toggle button elements, this event handler is invoked when the user activates the button with a mouse click or by keyboard traversal.

onfocus
> Invoked when the user gives keyboard focus to the element.

Description

An Input object represents an HTML `<input>` tag that defines a scriptable form input element. The three most important properties of an Input object are type, value, and name. These properties are described in the subsections that follow. See Chapter 18 for more information about HTML forms and form elements.

Input element types

The type attribute of the HTML `<input>` tag specifies the kind of input element that is to be created. This attribute is available to client-side JavaScript as the type property of the Input object and is useful to determine the type of an unknown form element, for example, when iterating through the elements[] array of a Form object.

The legal values of type are the following:

"button"

> The input element is a graphical push button that displays the plain text specified by the value property. The button has no default behavior and must be given an onclick event handler in order to be useful. For buttons that submit or reset a form, use a type of "submit" or "reset". Note that the HTML `<button>` tag can create buttons that display arbitrary HTML instead of plain text.

"checkbox"

> An input element of this type displays a toggle button that the user can check and uncheck. The checked property holds the current state of the button, and the onclick event handler is triggered whenever this value changes (browsers may also trigger the onchange handler). The value property is an internal value for submission to a web server and is not displayed to the user. To associate a label with a checkbox, simply place the label text near the `<input>` tag, optionally using a `<label>` tag. Checkbox elements often appear in groups, and the members of a group are sometimes given the same name property and different value properties, for the convenience of the web server to which the form is submitted.

"file"

> This type creates a "file upload" element. This element consists of a text input field for entering the name of a file, along with a button that opens a file-selection dialog box for graphical selection of a file. The value property holds the name of the file the user has specified, but when a form containing a file-upload element is submitted, the browser sends the contents of the selected file to the server instead of just sending the filename. (For this to work, the form must use "multipart/form-data" encoding and the POST method.)
>
> For security, the file-upload element does not allow HTML authors or JavaScript programmers to specify a default filename. The HTML value attribute is ignored, and the value property is read-only for this type of element, which means that only the user may enter a filename. When the user selects or edits a filename, a file-upload element triggers the onchange event handler.

"hidden"

> An input element of this type is, in fact, hidden. The value property of this invisible form element holds an arbitrary string to be submitted to the web server. Use an element of this type if you want to submit data that the user did not input directly.

"image"

> This type of input element is a form submit button that displays an image (specified by the src property) instead of displaying a textual label. The value property is unused. See the element type "submit" for further details.

"password"

> This text input field is intended for input of sensitive data, such as passwords. As the user types, her input is masked (with asterisks, for example) to prevent bystanders from reading the input value over her shoulder. Note, however that the user's input is not encrypted in any way: when the form is submitted, it is sent in clear text. As a security precaution, some browsers may prevent JavaScript code from reading the value property. In other respects, a password input element behaves like an element of type "text". It triggers the onchange event handler when the user changes the displayed value.

"radio"

> An input element of this type displays a single graphical radio button. A *radio button* is a button in a group of buttons that represents a set of mutually exclusive choices. When one button is selected, the previously selected button is deselected (as in the mechanical station preset buttons of old car radios). In order for a group of radio buttons to exhibit this mutually exclusive behavior, they must appear in the same <form> and must have the same name. For toggle buttons without mutual exclusion, use a type of "checkbox". Note that the HTML <select> tag can also be used for presenting exclusive or nonexclusive choices (see Select).

> The checked property indicates whether a radio button is selected. There is no way to determine which button in a mutually exclusive group of radio buttons is selected: you must examine the checked property of each one. Radio buttons trigger the onclick event handler when selected or deselected.

> The value property specifies a value to be submitted to a web server and is not displayed within the form. To specify a label for a radio button, do so externally to the <input> tag, such as with a <label> tag.

"reset"

> An input element of this type is like a push button created with type "button" but has a more specialized purpose. When a reset button element is clicked, the values of all input elements in the form that contains it are reset to their default values (specified by the HTML value attribute or the JavaScript defaultValue property).

> The value property specifies the text to appear in the button. A reset button triggers the onclick handler before resetting the form, and this handler may cancel the reset by returning false or by using other event cancellation methods described in Chapter 17. See also the Form.reset( ) method and the Form.onreset event handler.

"submit"

> An element of this type is a push button that submits the containing <form> when clicked. The value property specifies the text to appear in the button. The onclick event handler is triggered before the form is submitted, and a handler may cancel form submission by returning false. See also the Form.submit( ) method and Form.onsubmit event handler.

Client-Side
JavaScript
Reference

"text"

> This is the default value of the type property; it creates a single-line text input field. The HTML value attribute specifies the default text to appear in the field, and the JavaScript value property holds the currently displayed text. The onchange event handler is triggered when the user edits the displayed text and then transfers input focus to some other element. Use size to specify the width of the input field and maxLength to specify the maximum number of characters that may be entered. When a form contains only a single input element of type "text", pressing **Enter** submits the form.
>
> For multiline text input, use the HTML <textarea> tag (see Textarea). For masked text input, set type to "password".

Input element values

The value property of the Input object is a read/write string property that specifies the text that is sent to the web server when the form that contains the input element is submitted.

Depending on the value of the type property, the value property may also hold user-visible text. For input elements of type "text" and "file", this property holds whatever text the user has entered. For elements of type "button", "reset", and "submit", the value property specifies the text that appears in the button. For other element types, such as "checkbox", "radio", and "image", the contents of the value property are not displayed to the user and are used only for form submission purposes.

Input element names

The name property of the Input object is a String that provides a name for the input element. Its value comes from the HTML name attribute. The name of a form element is used for two purposes. First, it is used when the form is submitted. Data for each element in the form is usually submitted in the format:

    name=value

where *name* and *value* are encoded as necessary for transmission. If a name is not specified for a form element, the data for that element cannot be submitted to a web server.

The second use of the name property is to refer to a form element in JavaScript code. The name of an element becomes a property of the form that contains the element. The value of this property is a reference to the element. For example, if address is a form that contains a text input element with the name zip, address.zip refers to that text input element.

For input elements of type "radio" and "checkbox", it is common to define more than one related object, each of which have the same name property. In this case, data is submitted to the server with this format:

    name=value1,value2,...,valuen

Similarly, in JavaScript, each element that shares a name becomes an element of an array with that name. Thus, if four Checkbox objects in the form order share the name options, they are available in JavaScript as elements of the array order.options[].

Related form elements

The HTML <input> tag allows you to create a number of different form elements. But <button>, <select>, and <textarea> tags also create form elements.

See Also

Form, Form.elements[], Option, Select, Textarea; Chapter 18

Input.blur( )   DOM Level 2 HTML

remove keyboard focus from a form element

Synopsis

void blur( )

Description

The blur( ) method of a form element removes keyboard focus from that element without invoking the onblur event handler; it is essentially the opposite of the focus( ) method. The blur( ) method does not transfer keyboard focus anywhere, however, so the only time that it is actually useful to call this method is right before you transfer keyboard focus else-where with the focus( ) method, when you don't want to trigger the onblur event handler. That is, by removing focus explicitly from the element, you won't be notified when it is removed implicitly by a focus( ) call on another element.

Input.click( )   DOM Level 2 HTML

simulate a mouse click on a form element

Synopsis

void click( )

Description

The click( ) method of a form element simulates a mouse click on the form element but does not invoke the onclick event handler of the element.

The click( ) method is not often useful. Because it does not invoke the onclick event handler, it is not useful to call this method on elements of type "button"; they don't have any behavior other than that defined by the onclick handler. Calling click( ) on elements of type "submit" or "reset" submits or resets a form, but this can be more directly achieved with the submit( ) and reset( ) method of the Form object itself.

Input.focus( )   DOM Level 2 HTML

give keyboard focus to a form element

Synopsis

void focus( )

Description

The focus( ) method of a form element transfers keyboard focus to that element without calling the onfocus event handler. That is, it makes the element active with respect to

Client-Side
JavaScript
Reference

keyboard navigation and keyboard input. Thus, if you call focus( ) for an input element of type "text", any text the user subsequently types appears in that text element. Or, if you call focus( ) for an element of type "button", the user can then invoke that button from the keyboard.

Input.onblur   DOM Level 0

the handler invoked when a form element loses focus

Synopsis

Function onblur

Description

The onblur property of an Input object specifies an event-handler function that is invoked when the user transfers keyboard focus away from that input element. Calling blur( ) to remove focus from an element does not invoke onblur for that object. Note, however, that calling focus( ) to transfer focus to some other element causes the onblur event handler to be invoked for whichever element currently has the focus.

See Also

Element.addEventListener( ), Window.onblur; Chapter 17

Input.onchange   DOM Level 2 Events

event handler invoked when a form element's value changes

Synopsis

Function onchange

Description

The onchange property of an Input object specifies an event-handler function that is invoked when the user changes the value displayed by a form element. Such a change may be an edit to the text displayed in input elements of type "text", "password", and "file", or the selection or deselection of a toggle button of type "radio" or "checkbox". (Radio and checkbox elements always trigger the onclick handler and may also trigger the onchange handler.) Note that this event handler is invoked only when the user makes such a change; it is not invoked if a JavaScript program changes the value displayed by an element.

Also note that the onchange handler is not invoked every time the user enters or deletes a character in a text-entry form element. onchange is not intended for that type of character-by-character event handling; instead, onchange is invoked when the user's edit is complete. The browser assumes that the edit is complete when keyboard focus is moved from the current element to some other element—for example, when the user clicks on the next element in the form. See HTMLElement.onkeypress for character-by-character event notification.

The onchange event handler is not used by input elements of type "button", "hidden", "image", "reset", and "submit". Elements of those types use the onclick handler instead.

See Also

`Element.addEventListener( )`, `HTMLElement.onkeypress`; Chapter 17

Input.onclick

event handler invoked when a form element is clicked

Synopsis

`Function onclick`

Description

The onclick property of an Input object specifies an event-handler function that is invoked when the user activates the input element. This is typically done by clicking the element with the mouse, but the onclick handler is also triggered when the user activates the element using keyboard traversal. The onclick handler is not invoked when the click( ) method is called for the element.

Note that the input elements of type "reset" and "submit" perform a default action when clicked: they reset and submit, respectively, the form that contains them. You can use the onclick event handlers of each element to perform actions in addition to these default actions. You can also prevent these default actions by returning false or by using the other event-cancellation techniques described in Chapter 17. Note that you can do similar things with the onsubmit and onreset event handlers of the Form object itself.

See Also

`Element.addEventListener( )`; Chapter 17

Input.onfocus

event handler invoked when a form element gains focus

Synopsis

`Function onfocus`

Description

The onfocus property of an Input object specifies an event-handler function that is invoked when the user transfers keyboard focus to that input element. Calling focus( ) to set focus to an element does not invoke onfocus for that object.

See Also

`Element.addEventListener( )`, `Window.onfocus`; Chapter 17

Input.select( )

select the text in a form element

Synopsis

```
void select( )
```

Description

The select( ) method selects the text displayed in an input element of type "text", "password", or "file". The effects of selecting text may vary from platform to platform, but typically: the text is highlighted, it becomes available for cut and paste, and it is deleted if the user types another character.

JavaArray, JavaClass, JavaObject, JavaPackage

see Part III

JSObject   Java class in Java plug-in

Java representation of a JavaScript object

Synopsis

```
public final class netscape.javascript.JSObject extends Object
```

Methods

call( )
> Invokes a method of the JavaScript object.

eval( )
> Evaluates a string of JavaScript code in the context of the JavaScript object.

getMember( )
> Gets the value of a property of the JavaScript object.

getSlot( )
> Gets the value of an array element of the JavaScript object.

getWindow( )
> Gets a "root" JSObject that represents the JavaScript Window object of the web browser.

removeMember( )
> Deletes a property from the JavaScript object.

setMember( )
> Sets the value of a property of the JavaScript object.

setSlot( )
> Sets the value of an array element of the JavaScript object.

toString( )
> Invokes the JavaScript toString( ) method of the JavaScript object and returns its result.

Description

JSObject is a Java class, not a JavaScript object; it cannot be used in your JavaScript programs. Instead, the JSObject is used by Java applets that wish to communicate with JavaScript by reading and writing JavaScript properties and array elements, invoking JavaScript methods, and evaluating and executing arbitrary strings of JavaScript code. Obviously, since JSObject is a Java class, you must understand Java programming in order to use it.

Full details on programming with the JSObject can be found in Chapter 23.

See Also

Chapter 23, Chapter 12; JavaObject in Part III

JSObject.call( )

Java method in Java plug-in

invoke a method of a JavaScript object

Synopsis

```
public Object call(String methodName, Object args[])
```

Arguments

methodName
    The name of the JavaScript method to be invoked.

args[]
    An array of Java objects to be passed as arguments to the method.

Returns

A Java object that represents the return value of the JavaScript method.

Description

The call( ) method of the Java JSObject class invokes a named method of the JavaScript object represented by the JSObject. Arguments are passed to the method as an array of Java objects, and the return value of the JavaScript method is returned as a Java object.

Chapter 23 describes the data conversion of the method arguments from Java objects to JavaScript values, and the method return value from a JavaScript value to a Java object.

JSObject.eval( )

Java method in Java plug-in

evaluate a string of JavaScript code

Synopsis

```
public Object eval(String s)
```

Arguments

s   A string that contains arbitrary JavaScript statements separated by semicolons.

Returns

The JavaScript value of the last expression evaluated in *s*, converted to a Java object.

Description

The eval( ) method of the Java JSObject class evaluates the JavaScript code contained in the string *s* in the context of the JavaScript object specified by the JSObject. The behavior of the eval( ) method of the Java JSObject class is much like that of the JavaScript global eval( ) function.

The argument *s* may contain any number of JavaScript statements separated by semicolons; these statements are executed in the order in which they appear. The return value of eval( ) is the value of the last statement or expression evaluated in *s*.

JSObject.getMember( )   Java method in Java plug-in

read a property of a JavaScript object

Synopsis

```
public Object getMember(String name)
```

Arguments

name
> The name of the property to be read.

Returns

A Java object that contains the value of the named property of the specified JSObject.

Description

The getMember( ) method of the Java JSObject class reads and returns to Java the value of a named property of a JavaScript object. The return value may be another JSObject object or a Double, Boolean, or String object, but it is returned as a generic Object, which you must cast as necessary.

JSObject.getSlot( )   Java method in Java plug-in

read an array element of a JavaScript object

Synopsis

```
public Object getSlot(int index)
```

Arguments

index
> The index of the array element to be read.

Returns

The value of the array element at the specified *index* of a JavaScript object.

Description

The getSlot( ) method of the Java JSObject class reads and returns to Java the value of an array element at the specified *index* of a JavaScript object. The return value may be another JSObject object or a Double, Boolean, or String object, but it is returned as a generic Object, which you must cast as necessary.

JSObject.getWindow( )   Java method in Java plug-in

return initial JSObject for browser window

Synopsis

```
public static JSObject getWindow(java.applet.Applet applet)
```

Arguments

applet
> An Applet object running in the web browser window for which a JSObject is to be obtained.

Returns

A JSObject that represents the JavaScript Window object for the web browser window that contains the specified *applet*.

Description

The getWindow( ) method is the first JSObject method that any Java applet calls. JSObject does not define a constructor, and the static getWindow( ) method provides the only way to obtain an initial "root" JSObject from which other JSObjects may be obtained.

JSObject.removeMember( )   Java method in Java plug-in

delete a property of a JavaScript object

Synopsis

```
public void removeMember(String name)
```

Arguments

name
> The name of the property to be deleted from the JSObject.

Description

The removeMember( ) method of the Java JSObject class deletes a named property from the JavaScript object represented by the JSObject.

JSObject.setMember( )

set a property of a JavaScript object

Synopsis

```
public void setMember(String name, Object value)
```

Arguments

name
> The name of the property to be set in the JSObject.

value
> The value to which the named property should be set.

Description

The setMember( ) method of the Java JSObject class sets the value of a named property of a JavaScript object from Java. The specified *value* may be any Java Object. Primitive Java values may not be passed to this method. In JavaScript, the specified *value* is accessible as a JavaObject object.

JSObject.setSlot( )

set an array element of a JavaScript object

Synopsis

```
public void setSlot(int index, Object value)
```

Arguments

index
> The index of the array element to be set in the JSObject.

value
> The value to which the specified array element should be set.

Description

The setSlot( ) method of the Java JSObject class sets the value of a numbered array element of a JavaScript object from Java. The specified *value* may be any Java Object. Primitive Java values may not be passed to this method. In JavaScript, the specified *value* is accessible as a JavaObject object.

JSObject.toString( )

return the string value of a JavaScript object

Synopsis

```
public String toString( )
```

Returns

The string returned by invoking the toString() method of the JavaScript object represented by the specified Java JSObject.

Description

The toString() method of the Java JSObject class invokes the JavaScript toString() method of the JavaScript object represented by a JSObject and returns the result of that method.

KeyEvent   **Firefox and compatible browsers**

details about a keyboard event   Event → UIEvent → KeyEvent

Client-Side
JavaScript
Reference

Properties

readonly boolean altKey
> Whether the **Alt** key was held down when the event occurred.

readonly integer charCode
> This number is the Unicode encoding of the printable character (if any) generated by a keypress event. This property is zero for nonprinting function keys and is not used for keydown and keyup events. Use String.fromCharCode() to convert this property to a string.

readonly boolean ctrlKey
> Whether the **Ctrl** key was held down when the event occurred. Defined for all types of mouse events.

readonly integer keyCode
> The virtual keycode of the key that was pressed. This property is used for all types of keyboard events. Keycodes may be browser-, OS-, and keyboard-hardware-dependent. Typically, when a key displays a printing character on it, the virtual keycode for that key is the same as the encoding of the character. Key codes for nonprinting function keys may vary more, but see Example 17-6 for a set of commonly used codes.

readonly boolean shiftKey
> Whether the **Shift** key was held down when the event occurred. Defined for all types of mouse events.

Description

A KeyEvent object provides details about a keyboard event and is passed to event handlers for keydown, keypress, and keyup events. The DOM Level 2 Events standard does not cover keyboard events, and the KeyEvent object has not been standardized. This entry describes the Firefox implementation. Many of these properties are also supported in the IE event model; see the IE-specific properties described for the Event object. Note that in addition to the properties listed here, KeyEvent objects also inherit the properties of Event and UIEvent.

Chapter 17 includes several practical examples of working with KeyEvent objects.

Layer

See Also

Event, UIEvent; Chapter 17

Layer   Netscape 4 only; discontinued in Netscape 6

an obsolete Netscape API

Description

The Layer object was Netscape 4's technique for supporting dynamically positionable HTML elements. It was never standardized and is now obsolete.

See Also

Chapter 16

Link   DOM Level 0

a hyperlink or anchor in an HTML document   Node → Element → HTMLElement → Link

Properties

The most important property of a Link is its href, which is the URL to which it links. The Link object also defines a number of other properties that hold portions of the URL. For each of these properties, the example given is a portion of the following (fictitious) URL:

    http://www.oreilly.com:1234/catalog/search.html?q=JavaScript&m=10#results

String hash
> Specifies the anchor portion of the Link's URL, including the leading hash (#) mark—for example, "#results". This anchor portion of a URL refers to a named position within the document referenced by the Link. In HTML files, positions are named with the name attribute of the <a> tag. (see Anchor).

String host
> Specifies the hostname and port portions of a Link's URL—for example, "www.oreilly.com:1234".

String hostname
> Specifies the hostname portion of a Link's URL—for example, "www.oreilly.com".

String href
> Specifies the complete text of the Link's URL, unlike other Link URL properties that specify only portions of the URL.

String pathname
> Specifies the pathname portion of a Link's URL—for example, "/catalog/search.html".

String port
> Specifies the port portion of a Link's URL—for example, "1234".

String protocol
> Specifies the protocol portion of a Link's URL, including the trailing colon—for example, "http:".

`String search`

Specifies the query portion of a Link's URL, including the leading question mark—for example, "?q=JavaScript&m=10".

In addition to these URL-related properties, Link objects also define properties that correspond to the attributes for the HTML `<a>` and `<area>` tags:

Property	Attribute	Description
`String accessKey`	`accesskey`	Keyboard shortcut
`String charset`	`charset`	Encoding of the destination document
`String coords`	`coords`	For `<area>` tags
`String hreflang`	`hreflang`	Language of the linked document
`String name`	`name`	Anchor name; see Anchor
`String rel`	`rel`	Link type
`String rev`	`rev`	Reverse link type
`String shape`	`shape`	For `<area>` tags
`long tabIndex`	`tabindex`	Link's position in tabbing order
`String target`	`target`	Name of the frame or window in which the destination document is to be displayed
`String type`	`type`	Content type of the destination document

Methods

`blur( )`

Takes keyboard focus away from the link.

`focus( )`

Scrolls the document so the link is visible and gives keyboard focus to the link.

Event Handlers

The Link object has special behavior for three event handlers:

`onclick`

Invoked when the user clicks on the link.

`onmouseout`

Invoked when the user moves the mouse off the link.

`onmouseover`

Invoked when the user moves the mouse over the link.

HTML Syntax

A Link object is created with standard `<a>` and `</a>` tags. The `href` attribute is required for all Link objects. If the `name` attribute is also specified, an Anchor object is also created:

```
<a href="url"                        // The destination of the link
   [ name="anchor_tag" ]             // Creates an Anchor object
   [ target="window_name" ]          // Where the new document should be displayed
   [ onclick="handler" ]             // Invoked when link is clicked
   [ onmouseover="handler" ]         // Invoked when mouse is over link
```

```
    [ onmouseout="handler" ]    // Invoked when mouse leaves link
   >link text or image  // The visible part of the link
   </a>
```

Description

A Link object represents a hyperlink in a document. Links are usually created with <a> tags that have an href attribute defined, but they may also be created with <area> tags inside a client-side image map. When an <a> tag has a name attribute instead of an href attribute, it defines a named position in a document and is represented by an Anchor object instead of a Link object. See Anchor for details.

All links in a document (whether created with <a> or <area> tags) are represented by Link objects in the links[] array of the Document object.

The destination of a hypertext link is a URL, of course, and many of the properties of the Link object specify the contents of that URL. In this way, the Link object is similar to the Location object, which also has a full set of URL properties.

Example

```
// Get the URL of the first hyperlink in the document
var url = document.links[0].href;
```

See Also

Anchor, Location

Link.blur( )   DOM Level 0

take keyboard focus away from a hyperlink

Synopsis

```
void blur( );
```

Description

For web browsers that allow hyperlinks to have the keyboard focus, this method takes keyboard focus away from a hyperlink.

Link.focus( )   DOM Level 0

make a link visible and give it keyboard focus

Synopsis

```
void focus( );
```

Description

This method scrolls the document so the specified hyperlink is visible. If the browser allows links to have keyboard focus, this method also gives keyboard focus to the link.

Link.onclick

event handler invoked when a Link is clicked

Synopsis

```
Function onclick
```

Description

The onclick property of a Link object specifies an event-handler function that is invoked when the user clicks on the link. The browser default action after the event handler returns is to follow the hyperlink that was clicked. You can prevent this default by returning false or by using one of the other event-cancellation methods described in Chapter 17.

See Also

Element.addEventListener( ), MouseEvent; Chapter 17

Link.onmouseout

event handler invoked when the mouse leaves a link

Synopsis

```
Function onmouseout
```

Description

The onmouseout property of a Link object specifies an event-handler function that is invoked when the user moves the mouse off a hypertext link. It is often used with the onmouseover event handler.

See Also

Element.addEventListener( ), Link.onmouseover, MouseEvent; Chapter 17

Link.onmouseover

event handler invoked when the mouse goes over a link

Synopsis

```
Function onmouseover
```

Description

The onmouseover property of a Link object specifies an event-handler function that is invoked when the user moves the mouse over a hypertext link. When the user holds the mouse over a hyperlink, the browser displays the URL for that link in the status line. In older browsers, it is possible to prevent this default action and display your own text in the status line. For security reasons (to help prevent phishing attacks, for example) most modern browsers have disabled this capability.

See Also

`Element.addEventListener( )`, `Link.onmouseout`, `MouseEvent`; Chapter 17

Location

JavaScript 1.0

represents and controls browser location

Object → Location

Synopsis

```
location
window.location
```

Properties

The properties of a Location object refer to the various portions of the current document's URL. In each of the following property descriptions, the example given is a portion of this (fictitious) URL:

```
http://www.oreilly.com:1234/catalog/search.html?q=JavaScript&m=10#results
```

hash

> A read/write string property that specifies the anchor portion of the URL, including the leading hash (#) mark—for example, "#results". This portion of the document URL specifies the name of an anchor within the document.

host

> A read/write string property that specifies the hostname and port portions of the URL—for example, "www.oreilly.com:1234".

hostname

> A read/write string property that specifies the hostname portion of a URL—for example, "www.oreilly.com".

href

> A read/write string property that specifies the complete text of the document's URL, unlike other Location properties that specify only portions of the URL. Setting this property to a new URL causes the browser to read and display the contents of the new URL.

pathname

> A read/write string property that specifies the pathname portion of a URL—for example, "/catalog/search.html".

port

> A read/write string (not a number) property that specifies the port portion of a URL—for example, "1234".

protocol

> A read/write string property that specifies the protocol portion of a URL, including the trailing colon—for example, "http:".

search

> A read/write string property that specifies the query portion of a URL, including the leading question mark—for example, "?q=JavaScript&m=10".

Methods

`reload( )`
> Reloads the current document from the cache or the server.

`replace( )`
> Replaces the current document with a new one without generating a new entry in the browser's session history.

Description

The `location` property of the Window object refers to a Location object that represents the web address (the "location") of the document currently displayed in that window. The `href` property contains the complete URL of that document, and the other properties of the Location object each describe a portion of that URL. These properties are much like the URL properties of the Link object. When a Location object is converted to a string, the value of the `href` property is returned. This means that you can use the expression `location` in place of `location.href`.

While the Link object represents a hyperlink in a document, the Location object represents the URL, or location, currently displayed by the browser. However, the Location object does more than that: it also *controls* the location displayed by the browser. If you assign a string containing a URL to the Location object or to its `href` property, the web browser responds by loading the newly specified URL and displaying the document it refers to.

Instead of setting `location` or `location.href` to replace the current URL with a completely new one, you can modify just a portion of the current URL by assigning strings to the other properties of the Location object. This creates a new URL with one new portion, which the browser loads and displays. For example, if you set the `hash` property of the Location object, you can cause the browser to move to a named location within the current document. Similarly, if you set the `search` property, you can cause the browser to reload the current URL with a new query string appended.

In addition to its URL properties, the Location object also defines two methods. The `reload( )` method reloads the current document. The `replace( )` method loads a new document without creating a new history entry for it; the new document replaces the current one in the browser's history list.

See Also

Link, the `URL` property of the `HTMLDocument` object

Location.reload( )   JavaScript 1.1

reload the current document

Synopsis

```
location.reload( )
location.reload(force)
```

Arguments

force

An optional boolean argument that specifies whether the document should be reloaded even if the server reports that it has not been modified since it was last loaded. If this argument is omitted, or if it is false, the method reloads the full page only if it has changed since last loaded.

Description

The reload( ) method of the Location object reloads the document that is currently displayed in the window of the Location object. When called with no arguments or with the argument false, it uses the If-Modified-Since HTTP header to determine whether the document has changed on the web server. If the document has changed, reload reloads the document from the server, and if not, it reloads the document from the cache. This is the same action that occurs when the user clicks on the browser's **Reload** button.

When reload( ) is called with the argument true, it always bypasses the cache and reloads the document from the server, regardless of the last-modified time of the document. This is the same action that occurs when the user **Shift**-clicks on the browser's **Reload** button.

Location.replace( )   JavaScript 1.1

replace one displayed document with another

Synopsis

location.replace(*url*)

Arguments

url

A string that specifies the URL of the new document that is to replace the current one.

Description

The replace( ) method of the Location object loads and displays a new document. Loading a document in this way is different from simply setting *location* or *location*.href in one important respect: the replace( ) method does not generate a new entry in the History object. When you use replace( ), the new URL overwrites the current entry in the History object. After calling replace( ), the browser's **Back** button does not return you to the previous URL; it returns you to the URL before that one.

See Also

History

MimeType

represents a MIME datatype
Object → MimeType

Synopsis

```
navigator.mimeTypes[i]
navigator.mimeTypes["type"]
navigator.mimeTypes.length
```

Properties

description
A read-only string that provides a human-readable description (in English) of the data type described by the MimeType.

enabledPlugin
A read-only reference to a Plugin object that represents the installed and enabled plug-in that handles the specified MIME type. If the MIME type is not handled by any plug-ins (for example, if it's handled directly by the browser), the value of this property is null. This property is also null when a plug-in exists but has been disabled.

suffixes
A read-only string that contains a comma-separated list of filename suffixes (not including the "." character) that are commonly used with files of the specified MIME type. For example, the suffixes for the "text/html" MIME type are "html, htm".

type
A read-only string that specifies the name of the MIME type. This is a unique string such as "text/html" or "image/jpeg" that distinguishes the MIME type from all others. It describes the general type of data and the data format used. The value of the type property can also be used as an index to access the elements of the navigator.mimeTypes[] array.

Description

The MimeType object represents a MIME type (i.e., a data format) supported by a web browser. The format may be supported directly by the browser, or through an external helper application or a plug-in for embedded data. MimeType objects are members of the mimeTypes[] array of the Navigator object. In IE, the mimeTypes[] array is always empty, and there is no equivalent of this functionality.

Usage

The navigator.mimeTypes[] array may be indexed numerically or with the name of the desired MIME type (which is the value of the type property). To check which MIME types are supported by a browser, you can loop through each element in the array numerically. Or, if you just want to check whether a specific type is supported, you can write code like the following:

```
var show_movie = (navigator.mimeTypes["video/mpeg"] != null);
```

See Also

Navigator, Plugin

MouseEvent

details about a mouse event

Properties

`readonly boolean altKey`

Whether the **Alt** key was held down when the event occurred. Defined for all types of mouse events.

`readonly unsigned short button`

Which mouse button changed state during a mousedown, mouseup, or click event. A value of 0 indicates the left button, a value of 2 indicates the right button, and a value of 1 indicates the middle mouse button. Note that this property is defined when a button changes state; it is not used to report whether a button is held down during a mousemove event, for example. Also, this property is not a bitmap: it cannot tell you if more than one button is held down.

`readonly long clientX, clientY`

The X and Y coordinates of the mouse pointer relative to the *client area*, or browser window. Note that these coordinates do not take document scrolling into account; if an event occurs at the very top of the window, clientY is 0 regardless of how far down the document has been scrolled. These properties are defined for all types of mouse events.

`readonly boolean ctrlKey`

Whether the **Ctrl** key was held down when the event occurred. Defined for all types of mouse events.

`readonly boolean metaKey`

Whether the **Meta** key was held down when the event occurred. Defined for all types of mouse events.

`readonly Element relatedTarget`

Refers to an Element that is related to the target node of the event. For mouseover events, it is the Element the mouse left when it moved over the target. For mouseout events, it is the Element the mouse entered when leaving the target. relatedTarget is undefined for other types of mouse events.

`readonly long screenX, screenY`

The X and Y coordinates of the mouse pointer relative to the upper-left corner of the user's monitor. These properties are defined for all types of mouse events.

`readonly boolean shiftKey`

Whether the **Shift** key was held down when the event occurred. Defined for all types of mouse events.

Methods

`initMouseEvent( )`

Initializes the properties of a newly created MouseEvent object.

Description

This interface defines the type of Event object that is passed to events of types click, mouse-down, mousemove, mouseout, mouseover, and mouseup. Note that in addition to the properties listed here, this interface also inherits the properties of the UIEvent and Event interfaces.

See Also

Event, UIEvent; Chapter 17

MouseEvent.initMouseEvent( )   DOM Level 2 Events

initialize the properties of a MouseEvent object

Synopsis

```
void initMouseEvent(String typeArg,
                boolean canBubbleArg,
                boolean cancelableArg,
                AbstractView viewArg,
                long detailArg,
                long screenXArg,
                long screenYArg,
                long clientXArg,
                long clientYArg,
                boolean ctrlKeyArg,
                boolean altKeyArg,
                boolean shiftKeyArg,
                boolean metaKeyArg,
                unsigned short buttonArg,
                Element relatedTargetArg);
```

Arguments

The many arguments to this method specify the initial values of the properties of this MouseEvent object, including the properties inherited from the Event and UIEvent interfaces. The name of each argument clearly indicates the property for which it specifies the value, so they are not listed individually here.

Description

This method initializes the various properties of a newly created MouseEvent object. It may be called only on a MouseEvent object created with Document.createEvent( ) and only before that MouseEvent is passed to Element.dispatchEvent( ).

See Also

Document.createEvent( ), Event.initEvent( ), UIEvent.initUIEvent( )

Navigator

information about the browser in use

Synopsis

`navigator`

Properties

appCodeName

> A read-only string that specifies the code name of the browser. In all browsers based on the Netscape code base (Netscape, Mozilla, Firefox), this is "Mozilla". For compatibility, this property is "Mozilla" in Microsoft browsers as well.

appName

> A read-only string property that specifies the name of the browser. For Netscape-based browsers, the value of this property is "Netscape". In IE, the value of this property is "Microsoft Internet Explorer". Other browsers may identify themselves correctly or spoof another browser for compatibility.

appVersion

> A read-only string that specifies version and platform information for the browser. The first part of this string is a version number. Pass the string to parseInt( ) to obtain only the major version number or to parseFloat( ) to obtain the major and minor version numbers as a floating-point value. The remainder of the string value of this property provides other details about the browser version, including the operating system it is running on. Unfortunately, however, the format of this information varies widely from browser to browser.

cookieEnabled

> A read-only boolean that is true if the browser has cookies enabled and false if they are disabled.

mimeTypes[ ]

> An array of MimeType objects, each of which represents one of the MIME types (e.g., "text/html" and "image/gif") supported by the browser. This array may be indexed numerically or by the name of the MIME type. The mimeTypes[ ] array is defined by Internet Explorer but is always empty because IE does not support the MimeType object.

platform

> A read-only string that specifies the operating system and/or hardware platform on which the browser is running. Although there is no standard set of values for this property, some typical values are "Win32", "MacPPC", and "Linux i586".

plugins[ ]

> An array of Plugin objects, each of which represents one plug-in that is installed in the browser. The Plugin object provides information about the plug-in, including a list of MIME types it supports.

> The plugins[ ] array is defined by Internet Explorer but is always empty because IE does not support the Plugin object.

userAgent
> A read-only string that specifies the value the browser uses for the user-agent header in HTTP requests. Typically, this is the value of navigator.appCodeName followed by a slash and the value of navigator.appVersion. For example:
>
>   Mozilla/4.0 (compatible; MSIE 4.01; Windows 95)

Functions

navigator.javaEnabled( )
> Tests whether Java is supported and enabled in the current browser.

Description

The Navigator object contains properties that describe the web browser in use. You can use its properties to perform platform-specific customization. The name of this object obviously refers to the Netscape Navigator browser, but all browsers that implement JavaScript support this object as well. There is only a single instance of the Navigator object, which you can reference through the navigator property of any Window object.

Historically, the Navigator object has been used for "client sniffing" to run different code depending on what browser was in use. Example 14-3 shows a simple way to do this, and the accompanying text describes the many pitfalls of relying on the Navigator object. A better approach to cross-browser compatibility is described in Section 13.6.3.

See Also

MimeType, Plugin

Navigator.javaEnabled( )   JavaScript 1.1

test whether Java is available

Synopsis

navigator.javaEnabled( )

Returns

true if Java is supported by and enabled on the current browser; false otherwise.

Description

You can use navigator.javaEnabled( ) to check whether the current browser supports Java and can therefore display applets.

Node   DOM Level 1 Core

a node in a document tree

Subinterfaces

Attr, CDATASection, CharacterData, Comment, Document, DocumentFragment, DocumentType, Element, ProcessingInstruction, Text

Constants

All Node objects implement one of the subinterfaces listed above. Every Node object has a nodeType property that specifies which subinterface it implements. These constants are the legal values for that property; their names are self-explanatory. Note that these are static properties of the Node( ) constructor function; they are not properties of individual Node objects. Also note that they are not supported by Internet Explorer. For compatibilty with IE, you must use numeric literals directly. For example, use 1 instead of Node.ELEMENT_NODE:

```
Node.ELEMENT_NODE = 1;                         // Element
Node.ATTRIBUTE_NODE = 2;                       // Attr
Node.TEXT_NODE = 3;                            // Text
Node.CDATA_SECTION_NODE = 4;                   // CDATASection
Node.PROCESSING_INSTRUCTION_NODE = 7;          // ProcessingInstruction
Node.COMMENT_NODE = 8;                         // Comment
Node.DOCUMENT_NODE = 9;                        // Document
Node.DOCUMENT_TYPE_NODE = 10;                  // DocumentType
Node.DOCUMENT_FRAGMENT_NODE = 11;              // DocumentFragment
```

Properties

readonly Attr[] attributes
> If this is an Element node, the attributes property is a read-only, array-like object of Attr nodes that represent the attributes of that element. Note that this array is "live": any changes to the attributes of this element are immediately visible through it.
>
> Technically, the attributes[] array is a NamedNodeMap object. The NamedNodeMap interface is specified by the Level 1 DOM standard and defines a number of methods for querying, setting, and removing elements. The Element interface defines better methods for setting and querying element attributes, and there are no other uses of NamedNodeMap that are relevant to client-side JavaScript. For these reasons, therefore, NamedNodeMap is not documented in this book. Treat the attributes property as a read-only array of Attr objects, or use the methods defined by Element to query, set, and delete attributes.

readonly Node[] childNodes
> Contains the child nodes of the current node. This property should never be null: for nodes with no children, childNodes is an array with length zero. This property is technically a NodeList object, but it behaves just like a read-only array of Node objects. Note that the NodeList object is live: any changes to this element's list of children are immediately visible through the NodeList.

readonly Node firstChild
> The first child of this node, or null if the node has no children.

readonly Node lastChild
> The last child of this node, or null if the node has no children.

readonly String localName [DOM Level 2]
> In XML documents that use namespaces, specifies the local part of the element or attribute name. This property is never used with HTML documents. See also the namespaceURI and prefix properties.

readonly String namespaceURI *[DOM Level 2]*

In XML documents that use namespaces, specifies the URI of the namespace of an Element or Attribute node. This property is never used with HTML documents. See also the localName and prefix properties.

readonly Node nextSibling

The sibling node that immediately follows this one in the childNodes[] array of the parentNode, or null if there is no such node.

readonly String nodeName

The name of the node. For Element nodes, specifies the tag name of the element, which can also be retrieved with the tagName property of the Element interface. For other types of nodes, the value depends on the node type. See the upcoming table in the Description section for details.

readonly unsigned short nodeType

The type of the node—i.e., which subinterface the node implements. The legal values are defined by the previously listed constants. Since these constants are not supported by Internet Explorer, however, you may prefer to use hardcoded values instead of the constants. In HTML documents, the common values for this property are 1 for Element nodes, 3 for Text nodes, 8 for Comment nodes, and 9 for the single top-level Document node.

String nodeValue

The value of a node. For Text nodes, it holds the text content. For other node types, the value depends on the nodeType, as shown in the upcoming table in the Description section.

readonly Document ownerDocument

The Document object of which this node is a part. For Document nodes, this property is null.

readonly Node parentNode

The parent (or container) node of this node, or null if there is no parent. Note that the Document, DocumentFragment, and Attr nodes never have parent nodes. Also, nodes that have been removed from the document, or that are newly created and have not yet been inserted into the document tree, have a parentNode of null.

String prefix *[DOM Level 2]*

For XML documents that use namespaces, specifies the namespace prefix of an Element or Attribute node. This property is never used with HTML documents. See also the localName and namespaceURL properties.

readonly Node previousSibling

The sibling node that immediately precedes this one in the childNodes[] array of the parentNode, or null if there is no such node.

readonly String xml *[IE only]*

If the node is an XML Document or an Element within an XML document, this IE-specific property returns the text of the element or document as a string. Compare this property to the innerHTML property of HTMLElement, and see XMLSerializer for a cross-platform alternative.

Client-Side
JavaScript
Reference

Methods

appendChild( )

Adds a node to the document tree by appending it to the childNodes[] array of this node. If the node is already in the document tree, it is removed and then reinserted at its new position.

cloneNode( )

Makes a copy of this node, or of the node and all its descendants.

hasAttributes( ) *[DOM Level 2]*

Returns true if this node is an Element and has any attributes.

hasChildNodes( )

Returns true if this node has any children.

insertBefore( )

Inserts a node into the document tree immediately before the specified child of this node. If the node being inserted is already in the tree, it is removed and reinserted at its new location.

isSupported( ) *[DOM Level 2]*

Returns true if the specified version number of a named feature is supported by this node.

normalize( )

"Normalizes" all Text node descendants of this node by deleting empty Text nodes and merging adjacent Text nodes.

removeChild( )

Removes (and returns) the specified child node from the document tree.

replaceChild( )

Removes (and returns) the specified child node from the document tree, replacing it with another node.

selectNodes( ) *[IE only]*

This IE-specific method performs an XPath query using this node as the root and returns the result as a NodeList. See Document.evaluate( ) and Document.createExpression( ) for DOM-based alternatives.

selectSingleNode( ) *[IE only]*

This IE-specific method performs an XPath query using this node as the root and returns the result as a single node. See Document.evaluate( ) and Document.createExpression( ) for DOM-based alternatives.

transformNode( ) *[IE only]*

This IE-specific method applies an XSLT stylesheet to this node and returns the results as a String. See XSLTProcessor for a non-IE alternative.

transformNodeToObject( ) *[IE only]*

This IE-specific method applies an XSLT stylesheet to this node and returns the results as a new Document object. See XSLTProcessor for a non-IE alternative.

Description

All objects in a document tree (including the Document object itself) implement the Node interface, which provides the fundamental properties and methods for traversing and manipulating the tree. (In Internet Explorer, the Node interface also defines some IE-specific properties and methods for working with XML documents, XPath expressions, and XSLT transforms. See Chapter 21 for details.)

The parentNode property and childNodes[] array allow you to move up and down the document tree. You can enumerate the children of a given node by looping through the elements of childNodes[] or by using the firstChild and nextSibling properties (or the lastChild and previousSibling properties, to loop backward). The appendChild( ), insertBefore( ), removeChild( ), and replaceChild( ) methods allow you to modify the document tree by altering the children of a node.

Every object in a document tree implements both the Node interface and a more specialized subinterface, such as Element or Text. The nodeType property specifies which subinterface a node implements. You can use this property to test the type of a node before using properties or methods of the more specialized interface. For example:

```
var n;    // Holds the node we're working with
if (n.nodeType == 1) {      // Or use the constant Node.ELEMENT_NODE
    var tagname = n.tagName; // If the node is an Element, this is the tag name
}
```

The nodeName and nodeValue properties specify additional information about a node, but their value depends on nodeType, as shown in the following table. Note that subinterfaces typically define specialized properties (such as the tagName property of Element nodes and the data property of Text nodes) for obtaining this information:

nodeType	nodeName	nodeValue
ELEMENT_NODE	The element's tag name	null
ATTRIBUTE_NODE	The attribute name	The attribute value
TEXT_NODE	#text	The text of the node
CDATA_SECTION_NODE	#cdata-section	The text of the node
PROCESSING_INSTRUCTION_NODE	The target of the PI	The remainder of the PI
COMMENT_NODE	#comment	The text of the comment
DOCUMENT_NODE	#document	null
DOCUMENT_TYPE_NODE	The document type name	null
DOCUMENT_FRAGMENT_NODE	#document-fragment	null

See Also

Document, Element, Text, XMLSerializer, XPathExpression, XSLTProcessor; Chapter 15

Node.appendChild( ) DOM Level 1 Core

insert a node as the last child of this node

Synopsis

```
Node appendChild(Node newChild)
    throws DOMException;
```

Arguments

newChild

> The node to be inserted into the document. If the node is a DocumentFragment, it is
> not directly inserted, but each of its children are.

Returns

The node that was added.

Throws

This method may throw a DOMException with one of the following code values in the
following circumstances:

HIERARCHY_REQUEST_ERR

> The node does not allow children, it does not allow children of the specified type, or
> *newChild* is an ancestor of this node (or is this node itself).

WRONG_DOCUMENT_ERR

> The ownerDocument property of *newChild* is not the same as the ownerDocument property
> of this node.

NO_MODIFICATION_ALLOWED_ERR

> This node is read-only and does not allow children to be appended, or the node being
> appended is already part of the document tree, and its parent is read-only and does not
> allow children to be removed.

Description

This method adds the node *newChild* to the document, inserting it as the last child of this
node. If *newChild* is already in the document tree, it is removed from the tree and then reinserted at its new location. If *newChild* is a DocumentFragment node, it is not inserted itself;
instead, all its children are appended, in order, to the end of this node's childNodes[ ] array.
Note that a node from (or created by) one document cannot be inserted into a different
document. That is, the ownerDocument property of *newChild* must be the same as the
ownerDocument property of this node.

Example

The following function inserts a new paragraph at the end of the document:

```
function appendMessage(message) {
    var pElement = document.createElement("p");
    var messageNode = document.createTextNode(message);
    pElement.appendChild(messageNode);    // Add text to paragraph
    document.body.appendChild(pElement);  // Add paragraph to document body
}
```

See Also

`Node.insertBefore( )`, `Node.removeChild( )`, `Node.replaceChild( )`

Node.cloneNode( )

duplicate a node and, optionally, all of its descendants

Synopsis

```
Node cloneNode(boolean deep);
```

Arguments

deep
> If this argument is true, `cloneNode( )` recursively clones all descendants of this node. Otherwise, it clones only this node.

Returns

A copy of this node.

Description

The `cloneNode( )` method makes and returns a copy of the node on which it is called. If passed the argument true, it recursively clones all descendants of the node as well. Otherwise, it clones only the node and none of its children. The returned node is not part of the document tree, and its `parentNode` property is null. When an Element node is cloned, all of its attributes are also cloned. Note, however, that event-listener functions registered on a node are not cloned.

Node.hasAttributes( )

determine whether a node has attributes

Synopsis

```
boolean hasAttributes( );
```

Returns

true if this node has one or more attributes; false if it has none. Note that only Element nodes can have attributes.

See Also

`Element.getAttribute( )`, `Element.hasAttribute( )`, `Node`

Node.hasChildNodes( )

determine whether a node has children

Synopsis

```
boolean hasChildNodes( );
```

Returns

true if this node has one or more children; false if it has none.

Node.insertBefore( )

insert a node into the document tree before the specified node

Synopsis

```
Node insertBefore(Node newChild,
                  Node refChild)
    throws DOMException;
```

Arguments

newChild

> The node to be inserted into the tree. If it is a DocumentFragment, its children are inserted instead.

refChild

> The child of this node before which *newChild* is to be inserted. If this argument is null, *newChild* is inserted as the last child of this node.

Returns

The node that was inserted.

Throws

This method may throw a DOMException with the following code values:

HIERARCHY_REQUEST_ERR

> This node does not support children, it does not allow children of the specified type, or *newChild* is an ancestor of this node (or is this node itself).

WRONG_DOCUMENT_ERR

> The ownerDocument property of *newChild* and this node are different.

NO_MODIFICATION_ALLOWED_ERR

> This node is read-only and does not allow insertions, or the parent of *newChild* is read-only and does not allow deletions.

NOT_FOUND_ERR

> *refChild* is not a child of this node.

Description

This method inserts the node *newChild* into the document tree as a child of this node. The new node is positioned within this node's childNodes[] array so that it comes immediately before the *refChild* node. If *refChild* is null, *newChild* is inserted at the end of childNodes[], just as with the appendChild( ) method. Note that it is illegal to call this method with a *refChild* that is not a child of this node.

If *newChild* is already in the document tree, it is removed from the tree and then reinserted at its new position. If *newChild* is a DocumentFragment node, it is not inserted itself; instead, each of its children is inserted, in order, at the specified location.

Example

The following function inserts a new paragraph at the beginning of a document:

```
function insertMessage(message) {
    var paragraph = document.createElement("p");   // Create a <p> Element
    var text = document.createTextNode(message);   // Create a Text node
    paragraph.appendChild(text);                   // Add text to the paragraph
    // Now insert the paragraph before the first child of the body
    document.body.insertBefore(paragraph, document.body.firstChild)
}
```

See Also

Node.appendChild( ), Node.removeChild( ), Node.replaceChild( )

Node.isSupported( )   DOM Level 2 Core

determine if a node supports a feature

Synopsis

```
boolean isSupported(String feature,
                    String version);
```

Arguments

feature
> The name of the feature to test.

version
> The version number of the feature to test, or the empty string to test for support of any version of the feature.

Returns

true if the node supports the specified version of the specified feature, and false if it does not.

Description

The W3C DOM standard is modular, and implementations are not required to implement all modules or features of the standard. This method tests whether the implementation of this node supports the specified version of the named feature. See DOMImplementation.hasFeature( ) for a list of values for the *feature* and *version* arguments.

See Also

DOMImplementation.hasFeature( )

Node.normalize( )   DOM Level 1 Core

merge adjacent Text nodes and remove empty ones

Synopsis

```
void normalize( );
```

Client-Side
JavaScript
Reference

Description

This method traverses all descendants of this node and "normalizes" the document by removing any empty Text nodes and merging all adjacent Text nodes into a single node. This can simplify the tree structure after node insertions or deletions.

See Also

Text

Node.removeChild( )   DOM Level 1 Core

remove (and return) the specified child of this node

Synopsis

```
Node removeChild(Node oldChild)
    throws DOMException;
```

Arguments

oldChild
> The child node to remove.

Returns

The node that was removed.

Throws

This method may throw a DOMException with the following code values in the following circumstances:

NO_MODIFICATION_ALLOWED_ERR
> This node is read-only and does not allow children to be removed.

NOT_FOUND_ERR
> *oldChild* is not a child of this node.

Description

This method removes the specified child from the childNodes[] array of this node. It is an error to call this method with a node that is not a child. removeChild( ) returns the *oldChild* node after removing it. *oldChild* continues to be a valid node and may be reinserted into the document later.

Example

You can delete the last child of the document body with this code:

```
document.body.removeChild(document.body.lastChild);
```

See Also

Node.appendChild( ), Node.insertBefore( ), Node.replaceChild( )

Node.replaceChild( )

replace a child node with a new node

Synopsis

```
Node replaceChild(Node newChild,
                  Node oldChild)
    throws DOMException;
```

Arguments

newChild
> The replacement node.

oldChild
> The node to be replaced.

Returns

The node that was removed from the document and replaced.

Throws

This method may throw a DOMException with the following code values:

HIERARCHY_REQUEST_ERR
> This node does not allow children, it does not allow children of the specified type, or *newChild* is an ancestor of this node (or is this node itself).

WRONG_DOCUMENT_ERR
> *newChild* and this node have different values for ownerDocument.

NO_MODIFICATION_ALLOWED_ERR
> This node is read-only and does not allow replacement, or *newChild* is the child of a node that does not allow removals.

NOT_FOUND_ERR
> *oldChild* is not a child of this node.

Description

This method replaces one node of the document tree with another. *oldChild* is the node to be replaced and must be a child of this node. *newChild* is the node that takes its place in the childNodes[ ] array of this node.

If *newChild* is already part of the document, it is first removed from the document before being reinserted at its new position. If *newChild* is a DocumentFragment, it is not inserted itself; instead each of its children is inserted, in order, at the position formerly occupied by *oldChild*.

Example

The following code replaces a node n with a <b> element and then inserts the replaced node into the <b> element, which reparents the node and makes it appear in bold:

```
// Get the first child node of the first paragraph in the document
var n = document.getElementsByTagName("p")[0].firstChild;
var b = document.createElement("b");  // Create a <b> element
```

```
    n.parentNode.replaceChild(b, n);     // Replace the node with <b>
    b.appendChild(n);                    // Reinsert the node as a child of <b>
```

See Also

Node.appendChild( ), Node.insertBefore( ), Node.removeChild( )

Node.selectNodes( )   IE 6

select nodes with an XPath query

Synopsis

NodeList selectNodes(String *query*)

Arguments

query
> The XPath query string.

Returns

A NodeList containing nodes that match query.

Description

This IE-specific method evaluates an XPath expression, using this node as the root node of the query, and returns the result as a NodeList. The selectNodes( ) method exists only on the nodes of XML documents, not HTML documents. Note that since Document objects are themselves nodes, this method can be applied to entire XML documents.

For a cross-browser alternative, see Document.evaluate( ).

See Also

Document.evaluate( ), XPathExpression; Chapter 21

Node.selectSingleNode( )   IE 6

find a node matching an XPath query

Synopsis

Node selectSingleNode(String *query*)

Arguments

query
> The XPath query string.

Returns

A single Node that matches the *query*, or null if there are none.

Description

This IE-specific method evaluates an XPath expression using this node as the context node. It returns the first matching node found, or null if no nodes match. The selectSingleNode( ) method exists only on the nodes of XML documents, not HTML documents. Note that since Document objects are themselves nodes, this method can be applied to entire XML documents.

For a cross-browser alternative, see Document.evaluate( ).

See Also

Document.evaluate( ), XPathExpression; Chapter 21

Node.transformNode( )   IE 6

transform a node to a string using XSLT

Synopsis

String transformNode(Document *xslt*)

Arguments

xslt
    An XSLT stylesheet, parsed to a Document object.

Returns

The text produced by applying the specified stylesheet to this node and its descendants.

Description

This IE-specific method transforms a Node and its descendants according to the rules specified in an XSLT stylesheet and returns the result as an unparsed string. The transformNode( ) method exists only on the nodes of XML documents, not HTML documents. Note that since Document objects are themselves nodes, this method can be applied to entire XML documents.

For similar functionality in other browsers, see XSLTProcessor.

See Also

XSLTProcessor, Node.transformNodeToObject( ); Chapter 21

Node.transformNodeToObject( )   IE 6

transform a node to a document using XSLT

Synopsis

Document transformNodeToObject(Document *xslt*)

Arguments

xslt
>   An XSLT stylesheet, parsed to a Document object.

Returns

The result of the transformation, parsed to a Document object.

Description

This IE-specific method transforms a Node and its descendants according to the rules specified in an XSLT stylesheet and returns the result as a Document object. The transformNodeToObject( ) method exists only on the nodes of XML documents, not HTML documents. Note that since Document objects are themselves nodes, this method can be applied to entire XML documents.

For similar functionality in other browsers, see XSLTProcessor.

See Also

XSLTProcessor, Node.transformNode( ); Chapter 21

NodeList

DOM Level 1 Core

a read-only array of nodes

Object → NodeList

Properties

readonly unsigned long length
>   The number of nodes in the array.

Methods

item( )
>   Returns the specified element of the array.

Description

The NodeList interface defines a read-only, ordered list (i.e., an array) of Node objects. The length property specifies how many nodes are in the list, and the item( ) method allows you to obtain the node at a specified position in the list. The elements of a NodeList are always valid Node objects: NodeLists never contain null elements.

In JavaScript, NodeList objects behave like JavaScript arrays, and you can query an element from the list using square-bracket array notation instead of calling the item( ) method. However, you cannot assign new nodes to a NodeList using square brackets. Since it is always easier to think of a NodeList object as a read-only JavaScript array, this book uses the notation Element[] or Node[] (i.e., an Element array or Node array) instead of NodeList. The methods Document.getElementsByTagName( ), Element.getElementsByTagName( ), and HTMLDocument.getElementsByName( ) are all documented in this book as returning a Element[] instead of a NodeList object. Similarly, the childNodes property of the Node object is technically a NodeList object, but the Node reference page defines it as a Node[], and the property itself is usually referred to as "the childNodes[] array."

Note that NodeList objects are live: they are not static snapshots but immediately reflect changes to the document tree. For example, if you have a NodeList that represents the children of a specific node and you then delete one of those children, the child is removed from your NodeList. Be careful when you are looping through the elements of a NodeList: the body of your loop can make changes to the document tree (such as deleting nodes) that can affect the contents of the NodeList!

See Also

Document, Element

NodeList.item( ) DOM Level 1 Core

get an element of a NodeList

Synopsis

```
Node item(unsigned long index);
```

Arguments

index
> The position (or index) of the desired node in the NodeList. The index of the first node in the NodeList is 0, and the index of the last Node is length–1.

Returns

The node at the specified position in the NodeList, or null if *index* is less than zero or greater than or equal to the length of the NodeList.

Description

This method returns the specified element of a NodeList. In JavaScript, you can use the square-bracket array notation instead of calling item( ).

Option DOM Level 2 HTML

an option in a Select element Node → Element → HTMLElement → HTMLOptionElement

Constructor

Option objects can be created with Document.createElement( ), like any other tag. In the DOM Level 0, Option objects can also be dynamically created with the Option( ) constructor, as follows:

```
new Option(String text, String value,
        boolean defaultSelected, boolean selected)
```

Arguments

text
> An optional string argument that specifies the text property of the Option object.

value
> An optional string argument that specifies the value property of the Option object.

defaultSelected

> An optional boolean argument that specifies the defaultSelected property of the Option object.

selected

> An optional boolean argument that specifies the selected property of the Option object.

Properties

boolean defaultSelected

> The initial value of the selected attribute of the <option> element. If the form is reset, the selected property is reset to the value of this property. Setting this property also sets the value of the selected property.

boolean disabled

> If true, this <option> element is disabled, and the user is not allowed to select it. Mirrors the disabled attribute.

readonlyHTMLFormElementform

> A reference to the <form> element that contains this element.

readonly long index

> The position of this <option> element within the <select> element that contains it.

String label

> The text to be displayed for the option. Mirrors the label attribute. If this property is not specified, the plain-text content of the <option> element is used instead.

boolean selected

> The current state of this option: if true, the option is selected. The initial value of this property comes from the selected attribute.

readonly String text

> The plain text contained within the <option> element. This text appears as the label for the option.

String value

> The value submitted with the form if this option is selected when form submission occurs. Mirrors the value attribute.

HTML Syntax

An Option object is created by an <option> tag within a <select> tag, which is within a <form>. Multiple <option> tags typically appear within the <select> tag:

```
<form ...>
<select  ...>
<option
  [ value="value" ]   // The value returned when the form is submitted
  [ selected ] >      // Specifies whether this option is initially selected
  plain_text_label    // The text to display for this option
[ </option> ]
  ...
</select>
  ...
</form>
```

Description

The Option object describes a single option displayed within a Select object. The properties of this object specify whether it is selected by default, whether it is currently selected, the position it has in the options[] array of its containing Select object, the text it displays, and the value it passes to the server if it is selected when the containing form is submitted.

Note that although the text displayed by this option is specified outside the <option> tag, it must be plain, unformatted text without any HTML tags so it can be properly displayed in listboxes and drop-down menus that do not support HTML formatting.

You can dynamically create new Option objects for display in a Select object with the Option( ) constructor. Once a new Option object is created, it can be appended to the list of options in a Select object with Select.add( ). See Select.options[] for further details.

See Also

Select, Select.options[]; Chapter 18

Packages

see Packages in Part III

Password

see Input

Plugin

JavaScript 1.1; not supported by IE

describes an installed plug-in

Object → Plugin

Synopsis

```
navigator.plugins[i]
navigator.plugins['name']
```

Properties

description

> A read-only string that contains a human-readable description of the specified plug-in. The text of this description is provided by the creators of the plug-in and may contain vendor and version information as well as a brief description of the plug-in's function.

filename

> A read-only string that specifies the name of the file on disk that contains the plug-in program itself. This name may vary from platform to platform. The name property is more useful than filename for identifying a plug-in.

length

> Each Plugin object is also an array of MimeType objects that specify the data formats supported by the plug-in. As with all arrays, the length property specifies the number of elements in the array.

Client-Side
JavaScript
Reference

name

> The name property of a Plugin object is a read-only string that specifies the name of the plug-in. Each plug-in should have a name that uniquely identifies it. The name of a plug-in can be used as an index into the navigator.plugins[] array. You can use this fact to determine easily whether a particular named plug-in is installed in the current browser:
>
> ```
> var flash_installed = (navigator.plugins["Shockwave Flash"] != null);
> ```

Array Elements

The array elements of the Plugin object are MimeType objects that specify the data formats supported by the plug-in. The length property specifies the number of MimeType objects in this array.

Description

A *plug-in* is a software module that can be invoked by a browser to display specialized types of embedded data within the browser window. Plug-ins are represented by the Plugin object, and the plugins[] property of the Navigator object is an array of Plugin objects representing the installed plug-ins for the browser. IE does not support the Plugin object, and the navigator.plugins[] array is always empty on that browser.

navigator.plugins[] may be indexed numerically when you want to loop through the complete list of installed plug-ins, looking for one that meets your needs (for example, one that supports the MIME type of the data you want to embed in your web page). This array can also be indexed by plug-in name, however. That is, if you want to check whether a specific plug-in is installed in the user's browser, you might use code like this:

```
var flash_installed = (navigator.plugins["Shockwave Flash"] != null);
```

The name used as an array index with this technique is the same name that appears as the value of the name property of the Plugin.

The Plugin object is somewhat unusual in that it has both regular object properties and array elements. The properties of the Plugin object provide various pieces of information about the plug-in, and its array elements are MimeType objects that specify the embedded data formats that the plug-in supports. Don't confuse the fact that Plugin objects are stored in an array of the Navigator object with the fact that each Plugin object is itself an array of MimeType objects. Because there are two arrays involved, you may end up with code that looks like this:

```
navigator.plugins[i][j]            // The jth MIME type of the ith plug-in
navigator.plugins["LiveAudio"][0]  // First MIME type of LiveAudio plug-in
```

Finally, note that while the array elements of a Plugin object specify the MIME types supported by that plug-in, you can also determine which plug-in supports a given MIME type with the enabledPlugin property of the MimeType object.

See Also

Navigator, MimeType

ProcessingInstruction

a processing instruction in an XML document

Properties

String data
> The content of the processing instruction (i.e., the first nonspace character after the target up to but not including the closing ?>).

readonly String target
> The target of the processing instruction. This is the first identifier that follows the opening <?; it specifies the "processor" for which the processing instruction is intended.

Description

This infrequently used interface represents a processing instruction (or PI) in an XML document. Programmers working with HTML documents will never encounter a ProcessingInstruction node.

See Also

Document.createProcessingInstruction( )

Radio

see Input

Range

represents a contiguous range of a document

Constants

These constants specify how the boundary points of two Range objects are compared. They are the legal values for the *how* argument to the compareBoundaryPoints( ) method (see the Range.compareBoundaryPoints( ) reference page):

unsigned short START_TO_START = 0
> Compares the start of the specified range to the start of this range.

unsigned short START_TO_END = 1
> Compares the start of the specified range to the end of this range.

unsigned short END_TO_END = 2
> Compares the end of the specified range to the end of this range.

unsigned short END_TO_START = 3
> Compares the end of the specified range to the start of this range.

Properties

The Range interface defines the following properties. Note that all of these properties are read-only. You cannot change the start or end points of a range by setting properties; you must call setEnd( ) or setStart( ) instead. Note also that after you call the detach( ) method of a Range object, any subsequent attempt to read any of these properties throws a DOMException with a code of INVALID_STATE_ERR:

readonly boolean collapsed
> true if the start and the end of the range are at the same point in the document—that is, if the range is empty or "collapsed."

readonly Node commonAncestorContainer
> The most deeply nested Document node that contains (i.e., is an ancestor of) both the start and end points of the range.

readonly Node endContainer
> The Document node that contains the end point of the range.

readonly long endOffset
> The position of the range's ending point within endContainer.

readonly Node startContainer
> The Document node that contains the starting point of the range.

readonly long startOffset
> The position of the range's starting point within startContainer.

Methods

The Range interface defines the following methods. Note that if you call detach( ) on a range, any subsequent calls of any methods on that range throw a DOMException with a code of INVALID_STATE_ERR. Because this exception is ubiquitous within this interface, it is not listed in the reference pages for the individual Range methods:

cloneContents( )
> Returns a new DocumentFragment object that contains a copy of the region of the document represented by this range.

cloneRange( )
> Creates a new Range object that represents the same region of the document as this one.

collapse( )
> Collapses this range so that one boundary point is the same as the other.

compareBoundaryPoints( )
> Compares a boundary point of the specified range to a boundary point of this range and returns –1, 0, or 1, depending on their order. Which points to compare is specified by the first argument, which must be one of the constants listed in the Constants section.

deleteContents( )
> Deletes the region of the document represented by this range.

detach( )
> Tells the implementation that this range will no longer be used and that it can stop keeping track of it. If you call this method for a range, subsequent method calls or property lookups on that range throw a DOMException with a code of INVALID_STATE_ERR.

extractContents( )
>   Deletes the region of the document represented by this range, but returns the contents
>   of that region as a DocumentFragment object. This method is like a combination of
>   cloneContents( ) and deleteContents( ).

insertNode( )
>   Inserts the specified node into the document at the start point of the range.

selectNode( )
>   Sets the boundary points of this range so that it contains the specified node and all of
>   its descendants.

selectNodeContents( )
>   Sets the boundary points of this range so that it contains all the descendants of the
>   specified node but not the node itself.

setEnd( )
>   Sets the end point of this range to the specified node and offset.

setEndAfter( )
>   Sets the end point of this range to immediately after the specified node.

setEndBefore( )
>   Sets the end point of this range to immediately before the specified node.

setStart( )
>   Sets the start position of this range to the specified offset within the specified node.

setStartAfter( )
>   Sets the start position of this range to immediately after the specified node.

setStartBefore( )
>   Sets the start position of this range to immediately before the specified node.

surroundContents( )
>   Inserts the specified node into the document at the start position of the range and then
>   reparents all the nodes within the range so that they become descendants of the newly
>   inserted node.

toString( )
>   Returns the plain-text content of the document region described by this range.

Description

A Range object represents a contiguous range or region of a document, such as the region
that the user might select with a mouse drag in a web browser window. If an implementation supports the Range module (at the time of this writing, Firefox and Opera support it,
Safari has partial support, and Internet Explorer does not support it), the Document object
defines a createRange( ) method that you can call to create a new Range object. Be careful,
however: Internet Explorer defines an incompatible Document.createRange( ) method that
returns a nonstandard object similar to, but not compatible with, the Range interface. The
Range interface defines a number of methods for specifying a "selected" region of a document and several more methods for implementing cut-and-paste operations on the selected
region.

A range has two boundary points: a start point and an end point. Each boundary point is specified by a combination of a node and an offset within that node. The node is typically an Element, Document, or Text node. For Element and Document nodes, the offset refers to the children of that node. An offset of 0 specifies a boundary point before the first child of the node. An offset of 1 specifies a boundary point after the first child and before the second child. If the boundary node is a Text node, however, the offset specifies a position between two characters of that text.

The properties of the Range interface provide a way to obtain boundary nodes and offsets of a range. The methods of the interface provide a number of ways to set the boundaries of a range. Note that the boundaries of a range may be set to nodes within a Document or a DocumentFragment.

Once the boundary points of a range are defined, you can use deleteContents( ), extractContents( ), cloneContents( ), and insertNode( ) to implement cut, copy, and paste operations.

When a document is altered by insertion or deletion, all Range objects that represent portions of that document are altered, if necessary, so that their boundary points remain valid and they represent (as closely as possible) the same document content.

See Also

Document.createRange( ), DocumentFragment

Range.cloneContents( ) DOM Level 2 Range

copy range contents into a DocumentFragment

Synopsis

```
DocumentFragment cloneContents( )
    throws DOMException;
```

Returns

A DocumentFragment object that contains a copy of the document content within this range.

Throws

If this range includes a DocumentType node, this method throws a DOMException with a code of HIERARCHY_REQUEST_ERR.

Description

This method duplicates the contents of this range and returns the results in a Document-Fragment object.

See Also

DocumentFragment, Range.deleteContents( ), Range.extractContents( )

Range.cloneRange( )   DOM Level 2 Range

make a copy of this range

Synopsis

```
Range cloneRange( );
```

Returns

A new Range object that has the same boundary points as this range.

See Also

```
Document.createRange( )
```

Range.collapse( )   DOM Level 2 Range

make one boundary point equal to the other

Synopsis

```
void collapse(boolean toStart)
    throws DOMException;
```

Arguments

toStart
> If this argument is true, the method sets the end point of the range to the same value as the starting point. Otherwise, it sets the starting point to the same value as the end point.

Description

This method sets one boundary point of the range to be the same as the other point. The point to be modified is specified by the *toStart* argument. After this method returns, the range is said to be *collapsed*: it represents a single point within a document and has no content. When a range is collapsed like this, its collapsed property is true.

Range.compareBoundaryPoints( )   DOM Level 2 Range

compare positions of two ranges

Synopsis

```
short compareBoundaryPoints(unsigned short how,
                            Range sourceRange)
    throws DOMException;
```

Arguments

how
> Specifies how to perform the comparison (i.e., which boundary points to compare). Legal values are the constants defined by the Range interface.

sourceRange
> The range that is to be compared to this range.

Returns

The value −1 if the specified boundary point of this range is before the specified boundary point of *sourceRange*, 0 if the two specified boundary points are the same, or 1 if the specified boundary point of this range is after the specified boundary point of *sourceRange*.

Throws

If *sourceRange* represents a range of a different document than this range does, this method throws a DOMException with a code of WRONG_DOCUMENT_ERR.

Description

This method compares a boundary point of this range to a boundary point of the specified *sourceRange* and returns a value that specifies their relative order in the document source. The *how* argument specifies which boundary points of each range are to be compared. The legal values for this argument, and their meanings, are as follows:

Range.START_TO_START
 Compares the start points of the two Range nodes.

Range.END_TO_END
 Compares the end points of the two Range nodes.

Range.START_TO_END
 Compares the start point of *sourceRange* to the end point of this range.

Range.END_TO_START
 Compares the end point of *sourceRange* to the start point of this range.

The return value of this method is a number that specifies the relative position of this range to the specified *sourceRange*. Therefore, you might expect the range constants for the *how* argument to specify the boundary point for this range first and the boundary point for sourceRange second. Counterintuitively, however, the Range.START_TO_END constant specifies a comparison of the *end* point of this range with the *start* point of the specified *sourceRange*. Similarly, the Range.END_TO_START constant specifies a comparison of the *start* point of this range with the *end* point of the specified range.

Range.deleteContents( )   DOM Level 2 Range

delete a region of the document

Synopsis

```
void deleteContents( )
    throws DOMException;
```

Throws

If any portion of the document that is represented by this range is read-only, this method throws a DOMException with a code of NO_MODIFICATION_ALLOWED_ERR.

Description

This method deletes all document content represented by this range. When this method returns, the range is collapsed with both boundary points at the start position. Note that the deletion may result in adjacent Text nodes that can be merged with a call to Node. normalize( ).

See Range.cloneContents( ) for a way to copy document content and Range.extractContents( ) for a way to copy and delete document content in a single operation.

See Also

Node.normalize( ), Range.cloneContents( ), Range.extractContents( )

Range.detach( )   DOM Level 2 Range

free a Range object

Synopsis

```
void detach( )
    throws DOMException;
```

Throws

Like all Range methods, detach( ) throws a DOMException with a code of INVALID_STATE_ERR if it is called on a Range object that has already been detached.

Description

DOM implementations keep track of all Range objects created for a document because they may need to change the range boundary points when the document is modified. When you are certain that a Range object isn't needed any more, call the detach( ) method to tell the implementation that it no longer needs to keep track of that range. Note that once this method has been called for a Range object, any use of that Range throws an exception. Calling detach( ) is not required but may improve performance in some circumstances when the document is being modified. A Range object is not subject to immediate garbage collection.

Range.extractContents( )   DOM Level 2 Range

delete document content and return it in a DocumentFragment

Synopsis

```
DocumentFragment extractContents( )
    throws DOMException;
```

Returns

A DocumentFragment node that contains the contents of this range.

Throws

This method throws a DOMException with a code of NO_MODIFICATION_ALLOWED_ERR if any part of the document content to be extracted is read-only or a code of HIERARCHY_REQUEST_ ERR if the range contains a DocumentType node.

Description

This method deletes the specified range of a document and returns a DocumentFragment node that contains the deleted content. When this method returns, the range is collapsed, and the document may contain adjacent Text nodes (which can be merged with Node.normalize( )).

See Also

DocumentFragment, Range.cloneContents( ), Range.deleteContents( )

Range.insertNode( ) DOM Level 2 Range

insert a node at the start of a range

Synopsis

```
void insertNode(Node newNode)
    throws RangeException,
            DOMException;
```

Arguments

newNode

> The node to be inserted into the document.

Throws

This method throws a RangeException with a code of INVALID_NODE_TYPE_ERR if newNode is an Attr, Document, Entity, or Notation node.

This method also throws a DOMException with one of the following code values under the following conditions:

HIERARCHY_REQUEST_ERR

> The node that contains the start of the range does not allow children, it does not allow children of the specified type, or *newNode* is an ancestor of that node.

NO_MODIFICATION_ALLOWED_ERR

> The node that contains the start of the range or any of its ancestors is read-only.

WRONG_DOCUMENT_ERR

> newNode is part of a different document than the range is.

Description

This method inserts the specified node (and all its descendants) into the document at the start position of this range. When this method returns, this range includes the newly inserted node. If *newNode* is already part of the document, it is removed from its current position and then reinserted at the start of the range. If *newNode* is a DocumentFragment node, it is not inserted itself, but all of its children are inserted, in order, at the start of the range.

If the node that contains the start of the range is a Text node, it is split into two adjacent nodes before the insertion takes place. If *newNode* is a Text node, it is not merged with any adjacent Text nodes after it is inserted. To merge adjacent Text nodes, call Node.normalize( ).

See Also

DocumentFragment, Node.normalize( )

Range.selectNode( )

set range boundaries to a node

Synopsis

```
void selectNode(Node refNode)
    throws RangeException, DOMException;
```

Arguments

refNode

   The node to be "selected" (i.e., the node that is to become the content of this range).

Throws

A RangeException with a code of INVALID_NODE_TYPE_ERR if *refNode* is an Attr, Document, or DocumentFragment.

A DOMException with a code of WRONG_DOCUMENT_ERR if *refNode* is part of a different document than the one through which this range was created.

Description

This method sets the contents of this range to the specified *refNode*—i.e., it "selects" the node and its descendants.

See Also

Range.selectNodeContents( )

Range.selectNodeContents( )

set range boundaries to the children of a node

Synopsis

```
void selectNodeContents(Node refNode)
    throws RangeException, DOMException;
```

Arguments

refNode

   The node whose children are to become the contents of this range.

Throws

A RangeException with a code of INVALID_NODE_TYPE_ERR if *refNode* or one of its ancestors is a DocumentType, Entity, or Notation node.

A DOMException with a code of WRONG_DOCUMENT_ERR if *refNode* is part of a different document than the one through which this range was created.

Description

This method sets the boundary points of this range so that the range contains the children of *refNode*.

See Also

Range.selectNode( )

Range.setEnd( )   DOM Level 2 Range

set the end point of a range

Synopsis

```
void setEnd(Node refNode,
            long offset)
    throws RangeException, DOMException;
```

Arguments

refNode
> The node that contains the new end point.

offset
> The position of the end point within *refNode*.

Throws

A RangeException with a code of INVALID_NODE_TYPE_ERR if *refNode* or one of its ancestors is a DocumentType node.

A DOMException with a code of WRONG_DOCUMENT_ERR if *refNode* is part of a different document than the one through which this range was created, or a code of INDEX_SIZE_ERR if *offset* is negative or is greater than the number of children or characters in *refNode*.

Description

This method sets the end point of a range by specifying the values of the endContainer and endOffset properties.

Range.setEndAfter( )   DOM Level 2 Range

end a range after a specified node

Synopsis

```
void setEndAfter(Node refNode)
    throws RangeException, DOMException;
```

Arguments

refNode
> The node after which the end point of the range is to be set.

Throws

A RangeException with a code of INVALID_NODE_TYPE_ERR if *refNode* is a Document, DocumentFragment or Attr node, or if the root container of *refNode* is not a Document, DocumentFragment, or Attr node.

A DOMException with a code of WRONG_DOCUMENT_ERR if *refNode* is part of a different document than the one through which this range was created.

Description

This method sets the end point of this range to fall immediately after the specified *refNode*.

Range.setEndBefore( ) DOM Level 2 Range

end a range before the specified node

Synopsis

```
void setEndBefore(Node refNode)
    throws RangeException, DOMException;
```

Arguments

refNode
    The node before which the end point of the range is to be set.

Throws

This method throws the same exceptions in the same circumstances as Range.setEndAfter( ). See that method for details.

Description

This method sets the end point of this range to fall immediately before the specified *refNode*.

Range.setStart( ) DOM Level 2 Range

set the start point of a range

Synopsis

```
void setStart(Node refNode,
              long offset)
    throws RangeException, DOMException;
```

Arguments

refNode
    The node that contains the new start point.

offset
    The position of the new start point within *refNode*.

Throws

This method throws the same exceptions, for the same reasons, as `Range.setEnd( )`. See that reference page for details.

Description

This method sets the start point of this range by specifying the values of the `startContainer` and `startOffset` properties.

Range.setStartAfter( )   DOM Level 2 Range

start a range after the specified node

Synopsis

```
void setStartAfter(Node refNode)
    throws RangeException, DOMException;
```

Arguments

refNode
> The node after which the start point of the range is to be set.

Throws

This method throws the same exceptions in the same circumstances as `Range.setEndAfter( )`. See that reference page for details.

Description

This method sets the starting point of this range to be immediately after the specified *refNode*.

Range.setStartBefore( )   DOM Level 2 Range

start a range before the specified node

Synopsis

```
void setStartBefore(Node refNode)
    throws RangeException, DOMException;
```

Arguments

refNode
> The node before which the start point of the range is to be set.

Throws

This method throws the same exceptions in the same circumstances as `Range.setEndAfter( )`. See that reference page for details.

Description

This method sets the starting point of this range to be immediately before the specified *refNode*.

Range.surroundContents( )

surround range contents with the specified node

Synopsis

```
void surroundContents(Node newParent)
    throws RangeException, DOMException;
```

Arguments

newParent
> The node that is to become the new parent of the contents of this range.

Throws

This method throws a DOMException or RangeException with one of the following code values in the following circumstances:

DOMException.HIERARCHY_REQUEST_ERR
> The container node of the start of the range does not allow children or does not allow children of the type of *newParent*, or *newParent* is an ancestor of that container node.

DOMException.NO_MODIFICATION_ALLOWED_ERR
> An ancestor of a boundary point of the range is read-only and does not allow insertions.

DOMException.WRONG_DOCUMENT_ERR
> *newParent* and this range were created using different Document objects.

RangeException.BAD_BOUNDARYPOINTS_ERR
> The range partially selects a node (other than a Text node), so the region of the document it represents cannot be surrounded.

RangeException.INVALID_NODE_TYPE_ERR
> *newParent* is a Document, DocumentFragment, DocumentType, Attr, Entity, or Notation node.

Description

This method reparents the contents of this range to *newParent* and then inserts *newParent* into the document at the start position of the range. It is useful to place a region of document content within a <div> or <span> element, for example.

If *newParent* is already part of the document, it is first removed from the document, and any children it has are discarded. When this method returns, this range begins immediately before newParent and ends immediately after it.

Range.toString( )   DOM Level 2 Range

get range contents as a plain-text string

Synopsis

```
String toString( );
```

Returns

The contents of this range as a string of plain text without any markup.

RangeException   DOM Level 2 Range

signals a range-specific exception   Object → RangeException

Constants

The following constants define the legal values for the code property of a RangeException object. Note that these constants are static properties of RangeException, not properties of individual exception objects.

unsigned short BAD_BOUNDARYPOINTS_ERR = 1

   The boundary points of a range are not legal for the requested operation.

unsigned short INVALID_NODE_TYPE_ERR = 2

   An attempt was made to set the container node of a range boundary point to an invalid node or a node with an invalid ancestor.

Properties

unsigned short code

   An error code that provides some detail about what caused the exception. The legal values (and their meanings) for this property are defined by the constants just listed.

Description

A RangeException is thrown by certain methods of the Range interface to signal a problem of some sort. Note that most exceptions thrown by Range methods are DOMException objects. A RangeException is generated only when none of the existing DOMException error constants is appropriate to describe the exception.

Reset

see Input

Screen   JavaScript 1.2

provides information about the display   Object → Screen

Synopsis

```
screen
```

Properties

availHeight
> Specifies the available height, in pixels, of the screen on which the web browser is displayed. On operating systems such as Windows, this available height does not include vertical space allocated to semipermanent features, such as the task bar at the bottom of the screen.

availWidth
> Specifies the available width, in pixels, of the screen on which the web browser is displayed. On operating systems such as Windows, this available width does not include horizontal space allocated to semipermanent features, such as application shortcut bars.

colorDepth
> Specifies the color depth of the screen in bits per pixel.

height
> Specifies the total height, in pixels, of the screen on which the web browser is displayed. See also availHeight.

width
> Specifies the total width, in pixels, of the screen on which the web browser is displayed. See also availWidth.

Description

The screen property of every Window refers to a Screen object. The properties of this global object contain information about the screen on which the browser is displayed. JavaScript programs can use this information to optimize their output for the user's display capabilities. For example, a program can choose between large and small images based on the display size and between 8-bit and 16-bit color images based on the screen's color depth. A JavaScript program can also use the information about the size of the screen to center new browser windows on the screen.

See Also

The screen property of the Window object

Select

DOM Level 2 HTML

a graphical selection list

Node → Element → HTMLElement → Select

Properties

readonly Form form
> The <form> element that contains this <select> element.

readonly long length
> The number of <option> elements contained by this <select> element. Same as options.length.

readonly HTMLCollection options

> An array (HTMLCollection) of Option objects that represent the <option> elements contained in this <select> element, in the order in which they appear. See Select.options[] for further details.

long selectedIndex

> The position of the selected option in the options array. If no options are selected, this property is −1. If multiple options are selected, this property holds the index of the first selected option.

> Setting the value of this property selects the specified option and deselects all other options, even if the Select object has the multiple attribute specified. When you're doing listbox selection (when size > 1), you can deselect all options by setting selectedIndex to −1. Note that changing the selection in this way does not trigger the onchange( ) event handler.

readonly String type

> If multiple is true, this property is "select-multiple"; otherwise, it is "select-one". This property exists for compatibilty with the type property of the Input object.

In addition to the properties above, Select objects also mirror HTML attributes with the following properties:

Property	Attribute	Description
boolean disabled	disabled	Whether the user element is disabled
boolean multiple	multiple	Whether more than one option may be selected
String name	name	Element name for form submission
long size	size	The number of options to display at once
long tabIndex	tabindex	Position of Select element in the tabbing order

Methods

add( )

> Inserts a new Option object into the options array, either by appending it at the end of the array or by inserting it before another specified option.

blur( )

> Takes keyboard focus away from this element.

focus( )

> Transfers keyboard focus to this element.

remove( )

> Removes the <option> element at the specified position.

Event Handlers

onchange

> Invoked when the user selects or deselects an item.

HTML Syntax

A Select element is created with a standard HTML <select> tag. Options to appear within the Select element are created with the <option> tag:

```
<form>
    ...
<select
    name="name"  // A name that identifies this element; specifies name property
    [ size="integer" ]      // Number of visible options in Select element
    [ multiple ]            // Multiple options may be selected, if present
    [ onchange="handler" ]  // Invoked when the selection changes
>
<option value="value1" [selected]>option_label1
<option value="value2" [selected]>option_label2// Other options here
</select>
    ...
</form>
```

Description

The Select element represents an HTML <select> tag, which displays a graphical list of choices to the user. If the multiple attribute is present in the HTML definition of the element, the user may select any number of options from the list. If that attribute is not present, the user may select only one option, and options have a radio-button behavior—selecting one deselects whichever was previously selected.

The options in a Select element may be displayed in two distinct ways. If the size attribute has a value greater than 1, or if the multiple attribute is present, they are displayed in a list box that is size lines high in the browser window. If size is smaller than the number of options, the listbox includes a scrollbar so all the options are accessible. On the other hand, if size is specified as 1 and multiple is not specified, the currently selected option is displayed on a single line, and the list of other options is made available through a drop-down menu. The first presentation style displays the options clearly but requires more space in the browser window. The second style requires minimal space but does not display alternative options as explicitly.

The options[] property of the Select element is the most interesting. This is the array of Option objects that describe the choices presented by the Select element. The length property specifies the length of this array (as does options.length). See Option for details.

For a Select element without the multiple attribute specified, you can determine which option is selected with the selectedIndex property. When multiple selections are allowed, however, this property tells you the index of only the first selected option. To determine the full set of selected options, you must iterate through the options[] array and check the selected property of each Option object.

The options displayed by the Select element may be dynamically modified. Add a new option with the add( ) method and the Option( ) constructor; remove an option with the remove( ) method. Changes are also possible by direct manipulation of the options array.

See Also

Form, Option, Select.options[]; Chapter 18

Select.add( ) DOM Level 2 HTML

insert an \<option\> element

Synopsis

```
void add(HTMLElement element,
         HTMLElement before)
    throws DOMException;
```

Arguments

element
> The Option element to be added.

before
> The element of the options array before which the new *element* should be added. If this argument is null, *element* is appended at the end of the options array.

Throws

This method throws a DOMException with a code of NOT_FOUND_ERR if the *before* argument specifies an object that is not a member of the options array.

Description

This method adds a new \<option\> element to this \<select\> element. *element* is an Option object that represents the \<option\> element to be added. *before* specifies the Option before which *element* is to be added. If *before* is part of an \<optgroup\>, *element* is always inserted as part of that same group. If *before* is null, *element* becomes the last child of the \<select\> element.

See Also

Option

Select.blur( ) DOM Level 2 HTML

take keyboard focus away from this element

Synopsis

```
void blur( );
```

Description

This method takes keyboard focus away from this element.

Select.focus( ) DOM Level 2 HTML

give keyboard focus to this element

Synopsis

```
void focus( );
```

Description

This method transfers keyboard focus to this <select> element so the user can interact with it using the keyboard instead of the mouse.

Select.onchange

event handler invoked when the selection changes

Synopsis

```
Function onchange
```

Description

The onchange property of a Select object refers to an event-handler function that is invoked when the user selects or deselects an option. The event does not specify what the new selected option or options are; you must consult the selectedIndex property of the Select object or the selected property of the various Option objects to determine this.

See Element.addEventListener( ) for another way to register event handlers.

See Also

Element.addEventListener( ), Option; Chapter 17

Select.options[]

the choices in a Select object

Synopsis

```
readonly HTMLCollection options
```

Description

The options[] property is an array-like HTMLCollection of Option objects. Each Option object describes one of the selection options presented within the Select object.

The options[] property is not an ordinary HTMLCollection. For backward compatibility with the earliest browsers, this collection has certain special behaviors that allow you to change the options displayed by the Select object:

- If you set options.length to 0, all options in the Select object are cleared.
- If you set options.length to a value less than the current value, the number of options in the Select object is decreased, and those at the end of the array disappear.
- If you set an element in the options[] array to null, that option is removed from the Select object, and the elements above it in the array are moved down, changing their indices to occupy the new space in the array (see also Select.remove( )).
- If you create a new Option object with the Option( ) constructor (see Option), you can add that option to the end of the options list in the Select object by appending it to the options[] array. To do this, set options[options.length] (see also Select.add( )).

Select.remove( )

See Also

Option

Select.remove( )   DOM Level 2 HTML
remove an <option>

Synopsis

void remove(long *index*);

Arguments

index
>   The position within the options array of the <option> element to be removed.

Description

This method removes the <option> element at the specified position in the options array. If
the specified *index* is less than zero or greater than or equal to the number of options, the
remove( ) method ignores it and does nothing.

See Also

Option

Style

see CSS2Properties

Submit

see Input

Table   DOM Level 2 HTML
a <table> in an HTML document   Node → Element → HTMLElement → Table

Properties

HTMLElement caption
>   A reference to the <caption> element for the table, or null if there is none.

readonly HTMLCollection rows
>   An array (HTMLCollection) of TableRow objects that represent all the rows in the
>   table. This includes all rows defined within <thead>, <tfoot>, and <tbody> tags.

readonly HTMLCollection tBodies
>   An array (HTMLCollection) of TableSection objects that represent all the <tbody>
>   sections in this table.

TableSection tFoot
>   The <tfoot> element of the table, or null if there is none.

`TableSection tHead`
> The `<thead>` element of the table, or `null` if there is none.

In addition to the properties just listed, this interface defines the properties in the following table to represent the HTML attributes of the `<table>` element:

Property	Attribute	Description
`deprecated String align`	`align`	Horizontal alignment of table in document
`deprecated String bgColor`	`bgcolor`	Table background color
`String border`	`border`	Width of border around table
`String cellPadding`	`cellpadding`	Space between cell contents and border
`String cellSpacing`	`cellspacing`	Space between cell borders
`String frame`	`frame`	Which table borders to draw
`String rules`	`rules`	Where to draw lines within the table
`String summary`	`summary`	Summary description of table
`String width`	`width`	Table width

Methods

`createCaption()`
> Returns the existing `<caption>` for the table, or creates (and inserts) a new one if none already exists.

`createTFoot()`
> Returns the existing `<tfoot>` element for the table, or creates (and inserts) a new one if none already exists.

`createTHead()`
> Returns the existing `<thead>` element for the table, or creates (and inserts) a new one if none already exists.

`deleteCaption()`
> Deletes the `<caption>` element from the table, if it has one.

`deleteRow()`
> Deletes the row at the specified position in the table.

`deleteTFoot()`
> Deletes the `<tfoot>` element from the table, if it has one.

`deleteTHead()`
> Deletes the `<thead>` element from the table, if it has one.

`insertRow()`
> Inserts a new, empty `<tr>` element into the table at the specified position.

Description

The Table object represents an HTML `<table>` element and defines a number of convenience properties and methods for querying and modifying various sections of the table. These methods and properties make it easier to work with tables, but their functionality can also be duplicated with core DOM methods.

See Also

TableCell, TableRow, TableSection

Table.createCaption( )   DOM Level 2 HTML

get or create a <caption>

Synopsis

HTMLElement createCaption( );

Returns

An HTMLElement object representing the <caption> element for this table. If the table already has a caption, this method simply returns it. If the table does not have an existing <caption>, this method creates a new (empty) one and inserts it into the table before returning it.

Table.createTFoot( )   DOM Level 2 HTML

get or create a <tfoot>

Synopsis

HTMLElement createTFoot( );

Returns

A TableSection representing the <tfoot> element for this table. If the table already has a footer, this method simply returns it. If the table does not have an existing footer, this method creates a new (empty) <tfoot> element and inserts it into the table before returning it.

Table.createTHead( )   DOM Level 2 HTML

get or create a <thead>

Synopsis

HTMLElement createTHead( );

Returns

A TableSection representing the <thead> element for this table. If the table already has a header, this method simply returns it. If the table does not have an existing header, this method creates a new (empty) <thead> element and inserts it into the table before returning it.

Table.deleteCaption( )   DOM Level 2 HTML

delete the <caption> of a table

Synopsis

void deleteCaption( );

Description

If this table has a `<caption>` element, this method removes it from the document tree. Otherwise, it does nothing.

Table.deleteRow( )

delete a row of a table

Synopsis

```
void deleteRow(long index)
    throws DOMException;
```

Arguments

index
> Specifies the position within the table of the row to be deleted.

Throws

This method throws a DOMException with a code of INDEX_SIZE_ERR if *index* is less than zero or is greater than or equal to the number of rows in the table.

Description

This method deletes the row at the specified position from the table. Rows are numbered in the order in which they appear in the document source. Rows in `<thead>` and `<tfoot>` sections are numbered along with all other rows in the table.

See Also

TableSection.deleteRow( )

Table.deleteTFoot( )

delete the <tfoot> of a table

Synopsis

```
void deleteTFoot( );
```

Description

If this table has a `<tfoot>` element, this method removes it from the document tree. If the table has no footer, this method does nothing.

Table.deleteTHead( )

delete the <thead> of a table

Synopsis

```
void deleteTHead( );
```

Description

If this table has a <thead> element, this method deletes it; otherwise, it does nothing.

Table.insertRow( )

add a new, empty row to the table

Synopsis

```
HTMLElement insertRow(long index)
    throws DOMException;
```

Arguments

index
> The position at which the new row is to be inserted.

Returns

A TableRow that represents the newly inserted row.

Throws

This method throws a DOMException with a code of INDEX_SIZE_ERR if *index* is less than zero or greater than the number of rows in the table.

Description

This method creates a new TableRow representing a <tr> tag and inserts it into the table at the specified position.

The new row is inserted in the same section and immediately before the existing row at the position specified by *index*. If *index* is equal to the number of rows in the table, the new row is appended to the last section of the table. If the table is initially empty, the new row is inserted into a new <tbody> section that is itself inserted into the table.

You can use the convenience method TableRow.insertCell( ) to add content to the newly created row.

See Also

TableSection.insertRow( )

TableCell

a <td> or <th> cell in an HTML table   Node → Element → HTMLElement → TableCell

Properties

readonly long cellIndex
> The position of this cell within its row.

In addition to the cellIndex property, this interface defines the following properties, which correspond directly to the HTML attributes of the <td> and <th> elements:

Property	Attribute	Description
String abbr	abbr	See HTML specification
String align	align	Horizontal alignment of cell
String axis	axis	See HTML specification
deprecated String bgColor	bgcolor	Background color of cell
String ch	char	Alignment character
String chOff	choff	Alignment character offset
long colSpan	colspan	Columns spanned by cell
String headers	headers	id values for headers for this cell
deprecated String height	height	Cell height in pixels
deprecated boolean noWrap	nowrap	Don't word-wrap cell
long rowSpan	rowspan	Rows spanned by cell
String scope	scope	Scope of this header cell
String vAlign	valign	Vertical alignment of cell
deprecated String width	width	Cell width in pixels

Description

This interface represents <td> and <th> elements in HTML tables.

TableRow

DOM Level 2 HTML

a <tr> element in an HTML table   Node → Element → HTMLElement → TableRow

Properties

readonly HTMLCollection cells
    An array (HTMLCollection) of TableCell objects representing the cells in this row.
readonly long rowIndex
    The position of this row in the table.
readonly long sectionRowIndex
    The position of this row within its section (i.e., within its <thead>, <tbody>, or <tfoot> element).

In addition to the properties just listed, this interface also defines the following properties, which correspond to the HTML attributes of the <tr> element:

Property	Attribute	Description
String align	align	Default horizontal alignment of cells in this row
deprecated String bgColor	bgcolor	Background color of this row
String ch	char	Alignment character for cells in this row
String chOff	choff	Alignment character offset for cells in this row
String vAlign	valign	Default vertical alignment for cells in this row

Methods

deleteCell( )
> Deletes the specified cell from this row.

insertCell( )
> Inserts an empty <td> element into this row at the specified position.

Description

This interface represents a row in an HTML table.

TableRow.deleteCell( )   DOM Level 2 HTML

delete a cell in a table row

Synopsis

```
void deleteCell(long index)
    throws DOMException;
```

Arguments

index
> The position in the row of the cell to delete.

Throws

This method throws a DOMException with a code of INDEX_SIZE_ERR if *index* is less than zero or is greater than or equal to the number of cells in the row.

Description

This method deletes the cell at the specified position in the table row.

TableRow.insertCell( )   DOM Level 2 HTML

insert a new, empty <td> element into a table row

Synopsis

```
HTMLElement insertCell(long index)
    throws DOMException;
```

Arguments

index
> The position at which the new cell is to be inserted.

Returns

An TableCell object that represents the newly created and inserted <td> element.

Throws

This method throws a DOMException with a code of INDEX_SIZE_ERR if *index* is less than zero or is greater than the number of cells in the row.

Description

This method creates a new <td> element and inserts it into the row at the specified position. The new cell is inserted immediately before the cell that is currently at the position specified by *index*. If *index* is equal to the number of cells in the row, the new cell is appended to the end of the row.

Note that this convenience method inserts <td> data cells only. If you need to add a header cell into a row, you must create and insert the <th> element using `Document.createElement( )` and `Node.insertBefore( )`, or related methods.

TableSection   DOM Level 2 HTML

a header, footer, or body section of a table   Node → Element → HTMLElement → TableSection

Properties

readonly HTMLCollection rows

    An array (HTMLCollection) of TableRow objects representing the rows in this section of the table.

In addition to the rows property, this interface defines the following properties, which represent the attributes of the underlying HTML element:

Property	Attribute	Description
String align	align	Default horizontal alignment of cells in this section of the table
String ch	char	Default alignment character for cells in this section
String chOff	choff	Default alignment offset for cells in this section
String vAlign	valign	Default vertical alignment for cells in this section

Methods

deleteRow( )

    Deletes the specified numbered row from this section.

insertRow( )

    Inserts an empty row into this section at the specified position.

Description

This interface represents a <tbody>, <thead>, or <tfoot> section of an HTML table. The tHead and tFoot properties of a Table are TableSection objects, and the tBodies property is an array of TableSection objects.

TableSection.deleteRow( )   DOM Level 2 HTML

delete a row within a table section

Synopsis

```
void deleteRow(long index)
    throws DOMException;
```

Arguments

index
> The position of the row within this section.

Throws

This method throws a DOMException with a code of INDEX_SIZE_ERR if *index* is less than zero or is greater than or equal to the number of rows in this section.

Description

This method deletes the row at the specified position within this section. Note that for this method, *index* specifies a row's position within its section, not within the entire table.

See Also

Table.deleteRow( )

TableSection.insertRow( )   DOM Level 2 HTML

insert a new, empty row into this table section

Synopsis

```
HTMLElement insertRow(long index)
    throws DOMException;
```

Arguments

index
> The position within the section at which the new row is to be inserted.

Returns

A TableRow that represents the newly created and inserted <tr> element.

Throws

This method throws a DOMException with a code of INDEX_SIZE_ERR if *index* is less than zero or is greater than the number of rows in this section.

Description

This method creates a new empty <tr> element and inserts it into this table section at the specified position. If *index* equals the number of rows currently in the section, the new row is appended to the end of the section. Otherwise, the new row is inserted immediately before the row that is currently at the position specified by *index*. Note that for this method, *index* specifies a row position within a single table section, not within the entire table.

See Also

Table.insertRow( )

Text

a run of text in an HTML or XML document

Subinterfaces

CDATASection

Methods

splitText( )
>   Splits this Text node into two at the specified character position and returns the new Text node.

Description

A Text node represents a run of plain text in an HTML or XML document. Plain text appears within HTML and XML elements and attributes, and Text nodes typically appear as children of Element and Attr nodes. Text nodes inherit from CharacterData, and the textual content of a Text node is available through the data property inherited from CharacterData or through the nodeValue property inherited from Node. Text nodes may be manipulated using any of the methods inherited from CharacterData or with the splitText( ) method defined by the Text interface itself. Create a new Text node with Document.createTextNode( ). Text nodes never have children.

See Node.normalize( ) for a way to remove empty Text nodes and merge adjacent Text nodes from a subtree of a document.

See Also

CharacterData, Node.normalize( )

Text.splitText( )

split a Text node in two

DOM Level 1 Core

Synopsis

```
Text splitText(unsigned long offset)
    throws DOMException;
```

Arguments

offset
>   The character position at which to split the Text node.

Returns

The Text node that was split from this node.

Throws

This method may throw a DOMException with one of the following code values:

INDEX_SIZE_ERR
>   offset is negative or greater than the length of the Text or Comment node.

`NO_MODIFICATION_ALLOWED_ERR`
> The node is read-only and may not be modified.

Description

This method splits a Text node in two at the specified *offset*. The original Text node is modified so that it contains all text content up to, but not including, the character at position *offset*. A new Text node is created to contain all the characters from (and including) the position *offset* to the end of the string. This new Text node is the return value of the method. Additionally, if the original Text node has a `parentNode`, the new node is inserted into this parent node immediately after the original node.

The CDATASection interface inherits from Text, and this `splitText( )` method can also be used with CDATASection nodes, in which case the newly created node is a CDATA-Section rather than a Text node.

See Also

`Node.normalize( )`

Textarea
DOM Level 2 HTML

a multiline text input area
Node → Element → HTMLElement → Textarea

Properties

`String defaultValue`
> The initial content of the text area. When the form is reset, the text area is restored to this value. Setting this property changes the displayed text in the text area.

`readonly Form form`
> The Form object that represents the `<form>` element containing this Textarea, or `null` if this element is not inside a form.

`readonly String type`
> The type of this element, for compatibility with Input objects. This property always has the value "textarea".

`String value`
> The text currently displayed in the text area. The initial value of this property is the same as the `defaultValue` property. When the user types into this element, the `value` property is updated to match the user's input. If you set the `value` property explicitly, the string you specify is displayed in the Textarea object. This `value` property contains the text that is sent to the server when the form is submitted.

In addition to these properties, Textarea objects also mirror HTML attributes with the following properties:

Property	Attribute	Description
`String accessKey`	`accesskey`	Keyboard shortcut character
`long cols`	`cols`	The width in character columns
`boolean disabled`	`disabled`	Whether the Textarea is disabled

Property	Attribute	Description
String name	name	Textarea name for form submission and element access.
boolean readOnly	readonly	Whether the Textarea is noneditable
long rows	rows	Height of Textarea in lines
long tabIndex	tabindex	Position of Textarea in tabbing order

Methods

blur( )
>   Takes keyboard focus away from this element.

focus( )
>   Transfers keyboard focus to this element.

select( )
>   Selects the entire contents of the text area.

Event Handlers

onchange
>   Invoked when the user edits the text displayed in this element and then moves the keyboard focus elsewhere. This event handler is not invoked for every keystroke in the Textarea element but only when the user completes an edit.

HTML Syntax

A Textarea is created with standard HTML <textarea> and </textarea> tags:

```
<form>
   ...
  <textarea
    [ name="name" ]        // A name that can be used to refer to this element
    [ rows="integer" ]     // How many lines tall the element is
    [ cols="integer" ]     // How many characters wide the element is
    [ onchange="handler" ] // The onchange( ) event handler
  >
    plain_text             // The initial text; specifies defaultValue
  </textarea>
   ...
</form>
```

Description

A Textarea object represents an HTML <textarea> element that creates a multiline text input field (usually within an HTML form). The initial contents of the text area are specified between the <textarea> and </textarea> tags. You can query and set the text with the value property.

Textarea is a form input element like Input and Select. Like those objects, it defines form, name, and type properties.

See Also

Form, Input; Chapter 18

Textarea.blur( )   DOM Level 2 HTML

take keyboard focus away from this element

Synopsis

```
void blur( );
```

Description

This method takes keyboard focus away from this element.

Textarea.focus( )   DOM Level 2 HTML

give keyboard focus to this element

Synopsis

```
void focus( );
```

Description

This method transfers keyboard focus to this element so the user can edit the displayed text without having to first click on the text area.

Textarea.onchange   DOM Level 0

event handler invoked when input value changes

Synopsis

```
Function onchange
```

Description

The onchange property of a Textarea refers to an event-handler function that is invoked when the user changes the value in the text area and then "commits" those changes by moving the keyboard focus elsewhere.

Note that the onchange event handler is *not* invoked when the value property of a Text object is set by JavaScript. Also note that this handler is intended to process a complete change to the input value, and therefore it is not invoked on a keystroke-by-keystroke basis. See HTMLElement.onkeypress for information on receiving notification of every key press event and Element.addEventListener( ) for another way to register event handlers.

See Also

Element.addEventListener( ), HTMLElement.onkeypress, Input.onchange; Chapter 17

Textarea.select( )

select the text in this element

Synopsis

```
void select( );
```

Description

This method selects all the text displayed by this `<textarea>` element. In most browsers, this means that the text is highlighted and that new text entered by the user replaces the highlighted text instead of being appended to it.

TextField

see Input

UIEvent

details about user-interface events

Subinterfaces

KeyEvent, MouseEvent

Properties

readonly long detail
> A numeric detail about the event. For click, mousedown, and mouseup events (see MouseEvent), this field is the click count: 1 for a single-click, 2 for a double-click, 3 for a triple-click, and so on. For DOMActivate events, this field is 1 for a normal activation or 2 for a "hyperactivation," such as a double-click or **Shift-Enter** combination.

readonly Window view
> The window (the "view") in which the event was generated.

Methods

initUIEvent( )
> Initializes the properties of a newly created UIEvent object, including the properties inherited from the Event interface.

Description

The UIEvent interface is a subinterface of Event and defines the type of Event object passed to events of type DOMFocusIn, DOMFocusOut, and DOMActivate. These event types are not commonly used in web browsers, and what is more important about the UIEvent interface is that it is the parent interface of MouseEvent.

See Also

Event, KeyEvent, MouseEvent; Chapter 17

Client-Side
JavaScript
Reference

UIEvent.initUIEvent( )   DOM Level 2 Events

initialize the properties of a UIEvent object

Synopsis

```
void initUIEvent(String typeArg,
                 boolean canBubbleArg,
                 boolean cancelableArg,
                 Window viewArg,
                 long detailArg);
```

Arguments

typeArg
> The event type.

canBubbleArg
> Whether the event will bubble.

cancelableArg
> Whether the event may be canceled with preventDefault( ).

viewArg
> The window in which the event occurred.

detailArg
> The detail property for the event.

Description

This method initializes the view and detail properties of this UIEvent and also the type, bubbles, and cancelable properties inherited from the Event interface. This method may be called only on newly created UIEvent objects, before they have been passed to Element.dispatchEvent( ).

See Also

Document.createEvent( ), Event.initEvent( ), MouseEvent.initMouseEvent( )

Window   JavaScript 1.0

a web browser window or frame   Object → Global → Window

Synopsis

```
self
window
window.frames[i]
```

Properties

The Window object defines the following properties and also inherits all the global properties of core JavaScript (see Global in Part III):

closed

A read-only boolean value that specifies whether the window has been closed. When a browser window closes, the Window object that represents it does not simply disappear; it continues to exist, but its closed property is set to true.

defaultStatus

A read/write string that specifies the default message that appears in the status line. See Window.defaultStatus.

document

A read-only reference to the Document object that describes the document contained in this window or frame (see Document for details).

event *[IE only]*

In Internet Explorer, this property refers to the Event object that describes the most recent event. This property is used in the IE event model. In the standard DOM event model, the Event object is passed as an argument to event-handler functions. See Event and Chapter 17 for further details.

frames[]

An array of Window objects, one for each frame or <iframe> contained within this window. The frames.length property contains the number of elements in the frames[] array. Note that frames referenced by the frames[] array may themselves contain frames and may have a frames[] array of their own.

history

A read-only reference to the History object of this window or frame. See History for details.

innerHeight, innerWidth

Read-only properties that specify the height and width, in pixels, of the document display area of this window. These dimensions do not include the size of the menu bar, toolbars, scrollbars, and so on. These properties are not supported by IE. Instead use the clientWidth and clientHeight properties of document.documentElement or document.body (depending on the version of IE). See Section 14.3.1 for details.

location

The Location object for this window or frame. This object specifies the URL of the currently loaded document. Setting this property to a new URL string causes the browser to load and display the contents of that URL. See Location for further details.

name

A string that contains the name of the window. The name is optionally specified when the window is created with the open( ) method or with the name attribute of a <frame> tag. The name of a window may be used as the value of a target attribute of an <a> or <form> tag. Using the target attribute in this way specifies that the hyperlinked document or the results of form submission should be displayed in the named window or frame.

navigator

A read-only reference to the Navigator object, which provides version and configuration information about the web browser. See Navigator for details.

opener

> A read/write reference to the Window object that contained the script that called open( ) to open this browser window. This property is valid only for Window objects that represent top-level windows, not those that represent frames. The opener property is useful so that a newly created window can refer to properties and functions defined in the window that created it.

outerHeight, outerWidth

> These read-only integers specify the total height and width, in pixels, of the browser window. These dimensions include the height and width of the menu bar, toolbars, scrollbars, window borders, and so on. These properties are not supported by IE, and IE offers no alternative properties.

pageXOffset, pageYOffset

> Read-only integers that specify the number of pixels that the current document has been scrolled to the right (pageXOffset) and down (pageYOffset). These properties are not supported by Internet Explorer. In IE, use the scrollLeft and scrollTop properties of document.documentElement or document.body (depending on the version of IE). See Section 14.3.1 for details.

parent

> A read-only reference to the Window object that contains this window or frame. If this window is a top-level window, parent refers to the window itself. If this window is a frame, the parent property refers to the window or frame that contains it.

screen

> A read-only reference to a Screen object that specifies information about the screen: the number of available pixels and the number of available colors. See Screen for details.

screenLeft, screenTop, screenX, screenY

> Read-only integers that specify the coordinates of the upper-left corner of the window on the screen. IE, Safari, and Opera support screenLeft and screenTop, while Firefox and Safari support screenX and screenY.

self

> A read-only reference to this window itself. This is a synonym for the window property.

status

> A read/write string that specifies the current contents of the browser's status line. See Window.status for details.

top

> A read-only reference to the top-level window that contains this window. If this window is a top-level window itself, the top property simply contains a reference to the window itself. If this window is a frame, the top property refers to the top-level window that contains the frame. Contrast with the parent property.

window

> The window property is identical to the self property; it contains a reference to this window.

Methods

The Window object defines the following methods, and also inherits all the global functions defined by core JavaScript (see Global in Part III).

addEventListener( )
> Adds an event-handler function to the set of event handlers for this window. This method is supported by all modern browsers except IE. See attachEvent( ) for IE.

alert( )
> Displays a simple message in a dialog box.

attachEvent( )
> Adds an event-handler function to the set of handlers for this window. This is the IE-specific alternative to addEventListener( ).

blur( )
> Takes keyboard focus away from the top-level browser window.

clearInterval( )
> Cancels periodic execution of code.

clearTimeout( )
> Cancels a pending timeout operation.

close( )
> Closes a window.

confirm( )
> Asks a yes-or-no question with a dialog box.

detachEvent( )
> Removes an event-handler function from this window. This is the IE-specific alternative to removeEventListener( ).

focus( )
> Gives the top-level browser window keyboard focus; this brings the window to the front on most platforms.

getComputedStyle( )
> Determines the CSS styles that apply to a document element.

moveBy( )
> Moves the window by a relative amount.

moveTo( )
> Moves the window to an absolute position.

open( )
> Creates and opens a new window.

print( )
> Simulates a click on the browser's **Print** button.

prompt( )
> Asks for simple string input with a dialog box.

removeEventListener( )
> Removes an event-handler function from the set of handlers for this window. This method is implemented by all modern browsers except IE. IE provides detachEvent( ) instead.

Client-Side
JavaScript
Reference

resizeBy( )
>Resizes the window by a specified amount.

resizeTo( )
>Resizes the window to a specified size.

scrollBy
>Scrolls the window by a specified amount.

scrollTo( )
>Scrolls the window to a specified position.

setInterval( )
>Executes code at periodic intervals.

setTimeout( )
>Executes code after a specified amount of time elapses.

Event Handlers

onblur
>Invoked when the window loses focus.

onerror
>Invoked when a JavaScript error occurs.

onfocus
>Invoked when the window gains focus.

onload
>Invoked when the document (or frameset) is fully loaded.

onresize
>Invoked when the window is resized.

onunload
>Invoked when the browser leaves the current document or frameset.

Description

The Window object represents a browser window or frame. It is documented in detail in Chapter 14. In client-side JavaScript, the Window serves as the "global object," and all expressions are evaluated in the context of the current Window object. This means that no special syntax is required to refer to the current window, and you can use the properties of that window object as if they were global variables. For example, you can write document rather than *window*.document. Similarly, you can use the methods of the current window object as if they were functions: e.g., alert( ) instead of *window*.alert( ). In addition to the properties and methods listed here, the Window object also implements all the global properties and functions defined by core JavaScript. See Global in Part III for details.

The Window object has window and self properties that refer to the window object itself. You can use these to make the current window reference explicit rather than implicit. In addition to these two properties, the parent and top properties and the frames[] array refer to other Window objects related to the current one.

To refer to a frame within a window, use:

```
frames[i]       // Frames of current window
self.frames[i]  // Frames of current window
w.frames[i]     // Frames of specified window w
```

To refer to the parent window (or frame) of a frame, use:

```
parent         // Parent of current window
self.parent    // Parent of current window
w.parent       // Parent of specified window w
```

To refer to the top-level browser window from any frame contained (or nested multiple levels deep) within it, use:

```
top         // Top window of current frame
self.top    // Top window of current frame
f.top       // Top window of specified frame f
```

New top-level browser windows are created with the Window.open( ) method. When you call this method, save the return value of the open( ) call in a variable and use that variable to reference the new window. The opener property of the new window is a reference back to the window that opened it.

In general, the methods of the Window object manipulate the browser window or frame in some way. The alert( ), confirm( ), and prompt( ) methods are notable: they interact with the user through simple dialog boxes.

See Chapter 14 for an in-depth overview of the Window object, and see the individual reference pages for complete details on Window methods and event handlers.

See Also

Document; Global in Part III; Chapter 14

Window.addEventListener( )

see Element.addEventListener( )

Window.alert( )   JavaScript 1.0

display a message in a dialog box

Synopsis

window.alert(*message*)

Arguments

message
> The plain-text (not HTML) string to display in a dialog box popped up over *window*.

Description

The alert( ) method displays the specified *message* to the user in a dialog box. The dialog box contains an **OK** button the user can click to dismiss it. The dialog box is typically modal, and the call to alert( ) typically blocks until the dialog is dismissed.

Usage

Perhaps the most common use of the alert( ) method is to display error messages when the user's input to some form element is invalid in some way. The alert dialog box can inform the user of the problem and explain what needs to be corrected to avoid the problem in the future.

The appearance of the alert( ) dialog box is platform-dependent, but it generally contains graphics that indicate an error, warning, or alert message of some kind. While alert( ) can display any desired message, the alert graphics of the dialog box mean that this method is not appropriate for simple informational messages like "Welcome to my blog" or "You are the 177th visitor this week!"

Note that the *message* displayed in the dialog box is a string of plain text, not formatted HTML. You can use the newline character "\n" in your strings to break your message across multiple lines. You can also do some rudimentary formatting using spaces and can approximate horizontal rules with underscore characters, but the results depend greatly on the font used in the dialog box and thus are system-dependent.

See Also

Window.confirm( ), Window.prompt( )

Window.attachEvent( )

see Element.attachEvent( )

Window.blur( )

JavaScript 1.1

remove keyboard focus from a top-level window

Synopsis

window.blur( )

Description

The blur( ) method removes keyboard focus from the top-level browser window specified by the Window object. It is unspecified which window gains keyboard focus as a result. In some browsers and/or platforms, this method may have no effect.

See Also

Window.focus( )

Window.clearInterval( )

JavaScript 1.2

stop periodically executing code

Synopsis

window.clearInterval(*intervalId*)

Arguments

intervalId
    The value returned by the corresponding call to setInterval( ).

Description

clearInterval( ) stops the repeated execution of code that was started by a call to setInterval( ). *intervalId* must be the value that was returned by a call to setInterval( ).

See Also

Window.setInterval( )

Window.clearTimeout( )   JavaScript 1.0

cancel deferred execution

Synopsis

window.clearTimeout(*timeoutId*)

Arguments

timeoutId
> A value returned by setTimeout( ) that identifies the timeout to be canceled.

Description

clearTimeout( ) cancels the execution of code that has been deferred with the setTimeout( ) method. The *timeoutId* argument is a value returned by the call to setTimeout( ) and identifies which deferred code to cancel.

See Also

Window.setTimeout( )

Window.close( )   JavaScript 1.0

close a browser window

Synopsis

window.close( )

Description

The close( ) method closes the top-level browser window specified by *window*. A window can close itself by calling self.close( ) or simply close( ). Only windows opened by JavaScript can be closed by JavaScript. This prevents malicious scripts from causing the user's browser to exit.

See Also

Window.open( ), the closed and opener properties of Window

Window.confirm( ) JavaScript 1.0

ask a yes-or-no question

Synopsis

window.confirm(*question*)

Arguments

question

> The plain-text (not HTML) string to be displayed in the dialog box. It should generally express a question you want the user to answer.

Returns

true if the user clicks the **OK** button; false if the user clicks the **Cancel** button.

Description

The confirm( ) method displays the specified *question* in a dialog box. The dialog box contains **OK** and **Cancel** buttons that the user can use to answer the question. If the user clicks the **OK** button, confirm( ) returns true. If the user clicks **Cancel**, confirm( ) returns false.

The dialog box that is displayed by the confirm( ) method is *modal*. That is, it blocks all user input to the main browser window until the user dismisses the dialog box by clicking on the **OK** or **Cancel** buttons. Since this method returns a value depending on the user's response to the dialog box, JavaScript execution pauses in the call to confirm( ), and subsequent statements are not executed until the user responds to the dialog box.

There is no way to change the labels that appear in the buttons of the dialog box (to make them read **Yes** and **No**, for example). Therefore, you should take care to phrase your question or message so that **OK** and **Cancel** are suitable responses.

See Also

Window.alert( ), Window.prompt( )

Window.defaultStatus JavaScript 1.0

the default status line text

Synopsis

window.defaultStatus

Description

defaultStatus is a read/write string property that specifies the default text that appears in the window's status line. Web browsers typically use the status line to display the browser's progress while loading a file and to display the destination of hypertext links that the mouse is over. While it is not displaying any of these transient messages, the status line is, by default, blank. However, you can set the defaultStatus property to specify a default message to be displayed when the status line is not otherwise in use, and you can read the defaultStatus property to determine what the default message is. The text you specify may be temporarily overwritten with other messages, such as those that are displayed when the user moves the mouse over a hypertext link, but the defaultStatus message is always redisplayed when the transient message is erased.

The defaultStatus property has been disabled in some modern browsers. See Window.status for details.

See Also

Window.status

Window.detachEvent( )

see Element.detachEvent( )

Window.focus( ) JavaScript 1.1

give keyboard focus to a window

Synopsis

window.focus( )

Description

The focus( ) method gives keyboard focus to the browser window specified by the Window object.

On most platforms, a top-level window is brought forward to the top of the window stack so that it becomes visible when it is given focus.

See Also

Window.blur( )

Window.getComputedStyle( ) DOM Level 2 CSS

retrieve the CSS styles used to render an element

Synopsis

```
CSS2Properties getComputedStyle(Element elt,
                        String pseudoElt);
```

Arguments

elt
> The document element whose style information is desired.

pseudoElt
> The CSS pseudoelement string, such as ":before" or ":first-line", or null if there is none.

Returns

A read-only CSS2Properties object that represents the style attributes and values used to render the specified element in this window. Any length values queried from this object are always expressed as pixel or absolute values, not relative or percentage values.

Description

An element in a document may obtain style information from an inline style attribute and from any number of style sheets in the stylesheet "cascade." Before the element can actually be displayed in a view, its style information must be extracted from the cascade, and styles specified with relative units (such as percentages or "ems") must be "computed" to convert to absolute units.

This method returns a read-only CSS2Properties object that represents those cascaded and computed styles. The DOM specification requires that any styles representing lengths use absolute units such as inches or millimeters. In practice, pixel values are commonly returned instead, although there is no guarantee that an implementation will always do this.

Contrast getComputedStyle( ) with the style property of an HTMLElement, which gives you access only to the inline styles of an element, in whatever units they were specified, and tells you nothing about stylesheet styles that apply to the element.

In Internet Explorer, similar functionality is available through the nonstandard currentStyle property of each HTMLElement object.

See Also

CSS2Properties, HTMLElement

Window.moveBy( )   JavaScript 1.2

move a window to a relative position

Synopsis

    window.moveBy(dx, dy)

Arguments

dx   The number of pixels to move the window to the right.
dy   The number of pixels to move the window down.

Description

moveBy( ) moves the *window* to the relative position specified by *dx* and *dy*. See the security and usability considerations described under Window.moveTo( ).

Window.moveTo( )   JavaScript 1.2

move a window to an absolute position

Synopsis

    window.moveTo(x, y)

Arguments

x   The X coordinate of the new window position.

y   The Y coordinate of the new window position.

Description

moveTo( ) moves the *window* so its upper-left corner is at the position specified by *x* and *y*. For security resasons, browsers may restrict this method so it cannot move a window offscreen. It is usually a bad idea to move a user's browser window unless he explicitly request it. Scripts should typically use this method only on windows that they created themselves with Window.open( ).

Window.onblur   JavaScript 1.1

event handler invoked when the window loses keyboard focus

Synopsis

```
Function onblur
```

Description

The onblur property of a Window specifies an event-handler function that is invoked when the window loses keyboard focus.

The initial value of this property is a function that contains the semicolon-separated Java-Script statements specified by the onblur attribute of the <body> or <frameset> tags.

Usage

If your web page has animation or other dynamic effects, you can use the onblur event handler to stop the animation when the window doesn't have the input focus. In theory, if the window doesn't have the focus, the user probably can't see it or isn't paying attention to it.

See Also

Window.blur( ), Window.focus( ), Window.onfocus; Chapter 17

Window.onerror   JavaScript 1.1

error handler invoked when a JavaScript error occurs

Synopsis

You register an onerror handler like this:

```
window.onerror=handler-func
```

The browser invokes the handler like this:

```
window.onerror(message, url, line)
```

Arguments

message
> A string that specifies the error message for the error that occurred.

url
> A string that specifies the URL of the document in which the error occurred.

line
> A number that specifies the line number at which the error occurred.

Returns

true if the handler has handled the error and JavaScript should take no further action; false if JavaScript should post the default error message dialog box for this error.

Description

The onerror property of the Window object specifies an error-handler function that is invoked when a JavaScript error occurs and is not caught with a catch statement. You can customize error handling by providing your own onerror error handler.

You define an onerror handler for a window by setting the onerror property of a Window object to an appropriate function. Note that onerror is an error handler and differs from event handlers. In particular, an error handler cannot be defined with an onerror attribute on the <body> tag.

When the onerror handler is invoked, it is passed three arguments: a string specifying the error message, a string specifying the URL of the document in which the error occurred, and a number that specifies the line number at which the error occurred. An error handling function may do anything it wants with these arguments: it may display its own error dialog box or log the error in some way, for example. When the error-handling function is done, it should return true if it has completely handled the error and wants the browser to take no further action, or false if it has merely noted or logged the error in some fashion and still wants the browser to handle the error.

Window.onfocus
JavaScript 1.1

event handler invoked when a window is given focus

Synopsis

Function onfocus

Description

The onfocus property of a Window specifies an event-handler function that is invoked when the window is given keyboard focus.

The initial value of this property is a function that contains the semicolon-separated JavaScript statements specified by the onfocus attribute of the <body> or <frameset> tags.

Usage

If your web page has animation or other dynamic effects, you might use the onfocus event handler to start the animation and the onblur handler to stop it, so it runs only when the user is paying attention to the window.

See Also

Window.blur( ), Window.focus( ), Window.onblur; Chapter 17

Window.onload   JavaScript 1.0

event handler invoked when a document finishes loading

Synopsis

Function onload

Description

The onload property of a Window specifies an event handler function that is invoked when a document or frameset is completely loaded into its window or frame.

The initial value of this property is a function that contains the semicolon-separated JavaScript statements specified by the onload attribute of the <body> or <frameset> tags.

When the onload event handler is invoked, you can be certain that the document has fully loaded, and therefore that all scripts within the document have executed, all functions within scripts are defined, and all document elements have been parsed and are available through the Document object.

You can use Window.addEventListener( ) or Window.attachEvent( ) to register multiple event-handler functions for onload events.

See Also

Window.onunload; Section 13.5.7, "Manipulating the Document During Loading," Example 17-7, Chapter 17

Window.onresize   JavaScript 1.2

event handler invoked when a window is resized

Synopsis

Function onresize

Description

The onresize property of the Window object specifies an event-handler function that is invoked when the user changes the size of the window or frame.

The initial value of this property is a function that contains the JavaScript statements specified by the onresize attribute of the HTML <body> or <frameset> tag that defined the window.

Client-Side
JavaScript
Reference

Window.onunload
DOM Level 0

the handler invoked when the browser leaves a page

Synopsis

```
Function onunload
```

Description

The onunload property of a Window specifies an event-handler function that is invoked when the browser "unloads" a document in preparation for loading a new one.

The initial value of this property is a function that contains the semicolon-separated Java-Script statements specified by the onunload attribute of the <body> or <frameset> tags.

The onunload event handler enables you to perform any necessary cleanup of the browser state before a new document is loaded.

The onunload( ) handler is invoked when the user has instructed the browser to leave the current page and move somewhere else. Therefore, it is usually inappropriate to delay the loading of the desired new page by popping up dialog boxes (with Window.confirm( ) or Window.prompt( ), for example) from an onunload event handler.

See Also

Window.onload; Chapter 17

Window.open( )
JavaScript 1.0

open a new browser window or locate a named window

Synopsis

```
window.open(url, name, features, replace)
```

Arguments

url

An optional string that specifies the URL to be displayed in the new window. If this argument is omitted, or if the empty string is specified, the new window does not display a document.

name

An optional string of alphanumeric and underscore characters that specifies a name for the new window. This name can be used as the value of the target attribute of <a> and <form> HTML tags. If this argument names a window that already exists, the open( ) method does not create a new window, but simply returns a reference to the named window. In this case, the *features* argument is ignored.

features

A string that specifies which features of a standard browser window are to appear in the new window. The format of this string is specified in the Window Features section. This argument is optional; if it is not specified, the new window has all the standard features.

replace

> An optional boolean argument that specifies whether the URL loaded into the window should create a new entry in the window's browsing history or replace the current entry in the browsing history. If this argument is true, no new history entry is created. Note that this argument is intended for use when changing the contents of an existing named window.

Returns

A reference to a Window object, which may be a newly created or an already existing one, depending on the *name* argument.

Description

The open( ) method looks up an existing window or opens a new browser window. If the *name* argument specifies the name of an existing window, a reference to that window is returned. The returned window displays the URL specified by *url*, but the *features* argument is ignored. This is the only way in JavaScript to obtain a reference to a window that is known only by name.

If the *name* argument is not specified, or if no window with that name already exists, the open( ) method creates a new browser window. The created window displays the URL specified by *url* and has the name specified by *name* and the size and controls specified by *features* (the format of this argument is described in the next section). If *url* is the empty string, open( ) opens an empty window.

The *name* argument specifies a name for the new window. This name may contain only alphanumeric characters and the underscore character. It may be used as the value of the target attribute of an <a> or <form> tag in HTML to force documents to be displayed in the window.

When you use Window.open( ) to load a new document into an existing named window, you can pass the *replace* argument to specify whether the new document has its own entry in the window's browsing history or whether it replaces the history entry of the current document. If *replace* is true, the new document replaces the old. If this argument is false or is not specified, the new document has its own entry in the Window's browsing history. This argument provides functionality much like that of the Location.replace( ) method.

Don't confuse Window.open( ) with Document.open( ); the two methods perform very different functions. For clarity in your code, you may want to use Window.open( ) instead of open( ). In event handlers defined as HTML attributes, open( ) is usually interpreted as Document.open( ), so in this case, you must use Window.open( ).

Window Features

The *features* argument is a comma-separated list of features that appears in the window. If this optional argument is empty or not specified, all features are present in the window. On the other hand, if *features* specifies any one feature, any features that do not appear in the list do not appear in the window. The string should not contain any spaces or other whitespace. Each element in the list has the format:

feature[*=value*]

For most features, the *value* is yes or no. For these features, the equals sign and the *value* may be omitted; if the feature appears, yes is assumed, and if it doesn't, no is assumed. For the width and height features, *value* is required and must specify a size in pixels.

Here are the commonly supported features and their meanings:

height
> Specifies the height, in pixels, of the window's document display area.

left
> The X coordinate, in pixels, of the window.

location
> The input field for entering URLs directly into the browser.

menubar
> The menu bar.

resizable
> If this feature is not present or is set to no, the window does not have resize handles around its border. (Depending on the platform, the user may still have ways to resize the window.) Note that a common bug is to misspell this feature as "resizeable," with an extra "e."

scrollbars
> Enables horizontal and vertical scrollbars when they are necessary.

status
> The status line.

toolbar
> The browser toolbar, with **Back** and **Forward** buttons, etc.

top
> The Y coordinate, in pixels, of the window.

width
> Specifies the width, in pixels, of the window's document display area.

See Also

Location.replace( ), Window.close( ), the closed and opener properties of Window

Window.print( )   JavaScript 1.5

print the document

Synopsis

window.print( )

Description

Calling print( ) causes the browser to behave as if the user had clicked the browser's **Print** button. Usually, this brings up a dialog box that enables the user to cancel or customize the print request.

Window.prompt( )

get user input with a dialog box

Synopsis

```
window.prompt(message, default)
```

Arguments

message
> The plain-text (not HTML) string to be displayed in the dialog box. It should ask the user to enter the information you want.

default
> A string that is displayed as the default input in the dialog box. Pass the empty string ("") to make prompt( ) display an empty input box.

Returns

The string entered by the user, the empty string if the user did not enter a string, or null if the user clicked **Cancel**.

Description

The prompt( ) method displays the specified *message* in a dialog box that also contains a text input field and **OK** and **Cancel** buttons. Platform-dependent graphics in the dialog box help indicate to the user that her input is desired.

If the user clicks the **Cancel** button, prompt( ) returns null. If the user clicks the **OK** button, prompt( ) returns the text currently displayed in the input field.

The dialog box that is displayed by the prompt( ) method is *modal*. That is, it blocks all user input to the main browser window until the user dismisses the dialog box by clicking on the **OK** or **Cancel** buttons. Since this method returns a value depending on the user's response to the dialog box, JavaScript execution pauses in the call to prompt( ), and subsequent statements are not executed until the user responds to the dialog box.

See Also

Window.alert( ), Window.confirm( )

Window.removeEventListener( )

see Element.removeEventListener( )

Window.resizeBy( )

resize a window by a relative amount

Synopsis

```
window.resizeBy(dw, dh)
```

Client-Side
JavaScript
Reference

Arguments

dw The number of pixels by which to increase the width of the window.

dh The number of pixels by which to increase the height of the window.

Description

resizeBy( ) resizes *window* by the relative amounts specified by *dh* and *dw*. See the security and usability considerations discussed under Window.resizeTo( ).

Window.resizeTo( ) JavaScript 1.2

resize a window

Synopsis

window.resizeTo(*width, height*)

Arguments

width
>   The desired width for the window.

height
>   The desired height for the window.

Description

resizeTo( ) resizes *window* so it is *width* pixels wide and *height* pixels high. For security reasons, the browser may restrict this method to prevent scripts from making windows very small. For usability reasons, it is almost always a bad idea to change the size of a user's window. If a script created a window, the script can resize it, but it is bad form for a script to resize the window that it is loaded into.

Window.scrollBy( ) JavaScript 1.2

scroll the document by a relative amount

Synopsis

window.scrollBy(*dx, dy*)

Arguments

dx The number of pixels by which to scroll the document to the right.

dy The number of pixels by which to scroll the document down.

Description

scrollBy( ) scrolls the document displayed in window by the relative amounts specified by *dx* and *dy*.

Window.scrollTo( )

scroll the document

Synopsis

`window.scrollTo(x, y)`

Arguments

x   The document X coordinate that is to appear at the left edge of the window's document display area.

y   The document Y coordinate that is to appear at the top of the window's document display area.

Description

scrollTo( ) scrolls the document displayed within *window* so the point in the document specified by the *x* and *y* coordinates is displayed in the upper-left corner, if possible.

Window.setInterval( )

periodically execute specified code

Synopsis

`window.setInterval(code, interval)`

Arguments

code

A function to be periodically invoked or a string of JavaScript code to be periodically evaluated. If this string contains multiple statements, they must be separated from each other by semicolons. In IE 4 (but not later versions), this argument must be a string.

interval

The interval, in milliseconds, between invocations or evaluations of *code*.

Returns

A value that can be passed to `Window.clearInterval( )` to cancel the periodic execution of *code*.

Description

setInterval( ) repeatedly invokes or evaluates the function or string specified by *code*, at intervals of *interval* milliseconds.

setInterval( ) returns a value that can later be passed to `Window.clearInterval( )` to cancel the execution of *code*.

setInterval( ) is related to setTimeout( ). Use setTimeout( ) when you want to defer the execution of code but do not want it to be repeatedly executed. See `Window.setTimeout( )` for a discussion of the execution context of *code*.

See Also

`Window.clearInterval( )`, `Window.setTimeout( )`

Window.setTimeout( ) JavaScript 1.0

defer execution of code

Synopsis

window.setTimeout(*code, delay*)

Arguments

code

A function to be invoked, or a string of JavaScript code to be evaluated after the *delay* has elapsed. If this argument is a string, multiple statements must be separated from each other with semicolons. In IE 4, this argument must be a string; the function form of the method is not supported in that browser.

delay

The amount of time, in milliseconds, before the *code* should be executed.

Returns

An opaque value ("timeout id") that can be passed to the `clearTimeout( )` method to cancel the execution of *code*.

Description

The `setTimeout( )` method defers the invocation of a JavaScript function or the evaluation of a string of JavaScript code for *delay* milliseconds. Note that `setTimeout( )` executes *code* only once. If you want multiple invocations, use `setInterval( )` or have the *code* itself call `setTimeout( )` again.

When *code* is executed, it is executed in the context of the Window object. If *code* is a function, the Window object is the value of the `this` keyword. If *code* is a string, it is evaluated in the global scope with the Window object as the only object on the scope chain. This is true even if the call to `setTimeout( )` occurred within a function with a longer scope chain.

See Also

`Window.clearTimeout( )`, `Window.setInterval( )`

Window.status JavaScript 1.0

specify a transient status-line message

Synopsis

`String status`

Description

status is a read/write string property that specifies a transient message to appear in the window's status line. The message generally appears only for a limited amount of time, until it is overwritten by another message or until the user moves the mouse to some other area of the window, for example. When a message specified with status is erased, the status line returns to its default blank state or to the default message specified by the defaultStatus property.

At the time of this writing, many browsers have disabled scripting of their status lines. This is a security measure to protect against phishing attacks that hide the true destination of hyperlinks.

See Also

Window.defaultStatus

XMLHttpRequest
Firefox 1.0, Internet Explorer 5.0, Safari 1.2, Opera 7.60

An HTTP request and response   Object → XMLHttpRequest

Constructor

```
new XMLHttpRequest()                      // All browsers except IE 5 and IE 6
new ActiveXObject("Msxml2.XMLHTTP")       // IE
new ActiveXObject("Microsoft.XMLHTTP")    // IE with older system libraries
```

Properties

readonly short readyState

The state of the HTTP request. The value of this property begins at 0 when an XMLHttpRequest is first created and increases to 4 when the complete HTTP response has been received. Each of the five states has an informal name associated with it, and the table below lists the states, their names, and their meanings:

State	Name	Description
0	Uninitialized	This is the initial state. The XMLHttpRequest object has just been created or has been reset with the abort( ) method.
1	Open	The open( ) method has been called, but send( ) has not. The request has not yet been sent.
2	Sent	The send( ) method has been called, and the HTTP request has been transmitted to the web server. No response has been received yet.
3	Receiving	All response headers have been received. The response body is being received but is not complete.
4	Loaded	The HTTP response has been fully received.

The value of readyState never decreases, unless abort( ) or open( ) are called on a request that is already in progress. Every time the value of this property increases, the onreadystatechange event handler is triggered.

readonly String responseText

> The body of the response (not including headers) that has been received from the server so far, or the empty string if no data has been received yet. If readyState is less than 3, this property is the empty string. When readyState is 3, this property returns whatever portion of the response has been received so far. If readyState is 4, this property holds the complete body of the response.
>
> If the response includes headers that specify a character encoding for the body, that encoding is used. Otherwise, the Unicode UTF-8 encoding is assumed.

readonly Document responseXML

> The response to the request, parsed as XML and returned as a Document object. This property will be null unless all three of the following conditions are true:
>
> - readyState is 4.
> - The response includes a Content-Type header of "text/xml", "application/xml", or anything ending with "+xml" to indicate that the response is an XML document.
> - The response body consists of well-formed XML markup that can be parsed without errors.

readonly short status

> The HTTP status code returned by the server, such as 200 for success and 404 for "Not Found" errors. Reading this property when readyState is less than 3 causes an exception.

readonly String statusText

> This property specifies the HTTP status code of the request by name rather than by number. That is, it is "OK" when status is 200 and "Not Found" when status is 404. As with the status property, reading this property when readyState is less than 3 causes an exception.

Methods

abort( )

> Cancels the current request, closing connections and stopping any pending network activity.

getAllResponseHeaders( )

> Returns the HTTP response headers as an unparsed string.

getResponseHeader( )

> Returns the value of a named HTTP response header

open( )

> Initializes HTTP request parameters, such as the URL and HTTP method, but does not send the request.

send( )

> Sends the HTTP request, using parameters passed to the open( ) method and an optional request body passed to this method.

setRequestHeader( )

> Sets or adds an HTTP request header to an open but unsent request.

Event Handlers

onreadystatechange

> Event-handler function invoked each time the readyState property changes. It may also be invoked multiple times while readyState is 3.

Description

The XMLHttpRequest object allows client-side JavaScript to issue HTTP requests and receive responses (which need not be XML) from web servers. XMLHttpRequest is the subject of Chapter 20, and that chapter contains many examples of its use.

XMLHttpRequest is quite portable and well supported by all modern browsers. The only browser dependency involves the creation of an XMLHttpRequest object. In Internet Explorer 5 and 6, you must use the IE-specific ActiveXObject() constructor, as shown in the Constructor section earlier.

Once an XMLHttpRequest object has been created, you typically use it like this:

1. Call open() to specify the URL and method (usually "GET" or "POST") for the request. When you call open(), you also specify whether you want the request to be synchronous or asynchronous.
2. If you specified an asynchronous request, set the onreadystatechange property to the function that will be notified of the progress of the request.
3. Call setRequestHeader(), if needed, to specify additional request parameters.
4. Call send() to send the request to the web server. If it is a POST request, you may also pass a request body to this method. If you specify a synchronous request in your call to open(), the send() method blocks until the response is complete and readyState is 4. Otherwise, your onreadystatechange event-handler function must wait until the readyState property reaches 4 (or at least 3).
5. Once send() has returned for synchronous requests, or readyState has reached 4 for asynchronous requests, you can use the server's response. First, check the status code to ensure that the request was successful. If so, use getResponseHeader() or getResponseHeaders() to retrieve values from the response header, and use the responseText or responseXML properties to obtain the response body.

The XMLHttpRequest object has not been standardized, but work on a standard has begun at the W3C at the time of this writing. This documentation is based on working drafts of the standard. Current XMLHttpRequest implementations are quite interoperable but differ in minor ways from the standard. An implementation might return null where the standard requires the empty string, for example, or might set readyState to 3 without guaranteeing that all response headers are available.

See Also

Chapter 20

XMLHttpRequest.abort( )

cancel an HTTP request

Synopsis

```
void abort( )
```

Description

This method resets the XMLHttpRequest object to a readyState of 0 and aborts any pending network activity. You might call this method, for example, if a request has taken too long, and the response is no longer necessary.

XMLHttpRequest.getAllResponseHeaders( )

return unparsed HTTP response headers

Synopsis

```
String getAllResponseHeaders( )
```

Returns

If readyState is less than 3, this method returns null. Otherwise, it returns all HTTP response headers (but not the status line) sent by the server. The headers are returned as a single string, with one header per line. Lines are delimited by "\r\n" line terminators.

XMLHttpRequest.getResponseHeader( )

get the value of a named HTTP response header

Synopsis

```
String getResponseHeader(String header)
```

Arguments

header

> The name of the HTTP response header whose value is to be returned. You may specify this header name using any case: the comparison to response headers is case-insensitive.

Returns

The value of the named HTTP response header, or the empty string if no such header was received or if readyState is less than 3. If more than one header with the specified name is received, the values of those headers are concatenated and returned, using a comma and space as the delimiter.

XMLHttpRequest.onreadystatechange

event handler function invoked when readyState changes

Synopsis

```
Function onreadystatechange
```

Description

This property specifies an event-handler function that is invoked each time the readyState property changes. It may also be invoked (but this is not required) multiple times while readyState is 3 to provide notification of download progress.

An onreadystatechange handler typically checks the readyState of the XMLHttpRequest object to see if it has reached 4. If so, it does something with the responseText or responseXML properties.

It is unspecified whether any arguments will be passed to the function. In particular, there is no standard way for the event-handler function to get a reference to the XMLHttp-Request object it is registered on. This means that it is not possible to write a generic handler function that can be used for multiple requests.

The XMLHttpRequest object is supposed to follow the DOM event model and implement an addEventListener( ) method for registering handlers for readystatechange events. (See Event.addEventListener( ), for example.) Since IE does not support the DOM event model, and since it is rare to require more than one event handler per request, it is safer to simply assign a single handler function to onreadystatechange.

XMLHttpRequest.open( )

initialize HTTP request parameters

Synopsis

```
void open(String method,
          String url,
          boolean async,
          String username, String password)
```

Arguments

method

> The HTTP method to be used for the request. Reliably implemented values include GET, POST, and HEAD. Implementations may also support methods as well.

url

> The URL that is the subject of the request. Most browsers impose a same-origin security policy (see Section 13.8.2) and require that this URL have the same hostname and port as the document that contains the script. Relative URLs are resolved in the normal way, using the URL of the document that contains the script.

Client-Side
JavaScript
Reference

async

> Whether the request should be performed asynchronously or not. If this argument is false, the request is synchronous, and a subsequent call to send( ) will block until the response is fully received. If this argument is true or is omitted, the request is asynchronous, and an onreadystatechange event handler is typically required.

username, password

> These optional arguments specify authorization credentials for use with URLs that require authorization. If specified, they override any credentials specified in the URL itself.

Description

This method initializes request parameters for later use by the send( ) method. It sets readyState to 1; deletes any previously specified request headers and previously received response headers; and sets the responseText, responseXML, status, and statusText properties to their default values. It is safe to call this method when readyState is 0 (when the XMLHttpRequest object is just created, or after a call to abort( )) and when readyState is 4 (after a response has been received). The behavior of open( ) is unspecified when it is called from any other state.

Other than storing request parameters for use by send( ) and resetting the XMLHttpRequest object for reuse, the open( ) method has no other behavior. In particular, note that implementations do not typically open a network connection to the web server when this method is called.

See Also

XMLHttpRequest.send( ); Chapter 20

XMLHttpRequest.send( )

send an HTTP request

Synopsis

```
void send(Object body)
```

Arguments

body

> If the HTTP method specified by the call to open( ) is "POST" or "PUT", this argument specifies the body of the request, as a string or Document object, or null if no body is necessary. For any other method, this argument is unused and should be null. (Some implementations do not allow you to omit this argument.)

Description

This method causes an HTTP request to be issued. If there has been no previous call to open( ), or, more generally, if readyState is not 1, send( ) throws an exception. Otherwise, it issues an HTTP request that consists of:

- The HTTP method, URL, and authorization credentials (if any) specified in the previous call to open( )
- The request headers, if any, specified by previous calls to setRequestHeader( )
- The *body* argument passed to this method

Once the request has been issued, send( ) sets readyState to 2 and triggers the onreadystatechange event handler.

If the *async* argument to the previous call to open( ) was false, this method blocks and does not return until readyState is 4 and the server's response has been fully received. Otherwise, if the async argument is true or if that argument is omitted, send( ) returns immediately, and the server's response is processed, as described next, on a background thread.

If the server responds with an HTTP redirect, the send( ) method or the background thread follow the redirect automatically. When all HTTP response headers have been received, send( ) or the background thread sets readyState to 3 and triggers the onreadystatechange event handler. If the response is long, send( ) or the background thread may trigger the onreadystatechange more than once while in state 3: this can serve as a download progress indicator. Finally, when the response is complete, send( ) or the background thread sets readyState to 4 and triggers the event handler one last time.

See Also

XMLHttpRequest.open( ); Chapter 20

XMLHttpRequest.setRequestHeader( )

add a HTTP request header to the request

Synopsis

void setRequestHeader(String *name*, String *value*)

Arguments

name
> The name of the header to be set. This argument should not contain spaces, colons, linefeeds, or newlines.

value
> The value for the header. This argument should not contain linefeeds or newlines.

Description

setRequestHeader( ) specifies an HTTP request header that should be included in the request issued by a subsequent call to send( ). This method may be called only when readyState is 1—i.e., after a call to open( ) but before a call to send( ).

If a header with the specified *name* has already been specified, the new value for that header is the previously specified value, plus a comma, a space, and the *value* specified in this call.

If the call to open( ) specifies authorization credentials, XMLHttpRequest automatically sends an appropriate Authorization request header. You can append to this header with setRequestHeader( ), however. Similarly, if the web browser has stored cookies associated with the URL passed to open( ), appropriate Cookie or Cookie2 headers are automatically included with the request. You can append additional cookies to these headers by calling setRequestHeader( ). XMLHttpRequest may also provide a default value for the User-Agent header. If it does this, any value you specify for that header is appended to the default value.

Some request headers are automatically set by the XMLHttpRequest for conformance to the HTTP protocol and may not be set with this method. These include proxy-related headers as well as the following:

```
Host
Connection
Keep-Alive
Accept-Charset
Accept-Encoding
If-Modified-Since
If-None-Match
If-Range
Range
```

See Also

XMLHttpRequest.getResponseHeader( )

XMLSerializer   Firefox 1.0, Safari 2.01, Opera 7.60

serializes XML documents and nodes   Object → XMLSerializer

Constructor

new XMLSerializer( )

Methods

serializeToString( )
> This instance method performs the actual serialization.

Description

An XMLSerializer object enables you to convert or "serialize" an XML Document or Node object to a string of unparsed XML markup. To use an XMLSerializer, instantiate one with the no-argument constructor, and then call its serializeToString( ) method:

```
var text = (new XMLSerializer( )).serializeToString(element);
```

Internet Explorer does not support the XMLSerializer object. Instead, it makes XML text available through the xml property of the Node object.

See Also

DOMParser, Node; Chapter 21

XMLSerializer.serializeToString( )

convert an XML document or node to a string

Synopsis

```
String serializeToString(Node node)
```

Arguments

node
> The XML node to be serialized. This may be a Document object or any Element within the document.

Returns

A string of XML markup that represents the serialized form of the specified *node* and all its descendants.

XPathExpression   Firefox 1.0, Safari 2.01, Opera 9

a compiled XPath query   Object → XPathExpression

Methods

evaluate( )
> Evaluates this expression for a specified context node.

Description

An XPathExpression object is a compiled representation of an XPath query, returned by Document.createExpression( ). Evaluate the expression against a particular document node with the evaluate( ) method. If you need to evaluate an XPath query only once, you can use Document.evaluate( ), which compiles and evaluates the expression in a single step.

Internet Explorer does not support the XPathExpression object. For IE-specific XPath methods, see Node.selectNodes( ) and Node.selectSingleNode( ).

See Also

```
Document.createExpression( )
Document.evaluate( )
Node.selectNodes( )
Node.selectSingleNode( )
```
Chapter 21

XPathExpression.evaluate( )

evaluate a compiled XPath query

Synopsis

```
XPathResult evaluate(Node contextNode,
                     short type,
                     XPathResult result)
```

Arguments

contextNode
> The node (or document) against which the query should be evaluated.

type
> The desired result type. This argument should be one of the constants defined by XPathResult.

result
> An XPathResult object into which the results of the query should be stored, or null to have the evaluate( ) method create and return a new XPathResult object.

Returns

An XPathResult that hold the results of the query. This is either the object passed as the *result* argument or a newly created XPathResult object if *result* was null.

Description

This method evaluates the XPathExpression against a specified node or document and returns the results in an XPathResult object. See XPathResult for details on how to extract values from the returned object.

See Also

Document.evaluate( ), Node.selectNodes( ), XPathResult; Chapter 21

XPathResult   Firefox 1.0; Safari 2.01; Opera 9

the result of an XPath query   Object → XPathResult

Constants

The following constants define the possible types an XPath query can return. The resultType property of an XPathResult object holds one of these values to specify which kind of result the object holds. These constants are also used with Document.evaluate( ) and XPathExpression.evaluate( ) methods to specify the desired result type. The constants and their meanings are as follows:

ANY_TYPE
> Passes this value to Document.evaluate( ) or XPathExpression.evaluate( ) to specify that any type of result is acceptable. The resultType property is never set to this value.

NUMBER_TYPE
> numberValue holds the result.

STRING_TYPE
> stringValue holds the result.

BOOLEAN_TYPE
> booleanValue holds the result.

UNORDERED_NODE_ITERATOR_TYPE
> The result is an unordered set of nodes, which can be accessed sequentially by calling iterateNext( ) repeatedly until it returns null. The document must not be modified during this iteration.

ORDERED_NODE_ITERATOR_TYPE

 The result is a list of nodes, arranged in document order, which can be accessed sequentially by calling iterateNext( ) repeatedly until it returns null. The document must not be modified during this iteration.

UNORDERED_NODE_SNAPSHOT_TYPE

 The result is a random-access list of nodes. The snapshotLength property specifies the length of the list, and the snapshotItem( ) method returns the node at a specified index. The nodes may not be in the same order they appear in the document. Since this kind of result is a "snapshot," it remains valid even if the document is changed.

ORDERED_NODE_SNAPSHOT_TYPE

 The result is a random-access list of nodes, just like UNORDERED_NODE_SNAPSHOT_TYPE, except that this list is arranged in document order.

ANY_UNORDERED_NODE_TYPE

 The singleNodeValue property refers to a node that matches the query or null if no nodes matched. If more than one node matches the query, singleNodeValue may be any one of the matching nodes.

FIRST_ORDERED_NODE_TYPE

 singleNodeValue holds the first node in the document that matched the query, or null if no nodes matched.

Instance Properties

Many of these properties are valid only when resultType holds a particular value. Accessing properties that are not defined for the current resultType causes an exception.

readonly boolean booleanValue

 Holds the result value when resultType is BOOLEAN_TYPE.

readonly boolean invalidIteratorState

 Is true if resultType is one of the ITERATOR_TYPE constants and the document has been modified, making the iterator invalid, because the result was returned.

readonly float numberValue

 Holds the result value when resultType is NUMBER_TYPE.

readonly short resultType

 Specifies what kind of result the XPath query returned. Its value is one of the constants listed earlier. The value of this property tells you which other properties or methods you can use.

readonly Node singleNodeValue

 Holds the result value when resultType is XPathResult.ANY_UNORDERED_NODE_TYPE or XPathResult.FIRST_UNORDERED_NODE_TYPE.

snapshotLength

 Specifies the number of nodes returned when resultType is UNORDERED_NODE_SNAPSHOT_TYPE or ORDERED_NODE_SNAPSHOT_TYPE. Use this property in conjunction with snapshotItem( ).

stringValue

 Holds the result value when resultType is STRING_TYPE.

Methods

iterateNext( )
> Returns the next node in the node set. Use this method if the resultType is UNORDERED_
> NODE_ITERATOR_TYPE or ORDERED_NODE_ITERATOR_TYPE.

snapshotItem( )
> Returns the node at the specified index in the list of result nodes. This method may be
> used only if resultType is UNORDERED_NODE_SNAPSHOT_TYPE or ORDERED_NODE_SNAPSHOT_
> TYPE. Use the snapshotLength property in conjunction with this method.

Description

An XPathResult object represents the value of an XPath expression. Objects of this type are
returned by Document.evaluate( ) and XPathExpression.evaluate( ). XPath queries can evaluate to strings, numbers, booleans, nodes, and lists of nodes. XPath implementations can
return lists of nodes in several different ways, so this object defines a slightly complex API
for obtaining the actual result of an XPath query.

To use an XPathResult, first check the resultType property. It will hold one of the XPath-
Result constants. The value of this property tells you which property or method you need
to use to determine the result value. Calling methods or reading properties that are not
defined for the current resultType causes an exception.

Internet Explorer does not support the XPathResult API. To perform XPath queries in IE,
see Node.selectNodes( ) and Node.selectSingleNode( ).

See Also

Document.evaluate( ), XPathExpression.evaluate( )

XPathResult.iterateNext( )

return the next node that matches an XPath query

Synopsis

```
Node iterateNext( )
    throws DOMException
```

Returns

Returns the next node in the list of matching nodes, or null if there are no more.

Throws

This method throws an exception if the document has been modified since the XPath-
Result was returned. It also throws an exception if called when returnType is not
UNORDERED_NODE_ITERATOR_TYPE or ORDERED_NODE_ITERATOR_TYPE.

Description

iterateNext( ) returns the next node that matches the XPath query or null if all matching
nodes have already been returned. Use this method if resultType is UNORDERED_NODE_
ITERATOR_TYPE or ORDERED_NODE_ITERATOR_TYPE. If the type is ordered, nodes are returned in
the order they appear in the document. Otherwise, they can be returned in any order.

If the `invalidIteratorState` property is `true`, the document has been modified, and this method throws an exception.

XPathResult.snapshotItem( )

return a node that matches an XPath query

Synopsis

`Node snapshotItem(index)`

Arguments

index
The index of the node to be returned.

Returns

The node at the specified index, or `null` if the index is less than zero or greater than or equal to `snapshotLength`.

Throws

This method throws an exception if `resultType` is not `UNORDERED_NODE_SNAPSHOT_TYPE` or `ORDERED_NODE_SNAPSHOT_TYPE`.

XSLTProcessor

transform XML with XSLT stylesheets

Firefox 1.0, Safari 2.01, Opera 9

Object → XSLTProcessor

Constructor

`new XSLTProcessor( )`

Methods

`clearParameters( )`
Deletes any previously set parameters.

`getParameter( )`
Returns the value of a named parameter.

`importStyleSheet( )`
Specifies the XSLT stylesheet to be used.

`removeParameter( )`
Deletes a named parameter.

`reset( )`
Resets the XSLTProcessor to its initial state, clearing all parameters and stylesheets.

`setParameter( )`
Sets a named parameter to a specified value.

Client-Side
JavaScript
Reference

transformToDocument( )

> Transforms the specified document or node using the stylesheet passed to importStylesheet( ) and parameters passed to setParameter( ). Returns the result as a new Document object.

transformToFragment( )

> Transforms the specified document or node, returning the result as a DocumentFragment.

Description

The XSLTProcessor transforms XML document nodes using XSLT stylesheets. Create an XSLTProcessor object with the no-argument constructor, and initialize it with an XSLT stylesheet with the importStylesheet( ) method. If your stylesheet uses parameters, you can set those with setParameter(). Finally, perform an actual XSL transformation with tranformToDocument( ) or transformToFragment( ).

Internet Explorer supports XSLT but does not implement the XSLTProcessor object. See the IE-specific transformNode( ) and transformNodeToObject( ) methods of Node, and see Chapter 21 for XSLT examples and cross-platform utility functions.

See Also

Node.transformNode( ), Node.transformNodeToObject( ); Chapter 21

XSLTProcessor.clearParameters( )

delete all stylesheet parameter values

Synopsis

void clearParameters( )

Description

This method erases any parameter values that have been specified with setParameter( ). If a transformation is performed with no parameters set, the default values specified by the stylesheet are used.

XSLTProcessor.getParameter( )

return the value of a named parameter

Synopsis

String getParameter(String *namespaceURI*, String *localName*)

Arguments

namespaceURI

> The namespace of the parameter.

localName

> The name of the parameter.

Returns

The value of the parameter, or null if it has not been set.

XSLTProcessor.importStylesheet( )

specify an XSLT stylesheet for transformations

Synopsis

```
void importStylesheet(Node stylesheet)
```

Arguments

stylesheet
> The XSLT stylesheet to be used for transformations. This may be a Document of its own, or an <xsl:stylesheet> or <xsl:transform> Element.

Description

importStyleSheet( ) specifies the XSLT stylesheet to be used by future calls to transformToDocument( ) and transformToFragment( ).

XSLTProcessor.removeParameter( )

delete a parameter value

Synopsis

```
void removeParameter(String namespaceURI, String localName)
```

Arguments

namespaceURI
> The namespace of the parameter.

localName
> The name of the parameter.

Description

removeParameter( ) deletes the value of the named parameter, if any such parameter was previously set with setParameter( ). Subsequent transformations use the default value of the parameter that is specified in the stylesheet.

XSLTProcessor.reset( )

restore an XSLTProcessor to its default state

Synopsis

```
void reset()
```

Description

This method restores an XSLTProcessor to the state it was in when it was first created. After calling this method, there is no stylesheet and are no parameter values associated with the XSLTProcessor.

XSLTProcessor.setParameter( )

set a stylesheet parameter

Synopsis

```
void setParameter(String namespaceURI,
                  String localName,
                  String value)
```

Arguments

namespaceURI
>   The namespace of the parameter.

localName
>   The name of the parameter.

value
>   The value of the parameter.

Description

This method specifies a value for the named stylesheet parameter.

XSLTProcessor.transformToDocument( )

transform a node or document to a new document

Synopsis

```
Document transformToDocument(Node sourceNode)
```

Arguments

source
>   The document or node that is to be transformed.

Returns

A Document object that holds the result of the transformation.

Description

This method performs an XSLT transformation on the specified node, returning the result as a Document object. The transformation uses the XSLT stylesheet specified by importStylesheet( ) and the parameter values specified with setParameter( ).

XSLTProcessor.transformToFragment( )

transform a node or document to a DocumentFragment

Synopsis

```
DocumentFragment transformToFragment(Node sourceNode,
                                     Document ownerDocument)
```

Arguments

source

> The document or node that is to be transformed.

owner

> The document through which the returned DocumentFragment is created. The ownerDocument property of the returned DocumentFragment refers to this document.

Returns

A DocumentFragment object that holds the result of the transformation.

Description

This method performs an XSLT transformation on the specified node, returning the result as a DocumentFragment object. The transformation uses the XSLT stylesheet specified by importStylesheet( ) and the parameter values specified with setParameter. The returned fragment can be inserted into the specified *owner* document.

Index

We'd like to hear your suggestions for improving our indexes. Send email to *index@oreilly.com*.

L

L (left-to-right associativity), 63
label property, 876
<label> tag, 450
  for attribute, 312
labels, statement, 94
  for and break statements, 95
lambda functions, 33, 127
lang property, 311, 823
language attribute (<script>), 245
last character of strings, getting, 28
lastChild property, 319, 862
  Node object, 309
lastIndex property, 692
  RegExp object, 212
  String object methods and, 211
lastIndexOf( ) method (Array), 122
lastModified property
  HTMLDocument object, 816
  Document object, 301
Latin-1 character set, hexadecimal
    representation, escape
    sequences, 26
Layer object, 850
layers, DOM, 299
left attribute, 356, 365
left-to-right associativity (L), 63
length property, 745, 806, 874, 893
  Arguments object, 130, 601
  arguments[ ] array, 129
  arrays, 114, 116, 122
    looping through array elements, 116
    truncating and enlarging arrays, 117
  functions, 137
  HTMLFormElement interface, 312
  JavaScript and Java strings, 232
  Plugin object, 877
  String object, 700
  strings, 27
length type (CSS), 346
less-than operator (see < under Symbols)
less-than-or-equal operator (see < under
    Symbols)
letters, in identifier names, 18
levels, DOM, 239, 312
lexical scoping, 141
  functions shared between frames or
    windows, 293
  nested functions and, 143
lexical structure, JavaScript, 15
  case sensitivity, 16
  comments, 17

  identifiers, 18
  keywords, 19
  literals, 17
  semicolons, omitting between
    statements, 16
  Unicode character set, 15
  whitespace and line breaks, 16
lifetime
  cookies, 457, 459
  Window object and its properties, 255
line breaks, 16
  escape sequences and, 27
Link object, 850–854
  event handlers, 851
  onclick method, 394
  onclick property, 306
  properties corresponding to <a> and
    <area> tag attributes, 851
  properties, URL-related, 850
<link> tag
  disabled property, 382
  including CSS stylesheet into HTML
    page, 351
  specifying alternate stylesheet, 351
links
  buttons versus, 446
  cross-site scripting, 267
  HTML, 251
  links[ ] property, 303
  obscuring destination of, 264
  preventing browser from displaying
    URL, 395
  preventing deep-linking to your site, 302
  properties corresponding to HTML tag
    attributes, 305
  user confirmation for following, 394
links[ ] property, 816
listanchors( ) function, 306
listeners for events, 400
literals, 17
  array, 36
  in expressions, 59
  floating-point, 23
  function, 33, 127
  hexadecimal and octal, 23
  integer, 22
  numeric, 22
  object, 34, 106
  regular expression, 39, 199
  string, 25

objects (*continued*)
    HTML, event handlers defined as
        attributes, 249
    instance properties, 158
    Java
        accessing fields and methods in
            JavaScript, 221
        JavaObject class, 226, 232
        passed to JavaScript script or
            function, 221
        stored in Bindings object and
            converted to JavaScript, 218
    JavaScript
        conversion to Java, 231
        corresponding to HTML
            elements, 393
    manipulation by reference, 48
    methods, 32, 136
        common, 164–167
    properties, 33, 107–109
        checking existence of, 108
        creating, 108
        deleting, 109
        enumerating, 93, 108
        variables as properties, 56
    prototype, 138, 648, 680
    as reference types, 44
    registering as event handlers, 403
    storage, 55
    strings versus, 28
    wrapper, 40
    (see also classes)
    (see also Object class)
octal literals, 23
octal numbers, Latin-1 character escape
    sequences, 27
offscreen images, caching and, 533
offsetLeft and offsetTop properties, 283, 361
offsetParent property, 361
offsetWidth and offsetHeight properties, 361
offsetX, offsetY properties (IE Event
    object), 410
onabort event handler, 538
onblur event handler
    form elements, 445
    window losing keyboard focus, 923
onblur property (Input), 842
onchange event handler, 6, 250
    form elements, 445
        file, 448
        radio and checkbox, 447

Select, 449
    text fields, 448
Select object, 897
onchange property (Input), 842
onclick attribute, 392
onclick event handler, 6, 249, 390
    defining, 305
        for every link in a document
            (example), 394
    form elements, 445
        radio and checkbox, 447
    JavaScript URL as substitute for, 251
    links and buttons, 446
onclick method
    Link object, 394
    Submit object, 394
onclick property
    HTMLElement object, 828
    Input object, 843
    Link object, 305, 853
onerror event handler, 288, 538
onfocus event handler, 924
    form elements, 445
onfocus property (Input), 843
onkeydown event handler, 425, 448
onkeypress event handler, 425, 448
onkeyup event handler, 425, 448
onload event, 433
onload event handler, 250, 252, 253, 521
    Image object, 536
    triggering document modifications, 256
    Window object, 925
onlosecapture event, 413
onmousedown attribute, 424
onmousedown event handler, 249
onmouseout event handler, 250
    image rollover effect, creating, 532
onmouseout property (Link), 853
onmouseover event handler, 250, 390
    image rollover effect, creating, 532
    returning true to prevent display of link
        URL in status line, 395
onmouseover property (Link), 853
onmouseup event handler, 249
onreadystatechange event handler, 484, 491,
    937
onreset event handler, 438, 439
onresize event handler, Window object, 925
onsubmit attribute, 392
onsubmit event handler, 306, 390, 438
    returning false value, 395

About the Author

David Flanagan is a consulting computer programmer who spends much of his time writing books. His other O'Reilly books include *JavaScript Pocket Reference*, *Java in a Nutshell*, and *Java Examples in a Nutshell*. David has a degree in computer science and engineering from the Massachusetts Institute of Technology. He lives with his wife and children in the U.S. Pacific Northwest between the cities of Seattle, Washington, and Vancouver, British Columbia.

Colophon

The animal on the cover of *JavaScript: The Definitive Guide,* Fifth Edition, is a Javan rhinoceros. All five species of rhinoceros are distinguished by their large size, thick armor-like skin, three-toed feet, and single or double snout horn. The Javan rhinoceros, along with the Sumatran rhinoceros, is one of two forest-dwelling species. The Javan rhinoceros is similar in appearance to the Indian rhinoceros, but smaller and with certain distinguishing characteristics (primarily skin texture).

Rhinoceroses are often depicted standing up to their snouts in water or mud. In fact, they can frequently be found just like that. When not resting in a river, rhinos will dig deep pits in which to wallow. Both of these resting places provide a couple of advantages. First, they give the animal relief from the tropical heat and protection from blood-sucking flies. (The mud that the wallow leaves on the skin of the rhinoceros provides some protection from flies, also.) Second, mud wallows and river water help support the considerable weight of these huge animals, thereby relieving the strain on their legs and backs.

Folklore has long held that the horn of the rhinoceros possesses magical and aphrodisiacal powers, and that humans who gain possession of the horns will gain those powers, also. This is one of the reasons why rhinos are a prime target of poachers. All species of rhinoceros are in danger, and the Javan rhino population is the most precarious. Fewer than 100 of these animals are still living. At one time, Javan rhinos could be found throughout southeastern Asia, but they are now believed to exist only in Indonesia and Vietnam.

The cover image is is a 19th-century engraving from the Dover Pictorial Archive. The cover font is Adobe ITC Garamond. The text font is Linotype Birka; the heading font is Adobe Myriad Condensed; and the code font is LucasFont's TheSans Mono Condensed.

Better than e-books

Buy *JavaScript: The Definitive Guide*, 5th Edition, and access the digital edition FREE on Safari for 45 days.

Go to www.oreilly.com/go/safarienabled
and type in coupon code 6NGV-LJIF-APRG-7GFZ-Q4LG

Search thousands of top tech books

Download whole chapters

Cut and Paste code examples

Find answers fast

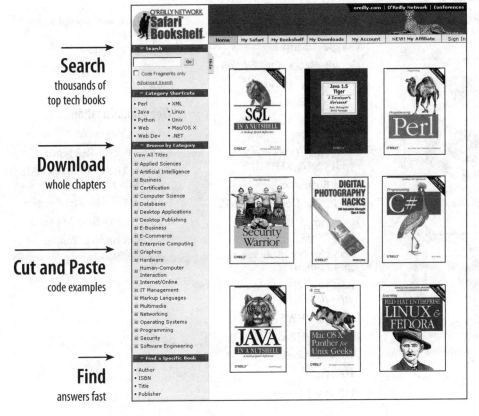

Search Safari! The premier electronic reference library for programmers and IT professionals.

O'REILLY NETWORK
Safari Bookshelf

 Addison Wesley

 Sun microsystems

 ALPHA

 Java

 Microsoft Press

 Peachpit Press

 O'REILLY

 New Riders

 Cisco Press

 macromedia PRESS

 PRENTICE HALL PTR

Adobe Press

SAMS

Related Titles from O'Reilly

Web Programming

ActionScript 3 Cookbook

ActionScript for Flash MX: The Definitive Guide, *2nd Edition*

Ajax Hacks

Dynamic HTML: The Definitive Reference, *2nd Edition*

Flash Hacks

Essential PHP Security

Google Advertising Tools

Google Hacks, *2nd Edition*

Google Map Hacks

Google Pocket Guide

Google: The Missing Manual, *2nd Edition*

Head First HTML with CSS & XHTML

Head Rush Ajax

HTTP: The Definitive Guide

JavaScript & DHTML Cookbook

JavaScript Pocket Reference, *2nd Edition*

JavaScript: The Definitive Guide, *4th Edition*

Learning PHP 5

Learning PHP and MySQL

PHP Cookbook

PHP Hacks

PHP in a Nutshell

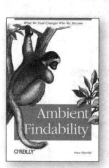

PHP Pocket Reference, *2nd Edition*

PHPUnit Pocket Guide

Programming ColdFusion MX, *2nd Edition*

Programming PHP, *2nd Edition*

Upgrading to PHP 5

Web Database Applications with PHP and MySQL, *2nd Edition*

Web Site Cookbook

Webmaster in a Nutshell, *3rd Edition*

Web Administration

Apache Cookbook

Apache Pocket Reference

Apache: The Definitive Guide, *3rd Edition*

Perl for Web Site Management

Squid: The Definitive Guide

Web Performance Tuning, *2nd Edition*

Our books are available at most retail and online bookstores.

To order direct: 1-800-998-9938 • *order@oreilly.com* • *www.oreilly.com*

Online editions of most O'Reilly titles are available by subscription at *safari.oreilly.com*

The O'Reilly Advantage

Stay Current and Save Money

Order books online:
www.oreilly.com/order_new

Questions about our products or your order:
order@oreilly.com

Join our email lists: Sign up to get topic specific email announcements or new books, conferences, special offers and technology news
elists@oreilly.com

For book content technical questions:
booktech@oreilly.com

To submit new book proposals to our editors:
proposals@oreilly.com

Contact us:
O'Reilly Media, Inc.
1005 Gravenstein Highway N.
Sebastopol, CA U.S.A. 95472
707-827-7000 or
800-998-9938
www.oreilly.com

Did you know that if you register your O'Reilly books, you'll get automatic notification and upgrade discounts on new editions?

And that's not all! Once you've registered your books you can:

» Win free books, T-shirts and O'Reilly Gear

» Get special offers available only to registered O'Reilly customers

» Get free catalogs announcing all our new titles (US and UK Only)

Registering is easy! Just go to
www.oreilly.com/go/register